L. F.

D1275140

Macroeconomic Models and Policy

Macroeconomics

MODELS & POLICY

Yiannis P. Venieris and Frederick D. Sebold
San Diego State University

John Wiley & Sons

Santa Barbara   New York   London   Sydney   Toronto

A Wiley/Hamilton Publication

ALBRIGHT COLLEGE LIBRARY

Copyright © 1977 by John Wiley & Sons, Inc.

All rights reserved. Published simultaneously in Canada.

No part of this book may be reproduced by any means,
nor transmitted, nor translated into a machine language
without the written permission of the publisher.

Library of Congress Cataloging in Publication Data

Venieris, Yiannis P.   1935–
   Macroeconomic models and policy.

   Includes index.
   1. Macroeconomics. 2. Macroeconomics—Mathematical
models. I. Sebold, Frederick D., joint author.
II. Title.
HB171.5.V4 1977   339   76–50592
ISBN 0–471–90560–7

Printed in the United States of America.

10 9 8 7 6 5 4 3 2 1

339
V459m

159275 ..

To Our Parents

13.15

About the Authors

Yiannis Venieris was educated in Europe and the United States, where he received his Ph.D. from the University of Oregon in 1969. He has consulted for several federal and state agencies and the National Science Foundation. He is presently professor of economics at San Diego State University.

His research interests encompass macro, monetary theory and consumer behavior, and he has published in various learned journals here and abroad including *Southern Economic Journal, The Review of Economics and Statistics* and the *Journal of Political Economy*.

Fred Sebold received his Ph.D. from Boston College in 1970. He is chairperson and professor of economics at San Diego State University. His main professional areas of interest are public finance and macroeconomics, and he has published in several economics journals, including *The Review of Economics and Statistics* and the *National Tax Journal*.

Preface

In writing this text, we have tried to imbue the reader with a sense of the excitement generated within the field of macroeconomics over the past few decades. Given the richness and breadth of ideas conceived and extended during this period, though, we were forced to exercise professional and pedagogical judgment in dealing with three interrelated choice problems. Recognizing the constraints of time and space, we had to choose from an almost boundless number of topics, several alternative levels of treatment and a variety of organizational formats. There is, of course, no ideal solution; but we hope that our efforts have resulted in a text which will serve the needs of a large number of students.

Our basic purpose in writing this book was to provide a systematic treatment of macroeconomic theory and policy, primarily for undergraduate students. Thus, our choice of topics was guided by the need to cover that body of macroeconomic literature which is considered by the majority of economists to be fundamental. In this connection, the reader will find that the two mainstreams of macroeconomic thought—neo-Keynesianism and monetarism—are given thorough coverage. Our approach in treating the controversy generated by these two viewpoints is an agnostic one. This does not mean that we are unmindful of the empirical evidence provided in support of (or against) each body of theory, or are unaware of the importance of the controversy. Rather, our treatment reflects the philosophy that textbook authors should be neither apologists for nor advocates of any particular school of thought.

The second choice problem involves the depth of coverage of each topic. In this context, it has often been alleged that there is a clear trade off between the rigorous pursuit of the fine points of theory and the provision of a general understanding of critical issues. While the dichotomy is sometimes very real, we find no inherent incompatibility between rigor and understanding. Our treatment does not necessitate any extensive mathematical background beyond college algebra; yet we feel that we have not subordinated rigor to simplicity. Each topic is developed verbally, graphically and algebraically in considerable detail. To fully appreciate the flow of ideas incorporated here, the student will find it necessary to sharpen a pencil or two and work through the numerical examples, pseudosimulations and exercises. The dividends in terms of understanding should be substantial.

Our choice of an organizational scheme rests on two basic principles. First, the presentation should develop the kind of understanding which allows students to generalize, extending the analysis to topics not specifically covered in the text. The reader will find many exercises incorporated into the text, each of which is designed to stimulate experimentation and further understanding. Second, each topic should be treated as an integral part of a continuous stream of thought. Our development of the first eleven chapters, for instance, constitutes a sequential construction of a comprehensive three-sector macro model. Simplifying behavioral assumptions are relaxed and substitutes are introduced at each step of the analysis, thus preserving a sense of continuity. These eleven chapters make up the core of the book and they are relatively devoid of digressions. To achieve this continuity, we have locked several topics into appendices. (The instructor might want to ignore them until the basic model has been completed.)

In building the basic model, we have used a simple Keynesian consumption function and have specified (with only a heuristic justification) "the" interest rate as the only argument of the investment function. This specification was a deliberate choice reflecting our classroom experience, which suggests that the early introduction of alternative consumption and investment theories turns attention from the fundamentals of macroeconomic models, and that the importance of these analyses is better understood later in the context of a full model. Obviously, though, some instructors might be more comfortable with a sequence different from the one we have used. If so, the chapters on consumption and investment (chapters 12 and 13) could be covered simultaneously with the core material.

We have reserved the last seven chapters of the text to analyze special topics: alternative theories of consumption, investment and money demand; monetarism; macroeconomic behavior in an international setting; growth models; and theories of inflation. The order in which we present these topics does not reflect any ranking with respect to importance, but rather what we thought was a convenient way to classify material. Each of these chapters is reasonably self-contained, and they can thus be covered in any order.

The treatment in early chapters is quite detailed, in the sense that we generally provide several alternative ways of analyzing each concept.

The pace of the book accelerates as we move through successive chapters, with progressively more of the analysis assigned to the reader in the form of exercises. We have found in our own teaching that this approach is an effective way of inducing a rising level of maturity in the student's ability to think in analytical terms. The extensive coverage of basic macroeconomic principles should also allow the instructor to devote relatively more classroom time to policy issues and special topics.

Although the text is designed primarily for undergraduate instruction, much of it (especially chapters 10 and on) would be appropriate as a basic text for a first-year graduate course in macroeconomics. With this in mind, we have included many advanced selections in the supplemental readings at the end of each chapter.

No project of this magnitude is completed without incurring a variety of debts. To be sure, we owe thanks to many people for their generous professional and personal contributions to the completion of our task. The concise and readable treatment of national income accounts is largely the handiwork of our colleague, Don Bridenstine. Both Douglas Stewart and Dean Popp contributed several helpful suggestions throughout the preparation of the manuscript. In addition, Ray Gilbert, Texas A & M University; Alan D. Hess, University of Washington; Michael C. Lovell, Wesleyan University; Kent Olson, Oklahoma State University; Ralph W. Pfouts, University of North Carolina; Lester D. Taylor, University of Arizona; Warren Weber, Virginia Polytechnic Institute and State University all did thorough jobs of evaluating earlier drafts of the manuscript and were responsible for many substantial improvements in content and style. We also offer thanks (and an apology, perhaps) to the many intermediate macro students who were commandeered to work through the text in the process of its preparation. We are likewise grateful to the editorial and production staffs of Wiley/Hamilton, P.J. Wilkinson, George Thomsen, Dick Palmer and Chuck Pendergast, for their confidence and patience throughout the completion of the text. We have also incurred a debt to Elizabeth Wolkonsky, Dana Stumpf and Cheryl Block, who have provided exceptional secretarial assistance throughout the preparation of the manuscript. And, finally, we acknowledge the unfailing moral support accorded by our wives, who at times must have felt the strain of being textbook widows.

January 1977   Yiannis P. Venieris

                                                      Frederick D. Sebold

Contents

PART ONE

Introductory Material

CHAPTER 1

The Anatomy
of an Economic Model

1.1 Introduction

Among a nation's many social goals are those which relate to the performance of the economy. In the United States, some of the most prominent economic objectives are the attainment of full employment, price stability, a reasonable balance of payments and an optimum rate of growth. Surprisingly, the substantial use of overt public policy to achieve these ends is a relatively recent phenomenon. Although the trend toward increased use of the tools of economic policy is the result in part of an evolution of economic thought, that process has accelerated so rapidly at times that we might better describe it as a revolution. The Great Depression of the 1930s and the subsequent publication of J. M. Keynes' *General Theory of Employment, Interest and Money,* in particular, revolutionized our perception of the role of the government in fostering economic prosperity.

In the context of the traditional goals of the nation, economic policy has been instrumental in promoting a remarkably good performance by the U.S. economy in the decades since World War II. To be sure, several recessions have appeared now and then on the postwar economic landscape; but none of them have assumed the dimensions of the Great Depression, when unemployment climbed to 25% and the mood of the nation plunged to almost unprecedented depths. And, in spite of occasional periods of inflation, we have managed to avoid the extreme price instability experienced by many other countries.

Yet the current widespread interest in economic policy is probably as much a result of perceived past and current failures as it is of recent

3

triumphs. The economics profession has come under fire on many counts in the past few years, but we can identify two major criticisms. First, it is argued that the recent incidence of relatively high unemployment rates coupled with substantial rates of inflation casts some doubt on the efficacy of standard policy prescriptions. It is true, of course, that the early 1970s have been anything but ideal from an economic perspective. Economic theory offers the tools to cope with the problem of inflation; moreover, traditional policy can deal effectively with widespread unemployment. But the fine tuning involved in dealing simultaneously with these two maladies has not yet been adequately incorporated into our policy kit. There are two general reasons for this shortcoming. First, the art of describing the complex relationships of a sophisticated economy is a difficult one, entailing the specification and quantification of almost innumerable economic relationships. Second, economic policies—like any others—are partially based on political considerations; in the face of some problem, economists may suggest a set of policies which are deemed to have too many political drawbacks to warrant adoption. This text is concerned primarily with the first issue, in the sense that we shall consider the way in which policy recommendations can be inferred from economic theory, with little regard for the likelihood that these policies will actually be adopted. But we do suggest that a general understanding by the public of the rationale behind these recommendations is a prerequisite for dispelling the political taboos which sometimes hinder the achievement of socioeconomic goals.

The second major charge against economics is that it does not respond to some of the crucial social problems of the day (e.g., the unequal distribution of income) and to changes in social priorities (e.g., the current shift to environmental concern). To a large extent, this criticism should be addressed to the political body of a society, which often exhibits difficulty in reading the signs of the public will. By extension, these charges could be extended to the single economic actor, who carries his decisions and biases into the voting booth. In this sense, economics has served and can continue to serve expressed needs. As a social science, it has dealt with problems according to the priorities suggested by the electorate. In fact, it has sometimes been a step or two ahead of the public mood. Economics entails a description of the economic actor as he is, not what we would like him to be. We leave this latter aspect to religion.

Regardless of the weight one places on each of the economic objectives of society, rational economic policy requires a firm understanding of the structure of the economy. Thus, the theoretical material presented in the remainder of this text should be of interest to individuals with a wide variety of values. The remainder of this chapter is devoted to introducing the reader to some of the methods and terminology we shall use in the development of that material.

1.2 Macroeconomics vs. Microeconomics

As an introduction to the material presented in subsequent chapters, it might be useful to discuss the general methodology to be used there. Obviously, our first task is to define the scope of our investigation. As is connoted by the term *macroeconomics,* we shall be attempting to describe broad economic relationships. We shall be concerned with the relations between aggregate economic variables like total consumption, total investment, national income and aggregate employment. It should be apparent that this type of analysis differs from *microeconomics,* which is the study of the market behavior of individual economic units (producers and consumers).

One should not get the impression that macroeconomics and microeconomics are inconsistent with each other. On the contrary, they are simply two ways of analyzing economic behavior, each approach having its own purpose and its own set of assumptions. Micro theory is an attempt to analyze the way in which relative prices and individual outputs are determined and distributed. This focus on particular markets is often simplified through a set of *ceteris paribus* assumptions relating to total income, total wealth and other aggregate variables. In macro theory, we are concerned about aggregate output and the general price level (among other variables), and thus often make simplifying assumptions about the distribution of individual outputs and income and the structure of relative prices.

The distinction between micro and macro analyses may, at times, be one of degree rather than kind. For instance, we generally characterize the study of individual markets as belonging to the sphere of microeconomics; but if those markets are defined to be sufficiently broad (e.g., the market for all investment goods), we traverse this category and enter the realm of macroeconomics. In some intermediate cases (e.g., the analysis of the market for durable consumption goods) there is considerable doubt concerning the jurisdiction of the two branches of economic theory. Actually, this problem should be of little concern to the reader, for it makes little difference what we call the analysis covering any "gray area." With few exceptions, the problems studied in this text will belong quite clearly to the auspices of macroeconomic theory. We shall sometimes make reference to microeconomic concepts, but the reference will almost always be used only to rationalize a counterpart notion contained in macro theory.[1]

1.3 The Meaning of an Economic Model

The student will soon find that much of our attention in macro analysis is focused on the construction of economic "models." A model is nothing but a set of relationships among economic variables. If put in algebraic form, an economic model will consist of a series of equations, each of which represents the association among certain variables. These theoretical constructs are used to formulate and analyze systematically hypotheses about the workings of the economy. Obviously, it would be impossible to capture the full complexity of the real world in any formal model of the economy; consequently, we are forced to abstract from some of these complexities. Any student who has had some contact with economic thinking should be well aware of the extensive use of "simplifying assumptions" made by economists. Although one has a natural tendency to be critical of any analysis based on what might be considered unrealistic assumptions, it should be emphasized that *some* degree of abstraction is generally necessary if we are to be able to specify workable and manageable models. Even the most sophisticated economic models—systems containing hundreds of relationships—are based on a series of assumptions. If we are to use our models for policy decision making, rather than for intellectual exercise, the assumptions should be as realistic as possible. But, still, assumptions must be made about such things as the motivation underlying the behavior of consumers and investors, the nature of technological improvements in production processes, the type of organizational structure in a particular market, and so on.

In our presentation of macroeconomic theory, assumptions will be used extensively. The reason for this practice is that it facilitates the exposition and learning of a great many concepts. As a general point, one could say that the difficulty or complexity of an economic model is inversely related to the number of assumptions underlying its specification, or alternatively that the realism of the model is directly associated

---

[1]As the reader will soon discover, many of the macroeconomic relations presented in subsequent chapters are based on microeconomic analyses. The development of a macro relation from a micro hypothesis involves numerous problems of aggregation. We shall refer to this type of problem in later chapters when it becomes necessary to do so.

with its complexity. Because of this, it seems plausible for us to begin with abstract (but simple) models based on many simplifying assumptions and to work in a stepwise fashion toward the specification of much more realistic (but more difficult) models necessitating far fewer assumptions. The analysis contained in subsequent chapters will not provide the reader with all of the answers to all policy questions; instead, it will hopefully illustrate the general procedures by which such answers can be obtained.

1.4 Types of Economic Variables

Stocks and Flows

In describing economic models, we shall often distinguish between alternative types of economic variables. The first distinction to be made is that between stocks and flows. Much of the controversy in economic literature has been spawned by a confusion over the classification of a variable into one or the other of these categories. A stock variable has no time dimension as such. Its value must be ascertained at some point in time, to be sure; however, the concept underlying the stock variable does not involve the specification of any particular length of time. A flow variable is one which must be defined with a specific time interval.

A series of examples might be useful to highlight the conceptual differences between flows and stocks. Consider a lake fed by a single mountain stream. The volume of water contained in the lake at any point in time is a stock; the volume of water passing into the lake is a flow. The contents of the lake can be measured without reference to a time dimension (e.g., in terms of millions of gallons). But the inflow of water must be put in terms of the amount per unit of time (e.g., in terms of millions of gallons per week or per day). Traffic on a highway has a stock and a flow counterpart. The number of autos on a particular stretch of roadway at some point in time is a stock; the number of autos passing under a bridge on the highway during some time interval is a flow. The number of units of good X purchased over a period of time is a flow; the inventories of good X held by producers at some point in time is a stock.

There is obviously a relation between stocks and flows. A stock may have different magnitudes at different points in time; the change in the value of a stock will constitute a flow, since such a change must be defined with reference to some time interval. The change in the volume of lake water over a week's time, the change in the number of autos on the roadway in an hour's time, the change in producer's inventories from one year to the next—all of these are flow variables requiring the specification of a unit of time.

In subsequent chapters, we shall be incorporating both stock and flow variables into our models of the economy. Each time we introduce a new variable into the analysis the student should take note of its classification as a flow or a stock. This procedure should aid in minimizing confusion as the analysis unfolds.

Endogenous and Exogenous Variables

In the course of our analysis, we shall make reference to variables as being endogenous or exogenous to the model under consideration. An exogenous variable is one whose value is assumed to be determined outside the model; that is, it is a variable whose value is presumed to be unaffected by the values of other variables in the model. On the other hand, an endogenous variable is one whose value is determined within the model, given the values of the relevant exogenous variables and given the relationships involved. It should be kept in mind that exogeneity (the characteristic of being exogenous) and endogeneity (the characteristic of being endogenous) are meaningful only in the context of a particular model. These are relative, rather than absolute, categorizations. It should also be apparent that the relegation of a variable into one of these two categories depends upon the scope of the model in question. If we were to specify a comprehensive model of the economy with the intention of describing all aspects of economic behavior, relatively few economic variables could be called truly "exogenous"; instead, almost every variable would be affected by some other variable in the system and would thus have to be characterized as "endogenous." At the other extreme, if we wanted to describe only one aspect of economic behavior, we might want to consider only one variable as "endogenous" and all the others as "exogenous." In general, we shall be concerned with cases lying between the two extremes. We shall begin with relatively simple models in which there are only a few endogenous variables. In order to focus on the determination of the values of these endogenous variables, we shall assume all others to be exogenous. Then, step by step, we shall expand our model to include successively more endogenous variables (and correspondingly, more relationships to "explain" them).

The reader might justifiably wonder why model-builders (the authors included) assume *any* variables to be exogenous. One fairly apparent reason for this convention is that the complexity of a model increases with the number of endogenous variables it contains. Each endogenous variable must be "explained" by an equation depicting its hypothesized relation to the other variables of the model. Thus, each model contains as many equations as it has endogenous variables. But no equations are needed to explain the values of the exogenous variables, insofar as these values are assumed to be determined outside of the model. Thus, some variables are often categorized as exogenous in an attempt to keep the model at a manageable size. This motive is especially important in the teaching of macroeconomics at the elementary and intermediate levels.

But pure simplification is not the only rationale underlying the assumption of exogeneity.[2] It is also very often the case that the builder of a particular model has no strong hypothesis as to the behavior of some variable in his model; lacking such a hypothesis, he may discretely assume that the value of the variable is unaffected by the other variables in the model. Or, one might wish to include in his model a variable which has its value determined by primarily noneconomic forces. For example, few economists would think of attempting to explain rainfall, even though rainfall can be predicted fairly well by scientific relations. Population growth (although probably affected somewhat by economic factors) is generally treated as an exogenous variable in economic models. Many variables fall into this type of classification in the sense that they affect economic activity but are not significantly affected by it. A third rationale is that an investigator may be interested only in one aspect (or a limited set of aspects) of economic behavior and may thus intentionally abstract from all other aspects. Thus, a model-builder attempting to focus on domestic economic behavior may take as exogenous the characteristics of foreign markets. If one of these rationales lies behind the assumption of exogeneity, then we often characterize the exogenous variable in question as datum (and the class of such exogenous variables as data).

In the course of our analysis, we shall dwell a great deal on another type of exogenous variable: instruments, or policy variables. These are variables whose values are assumed to be unaffected by the market mechanism itself, but which do fall under the control of policy authorities. Several examples come quickly to mind: the money supply, tax rates, government expenditures, tariff rates, import quotas, etc. Although the values of these variables are assumed to be given when

---

[2]For an excellent summary of the other reasons which follow, see Andreas G. Papandreou, *Fundamentals of Model Construction in Macroeconomics* Athens, Greece: (Center of Economic Research, 1962), chap. 3.

we derive the equilibrium values of the endogenous variables, we do take explicit recognition of the fact that their values are under the control of fiscal and monetary authorities. In fact, much of the controversy in macroeconomic literature has centered on the effects (on certain endogenous variables) of variations in the values of policy variables. One school of thought may contend that changes in the money supply have no impact on the level of income; others may argue that variation in government expenditures are impotent in inducing changes in income. As we shall see, the effects of policy actions (changes in the values of certain instruments) are dependent on the structure of the economy.

The endogenous variables of a model are also often divided into two subcategories: target variables and irrelevant variables. Target variables are those which are of special concern to the policy authorities; irrelevant variables, as the name would indicate, are those which are considered to have little direct importance by those people exercising economic policy.[3] One should not get the impression that there is necessarily anything intrinsic in an endogenous phenomenon which absolutely characterizes it as a target variable or an irrelevant variable. Each political administration has its own definition of the goals of the economy, and these can obviously vary from one administration to the next. Some of the variables more or less commonly accepted as target variables are the levels of income, employment and prices.

1.5 Types of Relationships Involved in Economic Models

So far we have defined an economic model to be a set of relationships among economic variables; but we have yet to explain the types of relationships with which we shall be concerned. We can distinguish four general classes of relations:

1. identities
2. behavioral relations
3. technical relations
4. equilibrium conditions

---

[3] This dichotomy between target variables and irrelevant variables is consistent with the jargon developed in the literature on economic policy. See, for instance, Papandreou, *Model Construction*, and Jan Tinbergen, *On the Theory of Economic Policy* (Amsterdam: North-Holland Publishing Co., 1966). Nevertheless, one could argue more generally that endogenous variables simply have various degrees of importance in the context of policy. The most important are singled out as target variables, and thus attract most of the attention of policymakers; the rest are assigned relatively little weight in the shaping of policy.

Identities

An identity is, quite simply, a definition. It is often useful to define one variable in terms of one or more other variables. Several examples from noneconomic analysis come to mind. A system of weights and measures, for instance, is just a system of identities relating units of measurements for weight and size. If we denote the unit "one foot" by the term F and the length "one inch" by I, we can write:

$$F \equiv 12I$$

which can be interpreted as saying that "one foot is defined to be equal to twelve inches." For another example, we could draw on micro theory by specifying the relationship between a firm's profits (P), total revenue (TR) and total cost (TC):

$$P \equiv TR - TC.$$

The above identity should be read as: "the level of profits is defined as total revenue minus total cost." Notice that we use the symbol ($\equiv$) to denote the term *is defined as*.

In devising an economic model, we need to establish certain "ground rules"; we use identities to establish the definitional relations among certain variables. The student should keep in mind that these identities are true for *any* values of the variables they involve. The relationships they embody are not contingent on behavior, technology or any other conditions.

Behavioral Relations

As is implied by the term, a behavioral relationship is one which describes a stimulus and a subsequent behavioral response. It suggests that one variable affects another through a process involving either an implicit or explicit decision by some individual or group of individuals. Behavioral equations, in short, incorporate our assumptions or speculations about the behavior of individuals. Suppose, for instance, that we are trying to describe the behavior of a consumer in a particular market. The decision as to how much of a good a person is willing to buy depends, *ceteris paribus*, upon the level of the price of that good. In a sense, the consumer receives a stimulus (the level of price) and, using some decision rule based, for example, on a process of utility maximization, determines his response (the amount he will purchase). Notice that some type of evaluation process is involved in the determination of an individual's demand function. Consequently, we categorize this function as a behavioral relationship between price and quantity demanded.

Another example can be found on the supply side of the market for some good. A producer operating in perfect competition receives a stimulus in the form of a market price. In response to this, he adjusts his output to the level he deems best, given the price in question. Again some evaluation of alternative responses is implied by the decision to choose some particular level of output. Some underlying motivation (e.g., profit maximization) generates the firm's supply relation. In this sense, a firm's supply equation is considered a behavioral relationship.

To generalize, a behavioral relation is one which implies a (rational) decision by some economic unit.[4] Given the general function:

$$y = f(x)$$

we could characterize this formulation as a behavioral relation if the value of the variable y is determined, through some behavioral response, by the value of x.

Technological Relations

Another class of economic relations can be categorized as technical, or technological, relationships. In this case, we specify that two or more variables are related through their physical properties. Any number of examples can be found in the physical sciences. For instance, Einstein's theory of relativity suggests that there is a technical relationship between energy (e), mass (m) and the speed of light (c) so that:

$$e = mc^2.$$

No decision process is involved in such a function; instead, mass and energy are related (via the speed of light) through their intrinsic physical properties. The law of gravity, Boyle's law, Bernoulli's law, Murphy's law (if anything can go wrong, it will)—all of these can be called technical relations.

One need not look only to the physical sciences for examples of technological relations; economic theory contains a few which are extremely important in model building. In economics, the most prominent example of a technical relation is the production function. In micro theory, we often specify that, given technology, the quantity of output produced by a firm (q) is related to the amounts of labor (n) and capital (k) used by that firm:

$$q = f(n, k).$$

---

[4]Some economic models are based on something called "limited rationality." We ignore this issue here in an attempt to avoid an extended philosophical discussion on the meaning of rationality in an economic context.

Again, no evaluation process lies behind the production function; once the amounts of labor and capital are given, the physical relationship between these inputs and output (given the state of technology) transfigures the amounts of inputs into the corresponding level of output.

Equilibrium Conditions

Although there are several ways of defining equilibrium, we shall adopt the one proposed by Fritz Machlup, who defines it as being "a constellation of selected interrelated variables so adjusted to one another that no inherent tendency to change prevails in the model which they constitute."[5]

There are several terms which should attract our attention immediately. First, equilibrium is defined in terms of a number of selected variables. This means that equilibrium is relevant only in the particular context of a set of variables chosen to be incorporated in the model in question. If this model is enlarged or truncated by increasing or decreasing the number of variables, then the statement of equilibrium may have to be modified to accommodate this change. The second characteristic of this definition is that the selected variables must also be interrelated. This implies that in equilibrium all the variables of the model must be simultaneously in a state of rest. Finally, these interrelated variables are adjusted to each other so that there is no inherent tendency for change. The implication of the term *inherent* is that this equilibrium, i.e., the balancing of the internal forces, occurs on the assumption that the values of the exogenous variables are given. Thus, for each set of values of the exogenous variables, there corresponds a distinct equilibrium or solution of the system. In view of the above, we can say then that an equilibrium condition is a constraint imposed on the model so that the values of the endogenous variables, given those of the exogenous, will be such that equilibrium will be satisfied.

1.6 Statics and Dynamics

Statics

In static analysis, attention is focused on the determination of equilibrium values of the endogenous variables. In a sense, the values of the

---

[5] F. Machlup, *Essays on Economic Semantics* (Englewood Cliffs, N.J.: Prentice-Hall, Inc., 1963).

exogenous variables are fed into the model and, together with the structural relationships comprising the model, determine a set of values for the endogenous variables. One of the structural relations will consist of a statement of an equilibrium condition; thus, the latter values will be equilibrium values.

If one of the exogenous variables changes in value, one can expect that the equilibrium values of at least some of the endogenous variables will also change. The analysis of such changes in equilibrium positions is referred to as comparative statics. By varying the value of a particular exogenous variable and observing the corresponding changes in the equilibrium values of each of the endogenous variables, we can obtain a feeling for the importance (both qualitatively and quantitatively) of the exogenous variable in question. Note that in comparative static analysis we ignore the path involved in moving from the old equilibrium to the new one; nor do we concern ourselves with the length of time passing during the period of adjustment.[6] The characteristics of the system in disequilibrium are not the province of static analysis.

It might prove useful at this point to offer an illustration of the use of static analysis. In doing so, we shall draw upon what should be the familiar body of microeconomic theory. Suppose that we define a market in which some good (X) is traded. Suppose further that the market is characterized by conditions of perfect competition, thus allowing us to define supply and demand relations. Let the workings of the market be described by the following equations:[7]

$$Q_D = f(p, Y) \qquad \text{(demand equation)}$$

$$Q_S = g(p) \qquad \text{(supply equation)}$$

$$Q_S = Q_D \qquad \text{(equilibrium condition)}$$

The first equation is the demand relation between quantity demanded (Q_D), the price of the good (p) and the level of consumers' income (Y). Traditionally, total consumer income is taken to be an exogenous variable in microeconomic analyses; the other two variables (Q_D and p) are considered endogenous. The second equation represents the supply relation between quantity supplied (Q_S) and the price of the good, both of which are endogenous to the model. Notice that both of these equa-

---

[6]In fact, as we shall see later, under some conditions, the system may not even tend toward a new set of equilibrium values. This issue involves an examination of dynamic analysis.

[7]Obviously, we have simplified the relations considerably in order to facilitate the presentation of an illustration designed to clarify, rather than complicate, the issues.

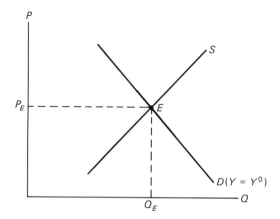

Figure 1.6.1 *Static Analysis*

tions are behavioral relations incorporating our assumptions or speculations in regard to the decision making on the part of consumers and
producers respectively. The third equation is an equilibrium condition
suggesting the values of the endogenous variables (Q_S, Q_D and p) will
come to rest when quantity demanded and quantity supplied are equal.
But the equilibrium values of quantity and price are dependent upon the
value assigned to the exogenous variable, Y. Once we have chosen (or
observed) the value of income, we can determine the values of quantity
and price which will satisfy the behavioral equations and the equilibrium condition of the market. The graphical analysis of this mechanism
should be familiar. In figure 1.6.1, we have sketched the demand
schedule (D) corresponding to a particular level of income, Y^0, and the
supply schedule (S). The equilibrium condition ($Q_D = Q_S$) is satisfied
at only one point in the diagram, point E. At E, we find the equilibrium
price (p_E) and quantity (Q_E) which would result from the model and
the given level of income. E is thus a static equilibrium position.

We could use the same model for an exercise in comparative statics. In
figure 1.6.2, we have sketched the supply schedule (S) and two demand
schedules: one (D) corresponding to the initial level of income (Y^0) and
the second (D') based upon a new, higher level of income (say, Y^1).
Notice that there are two equilibrium positions depicted—the initial
position at E and a new position at E'. The equilibrium values of price
and quantity change as the level of income changes. As is shown by the
diagram, an increase in income from Y^0 to Y^1 would cause the equilibrium price to rise from p_E to p'_E and the equilibrium quantity to increase

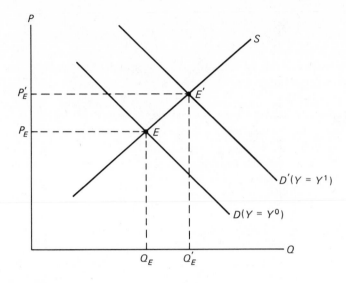

Figure 1.6.2   *Comparative Static Analysis*

from Q_E to Q'_E. The comparison of the two equilibrium positions constitutes a comparative static analysis of the effects of a change in income. Keep in mind that comparative static analysis tells us nothing about the behavior of the system in disequilibrium. In terms of the above analysis, we could tell nothing about the path which price and quantity would follow in moving from their initial equilibrium values (p_E and Q_E) to their eventual equilibrium values (p'_E and Q'_E) or the length of time this transition would require. In fact, static analysis cannot legitimately assure us that the new equilibrium will ever be reached!

Dynamics

As we pointed out earlier, dynamic analysis is concerned primarily with disequilibrium and change. It can be used to examine disequilibrium as well as equilibrium paths followed by the endogenous variables of the model.

Some dynamic models are specified in such a way as to focus on the behavior of certain phenomena in disequilibrium. With them, we can analyze the path taken by the endogenous variables over time as they move from an original equilibrium position to a new equilibrium position (if such a position exists). Or, if the initial equilibrium position remains fixed, we can use this type of dynamic model to determine the repercussions of a temporary departure from that equilibrium. In particular, we can examine the conditions under which the values of the endogenous variables will or will not return to their equilibrium values. If the system tends to move toward an equilibrium, we say that the equilibrium is stable; if such a tendency does not take place, we call the system unstable.

Perhaps an analogy from the physical sciences would yield an intuitive feeling for the meaning of stability and instability. Picture an experiment in which we place a marble in a salad bowl, and observe the marble at its place of rest (equilibrium position) at the bottom of the bowl. Presume that some outside force (your index finger) disturbs the marble's equilibrium by pushing it up the side of the bowl and then releasing it. The "system" (including the technological law of gravity) will tend to return the marble to its equilibrium position; thus, this equilibrium is stable. Now, change the experiment somewhat. Invert the salad bowl, placing it face down on a table. Place the marble (very carefully) on the top of the hump of the bowl in such a way that it is perfectly balanced. This, too, will be an equilibrium position, since there is no tendency for the marble to move in the absence of any outside force. Now, disturb this equilibrium by bumping the marble slightly. Notice that it will *not* return to its equilibrium position; thus, the equilibrium atop the bowl is unstable.

We can use our demand and supply model to illustrate the use of dynamic economic models in disequilibrium analysis. Until now, the demand and supply relations were specified without reference to time; all variables were implicitly presumed to be defined over the same time period. In order to make the model dynamic, we take recognition of the influence of time in the market place. Let's define a period of arbitrary length (say, one year) and denote the current period by the subscript t. The previous period will be signified by the subscript $t - 1$, the period before that by $t - 2$, etc. A subscript will be attached to each variable of the model and will refer to the period over which the variable in question is measured. Assume that consumers determine their current quantity demanded by considering the current market price and their current income (i.e., assume that there is no lag in the demand relation). Given this, we can write:

$$Q_t^D = f(p_t, Y_t)$$

where, as before, Y_t will be treated as an exogenous variable. But let's presume that there *is* a lag on the supply side of the market. In particular, suppose that it takes producers one full period to change their level of output, and that the quantity they produce this period is consequently determined by the *previous* period's price (p_{t-1}).[8] This would result in a supply function of the form:

$$Q_t^S = g(p_{t-1}).$$

To complete the model of the market, we can depict the equilibrium condition as the requirement that quantity demanded and quantity supplied be equal in each period, i.e.:

$$Q_t^D = Q_t^S.$$

Suppose that the level of income has been constant over several periods, and that both price and quantity have found their equilibrium levels at the intersection of the demand and supply schedules. This initial equilibrium position is depicted in figure 1.6.3 by point E, where price and quantity take on values p_0 and Q_0 respectively. Now, let's introduce a change in the system by allowing the level of income to increase in period 1. As this happens, the demand schedule shifts to the right to D', and the point of equilibrium moves to E'. The adjustment of the market to this point is not instantaneous, given the lagged response of quantity supplied to price changes. We can follow the time path of the endogenous variables (p and Q) by referring to the figure. In period 1, firms will produce Q_1 units of the good—the quantity supplied which corresponds to the previous period's price (p_0). But, given the new level of the demand schedule, producers can charge a price p_1 for the good (p_1 is the price consumers would be willing to pay at the level of output Q_1). Given this price, firms will produce Q_2 units of output in the second period (the output corresponding to p_1 along the supply schedule). But, as the transactions of the second period begin, producers will have to lower the price to p_2 in order to sell all they have produced. Because price is p_2 in the second period, firms produce only Q_3 in the third period; and this output can be sold at a price p_3. Insofar as the third period's price is p_3, producers will bring Q_4 to the market in the fourth period. This adjustment process continues through successive periods, and, according to the illustration, price and quantity converge to their new equilibrium values at point E'. Because the model results in a tendency to approach the new equilibrium, we can say that it (E') is a stable equilibrium. Had this tendency not been present, we would have characterized E' as an

---

[8]An interesting example is provided by agricultural markets. This year's harvest is dependent upon the price in existence before or during the planting season. Thus, the supply equation in these markets will embody the lag caused by the relevant gestation periods.

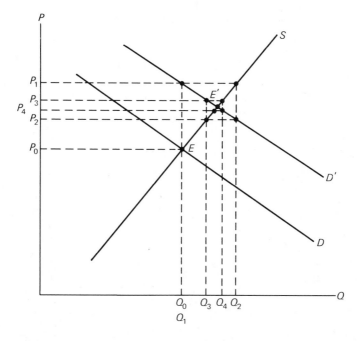

Figure 1.6.3 *Dynamic Analysis of Disequilibrium*

unstable equilibrium. (We shall not yet go through an illustration of an unstable equilibrium, but the curious student could rework the illustration presented above under the assumption that the supply schedule is much flatter than shown in figure 1.6.3.)

Notice carefully the mechanism through which the adjustment of price and quantity took place. Because of the lagged relationship between quantity supplied and price, each period's outcome depended on the outcome of the previous period. This link between the past and the present is the essence of dynamic analysis.

The student should not get the impression that dynamics is concerned only with disequilibrium analysis. Dynamic analysis also includes the specification and examination of models in which the endogenous variables take on a time path of equilibrium values. The study of balanced growth, for instance, is a dynamic analysis of the equilibrium time paths traced out by such critical variables as total income, employment, the stock of capital and other economic aggregates. In this type of model, we presume values (or time-streams of values) for the exogenous variables and examine the pattern of change exhibited by the endogenous variables under some equilibrium condition. We shall reserve further discussion of this use of dynamics until chapter 16, in which we take up the issue of economic growth.

1.7 Summary

It may be helpful at this point to synthesize our introductory comments by constructing an overview of a general economic model. Refer to figure 1.7.1 as a guide to the summary.

An economic model consists of a set of relationships among economic variables. Four types of relations can be distinguished: identities, which are definitional statements; technological relations, which are based on the physical properties of the variables; behavioral relations, which posit associations among variables based on evaluation by economic actors; and equilibrium conditions, which state the conditions under which the endogenous variables of the model have found their solution values.

Some of the variables contained in any economic model are considered exogenous, in the sense that their values are presumed to be determined outside of the model in question. These exogenous variables can be divided into instruments, or policy variables (those which are subject to the direct control of the authorities), and data (those which are beyond the control of the authorities). Both classes of exogenous variables can be further sorted into stocks and flows. The given values of all exogenous variables are substituted into the appropriate relations.

Given the values of the exogenous variables, the relationships in the model determine the equilibrium values of the endogenous variables (those variables whose values are determined within the model). Again, we can identify different classes of endogenous variables. Those we deem particularly important from a policy standpoint are referred to as target variables; those we deem relatively unimportant are called irrelevant variables. Both types of endogenous variables can include stocks and flows.

1.8 The Plan of Development

In order to set the tone for our theoretical development, a brief outline of the text is presented below. In the next chapter, we shall provide the student with an analysis of the aggregate identities used in macro-economics. We shall present there a brief analysis of the system of national income accounts used to define each of our economic variables.

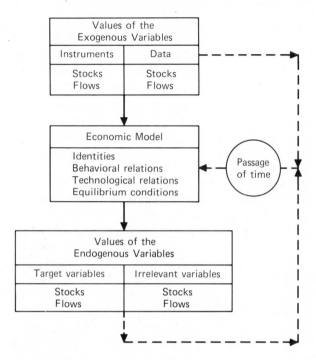

Figure 1.7.1 *Summary Analysis*

In chapter 3, an extremely simple model of the economy is developed and analyzed. The primary purpose of the discussion presented there is to introduce the student to the characteristics of a model in the context of macroeconomics. One aspect of this analysis is the specification of the conditions for and meaning of a product-market equilibrium. The model is then extended in chapter 4 to include the effects of government revenues and expenditures. Because of the inclusion of these instruments in the model, we are able to offer a "first view" of the rationale behind fiscal policy.

The analysis is further sophisticated in chapter 5, where we allow for the influence of interest rates on the level of investment. Given this extension of the model, the nature of product-market equilibrium is restated. In chapter 6, we turn to an investigation of the money market, concentrating on the determination of the demand for money. Using the results of that exposition, money-market equilibrium is defined and illustrated, and the concept of monetary policy is introduced. Then, in chapter 7, the conditions of product-market and money-market equilibrium are combined in order to establish an analysis of a general equilibrium of economic activity. With this new two-market framework, the impact of monetary and fiscal policy is reexamined. The analysis is extended in chapter 8, in which we attempt to reinforce understanding of the model by examining its extreme properties. More explicitly we consider the nature of equilibrium when it occurs at extremely low and, alternatively, extremely high levels of the rate of interest. Most importantly, we analyze the efficiency of monetary and fiscal policy under these alternative conditions.

In chapter 9, we introduce the labor market into the model. In that exposition, we consider the establishment of equilibrium values for employment and wages under alternative assumptions about the behavior of wage earners and the structural characteristics of the labor market. We concentrate there on the critical issues of whether or not full employment is an automatic and inevitable result of the labor-market mechanism.

In chapter 10, we discuss the key structural differences between the classical and Keynesian models. Then, in chapter 11, we develop the full Keynesian model, encompassing product-, money-, and labor-markets, and reexamine the impact of alternative monetary and fiscal policies.

Chapters 12, 13, 14 and 15 consider some of the recent contributions to macroeconomic theory. In chapter 12, we deal with some of the major works in the area of consumer behavior, focusing on the relative income, permanent income and life-cycle hypotheses. Chapter 13 presents a survey of some of the basic theories of investment behavior. In chapter 14, we discuss some of the modern theories of the demand for money. Then, in chapter 15 and appendix 15.A, we examine some of the basic writings of the monetarist school of thought.

In chapter 16 we relax the assumption that the economy is a closed system and examine its properties in an international environment. The conditions surrounding economic growth are investigated in chapter 17. A few simplified growth models are used to illustrate the process of balanced growth, and some attention is paid to the role of economic policy in obtaining an optimal rate of growth.

Chapter 18 offers a discussion of the nature and causes of inflation. In it, we analyze both "cost-push" and "demand-pull" theories and attempt to relate them to the appropriate policy dicta. Moreover, we consider the use of manpower programs and wage-price controls as means of alleviating inflation.

Suggested Further Reading

Fox, K. A.; Sengupta, J. K.; and Thorbecke, E. *The Theory of Quantitative Economic Policy with Applications to Economic Growth and Stabilization.* Amsterdam: North-Holland, 1966, chap. 1, pp. 3–19.

Frisch, R. "From National Accounts to Macroeconomic Decision Models." In *Income and Wealth,* series N4. International Association for Research in Income and Wealth. Edited by T. Gilbert and R. Stone. London: Bowes and Bowes, 1955, pp. 1–24.

Hansen, B. *Economic Theory and Fiscal Policy.* Translated by P. E. Burke. London: George Allen and Unwin, 1958, chap. 1, pp. 3–30.

Johansen, L. *Public Economics.* Chicago: Rand McNally, 1965, chaps. 1–3.

Tinbergen, J. *Economic Policy: Principles and Design.* Amsterdam: North-Holland, 1956.

————. *On the Theory of Economic Policy.* Amsterdam: North-Holland, 1952.

ALBRIGHT COLLEGE LIBRARY   159275

CHAPTER 2

National Income Accounting

2.1 Introduction

Throughout the analysis presented in this text, we shall investigate the properties of alternative macroeconomic models. These frameworks will differ from each other (sometimes considerably) due to the underlying differences in the assumptions or hypotheses on which they are based. Economic theory has evolved over the years through a process by which hypotheses are proposed, their theoretical merits are debated and actual data are used to test their validity. If we have two or more hypotheses purporting to explain the same aspect of economic behavior, the process of evaluation must be applied uniformly to each alternative.

Every economic model must be accompanied by a set of implicit or explicit definitions of terms to be used; otherwise, it would be extremely difficult to comment on the merits of that model. It should not be difficult to see that any analysis which deals with a number of economic models is greatly facilitated if the constructs in question are based on the same definitions of terms. In colloquial terms, it is extremely useful for the process of comparison and evaluation if all model-builders "speak the same language."

As we pointed out in the previous chapter, an identity is a type of definition, in that it defines one variable in terms of others. The field of macroeconomic accounting is concerned with the establishment of a full system of accounting relationships, or identities, linking together a complex of macroeconomic variables. Fortunately, there exists a standard and universally accepted system of accounts pertaining to the economic activity of the United States. Formulated and published by the U.S. Department of Commerce, the *National Income and Product Accounts* presents a comprehensive and extremely intricate overview of the flows of activity generated by the various sectors of the economy. These national accounts aid the development of macro theory in two important ways. First, they provide a standard set of identities which can be used by macro theorists in the formulation of economic models. In a sense, the accounts offer a superstructure of accounting relationships onto which the theorist can hang his hypotheses concerning economic behavior. Second, the accounts contain an invaluable source of data which can be used to test alternative economic theories. Because of the definitional value of the national income and product accounts, we shall devote most of this chapter to an explanation of the identities they contain.

The actual national income accounts maintained by the U.S. Department of Commerce are far more complex and detailed than those which will be discussed in the multisector models developed below. Our major purpose is to evolve a system of identities which can be employed throughout the text in helping to explain the relationships embodied in alternative economic theories. In that we shall be dealing with relatively basic models of the economy, we shall present the national accounts in correspondingly simplified form. To lean toward the side of simplicity, though, in no sense vitiates the usefulness of the identities derived. In fact, one might effectively argue that the given treatment of the national income accounts approximates that treatment actually desired by the Department of Commerce. The real world, with its complexities and encompassing subsectors delineated by penumbras rather than by distinct lines, proves a major obstacle to such an idealized approach. Thus, the student who desires a more thorough discussion of the actual national income accounts should refer to other sources.[1] On the other hand, we do hope to serve the needs of the student content with learning the quintessence of the accounts and the general procedures behind them.

In the next section, we shall attempt to offer an intuitive explanation of the meaning of some alternative measures of total business activity. Then, with these concepts in mind, we shall turn to an investigation of formal national accounting systems.

We begin by defining four sectors of the economy: the household, business, government and foreign sectors. We shall organize our development of the national accounts into three stages. In the first, we ignore

---

[1] For more detailed analyses of the national income accounts, see G. Ackley, *Macroeconomic Theory* (New York: Macmillan, 1961), chap. 3; and E. Shapiro, *Macroeconomic Analysis,* 3d ed. (New York: Harcourt, Brace and World, 1974), chap. 5.

governmental economic activities (both expenditures and taxes) and international trade and focus on the interaction between the household and business sectors of the economy. In the second stage, we include governmental expenditures and revenues explicitly in the accounting framework. The result is a three-sector accounting framework. Then, finally, we expand the analysis into a four-sector framework by recognizing the existence of international trade (transactions between the domestic economy and the "rest-of-the world" sector).

2.2 Variants of National Income and Product

As the name suggests, the national income and product accounts are concerned in part with the measurement of the aggregate level of production and the flow of factor income it generates. The overall volume of business activity—whether measured by production or factor income—is important from the standpoint of economic policy. In the phraseology of the previous chapter, national income (product) is generally considered to be a target variable. It is ordained as such because it is considered an indirect—although imperfect—indicator of the economy's state of material well-being. Certainly, high production is only one of many goals, and it is often accompanied by adverse by-products (inflation, pollution, etc.), but we shall have to return to these considerations later. For now, it seems sufficient to argue that the volume of business activity is important enough to measure and to analyze in a theoretical framework.

The term *national income and product* is a generic one in the sense that it denotes a class of measures of the flow of economic activity over some period of time. The specific measures with which we shall deal are called: gross national product (GNP), net national product (NNP), national income proper (NI), personal income (PI) and disposable personal income (DPI). In what follows, we shall attempt to give the student a general feeling for the conceptual differences among these alternative indicators.

Gross national product is defined to be the total volume of output of final goods and services, generally specified over the period of one year. Two types of "final" goods and services are included in the computation: those used to satisfy immediate needs and wants (consumption goods and services) and those used to add to the nation's stock of physical capital (capital goods).

Capital goods can be further divided into two categories: fixed capital, consisting of plant and equipment; and inventories of both finished and unfinished goods. The existence of inventories is a necessity for the operation of most firms, in that they act as a buffer between customer demands and the limitations on production (especially over short periods). Any change in the level of inventories is treated as investment, whether it is intended or unintended (i.e., whether firms changed the inventory stocks intentionally or an unexpected excess or deficiency of production relative to sales caused inventories to rise or fall from some desired level). Given the possibility of discrepancies between production and sales made possible by inventory accumulation or depletion, it becomes necessary to point out that national product figures are based on production rather than sales.

In that any diversified economy engages in the production of a whole array of goods and services, it is necessary to find some way of aggregating over these individual items to derive a total measure. In particular, we must be able to add cars and sewing machines and apples and oranges. With some exceptions (to be explained later), each item is weighted by its market price. That is, we take the number of units of each good, multiply this by the market price of the good and sum over all goods produced in the economy. The rationale for the use of market prices as weights is that they denote the importance, or intrinsic worth, of each good relative to others. Thus, a $2,000 car is presumed to be ten times as important as a $200 sewing machine, and a $20 watch is assumed twice as important as a $10 toaster. The process of weighting by market prices results in an aggregate of the total value of final goods and services (note that the number of units of a good, multiplied times its price, yields the value of production of the good in question).

Net national product is generally considered to be a more meaningful measure of economic activity than its counterpart, GNP. As we pointed out above, gross national product includes the value of output of consumption goods and investment goods. But the process of production uses up a certain amount of fixed capital. Some physical equipment wears out and dies a natural death of old age; other components of the capital stock are damaged or destroyed; still others are rendered obsolete through the process of technological change. This process is termed depreciation. The main reason for including the production of capital goods in any measure of final output is that this type of production adds to the community's stock of real wealth (even though capital goods are not final in the same sense as consumption goods). Thus, it would seem logical to deduct the amount by which fixed capital depreciates over the period from the amount produced to arrive at a measure of the *net* increase in the stock of capital. Unfortunately, we do not have a decent measure of the physical depreciation of the capital stock; thus, we are forced to use a proxy for it. Firms do report the total amount of funds placed in reserves for the replacement of existing capital. The amount so designated is called "capital-consumption allowances." Although there may be a distinct discrepancy between the rate at which capital actually wears out or becomes obsolete and the rate at which firms add to their replacement reserves, we use the latter as an indicator of the former. Thus, the transformation of gross national product into net national product is reflected in the identity:

$$NNP \equiv GNP - D$$

where D is depreciation, measured indirectly through the use of capital consumption allowances. For future purposes, it is important to keep in mind, then, that: gross national product is the total value of all consumption and investment goods produced; net national product is the total value of consumption goods produced plus the net addition to the aggregate capital stock.

The third measure of aggregate production is called national income proper (the term *proper* is used to distinguish this specific measure from the generic term *national income and product*). We know that output requires the services of factors of production: land, labor, capital and entrepreneurs. Insofar as the act of production generates factor income, we should be able to measure the value of final output in terms of the factor income it creates. Accordingly, the Department of Commerce computes national income as the income earned through participation in the production process: wages (inclusive of fringe benefits), interest, rents and profits.[2]

Notice that depreciation allowances are not included in the measure; thus, national income corresponds conceptually to net national product. But there are several reasons why national income differs from net national product. First, the market prices used to evaluate output for the purposes of computing net and gross national product include indirect business taxes (excise and sales taxes); this part of the receipts does not get allocated to factor payments, and is thus not included in national income. Second, firms often devote some funds to business transfers. Transfer payments, in general terms, are payments unassociated with the production of goods or services. If a firm contributes

---

[2]Notice carefully that profits are treated as factor payments in the context of this discussion.

$1,000 to a college, this transaction is registered in the national accounts under business transfers. Third, some firms make factor payments through the use of funds secured from some source other than the sale of output. Most important in this respect are government subsidies to private firms. In many agricultural industries, for example, farmers are paid subsidies to cover costs not recovered from the sale of their output. In this case, national product would include the sales of such industries, whereas national income would include the factor payments (some of which are financed by sales receipts, the rest of which comes from the government transfer).

It should be kept in mind that net national product and national income are both designed to measure the same phenomenon: the final output of the economy. However, the product approach implies the use of market prices for evaluation of output and the national income approach relies on the use of factor payments. As a consequence, national income is often called "total output evaluated at factor prices" and net national product is referred to as "total output evaluated at market prices."

Another concept found in the national accounts is personal income. Whereas gross national product, net national product and national income are all measures of final output, personal income is not. Personal income is simply a measure of the income received by noncorporate entities, regardless of whether or not the income is derived from the provision of factor services. For instance, undistributed corporate profits—the profits made by corporations but not distributed to shareholders in the form of dividends—are excluded from personal income. In addition, business contributions to employees' social security programs (captured in national income in the category of fringe benefits) are deducted on the grounds that they do not constitute present income. However, social security payments to individuals, as well as all other transfer payments from government and business to individuals, are included in personal income (but not in national income, insofar as these transfer payments are not made on the basis of present factor services).

The last variant of income to be considered is disposable personal income. This figure is designed to indicate the amount of income private (noncorporate) individuals actually have to spend or save. In order to derive disposable personal income, we simply subtract from personal income all personal tax payments. Disposable personal income can be further split into the two uses to which it can be put: consumption and saving. This allocation will be a central relationship in our later analysis.

2.3 Computation of National Income and Product

In the conceptual framework outlined above, we pointed out that the two measures of national product (gross national product and net national product) are intended to be valuations of the production of only *final* goods and services. This section deals with some of the problems and approaches involved in measuring the value of final production. To begin, we should remind the reader that the production of a final good often requires several stages of operation, each stage entailing the services of a particular set of firms. Most final goods are the end result of a series of transactions within the business sector which involve purchases of intermediate goods by some firms from others. Intermediate goods are those items which are not sold directly in the form of consumption or capital goods; they are, in some sense, unfinished goods which are used up in the production of other goods.

The stages of production can be illustrated by a specific example. The production of an automobile actually starts in industries which produce raw materials (e.g., iron ore, rubber, sand, hides, etc.) and proceeds through industries which refine these raw materials in some way to make semifinished products (sheet steel, tires, windows, leather upholstery, etc.); then finally, all of these semifinished goods are combined by auto-motive firms to yield the final product (an automobile).

Summation of the value of production of all firms taking part in the various stages of this process would not be an appropriate way of measuring national product, in that the value of goods produced at the earlier stages of production (e.g., those stages preceding the assembly of the autos) would be double-counted. In terms of the above example, the sales of raw materials to producers of semifinished goods and the subsequent sales of these goods to automotive companies would be counted in national product more than once. The value of an automobile already includes the value of the raw materials and semifinished goods used in its production. If we were to add the value of production of rubber, iron ore, sand, hides, sheet steel, tires, windows, upholstery and autos, we would obtain a gross overstatement of the value of final goods generated by the part of the economy comprised of all these firms.

In practice, there are two basic approaches to the evaluation of national product. The first alternative is to count only the value of production of firms producing final goods (those which have undergone the final stage of processing), excluding completely the value of production of firms producing intermediate goods (those which have not completed final processing). A second approach involves the summation of the value-added contributed by every firm in the economy. A firm's

Table 2.3.1.　*Value-Added Calculation*

Payments & Receipts	Wages (Labor)	Rent (Land)	Depreciation & Interest (Capital)	Purchases of Intermediate goods	Profits	Sales	Value-Added
Stages							
Stage I (Firm I) Raw Materials	$125	$ 20	$ 50	$ 0	$ 20	$ 215	$215
Stage II (Firm II) Semi-finished Good	175	15	70	215	25	500	285
Stage III (Firm III) Final Good	200	65	80	500	55	900	400
Totals	$500	$100	$200	$715	$100	$1615	$900
			TOTAL FACTOR PAYMENTS = 900				

value-added is defined as the total value of its production less its purchases of materials (raw and semiprocessed goods, or intermediate goods).

In order to explain the computation of national product, we shall construct a hypothetical case in which we view the activities of three firms, each one engaged in a different stage of production. Assume the following chain of production: the first firm produces a raw material; the second firm buys the raw material (and no others), processes it and sells it to a third firm; the third firm buys the semifinished good (and no others) and transforms it into a final product. Assume also that there are no taxes paid by the firms in question and no transfer payments to or from any of the firms. To further simplify the illustration, presume that all goods currently produced are sold (i.e., that there is no depletion or accumulation of inventories). Under these conditions, we can describe the activities of our three firms by the information given in table 2.3.1.

Referring to the column headings in table 2.3.1, note that each firm uses the three basic factors of production (labor, land and capital) and thus disburses payments to the owners of these factors. Profits, too, are considered factor payments in that they constitute a reward for entrepreneurial services. The other business expense listed in the table is the total value of purchases of intermediate goods. In our example, these are simply purchases by one firm from the firm preceding it in the three stages of production. The value of each firm's total sales (or, under the assumption that inventories are constant, the value of each firm's total product) is listed in the next column. Then, in the last column, we have depicted each firm's value-added; this figure is computed as the difference between total sales and purchases of intermediate goods.

In stage I, raw materials are produced. This type of production is assumed to require no intermediate goods; thus, the firm operating at this stage purchases nothing from the other firms.[3] It does, however, hire the services of land, labor and capital and makes total factor payments of $195 to them. When the raw material is sold to the firm operating in stage II, the producer of the raw material receives sales income of $215. Given total sales and the total cost, the firm makes a profit equal to the difference, or $20. In that this firm purchased no intermediate goods, its value-added is equal to its sales ($215).

The firm in stage II purchases the raw material at a cost of $215 and refines it in some way. This, too, requires factor services, and the firm pays the owners of land, labor and capital a total of $260. The semifinished good is then sold to firm III for a total sales amount of $500. Profit, the residual between total expenses and total sales, is thus $25 for the firm in question. The value-added in stage II is the difference between sales of the semifinished good and the purchases of materials used in its production. Conceptually, it is a measure of the "enhancement" of the good derived from the processing which takes place in stage II. In this example, the value-added in stage II would be $285(=$500 − $215).

In stage III, the final processing takes place. Firm III purchases the semiprocessed good from firm II, thus incurring an expense of $500. Then, in order to put the good in its final form, the firm operating in stage III applies the services of land, labor and capital. Its payments to these factors sums to $345. Taking into account these factor costs and the cost of procuring the semifinished good, the firm's total expenses are $845. Presuming that the sale of the final product yields $900 in total revenue, firm III makes a profit of $55. The value-added contributed by

---

[3]This firm would, of course, purchase capital goods from other firms; however, capital goods are treated as final goods in the national income and product accounts. We refer here to the fact that the raw-materials producer will use no other materials in the generation of his output.

stage III is, again, the residual between total sales and materials cost, or $400(=$900 − $500).

Suppose that we want to summarize the business activity involved in this three-stage production process by computing the gross national product it generates. If we sum the sales of all three firms, we find that total transactions amount to $1,615. But this figure overstages GNP, in that it double-counts the values of the raw material and the semi-finished good. The price of the final product includes the cost of the semiprocessed good, and the price of the latter good includes the cost of the raw material. Thus, we need to find a way of eliminating this redundancy in our computation. The most direct procedure would be to restrict our attention to the market value of the final good produced in stage III. Using the sales of this product, we derive the result that GNP = $900. An alternative approach would be to take the sum of the value-added over all stages of production. More specifically, we would sum the value-added of the firm in stage I ($215), the value-added of the second firm ($285) and the value-added in stage III ($400). As we would expect, the total of these three figures would be $900 — the exact amount derived through the previous approach. The consistency of these two approaches stems from the fact that the value of the final product consists of the value of materials, the value-added contributed by firms in stage II and the additional value generated through the completion of the process in stage III.

Given the simplifying assumptions underlying table 2.3.1, we could also use another approach to measuring GNP. Notice that, in each stage, value-added is exactly matched by the sum of wages, rent, interest, depreciation, and profits. It can be shown quite easily that this is no accident. First, recall that each firm's value-added is defined by the identity:

Value added ≡ Sales − Purchases of intermediate goods.

We have also implicitly defined profits by the identity:

Profits ≡ Sales − (Wages + Rent + Interest + Depreciation)

− Purchases of intermediate goods.

If we add wages, rent, interest and depreciation to both sides of the above identity, we obtain:

Wages + Rent + Interest + Depreciation + Profits ≡ Sales
− Purchases of intermediate goods.

Table 2.3.2.   *Consolidated Business Account*

Expenses		Receipts	
Wages	$500	Sales of Final Products	$900
Rent	100		
Depreciation and Interest	200		
Profits	100		
Total	$900	Total	$900

Notice, then, that according to the first and third relations, value-added in each stage of production is reflected (exactly, by definition) in the sum of factor payments. This discussion leads to the conclusion that GNP can also be computed in our simple model as the sum of factor payments made in each stage of production. According to table 2.3.1, total wage payments are $500, total rent is $100, total interest and depreciation is $200 and total profits are $100. The sum of these values is $900, the exact figure yielded by the other two approaches.[4]

In the following sections, we shall describe the business sector through the use of a consolidated income statement. This is an accounting summary of the transactions between the business sector and other sectors of the economy; it excludes transactions within the business sector. More pointedly, the consolidated business account excludes sales and purchases of intermediate goods and lists instead only sales of final goods. In terms of the above example, the consolidated business account would look like the one presented in table 2.3.2. The student should analyze this version and compare it to the totals listed in table 2.3.1.

2.4 National Accounts for a Two-Sector Economy

Let us imagine an economy neatly divided into a household, or personal, sector, and a business sector. The government is assumed to engage in no

---

[4]In practice, there are several complicating factors which come into play with this approach. The existence of business transfers, indirect and direct business taxes, and a host of other variables would have to be used to adjust actual factor payments in order to obtain a value for GNP with this approach. These complications are assumed away in the present analysis.

economic transactions whatsoever, and the economy is presumed to engage in no international trade. We further assume the following:

1. all production occurs in the business sector;
2. all business firms are incorporated;
3. businesses make no transfer payments to the household sector (i.e., all payments from business to households consist of factor income).

The two sectors interact through their respective roles in production. Households supply factors of production to the business sector and, in return, receive income payments from businesses. The factor income earned in production is then allocated between consumption expenditures (which constitute business income) and saving. This interaction is described in more detail below.

Our system of national income accounts for the hypothetical two-sector economy encompasses two interlocking income statements: one for the household sector and one for the business sector. We have added a third statement which summarizes the composition of and totals for saving and investment. The student will find that saving and investment are two extremely important variables in aggregate economic analysis, and that the special attention shown them here is well justified.

Before proceeding to construct these accounting statements, a brief explanation of the mechanics of income statements should prove helpful. Our income statements will be structured in traditional T-account form with receipts appearing on the right-hand side as credits and with costs, or expenditures, registered on the left-hand side as debits. Saving will serve on the debit side as a balancing or residual item for both the household-sector and the business-sector statements. One other preliminary word of advice is in order: in that we are dealing with a closed economy, every explicit outlay of one sector must appear as a receipt of the other sector. This point will become more apparent as we dissect the accounts.

Refer to table 2.4.1, where we have depicted the breakdown of business activity for the business sector. According to the figures presented in table 2.4.1, the business sector produced final goods and services equal in value to $67 million. This value of final product is broken down into the sales of consumption goods ($57 million), the sales of investment or capital goods ($8 million) and the increase in inventories ($2 million).

A brief digression on terminology is needed here. When we speak about "investment" in this and subsequent chapters, we refer to the sum

Table 2.4.1. *Two-Sector Accounts*

Household Sector

Debits		Credits	
Personal consumption	57	Wages	41
		Rents	10
Personal saving	4	Interest	8
		Dividends	2
Total charges against household receipts	61	Total receipts	61

Business Sector

Debits		Credits	
Wages	41	Personal consumption	57
Rents	10	Gross investment in fixed capital	8
Interest	8		
Depreciation	2	Change in inventories	2
Profits Dividends 2	6		
Retained earnings 4			
Total charges against final product	67	Total value of final product	67
Gross business saving	6		
Net business saving	4		

National Saving and Investment

Saving		Investment	
Personal saving	4	Gross investment in fixed capital	8
Gross business saving	6	Change in inventories	2
Gross saving	10	Gross investment	10
Net saving	8	Net investment	8

of inventory changes and purchases of new plant and equipment.[5] Plant and equipment will be called "fixed capital"; correspondingly, the purchase of fixed capital will be called "fixed investment." Both types (the narrow version implied by "fixed investment" and the broader type called "investment") will have net and gross counterparts.[6]

The production of $67 million worth of final goods and services lead the business sector to incur certain costs. These costs are depicted on the debit side of the ledger in the form of: wages ($41 million), rent ($10 million), interest payments ($8 million) and depreciation ($2 million). Profits were made during the period, and totaled $6 million.[7] Of this amount, part was given out to the shareholders in the form of dividends ($2 million) and the rest was kept as retained earnings ($4 million). Notice that, as a result of the inclusion of profits as a residual on the debit side, total credits and total debits are equal to each other.

The debits on the business accounts can be divided into outlays and saving. Net business saving is just retained earnings, which are defined to be the amount of income retained by the business sector after all deductions for factor payments (wages, interest, rent and depreciation) and dividend payments. According to the data contained above, net business saving is equal to $4 million. An associated term, gross business saving, is defined to be the sum of net business saving and depreciation. The latter concept reflects the fact that depreciation expenses do constitute a type of saving in the sense that they constitute income put aside for future replacement of capital goods. Given our figures, gross business saving would be equal to $6 million (net business saving of $4 million plus depreciation of $2 million). We have registered the amount of net and gross business saving in the T-account describing national saving and investment, and shall return to it later.

---

[5] The change in inventories is treated as investment to take account of the fact that inventories can be translated into sales of finished goods in some future period. The creation of additional inventories results from production (and hence factor payments) which will be recaptured in the form of sales receipts in some subsequent period.

[6] New residential construction is included as part of investment in the actual national income and product accounts. The rationale for this treatment is that residential housing constitutes a type of capital, in that it is used to generate housing services over a number of years. We ignore this type of investment in our discussion. An associated point is that the Department of Commerce includes in personal income an estimate of imputed rental income accruing to householders living in homes they own. Again, we have ignored this component in order to simplify the analysis.

[7] Profits as shown in table 2.4.1 do not correspond to the residual of sales minus factor costs. Instead, they are computed as the value of final product less factor costs. In other words, the change in the value of inventories is treated as business income and is used correspondingly in the computation of profits.

Now consider the credit side of the household-sector account. Notice that the income of the household sector consists of factor payments, including dividends.[8] Or, put another way, the income of the household sector comprises all of the debits of the business sector except gross business saving. Summing over wages, interest payments, rental income and dividend receipts, we find that household income is equal to $61 million. The disposition of household income is displayed by the debit side of that sector's ledger. In particular, note that personal consumption expenditures account for $57 million and the remainder, called personal saving, is recorded as $4 million. Since personal saving is defined as the residual between household income and personal consumption expenditures, total charges against household receipts equal total household receipts.

Notice that the consumption expenditures of the household sector appear as income in the business sector accounts. Some of the payments disbursed to factors thus return to business in the form of consumption purchases. Personal saving is also reflected in the business accounts, although in a subtle way. The business sector produced $67 million worth of final goods and services; $57 million dollars worth of these goods were purchased by households through consumption expenditures, thus leaving $10 million worth still unsold. This latter figure corresponds to the sum of two items: the part of business income retained in the form of gross business savings and thus never reaching the hands of the householders; and that part of factor payments received by the household sector but retained in the form of personal saving. These two savings components are thus that part of the value of total product which is not returned to the business sector through consumption purchases. But total savings (business plus personal) are partially returned to the business sector by purchases of fixed capital ($8 million). The remainder (total value of final product less consumption expenditures and expenditures on fixed capital) *must* appear as the change in inventories. Thus, business and personal saving will be exactly and identically matched by the sum of gross investment in fixed capital and the change in business inventories.

---

[8] See Ackley, *Macroeconomic Theory*, pp. 53–55. In the actual national-income accounts, interest income of the household sector represents a net figure. Payments of interest by the household sector to the business sector comprise a form of consumption spending. The business sector, on the other hand, makes interest payments to the household sector for the use of borrowed funds, but double counting is averted since interest outpayments of the business sector are netted against interest receipts from the household sector. Considerations of intrasector interest payments are omitted from our analysis.

This notion is shown more directly by the national saving and investment summary contained in table 2.4.1. On the saving side, we have personal saving ($4 million) and gross business saving ($6 million), the sum of which is gross national saving ($10 million). This amount is matched on the investment side by gross investment in fixed capital ($8 million) and the change in business inventories ($2 million). Notice that we can also verify that net national saving, defined as the sum of personal saving plus net business saving, is equal to net investment (gross investment less depreciation). These quantities are true by definition; they are *made* to be true by the inclusion of inventory changes in the computation of actual investment.

We now proceed to a more formal definition of the national income and product concepts outlined earlier. We shall use the following set of symbols in the specification of the various identities:

$$\text{GNP} \equiv \text{gross national product}$$
$$\text{NNP} \equiv \text{net national product}$$
$$\text{NI} \equiv \text{national income (proper)}$$
$$\text{PI} \equiv \text{personal income}$$
$$\text{DPI} \equiv \text{disposable personal income}$$
$$\text{C} \equiv \text{personal consumption expenditures}$$
$$S_p \equiv \text{personal saving}$$
$$S_b \equiv \text{net business saving}$$
$$\text{Pr} \equiv \text{business profits}$$
$$\text{D} \equiv \text{Depreciation}$$
$$\text{W} \equiv \text{wages}$$
$$\text{R} \equiv \text{rent}$$
$$i \equiv \text{interest payments}$$
$$\text{Dv} \equiv \text{dividends}$$
$$I_g^f \equiv \text{gross investment in fixed capital}$$
$$\Delta\text{H} \equiv \text{change in inventories}$$
$$I_g \equiv \text{total gross investment} \equiv I_g^f + \Delta\text{H}$$
$$I^f \equiv \text{net investment in fixed capital}$$
$$I \equiv \text{total net investment} \equiv I^f + \Delta\text{H}$$

The student should study these notations carefully before proceeding.

We begin with gross national product, which was defined earlier as the value of final product generated by the business sector over the period in question. In our two-sector model, final product consists of consumption goods sold, investment in fixed capital and the change in inventories. Thus, gross national product is given by the identity:

$$\text{GNP} \equiv C + I_g \qquad \text{where} \qquad I_g \equiv I + D \qquad (2.4.1)$$

or

$$\text{GNP} \equiv C + (I + D). \qquad (2.4.2)$$

And, as we illustrated earlier, gross national product can also be defined in terms of factor payments as:

$$\text{GNP} \equiv W + R + i + Pr + D. \qquad (2.4.3)$$

Be careful to note that depreciation allowances are included as a factor payment, although this disbursement is not paid to the household sector; correspondingly, part of business profits (retained earnings) does not become translated into household income.

Net national product, as we pointed out before, is equal to gross national product less depreciation. In our two-sector model, net national product is thus defined from the product side as:

$$\text{NNP} \equiv \text{GNP} - D \qquad (2.4.4)$$

or: $\text{NNP} \equiv C + I.$ \qquad (2.4.5)

From the factor-income side, we can also define NNP with the identity:

$$\text{NNP} \equiv W + R + i + S_b + Dv \qquad (2.4.6)$$

or $\text{NNP} \equiv W + R + i + Pr$ where $Pr \equiv S_b + Dv$ \qquad (2.4.7)

which gives net national product as the sum of all factor payments except depreciation. Keep in mind that the validity of this identity (and the others presented above) is contingent on our assumption of no government economic activity.

In the two-sector model, there are no indirect business taxes and no government transfers to business, so it makes no difference whether we evaluate production in market prices or in factor prices. Consequently, national income is identical in this model to net national product: i.e.,

$$\text{NI} \equiv \text{NNP} \equiv W + R + i + Pr. \qquad (2.4.8)$$

Whereas national income measures total product evaluated in factor prices, personal income includes only that income received by the household sector. But we have eliminated social security taxes corporate income taxes, and all types of transfer payments from consideration; hence, personal income will differ from national income and net national product only by the amount of business saving. More specifically, we have:

$$PI \equiv NI - S_b \tag{2.4.9}$$

or $\quad PI \equiv W + R + i + Dv.$ (2.4.10)

Finally, disposable personal income was conceptualized earlier as that part of personal income which is left in the hands of the household sector after all personal taxes. But, in the absence of taxes, we have:

$$DPI \equiv PI \equiv W + R + i + Dv. \tag{2.4.11}$$

And, as we pointed out previously, disposable personal income is exhausted by the sum of personal consumption expenditures and personal saving:

$$DPI \equiv C + S_p. \tag{2.4.12}$$

A Special Case for the Two-Sector Model

Even in the highly simplified two-sector model described above, several accounting relationships can be found. To most readers, a quick glance at the series of identities listed above will undoubtedly reveal what seems to be an overwhelming mass of equations and variables. Fortunately, the models presented in future chapters will ordinarily contain only a handful of the identities we analyze in this chapter.

In the case of the two-sector model, we shall make one additional simplifying assumption before summarizing the relevant equations. In particular, we assume that businesses distribute all profits in the form of dividend payments; or, in other words, that undistributed corporate profits (retained earnings) are equal to zero. Given this assumption, we shall define each of the variants of national income and product directly in terms of the value of production, ignoring the definitions in terms of the components of factor income. To begin, notice that the assumption of no undistributed corporate profits eliminates the difference between personal income and national income. Thus, under this and the other assumptions of the two-sector model, net national product, national income, personal income and disposable personal income will all be the same. Gross national product will differ from these other variants only by the amount of depreciation of capital equipment. Thus, we can summarize the system of accounts depicted above by the simple identities:

$$GNP \equiv C + I_g \tag{2.4.13}$$

and $NNP \equiv NI \equiv PI \equiv DPI \equiv C + I$ (2.4.14)

where $I_g = I + D.$

We have also specified another important identity which described the disposition of disposable personal income in the form of consumption and personal saving. If net business saving is assumed to be equal to zero, this means that disposable income is exhausted by consumption and net national saving. Given the equality of all forms of net income and product (NNP, NI, PI and DPI) and given the disposition of disposable income between consumption and net saving, we can write:

$$NNP \equiv NI \equiv PI \equiv DPI \equiv C + S. \qquad (2.4.15)$$

Thus, net national product can be specified as either the sum of actual consumption and net investment or as the sum of consumption and net saving. It thus becomes a simple matter to use these two identities to prove that actual net saving and actual net investment are equal by identity. Toward that end, we write:

$$NNP \equiv C + S \equiv C + I$$

which yields:

$$S \equiv I. \qquad (2.4.16)$$

This identity will be crucial for our later analyses, and should thus be remembered by the student.

2.5 National Accounts for a Three-Sector Economy

The approach employed above with a two-sector economy may also be employed with a three-sector economy. Again a system of interlocking income statements will permit us to visualize the circular flow of production and spending. Now a third sector, that of government, must be added, but we continue to assume that all production occurs in the business sector and that all business firms are corporations.

With the introduction of a government sector, we must consequently take into account the receipt and expenditure streams of government. First come receipts which for the present consist wholly of gross taxes (TX_g) since net transfer payments between nations need not be considered at this time. These tax revenues flow from the business and household sectors. Taxes contributed by business consist of remittances for social security benefits on behalf of employees (TX_{ssb}), corporate profits taxes (TX_{cp}), and indirect business taxes (TX_{ind}); e.g., sales and excise taxes. All these levies are dual in nature since they represent expenses to business and revenues to government. Similar reasoning applies to the household sector as it remits employee social security contributions (TX_{ssp}) and personal taxes (TX_p).

At the same time it receives tax payments, the government sector makes two major types of outlays. There are no government wage and salary payments in our model since we are assuming all production occurs in the business sector. Were government wage-salary expenditures to be admitted, their total would be utilized as a measure of the value of current government output. Thus we are left with government purchases of currently produced goods and services (G) and so-called transfer payments: i.e., outlays for other than current production and employee services. Benefits paid to veterans as well as interest payments on the government debt are major types of transfer payments.[9] We assume, again as a matter of simplicity, that the household sector holds all government debt and therefore receives the net interest earned as a part of government transfer payments to the household sector (TR_{gp}). A third type of government transfer payment is involved in our model. Some business firms cannot sell their output at prices high enough to cover production costs and are thus subsidized by government. These subsidy payments to business are designated as transfer payments from government to business (TR_{gb}). Notice that such outlays, in a behind-the-scenes fashion, expand national factor income, but do not influence gross national product.

Expansion of our model national-income accounting system to encompass three sectors necessitates some changes on the income statement of the business sector. Here taxes appear as expense items. First are business contributions for social security benefits on behalf of employees (TX_{ssb}). These outlays constitute so-called fringe benefits and thus make up a part of wages and national-factor income, albeit funneled on a delayed basis through government. Then come taxes on corporate profits (TX_{cp}) and indirect business taxes (TX_{ind}).[10] Transfer payments from government to business (TR_{gb}), i.e., subsidies, could appear on the receipt side of the business sector's income statement,

---

[9]Interest receipts by the household sector from government are also treated on a net basis. In the real world, the household sector does borrow from government and must consequently make interest payments to the government sector.

Government debt has been incurred largely for financing war expenditures rather than current production. Thus net interest on government debt is treated as a transfer rather than a factor payment.

[10]Transfer payments are also made by business firms to the household sector; e.g., charitable contributions or, if you choose, the purchase of tickets to the firemen's ball. These payments do not enter national-factor income as payments for current factor use, but they do enter the final selling prices of commodities as do indirect business taxes. In other words, both items are priced into the charges for goods and services as sold in the market. However, business transfers to the household sector are not specified in any of the models we shall be treating in this text; thus, we lose little by excluding them from consideration here.

but we want the total of the right-hand side of the statement to equal gross national product. These transfer payments are therefore shifted to the left-hand side as a minus or negative figure. Only one other magnitude has influenced the receipt side of the business sector's income statement: government expenditures on currently produced goods and services. We shall denote net taxes (T) as the sum of all taxes less the sum of all government transfer payments. And, accordingly, total government saving, the revenues minus the expenditures of the public sector, will be signified by $T - G$.

One can now quickly interpret the modest changes wrought in the household sector's income statement by the introduction of government into our model of the national-income accounts. Transfer payments from government appear as receipts while household social security contributions (TX_{ssp}) and personal taxes (TX_p) appear as outlays. In other respects, the household sector's income statement is the same as it was in the case of the two-sector model of the economy.

The T-accounts describing the transactions between the three sectors of the economy are presented in table 2.5.1. We can begin analyzing them by referring first to the credit side of the business ledger. The total value of final product consists of consumption goods sold to the household sector ($47 million), the sales of fixed capital within the business sector ($8 million), the change in inventories ($2 million), and the sales of goods to the government ($25 million). The sum of these four components yields gross national product ($82 million). From the product side, the formal accounting identity for GNP in the three-sector model is thus:

$$GNP \equiv C + I_g^f + \Delta H + G. \qquad (2.5.1)$$

Or, combining the components of gross investment, we have:

$$GNP \equiv C + I_g + G. \qquad (2.5.2)$$

We could also compute gross national product by adding all of the charges against the final product of the business sector (i.e., by adding all of the items on the debit side of the ledger) to get:

$$GNP \equiv W + TX_{ssp} + R + i + Pr + TX_{ind} - TR_{gb} + D.$$
$$(2.5.3)$$

Net national product is less than gross national product by the amount of depreciation. Subtracting depreciation from the above formulations, we obtain NNP $= 78$. The implied NNP identities are:

$$NNP \equiv GNP - D \qquad (2.5.4)$$

and, from the product side:

$$NNP \equiv C + I + G \qquad \text{where } I = I_g - D \qquad (2.5.5)$$

or, from the expenditure side:

$$NNP \equiv W + TX_{ssb} + R + i + Pr + TX_{ind} - TR_{gb}. \qquad (2.5.6)$$

National income, as we pointed out earlier, is the sum of factor payments resulting from production. According to the business sector's T-account, we find $NI = 75$. In formal terms, we can write:

$$NI \equiv NNP - TX_{ind} + TR_{gb} \qquad (2.5.7)$$

where TX_{ind} is subtracted in order to translate the value of business product into factor prices and TR_{gb} is added to account for the fact that some factor payments are made out of the government subsidies received by the business sector. A more direct measure of national income is found in the summation of factor payments; i.e.:

$$NI \equiv W + TX_{ssb} + R + i + Pr. \qquad (2.5.8)$$

In order to derive the income of the household sector, we can use the information contained in that sector's T-account. First, refer to the income (or credit) side of the ledger. Total payments to the household sector are comprised of factor payments received from business (W, R, i, Dv) and transfers from the government. Notice that three of the elements of total factor income (in particular, that part of profits going to business saving, social security taxes and corporate tax payments) are not included in personal income. Thus, we can express personal income in terms of national income as:

$$PI \equiv NI - TX_{cp} - S_b + TR_{gb} - TX_{ssb} \qquad (2.5.9)$$

or more directly:

$$PI \equiv W + R + i + Dv + TR_{gp}. \qquad (2.5.10)$$

And, according to the figures listed in table 2.5.1, $PI = 68$. Notice that we could also measure personal income by summing all of its uses, or dispositions. Using the debit side of the household accounts for a listing of these uses, we have:

$$PI \equiv C + S_p + TX_p + TX_{ssp}. \qquad (2.5.11)$$

Once we have personal income, disposable personal income can be obtained quite simply by subtracting personal taxes from the former measure to get:

Table 2.5.1. *Three-Sector Accounts*

Household sector

Debits		Credits	
C	47	W	44
S_p	8	R	10
DPI	55	i	8
		Dv	2
		TR_{gp}	4
TX_p	10		
TX_{ssp}	3		
PI	68	PI	68

Business Sector

Debits		Credits	
W	44	C	47
TX_{ssb}	3	I_g^f	8
R	10	ΔH	2
i	8	G	25
Pr	10		
TX_{cp}	6		
Dv	2		
S_b	2		
NI	75		
TX_{ind}	5		
$-TR_{gb}$	-2		
NNP	78		
D	4		
GNP	82	GNP	82

Government Sector

Debits		Credits	
G	25	TX_{ssp}	3
TR_{gp}	4	TX_{ssb}	3
TR_{gb}	2	TX_p	10
$T - G$	-4	TX_{cp}	6
		TX_{ind}	5
Claims against receipts	27	Receipts	27

National Saving and Investment

Debits		Credits	
I_g^f	8	S_p	8
ΔH	2	S_b	2
		$T - G$	-4
		D	4
Total net inv.: $I_g^f + \Delta H - D = 6$		Total net saving: $S_p + S_b + (T - G) = 6$	
Total gross inv.: $I_g^f + \Delta H = 10$		Total gross saving: $S_p + S_b + D + (T - G) = 10$	

$$DPI \equiv PI - TX_p - TX_{ssp} \qquad\qquad (2.5.12)$$

or: $DPI = C + S_p.$ $\qquad\qquad\qquad\qquad\qquad (2.5.13)$

Notice that, again, disposable income (that amount which is left over after personal tax payments) is allocated between saving and consumption. According to the figures used above, $DPI = 55$.

The student should also notice the details of the government accounts in table 2.5.1. As is shown there, total expenditures are decomposed into transfers and expenditures on goods and services. Total receipts consist of the various tax revenues generated by the authorities. The net difference between receipts and expenditures is listed as government saving, $T - G$. According to the data compiled in the table, the government had negative saving over the period; in this situation, we say that the government has incurred a deficit. Had receipts exceeded expenditures (i.e., had $T - G$ been positive), we would say that the government sector had a surplus.

The national investment and saving account is also of interest. Notice especially that total gross investment equals total gross saving, and that this equality also holds for the net counterparts. That is, we have:

$$I_g \equiv I_g^f + \Delta H = S_p + S_b + D + (T - G) \qquad (2.5.14)$$

and: $I \equiv I_g^f + \Delta H - D = S_p + S_b + (T - G).$ $\qquad (2.5.15)$

We shall return to the verification that these equalities are identically true (i.e., that they are identities) in the next section.

A Special Case for the Three-Sector Model

We can again make our lives a bit easier if we make the simplifying assumption that the business sector has no undistributed profits. Given this assumption, we can summarize those identities which will actually be used in subsequent chapters. First, we repeat the product-side identities for gross and net national product for the three-sector model:

$$GNP \equiv C + I_g + G \qquad\qquad\qquad (2.5.16)$$

$$NNP \equiv C + I + G \qquad\qquad\qquad\quad (2.5.17)$$

where $I_g \equiv I + D.$

And, using the identities for national income (2.5.7), personal income (2.5.9) and disposable personal income (2.5.12), we can derive:

$$NNP \equiv C + S + TX_p + TX_{ssp} + TX_{cp} + TX_{ssb} - TR_{gp} + TX_{ind} - TR_{gb}$$

$$\underbrace{}_{DPI}$$

$$\underbrace{\phantom{C + S + TX_p + TX_{ssp}}}_{PI}$$

$$\underbrace{\phantom{C + S + TX_p + TX_{ssp} + TX_{cp} + TX_{ssb} - TR_{gp}}}_{NI}$$

$$\underbrace{\phantom{C + S + TX_p + TX_{ssp} + TX_{cp} + TX_{ssb} - TR_{gp} + TX_{ind} - TR_{gb}}}_{NNP}$$

or, rewriting this expression by collecting the tax and government transfer items, we have:

$$NNP \equiv C + S + T \tag{2.5.18}$$

where $T \equiv TX_p + TX_{ssp} + TX_{cp} + TX_{ssb} + TX_{ind} - TR_{gp} - TR_{gb}.$
$- TR_{gp} - TR_{gb}.$

The above expression states that NNP is decomposed into consumption, saving and net taxes (taxes less government transfer payments). Combining 2.5.17 and 2.5.18, we find that:

$$C + S + T \equiv C + I + G \tag{2.5.19}$$

or: $\quad S + T \equiv I + G \tag{2.5.20}$

which suggests that savings plus taxes will, by definition, equal the sum of actual net investment and government expenditures. These identities (equations 2.5.16–2.5.20) will be used extensively in chapter 4 and the chapters following it. Study them carefully.

2.6 National Accounts for a Four-Sector Economy

We are now ready to integrate a fourth and final sector into our model of the national-income accounts. The economy begins to carry on transactions with other nations or with what we shall frequently refer to as the rest of the world (ROW). Some of the commodities currently purchased by domestic sectors are produced abroad and appropriately bolster or enlarge reported figures for consumption, investment, and government spending, but fail to reflect in national-factor income.[11] Having been produced abroad, these imported items generate expendi-

---

[11] In addition, some of the imported items are unfinished and semifinished goods to be used in domestic production of final goods. The value of these items should be subtracted from GNP to account for the fact that this part of the value of domestic final goods is not attributable to domestic production.

ture streams which go overseas rather than remain at home and consequently redound to the benefit of foreign nation income levels. Just the opposite sequence of events applies to exported commodities. These items generate factor income flows in the domestic economy which are not offset by or reflected in larger volumes of consumption, investment, and government spending although a compensating credit for exports is made to the product side of the business sector's income statement. It is this condition which forces us to think in terms of the net difference between commodity exports (Ex) and commodity imports (Im) as the magnitude which influences the ultimate size of gross national product.

Inclusion of the foreign sector introduces additional magnitudes which must be considered in setting up our system of model income statements and national saving-and-investment statement. Net transfer payments to foreigners by government and persons will influence both government saving and personal saving. Imports also enter the scene as, say, additions to consumption and government spending. Finally, exports will expand national factor income; we will assume wages, rent, net interest, and dividends are sufficiently enlarged. Another aspect or dimension of net exports (Ex − Im) requires emphasis. When positive, net exports expand gross national product and must be underwritten by some combination of three basic forms of financing: (1) net foreign investments (I_f), i.e., expenditures by foreigners out of their own current income or past savings for our commodities; (2) net government transfer payments to foreigners (TR_{gf}); and (3) net personal transfer payments to foreigners (TR_{pf}). Given this pattern of variables, we have the identity:

$$(Ex - Im) \equiv I_f + TR_{gf} + TR_{pf} \qquad (2.6.1)$$

With these modifications in mind, we can proceed to outline the transactions occurring among the four sectors of our expanded accounting system. In table 2.6.1, we have listed the T-accounts for each of the four sectors, and have included a statement of national saving and investment. As usual, we begin our analysis by referring to the credit side of the business-sector account.

Gross national product is again evaluated as the total value of domestic production. In our accounts, the value of domestic production is decomposed into total consumption purchases, gross fixed investment, the change in producers' inventories, sales to the government and net exports. This yields the identity:

$$GNP \equiv C + I_g + G + (Ex - Im) \qquad (2.6.2)$$

where of course I_g represents gross domestic investment, which includes

Table 2.6.1. *Four-Sector Accounts*

Household Sector

Debits		Credits	
C	49	W	48
S_p	13	R	12
TR_{pf}	1	i	9
		Dv	3
DPI	63	TR_{gp}	4
TX_{ssp}	3		
TX_p	10		
PI	76	PI	76

Business Sector

Debits		Credits	
W	48	C	49
TX_{ssb}	3	I_g^f	8
R	12	ΔH	2
i	9	G	26
Pr	11	Ex − Im	5
TX_{cp}	6		
Dv	3		
S_b	2		
Ni	83		
TX_{ind}	5		
$-TR_{gb}$	−2		
NNP	86		
D	4		
GNP	90	GNP	90

Government Sector

Debits		Credits	
G	26	TX_{ssp}	3
TR_{gp}	4	TX_{ssb}	3
TR_{gb}	2	TX_p	10
TR_{gf}	2	TX_{cp}	6
T − G	−7	TX_{ind}	5
Claims Against Receipts	27	Receipts	27

Foreign Sector

Debits		Credits	
Ex	8	IM	3
		TR_{gf}	2
		TR_{pf}	1
		I_f	2
Expenditures	8	Receipts	8

National Savings and Investment

Debits		Credits	
I_g^f	8	S_p	13
ΔH	2	S_b	2
I_f	2	T − G	−7
		D	4
Gross Investment	12	Gross Savings	12
Net Investment	8	Net Saving	8

domestic investment in fixed capital and inventory accumulation. As is shown in table 2.6.1, GNP in this case equals $90 million. As before, we can also define GNP in terms of the charges against the value of domestic production. Summing all of the elements on the debit side of the business account, we have:

$$\text{GNP} \equiv \text{W} + \text{TX}_{ssb} + \text{R} + \text{i} + \text{Pr} + \text{TX}_{ind} - \text{TR}_{gb} + \text{D}$$
(2.6.3)

the total of which also yields GNP = $90 million.

Net national product, as usual, is defined as gross national product less depreciation:

$$\text{NNP} \equiv \text{GNP} - \text{D}.$$
(2.6.4)

This basic identity can be used to specify the direct product-side and expenditure-side versions of NNP:

$$\text{NNP} \equiv \text{C} + \text{I} + \text{G} + (\text{Ex} - \text{Im})$$
(2.6.5)

where $\text{I} \equiv \text{I}_g - \text{D}$

and: $\text{NNP} \equiv \text{W} + \text{TX}_{ssb} + \text{R} + \text{i} + \text{Pr} + \text{TX}_{ind} - \text{TR}_{gb}.$
(2.6.6)

According to either approach, the hypothetical numbers contained in table 2.6.1 yield NNP = $86 million.

The transition from net national product to national income is given by:

$$\text{NI} \equiv \text{NNP} - \text{TX}_{ind} + \text{TR}_{gb}.$$
(2.6.7)

Or, more directly, we can substitute the previous definitions of NNP to get:

$$\text{NI} \equiv \text{C} + \text{I} + \text{G} + \text{Ex} - \text{Im} - \text{TX}_{ind} + \text{TR}_{gb}$$
(2.6.8)

and

$$\text{NI} \equiv \text{W} + \text{TX}_{ssb} + \text{R} + \text{i} + \text{Pr}.$$
(2.6.9)

Notice that the subtraction of indirect taxes and the addition of government transfers to business has the effect of translating the value of final product into terms of factor prices. In our example, NI = $83 million.

Personal income, as we have seen before, is the total income of the household sector. In deriving personal income, we need to deduct from national income social security payments made by businesses (none of these business charges are received by the household sector as current income) and add transfers to the household sector. In formal terms, this manipulation is captured by the identity:

$$PI \equiv NI - S_b - TX_{cp} - TX_{ssb} + TR_{gp}. \tag{2.6.10}$$

Substituting from 2.6.1 for national income (or what is the same, drawing from the receipt side of the household sector account), we thus obtain:

$$PI \equiv W + R + i + Dv + TR_{gp}. \tag{2.6.11}$$

The value of personal income in our example is $76 million; the student should be able to verify this by substituting the appropriate values into either 2.6.10 or 2.6.11.

Disposable personal income includes only those elements of personal income which are left for individuals after personal tax payments have been made. In our accounting system, individuals must pay both social security (employee contributions) and personal income taxes. Thus, we can write:

$$DPI \equiv PI - TX_{ssp} - TX_p. \tag{2.6.12}$$

Again, we can derive a more direct specification of DPI by substituting for personal income from 2.6.11 to get:

$$DPI \equiv W + R + i + Dv + TR_{gp} - TX_{ssp} - TX_p. \tag{2.6.13}$$

The disposition of income includes consumption, personal saving and personal transfers to foreigners:

$$DPI \equiv C + S_p + TR_{pf}. \tag{2.6.14}$$

As the student can observe from table 2.6.1, DPI is equal to $63 million in this hypothetical case.

The transactions of the government sector involve tax receipts from alternative sources and various types of government outlays. Total tax receipts add up to $27 million, as is shown by the credit side of the government account. Actual expenditures, comprised of purchases of goods and services and transfer payments to the other three sectors, total $34 million. As a result, the government runs a deficit of $7 million. This is recorded on the debit side as negative government saving, thus causing claims against government receipts to be $27 million.

In the foreign sector accounts, we record items from the standpoint of the foreign sector itself (ROW). Thus, the value of U.S. exports is counted as a debit and the value of U.S. imports is listed as a credit. Note that our direct payments to ROW ($Im + TR_{gf} + TR_{pf}$) totals only $6 million, whereas the foreign sector's payments to the United

States total \$8 million. The difference between these two figures (\$2 million) constitutes net foreign investment. In a sense, net foreign investment can be treated as a sale of debt by the foreign sector to the United States. It thus appears as a credit in the foreign sector account.

The national saving and investment account differs from the one presented in the previous section only in the respect that net foreign investment is now included on the investment side. Notice that, again, investment is equal to saving in both the net and the gross versions. In the next section, we shall verify again that this equality is true by definition.

A Special Case for the Four-Sector Economy

To simplify the students' task, we shall now summarize those identities which will be used in later chapters. Again, we shall do so under the simplifying assumption that there are no undistributed corporate profits. We shall also assume away personal and government transfers to the rest of the world. Begin with the product-side specifications for gross national product and net national product:

$$\text{GNP} \equiv C + I_g + G + (Ex - Im) \tag{2.6.15}$$

and

$$\text{NNP} \equiv C + I + G + (Ex - Im) \tag{2.6.16}$$

where, as usual,

$$I \equiv I_g - D.$$

Now, use the identities for national income (2.6.7), personal income (2.6.10) and the disposable personal income (2.6.12 and 2.6.14) to write:

$$\text{NNP} \equiv \underbrace{\underbrace{\underbrace{\underbrace{C + S}_{\text{DPI}} + TX_{ssp}\ TX_p + TX_{cp} + TX_{ssb} - TR_{gp}}_{\text{PI}}}_{\text{IN}} + TX_{ind} - TR_{gb}}_{\text{NNP}} \tag{2.6.17}$$

Remembering that total taxes less government transfers is designated as "net taxes" (T), equation 2.6.17 can be simplified to read:

$$\text{NNP} \equiv C + S + T. \tag{2.6.18}$$

Noting the NNP is defined by both 2.6.16 and 2.6.18, we can write:

$$C + I + G + (Ex - Im) \equiv C + S + T. \qquad (2.6.19)$$

And, subtracting consumption (C) from both sides, we have:

$$I + G + Ex - Im \equiv S + T$$

or:

$$I + (Ex - Im) \equiv S + (T - G). \qquad (2.6.20)$$

This last equation denotes that the sum of domestic and net foreign investment is identical to the sum of saving and the government surplus. This identity will be used in chapter 16 when we discuss the implications of international trade. Of the equations presented above, the students should be familiar with the following: 2.6.15, 2.6.16, 2.6.18 and 2.6.20; the others should be understood, but it is unnecessary to be able to duplicate them from memory.

2.7 Price Indices and Real Economic Magnitudes

In the discussion in subsequent chapters, we shall be analyzing the relationships among variables representing real economic magnitudes. Our investigation will be concerned with concepts like real consumption, real net national product, real investment, etc. The term *real* denotes that the variable in question has been adjusted, or deflated, for price changes taking place over time. It is important to focus on these real measures in order to be able to make meaningful conclusions about the interactions among certain key phenomena. For instance, it will be argued that the level of employment is closely tied to *real* output (an indicator of the amount of, rather than the value of, production). As preparation for this later analysis, then, we devote this section to a brief explanation of the process of deflation by which these real measures are derived.

In order to adjust some variable to represent its real value, an indicator of the general level of the relevant prices is needed. (For example, if we want to derive real consumption from the total dollar value of consumption expenditures, we would need some index of the prices of consumption goods.) Normally, this kind of price index (call it P_t) is defined in the following way:[12]

---

[12]Note that the symbol Σ means "the sum of." In general terms, Σx^i is used to denote $x^1 + x^2 + x^3 + \ldots$ over all values of i.

$$P_t = \frac{\Sigma p_t^i q_0^i}{\Sigma p_0^i q_0^i} \tag{2.7.1}$$

where p_t^i is the price of the ith good in the current period (period t), p_0^i is the price of the ith good in some base period (some period chosen for the sake of comparison of price levels), and q_0^i is the quantity of the ith good purchased in the base period. The denominator of equation 2.7.1 indicates the total value of the base-period bundle of commodities at the prices existing in the base year; the numerator measures what the total value of this same basket of goods would be if they were evaluated at current prices. Thus, the ratio of the two sums will be greater than one if the basket of goods would have a greater total cost at today's prices, less than one if the market basket would be less expensive at today's prices, and equal to one if the overall cost of the commodity bundle were the same at the price levels of the two periods. In general, then, we say that the higher the value of the index, the higher the general current level of prices (relative to the base year).

In looking at expression 2.7.1, note the following general characteristics: First, the price index is a *relative* measure, indicating the value of prices in the current period relative to their value in the base period. Second, each price is weighted (multiplied) by the quantity (purchased) of the good in question. The purpose of this weighting is to account for the fact that in terms of quantity some goods constitute a large part of the overall range of commodities and some constitute only a small part. The overall price of consumer goods, for instance, is more strongly affected by the price of milk than by the price of caviar (because very little caviar is consumed in comparison to milk). In general, the larger the quantity of a particular good, the larger the influence of a change in its price.[13] Base-period quantities are used as weights on *both* base-

---

[13] One of the shortcomings of the price indices we just described is that unfortunately they fail to take into account changes in the quality of the various commodities. For example, suppose that we compare the same car model in two periods in time, say, 1966 and 1974. Suppose also that these cars are the same in every respect except that the 1974 model has a pollution control device. Finally, let us assume that their respective prices are $5,000 and $7,500. One could suggest that the price of this model has increased by 50%. However, this would not take into consideration the fact that a certain technological improvement contributing to a better quality of the product was embodied in the 1974 model. Undoubtedly the reader can construct his own examples. The fact, however, is that the present state of the art in building price indices is not capable of dealing with such a problem. In other words, as long as price indices are not adjusted to take into consideration changes in the intrinsic characteristics of products they do not reflect the general movement of prices as accurately as we would like. Nevertheless, they still serve as reasonably good proxies for the overall level of prices of some bundle of goods and services.

period and current prices in order to focus the index strictly on price changes (as opposed to quantity changes).[14]

Once the value of the price index has been computed, it can then be used to derive a real measure of the variable in question. Suppose, for instance, that we want to compute real consumption from current-dollar consumption expenditures. The process would entail dividing the total expenditures by the price index for consumption goods, i.e.:

$$\text{real consumption} \equiv \frac{\text{current-dollar consumption expenditures}}{\text{price index for consumption goods}}$$

and this same general technique can be used to compute the real value of any variable, providing that we use the price index pertaining to the appropriate set of goods.

Table 2.7.1.   *Derivation of a Price Index*

	good 1		good 2		good 3	
	q^1	p^1	q^2	p^2	q^3	p^3
1967	100	20	40	10	10	3
1976	110	22	45	15	12	5

Let's consider an example of the application of the above analysis. Suppose (for simplicity) that total output consists of the production of only three goods, and that table 2.7.1 provides data on the prices and quantities of these goods for the current period (say, 1976) and the base period (say, 1967).

First, the total current-dollar value of output for the two years would be

total value of output in 1967:

---

[14]Although most popular price indices are computed with base-period quantities as weights, the reader should be aware that one could also construct a price index using current quantities as weights on current and past prices. The resultant price index will not, in general, take on the same value as the one described above. Nevertheless, the general principle is the same.

$$\Sigma p^i_{1967} q^i_{1967} = 100(20) + 40(10) + 10(3) = 2430$$

total value of output in 1976:

$$\Sigma p^i_{1976} p^i_{1976} = 110(22) + 45(15) + 12(5) = 3155.$$

Comparison for the two figures could be misleading if one wanted to analyze the growth of output over the time span, given that part of the increase was due to price increases. To standardize for the influence of price changes, then, we compute the value of the price index for the two years:[15]

$$P_{1967} = \frac{\Sigma p^i_{1967} q^i_{1967}}{\Sigma p^i_{1967} q^i_{1967}} = 1$$

$$P_{1976} = \frac{\Sigma p^i_{1976} q^i_{1967}}{\Sigma p^i_{1967} q^i_{1967}} = \frac{22(100) + 15(40) + 5(10)}{20(100) + 10(40) + 3(10)} = \frac{2850}{2430}$$

$$= 1.173.$$

Now, deflating the two current-dollar figures by the respective values of the price index, we obtain:

$$\text{real output in } 1967 = \frac{2430}{1} = 2430.$$

$$\text{real output in } 1976 = \frac{3155}{1.173} = 2690.$$

Comparison of these two figures now gives a reasonably good indication of the growth of output over the period 1967–76.

Suggested Further Reading

Edey, H. C. and Peacock, A. T. *National Income and Social Accounting.* London: Hutchison's University Library, 1954.

Kuznets, S. *Economic Change.* New York: W. W. Norton, 1953, chaps. 7, 8.

————. "Long-Term Changes in National Income of the U.S.A. since 1870." In *Income and Wealth,* series 2. International Association for Research in Income and Wealth. London: Bowes and Bowes, 1948.

---

[15]Conceptually, why is the price index for the base year (1967) equal to one?

National Bureau of Economic Research. "A Critique of the United States Income and Product Accounts." *Studies in Income and Wealth,* Vol. 22. Princeton, N.J., 1958.

Ruggles, R. and Ruggles, N. D. *National Income Accounts and Income Analysis.* 2d ed. New York: McGraw-Hill, 1956, part I.

U.S. Department of Commerce. *National Income and Product Accounts of the United States,* 1919–65, a supplement to the *Survey of Current Business* (1966).

————. *U.S. Income and Output, 1958.*

————. *Survey of Current Business,* August 1965.

PART TWO

Simple Aggregate Models

CHAPTER 3

A Simple Economic
Model

3.1 Introduction

The purpose of this chapter is to consider some of the most important
aspects of the theory of national income determination. The identities
relating alternative measures of national income and product and their
components are, by their intrinsic nature, valid for *any* level of business
activity. Thus, the accounting relationships we've looked at cannot be
expected to tell us *why* the level of income takes on a particular value at
any point in time. Actually, the economy is capable of producing any
number of alternative levels of output. The question, then, is what determines this level of income.

Although the economic model employed in this chapter is an extremely simple one, it should nevertheless help in bringing to light some
of the important causal relationships between income and its determining factors. In subsequent chapters, we shall investigate a series of other
models of the economy. At each step of our analysis, we shall relax some
of the restrictive assumptions used until that point. The final result will
be a macroeconomic model which integrates the main characteristics
of the economy as a whole.

In what follows, problems associated with price changes will not be
considered. Instead, all of our variables will be expressed in *real* terms,
that is, in constant dollars. We thus limit ourselves to an investigation of
the relationships among real economic magnitudes (e.g., real income,
real consumption, etc.).

3.2 The Concept of Equilibrium

In static analysis, we said in chapter 1, an equilibrium is some "position" from which there is no inherent tendency to move. In some sense, equilibrium denotes a balance of opposing pressures. We reviewed some microeconomic analyses in which equilibrium played a key role, and noted that the equilibrium of individual markets is sometimes cast in terms of the equality of quantity demanded and quantity supplied. In an analogous fashion, we shall argue that macroeconomic equilibrium necessitates the equality of aggregate demand and aggregate supply.

In what follows, aggregate supply will refer to the real value of all final goods and services produced over some period of time, and will be denoted by Y. In our analysis of the national income and product accounts, we noted that national income, net national product and gross national product—each specified in real terms—could qualify in some sense or another as measures of aggregate supply. In the models considered throughout the text, no distinction will be drawn between net national product and national income. That is, we shall not consider indirect business taxes and government transfers to business explicitly in our accounts of economic activity. We shall, however, distinguish between net and gross national product. Accordingly, aggregate supply will denote either national income or net national product, but will differ (by the amount of depreciation) from gross national product. With this in mind, we can incorporate some of the accounting relationships studied in chapter 2 into our economic models. Finally, aggregate demand will be used to refer to "desired" expenditures on final goods and services, and will be denoted as AD.

With these general comments in mind, we now set out to investigate an extremely simple macroeconomic model. We shall assume no governmental economic activity, no international economic relations, and no undistributed corporate profits. We based our two-sector accounting model of chapter 2 on the same set of assumptions, and found that under these conditions there would be no difference between net national product and disposable personal income. As a result, we can write both aggregate supply (net national product) and disposable personal income as:

$$Y \equiv Y_d \equiv C + S \qquad (3.2.1)$$

and

$$Y \equiv Y_d \equiv C + I \qquad (3.2.2)$$

where:

$Y \equiv$ aggregate supply, as measured by either real net national product or real national income

$Y_d \equiv$ real disposable personal income

$C \equiv$ real consumption expenditures

$S \equiv$ real saving by the household sector

$I \equiv$ net actual investment.

Identity 3.2.1 describes the fact that income is distributed between consumption expenditures and saving. Identity 3.2.2 reminds us that, by nature, the real value of production in the two-sector model can be sorted into consumption and net actual, or realized, investment. As we saw in the previous chapter, it can be shown that saving and actual investment are identical, regardless of the level of income. This point can be reiterated by combining identities 3.2.1 and 3.2.2 to get:

$$C + S \equiv Y \equiv C + I$$

or:

$$S \equiv I. \tag{3.2.3}$$

As will be remembered, this identity is made to be true by the inclusion of inventory changes in actual investment. We can expand investment into its two components by writing:

$$I \equiv I^f + \Delta H \tag{3.2.4}$$

where, as before, I^f refers to net purchases of fixed capital (plant and equipment) and ΔH denotes the change in inventories of all types of goods. Regardless of the values of saving and net fixed investment, the change in inventories will automatically adjust in such a way as to make the identity between saving and net actual investment come true.

But it should be apparent that producers may not be pleased with the change in inventories taking place. Some change may be desired, but part may also be deemed undesired. With the notable exceptions of a few firms engaged in a particular type of production (e.g., goods made to order), every firm has to carry a certain volume of inventories. First, the firms desire to smooth out the seasonal variations of sales with their production flow; second, they desire to speculate; and finally, they wish to secure an uninterrupted flow of sales against contingencies such as strikes. The result is that every firm, after a careful evaluation of the past and present behavior of the relevant variables, decides upon the amount of inventories it should carry in order to be able to face any contingency of the kind described. The level of inventories firms are willing to carry voluntarily is called the *desired* level, and we can expect that firms will insist on maintaining it by adjusting production levels and/or sales effort appropriately. Consequently, any deviation of inventories from the desired level can be called an *undesired* change, and may be due either to erroneous evaluation of circumstances (e.g., erroneous sales expectation) or to unexpected trouble within the production line. Of course, it is relatively obvious that this undesired change in inventories may be positive, negative, or zero depending on the relation between actual and desired changes.

We can capture the essence of the above discussion by respecifying actual net investment as:

$$I \equiv I^f + \Delta H^D + \Delta H^U \qquad (3.2.5)$$

where ΔH^D refers to *desired* inventory changes and ΔH^U denotes *undesired* variations. If we can presume that producers respond to undesired inventories by changing production levels, we have our first hint as to the way an equilibrium level of income is determined. More specifically, we can argue reasonably that producers will change their level of production whenever undesired inventory changes are either positive or negative. Thus, it is only when this term is zero that we can expect the current level of production to be sustained (or, better yet, to be an equilibrium level).

In order to focus more closely on the conditions for macroeconomic equilibrium we must first elaborate on the notion of aggregate demand. In our present model, we have only two sectors: the household and business sectors. Thus, we can distinguish between the demand by the household sector for consumption goods and the demand by the business sector for capital goods. Aggregate demand will be the sum of these two types of desired expenditures; that is, we can specify:

$$AD \equiv C + I^D \qquad (3.2.6)$$

where C is desired consumption expenditures and I^D is the desired level of net investment. Notice carefully that we have made no distinction between "actual" and "desired" consumption (the same term, C, is used in the aggregate supply and the aggregate demand identities). We thus implicitly assume that consumers automatically adjust their consumption expenditures to the desired level. But we *have* made an explicit distinction between actual and desired investment, and much of our analysis will revolve around this distinction. Desired investment is nothing but the amount of expenditures producers would *like* to have devoted to new capital goods during the period. It is given by the identity:

$$I^D \equiv I^f + \Delta H^D. \tag{3.2.7}$$

That is, we define desired investment as the sum of net purchases of fixed capital and the *desired* component of inventory change. A comparison of 3.2.7 with 3.2.5 should reveal the critical point that desired and actual investment differ by the amount of undesired change in inventories.

Now that we have investigated the supply and demand sides of the market for all final goods and services, we should be able to delve into the analysis of the equilibrium of that market. We begin by specifying the condition that aggregate demand and supply be equal:

$$Y = AD. \tag{3.2.8}$$

Regardless of how sophisticated we make our description of the product market, equation 3.2.8 will be maintained as a basic statement of equilibrium. Let us now use some of the supply and demand identities developed above in order to bring out more of the flavor of this condition. First, we can substitute for Y and AD from equations 3.2.2 and 3.2.6 respectively to transform 3.2.8 into:

$$C + I = C + I^D$$

or $I = I^D. \tag{3.2.9}$

The interpretation of this expression is fairly simple and quite straightforward. In that aggregate supply consists of consumption and *actual* investment and aggregate demand includes consumption and *desired* investment, it is necessary for equilibrium that these two versions of investment be equal. In a sense, it implies that producers have to be satisfied with their actual investment over the period if they are to continue producing at the same output. We can go a step further in our analysis by substituting into 3.2.9 the expressions for actual and desired investment to get:

$$I^f + \Delta H^D + \Delta H^U = I^f + \Delta H^D$$

which requires that:

$$\Delta H^U = 0. \tag{3.2.10}$$

That is, in order for actual and desired investment to be equal, it is necessary that there be no undesired changes in inventories, as pointed out earlier.

One more specification of the equilibrium condition will round out our preliminary analysis. If we again use the definition of aggregate demand as $C + I^D$ and use the identity describing the disposition of income through consumption and saving to rewrite aggregate supply, we find that equilibrium requires:

$$C + S = C + I^D$$

or:

$$S = I^D. \tag{3.2.11}$$

This version of our equilibrium condition suggests that saving and desired investment must be equal in order that the product market be in equilibrium. Although we shall analyze it in detail later on, perhaps we can offer a quick intuitive rationale for it here. Note that production entails a flow of income: producers hire factor services from the household sector and disburse factor payments to the owners of those services. In turn, the household sector uses some of its income to finance consumption expenditures on the products of business. But the household sector withdraws a certain amount from the flow of income; i.e., some factor income is absorbed in saving. Saving is thus that part of the value of production which is not returned to the business sector in the form of consumption expenditures. In order for businesses to go on producing at the current level, saving must then be matched by some other desired expenditures on business products. Desired investment expenditures can act in such a fashion, absorbing that part of production which is not consumed. As long as desired investment and saving are equal, the level of production is in equilibrium.

Below, for future use, we summarize the alternative versions of the product-market equilibrium condition in the two-sector model.

$$Y = AD = C + I^D \tag{3.2.8}$$

$$I = I^D \tag{3.2.9}$$

$$\Delta H^U = 0 \tag{3.2.10}$$

$$S = I^D \tag{3.2.11}$$

3.3 The Determinants of Aggregate Demand

In the previous section, we focused on the nature and meaning of equilibrium in our simple view of the economy. One of our conclusions was that macroeconomic equilibrium requires the equality of aggregate supply and aggregate demand. But our discussion did not actually reveal the way in which an equilibrium level of income is determined by economic forces. In a sense, we have seen how to define an equilibrium level of income, but have ignored until now the factors which determine the level of income at which equilibrium will take place.

We now proceed to examine the factors which influence aggregate demand and thus affect the equilibrium level of economic activity. As noted above, aggregate demand in the two-sector model consists of consumption and desired investment. For the present, we shall concentrate on consumption expenditures. This choice is not entirely arbitrary. The importance attached to consumption behavior by economists (including the late John Maynard Keynes) can be justified partially by the relative magnitude of consumption in total domestic expenditures. Indeed, depending on the country in question, expenditures on consumption amount to anywhere from two-thirds to four-fifths of net national product. Hence, the nature of behavior underlying consumption is extremely important from the standpoint of economic theory and policy.

Although there are still regions of ignorance, most economists nevertheless have agreed that the main factors influencing consumption expenditures can be classified into five general categories:

1. Income
2. Accumulated wealth
3. Demographic factors
4. Habits or standards of living attained in the past
5. Monetary factors

All of these factors can be (and have been) represented with variables which approximate them more or less satisfactorily. For the time being, we shall concentrate on the relation between aggregate income and aggregate consumption expenditures.

Economic literature reveals a running debate over the appropriate variant of income to be used in a consumption relation. We shall investigate some of these arguments in chapter 12. For now, we shall assume that current disposable personal income is the predominant driving force that determines the level of consumption expenditures. To give more content to this notion, we shall further assume two properties of the relationship. First, we presume that consumption varies directly with income. The higher (lower) the aggregate income level, the higher (lower) we expect consumption to be. In addition, we shall subscribe to what Keynes called "the fundamental psychological law" of consumption: "Men are disposed, as a rule and on the average, to increase their consumption as their income increases, but not by as much as the increase in their income."[1]

We can start to formalize the Keynesian propositions by using the national-income identity presented in the previous section:

$$Y_d \equiv C + S.$$

Now, suppose that disposable income increases by a small amount, say ΔY_d.[2] According to the Keynesian argument, people will choose to allocate this change in income between a small change in consumption, ΔC, and a small change in saving, ΔS. Hence, we may write that:

$$\Delta Y_d \equiv \Delta C + \Delta S. \tag{3.3.1}$$

If we divide both sides of the above identity by ΔY_d, we obtain:

$$1 \equiv \frac{\Delta C}{\Delta Y_d} + \frac{\Delta S}{\Delta Y_d}. \tag{3.3.2}$$

In the above relation, the term $\Delta C/\Delta Y_d$ shows the fraction of income increase which will be allocated to consumption expenditures, whereas the term $\Delta S/\Delta Y_d$ shows the corresponding allocation to savings. Obviously, the sum of these terms must be equal to unity. The first term is called the marginal propensity to consume (MPC), while the second is called the marginal propensity to save (MPS). Let us clarify these concepts in terms of an example. Suppose the disposable income of an economy is equal to $1,000 billion and that this is allocated into $800 billion in consumption expenditures and $200 billion in savings. Now let us assume that income increases to $1,100 billion, and that corresponding levels of consumption and savings are $880 and $220 billion respectively. It follows then that $\Delta Y_d = 100$; $\Delta C = 80$; and $\Delta S = 20$. Consequently, we obtain:

$$MPC = \frac{\Delta C}{\Delta Y_d} = .8; \quad \text{and} \quad MPS = \frac{\Delta S}{\Delta Y_d} = .2.$$

Now let us see what Keynes' hypothesis implies. Since he claims that the increase in consumption expenditures will be less than the increase in income, this means that $\Delta C < \Delta Y_d$, from which it follows that

---

[1] John M. Keynes, *The General Theory of Employment, Interest, and Money* (New York: Harcourt, Brace & World, 1964), p. 96.

[2] From now on, we shall maintain the convention of writing Δ to indicate a small but finite change in the value of a variable. Thus, a small change in income will be written as ΔY; in consumption as ΔC; in saving, as ΔS; and so on.

the ratio $\Delta C/\Delta Y_d$ will be less than unity. But since consumption expenditures also vary directly with income, it follows that the quantities ΔC and ΔY_d will have always the same sign. From this we can conclude that the ratio $\Delta C/\Delta Y_d$, the marginal propensity to consume, is always positive but less than unity. In other words, the MPC always obeys the double restriction:

$$0 < MPC < 1. \tag{3.3.3}$$

In addition to the above hypothesis, Keynes advanced one more in relation to the behavior of consumption expenditures, although he gave it less weight and confidence than the previous case. In particular, he argued that as income increases, the proportion of income allocated to consumption decreases. To see this more precisely, consider once more the disposable income identity (3.2.1) and divide both sides of this relation by disposable income to obtain:

$$1 \equiv \frac{C}{Y_d} + \frac{S}{Y_d}. \tag{3.3.4}$$

The term C/Y_d is called the average propensity to consume (APC). It shows the proportion of total income allocated to consumption expenditures. The term S/Y_d is called the average propensity to save (APS). It shows the proportion of income allocated to saving. What Keynes said is that as income increases, the APC will decrease and consequently its complement (APS) will increase.

The relation of consumption expenditures and income is called the consumption function. Although there are a great many functions which can satisfy the above hypotheses in regard to the marginal and average propensity to consume, we shall further restrict its shape by assuming for the sake of simplicity that the relation between C and Y_d is linear. This choice of a functional form allows us to write the behavioral relation as:

$$C = a + bY_d \tag{3.3.5}$$

where a and b are presumed to be constants. The right-hand side of this expression contains two terms, both of which can be interpreted intuitively. The first term, a, represents the value consumption would take on if the level of disposable income happened to be zero. Because it represents a minimum level of consumption unrelated to the value of disposable income, the constant a is sometimes called "autonomous consumption." The second term in the consumption equation is bY_d. This can be called "induced consumption" to reflect the fact that its value depends upon the level of disposable income.

The general linear consumption function (3.3.5) can be used to focus on the characteristics attributed to the consumption relation by Keynes. First, let us suppose that disposable income changes by the amount ΔY_d. As a result, we can expect consumption to change according to the specification:

$$\Delta C = b\Delta Y_d.$$

The above expression indicates that any change in Y_d is translated (through the term b) into a change in consumption. If we divide both sides of the equation by ΔY_d, we obtain:

$$\frac{\Delta C}{\Delta Y_d} = b.$$

The coefficient of disposable income, b, then gives us the change in consumption attributable to each dollar's change in income. But we have considered this concept before, and have defined it as the marginal propensity to consume (MPC). As a result, in the case of our linear consumption relation, we find that b *is* the MPC; i.e.,

$$MPC \equiv \frac{\Delta C}{\Delta Y_d} = b. \tag{3.3.6}$$

Given the restrictions we have placed on the MPC in equation 3.3.3, we must now restrict the value of b to satisfy the inequality:

$$0 < b < 1. \tag{3.3.7}$$

The average propensity to consume can also be specified in terms of the linear relation under consideration. If we divide both sides of the consumption relation, we find that b is the MPC; i.e.,

$$\frac{C}{Y_d} = \frac{a}{Y_d} + b.$$

But the term on the left side of the expression, C/Y_d, has already been defined as the average propensity to consume (APC); hence, we may write:

$$APC \equiv \frac{C}{Y_d} = \frac{a}{Y_d} + b. \tag{3.3.8}$$

Notice that the APC is written in terms of b (the MPC) and the ratio a/Y_d. As long as a is a positive contant, we can see that the APC will decline as Y_d increases. Furthermore, as Y_d becomes extremely large, the ratio a/Y_d approaches a zero value; hence, the APC approaches the

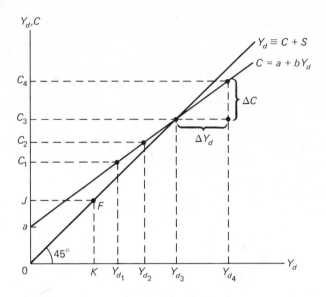

Figure 3.3.1   *The Keynesian Consumption Schedule*

MPC as income grows. We see then that the linear form of the consumption equation "fits" the Keynesian hypothesis provided that a is a positive number and b is a positive fraction.

The consumption relation can be investigated further through a graphical approach. In figure 3.3.1, we have sketched the hypothesized linear relation between consumption (measured along the vertical axis) and disposable income (measured along the horizontal axis *and* the vertical axis). We have also included a 45-degree line to be used as a frame of reference in the discussion. The essential property of a 45-degree line is that any point on it is equidistant from the horizontal and vertical axes. For example, consider point F. At F, the vertical distance, KF, is equal to the horizontal distance, JF. As we slide up along the 45-degree line, the same property is maintained. We have used this schedule as a graphical device to plot disposable income against itself. The value of this procedure is that it allows us to measure both consumption and disposable income as vertical distances and thus facilitates a comparison of the values of these two variables.

Refer now to the consumption schedule, labeled $C = a + bY_d$. Notice first that consumption takes on the value a when disposable income is zero; thus, a (autonomous consumption) is the vertical intercept of the consumption schedule. As income takes on successively larger values (Y_{d1}, Y_{d2}, Y_{d3}, Y_{d4}) consumption increases. The slope of the consumption schedule (the rise over the run) is nothing but the marginal propensity to consume, b. This can be shown by choosing any two values of disposable income and noting what happens to consumption as income increases from one value to the other. Consider, for instance, the movement from Y_{d3} to Y_{d4}. Notice that this change in income is denoted as ΔY_d in the diagram. As this change in income occurs, consumption increases from C_3 to C_4; this latter increment is represented as ΔC. We already know that the ratio of ΔC to ΔY_d is the marginal propensity to consume. On the other hand, the ratio $\Delta C/\Delta Y_d$ is the slope of the consumption schedule itself; thus, the MPC is represented graphically as the slope of the consumption schedule. The fact that the MPC is positive is reflected in the upward-sloping character of the consumption schedule. Moreover, the restriction that the MPC is less than one is shown by virtue of the fact that the consumption schedule is less steeply sloped than the 45-degree line.

We can also use the graphical representation in figure 3.3.1 to comment on the value of the average propensity to consume. As a starting point, consider the level of income Y_{d3}. Notice that, at this income, the consumption schedule crosses through the income (45-degree) line. This implies that income and consumption are equal at this point, referred to as the "break-even" point. In that $C = Y_d$ at the break-even point, the average propensity to consume takes on a value of one there. At incomes *below* Y_{d3}, we find that consumption exceeds income; the vertical distance to the income line is smaller than the distance to the consumption schedule. Or, what is the same, the consumption schedule lies above the income line over the range of incomes below Y_{d3}. Over this range, the average propensity to consume (C/Y_d) is thus greater than one. Now refer to the area to the right of Y_{d3}. Over these relatively high values of income, income exceeds consumption; the income line lies above the consumption schedule at all incomes higher than Y_{d3}. Thus, to the right of the breakeven point the average propensity to consume is less than one.

So far, we've considered the algebraic and graphical representations of a consumption function. But it should also be recognized that we have implicitly said something about saving, too. Given that consumption and saving are the two dispositions of disposable income, any relation which gives us the value of consumption at each level of income should also yield the corresponding levels of saving. Indeed, saving and consumption are just two views of the same behavior. To pursue this point, let's return to the national income identity relating disposable income, consumption, and saving:

$Y_d \equiv C + S.$

We can solve this expression for S and obtain:

$$S \equiv Y_d - C. \tag{3.3.9}$$

Notice that the consumption relation gives us pairs of values for Y_d and C; thus, for each of these pairs, we could use equation 3.3.9 to solve for the associated level of saving. Or we can use a more direct approach and utilize 3.3.9 and the consumption relation (3.3.5) to derive the relationship between saving and disposable income. Substitute the consumption function into 3.3.9 to obtain:[3]

$$S = Y_d - (a + bY_d).$$

Now, manipulate this expression by factoring out Y_d. The result is:

$$S = -a + (1 - b)Y_d. \tag{3.3.10}$$

Equation 3.3.10 is the saving function associated with our linear consumption function. Let's rationalize its nature by using concepts introduced in our discussion of the consumption function. First, recall that consumption supposedly takes on the value a when disposable income is zero. In order for any consumption to take place at a zero income, people must finance their expenditures by using past savings or by borrowing. In this event, we say that people *dissave,* or that they have negative saving. More specifically, if an amount a is spent on consumption at a zero income, then saving must be $-a$ (i.e., people must dissave the amount a). In a sense $-a$ could be called "autonomous saving." Second, let's consider what happens to saving as income starts to increase. For each extra dollar of income, some fraction b will be devoted to consumption. That leaves the residual fraction $(1 - b)$ for saving. We have already defined the ratio $\Delta S/\Delta Y_d$ as the marginal propensity to save; thus, in the saving relation above, the MPS is equal to $(1 - b)$. In that b (the MPC) is assumed to be a positive fraction, it also follows that $(1 - b)$ (the MPS) must obey also the restriction:

$$0 < (1 - b) < 1. \tag{3.3.11}$$

We can attach the same type of interpretation to the saving function as we applied to the consumption function. In particular, the linear saving equation consists of "autonomous saving" $(-a)$ plus "induced saving" (the MPS, $1 - b$, times the level of disposable income).

---

[3]Observe carefully that this expression is no longer an identity, in that we have obtained it by combining a behavioral relation (3.3.5) with an identity (3.3.9). It is now itself a behavioral relation.

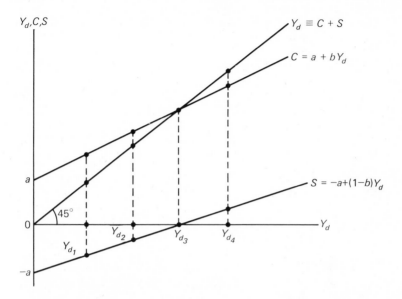

Figure 3.3.2 *The Keynesian Consumption and Saving Schedules*

The association between the saving and consumption functions can be illustrated diagrammatically as well as algebraically. In figure 3.3.2 we have presented a consumption schedule and an income line. These can be used to derive the associated saving schedule. Remember that the vertical distance to the consumption schedule represents the value of consumption at the chosen income level. Recall also that the vertical distance to the 45-degree line measures disposable income, which is the sum of consumption and saving. It follows, then, that the distance between the consumption schedule and the income line (again, measured vertically) represents saving. We could sketch the saving schedule just by choosing alternative values of income (e.g., Y_{d1}, Y_{d2} Y_{d3} and Y_{d4}) and plotting the amount of saving which would take place at each income. In fact, all we have done in figure 3.3.2 is plot saving explicitly after reading its values as the differences between Y_d and C. At Y_{d3}, consumption and income are equal; thus, saving is zero. At incomes below Y_{d3}, consumption exceeds income; consequently, saving will be negative over these values of income. At incomes above Y_{d3}, consumption is less than income; correspondingly, saving is positive.

A numerical example will undoubtedly aid the student in obtaining a better grasp of the concepts involved in the consumption and saving relations. Suppose the community spends on consumption 80% of its income plus \$100 billion. The latter term represents autonomous con-

Table 3.3.1. *The Relation of Disposable Income, Consumption and Savings for a Hypothetical Economy*
(in billions of dollars)

Disposable Income	Consumption Expenditures	Savings	APC	APS	MPC	MPS
0	100	− 100	—	—	—	—
100	180	− 80	1.80	− .80	.8	.2
200	260	− 60	1.30	− .30	.8	.2
300	340	− 40	1.13	− .13	.8	.2
400	420	− 20	1.05	− .05	.8	.2
500	500	0	1.00	0	.8	.2
600	580	20	.97	.03	.8	.2
700	660	40	.94	.06	.8	.2
800	740	60	.92	.08	.8	.2
900	820	80	.91	.09	.8	.2
1000	900	100	.90	.10	.8	.2

sumption, while the former is induced consumption. The function describing this behavior could be written as:

$$C = 100 + .8Y_d$$

where the marginal propensity to consume (b) is equal to .8. The corollary to the above relation is the saving equation. It can be derived from the disposable-income identity and the consumption equation as before:

$$S \equiv Y_d - C$$

and, substituting for C from the consumption equation, we obtain:

$$S = Y_d - (100 + .8Y_d)$$

or:

$$S = -100 + .2Y_d.$$

The relations between disposable income, consumption expenditures and saving used in our example are summarized in table 3.3.1. Focus first on the zero level of disposable income. Notice that autonomous consumption is equal to $100 billion and that this spending requires dissaving of the same amount. As income increases from 0 to $500 billion, consumption increases at each step by 80% of the increment in income. Correspondingly, saving increases (dissaving decreases) by 20% of the successive changes in income. The marginal propensities to consume

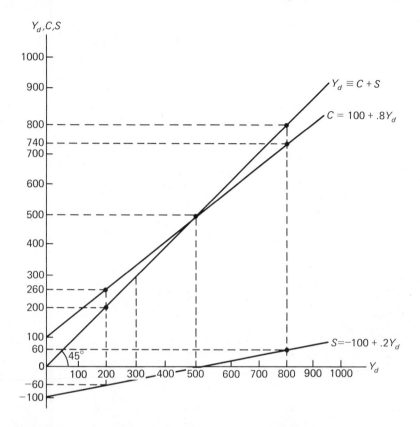

Figure 3.3.3   *Consumption and Saving: A Numerical Illustration*

and save thus take on the values of .8 and .2 respectively. Until we reach an income of $500 billion, consumption exceeds disposable income; as a result, the average propensity to consume is greater than one and the average propensity to save is negative. At an income of $500 billion, we reach a break-even point where consumption equals income and saving is zero. Beyond this income level, consumption and saving keep increasing; however, consumption is below income and saving is thus positive. Reflecting this, the APC falls below unity and the APS turns positive.

The numerical results of table 3.3.1 are plotted graphically in figure 3.3.3. The reader should use this diagram to verify all of the properties we have ascribed to the consumption and saving relations.

The most important points of this section are summarized below. We have outlined the determinants of consumption expenditures, but have narrowed our attention to the relation between consumption and disposable income. This consumption function can be specified in linear from as:

$$C = a + bY_d \qquad (3.3.5)$$

where a represents autonomous consumption and b is the marginal propensity to consume. The MPC is assumed to satisfy the double restriction that:

$$0 < MPC = b < 1. \qquad (3.3.7)$$

The corresponding saving function which is associated with the above consumption function is:

$$S = -a + (1 - b)Y_d \qquad (3.3.10)$$

where $-a$ is autonomous saving and $(1 - b)$ is the marginal propensity to save. The MPS must also satisfy the condition that:

$$0 < MPS = 1 - b < 1. \qquad (3.3.11)$$

These behavioral relations will be at the core of the economic model developed in the next section.

3.4 Equilibrium Restated

Now that we've examined the behavior underlying one of the components of aggregate demand, we can take our first glance at the process of income determination. This section will investigate the way in which a particular equilibrium level of income is established, given our hypothesis with regard to the behavior of consumption expenditure. We shall maintain our earlier assumptions of no government economic activity, no undistributed corporate profits and no international economic relations. Under these circumstances our model takes on the following form:

$$Y = AD \qquad (3.4.1)$$

$$AD \equiv C + I^D \qquad (3.4.2)$$

$$C = a + bY \qquad (3.4.3)$$

Each of these equations has been considered previously; however, it might be useful to review the interpretation of each one. The first expression (3.4.1) is an equilibrium condition. As noted in section 3.2, this is only one of the four versions we could use to state the general condition for equilibrium. Equation 3.4.2 is an identity defining aggregate demand in terms of its components. The last equation (3.4.3) is the consumption function. Notice that we have specified consumption as a function of net national product (Y) rather than disposable income (Y_d). The sole reason for this specification is that net national product and disposable income are identical under the assumptions set forth above.

The three equations above are written in four variables (Y, AD, C, and I^D). A system of this sort will not in general yield a unique solution for the values of the variables. Instead, there are an infinite number of values of Y, AD, C, and I^D which would satisfy the relationships contained in the model. But do not despair. We can choose one of the variables to be *exogenous* and solve for the equilibrium values of the other variables in terms of it. In particular, we can (and shall) assume that desired investment is determined by forces outside the model under consideration. Translated into less mechanical language, this means that we assume that firms wish to invest a certain amount regardless of the prevailing economic conditions we are attempting to describe. To signify that investment is exogenous, we use the expression:

$$I^D = I_0^D.$$

Given the value of desired investment, we can find the equilibrium values of income, consumption and aggregate demand by solving the system shown above. However, before we formalize our thinking on this point, it might be worthwhile to use an approach which entails more intuition and less rigor. Assume that the consumption equation takes the form:

$$C = 100 + .8Y$$

where C and Y are measured in billions of dollars. The above expression suggests that autonomous consumption is equal to $100 billion and that the marginal propensity to consume is .8. Or, in slightly different words, the community is assumed to spend on consumption an amount equal to 80% of its income plus $100 billion. We shall also assume that the desired level of investment is equal to $20 billion, and that the business community wants to invest this amount regardless of the prevailing economic conditions. From our earlier discussion, we know that the economy will be in equilibrium when current production (and hence income) is equal to aggregate demand (the sum of consumption and desired investment). Consequently, we can measure the level of aggregate

Table 3.4.1.   *Income Adjustments in the Product Market*
(in billions of dollars)

NNP = Y = Y_d	C	S	I^D	AD	ΔH^U
1	2	3	4	5	6
100	180	− 80	20	200	− 100
200	260	− 60	20	280	− 80
300	340	− 40	20	360	− 60
400	420	− 20	20	440	− 40
500	500	0	20	520	− 20
600	580	20	20	600	0
700	660	40	20	680	20
800	740	60	20	760	40

demand at each level of income and, by using a trial and error procedure, find the level of income which satisfies the equilibrium condition. Table 3.4.1 summarizes the results of this process.

The first column of table 3.4.1 lists alternative levels of net national product (which, by assumption, is equal to disposable income). The second and third columns show the levels of consumption and savings which, according to the consumption function specified above, correspond to each level of income. To illustrate the computation of the figures presented in the latter two columns, presume that income is equal to $600 billion. We can find the corresponding value of consumption by substituting $Y = 600$ into the consumption equation to obtain:

$$C = 100 + .8(600) = 580.$$

And saving would be the residual between income and consumption, i.e.,

$$S \equiv Y - C = 600 - 580 = 20.$$

In column 4, we write the exogenous level of desired investment, 20 billion. Notice that, by assumption, desired investment maintains this value regardless of the level of income. Column 5 provides the level of aggregate demand associated with each level of income. Each value of aggregate demand is computed as the sum of consumption (column 2) and the desired investment (column 4). Finally, the last column depicts the undesired change in inventories occurring at each income level; it is computed by subtracting aggregate demand (column 5) from production (column 1); that is:

$$\Delta H^U = Y - AD.$$

In using the results presented in this table, we shall attempt to focus on two points: the determination of the equilibrium level of income and the process by which the economy will tend to settle on this equilibrium position. In terms of the discussion on statics and dynamics contained in chapter 1, the first question will involve static analysis, whereas the second will require dynamic analysis. Although we shall not present a formal dynamic model, we shall still be using a dynamic view of the behavior of the business sector.

Start with the assumption that the community's net national product is equal to $100 billion. In accordance with our earlier assumption, the income distributed to the members of the community will also be $100 billion. From this income, consumers want to spend $180 billion on consumption goods; and, to do so, they must undergo dissaving of $80 billion. Businesses as a whole want to set investment equal to its desired level, $20 billion. Thus, aggregate demand is equal to $200 billion. This situation cannot be maintained, because aggregate demand exceeds aggregate supply by $100 billion. This excess demand can be satisfied only by making use of inventories which, in this case, play the role of a buffer. Since aggregate demand already included desired changes in inventories (in desired investment), the forced reduction in inventories shown in the last column is undesired. An undesired reduction in inventories will be intolerable to entrepreneurs if it persists and we would expect them to respond in some way to this adverse circumstance. Thus, $Y = 100$ is clearly *not* an equilibrium level of income. Static analysis itself cannot be used to analyze the type of action occurring as the result of disequilibrium situations. However, it seems reasonable to presume that a dynamic analysis of producer behavior would reveal a tendency to increase production in the face of undesired decreases in inventories. Thus, there should be a tendency for net national product to rise above its current level of $100 billion.

Now, as we can see from row 2, we assume that production (and hence income) rises to $200 billion. The corresponding level of consumption expenditures is equal to $260 billion, and hence savings is equal to the negative amount of $60 billion. The aggregate demand which corresponds to this level of income is 280. Thus, although firms increase their production and subsequently the income allocated to the members of the community by $100 billion, even this level of production is not sufficient to satisfy the current aggregate demand. The result will be a further undesired decrease in inventories by 80. Now we can see clearly the trial-and-error process through which firms, and consequently the economy, go in search of equilibrium.

At this stage we have to qualify two of our statements. First, the use of the concept of firms in the example may give the impression that all of the economy's firms undergo the process of increasing the volume of their production. This need not be so. Some firms may have to reduce their production levels if, for example, they produce a product with a declining demand. However, the *total* production of the economy does increase. We may compare the economy with a largely diversified firm which increases its overall production even though it decreases its output of certain products. Second, our example assumes a $100-billion dollar increase in each step of the adjustment. Again, this does not have to be so. The increase may be erratic or more modest and orderly.

Suppose that production keeps increasing and is eventually pushed up to the level of $500 billion. From the table, we can see clearly that the desired level of consumption expenditures is equal to the current level of production. Thus, at this level of income we witness the intersection of the consumption function and the 45-degree line. This is, of course, the break-even point mentioned in the previous section. The corresponding level of saving is equal to zero and aggregate demand amounts to 420. We see then that even at this level aggregate demand exceeds current production by 20 billion. Once more, inventories will suffer an undesired decline by an equivalent amount. Hence, firms will have to increase their production, say, to 600. This time, the desired level of consumption expenditures is equal to 580 and at this level of income the community appears to plan $20 billion of saving. The level of aggregate demand is thus 600 and it is equal to the current level of production. At this level, there are no further undesirable changes in inventories to necessitate changes in the production level. Thus, we may say that at this level of activity the firms (or the economy) have synchronized the flow of their production with aggregate demand. It must be recognized, however, that although current production is equal to current aggregate demand, a large portion of the firms' inventories has already been depleted during this trial-and-error process. Consequently, they may temporarily want to keep their production above the aggregate demand in order to restore the volume of inventories at the previous desired level. As soon as the restoration of the inventories is achieved, the economy will settle at a level of income which is equal to $600 billion.

Suppose now that instead of starting at a level of income and production equal to $100 billion, we start at a level of $800 billion. Now the process will be reversed, because at this level of production, the aggregate demand is only 760 and consequently, an undesirable accumulation of inventories will occur. It follows that the firms will want to decrease the rate of their production in order to reduce the level of inventories. If they reduce their production to $700 billion, they will still have the same problem. The only level of production and income which can be supported by an equal amount of aggregate demand is $600 billion. Now we may verify the equilibrium conditions we examined earlier. Indeed, at equilibrium: $Y = AD$, $S = I^D$, and $\Delta H^U = 0$. Notice also that actual investment (desired investment plus the undesired change in inventories) is equal to desired investment.

Another way to look at the concept of equilibrium is the following. Suppose that the firms produce a net national product equal to $700 billion. According to our assumption, disposable income will also be $700 billion. But since the marginal propensity to consume is less than one, the economy will absorb only $660 billion worth of goods, and will save the difference, in this case, $40 billion. This, however, means that firms do not sell $40 billion worth of the goods they have produced. Should desired investment be equal to zero, then the undesired accumulation of inventories would be equal to the amount that people decide to save, i.e., 40 billion. Now, even if the desired investments is not equal to zero, unless it is exactly equal to saving, firms will get stuck with undesirable increases or decreases in inventories. In other words, saving is always equal to the sum of the desired and undesired investment, the last item being the change in inventories that firms fail to anticipate. This is the meaning of an identity, and the reader may verify this by adding columns 4 and 6 to find that this sum is *always* equal to the volume of saving, which is given by column 3. But the existence of undesired investment ignites the mechanism we have described that will change the level of production. This process will stop when, and only when, saving is equal to the desired level of investment. This means that $\Delta H^U = 0$. This process can be visualized by the following analogy. Suppose that we want to maintain a certain water level in a tank where there is an outflow and inflow. The only way to achieve this will be to synchronize the flows in such a way that the inflow will equal the outflow.

We shall now attempt to solve the problem directly by utilizing the available information in regard to the behavior of the different variables. To do this, let us return to the algebraic statement of the model. The reader will remember that the model includes an equilibrium condition, the definition of aggregate demand in terms of consumption and desired investment, the consumption function and a statement defining the value of desired investment. For the sake of simplification, we shall follow the convention of combining the equilibrium condition and the aggregate demand identity. In particular, let us recall from our initial formulation of the two-sector model that:

$$Y = AD \tag{3.4.1}$$

$$AD \equiv C + I^D. \tag{3.4.2}$$

If we substitute the definition of aggregate demand (3.4.2) into the equilibrium condition (3.4.1), we obtain:

$$Y = C + I^D. \tag{3.4.4}$$

The use of this new version of the equilibrium condition allows us to "shrink" the model to the following relations:

$$Y = C + I^D \qquad \text{(equilibrium condition)} \tag{3.4.4}$$

$$C = a + bY \qquad \text{(consumption equation)} \tag{3.4.5}$$

$$I^D = I^D_0 \qquad \text{(specification of value of } I^D) \tag{3.4.6}$$

The model above contains three variables (Y, C, and I^D). Two of them (C and Y) are considered endogenous; the other (I^D) is exogenous. Equations 3.4.4 and 3.4.5 are called structural equations, because they show the basic structure of the economic system. Obviously, the more detailed our description of the basic structure of the economy, the larger the number of structural equations we shall need. These two structural equations alone would not yield a unique solution for the variables they relate; however, the assumption that desired investment is exogenous (3.4.6) allows us to solve uniquely for the values of income and consumption associated with each possible level of desired investment.

To show the explicit dependence of consumption and income on the value of desired investment, we can find the reduced form of the system of structural equations. A reduced-form equation specifies the value of an endogenous variable in terms of the exogenous variables of the model in question. There is a reduced-form equation for each endogenous variable in the system (in this case, one for C and one for Y). To obtain the reduced form of a system, we keep substituting the endogenous variables with their structural equations until every endogenous variable appears on the left-hand side of an equation with only exogenous variables on the right-hand side. This may sound like a complicated procedure (and it can be for large models), but it turns out to be quite simple in the present case.

First, let us turn to the solution for the equilibrium level of income. Substitute the consumption equation (3.4.5) into the equilibrium condition (3.4.4) to obtain:

$$Y = (a + bY) + I^D. \tag{3.4.7}$$

Now, collect terms and solve explicitly for Y:

$$Y - bY = a + I^D$$

$$(1 - b)Y = a + I^D$$

$$Y = \frac{a}{1 - b} + \frac{1}{1 - b} I^D. \tag{3.4.8}$$

Equation 3.4.8 is the reduced form for the endogenous variable income, which is expressed as an explicit function of the exogenous variable investment. Next, we may obtain the reduced form for the variable consumption by substituting equation 3.4.8 into the consumption function to obtain:

$$C = a + b \left[\frac{a}{1 - b} + \frac{1}{1 - b} I^D \right]$$

which, after a little algebraic manipulation, may be written as:

$$C = \frac{a}{1 - b} + \frac{b}{1 - b} I^D. \tag{3.4.9}$$

Equations 3.4.8–3.4.9 provide the reduced form of the system of structural equations given by 3.4.4–3.4.6. Now if we assume that investment is fixed at a certain level, say I_0^D, then the solution of the system will be:

$$Y_0 = \frac{a}{1 - b} + \frac{1}{1 - b} I_0^D \tag{3.4.10}$$

$$C_0 = \frac{a}{1 - b} + \frac{b}{1 - b} I_0^D \tag{3.4.11}$$

$$I^D = I_0^D. \tag{3.4.12}$$

Hence we see that given the value of the parameters of the system (a and b) and given the value of the investment, the value of consumption and income can be determined uniquely. The meaning of this solution is that given the demand for investment (I_0^D), if the economy produces output equal to Y_0, then this output will be an equilibrium output. No undesired change in inventories will occur; total demand will be exactly equal to total current production. This last proposition may be verified. The total demand which corresponds to Y_0 will be:

$$C_0 + I_0^D = \frac{a}{1-b} + \frac{b}{1-b} I_0^D + I_0^D$$

$$= \frac{a}{1-b} + \frac{b}{1-b} I_0^D$$

$$= Y_0.$$

A numerical example may help to secure these ideas. Suppose that autonomous consumption is equal to \$100 billion, autonomous investment is equal to \$20 billion and the marginal propensity to consume is equal to .8. Given these assumptions about the structure of the economy, we want to find the equilibrium level of income. Under these circumstances equations 3.4.4–3.4.6 become:

$$Y = C + I^D \tag{3.4.13}$$

$$C = 100 + .8Y \tag{3.4.14}$$

$$I^D = 20. \tag{3.4.15}$$

To derive the reduced form of the system, first substitute for consumption into the equilibrium condition (3.4.13) to obtain:

$$Y = 100 + .8Y + I^D.$$

Next, solve for Y in terms of I^D to obtain:

$$Y = \frac{100}{1-.8} + \frac{1}{1-.8} I^D. \tag{3.4.16}$$

Having the reduced-form equation for income, substitute 3.4.16 into the consumption function (3.4.14) to obtain the reduced form for consumption:

$$C = 100 + .8 \left[\frac{100}{1-.8} + \frac{1}{1-.8} I^D \right]$$

or $\quad C = \dfrac{100}{1-.8} + \dfrac{.8}{1-.8} I^D. \tag{3.4.17}$

Now we may use the value of investment to obtain the values for income and consumption:

$$Y = \frac{100}{1-.8} + \frac{1}{1-.8} (20) = 600 \tag{3.4.18}$$

$$C = \frac{100}{1 - .8} + \frac{.8}{1 - .8}(20) = 580. \qquad (3.4.19)$$

Hence, the equilibrium level of income is $600 billion.

Of course, the same result would be obtained if instead of using equation 3.4.13 as an equilibrium condition we used $I^D = S$. But for this, we need the savings function instead of the consumption function. For our numerical example the savings function can be found easily since we know that

$$S \equiv Y - C.$$

Substituting for C with the expression given in the numerical example we obtain:

$$S = Y - 100 - .8Y$$

or $\quad S = -100 + .2Y.$

Hence the system 3.4.13–3.4.15 becomes

$$I^D = S \qquad\qquad (3.4.20)$$

$$S = -100 + .2Y \qquad\qquad (3.4.21)$$

$$I^D = 20. \qquad\qquad (3.4.22)$$

Substituting the expression for saving and the assumed value for investment into the equilibrium condition we obtain:

$$20 = -100 + .2Y$$

which can be solved for income to give:

$$Y = 600.$$

The level of saving corresponding to this income will be:

$$S = -100 + .2(600) = 20$$

which is indeed equal to the level of investment. Since saving is equal to $20 billion, it follows that the sum of consumption and desired investment will be equal to the level of income. We see then that regardless of which equilibrium condition we use the results will be the same.

Now, let's cast the analysis in graphical terms, using an aggregate supply schedule, an aggregate demand schedule and the consumption and investment schedules. They will be related in such a way as to focus on the nature of equilibrium from a diagrammatic perspective.

Refer to figure 3.4.1, where we have plotted a linear consumption schedule like the one shown in the previous section. Notice that the

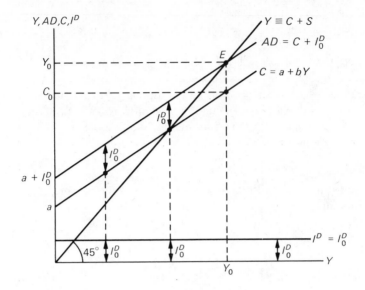

Figure 3.4.1   *Product-Market Equilibrium in the Two-Sector Model*

position of that schedule can be gauged by the intercept term, autonomous consumption (a), and that the slope is given by the marginal propensity to consume (b). In the same diagram, we have depicted an investment schedule. Notice that although investment is plotted against income, the schedule is a horizontal line parallel to the income axis. This is in conformity to our assumption that desired investment is exogenous. Regardless of what happens to the level of income, the level of desired investment stays the same. The consumption and investment schedules reflect the "behavior" of the two components of aggregate demand. We should then be able to combine them in order to sketch an aggregate demand schedule. In particular, we could choose alternative levels of income and add desired investment and the corresponding level of consumption to determine aggregate demand. If we were to follow this process for all conceivable values of income, the end result would be an aggregate demand schedule lying above the consumption schedule by the amount of desired investment. Geometrically, the aggregate demand schedule is simply the vertical sum of the consumption and investment schedules. Two characteristics are important enough to be stressed here. First, the intercept of the aggregate demand schedule is the sum of autonomous consumption and desired investment $(a + I_0^D)$; this corresponds to the fixed, or autonomous, part of aggregate demand. The slope of the aggregate demand schedule is the marginal propensity to consume (b). This should be apparent, in that the aggregate demand and consumption schedules are parallel and, as we have noted in the prior section, b is the slope of the consumption schedule. It should also be reasonable from a commonsense point of view. As income increases, consumption is the only element of aggregate demand subject to change; thus, the full change in AD from one income to the next will consist of extra consumption. And the extra consumption will be given by the MPC times the change in income. The equation of the aggregate demand schedule can be written as:

$$AD = a + bY + I_0^D. \tag{3.4.23}$$

The supply side of the economy is represented in the diagram by the 45-degree line.[4] To allow further elaboration, we have labeled that schedule with the aggregate supply identity. The equilibrium level of income can be found by noting that there is only one value of income at which aggregate supply and aggregate demand are equal. These two schedules intersect at point E, which corresponds to the level of income Y_0 and the level of consumption C_0. No other income can qualify as an equilibrium value. To illustrate this point, we have resketched the relevant schedules in panel (a) of figure 3.4.2 (leaving out some of the unnecessary details of the previous diagram and adding a few useful ones). First, consider an arbitrary level of income below Y_0, say Y_1. Notice that aggregate demand exceeds supply by the amount AB. As we have seen several times before, the excess demand could be satisfied only through an undesired decrease in inventories. Hence AB represents ΔH^U, which is negative in this instance. As we have argued earlier, such an unwanted decline in inventories should encourage firms to increase production in an effort to halt this movement and to replenish inventory stocks. This tendency will exist as long as aggregate demand exceeds aggregate supply at the existing level of income. Alternatively, consider those incomes above the equilibrium position. Choose Y_2 for the illustra-

---

[4]In Keynesian analysis, the 45-degree line is often characterized as an aggregate supply schedule. But it must be interpreted with caution. In this context, it is *not* a behavioral relation per se, in that it does not ascribe any particular motivation to producers. Instead, it shows the amount produced (supplied) at alternative income levels. More specifically, it reflects the *identity* that real income and real output (the aggregate amount supplied) are simply two views of the same phenomenon, and that the relation between them can thus be sketched as a 45-degree line. The equilibrium condition we introduced earlier *does* attribute a particular type of behavior to suppliers, though, in the sense that it says they will be satisfied only when undesired inventory changes are zero, and that they will adjust production whenever this condition is violated; but this behavioral assumption is hardly one that needs justification. A fuller view of the motivation and behavior of producers will be presented in later chapters.

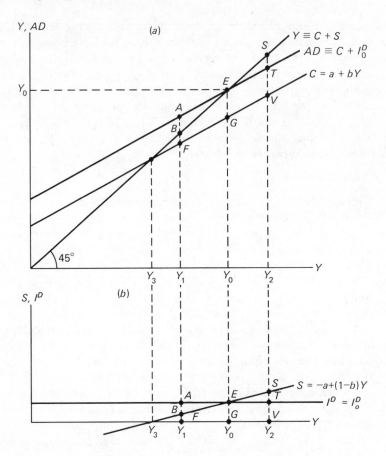

Figure 3.4.2   *Alternative Views of Product-Market Equilibrium*

tion. Notice that at Y_2 (and all others like it), aggregate demand falls short of aggregate supply. But if this condition holds, producers will experience undesired *increases* in inventories. The undesired change in inventories for this case is given by the distance ST. In response to excess supply conditions, producers will cut back production in an effort to curtail the unwanted rise in inventories.

As long as a given level of income causes an inherent tendency for change, that level of income is a disequilibrium value. Incomes Y_1 and Y_2 and all others like them fail to satisfy the conditions for equilibrium. It is only at Y_0 that aggregate demand and supply are equal. We can view the equilibrium condition from another direction by recasting the model explicitly in terms of saving and desired investment. In panel (b) of figure 3.4.2 we have sketched the saving and investment schedules. Before we use them to further illustrate the nature of equilibrium, it might be worthwhile to rationalize their relation with schedules of panel (a). First, consider the saving schedule, which can be drawn by plotting information contained in panel (a). In particular, we know from the aggregate supply identity $Y \equiv C + S$ that saving is just the residual between income and consumption. In that we have the income (aggregate supply) and consumption schedule plotted in panel (a), we can measure saving as the vertical distance between these two schedules. At a zero level of income, saving is equal to $-a$; at income Y_3, saving is zero ($Y = C$). When income is Y_1, the difference between income and consumption (and hence saving) is given by BF. At Y_2, saving is SV. And, finally, when income is at its equilibrium level, Y_0, saving is equal to EG. All of these distances have been incorporated into the saving schedule itself. Second, consider the investment schedule. Desired investment takes on a constant value given in panel (a) by the equal distances: AF at Y_1, EG at Y_0, TV at Y_2, etc. At the equilibrium level of income, saving and investment are equal. This can be seen from the relations in panel (a) or, more directly, those of panel (b). Thus, the saving and desired investment schedules can be used to depict an equilibrium position.

3.5 Multiplier Effects of Shifts in the Aggregate Demand Schedule

In the previous section, we analyzed the way in which a particular equilibrium level of income is determined. In doing so, we presumed that the one exogenous variable of the model (I^D) took on a fixed value. In this section, we shall investigate the repercussions stemming from a change in the value of desired investment. Our analysis falls into the category of comparative statics. We shall proceed to compare two successive equilibrium positions (solution sets) corresponding to two alternative values of desired investment. In the process of our analysis, we shall find that income is subject to a multiplier effect when desired investment changes. Then, in an identical fashion, we shall consider the implications of a change in the autonomous level of consumption.

First, suppose that the firms decide that they want to invest an amount equal to I_1^D ($I_1^D > I_0^D$) and again assume that this decision in regard to the new level of investment is independent of the prevailing economic conditions (i.e., investment is still considered to be exogenous). Substituting this new level of investment into the reduced-form system of our model (3.4.10–3.4.12), we find that equilibrium values of the variables of the system will be:

$$Y_1 = \frac{1}{1 - b} + \frac{1}{1 - b} I_1^D \tag{3.5.1}$$

$$C_1 = \frac{a}{1 - b} + \frac{b}{1 - b} I_1^D \tag{3.5.2}$$

$$I^D = I_1^D. \tag{3.5.3}$$

Comparison of the solution 3.5.1–3.5.3 with that of 3.4.10–3.4.12 reveals immediately that the difference in the equilibrium level of income is:

$$Y_1 - Y_0 = \frac{a}{1 - b} + \frac{1}{1 - b} I_1^D - \frac{a}{1 - b} - \frac{1}{1 - b} I_0^D$$

$$= \frac{1}{1 - b} [I_1^D - I_0^D]$$

or more briefly:

$$\Delta Y = k \, \Delta I^D \tag{3.5.4}$$

for $k \equiv \dfrac{1}{1 - b}$.

We thus establish that, given the assumption in regard to the marginal propensity to consume, the change in the equilibrium level of income due to a change in the autonomous investment will be equal to the change in investment multiplied by a quantity $k \equiv 1/(1 - b)$. This last term, k, is called the *multiplier* and it is equal to the reciprocal of the marginal propensity to save.[5] Insofar as the marginal propensity to save is greater than zero but less than unity (i.e., $0 < (1 - b) < 1$), it follows that the multiplier will be greater than one. In fact, the smaller the marginal propensity to save, or the closer the marginal propensity to consume is to unity, the larger the multiplier. The meaning of equa-

---

[5] The multiplier expressed by equation 3.5.4 ($k \equiv 1/(1 - b)$), registers the *total* increase (decrease) in the equilibrium level of income due to a corresponding increase (decrease) in the desired level of investment. For this reason it may be called the *total* income-investment multiplier. Furthermore, it is worth observing that this expression does not include any statement concerning the span of time which is necessary for the completion of the process of change. Neither does it tell us anything in regard to how this total change in income is distributed over the time span. For, as we have already suggested, the tracing of the time path of a variable (or, more generally, a system) belongs to the realm of dynamics. On this point see section 3.6 and in particular the comments associated with table 3.6.1 and figure 3.6.1.

tion 3.5.4 can now be explained easily: it tells us how much income should change in order to produce a change in saving which will be equal to the given change in investment. More explicitly, suppose that we start with a level of income Y_0 which corresponds to the equilibrium $S_0 = I_0^D$ and now investment increases by an amount ΔI^D to the level $I_1^D (I_1^D - I_0^D = \Delta I^D)$. At the new equilibrium the income has to provide saving S_1 such that $S_1 = I_1^D$. In other words, the change in saving, $\Delta S = S_1 - S_0$, has to be equal to the change in investment ($\Delta S = \Delta I^D$). We may compare equations 3.5.2 and 3.4.11. The change in consumption expenditures is equal to:

$$C_1 - C_0 = \frac{a}{1-b} + \frac{b}{1-b} I_1^D - \frac{a}{1-b} - \frac{b}{1-b} I_0^D$$

or $\quad C_1 - C_0 = \frac{b}{1-b}(I_1^D - I_0^D)$

or more briefly:[6]

---

[6]As in the case of 3.5.4, equation 3.5.5 gives us another total multiplier. In particular, it shows the total change in consumption expenditures due to a change in the desired level of investment. For this reason it may also be called the *total* consumption-investment *multiplier.*

Generalizing now, consider the reduced-form equations of the system 3.4.4–3.4.6:

$$Y = \frac{a}{1-b} + \frac{1}{1-b} I^D \qquad\qquad\qquad (3.4.8)$$

$$C = \frac{a}{1-b} + \frac{b}{1-b} I^D. \qquad\qquad\qquad (3.4.9)$$

There are two points to be made with regard to equations 3.4.8 and 3.4.9. First, these equations are linear, as is the original system of structural equations; and second, the coefficients of I^D give us directly the total multipliers of income and consumption respectively, due to a change in the level of the desired investment. Furthermore, from equations 3.4.8 and 3.4.9 we see that the same exogenous variable is associated with two different multipliers, depending on the equation in which it appears. In fact, since the reduced-form equations express the endogenous variables in terms of the exogenous, it follows that every exogenous variable will be related to every endogenous one via a total multiplier (unless an endogenous variable is already expressed in the structural system as a function of only some but not all the exogenous variables of the system). Therefore, in general the number of total multipliers will be equal to the number of exogenous variables times the number of endogenous.

We may conclude that when the structural equations are linear and static, the corresponding reduced-form equations are also linear and static. Under these conditions the coefficients of the exogenous variables will be total multipliers and will show directly the total change in the endogenous variable due to a corresponding change in the exogenous variable in question. In what follows, more often than not, we shall reserve the term *multiplier* for changes in income but we should understand that this multiplier is only one of many. Furthermore, since our system will be static (unless otherwise specified) the multipliers we present will be total multipliers.

$$\Delta C = \frac{b}{1 - b} \Delta I^D. \tag{3.5.5}$$

Now the change in saving will be:

$$\Delta S = \Delta Y - \Delta C. \tag{3.5.6}$$

Substituting ΔY and ΔC from equations 3.5.4 and 3.5.5 in 3.5.6 we find:

$$\Delta S = \frac{1}{1 - b} \Delta I^D - \frac{b}{1 - b} \Delta I^D$$

from which we can see immediately that

$$\Delta S = \Delta I^D.$$

It follows then that if income increases according to the multiplier equation (3.5.4), it will produce an increase in the volume of saving which will be equal to the change in investment.[7]

Diagramatically, the problem is posed in figure 3.5.1. C is the usual consumption schedule and $(C + I_0^D)$ is the initial aggregate demand schedule. Next we increase investment by ΔI^D to a new level, I_1^D. The corresponding change in income is given by ΔY and the new equilibrium level of income Y_1 is given by the intersection of the 45-degree line and the new aggregate demand schedule $(C + I_1^D)$.

We have shown how a change in the aggregate demand results in a change in the equilibrium level of income. Aggregate demand, however, can change not only through changes in the desired investment, but also through changes in the autonomous part of consumption, i.e., in the intercept of the consumption function.[8]

Suppose then that the autonomous part of consumption changes to a' $(a' > a)$. This implies a parallel shift in the consumption function, as figure 3.5.2 shows. If we now add desired investment, I_0^D, to both consumption schedules, we find that the corresponding equilibrium levels of income will be Y_0 and Y_0'. These equilibrium values are given by the intersection of the two levels of aggregate demand $(C + I_0^D)$ and

---

[7]More intuitively, we recall that saving increases by only $(1 - b)$ times the increase in income. It follows then that to induce an extra dollar of saving, we need $1/(1 - b)$ extra dollars of income. Further, insofar as we require $\Delta S = \Delta I^D$, it should be apparent that we need a change in income of the amount $[1/(1 - b)]\Delta I^D$.

[8]In addition, a change in the MPC would cause a change in the equilibrium level of income. However, we shall not consider this possibility, for two reasons: first, it is considerably more difficult to treat; second, unlike the case of a change in autonomous consumption, it would be of no use in our later analysis.

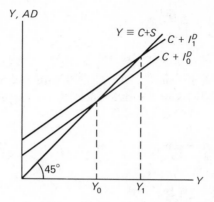

Figure 3.5.1 *The Multiplier Effect of a Change in Autonomous Investment*

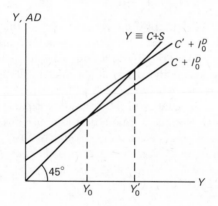

Figure 3.5.2 *The Multiplier Effect of a Change in Autonomous Consumption*

$(C' + I_0^D)$ with the 45-degree line. We may now determine algebraically the relation of Y_0 and Y_0' by finding the difference $\Delta Y = (Y_0' - Y_0)$. To this end we may substitute the new level of autonomous consumption into the system 3.4.10–3.4.12 to find the equilibrium values of the variables. These will be:

$$Y_0' = \frac{a'}{1 - b} + \frac{1}{1 - b} I_0^D \qquad (3.5.7)$$

$$C_0' = \frac{a'}{1 - b} + \frac{b}{1 - b} I_0^D \qquad (3.5.8)$$

$$I^D = I_0^D. \qquad (3.5.9)$$

Comparison of the solution 3.5.7–3.5.9 with that of 3.4.10–3.4.12 shows immediately that the difference in the equilibrium level of income is:

$$Y_0' - Y_0 = \frac{a'}{1 - b} + \frac{1}{1 - b} I_0^D - \frac{a}{1 - b} - \frac{1}{1 - b} I_0^D$$

$$Y_0' - Y_0 = \frac{1}{1 - b}(a' - a)$$

or more briefly:

$$\Delta Y = k \, \Delta a \text{ where } k \equiv \frac{1}{1 - b}. \qquad (3.5.10)$$

The change in the equilibrium level of income in this case is equal to the multiplier times the change in autonomous consumption. We may now combine the results given by equations 3.5.4 and 3.5.10 and say that any change in the autonomous part of our model will imply a change in the equilibrium level of income which will be equal to the product of the multiplier and the change of the autonomous part in question.

For a numerical example, suppose that autonomous consumption is $50 billion, autonomous investment is equal to $100 billion and the marginal propensity to consume is equal to .8. The equilibrium levels of the variables can be found by solving the system

$$Y = C + I^D$$

$$C = 50 + .8Y$$

$$I^D = 100.$$

The solution will be $Y = 750$, $C = 650$, and $I^D = 100$. Suppose now that investment increases from 100 billion to 150. The new equilibrium values of the variables will be $Y = 1,000$, $C = 850$, and $I^D = 150$. We thus see that the change in income is $\Delta Y = 250$ and that this is equal to the change in investment $\Delta I^D = 50$, times the multiplier, $k \equiv 1/(1 - .8) = 5$.

If, on the other hand, investment remains at the same level as before (100 billion) but autonomous consumption increases by 50 to 100 billion (i.e., the consumption function becomes $C' = 100 + .8Y$), then the new equilibrium values of the variables will be $Y = 1,000$, $C = 900$,

$I^D = 100$. Again the change of the equilibrium level of income is equal to $\Delta Y = 250$ which is equal to the product of $\Delta a = 50$ and the multiplier, $k = 5$.

3.6 The Dynamics of Response

So far, we have analyzed multipliers in terms of comparative statics. We compared two successive equilibrium levels of income and showed how these two levels of income are related to each other. The implicit assumption was that the adjustment of the economy from one equilibrium to another (represented by a move from, say, Y_0 to Y_1) would be instantaneous, or that the speed of adjustment would be infinite. In reality, though, change takes time. The transition of the economy from one equilibrium to another is not instantaneous; nor is it completed in one huge, sure-footed step. Instead, it builds gradually and is accomplished only after the system passes through conditions of disequilibrium. According to our earlier comments, any discussion of the time path which connects Y_0 and Y_1 clearly belongs to dynamic analysis. The formal model used so far is not intended to be dynamic; thus, it can provide no real insight into the nature of the adjustment process. In order to obtain this insight, we must introduce time explicitly into the analysis.

For the purposes of this section, assume that producers of consumer goods require one period in order to change their production levels. (The period can be of arbitrary length, as long as it is the same length throughout the analysis.) Further assume that the economy is initially in equilibrium in period t, and that income takes on a value of Y_0. Suppose that desired investment increases from I_0^D to I_1^D in period $t + 1$, thus disturbing the equilibrium. Also assume that the new level of investment (I_1^D) is maintained over the entire course of our analysis. As a result of the change in desired investment, the equilibrium level of income will obviously change. We will investigate the path traced out by the economy as it moves toward this new equilibrium position. In our discussion, we shall refer to the results presented in table 3.6.1. In that table, we have included a description of the general repercussions of the change in investment and, alongside, a numerical example drawn up under the assumption that the MPC equals .6 and the change in investment is equal to 100.

Let's begin our analysis in period $t + 1$. Desired investment increases, and producers attempt to satisfy the extra demand for capital goods by increasing production correspondingly. Thus, the first period yields a

Table 3.6.1.   *The Dynamics of the Investment Multiplier*

Period	Change in income by period (general form)	Change in income by period (numerical form, $\Delta I^D = 100$; $b = .6$)
$t + 1$	$\Delta Y_{t+1} = \Delta I^D_{t+1}$	$\Delta Y_{t+1} = 100$
$t + 2$	$\Delta Y_{t+2} = \Delta C_{t+1} = b\Delta Y_{t+1} = b\Delta I^D_{t+1}$	$\Delta Y_{t+2} = .6(100) = 60$
$t + 3$	$\Delta Y_{t+3} = \Delta C_{t+2} = b\Delta Y_{t+2} = b^2\Delta I^D_{t+1}$	$\Delta Y_{t+3} = .6^2(100) = 36$
$t + 4$	$\Delta Y_{t+4} = \Delta C_{t+3} = b\Delta Y_{t+3} = b^3\Delta I^D_{t+1}$	$\Delta Y_{t+4} = .6^3(100) = 21.6$
$t + 5$	$\Delta Y_{t+5} = \Delta C_{t+4} = b\Delta Y_{t+4} = b^4\Delta I^D_{t+1}$	$\Delta Y_{t+5} = .6^4(100) = 12.96$
$\vdots$	$\vdots$	$\vdots$
$t + n$	$\Delta Y_{t+n} = \Delta C_{t+n-1} = b\Delta Y_{t+n-1} = b^{n-1}\Delta I^D_{t+1}$	$\Delta Y_{t+n} = .6^{n-1}(100) \simeq 0$

Total change in income: $\Delta Y = \Delta I^D + b\Delta I^D + b^2\Delta I^D + b^3\Delta I^D + b^4\Delta I^D + \ldots + b^{n-1}\Delta I^D$

$$\Delta Y = 100 + (.6)100 + (.6)^2 100 + (.6)^3 100 + (.6)^4 100 + \ldots + (.6)^{n-1} 100$$

$$\Delta Y = \frac{1 - .6^n}{1 - .6}(100)$$

$$\Delta Y \simeq \frac{1}{1 - .6}(100)$$

$$\Delta Y = 250$$

change in production equal to the change in investment (in terms of the numerical example, 100). Due to the increase in production, additional income (100) is generated. The recipients of this additional income want to use some of it to finance additional consumption expenditures. But, due to our assumption about the one-period lag in the production of consumer goods, producers will have to satisfy the extra consumption demand by selling out of inventory stocks. Thus, production (and hence income) increases by only $\Delta I^D(100)$ in the first period. In period $t + 2$, producers step up production even further in an attempt to satisfy the increase in desired consumption experienced in the previous period. Using the consumption function specified earlier, we know that desired consumption increased in period $t + 1$ by the product of the marginal propensity to consume (b) and the change in income. So we have $\Delta C_{t+1} = b\Delta Y_{t+1}(=60)$. But the previous period's change in income was equal to the increment in desired investment: $\Delta Y_{t+1} = \Delta I^D_{t+1}$; consequently, production (and income) in period $t + 2$ will increase by the MPC times the change in I^D. But this change in income induces another increase in desired consumption expenditures (by $b\Delta Y_{t+2}$), and thus forces producers to adjust production again in the next period.

In period $t + 3$, producers expand production by the increase in consumption experienced in period $t + 2$. We have seen that this rise in consumption was $\Delta C_{t+2} = b\Delta Y_{t+2}$; in addition, we know that $\Delta Y_{t+2} = b\Delta I_t^D$. Hence, the extra production generated in period $t + 3$ will be $\Delta Y_{t+3} = b^2(\Delta I_t^D)$. Part of the extra income generated by this change is again translated into a desired change in consumption expenditures, and this forces another increment in production in period $t + 4$.

This process goes on continually, from period to period, until the impetus for further changes in production dissipates. In general terms, production goes through a series of increases. The first increase (in period $t + 1$) is directly due to the extra demand for investment; all subsequent changes in production are fostered by induced increases in consumption expenditures. Through the relation between income and consumption, each period's change in income elicits change in production in the subsequent period. But notice that the successive increments in production get smaller and smaller as we pass through time. This is due to the fact that only part of each period's change in income is translated into an increase in consumption (that part given by the MPC). Thus, if we consider enough periods, the additional change in production will eventually drop very close to zero. In a sense, the process "wears itself out."

Now that we know the chain of response taking place when desired investment changes, we can turn to the task of finding the eventual *total* increase in income as we move from the initial equilibrium to the new one. This total change (ΔY) will be the sum of the changes occurring in successive periods, or:

$$\Delta Y = \Delta Y_{t+1} + \Delta Y_{t+2} + \Delta Y_{t+3} + \Delta Y_{t+4} + \ldots \Delta Y_{t+n}.$$

Substituting the values of $\Delta Y_{t+1}, \Delta Y_{t+2}, \ldots, \Delta Y_{t+n}$ from the second column of table 3.6.1, we obtain an expression for ΔY in terms of the assumed change in investment:

$$\Delta Y = \Delta I_{t+1} + b\Delta I_{t+1}^D + b^2\Delta I_{t+1}^D + b^3\Delta I_{t+1}^D + \ldots + b^{n-1}\Delta I_{t+1}^D.$$

Or, factoring out ΔI_{t+1}^D (and dropping the time subscript from this term) we find:

$$\Delta Y = (1 + b + b^2 + b^3 + \ldots + b^{n-1})\Delta I^D. \qquad (3.6.1)$$

This expression looks rather formidable, but it can be simplified considerably. First, multiply 3.6.1 by b to get:

$$b\Delta Y = (b + b^2 + b^3 + b^4 + \ldots b^n)\Delta I^D. \qquad (3.6.2)$$

Now, subtract 3.6.2 from 3.6.1 to obtain:[9]

$$\Delta Y - b\Delta Y = (1 - b^n)\Delta I^D.$$

And now, solving for ΔY, we have:

$$\Delta Y = \frac{1 - b^n}{1 - b}\Delta I^D.$$

Keep in mind that the MPC (b) is assumed to be less than one. If we have included enough terms in our computation of successive changes in income, the value of n will have been chosen is a number large enough so that b^n is extremely small.[10] In fact, as we choose successively larger values of n, the term b^n approaches zero. Thus, we can exclude this term and write:

$$\Delta Y = \left(\frac{1}{1 - b}\right)\Delta I^D. \tag{3.6.3}$$

We now see from another perspective why the coefficient of ΔI^D in equation 3.5.4 was termed a total multiplier. To be sure, equation 3.6.3 gives the sum of the per-period changes in income due to a change in I^D as expressed by equation 3.6.1. Thus, these two equations, taken in conjunction, provide us not only with the total change in income but also with its distribution over time. Indeed, it was already shown in table 3.6.1 that each of the components of the expression in parentheses in equation 3.6.1 corresponds to the increase in income which took place during a certain time period. More specifically, we saw that, given our assumptions, the initial change in the level of desired investment was accompanied by an equal change in income during the same period. In other words, the change in the level of income due to a one-dollar change in the level of desired investment during the same period is equal to unity (i.e., $\Delta Y_{t+2}/\Delta I^D_{t+1} = 1$). During the second period, the initial change in investment triggers another change in income which is equal to b (i.e., $\Delta Y_{t+2}/\Delta I^D_{t+1} = b$). Similarly, we see that the change in income after $(n - 1)$ periods per dollar change in the level of the desired investment is equal to b^{n-1} (i.e., $\Delta Y_{t+n}/\Delta I^D_{t+1} = b^{n-1}$). These quantities (i.e.,

---

[9]Notice that all the terms in the parentheses except 1 and b^n cancel out.

[10]In fact, the series of terms in 3.6.1 and 3.6.2 is infinite; we have chosen an end period only to simplify the analysis. In the process of choosing a value of n, we can arbitrarily choose one which is as large as we need to capture the full impact of the multiplier effect. All of this hinges on the assumption that $0 < b < 1$. If b were greater than one, the income adjustments in each period would be *larger* than the last, and the total change in income would be infinite.

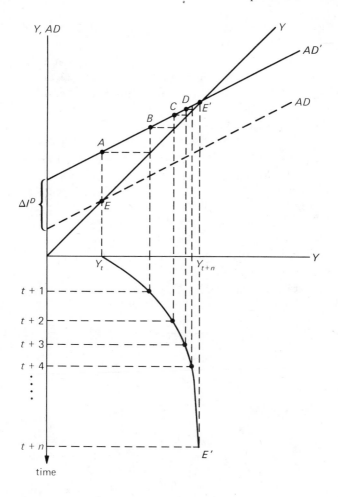

Figure 3.6.1   *The Dynamics of the Investment Multiplier*

the consecutive per-period change in income) are called *dynamic* or *interim* income-investment *multipliers*. Thus, another way of reading equation 3.6.3 is to suggest that the sum of dynamic income-investment multipliers is equal to the *total* income-investment multiplier. Traditionally the first or concurrent interim multiplier is also called the *impact* multiplier (in the present case this will be $\Delta Y_{t+1}/\Delta I_{t+1}^D = 1$).[11]

---

[11]Exercise: Use table 3.6.1 to determine the impact, dynamic and total consumption-investment multipliers.

Figure 3.6.1 shows the diagrammatic interpretation of the multiplier process outlined above. Start at point E, which represents the equilibrium position associated with the aggregate demand schedule AD (shown as a dotted line). Then, presume that desired investment increases, causing an upward shift in the aggregate demand schedule to AD′ (solid line). In period t + 1, producers adjust production to Y_{t+1} to allow for the increase in investment demand. But as income moves from Y_t to Y_{t+1} consumption increases. This is shown as a movement *along* the aggregate demand schedule from A to B. In period t + 2, producers take account of this increase in consumption and raise production to Y_{t+2}. But, again, this latter change in income causes a further increase in consumption, represented by the movement from B to C. This adjustment process continues until the economy eventually reaches the new equilibrium position, E'.

It is interesting to notice that figure 3.6.1 provides not only the static equilibrium of the model we have used so far but also the stationary solution of the dynamic model which underlines our analysis. According to this dynamic law of motion the quantity adjusts to clear the market and the reader can easily verify these two solutions coincide at point E'. Notice that in the southeast quadrant we have also introduced explicitly a time dimension.

3.7 Summary

This chapter has presented the reader with a first view of a macroeconomic model. We have concentrated on a hypothetical economy comprised of only two sectors, households and business, and have attempted to show how the interaction of these sectors generates an equilibrium level of economic activity. We found that the structural equations of our model could be used to find the equilibrium level of income and consumption associated with any assumed value of desired investment. Furthermore, we examined the impact on the economy stemming from a change in the level of desired investment. Our treatment has taken us into the fields of pure statics (equilibrium determination), comparative statics (specification of the multiplier effect in terms of only the two successive equilibrium positions) and dynamics (our analysis of the behavior of the economy in disequilibrium).

Now that the reader has gained a degree of familiarity with some of the tools and concepts involved in macroeconomic analysis, we can proceed to build upon this knowledge in subsequent chapters.

Suggested Further Reading

Ackley, G. "The Multiplier Time Period: Money, Inventories, and Flexibility." *American Economic Review* 41 (June 1951, 350–68.

Keynes, J. M. *The General Theory of Employment, Interest and Money.* New York: Harcourt, Brace, 1936, chap. 10.

Lerner, A. P. "Saving and Investment: Definitions, Assumptions, Objectives," American Economic Association, *Readings in Business Cycle Theory.* Homewood, Ill.: R. D. Irwin, 1944.

Machlup, F. "Period Analysis and Multiplier Theory." *Quarterly Journal of Economics* 54 (November 1939), 1–27.

Samuelson, P. "The Simple Mathematics of Income Determination." In *Income, Employment, and Public Policy: Essays in Honor of Alvin Hansen.* New York: Norton, 1948, pp. 133–55.

CHAPTER 4

Introducing Governmental Economic Activity Into The Model

4.1 Introduction

The analysis of the preceding section was based on two main assumptions, a closed economy, and no government economic activity. We shall continue to assume a closed economy, but we now introduce governmental economic activity into the analysis. In this chapter, government spending and taxation are integrated into the model to allow a preliminary examination of the role of these variables in policy making. Our analysis is limited, however, by the simplicity of the model, with our assumption of an exogenous level of investment as the key to this simplicity. For the time being, it allows us to ignore a variety of monetary conditions and the potential impact of fiscal policy on financial markets (an impact which may have feedback effect on net investment). For now, our purpose is simply to offer some insights into the basic mechanism of fiscal policy.

Basically, the economic activity of the government may be divided into six categories, as shown in table 4.1.1. These six categories envelop all of the economic activities of the government which may give rise to expenditures and receipts. On the other hand, all transactions of the government with the private sector can be classified into two broad classes: exchanges and transfers. The government, like any other organization, engages in the purchase of goods and services. Exchanges are two-way, or bilateral, transactions and are similar to the business

Table 4.1.1.   *Categories of Government Expenditures and Receipts*

Expenditures	Receipts
1. purchase of goods and services	4. sales of goods and services
2. net transfer payments and subsidies	5. taxes
3. retirement of public debt	6. creation of public debt

activity of the private sector. Transfer transactions derive from two governmental powers which private organizations do not possess: the power to create money and the power to tax. Tax receipts constitute transfer payments from the private sector to the government. Net transfers from the government to the private sector (e.g., grants, subsidies, pensions, etc.) are recorded as expenditures.

Government debt usually arises when the receipts of the government, in the form of taxes and sales of goods and services, fall short of government expenditures. The difference between receipts and expenditures is covered in general by the creation of public debt. More specifically, the government may fill the gap in question either by issuing new money or by selling government bonds to the banks or the public.

The question of the impact of budgetary adjustments (in both the structure and the level) on the economy as a whole is very recent. Indeed, not long ago, the economic role of the government was so small that it attracted little analytical attention. Since the *New Deal,* however, its economic role has increased at a very fast pace and one should reasonably expect that it will further increase in the future. Governmental expenditures and receipts now have a major impact on the economic process. It is only a short step forward to attempt to use budget adjustments deliberately in order to achieve predetermined goals (e.g., to influence the course and level of national income, prices, and unemployment). The power of the government to adjust the level of economic activity through manipulations of its receipts and expenditures is real and it neither vanishes if we choose to ignore it, nor increases if we decide to acknowledge it.

The use of overt economic policy begins with the specification of a series of goals. It would be an enormous task to present a comprehensive list of the economic goals of any modern society. Policy planners are, in fact, faced with a menu of objectives from which they can choose. Unfortunately, there is—even among economists—a great deal of disagreement over the ranking of goals. The traditional list of objectives, those which have guided the course of economic policy over recent U.S. history, includes: full employment, price stability, economic growth, income redistribution and a favorable balance of payments. But there are many signs of a revision of societal objectives in the direction of more basic improvements in the quality of life. Environmental protection, population control, and several other new goals may well supplant some of the old values.

The existence of opposing views about the ends of policy complicates the exercise of policy. But even in a society in which there is general agreement as to the nature of the goals, there still remains the problem of ranking those goals in order of priority. Given a near consensus on some macroeconomic objectives, one might be tempted to think that all of these goals could be reached simultaneously. But, alas, if we view these goals in their complete sense—as the attainment of full employment, maximum price stability, an ideal distribution of income, and an optimum rate of growth—this is not the case at all. Instead, our current state of knowledge about the functioning of the economy forces us into a series of dilemmas. A movement toward any one of the economic goals is often accompanied by a movement away from one or more of the others. For instance, a policy designed to reduce unemployment might aggravate inflation; or, an attempt to correct a persistent balance-of-payments deficit could create massive unemployment. Given the multiplicity of a society's objectives, certain trade-offs must be made. At best, economists can make the trade-offs as favorable as possible. Still, someone must decide how much inflation we are willing to accept in order to expand employment, or how much additional unemployment we can allow in our effort to make the balance of payments more palatable. These decisions are, of course, subject to the political process, and are not exclusively economic in nature.

There are two types of policy ordinarily associated with stabilization efforts: monetary and fiscal policy. Monetary policy entails the use of variations in the money supply, interest rates and credit conditions in order to regulate economic activity. Fiscal policy involves the manipulation of government expenditures and taxes for the same general purpose. In formal terms, Congress holds the legislative power that forms the foundation for fiscal measures; and Congress has delegated the power for monetary policy to the Federal Reserve System. The executive branch has the duty of administering congressional legislation. But these formal divisions tell only a small fraction of the story. A brief glance at the mechanics of fiscal policy formulation will shed more light on the subject. An analysis of the exercise of monetary policy will be presented in chapter 6.

The responsibilities for the exercise of fiscal policy are shared by the executive and legislative branches of the government. The president, as the chief executive, customarily acts as the initiator of legislation in this area. Aided by a host of councils and agencies, the president draws up a comprehensive program for government expenditures and taxation and submits this program to the legislature.

The Office of Management and the Budget (OMB) organizes the expenditure proposals of individual agencies and performs the first screening of these spending plans. After considerable interplay between the OMB and individual agencies, the OMB presents a comprehensive budget to the president. The Treasury Department has a broad range of duties: raising finances for expenditures through a combination of taxes and loans when necessary, preparing proposals for tax legislation, and monitoring international monetary policy. The Council of Economic Advisors (CEA) is strictly an advisory committee, with the primary responsibility of advising the president in implementing the pursuit of stated policy goals. Its power is informal, and thus depends almost exclusively on the relationship between the president and the council members.

Before the president submits his budget proposals to Congress, he consults with the heads of the Treasury, OMB and the CEA. Because of the high-level nature of these conferences, the group has been called the "troika." Whereas individual agencies are concerned primarily with their own particular objectives, the "troika" deals with the budget from the standpoint of its effect on overall economic activity. Thus, the final budget proposals emanating from the executive branch are the result of an incredibly complex interplay of pressures and priorities.

Under the provisions of the 1974 Congressional Budget Act, Congress establishes budget totals before it acts on specific appropriations requests. Budget ceilings are recommended by the House and Senate Budget Committees and acted upon by both chambers. In this process, the overall fiscal impact of alternative budgetary levels is a prime consideration. Thus, Congress is now more formally involved in the discussion of stabilization priorities than it previously was.

By law, formal legislation dealing with taxes originates in the House of Representatives; and, by tradition, expenditures, or appropriations bills, also come from the House. An appropriations measure's first stop in the legislative mill is in the House Appropriations Committee. Each proposal is referred to one of the thirteen subcommittees of the committee, and undergoes considerable scrutiny. The subcommittee recommendation carries substantial weight in full committee deliberations; thus, the chairmen of these subcommittees are legitimately considered to be some of the most influential members of government. Once the appropriations bill has been reformulated and approved by the full Appropriations Committee, it is submitted to the House, where it is generally passed with little debate.

The appropriations procedure in the Senate is similar to that of the House. Here, the screening process is done by the twelve subcommittees of the Senate Appropriations Committee, and a bill then passes from a subcommittee to the full committee to the Senate floor. Although generalizations about political behavior are seldom without exceptions, there is a strong tendency for the Senate version of the appropriations measure to be more generous than the House version.

When discrepancies exist between the bills passed by the two houses of Congress, the issue is referred to a joint conference committee. A compromise measure is drafted by this committee and is submitted for both houses' approval. Generally, the conference committee's recommendation is accepted by both houses; if not, the bill goes back to the joint committee for further work. Eventually, agreement is reached and the bill is submitted to the president for his signature (or veto). Needless to say, the bill in question may differ substantially from the original request handed to the legislature. If the appropriations bill is signed into law, the agency in question then submits a proposal for apportionment (a designation of the *timing* of authorized expenditures) to the OMB. The OMB then approves or modifies the request and authorizes it.

Until 1974, the president had considerable latitude in determining the apportionment (or timing) of expenditures. However, the Budget and Impoundment Control Act of 1974 stipulates that deferrals of authorized expenditures may not extend past the end of the fiscal year, and can be reversed by either House of Congress. Complete recissions (cancellations of budget authority) must be approved by the full Congress.

Tax measures proposed by the executive branch must also run the gauntlet of congressional screening. They are initially referred to two legislative committees: the House Ways and Means Committee and the Senate Finance Committee. These committees, like others, play crucial roles in shaping the types of policies placed before the houses of Congress. Their recommendations to the two legislative bodies carry considerable influence. Once the House and Senate pass their respective versions of a tax bill, any differences are ironed out in a conference committee and resubmitted to the houses for passage. And, again, the bill is presented in final form to the president for his signature.

Some mention must be made of two other committees wielding influence on macro policy issues. The House Rules Committee is responsible for establishing the legislative agenda for the House. This duty may seem trivial, but it is not. A bill can be defeated by "benign neglect" as easily as by an adverse vote. The Joint Economic Committee has no legislative powers per se; instead, it was established by the Employment Act of 1946 to advise Congress on economic policy issues. It holds hearings on such matters, evaluates the Economic Report of the President, and offers recommendations to the legislature. In that its responsibilities are informal and educational, much of its influence depends on the atittudes of legislators and the persuasiveness of committee members.

The political process associated with economic policy is, according to anyone's definition, a complicated and imperfect one. But it seems reasonable to argue that the results of this political process are bound to improve as the tools of policy making become more sophisticated. One would think that most analytical propositions concerning the effects of alternative budget policies would have been tested by now and a consensus of opinion reached. To a certain extent, this is true. Economists do generally agree that budgetary policy is a viable tool for regulating economic activity. Unfortunately, though, the business community and the general public often believe that the budget should remain an accounting device designed to keep the government's house in order. Indeed, any association of budget adjustment with economic goals was once judged as fiscal heresy.

Because the budget can, and does, exert an influence on the economic process, it is important to attempt to acquire an analytical understanding of this influence. This should be true regardless of one's attitude about the political philosophies of the people using this power, since only through this understanding may one truncate or reinforce its influence.

4.2 Introduction of Government Activity into the Model

To begin, we maintain our assumptions that there is no international economic activity and that there are no undistributed corporate profits. But we shall now introduce governmental activity into our model. Let G stand for government expenditures (local, state, and federal) on goods and services, T_r for transfer payments to the private sector, and T_x for all tax revenues. Let us also define T to be the net receipts of the government, or the difference between tax revenues and net transfer payments:

$$T \equiv T_x - T_r \tag{4.2.1}$$

To take account of the government's role, we must change three of the identities used in the previous chapter. First, the existence of taxes forces us to distinguish between net national product (Y) and disposable income (Y_d). Disposable income is now that part of NNP "left over" after all tax payments and transfer payments have been made; i.e.:

$$Y_d \equiv Y - T. \tag{4.2.2}$$

Second, aggregate supply can now be decomposed into *three* uses: consumption, saving and net taxes. Recall from chapter 3 that disposable income is divided by identity into consumption and saving $(Y_d \equiv C + S)$; add to this the new definition of net national product as the sum of disposable income and net taxes $(Y \equiv Y_d + T)$. The resultant aggregate supply identity is then:

$$Y \equiv C + S + T. \tag{4.2.3}$$

The third alteration pertains to the demand side of the economy. In that government expenditures on goods and services constitutes another component of aggregate demand, we must now write:

$$AD \equiv C + I^D + G. \tag{4.2.4}$$

Aggregate demand is thus defined as the demand of the private sector $(C + I^D)$ plus that of the government sector (G).

Now let us turn to the specification of the conditions for equilibrium. The most general statement of equilibrium is that aggregate supply and aggregate demand must be equal in order that the economy "come to rest"; i.e.,

$$Y = AD. \tag{4.2.5}$$

This much remains as it was in the previous chapter. But the other statements of this general condition will change in accordance with the expanded definitions of aggregate demand and aggregate supply. Using the definition of AD from 4.2.4, we now have:

$$Y = C + I^D + G \tag{4.2.6}$$

which suggests that aggregate supply must equal the sum of the components of aggregate demand. Using the new definition of aggregate supply from 4.2.3, we can rephrase 4.2.6 as:

$$C + S + T = C + I^D + G$$

or $\quad S + T = I^D + G.$ \hfill (4.2.7)

This expression is analogous to our previous condition involving the equality of saving and desired investment. But we now have a more general view in which total "leakages" from the flow of income $(S + T)$ must be equal to total "injections" $(I^D + G)$.[1]

Equation 4.2.7 can be rewritten as:

$$I^D = S + (T - G) \qquad (4.2.8)$$

which suggests that desired investment must equal the sum of private savings (S) and government saving $(T - G)$. In chapter 2, we showed that actual investment (I) is identically equal to the sum of private and government saving. Thus, we can also write our equilibrium condition as:

$$I^D = I \qquad (4.2.9)$$

i.e., desired investment must equal actual investment in order for the economy to be in equilibrium. And, again, we can make use of the fact that any discrepancy between desired and actual investment is an undesired change in inventories and can thus write:

$$\Delta H^U = 0 \qquad (4.2.10)$$

as our final equlibrium condition. Under the assumptions of this section, equations 4.2.5–4.2.10 are mirror images of each other. In our following discussion, we shall cast most of our analysis in terms of the specifications contained in 4.2.6 and 4.2.7; but the reader should keep the other versions in mind throughout our discussion.

4.3 The Properties of the Model

In our investigation of the analytical properties of the model, our assumptions will be that the tax revenue is obtained through a lump-sum or head tax so that its level is independent of the level of income, and that the government expenditures and net tax revenues are fixed by the government at the levels $G = G_0$ and $T = T_0$ respectively. We still maintain the assumption that investment is fixed exogenously at a level $I^D = I_0^D$ regardless of the prevailing economic conditions.

Under these assumptions our simple model of income determination becomes:

---

[1] The term *leakages* in this context refers to that part of income which is not channeled back into the business sector in the form of consumption. The connotation is that these funds $(S + T)$ "leak" out of the flow of income between the business sector and the household sector. Similarly, the expression *injections* indicates expenditures other than consumption on the output of the business sector. These expenditures $(I^D + G)$ are, in a sense, "injected" into the flow of income.

$$Y = C + I^D + G \tag{4.3.1}$$

$$C = a + bY_d \tag{4.3.2}$$

$$Y_d \equiv Y - T. \tag{4.3.3}$$

Note that equation 4.3.1 is the equilibrium condition, which specifies that demand has to be equal to current production. Equation 4.3.2 depicts the behavioral assumption that the consumption expenditures depend upon the level of the disposable income, while 4.3.3 is an identity used to define disposable income. As one can see, the above system contains six variables from which three (Y, C, Y_d) are endogenous and the rest I^D, G, T) are exogenous. We may derive the reduced form of the system, and by substituting the given values of the exogenous variables, we find the solution to be:[2]

$$Y_0 = \frac{a}{1-b} + \frac{1}{1-b}I_0^D + \frac{1}{1-b}G_0 - \frac{b}{1-b}T_0 \tag{4.3.4}$$

$$C_0 = \frac{a}{1-b} + \frac{b}{1-b}I_0^D + \frac{b}{1-b}G_0 - \frac{b}{1-b}T_0 \tag{4.3.5}$$

$$Y_{d0} = \frac{a}{1-b} + \frac{1}{1-b}I_0^D + \frac{1}{1-b}G_0 - \frac{1}{1-b}T_0. \tag{4.3.6}$$

Let us now concentrate on equation 4.3.4 to analyze the results of an adjustment in the government budget. This adjustment may take several forms. It may involve only a change in the expenditures G or a change in the net revenues T (which will be the result of a change in either T_x or T_r or both), or finally it may be a combination involving both expenditures and revenues.

Suppose first that the government readjusts the budget by changing expenditures from the level G_0 to the level, say, G_1 ($G_1 > G_0$) while holding T constant at the level T_0. Substituting this new level of government expenditures (G_1) into the solution 4.3.4–4.3.6 we find the corresponding equilibrium values of the endogenous variables. In particular, the new equilibrium level of income will be:

$$Y_1 = \frac{a}{1-b} + \frac{1}{1-b}I_0^D + \frac{1}{1-b}G_1 - \frac{b}{1-b}T_0. \tag{4.3.7}$$

Comparison of the new solution given by equation 4.3.7 with that given by equation 4.3.4 reveals immediately that:

---

[2]Exercise: Write down the reduced-form equations underlying the solution 4.3.4–4.3.6 and determine the number and magnitude of all total multipliers involved in the system.

$$Y_1 - Y_0 = \frac{1}{1-b}(G_1 - G_0)$$

or more briefly:

$$\Delta Y = k\Delta G \qquad\qquad (4.3.8)$$

where $k \equiv 1/(1-b)$ is the government expenditures multiplier associated with the model.

We have thus established that, given the marginal propensity to consume, the change in government expenditures by an amount equal to ΔG will result in a change in the equilibrium level of income which will be equal to the product of the multiplier, $1/(1-b)$, times the change in the government expenditures, ΔG. In addition, we may find the impact of the change in G on C and Y_d by referring to the reduced-form equations for the latter two variables.

Looking at equations 4.3.5 and 4.3.6, we find by inspection that the change in G will result in a change of consumption and disposable income which is equal to:

$$\Delta C = \frac{b}{1-b}\Delta G = kb\Delta G \qquad\qquad (4.3.9)$$

and $$\Delta Y_d = \frac{1}{1-b}\Delta G = k\Delta G \qquad\qquad (4.3.10)$$

respectively. Indeed, since net national product changes by $k\Delta G$ it follows from the definition of disposable income (equation 4.3.3), that, given the value of T, disposable income should change by the same amount. But from the consumption function (equation 4.3.2) we see that a change of Y_d by an amount ΔY_d will result in a change in consumption which will be equal to $\Delta C = b\Delta Y_d$. Since, the change in Y_d is equal to $k\Delta G$, it follows that the change in consumption will be $\Delta C = bk\Delta G$ which is given by equation 4.3.9 directly. Notice that in equation 4.3.2, b is defined to be the marginal propensity to consume out of disposable income. Also, the change in saving will be equal to the difference of the change in the disposable income and the change in consumption. Thus we find that:

$$\Delta S = \Delta Y_d - \Delta C$$

$$= k\Delta G - kb\Delta G$$

or $$\Delta S = (1-b)k\Delta G = \Delta G \qquad\qquad (4.3.11)$$

since $k = 1/1 - b$.

Table 4.3.1. *The Effects of a Change in Government Expenditures*

	Y	T	Y_d	C	S	I^D	G
$1/G_0 = 100$	960	110	850	780	70	80	100
$2/G_1 = 120$	1060	110	950	860	90	80	120
Change (Δ)	100	0	100	80	20	0	20

Suppose that the parameters and exogenous variables of the system 4.3.1–4.3.3 take the following values: $a = 100, b = .8, I^D = 80, T = 110$, and $G = 100$. Substituting these values into the system and solving for Y, C, Y_d we find:

$$Y = 960, Y_d = 850 \text{ and } C = 780.$$

Next, suppose that government expenditures increase from \$100 billion to \$120 billion. Substituting the new value for G into the system we find that the solution values for Y, C, and Y_d are $Y = 1060, Y_d = 950$ and $C = 860$. For the sake of comparisons table 4.3.1 summarizes the solution of the system for $G = 100$ and $G = 120$. To make sure that $Y = 960$ and $Y = 1060$ are the correct values of the equilibrium level of income, notice that the condition $Y = C + I^D + G$ is satisfied in both cases. Also, one may find saving, given under column S, by subtracting consumption from disposable income. We also know that at equilibrium $S + T = I^D + G$. Again, $70 + 110 = 80 + 100$ for the level $Y = 960$ and also, $90 + 110 = 80 + 120$ for $Y = 1060$. Now we see that the change in income is equal to 100 which is equal to the change in government expenditures, 20, times the multiplier, which in our case is equal to 5. This result could have been found by using the formula 4.3.8 directly, as one should, instead of solving the system twice. Also, the change in disposable income is equal to 100 (see equation 4.3.10); and finally, the change in consumption is equal to the change in disposable income times the marginal propensity to consume.

We may now attempt to solve the problem graphically. First, notice that the introduction of the governmental economic activity resulted in the inequality of disposable income and the net national product. Substituting then the definition of disposable income from 4.3.3 into 4.3.2, we find that:

$$C = a - bT + bY. \tag{4.3.12}$$

On the other hand, the saving function was found to be:

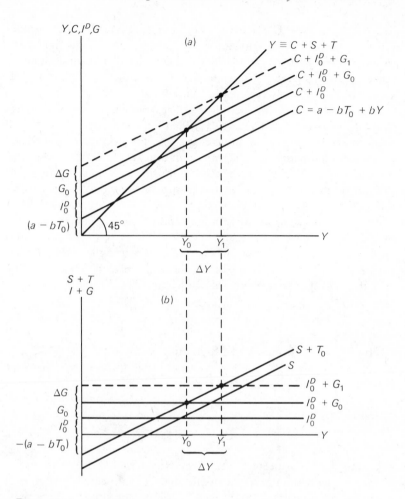

Figure 4.3.1 *The Effect of a Change in Government Expenditures*

$$S = -a + (1 - b)Y_d.$$

Substituting the definition of Y_d into the saving function, we find:

$$S = -a - (1 - b)T + (1 - b)Y. \tag{4.3.13}$$

The consumption and saving schedules are plotted in figure 4.3.1. Notice carefully that the intercepts of these schedules depend upon the level of net taxes. First, concentrate on panel (a). If we add the given level of desired investment (I_0^D) and some initial value of government expenditures (G_0) to the consumption schedule, we obtain the aggregate demand ($C + I_0^D + G_0$) schedule. The change in government expenditures from G_0 to G_1 is represented as a vertical shift of the aggregate demand schedule by an amount ΔG. Thus, the equilibrium value of income rises from Y_0 to Y_1. The same phenomenon is depicted in panel (b). There, we have plotted total leakages ($S + T_0$) and total injections ($I_0^D + G$) with the initial set of assumed values. These two schedules intersect each other at Y_0, which is the same equilibrium level of income as the one found in panel (a). This follows immediately from the construction of the two diagrams. On the other hand, as G rises, the injections schedule shifts upward by ΔG to $I_0^D + G_1$. Again, the equilibrium value of income rises by the multiplier times the change in G to the value Y_1.

Now, let's consider an alternative type of budget policy. Suppose that the government changes net taxes from T_0 to T_1 ($T_1 > T_0$) while holding G constant at its original levels. Substituting the new level of net taxes (T_1) into the reduced-form income equation (4.3.4), we find that the corresponding new level of income (Y_1) will be:

$$Y_1 = \frac{a}{1 - b} + \frac{1}{1 - b}I_0^D + \frac{1}{1 - b}G_0 - \frac{b}{1 - b}T_1. \qquad (4.3.14)$$

Subtracting 4.3.4 from 4.3.14, we obtain:

$$Y_1 - Y_0 = \frac{-b}{1 - b}(T_1 - T_0)$$

or more briefly:

$$\Delta Y = -bk\Delta T. \qquad (4.3.15)$$

Consider the magnitude of this effect. Notice that, dollar for dollar, a change in net taxes induces a smaller change in income than does a change in government expenditures. That is, the produce bk is less than k as long as b (the MPC) is less than one. This result can be interpreted along intuitive lines by referring to the path of impact exerted by changes in these two policy variables. Notice that a change in government expenditures causes the aggregate demand schedule to shift by the full amount (ΔG). The reason for this is that government expenditures constitute a *component* of aggregate demand. But a change in net taxes affects the position of the aggregate demand schedule only indirectly, through its influence on consumption spending. As net taxes increase, only *part* of this change is translated into a decrease in consumption at a given level of NNP; the rest is absorbed by a decline in saving. More specifically, the consumption schedule shifts now downward only by

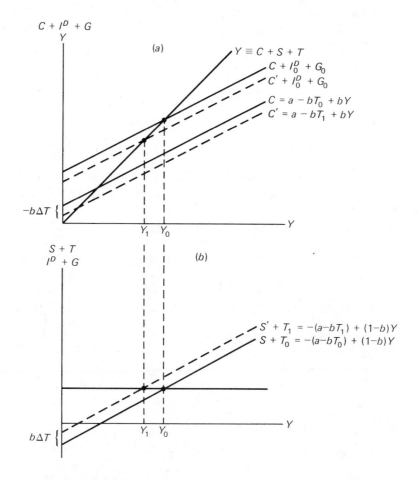

Figure 4.3.2   *The Effect of a Change in Net Taxes*

b (the MPC) times the change in net taxes. See figure 4.3.2 for a graphical illustration of this point. Thus, a change in taxes has less impact than a change in government expenditures.

A point should also be raised about the quantitative effect of a change in net taxes. In that the marginal propensity to consume appears twice in expression 4.3.15, it is unclear whether ΔY will be greater than, equal to or less than ΔT. The answer, of course, depends upon the value of b. The following inequalities describe the relevant range of values for the MPC as well as the resulting relation between change in taxes and income.

1. if $b > .5$, then $b\left(\dfrac{1}{1-b}\right) > 1$ and $\Delta Y > \Delta T$

2. if $b = .5$, then $b\left(\dfrac{1}{1-b}\right) = 1$ and $\Delta Y = \Delta T$

3. if $b < .5$, then $b\left(\dfrac{1}{1-b}\right) < 1$ and $\Delta Y < \Delta T$.

The above analysis shows that, *ceteris paribus,* an increase in government expenditures has an expansionary effect on the income while the effect of an increase in net taxes is contractionary. Furthermore, changes in government expenditures (see equation 4.2.13) are associated with full multiplier effects, whereas changes in net taxes (stemming from variations in tax revenues or transfer payments) induce something less than full multiplier effects. We have established a very interesting conclusion about the use of these variables as policy instruments: the potency of government expenditures is greater than that of taxes or government transfers. The preceding analysis considered the effects of changes in alternative policy variables in isolation from one another. We shall now concentrate on the effects of simultaneous and corresponding changes in revenues and expenditures.

Suppose that the government decides to change expenditures on goods and services and net taxes by equal amounts in such a way that the deficit or surplus of the budget remains constant. This can happen, for example, when the government decides to finance the increase in expenditures by raising taxes, so that $\Delta G = \Delta T$. To find the impact of such a policy upon the equilibrium level of income let us assume that net taxes and government expenditures change from the levels T_0 and G_0 to T_1 and G_1 respectively ($T_1 > T_0$; $G_1 > G_0$) so that $\Delta T = \Delta G$. Substituting the new levels of G and T in equation 4.3.4, we find that the corresponding equilibrium level of income will be:

$$Y_1 = \frac{a}{1-b} + \frac{1}{1-b}I_0^D + \frac{1}{1-b}G_1 - \frac{b}{1-b}T_1. \quad (4.3.16)$$

Comparison of 4.3.16 with 4.3.4 leads to

$$Y_1 - Y_0 = \frac{1}{1-b}(G_1 - G_0) - \frac{b}{1-b}(T_1 - T_0)$$

or in a more compact form:

$$\Delta Y = \frac{1}{1-b}\Delta G - \frac{b}{1-b}\Delta T. \quad (4.3.17)$$

But by hypothesis $\Delta G = \Delta T$; hence it follows that:

$$\Delta Y = \frac{1}{1 - b}(1 - b)\Delta G = \frac{1}{1 - b}(1 - b)\Delta T,$$

from which we obtain:

$$\Delta Y = \Delta G = \Delta T. \tag{4.3.18}$$

We thus have established the proposition that an increase in government expenditures on goods and services which is financed by an increase in taxes has a multiplier effect which is equal to one. This proposition is known as the Haavelmo theorem or the balanced budget multiplier theorem, and although its validity depends on rather restrictive assumptions, it should be observed that it holds regardless of the magnitude of the marginal propensity to consume and the form of the consumption function, provided that all taxpayers have the same marginal propensity to consume.[3] The interpretation of the above theorem is quite simple. The increase of expenditures initially will be equal to G, while the decrease in consumption due to the imposition of higher taxes will be only $b\Delta T$. Thus, savings will be reduced by $(1 - b)\Delta T$. But since $\Delta G = \Delta T$ it follows that the initial change in expenditures will be $\Delta G - b\Delta G = (1 - b)\Delta G$. The last quantity multiplied times the multiplier $(k = 1/1 - b)$ provides us with the total change in income which, of course, will be equal to ΔG.

While the balanced-budget multiplier is a very special case, its implications are interesting since it disproves the common fallacy that as long as the government budget is balanced, fiscal policy does not affect the level of economic activity, or, to put it in another way, that budgetary adjustments which maintain a *status quo* deficit level have neutral effects on the level of economic activity.

We may now summarize our findings in terms of an example, using the same numerical values displayed in table 4.3.1. In particular, let a = 100, b = .8, I^D = 80, T = 110 and G = 100. The solution values of the endogenous variables are given in row 1, which also gives, for the sake of convenience, the values of the exogenous variables. Row 2 is associated with the solution resulting from a change in taxes by $10 billion. Row 3 describes the situation in which the government simultaneously increases both taxes and expenditures by $10 billion.

---

[3] See T. Haavelmo, "Multiplier Effects of a Balanced Budget," *Econometrica* 13 (October 1945), 311–18.

Table 4.3.2. *The Impact of Alternative Policies*

	Y	T	Y_d	C	S	I^D	G
1/Initial Solution	960	110	850	780	70	80	100
2/$\Delta T = 10$	920	120	800	740	60	80	100
3/Haavelmo's theorem: $\Delta G = 10$ $\Delta T = 10$	970	120	850	780	70	80	110

4.4 Inflationary and Deflationary Gaps

In the previous section, we illustrated the potency of changes in government expenditures and taxes. We turn now to the overt use of fiscal tools to bring about desired changes in economic conditions. The desire to influence economic activity stems from the fact that the economy's current equilibrium position may be associated with a variety of maladies. Consider figure 4.4.1, where we have sketched two alternative problems with which an economy could be confronted. Refer first to panel (a). Suppose the economy is currently in equilibrium at point E, with a net national product of Y_0. But presume in addition that the level of production which would allow full employment of the labor force is Y^F. Because income (Y_0) is below its full-employment position, unemployment results. The root of the problem is that aggregate demand is not high enough to sustain full employment. We often characterize such a problem by referring to the deficiency of aggregate demand at the full-employment level of income. In terms of our diagram, aggregate demand would be less than aggregate supply by the amount AB at full employment. This amount is called the *deflationary gap*. In order to close the gap and bring income up to its full-employment level, policy would be directed at shifting the aggregate demand schedule upward so that it would cut the aggregate supply schedule at point A. As we have seen, this objective could be accomplished through an increase in government expenditures, a decrease in taxes, or the application of a balanced-budget policy involving a substantial increase in expenditures and taxes.

In panel (b), we have depicted an alternative problem. In particular, equilibrium may occur at a point *above* the full-employment level of

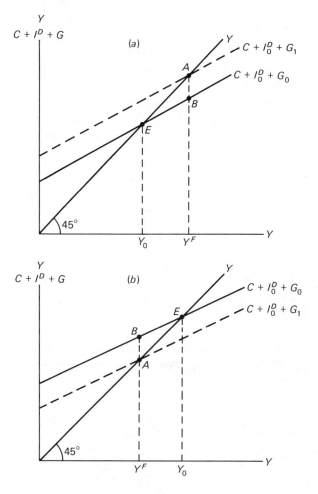

Figure 4.4.1 *Deflationary and Inflationary Gaps*

income. Ordinarily, the economy cannot sustain operation at such a point, in that it entails the use of more resources (labor, capital, etc.) than are currently available. Thus, the full-employment level of income acts as a barrier to the attainment of equilibrium. But if the economy is stuck in a disequilibrium position (like Y^F), something has to give. Excess aggregate demand can be expected to bring about inflationary pressures across the economy, and these tendencies are likely to persist until the disequilibrium is corrected. Because of the inflationary consequences of the situation shown in panel (b), the excess of aggregate

demand over aggregate supply at full employment is called an *inflationary gap*. Ignoring changes in productive capacity, the gap can be
eliminated and the economy brought back to a full-employment equilibrium only if the aggregate demand schedule falls until it cuts aggregate supply at *A*. Fiscal policy designed to prompt such a contraction
in demand could take several shapes. The ones we have studied would
be: a decrease in government expenditures, an increase in taxes, or a
balanced-budget policy consisting of corresponding decreases in
spending and taxes.

Given a discrepancy between the equilibrium level of income and the
current full-employment level, policymakers will attempt to find those
policies which would restore full-employment equilibrium. In quantitative terms, the policy would be contingent upon the relevant multipliers associated with the policy instruments to be used. Suppose, for
instance, that the authorities decided to use a change in government
expenditures to correct a deflationary or an inflationary gap. The effect
of a change in G is given by:

$$\Delta Y = \frac{1}{1 - b} \Delta G \qquad (4.4.1)$$

But we can specify ΔY to be the desired change in income from its
current equilibrium level (Y_0) to a new full-employment equilibrium
level (Y^F), thus obtaining:

$$Y^F - Y_0 = \frac{1}{1 - b} \Delta G \qquad (4.4.2)$$

The policy problem can now be viewed as solving 4.4.2 for the change
in G which would bring about the desired change in income. Multiplying both sides of 4.4.2 by $(1 - b)$, we find that solution to be:

$$\Delta G^0 = (1 - b)(Y^F - Y_0) \qquad (4.4.3)$$

Thus, we can sometimes use our knowledge of the effects of changes in
policy instruments in order to find the policy which would accomplish
our economic objectives.[4]

---

[4] Exercise: Find the expression for the change in taxes which would correct a discrepancy
between Y^F and Y_0. Find the balanced-budget policy which would accomplish the same
objective.

Exercise: Assume that $b = .75$, and the equilibrium level of income falls short of the
full-employment level by $11 billion. Find three types of policies which could restore full
employment.

4.5 Income Taxation in the Economic Model

The two preceding sections presented the solution values of our macro-economic model and investigated its properties on the assumption that the levels of taxes (T_x) and transfers (T_r) were determined exogenously. The reader may justifiably object that these assumptions are gross oversimplifications of reality.

This section will modify those assumptions to achieve a better approximation of reality. In particular, we will consider an economic system in which government revenues are raised from an income tax. To avoid unnecessary complications, we assume that tax revenues depend upon net national product (i.e., that NNP is the base for the tax) and that there is a uniform tax rate set by the government. This restructuring of the model constitutes a major change, in that it introduces another "feedback" into the system. More explicitly, it takes account of the fact that variations in income will induce automatic changes in tax receipts. As we will see, the introduction of the income tax substantially alters the overall properties of the economic model.

In formal terms, we assume that tax revenues are given by the equation $T_x = t_1 Y$ where t_1 is the tax rate. We also assume that transfers are fixed at a level $T_r = t_0$. Net taxes (T) were earlier defined by the identity:

$$T \equiv T_x - T_r.$$

Given our assumptions with regard to T_x and T_r, we now have:

$$T = -t_0 + t_1 Y \qquad (4.5.1)$$

where the tax rate satisfies the double restriction:

$$0 < t_1 < 1.$$

Apart from changes in G, fiscal policy can be expressed in terms of changing either the level of transfers (t_0) or the tax rate (t_1) or both. Graphically, a change in the level of transfers will shift the tax function up or down in a parallel fashion, whereas a change in the tax rate will result in a rotation of the function around the point *A* as figure 4.5.1 shows. Notice that point *B* is a "break-even" point for the government in the sense that the net tax collection is equal to zero. To find the level of income which provides tax yield equal to transfers we set $T = 0$. Hence, $0 = -t_0 + t_1 Y$ from which we obtain that $T = 0$ when income is equal to t_0/t_1.

As we saw earlier, variations in taxes affect the expenditures of consumption. Let us now see the effect of our assumptions on the consumption function. For this we may write:

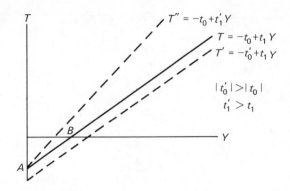

Figure 4.5.1 *Policy-Induced Movements of the Tax Function*

$$C = a + bY_d$$

$$Y_d \equiv Y - T$$

$$T = -t_0 + t_1 Y.$$

Substituting the expression for T into the definition of disposable income we obtain:

$$Y_d = t_0 + (1 - t_1)Y. \tag{4.5.2}$$

Equation 4.5.2 shows clearly that, given the level of NNP, disposable income will increase whenever transfer payments (t_0) increase and will decrease whenever the tax rate increases. Finally, substituting equation 4.5.2 into the consumption function, we express consumption expenditures in terms of national income:

$$C = (a + bt_0) + b(1 - t_1)Y \tag{4.5.3}$$

We may then note that a change in transfers (t_0) implies a parallel shift of the consumption function, whereas a change in the tax rate will force the consumption schedule to rotate. The implications of these changes are shown in figure 4.5.2.

The consumption function expressed in equation 4.5.3 lends itself to some interpretation. The first term on the right ($a + bt_0$) denotes the level of consumption associated with a zero level of net national product. The second term is again the "induced" consumption. The parameter b is the marginal propensity to consume out of *disposable income:*

$$b = \frac{\Delta C}{\Delta Y_d}.$$

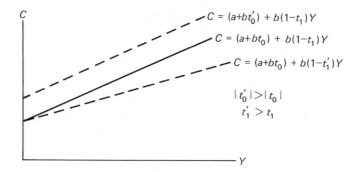

Figure 4.5.2 *The Effects of Tax Policy on the Consumption Schedule*

The term $b(1 - t_1)$ can be viewed as the marginal propensity to consume out of NNP, or:

$$b(1 - t_1) = \frac{\Delta C}{\Delta Y}.$$

We shall now investigate the effects of fiscal policy on the solution of our system assuming that the net tax yield takes the form of equation 4.5.1 and that government expenditures and investment are fixed at the level $G = G_0$ and $I^D = I_0^D$ respectively. Let us then write

$$Y = C + I^D + G \tag{4.5.4}$$

$$C = a + bY_d \tag{4.5.5}$$

$$Y_d \equiv Y - T \tag{4.5.6}$$

$$T = -t_0 + t_1 Y. \tag{4.5.7}$$

The above system 4.5.4–4.5.7 has six variables from which Y, C, Y_d, and T are endogenous and the remaining two (G, I^D) are exogenous. To find the solution values of the endogenous variables, we derive the reduced form of the system and then substitute the given values of the exogenous variables. Although the reader should attempt to derive the reduced form of the system and subsequently the solution values of the endogenous variables, here we provide only the solution value of the variable income. This is:

$$Y_0 = \frac{a + bt_0}{1 - b(1 - t_1)} + \frac{1}{1 - b(1 - t_1)} I_0^D + \frac{1}{1 - b(1 - t_1)} G_0. \tag{4.5.8}$$

From the above expression we can see that the assumption of an income tax results in a multiplier which is smaller than in the case of lump-sum taxes. Indeed, since $(1 - b) < 1 - b(1 - t_1)$ it follows that $1/(1 - b) > 1/[1 - b(1 - t_1)]$. This smaller multiplier has the impact of tempering the effects of changes in the values of the exogenous variables.

First, we consider the effect of a change in desired investment. Suppose that investment increases from I_0^D to a new, higher, value, I_1^D. The new equilibrium level of income would be given by:

$$Y_1 = \frac{a + bt_0}{1 - b(1 - t_1)} + \frac{1}{1 - b(1 - t_1)}I_1^D + \frac{1}{1 - b(1 - t_1)}G_0.$$

$$(4.5.9)$$

Subtraction of 4.5.8 from 4.5.9 gives us:

$$\Delta Y = k'\Delta I^D \qquad\qquad (4.5.10)$$

where $k' \equiv \dfrac{1}{1 - b(1 - t_1)}$.

Notice that, dollar for dollar, a change in investment induces a smaller change in income than was the case in our previous analysis where taxes were collected on a lump-sum basis. The reduction in the multiplier (from k to k′) stems from the fact that the income tax instills a feedback mechanism which diminishes the effects of exogenous "shocks" to the system. To put it another way, as long as the tax rate, t_1, remains unchanged, a larger income generates larger tax yield, T_x. Given a constant amount of transfers, t_0, the net tax revenue, T, increases. This last increase partially offsets the expansionary effects of the increase in investment. We can see then clearly that the introduction of an income tax implies an automatic brake on expansion. The larger the tax rate, t_1, the smaller the multiplier, and the stronger the brake on expansion. On the other hand, this system implies also that when income declines, due to a reduction of investment, for example, taxes will fall, automatically dampening the income decrease.

It follows then that the income tax introduces into our model a built-in flexibility of net taxes and thus acts as an automatic stabilizer of economic activity. In this connection the following comment made in a report of a subcommittee of the Joint Economic Committee, the so-called Douglas Report, is of particular interest:

> The maintenance of unchanged tax rates and expenditures programs will produce, as a response to fluctuations in the national income, an automatic flexibility of revenues and actual expenditures, which will exert a stabilizing effect on the economy. . . . We believe that this

automatic flexibility is a valuable contribution to stability and that the degree of automatic flexibility in our fiscal system should, if possible, be increased.[5]

Let us now find the effects of the different budgetary adjustments upon the equilibrium level of income. Suppose that government expenditures on goods and services change from, say, G_0 to G_1 ($G_1 > G_0$) while t_0 and t_1 remain at the same level.

Substituting the new value of G into equation 4.5.8 we obtain

$$Y_1 = \frac{a + bt_0}{1 - b(1 - t_1)} + \frac{1}{1 - b(1 - t_1)}I_0^D + \frac{1}{1 - b(1 - t_1)}G_1.$$
$$(4.5.11)$$

Subtraction of 4.5.8 from 4.5.11 yields

$$\Delta Y = k'\Delta G. \tag{4.5.12}$$

We may then conclude that although the formula which relates changes in the equilibrium level of income to changes in the government expenditures has remained similar, the resulting increase in income is smaller than that which corresponds to a constant level of taxes. This is, of course, the result of the smaller multiplier.

Next, consider a change in transfers from t_0 to t_0' ($t_0' > t_0$) while t_1 and G remain constant. Substituting t_0' into equation 4.5.8 we obtain:

$$Y_0' = \frac{a + bt_0'}{1 - b(1 - t_1)} + \frac{1}{1 - b(1 - t_1)}I_0^D + \frac{1}{1 - b(1 - t_1)}G_0.$$
$$(4.5.13)$$

Comparison of equation 4.5.13 with 4.5.8 reveals that:

$$\Delta Y = \frac{b}{1 - b(1 - t_1)}\Delta t_0 = bk'\Delta t_0. \tag{4.5.14}$$

From equation 4.5.14 we see that an increase of transfers will result in an income increase and that for equal changes in government expenditures and transfers, the changes of income which correspond to changes in government expenditures are larger than those which correspond to transfers. Thus, given our assumptions, we have established that government expenditures are a more potent fiscal tool than transfers (see equation 4.5.12). Government expenditures on goods and services

---

[5] See U.S. Congress, Joint Committee on the Economic Report, *Report of the Subcommittee on Monetary, Credit, and Fiscal Policies*, 81st Cong., 2d sess., 1950, Document 129, p. 16.

are registered in NNP (Y) when they are made, so the full initial expenditure becomes part of the multiplier effect on NNP. On the other hand, transfer payments are not considered part of NNP when they are disbursed, and hence have only an indirect multiplier effect stemming from the consumption expenditures they are used to finance. More specifically, only some part equal to the MPC (b) times the added transfers will be translated into aggregate demand at each level of NNP, so the transfer multiplier is only b times the government expenditures multiplier.

Finally, suppose that the government chooses to change the tax rate from t_1 to t_1' ($t_1' > t_1$). Let us examine what happens to the equilibrium level of income. As the tax rate increases, disposable income will decrease (see equation 4.5.2) and as a result the spending out of each dollar of income will be less (see equation 4.5.3). This, however, implies that the multiplier will be smaller, as will the equilibrium level of income. This can be easily seen if we substitute t_1' in equation 4.5.8. Although none of the numerators changes, the larger value of t_1 implies a smaller value for the multiplier and, consequently, for the equilibrium level of income.

To find the implied change in income we substitute t_1' in 4.5.8 to obtain:

$$Y_0' = \frac{a + bt_0}{1 - b(1 - t_1')} + \frac{1}{1 - b(1 - t_1')}I_0^D + \frac{1}{1 - b(1 - t_1')}G_0.$$
$$(4.5.15)$$

Subtracting equation 4.5.15 from 4.5.8 we obtain:

$$\Delta Y = \left[\frac{1}{1 - b(1 - t_1)} - \frac{1}{1 - b(1 - t_1')}\right][a + bt_0 + I_0^D + G_0]$$

which with a little algebraic manipulation becomes:

$$\Delta Y = \frac{-[a + bt_0 + I_0^D + G_0]}{[1 - b(1 - t_1)][1 - b(1 - t_1')]}b\Delta t_1.$$

But, given equation 4.5.8, the above expression can be simplified to read:

$$\Delta Y = \frac{-bY_0}{1 - b(1 - t_1')}\Delta t_1.$$
$$(4.5.16)$$

According to equation 4.5.16, the change in income depends not only on the change in the tax rate but also on the equilibrium level of income which prevailed initially: the larger the initial equilibrium level of income, *ceteris paribus,* the larger the change will be.

4.6 The Effects of Fiscal Policy on the Budget

In this section, we shall investigate the impact on the government's budget stemming from the exercise of fiscal policy. We often describe a budgetary situation by referring to the "surplus" or the "deficit" of the government account. We can define the budget deficit (D) as the excess of expenditures over net receipts:

$$D \equiv G - T. \tag{4.6.1}$$

The budget surplus (R) will be the negative of the deficit, or the excess of taxes over expenditures:

$$R \equiv -D \equiv T - G. \tag{4.6.2}$$

If taxes were levied on a lump-sum basis, any change in government expenditures or tax liabilities would have a rather obvious effect on the budget deficit. In particular, a \$1 increase in G (T constant) would increase the deficit by \$1; and a \$1 increase in T (G constant) would decrease the deficit by an identical amount. But much more interesting results are obtained when we consider the more realistic case where tax revenues are generated by a proportional income tax. Below, we shall examine the budgetary repercussions of variations in government expenditures, the tax rate and transfer payments with an income tax in the system.

Using the definition of the deficit (4.6.1) and substituting the expression for net taxes (4.5.1), we obtain a specification for the deficit in terms of the policy instruments and the level of income:

$$D = G + t_0 - t_1 Y. \tag{4.6.3}$$

Because income itself is affected by variations in any one of the instruments, a change in G, t_0 or t_1 will have a direct and an indirect effect on the level of the deficit.

First, suppose that government expenditures increase ($\Delta G > 0$) and that transfers and the tax rate remain constant ($\Delta t_0 = \Delta t_1 = 0$). Remembering that a change in G induces a change in Y, we can use 4.6.3 to express the change in D as:

$$\Delta D = \Delta G - t_1 \Delta Y. \tag{4.6.4}$$

But we can now substitute for ΔY from the multiplier expression of the previous section (4.5.12) to obtain:

$$\Delta D = \Delta G - t_1 k' \Delta G. \tag{4.6.5}$$

The first term on the right-hand side of 4.6.5 indicates the change in D due to the increase in G with total tax revenues constant; the second term reflects the change in taxes stemming from the expansion of income. The net change in D is the difference between these two terms. Factoring ΔG from 4.6.5, we have:

$$\Delta D = (1 - t_1 k')\Delta G. \tag{4.6.6}$$

It can be shown that $t_1 k'$ is a positive fraction as long as the tax rate is between zero and one[6] (something we have already assumed); thus, the term $(1 - t_1 k')$ is also a positive fraction. The implication is that a change in G will induce a lesser change in the deficit (in the same direction). Furthermore, it should be noted that the extent to which government expenditures affect the budget deficit depends on the tax rate. In general, the larger the tax rate, the stronger the indirect effect of induced changes in tax revenues and the smaller the impact on the deficit. We see, then, that in the context of the model presented above, an increase in government expenditures does *not* lead to an equal increase in the budget deficit.

Next, suppose that transfer payments are increased ($\Delta t_0 > 0$) and that government expenditures and the tax rate are left unchanged ($\Delta t_1 = \Delta G = 0$). The change in the deficit would be:

$$\Delta D = \Delta t_0 - t_1 \Delta Y. \tag{4.6.7}$$

---

[6]We can show this by expanding the expression for k' to get:

$$0 < t_1 \left[\frac{1}{1 - b(1 - t_1)} \right] < 1.$$

Multiply the inequality by $1 - b(1 - t_1)$, a positive quantity, to get:

$$0 < t_1 < 1 - b(1 - t_1).$$

Now, note that the first part of the inequality is obviously true, in that the tax rate is non-negative. Concentrating then on the second part of the inequality, we must prove that:

$$t_1 < 1 - b(1 - t_1).$$

Adding $b(1 - t_1)$ to both sides, we have:

$$t_1 + b(1 - t_1) < 1$$

or

$$t_1(1 - b) + b < 1.$$

Now, subtract b from both sides to obtain:

$$t_1(1 - b) < 1 - b.$$

And now divide both sides by $(1 - b)$ to get:

$$t_1 < 1.$$

This proves the assertion made in the text.

Again, we can interpret 4.6.7 as breaking ΔD into a direct effect (Δt_0) and an indirect effect $(-t_1 \, \Delta Y)$ stemming from the change in transfers. Remembering the multiplier expression for a change in Y due to a change in transfer payments, we can rewrite 4.6.7 as:[7]

$$\Delta D = \Delta t_0 - t_1 bk' \, \Delta t_0$$

or: $\Delta D = (1 - t_1 bk') \, \Delta t_0.$ (4.6.8)

We have already pointed out that $t_1 k'$ is a positive fraction; thus, given the permissible range of values of b, it should be apparent that $t_1 bk'$ also lies between zero and one. It follows that the expression $(1 - t_1 bk')$ is a positive fraction, and that the change in the deficit will be smaller than the change in transfers.

As a final exercise, consider the case where the tax rate increases $(\Delta t_1 > 0)$ with government expenditures and transfers held constant $(\Delta t_0 = \Delta G = 0)$. The budgetary change would be given by:

$$\Delta D = -\Delta(t_1 Y).$$ (4.6.9)

In this case, the budget deficit is decreased by the amount of increase in total tax revenues. If we assume that the change in t_1 and the associated change in Y are extremely small, we can approximate 4.6.9 as:

$$\Delta D = -(Y \, \Delta t_1 + t_1 \, \Delta Y).$$ (4.6.10)

Equation 4.6.10 decomposes the change in tax revenues into two separable effects: the increase in revenues stemming directly from the raising of the tax rate, evaluated at the original level of income $(Y \Delta t_1)$; and the indirect increase in revenues resulting from the induced change in income, evaluated at the original tax rate $(t_1 \, \Delta Y)$. Again, we can make use of the multiplier expression from the previous section (4.5.16) to rewrite 4.6.10 as:

$$\Delta D = -(Y \, \Delta t_1 - t_1 bk'Y \, \Delta t_1)$$

or, factoring out Δt_1 and Y:

$$\Delta D = -Y(1 - t_1 bk') \, \Delta t_1.$$ (4.6.11)

Noting again that $(1 - t_1 bk')$ is between zero and one, we find that an increase in the tax rate brings about a decrease in the deficit which is less than the decrease which would be indicated by applying the change in the tax rate to the original level of income $(-Y \, \Delta t_1)$.

---

[7] Exercise: Prove that a change in transfers induces a larger change in the deficit than an equal change in government expenditures.

4.7 Some Implications of Balanced-Budget Policy

We have considered the effects of variations in government expenditures and taxes without regard to any restrictions on the size of the government's budget deficit (or surplus). But there is still a strong feeling in some quarters that the government should "keep its house in order" either by balancing the budget (in the extreme) or by guarding against any increase in the deficit. In this section, we treat some of the implications of a policy aimed at holding the deficit at a constant value regardless of the state of economic affairs.

First, let's allow for changes in government expenditures (G), transfers (t_0), the tax rate (t_1) and the level of investment (I^D). The change in income associated with these simultaneous fluctuations in the exogenous variables would be the sum of the multiplier effects derived in section 4.5.[8] That is, we have:

$$\Delta Y = bk'\Delta t_0 + k'\Delta G + k'\Delta I^D - bk'Y\Delta t_1. \qquad (4.7.1)$$

Now, we can introduce changes in the budget deficit as G, t_0, t_1 and I^D vary by combining the results of section 4.6 to get:[9]

$$\Delta D = \Delta G + \Delta t_0 - t_1 \Delta Y - Y \Delta t_1. \qquad (4.7.2)$$

According to the purpose of this section, we want to investigate the properties of the model under the assumption that $\Delta D = 0$; thus, we can write:

$$\Delta D = \Delta G + \Delta t_0 - t_1 \Delta Y - Y \Delta t_1 = 0. \qquad (4.7.3)$$

Equations 4.7.1 and 4.7.3 may now be treated as a system in which there are two equations and two endogenous variables. It should be obvious that income, Y, is endogenous, but where is the other endogenous variable? Aren't all of the other variables either policy instruments or autonomous investment? The answer is that the constant-deficit assumption forces one of the policy variables to become endogenous. The adherence to a balanced budget forces the authorities to change one of their policy instruments in response to economic conditions. In a real sense, then, the state of economic affairs *determines* the value of one of the policy variables. Suppose that the authorities maintain a constant deficit

---

[8] See equations 4.5.10, 12, 14 and 16, and note that the investment multiplier is the same as the government expenditures multiplier.

[9] See equations 4.6.4, 4.6.7 and 4.6.10. Note also that the influence on income of changes in desired investment (as well as the joint influence of variations in the policy instruments) is reflected in the term ΔY.

by adjusting the tax rate (t_1) as economic activity varies. Then the endogenous variables of the system would be Y and t_1. We can solve the system for the changes in Y and t_1 by using the information contained in 4.7.1 and 4.7.3.

First, use 4.7.3 to solve for Δt_1 as:

$$\Delta t_1 = \frac{\Delta G + \Delta t_0 - t_1 \Delta Y}{Y}. \tag{4.7.4}$$

Substituting for Δt_1 from 4.7.4 into 4.7.1 we find:

$$\Delta Y = bk' \Delta t_0 + k' \Delta G + k' \Delta I^D - bk'Y \left[\frac{\Delta G + \Delta t_0 - t_1 \Delta Y}{Y} \right]. \tag{4.7.5}$$

Now, assume that transfers remain unchanged ($\Delta t_0 = 0$) and solve 4.7.5 for ΔY to get:

$$\Delta Y = \frac{k'(1 - b)}{1 - bk't_1} \Delta G + \frac{k'}{1 - bk't_1} \Delta I^D. \tag{4.7.6}$$

Noting that $k' = 1/[1 - b(1 - t_1)]$, the above expression can be simplified to read:

$$\Delta Y = \Delta G + \frac{1}{1 - b} \Delta I^D. \tag{4.7.7}$$

We have then derived the following very interesting result: if the government follows a policy of a balanced budget or aims at maintaining the same deficit or surplus, then the government expenditures multiplier is unity. In addition, any fluctuation of investment will be associated with more violent fluctuations in income if the government insists on a balanced budget than if the government relaxes this requirement. Indeed, we can easily see that if $\Delta I^D = 0$ then the change in income due to a change in G is equal to that change of G. Hence under our assumptions the Haavelmo theorem still holds. On the other hand, if $\Delta I^D \neq 0$ we see that its coefficient is independent of the tax rate and in particular is equal to the multiplier we derived in the case of the simple model without governmental economic activity or with a lump-sum tax.

On the other hand, the implication of the theorem that a balanced budget reinforces expansionary or contractionary forces is of fundamental importance from the point of view of fiscal policy which seeks to stabilize income and employment. To be more explicit, the theorem implies that income stabilization is quite incompatible with attempts to balance the budget in each period. This last point is clearly expressed in the aforementioned Douglas report:

A policy based on the principle of an annually balanced budget regardless
of fluctuations in the national income does not meet these tests (i.e., to
avoid aggravating economic instability, etc.), for if actually followed it
would require drastic increases of tax rates or drastic reductions of government expenditures during periods of deflation and unemployment,
thereby aggravating the decline, and market reductions of tax rates or
increases of expenditures during periods of inflationary boom, thereby
aggravating the inflation.

From the above, the following conclusion is derived: "A policy that
will contribute to stability must produce a surplus of revenues over
expenditures in periods of high prosperity and comparatively full
employment and a surplus of expenditures over revenues in periods of
deflation and abnormally high unemployment."[10]

4.8 Full-Employment Surplus and Fiscal Drag

Fortunately, the incompatability of a balanced budget with a reasonable
exercise of fiscal policy now seems to be accepted by all those in policymaking positions. Recent presidents have recognized the irrationality of
forcing budgetary balance each year in spite of economic conditions.
A deficit in any given year may reflect low levels of income (and low tax
revenues), rather than overspending on the part of the government;
and a surplus may indicate vigorous economic activity (and high tax
receipts), rather than thriftiness at the federal level. In short, the relation
between taxes and income makes the current budget deficit a poor
indicator of the fiscal posture of policymakers. The recognition of this
point gave rise to the concept of the full-employment surplus. This last
concept is defined as the difference between net taxes and government
revenue evaluated at the full-employment level of income.

In figure 4.8.1, we have sketched the government expenditures and
tax schedules corresponding to a given set of values for G, t_0 and t_1.
The basic disposition of policymakers is indicated by the relation between the tax schedule and the government expenditures line. But to use
the actual deficit at the current equilibrium level of income as a measure
of policy attitude is generally misleading. If income is at Y_1, for instance,
the government deficit would be given by AB. But this deficit is partially
the result of the fact that Y_1 is far below the full-employment level of
income, Y_F. If income were at Y_2, the budget would be "balanced,"

---

[10]U.S. Congress, Joint Committee on the Economic Report, pp. 11–12.

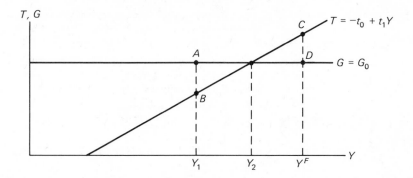

Figure 4.8.1 *The Full-Employment Surplus*

even though tax rates and expenditure policies would be the same as they were at Y_1. Obviously, any measure of policy behavior should be defined with some standardized level of income as a reference point. Because full-employment income constitutes such a reference point, the full-employment surplus (CD) is often used as the basis for a standardized measure of policy direction.

We have characterized fiscal policy in previous pages as the utilization of *changes* in government expenditures and tax structures. In a like manner, the most meaningful single measure of overall policy posture would be the *change* in the full-employment surplus. Thus, an increase in the surplus (or a decrease in the deficit) signals an effort to restrain economic activity. And a decrease in the surplus (or an increase in the deficit) reflects an attempt to expand the economy.

Table 4.8.1 reports the full-employment surplus estimates for the years 1960–70. Notice that we can pick out certain policy changes with reference to the change in the surplus (deficit). For example, the expansionary policy of the middle 1960s is reflected by the decreases in the surplus evidenced in 1964 through 1968. The most drastic fall came in 1964 with the tax cut of that year. The emphasis on restraint evidenced in the early Nixon years is signified by the sharp rises in the surplus in 1968–69.

The incorporation of income taxation into our model also brings into focus the issue of fiscal drag. Whereas the role of the income tax as an automatic stabilizer is desirable from the standpoint of short-run fluctuations in income, the relation between total taxes and income may have an undesirable effect in the long run. Recent policy has been aimed at guiding the economy along a smooth path of expansion. Automatic stabilizers (like the income tax analyzed here) do tend to

Table 4.8.1. *The Full-Employment Receipts and Expenditures Estimates, 1960–70*
Billions of dollars

Calendar year	Receipts	Expenditures	Surplus or deficit ($-$)	Change in surplus from preceding year
1960	105.0	92.0	13.0	8.3
1961	109.2	100.4	8.8	-4.2
1962	113.8	109.4	4.4	-4.4
1963	121.8	112.8	9.0	4.6
1964	119.2	117.5	1.8	-7.2
1965	124.2	123.2	1.0	-0.8
1966	139.3	142.9	-3.6	-4.6
1967	153.1	163.6	-10.5	-6.9
1968	175.7	181.7	-6.0	4.5
1969	203.3	191.7	11.7	17.7
1970	212.0	205.3	6.7	-5.0

Source: *Economic Report of the President*, 1971, p. 73.

dampen short-run fluctuations of income and thus help to minimize conditions of extreme unemployment or inflation. However, the response of tax revenues to the long-run growth in income may also tend to restrain the rate of growth itself. This characteristic of the income tax (and others like it) is called fiscal drag.

The notion of fiscal drag is illustrated in figure 4.8.2. Suppose that the initial equilibrium and full-employment levels of income, Y_1 and Y_1^F respectively, coincide. As the productive capacity of the economy expands, the full-employment level of income will increase (say, to Y_2^F). But as the equilibrium level of income starts to expand, taxes rise relative to government expenditures. In order for income to keep pace with its full-employment counterpart, investment would have to rise relative to saving by enough to offset the difference between net taxes and government expenditures at full employment. If this relative increase in investment is not forthcoming, the equilibrium level of income will encounter a "drag" which prohibits it from following a full-employment path (growing, say, to Y_2 rather than to Y_2^F). In a sense, the income tax builds into the system an automatic contractionary policy as taxes rise relative to government expenditures. This can be seen by referring to the automatic increase in the full-employment surplus (from AB to CD) resulting from the growth of full-employment output. Under these circumstances, there may be a tendency for growing unemployment to result as Y^F expands.

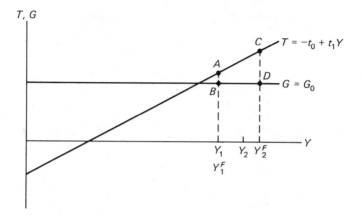

Figure 4.8.2 *Fiscal Drag*

In order to alleviate fiscal drag[11] (presuming that this is deemed desirable), policymakers should respond to long-term trends in tax revenues by either adjusting the tax schedule downward or by shifting the government expenditures schedule upward over time or by some combination of these measures. Tax and expenditures policies must be flexible enough to adjust to long-run, as well as short-run, problems.

4.9 A Numerical Example of the Effects of Fiscal Policy

For a numerical example illustrating the above ideas, suppose that the MPC out of disposable income is .8, a = 100, and that transfer payments and the tax rate are set at 50 billion and .25 respectively. Then the system 4.5.4–4.5.7 takes the following form:

$$Y = C + I^D + G$$

$$C = 100 + .8Y_d$$

$$Y_d \equiv Y - T$$

$$T = -50 + .25Y.$$

---

[11]This discussion should not be considered an argument for growth per se. But it should be clear that limiting growth is much more wisely accomplished by restricting the growth of full-employment output (Y^F) than by allowing the equilibrium level of income to fall far behind Y^F, insofar as the latter approach would induce increases in unemployment— whereas the former could be made compatible with full employment.

Table 4.9.1.   *Illustration of the Impact of Alternative Fiscal Policies*

Variable	1 Initial Solution	2 G = 140	3 $t_0 = 70$	4 $t_1 = .375$
Y	1,000	1050.0	1040	800
T	200	212.5	190	250
Y_d	800	837.5	850	550
C	740	770.0	780	540
S	60	67.5	70	10
G	120	140.0	120	120
I^D	140	140.0	140	140
D	−80	−72.5	−70	−130

The reduced form for income is:

$$Y = 350 + 2.5I^D + 2.5G.$$

To find the solution value or equilibrium level of income let us further assume that investment is equal to 140 billion and that the government expenditures are fixed at the level of 120 billion. Substituting these values in the above equation we find that $Y = 1,000$. Next we see that taxes corresponding to this level of income are equal to $T = -50 + .25(1,000) = 200$ billion and hence by using the definition of disposable income we find that $Y_d = 800$. Now, having found the level of disposable income, consumption expenditures can be determined. These are equal to 740 billion. It follows, then, that given the values of I^D and G all the endogenous variables can be determined. Table 4.9.1 summarizes the results.

From column 1 we can see immediately that our solution satisfies the equilibrium condition since $Y = 1,000$ and $C + I^D + G = 1,000$ or $S + T = I^D + G = 260$. Notice also that the government runs a budget surplus $(T - G)$ which is equal to 80 billion (a budget deficit of −80 billion).

Suppose that government expenditures increase from 120 to 140 billion. Column 2 gives the solution values of the variables. There are some interesting comments to be made by comparing columns 1 and 2. First, net national product has increased by 50 billion (the product of the multiplier, 2.5, times the change in the government expenditures, 20; see equation 4.5.12 above). As income increases, tax revenues increase by an amount, 12.5, which is equal to the tax rate, .25, times the change in income, 50. Thus, disposable income will increase by an amount which will be equal to the difference of the income increase, 50, and the increase in tax revenue, 12.5, i.e., 37.5. On the other hand, consumption will increase by the increase in the disposable income (37.5) times the marginal propensity to consume (.8), whereas saving will increase by 7.5 (the product of the increase in the disposable income and the marginal propensity to save, .2). Notice also that these propensities to consume and save refer to disposable income rather than net national product. Finally, it is interesting to observe that the surplus does not decrease by the whole amount of the increase in the government expenditures, 20 billion, but rather by only 7.5 billion, the difference between the increase in government expenditures and the increase in tax yield. This last result is given by equation 4.6.6 directly.

Column 3 of table 4.9.1 presents the set of equilibrium values resulting from a change in transfers from 50 billion to 70 billion. Compare columns 3 and 1 in order to verify the foregoing analysis of the effects of a change in transfer payments. In addition, the effects of a change in the tax rate from .25 to .375 may be traced by comparing columns 4 and 1.

Finally, consider the case of the Haavelmo theorem. Assume that the policymaker is confronted with the same system as in the previous example:

$$Y = C + I^D + G$$

$$C = 100 + .8Y_d$$

$$Y_d \equiv Y - T$$

$$T = -50 + .25Y$$

where G and I^D are assumed exogenous, as usual, and are fixed at the levels of $120 and $140 billion respectively. In addition, we also assume that although the policymaker is already committed to increase government expenditures, at the same time, either because of his own political philosophy and/or restrictions imposed by different social institutions, he requires that the budget shows the same surplus as before (in our example $80 billion) despite the increase in government expenditures. At the risk of being repetitious, it will be instructive to present in the same table the solution of the above system with and without the imposed restriction in regard to the surplus in the budget. In table 4.9.2, column 1 depicts the initial solution of the system. Column 2 is constructed on the assumption that government expenditures increase by 20 billion, and that the policymaker imposes *no* restrictions on the level of the surplus (deficit). Given these assumptions, we see that the surplus changes from 80.00 billion in the initial case to 72.50 billion at the new level of government expenditures. This change can be explained

Table 4.9.2.   *The effects of a Change in Government Expenditures, with and without the Balanced-Budget Requirement*

Variables	Initial Solution 1	$\Delta G = 20$ Unrestricted 2	$\Delta G = 20$ Restricted 3
Y	1,000.00	1,050.00	1,020.00
T	200.00	212.50	220.00
Y_d	800.00	837.50	800.00
C	740.00	770.00	740.00
S	60.00	67.50	60.00
G	120.00	140.00	140.00
I^D	140.00	140.00	140.00
D	-80.00	-72.50	-80.00
t_1	.25	.25	.265

easily. As G rises, income increases by 50, which is equal to the product of the multiplier (2.5) and the change in G. The corresponding change in taxes will be $\Delta T = .25 \; \Delta Y = 12.5$ billion. It follows that the impact of such a change on the budget will be the residual $\Delta T - \Delta G = 12.5 - 20.0 = -7.50$ billion. Hence, the surplus will change by this amount, as column 2 indicates. Since the solution depicted in column 2 is based on the assumption that the policymaker has imposed no restriction on the outcome of these changes on the budget, we have called it the unrestricted solution. Column 3 depicts the impact of the same change in government expenditures under the assumption that the policy-maker, for reasons of his own, imposes the restriction that the surplus remain at $80 billion. This solution assumes that the government fulfills its commitments by increasing the expenditures from 120 to 140 billion. But since the imposed restriction requires that the surplus remain at the same level of $80 billion, it follows that induced taxes have to increase by the same amount i.e., $\Delta T = 20$. Clearly, this is the case of the Haavelmo theorem. Thus, income increases by an amount which is equal to the change in government expenditures: i.e., $\Delta Y = \Delta G = 20$ billion. But in this case, if the government were to maintain the same tax rate, the tax yield would increase by an amount less than 20. It follows then that the tax rate will have to increase. Formally, to find the corresponding changes in income and tax rate which satisfy the re-quirements of the policymaker, one should use the system 4.7.1 and 4.7.3 from above:

$$\Delta Y + bk'Y \Delta t_1 = bk' \Delta t_0 + k' \Delta I^D + k' \Delta G$$

$$t_1 \Delta Y + Y \Delta t_1 = \Delta t_0 + \Delta G.$$

We now substitute the values $b = .8, k' = 2.5, Y = 1,000$ and, according to our assumptions, $\Delta t_0 = \Delta I^D = 0$. The above system becomes:

$$\Delta Y + 2,000 \Delta t_1 = 50$$

$$.25 \Delta Y + 1,000 \Delta t_1 = 20$$

which can be solved simultaneously for ΔY and Δt_1. The solution values are $\Delta Y = 20$ and $\Delta t_1 = .015$. Hence, the new level of income and the tax rate will be 1020 and .265 respectively. The remainder of column 3 shows the new values of the other endogenous variables of the system. Comparison of columns 1 and 3 reveals that the only variables which change are net national product, Y, the tax yield, T, and government expenditures, G. All of the other variables remain unchanged. This is in accordance with what we should have expected. Although net national product increased by \$20 billion, disposable income remains the same and consequently the expenditures associated with it stay at their previous levels.[12]

4.10 Government Spending as an Endogenous Variable

We have assumed until this point that government expenditures act *as if* they are determined exogenously—i.e., outside the confines of the economic system. This view, however, constitutes either an underestimation of the complexities of economic relations or an overestimation of the power of the government. In the first place, the expenditures of the government depend upon its receipts. The strength of this relation, however, is not invariant. It rather depends on the particular views of each government about fiscal policy. In other words, it depends on the way the government views the problem of running a deficit, or for that

---

[12]Exercise: Consider the numerical example of this section and suppose that the level of investment decreases by \$60 billion. Find the solution values of the endogenous variables of the system. Now suppose that for compensatory reasons the government contemplates an increase in its own spending.

1. Find the amount by which G must change so that Y will be restored to its previous level (i.e., in its initial solution).

2. Find the amount by which G has to change so that Y will be restored its previous level on the assumption that the policymaker insists that $\Delta D = 0$.

matter, increasing the public debt. In the second place, government expenditures depend on general economic and socio-environmental conditions.

Although our concern so far has been directed toward the level of governmental expenditures and their impact on general economic activity, it should be quite obvious that their structure, reflecting the relative power of different economic and political interests, also plays an important part in the evolution of any economy. Our implicit assumption has been that while government expenditures will affect the level of GNP in one way or another, this influence is invariant to the form they assume. This assumption, unfortunately, overlooks the fact that this variable has some very important intrinsic characteristics emanating from its own structure. Government expenditures may assume the form of digging holes, building pyramids, constructing schools, or battling pollution problems. However, one should not argue that all of the above forms of governmental spending will have the same impact on the economy. The distribution of government expenditures may not only generate different long-run paths in the economic evolution of the state, but also exert different short-run impacts on the level of income. Since the model used so far is not designed to shed light on the long-run problems of the economy, we may forgo this side of the problem. However, changes in the distribution of government expenditures (across economic sectors) will cause differences in the associated short-run effects of a given level of spending. Our excuse for ignoring this aspect of the problem is only to keep the size of the model within manageable terms. Therefore the short-run government expenditures multiplier used here should be considered as a weighted average of all "sectoral" multipliers. With this comment in mind we shall ignore the distributional aspects of government expenditures and shall assume that regardless of where these expenditures occur, they always result in higher employment and consequently a higher level of income.

In addition, we may observe that as income increases, the public demands an ever-improved quality and increased quantity of public goods. Indeed, it would be reasonable to argue that there is a close correlation between increases in income and the sophistication of various segments of the constituency in awareness of their prerogatives and rights. This phenomenon results in a decrease of freedom available to the policymaker in determining the level and the distribution of the federal budget. This increase in awareness by various groups usually assumes the form of demands on the structure of the budget. In other words, the increased sophistication of various social groups, combined with their rising expectations, makes it increasingly more difficult for the policymaker to substitute dollars of one budgetary item for those of another.

For example, it has become considerably more difficult to reduce the size of the defense budget in favor of, say, urban renewal. The greater the political leverage of various social groups, the smaller the degree of substitutability between the budget items expressing their interests. It also follows, therefore, that the increased complementarity among the various items of the budget will imply that as income increases almost every item of the budget will increase, but at a different rate. All this, however, points to the fact that the level of governmental spending will tend to increase over time as income grows.

Recent studies have begun recognizing this relationship between income and governmental spending and have moved to incorporate this functional relation into economic models. Although our functional relation of G and Y leaves much to be desired, it nevertheless constitutes a step towards the right direction by recognizing that G may be divided into two parts The first is assumed to be autonomously determined, while the second is induced by the level of income, i.e.,

$$G = v_0 + v_1 Y \qquad\qquad (4.10.1)$$

where v_0 stands for the exogenous government expenditures and v_1 for government marginal propensity to spend. In regard to the structure of v_0, it appears that in the short run the largest predetermined items are the salaries of bureaucrats, agricultural subsidies, military salaries, interest of public debt and veteran benefits. Our assumption in regard to these parameters will be that both are positive and, in addition, that v_1 satisfies the double restriction that $0 < v_1 < 1$. But this additional change in the model, trivial as it appears at first glance, has much more far-reaching effects than we suspect. Indeed, the introduction of G as an endogenous variable in the model implies that the government is able to exert only partial control on the level of G, via manipulating the parameters v_1 and, to far smaller extent, v_0. On the other hand, the effectiveness of all the other exogenous variables is increased since the introduction of induced government expenditures implies in the last analysis that the multiplier as such increases.

It follows then that, although the government loses some influence since part of the G becomes induced, due to the greater multiplier, the autonomous parts of the model, including v_0, become more potent.[13]

---

[13]Prove the assertion that the introduction of induced government expenditures as exemplified by equation 4.10.1 implies an increase in the value of the multiplier.

4.11 Summary

In this chapter, we have developed a number of policy conclusions based upon what is still a relatively simple economic model. As a refresher, we list these conclusions below:

1. A change in any one of the policy variables causes a multiplier effect on the equilibrium values of the endogenous variables. If we assume taxes to be of a lump-sum nature, the government expenditures multiplier is $1/(1 - b)$ and the net tax multiplier is $-b/(1 - b)$. If we use an income tax in the system, the government expenditures multiplier shrinks to $1/[1 - b(1 - t_1)]$ and we obtain a tax-rate multiplier of $-bY_0/[1 - b(1 - t_1')]$ and a transfers multiplier of $b/[1 - b(1 - t_1)]$.

2. Because of the feedback it introduces, the income tax acts as an automatic stabilizer.

3. Dollar for dollar, a change in government expenditures is more potent than a change in net taxes. As a consequence, we find that a balanced-budget policy can still have some effect on the level of economic activity. However, the associated policy multiplier is small, thus indicating that the achievement of certain goals may take extremely large changes in expenditures and taxes if the balanced budget is to be preserved.

4. Given an income tax in the system, a change in government expenditures, transfers or the tax rate will induce a change in the government's budgetary position (deficit or surplus), but that change will be the net result of direct and indirect effects.

In subsequent chapters, we shall sophisticate our analysis by investigating the behavior of the economy and the impact of alternative fiscal policies in more realistic settings. We shall find, though, that *qualitatively* the conclusions of this chapter will be reinforced at each step of the way.

Suggested Further Reading

Keynes, J. M. *The General Theory of Employment, Interest and Money.* New York: Harcourt, Brace, 1936, chap. 24.

Musgrave, R. A. *The Theory of Public Finance.* New York: McGraw-Hill, 1959, chap. 18.

Salant, W. "Taxes, Income Determination and the Balanced Budget Theorem." *Review of Economics and Statistics* 39 (May 1957), 152–61.

Samuelson, P. "The Simple Mathematics of Income Determination." In *Income, Employment, and Public Policy: Essays in Honor of Alvin Hansen.* New York: Norton, 1948, pp. 133–55.

PART
THREE

General
Equilibrium

CHAPTER 5

The Equilibrium
of the Expenditure
Sector

5.1 Introduction

Up until now, we have treated investment as an exogenous variable, presuming that investment plans do not depend on the other economic variables of our model. Under this assumption, we have focused on the multiplier effects via which investment and the other exogenous variables of our model affect the level of income. Ignoring explicit policy measures (variations in government expenditures and taxes), investment can be cast in the role of the active force involved in the process of income determination. The level of investment determines the total saving (private plus government) the economy is capable of offsetting. And, given the association between saving and income, it establishes the level of income at which the economy will reach equilibrium.

Given the crucial nature of investment, it should be obvious that any serious description of the economy should be accompanied by an analysis of the determinants of investment behavior. We cannot really hope to understand the roots of income fluctuations without at least a basic knowledge of the reasons for changes in the level of investment.

Unfortunately, the theory of investment makes up one of the most difficult and controversial chapters of economic theory. It would take an immense digression in order to treat the issues involved in that branch of economic analysis. We thus mortgage chapter 13 for the detailed discussion of the determinants of private investment and reserve this chapter for a far less ambitious purpose. We shall now relax the assumption that investment is exogenous and replace it with the simple hypothesis that investment is a function of the rate of interest and the level of economic activity. Then, having expressed investment in terms of a functional relation, we shall attempt a fairly detailed investigation of the effects of this hypothesis upon the properties of our economic model. In our analysis, we shall find that the endogenous nature of investment has several crucial implications for the exercise of economic policy.

5.2 Capital, Gross and Net Investment

Before we begin our analysis, we shall elaborate on the meaning of capital, gross investment and net investment. For our purposes, capital is defined as the physical productive wealth of an economy. Notice that our definition emphasizes the "physical" and "productive" characteristics of capital. We ignore what is often called "human capital," i.e., the store of skills and training embodied in individuals. Although this concept is extremely important in long-run analyses and has received considerable attention in recent economic literature, we shall abstract from any changes in human capital. Furthermore, the student must note carefully that our definition differs from the colloquial usage of the term *capital*. In particular, we do *not* include money, or bonds, or any other strictly financial asset in our concept of capital.

Capital is a stock variable. And, like any other variable we have introduced, it is subject to changes because of either deliberate acts or random events. Expenditures on capital are referred to as gross investment. Note again that gross investment denotes *only* the purchase of physical, productive wealth (plant and equipment or inventories); it does not include the purchase of strictly financial assets like bonds or savings accounts. Net investment is defined to be the net addition to the stock of capital taking place during some period of time. It is the difference between gross investment and replacement investment, where replacement investment is defined to be those purchases of capital which are carried out in order to maintain the existing stock of capital in view of its wear and/or destruction due to either natural phenomena or technological change. It should be apparent that net investment will be positive (i.e., the stock of capital will increase) if gross investment is larger than replacement investment.

Although in principle distinguishing between gross and net investment should be quite simple, unfortunately in practice this becomes a rather difficult task. The reason for this difficulty is that investment usually plays a dual role in the functioning of the economic system.

Investment is not only an important component of aggregate demand, but it is also the vehicle via which new technology is introduced in the system. A worn-out piece of equipment is not usually replaced by another exactly like it. The likelihood is that the replacement will embody the latest technology, which may or may not have been embodied in the piece being replaced. It is clear then that replacement—via changes in technology—may increase the productivity of capital which, of course, is the same as an increase of the productive capacity of the old stock without the productivity changes. But this implies that replacement investment includes an element of new investment and consequently it is rather difficult to separate them from each other.

In what follows, we shall concentrate our attention on the determinants of net investment, ignoring any explicit analysis of replacement investment. Furthermore, we shall concern ourselves only with the role of net investment as a component of aggregate demand. This latter approach is one taken by Keynes and most other economists in analyzing the short-run behavior of the economy. Unfortunately, it is handicapped by an internal inconsistency, since, in effect, it is based on the faulty assumption that net investment has no "supply-side" effects. More explicitly, we shall treat the capital stock as a constant and at the same time allow net investment to take on positive or negative values. This approach is ordinarily justified on the grounds that net investment is an extremely important component of aggregate demand but that net investment during a short-run period does not affect the capital stock to an appreciable degree. We shall discard this unrealistic assumption when we treat the dual nature of investment extensively in our analysis of growth.

One more prefatory remark is in order. We shall hereafter denote net desired investment by the letter I without the superscript D. Hopefully, the reader is now fully aware of the conceptual distinction between actual and desired investment and will keep this difference in mind.

5.3 Investment as a Function of the Rate of Interest

We now relax the assumption in regard to the exogenous character of investment and consider it in the form of a schedule rather than a given quantity. Our basic hypothesis is that the level of investment is a function of the rate of interest. Before we attempt any specification of this functional relation, however, we shall give a rather heuristic explanation of this dependence.

The schedule we referred to may be considered as a demand for resources to be used in order to increase the physical productive wealth or, what is the same, the capital of an economy. These additions to the existing capital stock are undertaken because of the expectations that they will yield some net returns. Against these returns one has to weigh either the cost of financing the investment through borrowing—if the firm has to assume a loan—or of alternative uses and consequently alternative net returns if the firm finances this investment program through liquid assets already under its control. In other words, the decision to invest does take into consideration either the real or the opportunity cost (that is, what the firm has to forgo by making this commitment as opposed to another one). This leads us to the conclusion that the volume of investment a firm will consider reasonable to undertake at any point of time will be determined through a comparison of the expected net returns for this investment with the opportunity or real cost of raising the necessary funds to finance it. It follows then that the rational firm has to rank its investment opportunities according to their net expected returns (profitability) and, depending on the circumstances and market conditions, cut off those projects which are associated with a net expected return which is lower than the market rate of interest.

Accordingly, by using the simplifying assumption that all the aspects of the financial cost of investment decisions can be expressed quantitatively, we shall choose the rate of interest to play this role in our model as a proxy variable. Furthermore, to the extent that there is a high correlation among the various interest rates we shall be able to talk about "the" rate of interest with the explicit understanding that this proxy variable incorporates all the qualitative characteristics and reflects the conditions of financial markets.

In relation to choices concerning the variables we shall use, there is one more qualification which should be mentioned. Although in this section we shall be talking in terms of "investment" in general as if it were a homogeneous entity, recent studies have suggested that the sensitivity of the various segments of investment to fluctuations of the rate of interest is not the same. In a larger, and consequently less aggregated model, one usually recognizes the various types of investment separately and associates each segment with the corresponding rate of interest. For the sake of simplicity, however, we shall treat investment as a homogeneous entity and thus our analysis will evolve around the concepts of "the" rate of interest and "the" level of investment.

To appreciate the above argument suppose that the economy consists of three firms A, B and C, each of which considers a number of investment opportunities. For the sake of concreteness, also assume that the amount required by each investment project is known and that careful market research has determined the net rate of return each firm should

Table 5.3.1. *Ranking of Investment Projects by Expected Net Return*

	Firm A		Firm B		Firm C	
No. of Proj.	Required Investment in $	Expected Net Return	Required Investment in $	Expected Net Return	Required Investment in $	Expected Net Return
1	1,000,000	10%	500,000	15%	2,000,000	11%
2	1,000,000	8%	1,500,000	10%	1,000,000	8%
3	2,000,000	6%	500,000	5%	500,000	6%
4			100,000	3%	500,000	4%
5					1,000,000	3%

reasonably expect from these projects. Obviously, if these projects are financed by internally accumulated funds, the least each firm expects in rates of return is the market rate of interest which they would receive if they placed their funds in the financial markets. This is, of course, their opportunity cost.

For simplicity here we assume that these projects are to be financed by borrowing. Table 5.3.1 summarizes all pertinent information about the amounts required by each investment project and their corresponding net expected return. We can see that if the market rate of interest is equal to 12%, the desired amount of investment will be only $500,000; i.e., only the first project of Firm B is profitable enough to be undertaken. Suppose now that the market rate decreases to 9%. The demand for investment will increase, since the first project of A, the first and second of B and the first of C all become worthwhile propositions. Indeed, if the interest rate is 9% then the corresponding demand for investment will amount to $5,000,000. Table 5.3.2 summarizes the desired level of investment which corresponds to a series of market rates of interest.

Table 5.3.2 summarizes the desired level of investment which corresponds to a series of market rates of interest.

The above heuristic analysis leads directly to the conclusion that the level of investment and the rate of interest are related functionally to each other. We may express this dependence as:

$$I = f(r) \tag{5.3.1}$$

where r stands for the rate of interest. In addition, to be consistent with the ideas suggested above, equation 5.3.1 has to show high investment activity associated with low interest rates and low activity associated with high interest rates. A plausible graph of equation 5.3.1 is suggested in figure 5.3.1.

Table 5.3.2. *Relationship between Desired Investment and the Rate of Interest*

Desired level of Investment (I)	Market rate of interest (r)
500,000	12
5,000,000	9
7,000,000	7
9,500,000	5
10,500,000	4
11,600,000	3

The schedule II′ indicates the level of investment which will be demanded at each level of the rate of interest. In other words, given a certain set of expectations about future economic developments, a decrease in the rate of interest from r_0 to r_1 will result in an increase of the level of investment from I_0 to I_1. These types of movements along the curve II′ are usually expressed in terms of elasticity, which is a normalized index of the sensitivity of investment to the fluctuations of the rate of interest. This is measured by the equation:

$$e_{I,r} = \frac{\Delta I}{I} \bigg/ \frac{\Delta r}{r} = \frac{\Delta I}{\Delta r} \cdot \frac{r}{I}$$

i.e., the interest elasticity of investment is defined to be the ratio of the percentage change in investment to the corresponding percentage change of the rate of interest.

On the other hand, movements along an investment schedule should not be confused with shifts of the schedule itself. The latter may be the product of a change in the general economic conditions (e.g., a change in the mood of the entrepreneurs or the introduction of a technological change), in which case firms, and consequently the economy as a whole, are willing to invest more (less) at each level of interest, as figure 5.3.2 shows. Although there are many functions which can satisfy the qualitative characteristics imposed on equation 5.3.1, we shall further assume that the relation of investment with the rate of interest is a linear one:

$$I = g_0 - g_1 r \tag{5.3.2}$$

where g_0 and g_1 are constants. Notice that the coefficient of r (g_1), gives the amount of change in the level of investment due to a small change in the rate of interest; i.e., $\Delta I/\Delta r = g_1$. Thus, in the case of a completely inelastic investment schedule, g_1 is equal to zero. In such a case equation 5.3.2 collapses into $I = g_0$ which, of course, is the autonomous type of investment we have been dealing with in the previous chapters. Notice

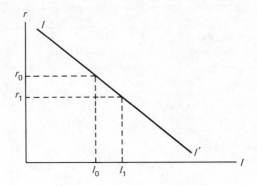

Figure 5.3.1   *The Investment Schedule*

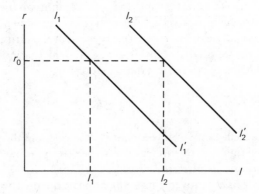

Figure 5.3.2   *A Shift in the Investment Schedule*

also that changes in g_0 imply shifts of the investment function itself. Indeed, if g_0 changes to g_0' ($g_0' > g_0$) then the whole investment schedule shifts from $I_1 I_1'$ to $I_2 I_2'$, as figures 5.3.2 shows.

5.4 The Expenditure Sector

We may now introduce equation 5.3.2 in our model and see how this affects the model. We shall assume once more no governmental economic activity, no undistributed corporate profits and no international economic relations on either the trade or the capital account. We shall further assume that the rate of interest can be influenced by the authorities, say, the Federal Reserve, and since its value is determined outside the system we shall consider it as an exogenous variable. With these qualifications we are prepared to show how the equilibrium level of income is determined when both components of aggregate demand, i.e., consumption and investment expenditures, assume functional forms.

Under these conditions the system of structural equations takes the following form:

$$Y = C + I \tag{5.4.1}$$

$$C = a + bY \tag{5.4.2}$$

$$I = g_0 - g_1 r. \tag{5.4.3}$$

From the above system, equation 5.4.1 describes the equilibrium condition; whereas equations 5.4.2 and 5.4.3 are the behavioral equations depicting our hypotheses in regard to the behavior of consumption and investment expenditures respectively. Notice that equations 5.4.1–5.4.3 compose a system of three equations in four unknowns, i.e., Y, C, I, and r. From them we have already assumed that only the rate of interest is an exogenous variable. It follows then that for each value we assign to the exogenous variable there will be a corresponding solution of the system. Another way of looking at this is that three equations in four unknowns do not under normal circumstances determine any of the unknowns. They can, however, be combined into a single equation containing any two unknowns. This is the first of the differences implied by the introduction of the investment function (5.4.3). There is, however, one more important difference between the solutions we have already presented in earlier chapters and the one we currently seek: now the changes in income are caused not by arbitrary changes in the level of investment, but instead by changes in the rate of interest. In other words, the line of causation runs this time from the rate of interest to investment, to income, and finally to consumption.

To obtain the reduced form of the system, we express the endogenous variables in terms of the exogenous ones. For this we substitute equations 5.4.2 and 5.4.3 into the equilibrium condition 5.4.1 and solve for the endogenous variable (Y) in terms of the exogenous (r) to find:

$$Y = \frac{a + g_0}{1 - b} - \frac{g_1}{1 - b} r. \tag{5.4.4}$$

Next, substituting the value of Y obtained from 5.4.4 into the consumption function, we find:

$$C = \frac{a + g_0 b}{1 - b} - \frac{bg_1}{1 - b}r. \tag{5.4.5}$$

Notice that the solution of the system depends on the value r assumes. And since the rate of interest itself is not a fixed quantity but a variable, it follows that Y and C, like I, are all expressed now in terms of schedules.

From the above equations we shall concentrate on equation 5.4.4, the reduced form of the variable income. This equation expresses the equilibrium level of income as a function of the rate of interest. To better appreciate this functional relationship consider once more the whole system 5.4.1–5.4.3. For each level of the rate of interest there is a corresponding level of investment. In turn, for each level of investment, a different level of income can be determined. Thus, we may say that equation 5.4.4 ties directly the cause (r) with the effect (Y). More explicitly, suppose that the rate of interest is equal to r_0. From equation 5.4.3 we immediately see that investment will be equal to:

$$I_0 = g_0 - g_1 r_0.$$

Now, if we reduce the rate of interest from r_0 to r_1, the level of investment will increase to:

$$I_1 = g_0 - g_1 r_1.$$

Subtracting I_0 from I_1, we find that the increase in investment due to the decrease in the rate of interest by Δr is equal to:

$$\Delta I = -g_1 \, \Delta r.$$

But since investment has increased by ΔI, it follows that income will increase by a quantity which is equal to the multiplier times the change in investment, i.e., $\Delta Y = [1/(1 - b)]\Delta I$. Substituting ΔI with the expression given above we find that:

$$\Delta Y = \frac{-1}{1 - b}g_1 \, \Delta r.$$

This last quantity is given directly by the coefficient of the rate of interest in equation 5.4.4. It is then quite obvious that as the rate of interest decreases, the level of investment increases, which in turn implies that the equilibrium level of income increases. Thus, the lower (higher) the rate of interest, the higher (lower) the equilibrium level of income. This is expressed by the negative slope of equation 5.4.4. The graph of this equation is given in figure 5.4.1.

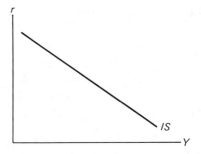

Figure 5.4.1   *Product-Market Equilibrium:*
The IS Schedule

Notice that since the independent variable is measured along the vertical axis, it follows that the slope of this functional relationship, $[1/(1 - b)]g_1$, is referred to the same axis as well.

Another way of deriving equation 5.4.4 is to use the equilibrium condition which is cast in terms of the equality between the desired levels of saving and investment; namely,

$$I = S \tag{5.4.6}$$

$$S = -a + (1 - b)Y \tag{5.4.7}$$

$$I = g_0 - g_1 r. \tag{5.4.8}$$

Substituting now the behavioral equations 5.4.7 and 5.4.8 into the equilibrium condition 5.4.6, we obtain:

$$-a + (1 - b)Y = g_0 - g_1 r.$$

Solving the above equation for Y in terms of r, we derive once more equation 5.4.4:

$$Y = \frac{a + g_0}{1 - b} - \frac{g_1}{1 - b} r.$$

Consequently, we see that another interpretation of equation 5.4.4 is that it provides the level of income at each rate of interest for which the desired levels of saving and investment are equal to each other. For this reason the graph of equation 5.4.4 as depicted in figure 5.4.1 is called the IS curve. The IS curve and the equations underlying it, i.e., 5.4.1–5.4.3 or equivalently 5.4.6–5.4.8, will be referred to as the "expenditure sector" of the economy. In particular, we shall define the

Table 5.4.1.   *Equilibrium values (solution) of the expenditure sector as depicted by the system 5.4.9–5.4.11 for various levels of the rate of interest in range 3–10% (in billions of dollars)*

r (1)	Y (2)	C (3)	I (4)	S (5)	C + I (6)
.03	940	852	88	88	940
.04	920	836	84	84	920
.05	900	820	80	80	900
.06	880	804	76	76	880
.07	860	788	72	72	860
.08	840	772	68	68	840
.09	820	756	64	64	820
.10	800	740	60	60	800

IS curve to be the locus of pairs of income and interest rates for which the expenditure sector is at equilibrium.

At this stage a numerical example may help to secure these ideas. Suppose that the behavioral equations for consumption and investment assume the following forms:

$$C = 100 + .8Y \qquad (5.4.9)$$

$$I = 100 - 400r \qquad (5.4.10)$$

which along with the equilibrium condition

$$Y = C + I \qquad (5.4.11)$$

complete the expenditure sector of the economy. Substituting equations 5.4.9 and 5.4.10 into the equilibrium condition 5.4.11 we obtain:

$$Y = 100 + .8Y + 100 - 400r$$

which can be solved for Y in terms of r to give

$$Y = 1,000 - 2,000r. \qquad (4.3.12)$$

Equation 5.4.12 is of course the formula of the IS curve. Table 5.4.1 provides a bird's-eye view of the equilibrium values of the various variables of our example corresponding to a series of hypothetical rates of interest.

In the above table, column 1 gives the assumed values for the rate of interest, and columns 2 and 3 the corresponding values of income and consumption expenditures respectively. On the other hand, columns 4,

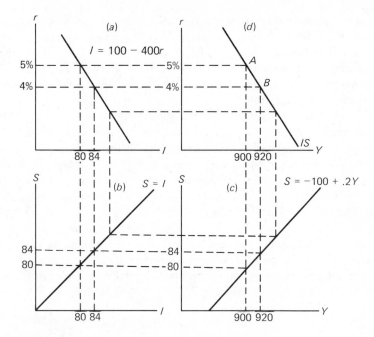

Figure 5.4.2 *Graphical Derivation of the IS Schedule*

5, and 6 provide the corresponding values of the desired levels of investment, saving, and, finally, aggregate demand. Notice that for each rate
of interest the implied level of income is an equilibrium level since it is
equal to its corresponding aggregate demand; or, equivalently, the
corresponding saving is equal to the level of investment induced by the
rate of interest in question. Notice also that for each increase of the rate
of interest by 1%, the equilibrium level of income decreases by $20
billion. This can be traced back to the slope of the IS curve, which is
equal to −2,000. More explicitly, as we can see from the investment
function, each increase of the rate of interest by 1% will result in a decrease of the desired level of investment by $4 billion and, since the multi-
plier in our example is equal to 5, it follows that the equilibrium level of
income will decrease by $20 billion (or the slope of IS times the change
in the rate of interest, 1%).

Let us now retrace our argument and try to solve our problem graphically. For the sake of concreteness we shall use the values of our numerical example as they are given in table 5.4.1 above. Figure 5.4.2
describes the geometric solution of the problem. In particular, panel (a)

depicts the investment function (equation 5.4.10), whereas panel (c) gives the graph of the saving function which corresponds to the consumption function of our example, i.e., $S = -100 + .2Y$. The equality of saving and investment, that is to say the equilibrium condition, is secured in panel (b). Finally, panel (d) depicts the solution of the system, giving the IS curve itself.

To appreciate the mechanics of the above diagram, let us assume that the rate of interest is equal to 5%. From panel (a) the reader can see that the corresponding level of investment is equal to $80 billion. For equilibrium saving has to be at the same level and by using panel (b), we are able to read from panel (c) directly that the economy is capable of producing this much saving only if income is at $900 billion. Extending the lines of Y and r, as the diagram indicates, we find point A, which has as coordinates the pair ($Y = 900$, $r = .05$), the level of income and rate of interest for which investment is equal to saving. This same process is repeated to obtain point B, whose coordinates are ($Y = 920$, $r = .04$). Repeating the same procedure for all possible values of the rate of interest and joining together the resulting points like A and B, we derive the IS curve.[1]

5.5 Properties of the Model When Governmental Economic Activity Is Introduced

In the previous section we derived the IS curve assuming to governmental economic activity and no economic relations with foreign countries. While we shall still maintain the assumption of a closed economy, we now relax the assumption about governmental economic activities. Under these circumstances the model of the previous section assumes the following form:

$$Y = C + I + G \qquad (5.5.1)$$

$$C = a + bY_d \qquad (5.5.2)$$

$$I = g_0 - g_1 r \qquad (5.5.3)$$

$$Y_d \equiv Y - T \qquad (5.5.4)$$

$$T = -t_0 + t_1 Y. \qquad (5.5.5)$$

To find the solution values of the endogenous variables, we derive the reduced form of the system and then we substitute the given values of the

---

[1] Exercise: Derive the IS curve as geometric solution of the system 5.4.9–5.4.11.

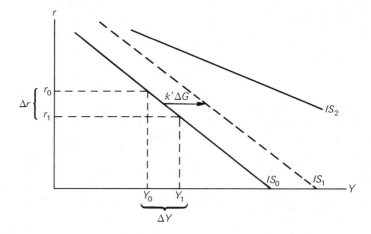

Figure 5.5.1 *Policy-Induced Shifts in the IS Schedule*

exogenous variables. Although the reader should attempt to derive the reduced form of the whole system, here we provide only the functional relation of income with the rate of interest, assuming that $G = G_0$. This is

$$Y = \frac{a + g_0 + bt_0 + G_0}{1 - b(1 - t_1)} - \frac{g_1}{1 - b(1 - t_1)}r. \qquad (5.5.6)$$

The graph of equation 5.5.6 is given in figure 5.5.1 and is labeled IS_0.

Let us now study the effects of changes in the various parameters and exogenous variables on the equilibrium level of income. Suppose for a moment that the rate of interest is fixed at the level r_0. Then the corresponding equilibrium level of income is given by:

$$Y_0 = \frac{a + g_0 + bt_0 + G_0}{1 - b(1 - t_1)} - \frac{g_1}{1 - b(1 - t_1)}r_0. \qquad (5.5.7)$$

This pair of equilibrium values of income and the rate of interest is shown in figure 5.5.1. If the rate of interest now changes to $r_1 (r_1 < r_0)$, then by substituting this new value into equation 5.5.6, we find that the corresponding new equilibrium level of income will be:

$$Y_1 = \frac{a + g_0 + bt_0 + G_0}{1 - b(1 - t_1)} - \frac{g_1}{1 - b(1 - t_1)}r_1. \qquad (5.5.8)$$

Comparison of the new solution given by equation 5.5.8 with that given by equation 5.5.7 reveals immediately that

$$Y_1 - Y_0 = \frac{-g_1}{1 - b(1 - t_1)}(r_1 - r_0)$$

or more briefly

$$\Delta Y = -g_1 k' \Delta r \tag{5.5.9}$$

where $k' \equiv 1/[1 - b(1 - t_1)]$ is of course the value of the multiplier. This change represents a movement along the IS curve, as figure 5.5.1 shows.

Suppose next that the government changes its own level of expenditures from G_0 to G_1 ($G_1 > G_0$) while the interest rate remains constant. Substituting this new value for government expenditures into 5.5.6 and subtracting the resulting value of Y from equation 5.5.7, we find that the change in income is equal to:

$$Y_1 - Y_0 = k'(G_1 - G_0)$$

or $\Delta Y = k' \Delta G.$ \hfill (5.5.10)

Thus, we see that the change in income due to a change in government expenditures is the same as the one we found in chapter 4 (see equation 4.5.12) as far as magnitude is concerned. The implication of such a change on the IS curve however, is that the curve itself shifts in a parallel fashion (since the slope does not change) to a new position given by IS_1 (figure 5.5.1). Similar effects result if we change the autonomous part of consumption (a), investment (g_0), or transfer payments (t_0). These changes will be

$$\Delta Y = k' \Delta a \tag{5.5.11}$$

$$\Delta Y = k' \Delta g_0 \tag{5.5.12}$$

$$\Delta Y = k'b \, \Delta t_0. \tag{5.5.13}$$

Next, suppose that the government chooses to change the tax rate from t_1 to t_1' ($t_1' < t_1$). Let us see what happens to the equilibrium level of income and for that matter to the IS curve. Since the tax rate has decreased, disposable income will increase (see equations 5.5.4 and 5.5.5). As a result, the spending out of each dollar earned will increase. This implies that the multiplier will become larger and consequently the equilibrium level of income will rise. To find the implied change we substitute t_1' in 5.5.7 to obtain:

$$Y' = \frac{a + g_0 + bt_0 + G_0}{1 - b(1 - t_1')} - \frac{g_1}{1 - b(1 - t_1')}r_0. \tag{5.5.14}$$

Subtracting 5.5.14 from 5.5.7, we obtain:

$$\Delta Y = \left[\frac{1}{1 - b(1 - t_1')} - \frac{1}{1 - b(1 - t_1)} \right] [(a + g_0 + bt_0 + G_0) - g_1 r_0]$$

which yields:

$$\Delta Y = \frac{b \, \Delta t_1}{1 - b(1 - t_1')} \left[\frac{a + g_0 + bt_0 + G_0}{1 - b(1 - t_1)} - \frac{g_1}{1 - b(1 - t_1)} r_0 \right].$$

Recalling that the expression in brackets is equal to the initial value of Y (see equation 5.5.7), the above expression can be simplified to read:

$$\Delta Y = \frac{bY_0}{1 - b(1 - t_1')} \Delta t_1. \tag{5.5.15}$$

From equation 5.5.15 we can see that the change in income depends not only on the change in the tax rate but also on the initial equilibrium level of income. The larger the initial equilibrium level of income, *ceteris paribus*, the larger the change will be.

In addition, we can observe from equation 5.5.6 that since the multiplier is a factor in both intercept as well as the slope of the IS curve, it follows that the implied change in the multiplier will affect both of these parameters with the result that this schedule will rotate, taking on a larger slope. This implies that the sensitivity of the equilibrium level of income to fluctuation of the rate of interest will be greater than it was before. This change is depicted in figure 5.5.1 by the line labeled IS_2.

We may now illustrate these ideas by means of a numerical example. To this end, suppose that the foregoing model takes the following form:

$$Y = C + I + G \tag{5.5.16}$$

$$C = 30 + .8Y_d \tag{5.5.17}$$

$$I = 100 - 400r \tag{5.5.18}$$

$$T = -50 + .25Y \tag{5.5.19}$$

$$Y_d \equiv Y - T \tag{5.5.20}$$

$$G = 130. \tag{5.5.21}$$

To solve the above system we may start by expressing disposable income as a function of NNP. This can be done easily enough by substituting equation 5.5.19 into 5.5.20 to find

$$Y_d = 50 + .75Y. \tag{5.5.22}$$

Substituting this expression into the consumption function (equation 5.5.17), we find

$$C = 70 + .6Y. \tag{5.5.23}$$

Table 5.5.1.   *Solution Values of the System under Alternative Values of the Tax Rate and the Rate of Interest*

No.	Variable	(1) Initial Equilibrium r = .05	(2) New Equilibrium r = .15	(3) New Equilibrium r = .03	(4) New Equilibrium r = .03 t_1 = .375
1	Y	700	600	720	576
2	T	125	100	130	166
3	Y_d	575	500	590	410
4	C	490	430	502	358
5	I	80	40	88	88
6	G	130	130	130	130
7	r	.05	.15	.03	.03
8	$D \equiv T - G$	-5	-30	0	$+36$
9	$S = Y_d - C$	85	70	88	52

Finally, equations 5.5.23, 5.5.18 and 5.5.21 are substituted into the equilibrium condition to obtain the equation of the IS curve, which assumes the form:

$$Y = 750 - 1{,}000r. \tag{5.5.24}$$

Notice that the multiplier in our example is equal to $k' = 1/[1 - .8(1 - .25)] = 2.5$. Assuming that the rate of interest is equal to 5%, the equilibrium values of the system are given in column 1 of table 5.5.1. Column 2 demonstrates the concept of a movement along the IS curve for a change in the rate of interest from 5% to 15%. The result is a new equilibrium of the expenditure sector. Notice that the government has to accept a larger deficit than before despite a passive role, i.e., without a deliberate change in either the tax rate or government expenditures. We emphasize this point because of the common error many commit by confusing the level of taxes (T), which is an uncontrolled endogenous variable depending on income, with the tax rate (t_1), which is in effect a policy parameter controlled by the government. We may now investigate the reason for these results, which the student should study carefully with the appropriate equations of the text. The change in the interest rate affects directly the level of investment and, since the latter variable is a component of aggregate demand, net national product eventually falls. This decrease in Y is reflected also in the governmental collection of taxes and, since the government's purchases of goods and services remains at the same level as before, the deficit increases. At the same time the decrease in net national product results in a decrease in disposable income, which manifests a decrease in both consumption and its complement, saving.

In connection with the above analysis, there is a common fallacy that if the government runs a deficit and wishes to close it, the only ways of achieving this are to decrease the purchases of goods and services (G), increase the tax rates (t_1), or do both. These are not the only ways and under some circumstances not the best ways, either. For example, suppose that the government has a commitment to a certain level of expenditures. Suppose also that the economy experiences some unemployment and that the full-employment level of income is 720. At the present time, we shall also assume that the structure of the economy is depicted by column 2 of table 5.5.1, with a level of income of 600 and a deficit of 30. Let us now suppose that the political philosophy of the government is firmly opposed to a deficit. Then one solution to such a problem could be to increase the tax rate, since there is already a commitment to a certain level of government expenditures. However, such a solution would be naive and against the best interest of the economy, since it would aggravate the problem of unemployment.

The government could cope with both the deficit and unemployment at the same time. This can be done by increasing income as such, thereby closing the deficit via an increase in the tax revenue. In our example, it suffices to decrease the rate of interest from 15% to 3%. To see this consider once more the definition of the deficit:

$$D \equiv G - T$$

and substitute for T and G with equations 5.5.19 and 5.5.21 to find:

$$D = 50 - .25Y + 130.$$

According to our example the deficit can change only as a result of a change in income. Thus, we may write

$$\Delta D = -.25 \, \Delta Y.$$

In fact, since our target is no deficit, it follows that ΔD should be equal to -30 and therefore

$$30 = .25 \, \Delta Y$$

from which we obtain that $\Delta Y = 120$. But from equation 5.5.24 we can see that

$$\Delta Y = -1,000 \, \Delta r$$

and since the desired change in income is 120, substitution of this value in the above expression yields

$\Delta r = -.12.$

Therefore, we find that the governmental deficit will close provided that the rate of interest decreases to 3%. It will be left for the student to go through the rest of the associated changes.

The above analysis demonstrates a very interesting piece of policy making and is based on the implicit assumption that the expenditure sector is sensitive to changes in the rate of interest. In principle, if this were the case, one would never need to use the fiscal instruments. However, it is not wise to let one policy variable carry the whole burden of the desired change. If one insists on commiting only one variable to carry out a policy, one may encounter difficulties imposed by economic constraints, but even more so by the structure and norms of the various social institutions. Notice, for example, that the change in the equilibrium values of the variables in columns 2 and 3 is due to an enormous change in the rate of interest, but such changes may not be compatible with the norms of a society at a certain point of time. In addition, there is usually a time lag between adopting a certain policy and committing an instrument variable and final achievement of the goal. One may be able to shorten this lapse of time by using a mixture of policy tools rather than by forcing one to do the job by itself. Implementation of policies usually gets better results when we work, to use loose terms, from both ends.

Referring back to table 5.5.1, column 4 describes the case in which the IS rotates, or what is the same, the case in which both the slope and the intercept of the IS change simultaneously. Before we analyze it, however, it will be helpful to state explicitly the assumptions which lead to such a solution. Consider once more column 3 and assume that the government wishes not only to close the gap between expenditures and revenues, but in addition seeks a certain level of surplus. Furthermore, assume that government expenditures cannot be used as a policy instrument and that there is some uncertainty about the effectiveness of the rate of interest. As a result, the government will attempt to reach the target by manipulating the tax rate. Assume that the tax rate is set at the level $t_1 = .375$. The new tax equation takes the form

$$T = -50 + .375Y$$

Inserting this equation into the model, we find that the new equation for the IS curve is:

$$Y = 600 - 800r$$

Notice that the value of the new multiplier is 2 as compared to 2.5 of the initial model, and see how different are the results we obtain although the intention of the government is basically the same (namely, closing the gap or even creating a slight budgetary surplus). Using columns 3 and 4 for our comparison, we find that the change in the tax rate proves to be a powerful policy instrument.

5.6 Income as an Explanatory Factor in the Investment Equation

In the simple analysis of income determination developed in chapter 3, we supposed that investment assumed an exogenous character. This assumption was subsequently modified and we have introduced the rate of interest as an explanatory factor of the behavior of investment. In the process of providing a heuristic explanation of this relation between the level of investment and rate of interest, we used the concept of expectations of the entrepreneurial class. Expectations are one of the main factors causing optimism or pessimism, which are important springs of the entrepreneurial decision-making process. Expectations, like any other psychological motive, are hard to quantify. But if one wishes to use a single index which embodies the general economic conditions generating the various tones of expectations, a natural choice would be either the change in or the level of income itself. However, using the change in income as an explanatory factor in the investment equation would take us in a hurry into the realm of dynamic models. Thus, it seems that within our framework of comparative statics the level of current income appears to be a more appropriate choice. In particular, it seems reasonable to assume that the higher the level of income, the more buoyant the expectations and consequently the higher the level of investment. In accordance, the investment equation can be further modified to read:

$$I = g_0 - g_1 r + g_2 Y \qquad (5.6.1)$$

where the parameter g_2 is defined to be the marginal propensity to invest and, as in the case of consumption function, it shows the amount by which investment will change due to a change in income by one dollar, i.e.:

$$g_2 = \Delta I / \Delta Y. \qquad (5.6.2)$$

In other words, g_2, which will be assumed to obey the double restriction $0 < g_2 < 1$, is the ratio of the change in investment to the change in income.

From a diagrammatic point of view the introduction of income in the investment function presents some problems. Indeed, since equation 5.6.1 expresses investment as a function of two variables, we have lost the simplicity of using two-dimensional diagrams and a three-dimensional one should be employed instead to depict this relation. However, we can still plot the investment schedule in two dimensions provided that we adopt the convention of fixing one of the independent variables at a certain level and plot the relation of the other two. This procedure will produce, obviously, not one but instead a family of investment schedules, one for each value the fixed variable assumes. For example, if we suppose that the level of income is fixed at Y_0, substituting this value into equation 5.6.1 we obtain:

$$I = (g_0 + g_2 Y_0) - g_1 r \qquad (5.6.3)$$

where the expression in parenthesis—the intercept of the investment schedule—is a known number. By now allowing income to vary, say from Y_0 to Y_1, we change in effect the intercept of the investment schedule. Figure 5.6.1 depicts the graph of equation 5.6.1 for a set of assumed values for the level of income. Notice that the larger the assumed value for income, the larger the intercept of the investment schedule will be. Consequently, for $Y_1 > Y_0$, the investment schedule which is associated with Y_1 will be found to the right of the one associated with the level of income Y_0, etc.[2]

From a theoretical point of view it should be recognized that as far as the long run is concerned, it seems rather doubtful that investment is related to a stationary level of income. But since our main interest here is the analysis of comparative statics, this assumption appears to be quite satisfactory. On the other hand, the inclusion of income as an explanatory variable of the level of investment presents no formal analytical difficulty. To see that, we may substitute equation 5.6.1 for equation 5.5.3 into the model of the previous section to obtain:

$$Y = C + I + G \qquad (5.6.4)$$

$$C = a + bY_d \qquad (5.6.5)$$

$$I = g_0 - g_1 r + g_2 Y \qquad (5.6.6)$$

$$Y_d \equiv Y - T \qquad (5.6.7)$$

$$T = -t_0 + t_1 Y. \qquad (5.6.8)$$

---

[2]Try another way of plotting equation 5.6.1 in a two-dimensional space, which is to fix the rate of interest at various levels and concentrate on the relation between investment and the level of income.

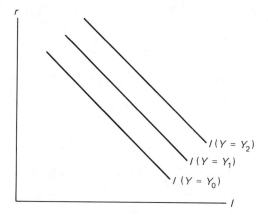

Figure 5.6.1   *Relationship Between Investment and the
Rate of Interest at Alternative Values of
Income*

The only difference between the above system and that of the previous
section is the introduction of the variable income into the investment
equation. But since we have not introduced any new variable in the
model and the number of equations has not changed, it follows that
the procedure for finding the reduced-form equations is unchanged.
Solving then for income in terms of the rate of interest and substituting
$G = G_0$, we obtain once more the equation for the IS curve:

$$Y = \frac{a + g_0 + bt_0 + G_0}{1 - b(1 - t_1) - g_2} - \frac{g_1}{1 - b(1 - t_1) - g_2}r. \qquad (5.6.9)$$

The main feature of the new equation of the equilibrium of the expenditure sector is the presence of the marginal propensity to invest in the
expression of the multiplier, which as a result increases the multiplier
relative to the one which corresponds to the system 5.5.1–5.5.5.

There is, however, one respect in which the analytical properties of
the system 5.6.4–5.6.8 and those of equation 5.6.9 may have been
altered. To be more specific, if both consumption and investment depend
upon income, there seems to be no real basis for asserting, as a general
proposition, that the marginal propensity to spend, i.e., the sum of
marginal propensities to consume and invest out of NNP, is less than
one. The difference in the analytical properties of the expenditure
sector appears as soon as we give up this restriction. Indeed, if we assume
that the marginal propensity to spend, $[b(1 - t_1) + g_2]$, is equal to or
greater than one, a host of special problems of interpretation emerge.
More specifically, if $1 < [b(1 - t_1) + g_2]$ then the sign of the coefficient

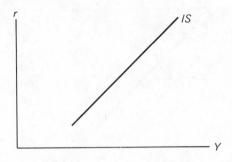

Figure 5.6.3   *The Case of an Upward-Sloping IS Schedule*

of the rate of interest in the equation of the equilibrium of the expenditures sector becomes positive and thus the curve itself slopes upwards, as figure 5.6.3 shows.

To appreciate this point let us define η to be the marginal propensity to spend. Let us also assume that the rate of interest decreases by a small quantity. Since the rate of interest decreases this will generate some additional investment and at first the income will increase by an amount which is equal to the change in investment. This increase in income will result in an increase of the level of consumption as well as investment by an amount which will be equal to $b(1 - t_1) \Delta Y + g_2 \Delta Y = \eta \Delta Y$, which in turn will increase the level of income, etc. Table 5.6.1 gives a bird's-eye view of this chain reaction.

To find the total change in income we sum the change occurring in each successive period to obtain:

$$\Delta Y = \Delta Y_t + \Delta Y_{t+1} + \Delta Y_{t+2} + \ldots \ldots + \Delta Y_{t+j} + \ldots .$$

Substituting now the various values of ΔY_t's from the above table, we obtain:

$$\Delta Y = \Delta I_t + \eta \Delta I_t + \eta^2 \Delta I_t + \ldots \ldots + \eta^j \Delta I_t + \ldots .$$
$$= \Delta I_t (1 + \eta + \eta^2 + \ldots \ldots + \eta^j + \ldots \ldots) \quad (5.6.10)$$

But since η by hypothesis is equal to or greater than one, it follows that the expression in parenthesis can become and remain larger than any predetermined large number. Indeed, this sum is a divergent geometric series which at the limit approaches infinity. Thus, the multiplier in this case is said to be infinite. Consequently, if the marginal propensity to spend is equal to or greater than unity, the multiplier is no longer given by the formula $1/1 - \eta$.

Table 5.6.1.

Period	Change in Income
t	$\Delta Y_t = \Delta I_t$
t + 1	$\Delta Y_{t+1} = (\Delta C_t + \Delta I_t) = \eta\,\Delta Y_t = \eta\,\Delta I_t$
t + 2	$\Delta Y_{t+2} = (\Delta C_{t+1} + \Delta I_{t+1}) = \eta\,\Delta Y_{t+1} = \eta^2\,\Delta I_t$
t + 3	$\Delta Y_{t+3} = (\Delta C_{t+2} + \Delta I_{t+2}) = \eta\,\Delta Y_{t+2} = \eta^3\,\Delta I_t$
....	....
....	....
....	....
t + j	$\Delta Y_{t+j} = (\Delta C_{t+j-1} + \Delta I_{t+j-1}) = \eta\,\Delta Y_{t+j-1} = \eta^j\,\Delta I_t$
....	....

Another way of looking at the same thing is to consider the denominator of equation 5.6.10 and observe that a marginal propensity to spend greater than one implies that $1 - b(1 - t_1) < g_2$, i.e., the marginal propensity to save out of NNP $[1 - b(1 - t_1)]$, is less than the marginal propensity to invest, g_2. We know, however, than in equilibrium, an increase in saving due to an increase in the level of income should be accompanied by an equal increase in investment. In view of our assumption about the relation of marginal propensities, as income increases, the rise of saving keeps lagging behind the increase in investment continuously or, what is the same, the aggregate demand is continually greater than the current production. Consequently, the income keeps increasing ad infinitum and an equilibrium of the expenditures sector cannot be attained. The only way to discourage investment from increasing at a faster pace than saving will be to let the rate of interest increase. This is exactly the meaning of the rising IS curve, i.e., if income increases, for equilibrium, the rate of interest has to increase as well.

5.7 Summary

In this chapter, we laid some groundword for subsequent analyses by specifying investment as an endogenous variable. In our first treatment, we hypothesized that investment is inversely related to the rate of interest. On the basis of this assumption, we found that, given the values of all other exogenous variables (government expenditures, transfers and the tax rate), the equilibrium level of income itself depends upon the rate of interest. The product-market equilibrium relation between Y and r was formalized graphically as an IS schedule. We also discussed the impact of a change in each of the policy variables, and noted the following conclusions: a change in either government expenditures or transfers will cause the IS schedule to shift in a parallel fashion by the change in question times the relevant multiplier; and an alteration in the tax rate will cause the IS schedule to rotate, with the change in income at each tax rate depending upon the tax-rate multiplier. In analyzing the effects of these alternative policies, we held the rate of interest constant (by assumption). But in our later expositions, we shall recognize that such policies may *not* leave the rate of interest unaffected. When we come to that point, we shall find the notion of the IS schedule indispensible in treating policy questions.

In the last section, we further elaborated on the model by including the level of income as a determinant of investment. We found that the model could still be "solved" in the same fashion as before to obtain an IS schedule, and that the interpretation of that schedule remained the same. But we did note that, if the marginal propensity to spend exceeds one, the IS schedule becomes upward-sloping and the total multipliers become infinite. This latter problem is a dynamic one, and there is little evidence that it is particularly relevant in what we endearingly refer to as the "real world." Thus, the inclusion of the income term in the investment function yields no important changes in the overall model. As a result, we shall simplify our later presentation by excluding that term from the analysis of investment.

Suggested Further Reading

Bailey, M. J. *National Income and the Price Level.* London: McGraw-Hill, 1962, chap. 2.

Hansen, A. *A Guide to Keynes.* New York: McGraw-Hill, 1953.

Hicks, J. R. "Mr. Keynes and the Classics." *Econometrica* 5 (April 1937), 147–59. Reprinted in American Economic Association, *Readings in the Theory of Income Distribution.* Homewood, Ill.: R. D. Irwin, 1951, pp. 461–76.

Laidler, D. *The Demand for Money: Theories and Evidence.* Scranton, Pa: International Textbook Co., 1969, part I, chap. 1.

CHAPTER 6

Money and the Rate of Interest

6.1 Introduction

So far, the models we have introduced were nonmonetary ones in the sense that all variables involved represented aggregates of goods. Thus implicitly we assumed that goods were exchanged for goods and consequently the models reflected in effect a barter economy.

Barter—the exchange of goods for goods—has played an important role in primitive societies and is never entirely absent even in the most sophisticated ones. The specialization of production, however, and the subsequent development of the market called for a more efficient means of exchange. The bilateral arrangement of barter is characterized by the necessity of accommodating simultaneously the needs of both parties involved in the transaction. This means that bilateral barter requires a double coincidence of wants of both seller and buyer. Should this transaction scheme fail, a multilateral arrangement takes place and new persons are introduced into the picture until the exchange eventually satisfies the wants of all parties involved. This awkwardness associated with barter arrangements can be avoided by using any particular good as a common medium of exchange. Once such a medium is adopted, the single affair of barter is decomposed into two separate transactions: a sale for and a purchase with this medium of exchange.

The introduction of a medium of exchange not only facilitates the economic process by decomposing barter into two separate affairs, it also lifts another restriction inherent in a barter economy. Although exchange ratios on a barter basis may be quoted symmetrically for every good in terms of every other, as soon as the market grows to include a reasonable number of goods, the volume of these exchange ratios assumes astronomical dimensions. To appreciate this point, consider a ten-good market place. The number of trading ratios will be 100 (each good would have an exchange ratio with each of the other nine goods, plus a trivial exchange ratio of one with itself). Of course, forty-five of these exchange ratios will be simply reciprocals of others (e.g., the price of good 1 in terms of good 2 will be the reciprocal of the price of good 2 in terms of good 1). However, the number of exchange ratios is still very large relative to the number of goods. Indeed, in an economy with only fifty goods, there would be 2,500 such ratios, and in a modern economy with literally thousands of goods there would be millions of exchange ratios. But this problem can be solved immediately if every good is quoted in terms of the medium of exchange, reducing the dimensions of the problem considerably. The number of exchange ratios, for example, in the case of a ten-good system would be only nine, and in a fifty-good market the number of ratios would be only forty-nine.

Therefore we may be tempted to define money as being that commodity which performs the functions of medium of exchange and unit of account. However, the last function, although technical and important, is neither a necessary nor a sufficient condition for the definition of money. It is possible to have a unit of account which does not appear to have any monetary and/or physical form like the ones we implied here, such as England's guinea. The British guinea, however, is an exception, and as a general rule, the unit of account corresponds with the monetary unit, or what is the same, with the unit of the medium of exchange.

The introduction of this exchange lubricant and the subsequent decomposition of the function of barter into two separate transactions affords time to lapse between the sale and the purchase of the exchange medium. Since the medium of exchange is generally accepted in transactions, the seller of a certain commodity (the buyer of the exchange medium) does not have to use it immediately, as in the case of bilateral or multilateral barter. He may very well hold it over time and make use of it whenever the occasion arises. In other words, the introduction of the exchange medium invites time to lapse between payments and receipts. Thus, we can see one more function of money emerging: its role as a store of value. Once more, like its function as an accounting unit, it is only a consequence of its use as an exchange medium rather than a crucial element of its definition.

Money, then, can be defined as any economic good which can function as an exchange medium. Depending on the norms of the society and the structure of production, through history a great variety of commodities have been used for such a purpose. On the other hand, only a few have actually passed the test of time. One important set of reasons is that the medium of exchange has to be easily transportable, divisible, and fairly durable, and it must be something which is limited in supply (so that it is valuable in exchange). Another equally important reason is that the ultimate test a commodity has to pass is its general acceptability in settling debts. One may argue that this last property is a necessary condition for accepting a certain commodity to play the role of money.[1]

The definition of money supply in this context becomes very crucial. In contemporary banking systems the money supply is defined as the sum of cash in circulation and commercial bank deposits. In addition, commercial banks differentiate between demand and time deposits. Demand deposits or checking accounts are those obligations which are not associated with any interest payment and are made available by them and accepted by the public as a means of exchange. These deposits can be withdrawn, without any notice, either directly or by the means of a check. On the other hand, time deposits are those obligations of the banks on which interest is paid and which, at least potentially or formally, can be made available to the depositors after some delay and notice. In regard to which deposits are to be used in the definition of money supply, there is a substantial difference in opinion. One school of thought includes only demand deposits and thus, according to this view, the money supply consists only of the sum of currency in circulation and demand deposits at commercial banks. Another view insists that a more appropriate definition of money supply should include, above and beyond these two items, time deposits as well. Furthermore, a more far-reaching alternative definition expands the concept of money supply to include a variety of the so-called near monies, like deposits in saving and loan associations.

The choice among these alternative definitions may be based on two criteria. First, one may want to define money in such a way that it envelops all the relevant segments of financial assets on which, given

---

[1]It is worth mentioning that any barter transaction, be it bilateral or multilateral, involves the use of some resources the magnitude of which may very well depend upon the nature of goods one wishes to exchange. We cannot ignore the fact, for example, that time—an economic good—has to be used for collecting and processing information concerning market conditions and transactions. Therefore, once money is introduced as a common medium of exchange, the cost of gathering and processing relevant information as well as transacting (e.g., transporting) is reduced; consequently the process becomes more efficient in the sense that it minimizes the use of limited resources. On this point see K. Brunner and A. H. Meltzer, "The Uses of Money: Money in the Theory of an Exchange Economy," *American Economic Review* 61 (December 1971), 784–805.

the monetary institutions and systems, the monetary authorities can and do exert direct influence. Second, one may wish to define money in such a way that the analysis of various motives for holding money is facilitated.

The problem of defining money is still associated with a considerable degree of controversy. The important thing is that once a definition is adopted, a consistent use of this definition is required. For our purposes in what follows, we shall define the money supply as the sum of currency in circulation and demand deposits at commercial banks.

We now attempt to see briefly some of the factors which contribute to establishing this general acceptability of money. The first factor has already been suggested implicitly above: it is acceptable because it is used by others. This is, however, circular reasoning which involves a very interesting indeterminate process. Money is a peculiar and fascinating thing, insofar as its use is justified not by its physical properties but instead by its very arbitrary function. If this is the case then one may say that the driving force of its acceptability is mainly custom; consequently, what emerges from such an arrangement is called customary money. On the other hand, what is to be used as money may be the product of deliberate action of the legal institutions, in which case money assumes a legal status. Under these circumstances money becomes legal tender in the sense that payment in this commodity is accepted by the courts as a lawful and complete satisfaction of debts. Money which assumes such a legal status is called legal money.

From our point of view, the distinction of money in terms of commodity and token is also important. The first refers to that medium of exchange which has its own intrinsic value as a commodity above and beyond its acquired value as an exchange medium. Precious metals belong in this category. On the other hand, token money, at its extreme, lacks entirely any intrinsic value and instead its value is derived from the fact that it is accepted in exchange for other goods.

6.2 Monetary Systems and Authorities

In modern economies, monetary systems—the set of regulations and principles governing the functions of money supply—are to a large extent determined by governmental actions. Thus, one may easily argue that the government, and by extension the political institutions, carry the responsibility for the functioning of the monetary system within the confines of the goal-oriented behavior of the market economy. And since the monetary system, by virtue of its legal and political status, can become the subject of pressures imposed by the various political institutions, and, often enough, vested interests, it is an obvious question to ask what is considered to be a good performance of it.

As was pointed out above, in a barter economy the exchange of goods establishes implicit exchange ratios. In a monetary economy these ratios become prices which express the value of commodities in terms of monetary units. Consequently, we may say that money is a measure of value or a measure of purchasing power. But money also plays the role of a store of value. Suppose that two parties write a contract of a loan in terms of money according to which the first party will pay to the second after a predetermined lapse of time the amount designated in the contract. One may view this loan contract as an arrangement according to which the second party will receive purchasing power at some future date. Such a contractual agreement seems to be quite similar to contracts promising future delivery of various goods. But this similarity is only superficial.

Contracts promising future delivery of goods are expected to be satisfied by using the same unit of measure which is identified by the contractual agreement; in the case of money, however, this may or may not be so. If someone lends 1,000 yards of a certain type of cloth material to be repaid in one year, he expects that he will receive back the same amount of yards of the same type of material. However, if one lends $1,000, the value of this amount at the terminal time of the contract may or may not be the same, since the purchasing power of this amount may be different at these two dates. This difference can be attributed to the fact that although the yard is an abstract unit of measure disembodied from the good itself, the monetary unit of value is usually a good in its own right which is demanded by the economic units for its functions and supplied by the monetary system and is consequently subject to their corresponding pressures. Thus, one may argue that a monetary system performs well when it operates so that it maintains a stable unit of value, so that contracts promising delivery of money on some future date represent the same purchasing power. This means that the monetary system should react in such a way that it maintains a stable overall level of commodity prices.

More generally though, it will become apparent that monetary authorities are also delegated the responsibility of assisting, or at least not frustrating, the society's efforts to achieve high employment, economic growth and a reasonable outcome in the balance of payments.

Having discussed the functions of money, we shall use the above concepts to include money in our model. In the process, we shall see how the supply of and the demand for money affect the rate of interest. The next section analyzes the factors underlying the demand for money.

6.3 The Demand for Money

In static microeconomic theory at each point in time the consumer is confronted by a set of available goods and his choice problem is the maximization of his satisfaction, given the prices of goods and his money income. Likewise, in macroeconomics the demand for money can be viewed as a problem within the framework of the theory of rational choice. More explicitly, in this context our consumer is confronted with a given level of wealth and his problem is how to allocate this wealth among the various alternatives available to him. For example, to the extent that people desire to hold some cash and/or demand deposits (checking accounts), an obvious question arises: why should they demand these assets in view of the fact that they earn no yield and when any alternative allocation of their wealth among other financial assets would imply an increase in their earnings?

The list of factors affecting the demand for money, as given by various economists, includes a rather wide selection. It is agreed, however, by the majority of them that the fundamental reasons for holding (demanding) money are two: first, the existence of time and the fact that human actions do take time; and second, the uncertainty of economic conditions, in particular the future value of fixed-interest-bearing assets conveniently called "bonds." Since Keynes' *General Theory,* it has become a rather common practice to classify the motives for holding money into three categories: the transaction motive, the precautionary motive, and the speculative motive.[2] We proceed now to analyze each of them in turn.

---

[2] However, we should warn the reader that the recognition of these three motives for demanding money and the resultant partitioning of its total demand into three components is, at least at the present, merely a useful pedagogical device. It allows us to isolate the factors which influence each component and consequently to better appreciate the relationship of these factors with the total demand for money. Indeed, these separate components are not observable variables; but their identification facilitates the discussion of the alternative theories of the demand for money. For an ingenious attempt to identify one component of the total demand for money see James Tobin's article, "Liquidity Preference and Monetary Policy," *Review of Economics and Statistics* 29 (May 1947), 124–31.

The Transaction Motive

As was pointed out above, one of the functions of money is to play the role of a medium of exchange. As long as there is a perfect synchronization of the flow of receipts with that of expenditures, people need not demand money to hold for transaction purposes. If everyone, for example, were paid wages at the end of each day, there would be almost a perfect coincidence between receipts and expenditures. But due to various technological and institutional reasons there is always a time gap between receipts and payments. It follows then, that since receipts take place at predetermined intervals in time (for example, weekly, bimonthly, monthly, etc.), while expenditures are made continuously during the time interval between these points, a typical wage-earner in a monetary economy will have to hold some money to bridge this gap. The amount of money a typical individual or household wishes to hold to cover the cost of purchases during the interval between receipts is called the transaction demand for money.

Of course, one may argue that under the present conditions of the credit markets, it is possible for an individual to exhibit a zero demand for transaction balances, simply by using credit cards and paying off the accumulated debt at the end of each payment period (for example, at the end of each month). Indeed, such a possibility exists and we may witness such developments taking place to a larger extent in the future. But the majority of consumers still prefer to hold some transaction balances, since purchases on credit imply inconvenience and, more often than not, additional cost. For these reasons, households demand cash balances for transaction purposes and it will be instructive to take a closer look at their behavior.

Let us then consider the case of the "typical" consumer who earns $1,000 per month. Assuming away any saving, his balances might look somewhat like those in figure 6.3.1. According to this diagram we see that at the beginning of each month he receives $1,000, which he spends uniformly during this period, reducing his cash balances to zero by the end of the month.

Thus, we can say that, provided that cash balances are used according to our straight-line assumption, our consumer, on the average, will demand to hold an amount equal to $500, or half of his monthly income. Another way of describing the behavior of his cash balances is to say that a dollar is held in his accounts for an average of fifteen days.

We may now try to establish the factors which determine the average level of cash balances. For the individual consumer with a given income

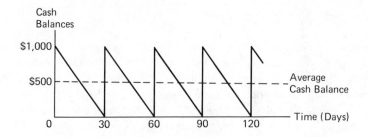

Figure 6.3.1 *Time-Pattern of an Individual's Transactions Balances, for a Thirty-Day Pay Period*

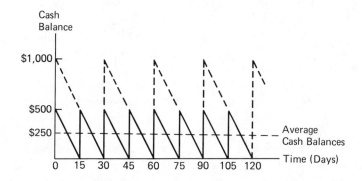

Figure 6.3.2 *The Effect of a Shortening of the Pay Period*

we may argue that the factors which determine the average level of cash balances are basically the time pattern of receipts and the payments interval which together determine the so-called income-expenditure period. The payments interval is defined to be that interval which lies between successive payments. Although in the case of our example this interval is one month, it could very well be equal to one week, two weeks, a quarter of a year, etc.

Let us now see how the behavior of cash balances changes as a result of a change in the payment interval. To this end suppose that our consumer receives his salary semimonthly instead of monthly. The new pattern is depicted in figure 6.3.2. For comparison we have superimposed in dotted lines the cash balances from figure 6.3.1. Figure 6.3.2 shows that although monthly income has remained constant, the frequency of payments has increased. As a result, the level of the average cash balances has declined from $500 to $250. Thus, we conclude that,

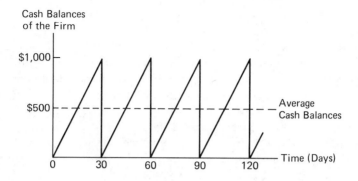

Figure 6.3.3   *Time-Pattern of the Firm's Transactions Balances*

ceteris paribus, the level of the average balances required declines as the frequency of payments increases (as the payment interval decreases).

To complete the analysis we must bring into the picture the activities of firms. For this it is necessary to slightly alter our assumptions. Suppose that the behavior depicted in diagram 6.3.1 refers not to the individual consumer, but to the aggregate of income recipients in the economy. Let us also assume for simplicity that all these income recipients are paid on the same day and that the whole productive activity of the economy is carried out by only one firm. Obviously, whatever is registered as income for consumers is at the same time an expenditure for the firm. It follows that the behavior of the cash balances of the firm will be the mirror image of that of the consumers, as figure 6.3.3 shows.

In figure 6.3.3 it is assumed that at time "0" the firm pays out to individuals wages, salaries, profits, interest, etc., and thus its cash balances fall to zero. As consumers start purchasing goods from the firm, their cash balances decline and at the same time the cash balances of the firm increase by the same amount. At the end of the payment period, the cash balances of consumers decline to zero, whereas those of the firm reach a maximum level which again is, of course, equal to $1,000. Thus, at any point in time, the total demand for money for transaction purposes is equal to the sum of cash balances at the hands of consumers and the firm. The above example suggests that consumers sold to the firm $1,000 worth of productive services for twelve months, i.e., $12,000, and they bought back from the firm the same amount of goods and services. Thus, since the available amount of money in this example is equal to $1,000, it follows that on the average, each dollar bounced back and forth from the firm to the individuals to the firm twelve times.

Consequently, if we assume that the output of this economy is equal to the total amount the firm produced (the total amount of goods the consumers purchased), we see that the transaction demand for money (the amount of money required to accommodate the total volume of transactions) is a fraction of the value of net national product. Of course, in our case, since we assumed that the productive activity of the economy is organized in one firm, we have excluded problems associated with the degree of vertical integration of the economy. If the production of the economy had been organized in such a way that each stage of production was carried out by a different firm, then the value of the total volume of transactions would have exceeded that of NNP. We have already shown this in chapter 2.

Thus, the transaction demand for money also depends on the organizational structure of the economy itself. However, despite the fact that the total volume of transactions in reality is bound to be larger than the NNP, to the extent that their relation remains fairly stable, at least in the short run, one may establish, as a first approximation, a functional relation between the amount of money demanded for transaction purposes and NNP, i.e.:

$$M_{t,d} = F(P \cdot Y) \tag{6.3.1}$$

where $M_{t,d}$ stands for the amount of money demanded for transaction purposes, P stands for the implicit NNP price deflator and Y stands for the NNP itself expressed in constant prices. Thus, the product $P \cdot Y$ reflects NNP in current prices and consequently equation 6.3.1 expresses the "nominal" demand for money for transaction purposes as a function of NNP in current prices. We shall assume that the above functional relation is one of proportionality, namely:

$$M_{t,d} = l_1 PY \tag{6.3.2}$$

where l_1 stands for the factor of proportionality. When our variables are expressed in terms of annual rates, l_1 is a positive number between zero and one, i.e., $0 < l_1 < 1$. From the above equation, we can see that the demand for money for transaction purposes $(M_{t,d})$ increases (decreases) as a result of an increase (decrease) in the price level (P) and/or real NNP.

We may now make use of the presence of the variable P and express the variables which appear in equation 6.3.2 in real terms as opposed to nominal terms. This can be done by dividing both sides of 6.3.2 by P to obtain:

$$\frac{M_{t,d}}{P} = l_1 Y. \tag{6.3.3}$$

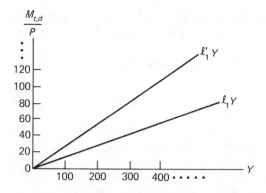

Figure 6.3.4 *The Real Transactions Demand for Money*

A heuristic interpretation of equation 6.3.3 is that the amount of constant value dollars the economic units demand for transaction purposes depends on the real value of NNP. To say the same thing a bit differently: if the factor of proportionality l_1 as well as real income are constant, an increase in the price level by a certain percent will be accompanied by an equal percentage increase in the nominal demand for money for transaction purposes. The reason for this, of course, is that since the volume of goods and services to be transacted remains the same and since the price level increases, it follows that the economy will need proportionally higher balances to effect transactions.

Now suppose that the factor of proportionality, l_1, assumes the value .2. This implies that $5 worth of transactions of real NNP can be accommodated by $1 of constant value. Another way of looking at the same thing is to say that each constant value dollar changes hands an average of five times within the period in consideration, which is in our case equal to one year.

Figure 6.3.4 depicts this relation between NNP and the real transactions for cash balances. From figure 6.3.4 we can see that, *ceteris paribus,* the higher the level of real income the larger the required amount of constant-value money necessary to accommodate the transactions. On the other hand, as was pointed out above, habits, institutional factors and modes of organization of the productive effort exert various degrees of influence on the relation of $M_{t,d}/P$ with Y. According to our assumptions, this relation is expressed via the parameter l_1 which can be subjected to changes as a result of changes in any of the above factors. For example, diagram 6.3.4 indicates a shift of the relation between $M_{t,d}/P$ and Y from the initial position $l_1 Y$ to $l_1' Y$. This shift, obviously, is characterized by the fact that $l'_1 > l_1$; i.e., for the same volume of net national product there is more demand for money for transaction purposes. This may be the result of a reduction of the degree of vertical integration of the economy or a decrease in the frequency of receipts.

The Precautionary Motive

The precautionary motive for holding money stems from the desire to weather unforeseen contingencies as well as to take advantage of future opportunities. Since money is used as a means of transaction, it involves a minimum of commitment and provides a maximum of flexibility in meeting emergencies and taking advantage of various bargains which appear in the market place. Furthermore, one may argue that the greater the uncertainty in regard to the future, the higher the desire for flexibility and consequently the greater the precautionary demand for money.

The evolution of our knowledge and institutions over time results in an almost continuous conversion of uncertainty into risk for which mathematical expectations can be determined and for which insurance policies can be negotiated and purchased. For example, today one may purchase health insurance which covers at least a substantial portion of potential medical expenses. This, however, implies that while the individual economic unit ceases to demand to hold money for health contingencies and therefore precautionary demand decreases, at the same time the transaction demand increases by an amount which is related to the premium on the policy in question. Furthermore, the emerging institution of the extensive use of credit cards has undoubtedly reduced the demand to hold cash balances for precautionary purposes.

The reliability of obtaining cash through either bank borrowing or disposition of other marketable securities plays a considerable role in the determination of the precautionary demand for money. This is also quite true for the business world where assets are held in cash balances in order to meet future financial obligations and/or to satisfy requirements of future expansionary programs. A firm's ability to obtain external capital on satisfactory terms for further expansion or even to preserve the amenities of life for its management may very well depend on its ability to maintain an uninterrupted stream of dividends to shareholders despite some temporary adverse economic conditions. Therefore firms may desire to hold reserves in cash balances which can be used to iron out large fluctuations in the distribution of dividends.

To the extent that convenience and security against unforeseen contingencies, as measured by the size of cash balances held for these purposes by economic units, can be considered as economic goods, it can be argued that the demand for these goods depends on both the income of the individual economic unit and the cost of holding money. As in the case of any other normal good, the amount of money demanded for precautionary purposes will vary directly with the income or scale of operation of the individual economic units and inversely with its cost. To appreciate the nature of the cost in this case, consider that one must weigh the convenience and security provided by the holding of cash balances against the fact that idle money in the vaults of a firm does not earn any yield which alternative uses could certainly provide. Thus, the holdings of cash balances implies an opportunity cost which can be expressed by the interest forgone. Therefore the price in question is the market rate of interest, and there is an inverse relationship between this rate of interest and the amount of money held for precautionary purposes.

Although in principle the precautionary demand for money could be separated from the transaction demand, nevertheless in practice this becomes a rather formidable task. Therefore we shall ignore for the time being the functional relation between the precautionary demand and the rate of interest and we shall instead assume that it is a function of income alone. Consequently, since both transaction and precautionary demand for money are assumed to be functions of income alone, the two may be combined in one equation which will relate their sum to NNP. For the sake of simplicity we shall further assume that this functional relation may be expressed in terms of equation 6.3.3 with the understanding that now the variable $M_{t,d}$ will represent the sum of these two segments of the demand for money.

The Speculative Motive

At this point someone may suggest that the previous two motives exhaust the cash needs of all economic units and consequently that there is no further reason for demanding money to hold. This would be a legitimate argument if it were not for "all sorts of vague doubts and fluctuating states of confidence and courage" concerning future economic developments. This observation leads us to the examination of the third reason for holding cash, the speculative motive. We shall investigate this motive in a more detailed fashion not only because it is a bit more difficult to appreciate but also because, according to some views, it is one of the basic channels via which the effects of changes in money supply are transmitted into the economy.

Individual economic units must make decisions about the allocation of their wealth among various real and financial assets, i.e., how much of each of these assets they want to include in their portfolio.[3] To keep our discussion in rather simple terms we shall recognize three basic categories of financial assets: money, various forms of marketable debt claims, and equities. From the above categories we shall focus the analysis on money and marketable debt claims since the decision to acquire equities (which represent in effect a fractional ownership and participation in the outcome of the entrepreneurial effort) in some sense can be considered as obeying the same rules and exhibiting the same characteristics as investment in real goods.

In addition, for historical reasons as well as for the sake of simplicity, we shall assume that the marketable debt claims consist of identical nonmaturing government bonds—the so-called consols—and thus the interest rate we shall discuss will be the long-run one. Assuming then that the composition of the portfolio may consist of cash and/or marketable debt claims (consols), the reader may wonder about the rationality of an economic unit which decides to hold cash balances instead of consols, which would increase the expected return of its portfolio.

While the inclusion of money in this portfolio may appear at first glance as irrational, closer examination of the properties of the various assets reveals that this may not be so. Under the present organization of financial markets, it appears that marketable debt claims are almost as liquid as money. However, they also have two serious shortcomings which money does not possess. First, they are not a medium of exchange; second, these assets are riskier than money since their price is subject to fluctuations. Thus, the exchange of consols with money involves both an objective as well as a subjective cost. Ignoring for a moment that their price may fluctuate and focusing only on the cost of transaction, we should expect that economic units would be induced to invest in marketable forms of debt as long as the market rate of interest would at least cover the objective cost of transactions. Thus, given the level of these costs, one would expect that the higher the rate of interest the higher the demand for these securities and consequently the lower the demand

---

[3] In this connection it should be recognized that the majority of wage earners demand money predominantly for transaction purposes. It appears then that it would be quite superficial to implicate them with the aspects of the theory of asset choice. On the other hand, there are financial institutions which demand money predominantly for the purpose of investment and consequently a large portion of their demand for money could be justified by the speculative motive. Thus although we shall continue our analysis in terms of the individual economic units, the reader will find it useful to bear the above distinction in mind. Furthermore, the reader should be warned that our analysis of speculative demand is only one possible treatment of it. In chapter 14, we consider an alternative derivation of the relationship, one which was first presented by James Tobin.

for money. Conversely, one would expect that a decrease in the rate of interest not accompanied by a decrease in the transaction cost would force some prospective investors to abstain from purchasing securities and instead keep their assets in the form of money. In other words, a decline in the rate of interest will be associated with an increase in the demand for money as an asset (the speculative motive) due to the fact that the expected earnings either do not justify the subjective cost of inconveniences, or they imply outright losses.

On the other hand, the current rate of interest may be considered as the opportunity cost of holding money instead of securities. A decline in the rate of interest implying a decrease in the opportunity cost— measured in terms of income forgone—makes the holding of money as an asset more attractive, thus resulting in an increase in the demand for it. This line of argument suggests that the demand for money as an asset should vary inversely with the rate of interest.

Although the above discussion establishes a negative relationship between the rate of interest and the demand for money as an asset, unfortunately, it does not make clear the speculative character of this demand. To drive the argument home it is necessary to consider the relation between the price of a consol and the market rate of interest. This is given by the following equation (see Appendix 6.A):

$$V = \frac{C}{r} \tag{6.3.4}$$

where V stands for the market price of the consol in question, C stands for its coupon and r for the long-run market rate of interest. Notice that since the amount of dollars represented by the coupon do not change, it follows that the market value of the consol can change only as a result of a change in the market rate of interest. In fact, from equation 6.3.4 we can see that there is an inverse relationship between the market rate of interest and the price of this consol. We may now use this concept to relate the various amounts of money demanded for speculative purposes with the different levels of the market rate of interest.

Depending on historical trends, at any point in time there is a range, as well as a level, of the rate of interest which is considered normal by the economic units of a community. The range within which the rate of interest is supposed to fluctuate may or may not be quite the same for each individual unit. However, although the interpretation of historical trends depends quite heavily on one's perception, the wide use and effectiveness of the communication media tend to diminish differences in opinion about the upper and lower bounds of this interval. On the other hand, the size of this interval depends upon the time and place reference of the economic units. The views of the economic units may differ depending on whether the range of the rate of interest refers to the period 1960–65 or 1966–71, or if it refers to the same period but for different countries. At any rate, the range will have to be large enough to envelop the most extreme expectations of the community. The normal level of the rate of interest may be considered as a weighted average of the rates which prevail in the immediate history of the community in question.

Now, as long as the rate of interest fluctuates near its *normal* level there are always in effect two poles of opinion in regard to its future level: the "bears," who expect that the rate will increase, and thus that the market value of consols will decrease; and the "bulls," who expect that the rate will decrease and consequently that the price of consols will increase. However, as soon as the rate of interest starts moving in one direction, these two poles of opinion begin to converge in such a way that in the end there is only one opinion in regard to expected values in the immediate future. In other words, as long as two poles of opinion exist in the market there will be transactions of securities which reflect the willingness and courage of the individual economic units to use their cash balances to back their respective expectations. For example, the bears, on the assumption that the rate of interest will increase, would like to sell; whereas the bulls, with opposite expectations, would be interested in buying. However, as soon as the rate of interest starts moving away from its normal value, the amount of transactions decreases since the mechanism of convergence of opinions begins to operate.

Suppose that the normal range and level of interest are 2%–9% and 5% respectively, as figure 6.3.5 indicates. Assume also that there are x number of players in the market and that half of them believe that the rate of interest is going to increase in the near future (that the price of consols will decrease), whereas the other half hold exactly the opposite set of expectations. Furthermore, let us assume that various individuals or groups of individuals expect that the rate of interest will fluctuate within different ranges covering all points of the space between 2% and 9% and that all these ranges are enveloped by the range of our example. Consequently, as the rate of interest moves from 5% to its expected extreme values, we meet the various upper and lower limits of the range various individuals have set, depending on their interpretation of historical trends and their perception of current economic developments. Finally, it will be assumed that opinions about the normal rate and range remain unchanged during the period in consideration. This is, of course, another way of recognizing that our analysis is strictly a short-run one.

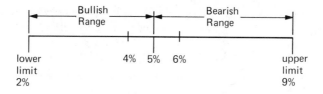

Figure 6.3.5 *The "Normal" Range of Values of the Rate of Interest*

We may now start by assuming that the long-run market rate of interest is currently at 5%. As long as some of the economic units expect that the rate will increase and the others think that it will decrease, it follows that transactions will take place reflecting this difference in expectations. Now suppose that the rate of interest changes by very small but finite quantities monotonically toward 4% until it assumes that value, but that these changes are not considered by the economic units as enough to establish a trend. This means that the price of consols will increase and the bulls will keep purchasing on the assumption of further increases in the price of consols. At 4%, however, the expectations of some of the bulls have already been realized. This implies that these economic units do not expect that the rate of interest will further decrease. Thus, the only alternative open to them is to become bears and try to sell their consols to realize the profit which resulted from the increase in the price of consols. Thus, we see that, given the distribution of individual economic units with lower limits higher than 2%, as indicated by figure 6.3.5 above, a decrease in the rate of interest induces an increase in the quantity of cash balances demanded.

If the rate of interest keeps its monotonic course from 4% to 2%, more and more bulls become bears until at 2% (the limit itself) even the most hard-nosed bull will have realized his expectation.[4] At this point, the market would have no bullish attitude left. Everybody will have become a bear. Thus, everyone would like to sell his consols at this very price since there is nobody expecting that the rate of interest will further decline, or that the price of consols will further increase to a higher level.

---

[4]At this point the reader may wonder if, and to what extent, the increasing number of bears can indeed find willing bulls to unload their securities. As strange as it may sound this is irrelevant. What is at stake here is not whether the transactions in effect take place but the interactions of the players in the market. It would be more accurate to say that at a 4% rate of interest the demanded quantity of money is larger than that at 5%. Here, we have wishful thinking and it is immaterial if it is satisfied or not. In the final analysis this is the exact meaning of all demand curves.

In other words, economic units would like to liquidate the whole amount of holdings of marketable debt claims, or to replace consols with money.

The behavior we have just described clearly suggests that as the rate of interest decreases, increasingly larger amounts of money will be demanded for speculative purposes. In this connection it is interesting to notice that the value of a coupon, or for that matter the yield associated with a certain consol, is usually eclipsed by the fluctuations of the price of the consol itself. Thus, in order to protect their capital and/or to realize the profits resulting from these fluctuations, economic units may very well forgo the nominal yield associated with these marketable claims of debt and express their desire to hold cash balances instead.[5]

Had the rate of interest started changing from 5% toward 9%, the above analysis would have produced dramatically opposite results. In other words, as the rate of interest changes from 5% to 6% the price of consols decreases and some bears become bulls. The limit will be that at a 9% rate of interest nobody believes that the interest can increase to even higher levels (that the price of consols will decline any more). However, this suggests that the price of consols can only increase and that profits (capital gains) will be realized. Thus, at this point, there is a unanimous desire to purchase consols, and the desire to hold (demand) cash balances for speculative purposes diminishes to zero.

The above analysis leads directly to the conclusion that the demand for money for speculative purposes and the rate of interest are related functionally to each other. We may then express this dependence as:

$$\frac{M_{s,d}}{P} = g(r) \tag{6.3.5}$$

where $M_{s,d}$ stands for the nominal demand for speculative balances, P is the implicit NNP price deflator and r is the long-run rate of interest.

To be consistent with the ideas advanced earlier, the properties of equation 6.3.5. depend on the values of the rate of interest. More ex-

---

[5]For example, suppose that the current rate of interest is 5% and that the coupon of a consol is $50. Then according to equation 6.3.4 the market value of this consol will be equal to its par value, i.e., $1,000. Now if the market rate of interest declines from 5% to 4% to 2% then the corresponding market values of this consol will be $1,250 and $2,500 respectively. Thus, we can clearly see that the yield of consols can easily be dwarfed by fluctuations of their prices which are due to changes in the rate of interest. The speculative motive thus is expressed by the fact that although by holding the consol the economic unit may earn $50 annually, or 5% of its par value, this behavior may be considered utterly irrational from a financial point of view since by selling the consol (i.e., demanding cash balances), the economic unit could realize profit amounting to 25% or 150% depending on whether the rate of interest is at 4% or 2% respectively.

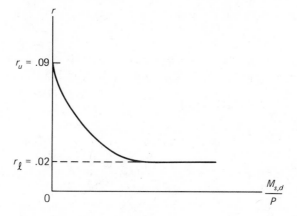

Figure 6.3.6 *The Speculative Demand for Money Schedule*

plicitly, if r_u and r_l stand for the upper and lower values respectively of what is considered the normal range, then our earlier discussion suggests:

$$\frac{M_{s,d}}{P} = 0 \qquad \text{if } r \geqq r_u \tag{6.3.5a}$$

and

$$\frac{M_{s,d}}{P} \to \infty \qquad \text{if } r = r_l. \tag{6.3.5b}$$

Equation 6.3.5a describes the fact that when the rate of interest is equal to or higher than the upper value of its normal range, i.e., r_u, then the demand for speculative cash balances becomes zero. On the other hand, equation 6.3.5b describes the diametrically opposite case: when the rate of interest becomes equal to the lower value of the normal range, i.e., r_l, then the demand for speculative cash balances becomes infinitely large. For obvious reasons equations 6.3.5a and b depict the extreme properties of the demand for money for speculative purposes. If the rate of interest is between these two extreme values (in our example, 2% and 9%), equation 6.3.5 expresses this inverse relation with the demand for speculative cash balances. A plausible graph of equation 6.3.5 is given in figure 6.3.6.

In what follows we shall ignore the extreme properties of the speculative demand for money. In addition, without any loss of generality and for the sake of convenience, we shall assume that the speculative demand

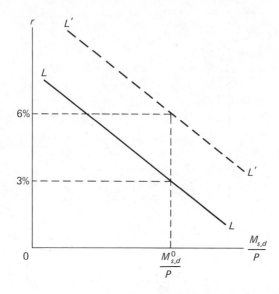

Figure 6.3.7   *A Linear Real Speculative Demand for Money Schedule*

for money is a linear function of the rate of interest. Figure 6.3.7 provides us with the graph of the equation 6.3.5 on the assumption that the variables involved are related linearly.

In the above diagram LL shows the short-run speculative demand for money. In other words, this line is drawn on the assumption of a given set of opinions about the normal range and level of the rate of interest. Suppose, however, that the rate of interest loses its gravity and instead keeps fluctuating around generally higher values. This may very well lead to a revision of the community's opinion of what is normal. Should this be the case, the speculative demand schedule could shift upward, implying either that larger amounts of speculative balances are demanded at the same rate of interest i.e., (that the same amounts of such balances are demanded at higher rates of interest).

So far the development of the argument has followed the traditional lines of the Keynesian theory of liquidity preference. However, the reader has undoubtedly observed that according to this theory the economic units are left with the choice between risky bonds and riskless cash balances in a mutually exclusive fashion. In other words, according to the liquidity preference theory the economic units behave *as if* they choose to hold all their financial assets either in cash balances or in long-run marketable forms of debt claims. In reality, however, the choices open to them are by far wider than those recognized by this theory. An individual economic unit may choose among time deposits, savings and loan shares, commercial paper, Treasury bills, and other varieties of debt claims, all of which are associated with a rate of return and, with the exception of Treasury bills, all of which are associated with nonfluctuating market values. Thus, the choice between all or nothing posed by the Keynesian theory loses its sharpness since economic units have the open alternative of choosing short-run claims (which, however, are usually associated with a lower yield than the long-run ones). The relevant question is not whether the economic units are induced to hold cash or risky bonds but instead how they allocate the relevant portion of their wealth among the various debt instruments.

Although the recognition of short-term debt claims may reduce our confidence in the theory of liquidity preference, this should not shake our belief in the inverse relation between demand for money and rate of interest. On the contrary, this relation still exists but its rationale has shifted from the demand for speculative balances to the demand for precautionary and transaction ones. However, in order to appreciate recent developments and place them in the appropriate historical perspective, for the time being we shall continue to disregard the extreme cases of the demand for speculative balances.

6.4 The Total Demand for Money

The main conclusion of the previous section was that the demand for transaction and precautionary balances depends on the level of income, whereas the demand for speculative balances depends on the long-run rate of interest (r). It follows then that the total demand for money could be considered as a function of the level of income and the rate of interest, i.e.,

$$\frac{M_d}{P} = F(Y, r). \tag{6.4.1}$$

But since the total demand for money is the sum of transactions, precautionary and speculative balances, it follows that we can write

$$M_d \equiv M_{t,d} + M_{s,d} \tag{6.4.2}$$

where M_d stands for the total demand for money and $M_{t,d}$ is defined to include both transactions and precautionary balances. Recalling now that we have already specified:

$$M_{t,d} = l_1 PY$$

and: $M_{s,d} = Pg(r)$

identity 6.4.2 can be rewritten as:

$$M_d = l_1 PY + Pg(r). \tag{6.4.3}$$

From 6.4.3 we can see that if the price level remains constant the nominal demand for money depends on the level of real income and the rate of interest. On the other hand, if the price level, P, varies while the other variables remain constant, the nominal demand for money will vary in exact proportion with the price level.[6] Dividing both sides of equation 5.4.3 by P, we obtain

$$\frac{M_d}{P} = l_1 Y + g(r). \tag{6.4.4}$$

To make any further progress it is necessary for us to specify the relation between speculative demand and the rate of interest in more concrete terms. While there are various ways of expressing this relationship, our assumption will be that it is linear. Thus we shall write:

$$\frac{M_{s,d}}{P} = g(r) = l_0 - l_2 r \tag{6.4.5}$$

where l_0 and l_2 are parameters.

Substituting equation 6.4.5 into 6.4.4, we obtain the expression for the total demand for money:

$$\frac{M_d}{P} = l_0 + l_1 Y - l_2 r. \tag{6.4.6}$$

Diagramatically, equation 6.4.6 presents the same problems as our equation of the demand for investment (see equation 5.6.1). Since equation 6.4.6 expresses the total demand for money as a function of two variables, we no longer can use a two-dimensional diagram unless we adopt the convention of fixing one of the independent variables at a certain level and plot the relation of the other two. This procedure will produce, as in the case of the investment equation, not one, but instead a family of demand for money schedules, one for each value the fixed variable assumes.

---

[6] This formulation of the demand for money follows D. Patinkin's argument as expressed in his "Keynesian Economics and the Quantity Theory" in *Post-Keynesian Economics,* ed. K. K. Kurihara (New Brunswick, N.J.: Rutgers University Press, 1954).

For example, let us suppose that $l_0 = 110$, $l_1 = .15$ and $l_2 = 500$. Substituting these values for the parameters in equation 6.4.6, we obtain

$$\frac{M_d}{P} = 110 + .15Y - 500r. \tag{6.4.7}$$

Let us also assume that the income is fixed at the level of $1,000 billion. Substituting this value of income in 6.4.7 we find

$$\frac{M_d}{P} = (110 + .15 \times 1,000) - 500r$$

or

$$\frac{M_d}{P} = 260 - 500r. \tag{6.4.8}$$

Equation 6.4.8 can be plotted easily in two dimensions. On the other hand, should income assume the value of 1,100, then 6.4.7 would become

$$\frac{M_d}{P} = 275 - 500r. \tag{6.4.9}$$

Notice that the effect of assuming various values for income is that the intercept of equation 6.4.7 changes, implying a parallel shift of the graph of this function.

Figure 6.4.1 presents the relationship of the demand for money with the rate of interest for three different assumed values of income.

6.5 The Supply of Money

Having analyzed the nature and the properties of the demand for money, we now bring into the picture the money supply in an attempt to determine the level of the rate of interest.

The supply of money is defined as the total cash and demand deposits held by the public. To keep the analysis simple, we shall assume that the central bank is capable of exerting complete control over the available stock of money. This is another way of saying that the supply of money is determined outside the confines of our structural system of equations and consequently can be considered as an exogenous variable. This assumption implies that there is no relationship between the rate of interest and the money supply. This is illustrated in figure 6.5.1, where the supply of money is expressed in terms of a vertical line which shifts to the right

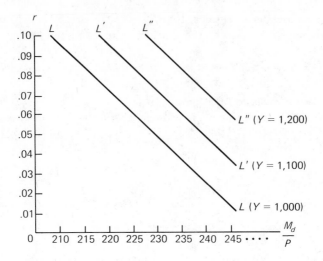

Figure 6.4.1   *The Real Total Demand for Money at Alternative
Income Levels*

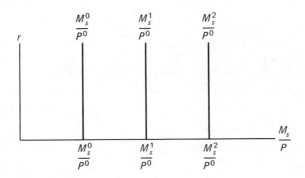

Figure 6.5.1   *The Real Money Supply*

(left) as the monetary authorities increase (decrease) its amount. In this
diagram, we have plotted the real money supply against the long-run
rate of interest. We assume implicitly that the monetary authorities
control only the nominal amount of money which will be available to
the community. Thus, given the price level and the exogenously
determined nominal amount of money supply, one can immediately
determine the real money supply (the supply of money measured in
units of constant purchasing power).

It is also worth observing that the above diagram has been drawn on the assumption that the real money supply changes only as a result of changes in the nominal money supply. However, the real money supply can also change due to changes in the price level alone and without any changes in the nominal money supply. For example, suppose that the nominal money supply remains constant at the level M_s^0 and that the price level declines by 50%, i.e., from P^0 to $(1/2)P^0$. Then the real money supply will increase by 100%, i.e., from M_s^0/P^0 to $2M_s^0/P^0$. If this is the case the vertical line designated as M_s^0/P^0 will shift to the right as if the nominal money supply had doubled without any change in the price level. For the present, though, we shall assume that the price level is an exogenous variable and shall largely ignore variations in its value. At a later point, of course, we shall relax this unrealistic assumption.

6.6 The Determination of the Rate of Interest: First Attempt

We are now prepared to show how the rate of interest can be determined. Superficially, this problem should not be a difficult one since we know that the demand for and supply of a commodity can be combined to determine the price which, under normal conditions, will clear its market.

To this end let us suppose that the level of income and prices are fixed by Y^0 and P^0 respectively. Then, equation 6.4.6 can be written as:

$$\frac{M_d}{P^0} = (l_0 + l_1 Y^0) - l_2 r. \tag{6.6.1}$$

Thus, the total demand for real cash balances appears to be a function of only its cost, the rate of interest (i.e., the rent paid/received for the temporary use of money).

Suppose also that the monetary authorities set the stock of money available to the community at the level of M_s^0. Thus, the real money supply can be written as:

$$\frac{M_s}{P} = \frac{M_s^0}{P^0}. \tag{6.6.2}$$

At equilibrium, the rate of interest should be at such a level that the demand for money will be equal to the supply of money:

$$\frac{M_d}{P} = \frac{M_s}{P}. \tag{6.6.3}$$

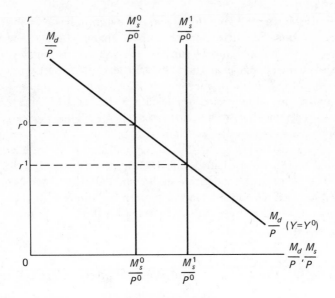

Figure 6.6.1   *The Effects of a Change in the Real Money Supply at a Given Income Level*

Substituting the equations for the supply of and demand for money into the equilibrium condition, we find:

$$l_0 + l_1 Y^0 - l_2 r = \frac{M_s^0}{P^0}. \qquad (6.6.4)$$

Equation 6.6.4 contains only one unknown, the rate of interest. Thus, we may solve for r in terms of the other parameters and variables to obtain:

$$r^0 = \frac{l_0}{l_2} - \frac{M_s^0/P^0}{l_2} + \frac{l_1}{l_2} Y^0. \qquad (6.6.5)$$

Equation 6.6.5 provides us with the equilibrium rate of interest, i.e., the rate of interest which clears the money market.

Diagrammatically, the equilibrium rate of interest can be found by combining the diagrams of the supply of and demand for money. This is done in figure 6.6.1. Examining that diagram, we see that the equilibrium rate of interest is determined by the intersection of the supply and demand schedules.

The meaning of this equilibrium can be explained by recalling the underlying assumptions. Indeed, since we have assumed that real income and the price level are fixed at Y^0 and P^0, it follows that the demand for real transaction and precautionary balances can be determined by substituting these values into equation 6.3.3, i.e.:

$$\frac{M_{t,d}^0}{P^0} = l_1 Y^0.$$

In view of the fact that the total real money supply is equal to M_s^0/P^0, it follows that the difference

$$\frac{M_s^0}{P^0} - \frac{M_{t,d}^0}{P^0} = \frac{M_s^0}{P^0} - l_1 Y^0 \qquad (6.6.6)$$

is what remains to satisfy the demand for real speculative balances, $M_{s,d}^0/P^0$. Thus, under these circumstances the rate of interest has to assume that value which will induce the economic units of the community to hold exactly this amount in speculative balances. Substituting this value for real speculative demand into equation 6.4.5, we find

$$\frac{M_{s,d}^0}{P^0} = l_0 - l_2 r$$

and since

$$\frac{M_{s,d}^0}{P^0} = \frac{M_s^0}{P^0} - l_1 Y^0$$

we have:

$$\frac{M_s^0}{P^0} - l_1 Y^0 = l_0 - l_2 r \qquad (6.6.7)$$

which can be solved for the rate of interest to yield the solution we have already determined in equation 6.6.5.

Now, let us assume that the central bank increases the nominal money supply from M_s^0 to M_s^1. Assuming that the price level remains constant at P^0, it follows that the real money supply increases from M_s^0/P^0 to M_s^1/P^0 (see figure 6.6.1). Let us also assume that the level of real income remains constant at Y^0. This implies that the demand for real transaction and precautionary balances remains the same as before, i.e.,

$$\frac{M_{t,d}^0}{P^0} = l_1 Y^0$$

Thus, the amount available for real speculative balances is now

$$\frac{M_s^1}{P^0} - l_1 Y^0$$

which is obviously greater than in the previous case. Since the demand for real transaction and precautionary balances does not change, it follows that the increase in the real money supply has to be absorbed by the speculative real demand. But to induce the community to hold (demand) greater amounts of money for speculative purposes the rate of interest has to decline. This can be seen by solving once more the equation

$$\frac{M_s^1}{P^0} - l_1 Y^0 = l_0 - l_2 r$$

to find

$$r^1 = \frac{l_0}{l_2} - \frac{M_s^1/P^0}{l_2} + \frac{l_1}{l_2} Y^0.$$

This is shown in figure 6.6.1, where an increase in the real money supply from M_s^0/P^0 to M_s^1/P^0 has resulted in a decline in the equilibrium level of the rate of interest from r^0 to r^1.

According to the above discussion, the determination of the rate of interest is purely a matter of the money market; that is, it is determined by the forces of the demand for and supply of money, or even more accurately, by the equality of the real demand for money as an asset (speculative demand) and the residual of the total real money supply less the demand for real transaction and precautionary balances. We shall call this theory the crude Keynesian version, in that it is the one which was used by Keynes in his *General Theory* as well as in the immediately ensuing economic literature.

While in later journal articles Keynes made several concessions and modifications of the crude money-market model, he nevertheless did not come close to answering all the charges advanced against this view. This was to be done in what we shall call the neo-Keynesian version or the modern theory of the rate of interest, developed by John R. Hicks.

6.7 The Determination of the Rate of Interest: Second Attempt

The trouble with the version presented in the previous section is that, despite claims to the contrary, it cannot determine the equilibrium rate of interest. More explicitly, the determination of the equilibrium rate required that the level of income, as well as that of prices, was given. This *ceteris paribus* assumption was crucial since it enabled us to

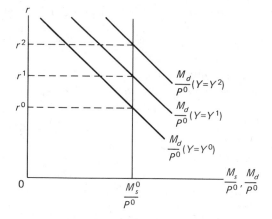

Figure 6.7.1   *Money-Market Equilibria at Alternative
Levels of Income*

determine a unique schedule of the demand for cash balances. However, from section 6.4 we know that as real income changes the demand for real cash balances changes. Thus, for each level of income there is a corresponding separate demand schedule for real cash balances, and consequently, given the money supply and the price level, a separate equilibrium rate of interest. It follows then that the crude Keynesian version cannot determine the equilibrium level of interest on a *mutatis mutandis* basis in regard to the level of income. Figure 6.7.1 makes this point clear. In diagram 6.7.1 we have drawn three demand schedules for real cash balances which correspond to three levels of real income, Y^0, Y^1, Y^2, ($Y^0 < Y^1 < Y^2$). As the reader can see, their intersection with the constant real money supply determines three different equilibrium levels of the rate of interest. In effect, the only point we can unequivocally make from figure 6.7.1 is that as income increases so does the money-market equilibrium rate of interest.

Thus, the crude Keynesian version cannot determine a unique equilibrium rate of interest. To appreciate this lack of a unique solution in regard to the equilibrium rate of interest, let us consider once more the equations of the money market; namely:

$$\frac{M_d}{P} = l_0 + l_1 Y - l_2 r \tag{6.7.1}$$

$$\frac{M_d}{P} = \frac{M_s}{P}. \tag{6.7.2}$$

The system 6.7.1–6.7.2 contains five variables, i.e., M_d, M_s, P, Y, r; of these, we shall assume that two, M_s and P, are determined exogenously. Thus, there still remain three endogenous variables, M_d, Y and r, cast in only two equations. It follows then that under normal circumstances we cannot obtain a unique solution for the variables involved. Under these conditions, the best we can do is to reduce the system into one equation containing two variables. This can be done by substituting equation 6.7.1 into 6.7.2 to obtain:

$$\frac{M_s}{P} = l_0 + l_1 Y - l_2 r. \tag{6.7.3}$$

Assuming that the values of the exogenous variables are, say, M_s^0 and P^0, the above equation reduces to:

$$\frac{M_s^0}{P^0} = l_0 + l_1 Y - l_2 r \tag{6.7.4}$$

which contains two unknowns, Y and r. Solving for r in terms of Y we find:

$$r = \frac{l_0}{l_2} - \frac{M_s^0/P^0}{l_2} + \frac{l_1}{l_2} Y. \tag{6.7.5}$$

The above equation expresses the equilibrium rate of interest as a function of the level of income. As the reader should be able to see, it is a generalized version of equation 6.6.5, the crude Keynesian version (which could be obtained by assuming that the level of income is equal to Y^0).

The graph of equation 6.7.5, as depicted in figure 6.7.2, is called an LM schedule. It is defined to be the locus of all pairs of income and interest rates for which the monetary sector is at equilibrium, or for which the demand for money is equal to its supply.

The LM curve and the equations underlying it, 6.7.1–6.7.2, will be referred to as the monetary sector of the model. Notice that since income can assume, at least theoretically, any value on the positive axis, so can the rate of interest. Thus, contrary to the Keynesian claim, we have a unique relation between the rate of interest and the level of income capable of being satisfied by an infinite number of combinations of Y and r.

In addition, we can see clearly now that: first, the factors which determine the rate of interest are not exclusively stock variables, as in the crude version; and, second, the determination of the equilibrium rate of interest does not exclusively depend on monetary factors.

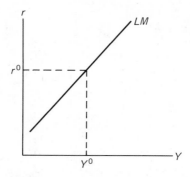

Figure 6.7.2 *Money-Market Equilibrium:*
the LM Schedule

We may now attempt to derive the LM curve graphically. This is done in figure 6.7.3, where we have drawn in separate panels the equations of the monetary sector. Panel (a) and (c) depict the demand for speculative and transaction balances, whereas panel (b) graphs the equilibrium condition of the money market and (d) depicts the LM curve. Notice that in the case of panel (b), the segments OA and OB are constructed to be equal to each other and to the real money supply. For the sake of the example, we shall assume that the nominal money supply and the price level are both determined exogenously at M_s^0 and P^0 respectively.

The graphical derivation of LM may start either from panel (c), assuming a certain level of income, or alternatively from panel (a), assuming a certain rate of interest. Suppose that the level of income is Y^0. From panel (c) we see that the corresponding demand for real transaction balances is equal to $M_{t,d}^0/P^0$. This amount is shown in the vertical axis of panel (b) as the distance OC. But since by construction the total real money supply is equal to OA, it follows that the difference between total real money supply and demand for real transaction balances (i.e., $AC = OA - OC$) has to be absorbed by speculative balances. Thus, the problem is now to find that rate of interest which will induce people to hold AC amount of real speculative balances. Notice that $AC = OE$ since both of them are equal to CG. (AC is equal to CG because the traingle ACG is isosceles and OE equals CG because of the rectangular paralellogram $OEGC$.) Finally, from panel (a) we find that the rate of interest in question is equal to r^0.

Our construction is summarized in panel (d). Indeed, point E^0 gives us the combination of income and interest rate at which the demand

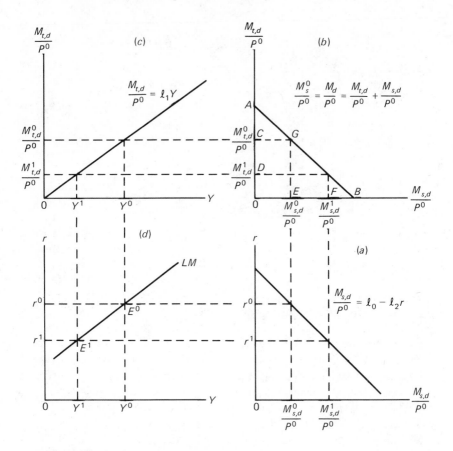

Figure 6.7.3   *Graphical Derivation of the LM Schedule*

for money is equal to the supply of money. More explicitly, if the level of income is Y^0 and the rate of interest r^0, then the demand for real transaction and speculative balances is equal to $(M_{t,d}^0/P^0) + (M_{s,d}^0/P^0)$, which by construction is equal to the real money supply.

In a similar fashion we find that if the level of income is Y^1 then the rate of interest must be r^1 for the monetary sector to be in equilibrium. This new combination is given by point E^1. The locus of all points like E^0 and E^1 makes up the LM curve.

From the above LM diagram as well as its corresponding equation, we see that as income increases or decreases, so must the rate of interest. Mechanically, this is of course the meaning of the positive slope (i.e., l_1/l_2) of the equation of the LM curve. But the reader may still wonder about the economic interpretation of such a positive slope. To appreciate this, consider the equation of the demand for transaction balances, i.e.,

$$\frac{M_{t,d}}{P} = l_1 Y$$

and suppose that the level of prices is equal to P^0 and that the level of income changes from Y^0 to Y^1. The corresponding levels of demand for transaction balances will be

$$\frac{M_{t,d}^0}{P^0} = l_1 Y^0 \tag{6.7.6}$$

and

$$\frac{M_{t,d}^1}{P^0} = l_1 Y^1 \tag{6.7.7}$$

respectively. Subtracting 6.7.6 from 6.7.7, we find that the change in the demand for transaction balances due to the above change in income is equal to:

$$\frac{\Delta M_{t,d}}{P^0} = l_1 \Delta Y. \tag{6.7.8}$$

Since the money supply remains constant, it follows that this increase in the demand for transaction balances will have to be satisfied at the expense of the speculative balances. That is, this demand for speculative balances must decline by exactly the same amount as the increase in the demand for transaction balances. However, to induce such a reduction in the demand for speculative balances, as we know from section 3 above, the rate of interest will have to increase. Then the question is how much the interest rate has to increase to induce the community to release the required amount. This can be found immediately by using equation 6.4.5, i.e.:

$$\frac{M_{s,d}}{P} = l_0 - l_2 r. \tag{6.7.9}$$

Assuming again that the price level is set at P^0 and that the interest rate increases from r^0 to r^1 we find that the corresponding levels of demand for speculative balances will be:

$$\frac{M_{s,d}^0}{P^0} = l_0 - l_2 r^0 \tag{6.7.10}$$

and

$$\frac{M_{s,d}^1}{P^0} = l_0 - l_2 r^1 \tag{6.7.11}$$

from which we can see immediately that the reduction of speculative demand due to the above increase in the rate of interest will be

$$\frac{\Delta M_{s,d}}{P^0} = -l_2 \,\Delta r. \tag{6.7.12}$$

But as we pointed out above, the change (reduction) in the demand for speculative balances will have to be equal to the change (increase) in the demand for transaction balances since the money supply remains constant. Thus, their sum has to be equal to zero, i.e.:

$$\frac{\Delta M_{t,d}}{P^0} + \frac{\Delta M_{s,d}}{P^0} = 0 \tag{6.7.13}$$

and substituting their values from equations 6.7.8 and 6.7.12, we find

$$l_1 \,\Delta Y - l_2 \,\Delta r = 0$$

from which we can immediately derive that

$$\Delta r = \frac{l_1}{l_2} \Delta Y. \tag{6.7.14}$$

The last expression could have been obtained directly from equation 6.7.5, the equation of the LM curve. It verifies that given a constant money supply, any increase in the level of income must be accompanied by an increase in the rate of interest in order for money-market equilibrium to be maintained.

We now turn to study the impact of changes in the exogenous variables on the equilibrium rate of interest. Suppose that the central bank changes the nominal money supply from M_s^0 to M_s^1 ($M_s^0 < M_s^1$) while the price level remains constant at P^0. Then the corresponding values of the rate of interest will be:

$$r^0 = \frac{l_0}{l_2} - \frac{M_s^0/P^0}{l_2} + \frac{l_1}{l_2} Y^0 \tag{6.7.15}$$

and

$$r^1 = \frac{l_0}{l_2} - \frac{M_s^1/P^0}{l_2} + \frac{l_1}{l_2} Y^0. \tag{6.7.16}$$

Subtracting now 6.7.15 from 6.7.16, we find that

$$\Delta r = \frac{-\Delta M_s/P^0}{l_2}. \tag{6.7.17}$$

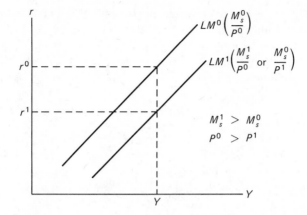

Figure 6.7.4 *The Effects of Changes in the Real Money Supply*

Thus, equation 6.7.17 establishes that if the money supply increases, given the level of income, this will be accompanied by a decrease in the rate of interest. The student should be able to determine why this is so.

Next, suppose that the price level changes from P^0 to P^1 ($P^1 < P^0$) while the nominal money supply remains constant. Substituting these new values for the price level into equation 6.7.5 we find

$$r^0 = \frac{l_0}{l_2} - \frac{M_s^0/P^0}{l_2} + \frac{l_1}{l_2} Y^0 \tag{6.7.18}$$

and

$$r^1 = \frac{l_0}{l_2} - \frac{M_s^0/P^1}{l_2} + \frac{l_1}{l_2} Y^0. \tag{6.7.19}$$

Subtracting 6.7.18 from 6.7.19, we find that:

$$\Delta r = \frac{M_s^0/P^0}{l_2} \cdot \frac{\Delta P}{P^1}. \tag{6.7.20}$$

Thus, equation 6.7.20 establishes the fact that if the price level decreases (increases), again given the level of income, the rate of interest will decrease (increase). This should not be difficult to appreciate since a reduction of the price level, given the nominal supply, should be equivalent to an increase in the nominal supply given the price level. In both cases the real money supply will increase.

The above two changes affect only the intercept of the LM equation (6.7.5), while they leave the slope the same. Consequently, they imply parallel shifts of the LM curve. Figure 6.7.4 shows this.

The reader is invited to derive the impact on LM, and for that matter on the rate of interest, of changes in the parameters l_1 and l_2.

At this juncture a numerical example may be a welcome change of pace. Let the transaction and speculative demand for cash balances assume the following forms:

$$\frac{M_{t,d}}{P} = .15Y \qquad (6.7.21)$$

$$\frac{M_{s,d}}{P} = 110 - 500r. \qquad (6.7.22)$$

Thus, the total demand for real cash balances can be written as:

$$\frac{M_d}{P} = 110 + .15Y - 500r. \qquad (6.7.23)$$

Let us also assume that the monetary authorities fix the money supply at $M_s = \$235$ billion and that, for the sake of convenience, $P = 1$. Thus $M_s/P = 235$. For equilibrium we need:

$$\frac{M_s}{P} = \frac{M_d}{P}$$

and substituting the corresponding expression and values, we find

$$110 + .15Y - 500r = 235$$

from which we derive that:

$$r = -.25 + .0003Y. \qquad (6.7.24)$$

Next, suppose that the nominal supply changes from \$235 to \$210 billion while all the other parameters remain constant. The new equation for the LM curve becomes

$$r = -.20 + .0003Y. \qquad (6.7.25)$$

As an exercise, plot equations 6.7.24 and 25 and note the implied shift in the LM curve.

6.8 Summary

In this chapter, we analyzed on a preliminary basis the determination of an equilibrium rate of interest. We found that the money market does not by itself determine a unique equilibrium value for the interest rate; instead, it yields only an equilibrium relation between income and the interest rate. Thus, to determine the rate of interest we must know the level of income. In the previous chapter we found that to determine the level of income we should know the rate of interest. The next chapter determines both by combining the information accumulated in these two chapters. But then we see that this interrelation of the rate of interest with income negates the claim that the rate of interest is a monetary phenomenon and that it consequently can be determined only by monetary factors acting in the money market.

Suggested Further Reading

Bailey, M. J. *National Income and the Price Level.* London: McGraw-Hill, 1962, chap. 2.

Gilbert, J. C. "The Demand for Money: The Development of an Economic Concept." *Journal of Political Economy* 61 (April 1953), 144–59.

Hansen, A. *A Guide to Keynes.* New York: McGraw-Hill, 1953.

Hicks, J. R. "Mr. Keynes and the Classics." *Econometrica* 5 (April 1937), pp. 147–59. Reprinted in American Economic Association, *Readings in the Theory of Income Distribution.* Homewood, Ill.: R. D. Irwin, 1951, pp. 461–76.

Keynes, J. M. *The General Theory of Employment, Interest and Money.* New York: Harcourt, Brace, 1936.

Laidler, D. *The Demand for Money: Theories and Evidence.* Scranton, Pa: International Textbook Co., 1969, part I, chap. 2; part II, chap. 3 and 6.

Latané, H. A. "Cash Balances and the Interest Rate—A Pragmatic Approach." *Review of Economics and Statistics* 36 (November 1954), 456–60.

Newlyn, W. T. *Theory of Money.* Oxford: Clarendon Press, 1971, chap. 1–3.

Appendix 6.A

The Arithmetic of Interest-Bearing Assets

A bond is an interest-bearing contractual obligation issued by a private or public institution which promises to pay the holder a specified amount of money on a specified date. Usually, bond prices are quoted in terms of a percent of their par value, which is the amount of obligation the issuing institution will pay back at the time of maturity. As a rule, the par value of such an obligation is mentioned explicitly in the body of the bond itself. For example, if a 4% bond is selling for 80, this means that a bond with a par value of $1,000 and an annual interest of $40 is currently selling (can be purchased) in the market for $800.

In this case although the nominal yield (i.e., the rate of interest which is mentioned in the body of the certificate) is only 4% of the par value, the actual yield is higher than 4%. Since the purchase price is $800 and the annual interest is $40, it follows that the real return of this particular investment is equal to $40/800 = .05$. To appreciate this suppose that Treasury bonds (call them series A) are currently selling on a 4% basis. This actually means that the conditions in the financial markets are such that the Treasury can sell at par value a $1,000 bond with a 4% coupon. In other words, the Treasury will pay $40 annual interest on each bond of series A.

Now assume that Mr. Y buys such a bond and that a few days after his purchase the market rate of interest increases to 5%. Assume furthermore that the Treasury offers another issue (series B) which carries a 5% coupon (which, of course, means that it will pay $50 annually).

These circumstances present an interesting case in which the same amount of investment yields substantially different returns. Such a case could be justified in other types of investments but not in the present one. Bonds are highly liquid assets and an owner does not have to get locked in once he has invested in them. It takes only a phone call to his broker to liquidate them into cash. Consequently, the question now is what does happen to the price of the bond of series A that was purchased by Mr. Y, assuming that the date of maturity (repayment) of both series is far enough in the future.

Heuristically, one would argue that since there is this difference in the yields, Mr. Y will attempt to replace his bond of series A with a corresponding one of series B so that he can enjoy the higher yield. However, under these circumstances there will be no buyer willing to pay him $1,000 since one can do considerably better by investing money in a bond of series B. In fact, all Mr. Y can expect to receive is an amount which will allow the buyer of his bond to earn 5% on his investment. Thus, the price of the bond will be that amount on which a return of 5% is equal to $40, i.e.,

$$X \cdot (.05) = \$40$$

where X denotes the unknown price of this particular bond.

Solving the above equation for X we find:

$$X = \frac{\$40.00}{.05} = \$800.$$

In other words, it appears that $800 (or a quoted price of 80), is all he can expect to receive from the sale of his bond.

Let us now examine the pricing of bonds in a more general context. Since the price of a bond is related to the series of interest payments attached to it, we need to derive a formula for computing the present value of a future stream of returns. Suppose that we calculate the value which a simple payment of $50 made today will have after one year at 5% rate of interest. Obviously, the future value of such a payment will consist of two parts: the principal and the interest earned in the year's interval. Thus,

$$\text{Future value} = 50 + (50)(.05) = 50(1 + .05) = \$52.50.$$

or in more general terms:

$$P_1 = P_0(1 + r) \tag{6.A.1}$$

where P_1 denotes the value of the payment in question after one year, P_0 its present value and r the market rate of interest. By the same token we can also find that the value of this payment at the end of the second year will be

$$P_2 = P_1 + rP_1 = P_1(1 + r).$$

Expressing P_1 in terms of P_0, the above equation can be rewritten as

$$P_2 = P_0(1 + r)(1 + r) = P_0(1 + r)^2. \tag{6.A.2}$$

Following the same procedure we find that the value of the initial payment P_0 at the end of the third, fourth, and t-th year will be:

$$P_3 = P_0(1 + r)^3$$
$$P_4 = P_0(1 + r)^4$$
$$\cdot \cdot \quad \cdot \cdot \cdot \cdot$$
$$P_t = P_0(1 + r)^t. \tag{6.A.3}$$

In terms of our original example these values are approximately:
$P_2 = 50(1 + .05)^2 = 55.125;$ $P_3 = 50(1 + .05)^3 = 57.88;$
$P_4 = 50(1 + .05)^4 = 60.77,$ etc.

Suppose now that we wish to calculate the present value of a simple payment of $52.50 which is to be made one year from today. We may use equation 6.A.1 to solve for P_0 in terms of P_1, i.e.

$$P_0 = \frac{P_1}{(1 + r)}. \tag{6.A.4}$$

In terms of our example, the answer is:

$$P_0 = \frac{\$52.50}{1.05} = \$50$$

or in more general terms, equation 6.A.3 suggests that:

$$P_0 = \frac{P_t}{(1 + r)^t}. \tag{6.A.5}$$

Equation 6.A.5 gives the present value of a single payment which is to be made after t years. The transformation of future values into present ones is called discounting. From the above analysis, it follows that if a financial asset carries the obligation to pay C dollars per year for the next t years, and a final payment of the principal of P dollars at the end of the t-th year, then the present value of such a stream of income discounted at an interest rate of r per year will be

$$V_r = \frac{C}{(1 + r)} + \frac{C}{(1 + r)^2} + \cdots \cdot \frac{C}{(1 + r)^t} + \frac{P}{(1 + r)^t}$$
$$\tag{6.A.6}$$

Suppose for example that we are interested in finding the value of a bond with a par value of $1,000 which will pay $50 annually, maturing in five years. Let us also assume three alternative interest rates: 4%, 5% and 6%. The corresponding present values of this stream of income will be

$$V_{.04} = \frac{50}{(1 + .04)} + \frac{50}{(1 + .04)^2} + \frac{50}{(1 + .04)^3} + \frac{50}{(1 + .04)^4}$$

$$+ \frac{50}{(1 + .04)^5} + \frac{1000}{(1 + .04)^5}$$

$$= 48.08 + 46.23 + 44.44 + 42.74 + 41.10 + 821.96$$

$$= 1,044.55$$

$$V_{.05} = \frac{50}{(1 + .05)} + \frac{50}{(1 + .05)^2} + \frac{50}{(1 + .05)^3} + \frac{50}{(1 + .05)^4}$$

$$+ \frac{50}{(1 + .04)^5} + \frac{1000}{(1 + .04)^5}$$

$$= 47.62 + 45.35 + 43.19 + 41.14 + 39.18 + 783.51$$

$$= 1{,}000$$

$$V_{.06} = \frac{50}{(1 + .06)} + \frac{50}{(1 + .06)^2} + \frac{50}{(1 + .06)^3} + \frac{50}{(1 + .06)^4}$$

$$+ \frac{50}{(1 + .06)^5} + \frac{1000}{(1 + .06)^5}$$

$$= 47.17 + 44.50 + 41.98 + 39.60 + 37.36 + 747.27$$

$$= 957.88$$

The above equations suggest that the higher (lower) the rate of interest we use to discount this stream of the expected returns, the smaller (larger) the present value of this stream will be. We can also see that variations of the market price of these instruments align their real yields with the current market rate of interest. It is also interesting to observe that when the market rate is equal to the rate quoted in this financial obligation (in terms of our example, 5%), the bond price is equal to its par value itself. Furthermore, when the market rate is greater than the coupon rate, the bond in question commands a price which is smaller than its par value. Conversely, in the case in which the market rate is smaller than the coupon rate, the bond sells above its par value. The general conclusion we may derive from the above example is that the price of bonds varies *inversely* with the market rate of interest.

Finally, since bonds with a longer term to maturity are discounted more heavily—the denominators contain larger powers of $(1 + r)$ as we move further in the future—it follows that their market price is affected more by a change in the market rate of interest than the corresponding price of the short-term debts. That is, the longer a bond's term to maturity, the higher will be its sensitivity to fluctuations of the rate of interest, and consequently the greater its potential for capital gains and losses.

An interesting but infrequently used instrument of financial intermediation is the so-called consol. The main characteristic of such a bond is that it does not have a maturity date; it follows then that the present value of such an instrument will be

$$V = \frac{C}{(1 + r)} + \frac{C}{(1 + r)^2} + \ldots\ldots + \frac{C}{(1 + r)^t} + \ldots$$

Multiplying both sides of the above equation by $1/(1 + r)$ we obtain

$$\frac{1}{1 + r}V = \frac{C}{(1 + r)^2} + \frac{C}{(1 + r)^3} + \ldots\ldots + \frac{C}{(1 + r)^{t+1}} + \ldots$$

Subtracting now the latter expression from the former, we further obtain

$$\left[1 - \frac{1}{1 + r}\right]V = \frac{C}{1 + r} - \frac{C}{(1 + r)^{t+1}}$$

The above expression can be further simplified to read

$$V = \frac{C}{r}\left[1 - \frac{1}{(1 + r)^t}\right]. \qquad (6.A.7)$$

From the last equation, we can clearly see that for arbitrarily large values of t the term $1/(1 + r)^t$ approaches zero and thus we may ignore it. Consequently, we can write

$$V = \frac{C}{r}. \qquad (6.A.8)$$

The above expression shows that the present value of a consol is proportional to the inverse of the rate of interest, the factor of proportionality being the annual interest or coupon C. In fact, this equation is exactly the same as the one we used in chapter 6.

Appendix 6.B

The Federal Reserve and Its Influence on the Money Supply

In the previous chapter we showed that the supply of money—the sum of currency and demand deposits in the hands of the public[1]—is a very important factor, not only for the efficient functioning of the economy but also for the determination and regulation of economic activity as well. The assumption we used there was that the money supply is an exogenous variable controlled by the monetary authorities, operating through the Federal Reserve System. In discussing how the Federal Reserve System exercises control over the money supply, our intention is not to provide an exhaustive analysis of the intricate mechanism involved in managing the money supply. Instead we shall paint an impressionistic picture so that the readers' view of the economy will be more spherical.

Each country has a central bank whose main responsibility is the management of the money supply. Central banks are for the most part specialized banks whose customers are the national treasury and the commercial banks. In addition, they do not, under normal circumstances, accept private customers and as a result they do not compete with commercial banks in financial markets. The central bank of the United States is the Federal Reserve System.[2]

In order to appreciate the working of the system, we should start with the fact that commercial banks are manufacturers of money.[3] This role is enjoyed by virtue of their ability to issue checking deposits which enable them to create means of payment by making appropriate entries in their accounting books. To see how this is done, take a look at

---

[1] For other definitions of money see chapter 6, section 1.

[2] The Federal Reserve System consists of twelve regional banks whose purpose is to carry out the policy designed by its Board of Governors, an independent government agency in Washington, D.C. The Federal Reserve System, in the process of discharging its responsibilities as a manager of the money supply, realizes profits. Of these profits, 90% is funneled to the Department of Treasury and the residual 10% is used to increase the assets of the Fed.

[3] At the present, the main distinguishing characteristic of commercial banks, as opposed to savings and loan institutions, is that the former are allowed to issue checking deposits whereas the latter are not. This distinction seems to be fading at the time of writing of this text, and may have largely disappeared by the time the student reads this section.

the balance sheet of a commercial bank. Suppose that the balance sheet of the First National Bank of Los Angeles on December 31, 1975, reads as follows:

Table 6.B.1.   *First National Bank of Los Angeles Balance Sheet, December 31, 1975*

Assets	
1. Cash on hand and due from banks	$ 500
2. Loans and discounts	1,500
3. U.S. Government securities	330
4. Other securities	150
5. Stock in Federal Reserve Bank	10
6. Real estate	5
7. Other assets	5
	$2,500

Liabilities	
1. Demand deposits	$1,600
2. Time deposits	400
3. Dividends declared but unpaid	10
4. Reserves for tax obligations	40
5. Capital stock	140
6. Undistributed profits	80
7. Other liabilities	230
	$2,500

From the above statement we shall focus only on cash on hand, etc., demand deposits and time deposits. In particular, the item *cash on hand and due from banks* includes currency in the vault of the bank, deposits with other commercial banks and the Federal Reserve Bank, and checks in the process of collection. Thus for all practical purposes this is the most liquid asset of the bank. On the other hand, demand deposits are an obligation of the bank and can be drawn through the writing of checks. Demand deposits do not pay any interest, by law. Finally, time deposits do bear interest, but unlike demand deposits, the bank can insist that an advance notice is given before it will redeem them.[4] The

---

[4]This notice is usually filed with the institution thirty days before the redemption time.

reader should notice that according to the definition of money we have adopted in this book, time deposits do not count as a part of the money supply despite the fact that they constitute a highly liquid form of assets.

For obvious reasons a bank must always be ready to redeem its deposits in currency. For this purpose it maintains a reserve consisting of currency in the vault and deposits at the Federal Reserve Bank. Thus the ability of the bank to honor its obligations depends mainly on how much reserves are maintained in various forms vis-à-vis the deposits, which is usually measured by a ratio of cash reserves to deposits, the so-called reserve ratio.

Although for a long time reserve ratios of commercial banks reflected mostly the psychological makeup of the individual banker as well as his expectations about future economic developments, today in the United States minimum reserve requirements are determined by the monetary authorities. Given the minimum reserve ratios required by law, the total actual reserves of a commercial bank will always be equal to the algebraic sum of required reserves and excess reserves. It follows that the reserve requirement will be satisfied if the actual reserves are at least equal to those required. Suppose that the reserve ratio is 20%, i.e., the required reserves are 20% of the demand deposits.[5] Lump all the items but cash reserves into the entry "earning assets" and assume that liabilities are comprised of only demand deposits. Then the balance sheet of the First National Bank of Los Angeles would assume the following form:

Table 6.B.2.

Assets			Liabilities	
Cash Reserves		$ 500	Demand Deposits	$2,500
Required	500			
Excess	. . .			
Other Earning Assets		2,000		
		$2,500		$2,500

---

[5] Demand deposits subject to reserve requirements are gross demand deposits minus cash items in the process of collection and demand balances due from domestic banks.

Effective November 9, 1972, requirements for reserves against net demand deposits of member banks were restructured to provide that each bank maintain reserves which are related to the size of its net demand deposits. According to this rule, the reserve requirements are 8%, 10%, 12%, 13%, and 17.5% for banks with net demand deposits falling in the ranges of 0–2, 2–10, 10–100, 100–400, and over $400 million, respectively.

Since the required reserves are assumed to be 20% of the demand deposits, this bank complies with the law, i.e., actual reserves are equal to required reserves (500/2,500 = 20%), leaving no excess reserves.

Next, suppose that a customer makes a deposit of $500, and in addition assume that this amount does not come out of the reserves of any other commercial bank. Then the new balance sheet of the bank in question is depicted in table 6.B.3.

Table 6.B.3.

Assets			Liabilities	
Cash Reserves		$1,000	Demand Deposits	$3,000
Required	600			
Excess	400			
Other Earning Assets		2,000		
		$3,000		$3,000

Notice that since the deposits have increased by $500, it follows that the required reserves have increased by $100 ($500 × .20). Thus, the bank now has available some excess reserves, which of course amount to the difference between the change in the actual reserves and reserves required by the law, i.e., $500 − $100 = $400. These excess reserves now constitute unutilized lending power, and in view of the fact that commercial banks are profit-oriented institutions, it is reasonable to assume that they will attempt to use this lending power to increase the amount of earning assets. Further assume that the bank acquires additional earning assets, either by buying securities or by lending to a customer in exchange for his promissory note. The question now becomes: by how much can the bank increase the amount of earning assets? The answer to this question depends on whether the bank pays in cash or opens a demand deposit account. If, for example, the bank acquires these new earning assets by paying cash, then obviously the earning assets can increase only by an amount which is equal to excess reserves, i.e., $400, and the balance sheet of the bank will assume the following form:

Table 6.B.4.

Assets		Liabilities	
Cash Reserves	$ 600	Demand Deposits	$3,000
Required 600			
Excess . . .			
Other Earning Assets	2,400		
	$3,000		$3,000

In this case the bank's actual reserves are equal to the required ones and we say that the bank is loaned-up. If, however, the bank can convince the seller of securities or its customers (as usual) to accept payment by opening a demand deposit account, then the bank will be able, at least superficially, to expand its earning assets by such an amount that the whole excess reserve will be converted into required reserves. In this case the bank will be able to expand its earning assets by $2,000. Notice that an addition of $2,000 in demand deposits necessitates a $400 increase in the required reserves. Thus, if the bank transfers the amount of excess reserves into required reserves, it will once again comply with the requirements of the law. In the last case the balance sheet of the bank will be as follows:

Table 6.B.5.

Assets		Liabilities	
Cash Reserves	$1,000	Demand Deposits	$5,000
Required 1,000			
Excess . . .			
Other Earning Assets	4,000		
	$5,000		$5,000

Once more the bank has zero excess reserves and consequently no unutilized lending power whatsoever. Thus, again the bank is fully loaned-up.

The balance sheet depicted in table 6.B.5 is nevertheless misleading. It is based on the implicit assumption that the owners of newly created deposits, i.e., the seller of securities or the customer who borrowed the amount of $2,000, will not write checks against the bank. This, however, is unrealistic since nobody borrows money just for the sake of doing it and leaves it in the hands of the bank. There are only two cases, both of which are rather unrealistic, where the bank in question will be able to acquire earning assets in the amount of $2,000: first, if all checks drawn against the newly created deposits are payable to individuals who are already customers of the same bank and consequently maintain demand deposits, and second, if none of the owners of the newly created deposits wishes to withdraw additional currency for, say, hand-to-hand use.

As long as neither of these conditions is satisfied, it would be more realistic to assume that table 6.B.6 is more likely to depict the actual picture. Under normal circumstances this bank can afford to lose an amount which is equal to its excess reserves, and therefore it can create deposits and increase its loans or other earning assets by $400. Thus, the bank will grant a loan, say, for $400, and it will create the equivalent amount of demand deposits as table 6.B.6 indicates.

Table 6.B.6.

Assets			Liabilities	
Cash Reserves		$1,000	Demand Deposits	$3,400
Required	680			
Excess	320			
Other Earning Assets		2,400		
		$3,400		$3,400

Notice that although the First National Bank shows excess reserves of $320, this will be only a temporary picture, since by virtue of our assumption its customer will be withdrawing $400 by writing checks against his demand deposits. Should this be the case, then the bank will have to pay $400 and thereby use up the $320 of excess reserves. In addition, since the volume of demand deposits will be reduced by $400, it follows that the required reserves would decline by $80, which the bank will use to pay off the checks of its customer. Thus once more the situation is depicted by table 6.B.4 above.

The process, however, does not terminate at this point. Provided that the amount of $400 is deposited in another bank, the demand deposits of this bank increase. Assuming that this second bank is fully loaned-up, it follows that its required reserves will increase by $80, and its excess reserves by $320. This bank now will be able to generate new earning assets in the amount of $320 and an equal amount of deposit liabilities. The rounds will continue until all excess reserves of the system have been converted into earning assets of one sort or another. Table 6.B.7 provides a bird's-eye view of this process by depicting the chain reaction generated by the increase in the deposits of the First National Bank of Los Angeles.

Table 6.B.7.

Bank # or # of Rounds	Changes in Reserves and Assets		
	ΔDD	ΔRR	ΔEA
Bank #1	$ 500.00	$100.00	$ 400.00
Bank #2	400.00	80.00	320.00
Bank #3	320.00	64.00	256.00
Bank #4	256.00	51.20	204.80
Bank #5	204.80	40.96	163.84
Bank #6	163.84	32.77	131.07
. . .	. . .	. . .	. . .
Total	$2,500.00	$500.00	$2,000.00

In the above table the first column shows the amount by which the demand deposits change in each round and the second column shows the change in the required reserve, whereas the third shows the corresponding changes in the earning assets.

Thus, we see that an initial increase in demand deposits by $500 has generated an increase in the money supply equal to $2,500. This was done by the interaction of the whole system of commercial banks and not by one bank alone. Thus, if we lump together the whole system of commercial banks and assume that assets and liabilities of all the other banks but the First National are zero, the picture will be the same as the one of table 6.B.5. Of course, the opposite chain reaction would occur if someone were to withdraw $500 from the system.

Let us now see how the monetary authorities may change the money supply, i.e., the amount of currency and demand deposits available to the public. Basically, there are three ways by which the monetary authorities, through their acting agents, the Federal Reserve banks, exercise control over the behavior of credit in general and that of the money supply in particular. Manipulation of the money supply may be the result of: first, changing the discount rate; second, varying required reserve ratios; the third, buying or selling securities and bills of exchange in the open market. Let us first see how the open market operations— the buying and selling of securities by the Federal Reserve System— change the stock of money available in the economy. Suppose that the consolidated balance sheet of all Federal Reserve banks (taken together) is described by table 6.B.8.

Table 6.B.8.

Assets		Liabilities	
Gold certificates	$ 300	U.S. Treasury gen'l. account	$ 50
Discounts & advances	10	Member banks' reserves	300
U.S. Gov't. securities	690	Federal Reserve notes	650
	$1,000		$1,000

Next, suppose that the consolidated statement of all commercial banks is as follows:

Table 6.B.9.

Assets		Liabilities	
Actual reserves	$ 600	Demand deposits	$3,000
Required 600			
Excess . . .			
Other earning assets	2,400		
	$3,000		$3,000

From table 6.B.9 we see that actual reserves of the commercial banks are exactly equal and required.[6] It follows, therefore, that there is no unutilized lending capacity in the system.

---

[6]It is assumed that the actual reserves include the $300 reserve deposits at the Federal Reserve banks.

Now suppose that the monetary authorities decide to increase the money supply. To this end the Federal Reserve purchases $1 billion worth of government securities in the open market. These securities are purchased with checks drawn against the Federal Reserve and in favor of the various sellers. Assuming now that the sellers deposit these checks in their banks, we see that the purchase of the securities implies an increase in the demand deposits of the commercial banks by an equal amount. But since the demand deposits have increased by $1 billion, it follows that the banks can use this amount as reserves and expand their earning assets by creating additional demand deposits of $4 billion. That is, the commercial banking system will attempt to convert the whole amount of $1 billion into required reserves. The reader should notice that our analysis runs in terms of the commercial banking system as a whole, not individual commercial banks. In other words, we are referring to the chain reaction which was depicted in table 6.B.7.

Thus, the new balance sheet of the Federal Reserve banks as a whole will read:

Table 6.B.10.

Assets		Liabilities	
Gold certificates	$ 300	U.S. Treasury gen'l. account	$ 50
Discounts & advances	10	Member banks' reserves	301
U.S. Gov't. securities	691	Federal Reserve notes	650
	$1,001		$1,001

On the other hand, the consolidated picture of the commercial banks will read:

Table 6.B.11.

Assets			Liabilities	
Actual reserves		$ 601.00	Demand deposits	$3,001.00
Required	600.20			
Excess	.80			
Other earning assets		2,400.00		
		$3,001.00		$3,001.00

Assuming now that the commercial banks convert the excess reserves into required by increasing their liabilities in terms of demand deposits, we obtain:

Table 6.B.12.

Assets		Liabilities	
Actual reserves	$ 601	Demand deposits	$3,005
Required 601.00			
Excess . . .			
Other earning assets	2,404		
	$3,005		$3,005

Conversely, had the monetary authorities decided to decrease the money supply, they would have generated the reverse set of motions by selling $1 billion worth of government securities. In this case the buyers of these securities would write checks against their commercial banks and in favor of the Federal Reserve banks, thereby destroying the equivalent of $5 billion worth of demand deposits. Since the customers write $1 billion in checks against the commercial banking system, it follows that the actual reserves as well as the demand deposits decrease by the same amount. Thus, the actual reserves will be $600.00, the demand deposits $3,004.00 and the required reserves $600.80 (i.e., $3,004.00 × .20). Since the actual reserves are smaller than the required by $.80 billion, it follows that some commercial banks in the system are breaking the law. In this case the commercial banks will find it necessary to borrow this amount from the Federal Reserve banks on a temporary basis and at the same time try to reduce their earning assets and demand deposits by $4 billion. This will bring the demand deposits once more in line with the actual and required reserves.

Introducing the concept of borrowing by the commercial banks from the Federal Reserve banks hints upon the next tool by which the monetary authorities exert control over the money supply—i.e., the discount rate, which is the rate of interest commercial banks pay on loans from the Federal Reserve banks. These loans are explicitly made to bring their depleted actual reserves in line with the required ones. Therefore an increase in the discount rate increases the cost of borrowing funds from the Federal Reserve banks, thereby encouraging the member banks to repay their debts.[7] However, repayment of debts to the Fed means that the deposits (and consequently the required reserves) will have to decrease. This can be achieved either by calling in loans or by selling other assets.

Although the above two policies can and do exert considerable influence on the level of money supply separately, the monetary authorities typically use them simultaneously. As we saw earlier, the sale of securities by the Federal Reserve in the open market decreases the actual reserves of the commercial banks. To be sure, the commercial banks may restore their actual reserves up to the required ones by borrowing from the system. Thus, the first result of open market operations in this case is to force the commercial banks to the "discount window" and put them in debt to the Federal Reserve banks. By raising the discount rate and thereby making borrowing expensive, commercial banks will attempt to repay their debt by contracting their deposits and reducing their earning assets. It follows, therefore, that open market operations and discount rates reinforce each other in the exercise of monetary policy.

The complementarity of these two tools is also useful when the monetary authorities wish to prevent any further expansion of the money supply. For example, assume a great deal of excess reserves at the hands of the commercial banks. To check any further expansion, the monetary authorities decide on an increase in the discount rate. But as long as the commercial banks have available excess reserves, this increase in the rediscount rate does not have any teeth. Consequently, the system may sell securities to absorb the excess reserves. As a result commercial banks will have to refuse new loans and/or sell securities themselves. In this case the other rates of interest will have to follow the rise in the discount rate. This is usually known as making the discount rate effective, giving the policy some teeth.

Thus, we can see how open market operations can be used to influence market rates of interest. More explicitly, when the monetary authorities wish to increase the money supply, the Federal Reserve, by purchasing securities, will attempt to induce the public to hold (demand) more money. However, as we already know, this can be done only if the interest rate declines (the price of securities increases). Conversely, when the open market sales are used to absorb funds and thereby

---

[7]Member banks can borrow funds from the Federal Reserve banks by giving either their own promissory notes which are secured by either U.S. government bonds or other acceptable collateral, or alternatively, by rediscounting commercial paper. The first type of borrowing is usually called *advances* whereas the second is better known as *discounts*.

decrease the money supply, the interest rate increases (the price of securities decreases). We may then conclude that commercial banks, by operating within a framework of rather rigid rules regarding the required reserves, behave in such a way that the monetary authorities are able to exercise rather tight control upon the money supply and rates of interest.

Finally, the monetary authorities have the power to set the minimum required reserve ratios. In the above discussion, for example, we assumed that the required reserves were set at 20% of the demand deposits. It should be quite obvious that an increase in this ratio will imply, *ceteris paribus,* a decrease in the extent to which the commercial banking system can increase the money supply by creating deposit liabilities. Of course, the opposite is also true. If the monetary authorities wish to increase the money supply, they can achieve this objective by lowering the required reserve ratio, thereby increasing the extent to which the commercial banking system can expand the money supply.

The preceding discussion assumed that the amount of the banks' deposit liabilities is independent of the level of the rate of interest which the banks charge on loans to customers or earn from other assets. In reality, however, banks do hold (demand) excess reserves which, incidentally, behave in the same fashion as the demand for speculative balances on the part of individuals in the community; that is, their magnitude varies inversely with the rate of interest. It follows then that the creation of deposit liabilities will vary directly with the rate of interest. This last proposition amounts to arguing that the money supply is an increasing function of the rate of interest, i.e.,

$$\frac{M_s}{P} = f(r), \qquad \frac{\Delta(M_s/P)}{\Delta r} > 0.$$

Graphically, this functional relation could be depicted by an upward-sloping curve. However, although this may not be quite consistent with our treatment of money supply (i.e., vertical lines exhibiting zero interest elasticity), it does not introduce any new analytical difficulty. Consequently the reader may assume either that the money supply is an exogenous variable or that it is a linear function of the rate of interest. In what follows we shall maintain the assumption that the money supply is exogenous.[8]

---

[8] Exercise: Derive the LM curve on the assumption that the real money supply depends upon the interest rate and compare your results with the LM curve of the text derived on the assumption that the money supply is exogenous.

CHAPTER 7

The Equilibrium of the Expenditure and Monetary Sectors

7.1 Introduction

The two previous chapters have indicated that neither the expenditure nor the monetary sector could separately determine the equilibrium values of the relevant endogenous variables. We found that each sector contained one more endogenous variable than it had equations; thus, the most we could do was to reduce the description of each sector to a single equilibrium equation containing two endogenous variables: the level of income and the rate of interest. In fact, our money-market analysis even made use of the simplifying assumption that the price level (P) was an exogenous variable. Had we treated P as being endogenous, our final money-market equilibrium equation would have contained three, rather than two, endogenous variables.

Under the assumption that the price level was given, we were able to sketch an LM schedule representing all the combinations of values of Y and r which would leave the money market in equilibrium. Of course, each different value of P gave us a different LM schedule. In our product-market analysis in chapter 5, we derived an IS schedule, which was the locus of combinations of values of Y and r for which the product market would be in equilibrium. The purpose of this chapter is to integrate the analysis of the product and money markets. We shall show that, given the price level, these two markets *acting together* will simultaneously determine unique equilibrium values for income and the rate of interest. That is, we shall go one step further by asking if there is a unique pair of values for Y and r for which both sectors will be at equilibrium

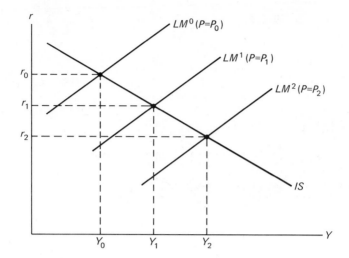

Figure 7.1.1   *General Equilibrium at Alternative Price Levels*

simultaneously. Graphically, the answer to this question is quite simple. It can be found by combining the IS and the LM schedules derived in the previous two chapters. Insofar as each of these schedules represents alternative equilibrium positions for its corresponding sector, it follows that their intersection (provided that there is one) will give the one pair of values for Y and r at which *both* sectors are simultaneously in equilibrium for *each* price level. In other words, the equilibrium values of Y and r depend uniquely on the value of the price level. Once we know the general price level, we can find the corresponding equilibrium values of Y and r.

The points made above are illustrated graphically in figure 7.1.1. We have depicted here an IS schedule and three LM schedules (one for each of three possible values of the price level). According to figure 7.1.1, there is an intersection of the IS and LM for each different price level P_0, P_1, and P_2 ($P_2 < P_1 < P_0$). Thus, if $P = P_0$, the equilibrium values of Y and r would be Y_0 and r_0 respectively. If the price level fell to P_1 (and hence the real money supply expanded), the relevant equilibrium values would be Y_1 and r_1. A further decrease in price to P_2 would leave the economy at Y_2, r_2. And so on. . . .

Perhaps the best way to illustrate the character of the general equilibrium of the money and product markets is to examine the nature of disequilibrium. In figure 7.1.2, we have depicted the IS and LM schedules under the assumption that $P = P_0$. Notice that the general equilibrium

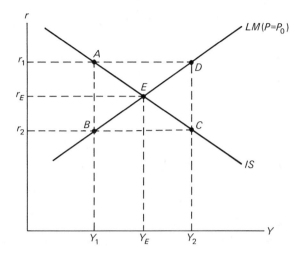

Figure 7.1.2 *General Equilibrium and Disequilibrium*

occurs at point E, with $Y = Y_E$ and $r = r_E$. We have also designated four other points ($A, B, C,$ and D) on the diagram, and shall use them as points of reference for our illustration. First, consider point A where $r = r_1$ and $Y = Y_1$. Insofar as A lies along the IS schedule, the corresponding pair of values for income and the rate of interest satisfy the equilibrium condition in the product market. That is, r_1 and Y_1 are values which equate aggregate demand and aggregate supply. But point A does *not* lie on the LM schedule; thus, at the values r_1 and Y_1, the money market is not in equilibrium. We can qualitatively characterize the conditions in the money market by noting the position of point A relative to point B, one of the points on the LM schedule. Notice that points A and B reflect the same level of income, but that the interest rate is higher at A than at B. Insofar as money demand and money supply are equal at point B, it follows that the interest rate r_1 is "too high" for money-market equilibrium at the given level of income. But if the rate of interest is "too high" at A, this just means that the demand for money will be less than the supply of money at that position. (Remember that money demand is inversely related to the interest rate.)

As an alternative approach, compare point A to point D. Both positions indicate the same rate of interest, but the level of income is higher at D than at A. Insofar as D *does* reflect money-market equilibrium we could say that Y_1 is "too low" for the equality of money demand and supply at the interest rate r_1. But if income is "too low" at A, this can be translated as an indication that money demand is less than money supply at A. (Remember that money demand is positively associated with the level of income.) This, of course, is the same conclusion we reached in comparing points A and B. Generalizing somewhat from this exercise, we can say that, given an upward-sloping LM schedule, any combination of values for r and Y which lies above (and to the left of) the LM schedule reflects an excess of money supply over money demand. It will be left to the student to prove that the opposite is also true: that is, that any point below (and to the right of) the LM schedule indicates an excess of money demand over money supply.

Now, let's consider a point which lies on the LM schedule but not on the IS. Position B, for example, satisfies the equilibrium condition in the money market, but fails to yield a product-market equilibrium. But what is the nature of the disequilibrium in the product market at B? To obtain an answer, compare points B and A again. The level of income is the same at both positions, but the rate of interest is lower at B than at A. Since r_1 was the appropriate interest rate for the attainment of product-market equilibrium at the income level Y_1, it follows that r_2 is "too low" for the equality of aggregate demand and aggregate supply at that income. But if r_2 is "too low," then we can deduce that aggregate demand is greater than aggregate supply. The reason is simple: investment, one of the components of aggregate demand, is inversely related to the rate of interest. To say that the interest rate is "too low" at some level of income is tantamount to saying that investment (and hence aggregate demand) is too high. We might also compare points B and C, the latter a product-market equilibrium position. Both points share the same interest rate (r_2), but the level of income is higher at C than at B. But this means that, given r_2, the level of income is "too low" at B. As the student should remember from chapter 5, this means that aggregate demand exceeds aggregate supply at B. Again, we should be able to generalize: any point below (and to the left of) the IS schedule will reflect an excess of aggregate demand over aggregate supply. And, for the sake of space preservation, we shall allow the student to prove that the opposite is also true: that is, that any point above (and to the right of) the IS schedule will be associated with excess aggregate supply.

7.2 The Expenditures and Monetary Sectors Considered Simultaneously

We now investigate the properties of the model, maintaining the assumption of a closed economy. In addition, we confine our analytical tour to underemployment situations so that we do not have to deal with problems associated with price changes.

We proceed by using the equations of the expenditure sector—in conjunction with those of the monetary sector—to form the following system.

$$Y = C + I + G \qquad\qquad (7.2.1)$$

$$C = a + bY_d \qquad\qquad (7.2.2)$$

$$I = g_0 - g_1 r \qquad\qquad (7.2.3)$$

$$Y_d \equiv Y - T \qquad\qquad (7.2.4)$$

$$T = -t_0 + t_1 Y \qquad\qquad (7.2.5)$$

$$M_d/P = l_0 + l_1 Y - l_2 r \qquad\qquad (7.2.6)$$

$$M_d/P = M_s/P. \qquad\qquad (7.2.7)$$

From the above system equations 7.2.1–7.2.5 compose (as usual) the expenditure sector, whereas 7.2.6 and 7.2.7 make up the monetary sector. As the reader can easily verify, the system 7.2.1–7.2.7 contains ten variables (i.e., $Y, C, I, r, G, Y_d, T, M_d, P, M_s$), from which three (i.e., G, M_s, P) are assumed to be exogenous. Under normal circumstances we should be able to determine the solution values of the endogenous variables without any difficulty. To this end, we can first derive the reduced form of the system by combining the equations of the expenditure and monetary sector to derive the equations of IS and LM; we then solve explicitly for the values of the endogenous variables Y and r in terms of the exogenous.

Combining equations 7.2.1–7.2.5 as usual, we obtain:

$$[1 - b(1 - t_1)]Y + g_1 r = a + g_0 + bt_0 + G. \qquad (7.2.8)$$

The reader should recognize immediately that equation 7.2.8 is the equation of the IS curve cast in another form. Indeed, there is now no reason for expressing Y in terms of r, as we did in chapter 5, since both these variables are considered to be endogenous. Instead, in equation 7.2.8, we have separated the endogenous (Y and r) from the exogenous (G) as well as the parameters (a, g_0, b, t_0). On the other hand, substitution of 7.2.6 into the equilibrium condition 7.2.7 gives us:

$$l_0 + l_1 Y - l_2 r = \frac{M_s}{P}$$

which can be rewritten as:

$$l_1 Y - l_2 r = \frac{M_s}{P} - l_0. \qquad\qquad (7.2.9)$$

Once more the reader should be able to recognize that expression 7.2.9 is another way of writing the equation for the LM curve.

Thus, the above system, 7.2.1–7.2.7, has collapsed into a system of two endogenous variables in two equations. Once we have determined the reduced forms for Y and r, we can proceed to substitute them directly into the original system, 7.2.1–7.2.7, to obtain the corresponding reduced forms of the rest of the endogenous variables.

Pulling equation 7.2.8 and 7.2.9 together, we form the system:

$$[1 - b(1 - t_1)]Y + g_1 r = a + g_0 + bt_0 + G$$

$$l_1 Y - l_2 r = \frac{M_s}{P} - l_0.$$

To solve the above system we may use the second equation to solve for r in terms of Y; i.e.,

$$r = -\frac{M_s/P - l_0}{l_2} + \frac{l_1}{l_2}Y. \tag{7.2.10}$$

Substituting the value of r given by 7.2.10 into the first equation of the system, we find:

$$[1 - b(1 - t_1)]Y + g_1 \left[\frac{l_0 - M_s/P}{l_2} + \frac{l_1}{l_2}Y \right] = a + g_0 + bt_0 + G.$$

Since the above equation contains only one endogenous variable (Y), we may solve it by expressing Y in terms of the exogenous variables to obtain:

$$Y = \frac{1}{1 - b(1 - t_1) + g_1 \dfrac{l_1}{l_2}} \left[a + g_0 + bt_0 + G - \frac{g_1}{l_2} l_0 + \frac{g_1}{l_2} \frac{M_s}{P} \right]. \tag{7.2.11}$$

Next, since we have already obtained the reduced form for Y we may use it to substitute in equation 7.2.10 in order to find the corresponding reduced form for the rate of interest. This is found to be:

$$r = -\frac{M_s/P - l_0}{l_2}$$

$$+ \frac{l_1}{l_2} \frac{1}{1 - b(1 - t_1) + g_1 \dfrac{l_1}{l_2}} \left[a + g_0 + bt_0 + G - \frac{g_1}{l_2} l_0 + \frac{g_1}{l_2} \frac{M_s}{P} \right]$$

which can be further simplified to read:

$$r = \frac{l_1[a + g_0 + bt_0 + G] + [1 - b(1 - t_1)]\left(l_0 - \dfrac{M_s}{P}\right)}{l_2\left[1 - b(1 - t_1) + g_1 \dfrac{l_1}{l_2}\right]}.$$

(7.2.12)

Next, one may proceed to substitute the variables Y and r as expressed by 7.2.11 and 7.2.12 into the other equations of the system to obtain the corresponding reduced-form equation for all the endogenous variables. Here we shall concentrate only on equations 7.2.11 and 7.2.12.

Assume that $G = G^0$, $M_s = M_s^0$ and $P = P^0$. Substitution of these values in the above expressions allows us to determine the equilibrium values for income and rate of interest. These are found to be:

$$Y^0 = \frac{1}{1 - b(1 - t_1) + g_1 \dfrac{l_1}{l_2}}\left[a + g_0 + bt_0 + G^0 - \frac{g_1}{l_2}\left(l_0 - \frac{M_s^0}{P^0}\right)\right]$$

(7.2.13)

and

$$r^0 = \frac{l_1[a + g_0 + bt_0 + G^0] + [1 - b(1 - t_1)]\left(l_0 - \dfrac{M_s^0}{P^0}\right)}{l_2\left[1 - b(1 - t_1) + g_1 \dfrac{l_1}{l_2}\right]}$$

(7.2.14)

Having found the equilibrium values for income and rate of interest, we proceed to examine the qualitative and quantitative implications of changes in the parameters and exogenous variables of the model.

Suppose that the government changes its own level of expenditures on goods and services from G^0 to G^1 $(G^1 > G^0)$ while everything else remains constant. Substituting this new value for government expenditure into 7.2.11 and 7.2.12, we obtain the new equilibrium levels of income and rate of interest:

$$Y^1 = \frac{1}{1 - b(1 - t_1) + g_1 \dfrac{l_1}{l_2}}\left[a + g_0 + bt_0 + G^1 - \frac{g_1}{l_2}\left(l_0 - \frac{M_s^0}{P^0}\right)\right]$$

(7.2.15)

and

$$r^1 = \frac{l_1[a + g_0 + bt_0 + G^1] + [1 - b(1 - t_1)]\left(l_0 - \dfrac{M_s^0}{P^0}\right)}{l_2\left[1 - b(1 - t_1) + g_1 \dfrac{l_1}{l_2}\right]}.$$

(7.2.16)

Subtracting 7.2.13 and 7.2.14 from 7.2.15 and 7.2.16 respectively, we find the change in the equilibrium values of Y and r due to the given change in the level of governmental expenditures:

$$\Delta Y = m \, \Delta G \tag{7.2.17}$$

and

$$\Delta r = \frac{l_1}{l_2} m \, \Delta G \tag{7.2.18}$$

where

$$m \equiv \frac{1}{1 - b(1 - t_1) + g_1 \dfrac{l_1}{l_2}}$$

is, of course, the new value of the multiplier. Thus, we immediately see that an increase in governmental expenditures implies an increase in the equilibrium level of both income and the interest rate (provided that $b(1 - t_1) - g_1(l_1/l_2) < 1$).

Similar effects will result in the case of a change in the autonomous part of consumption (a), investment (g_0), and transfer payments (t_0). More explicitly, these changes will be:

$$\Delta Y = m \, \Delta a \tag{7.2.19}$$

$$\Delta r = \frac{l_1}{l_2} m \, \Delta a \tag{7.2.20}$$

$$\Delta Y = m \, \Delta g_0 \tag{7.2.21}$$

$$\Delta r = \frac{l_1}{l_2} m \, \Delta g_0 \tag{7.2.22}$$

$$\Delta Y = mb \, \Delta t_0 \tag{7.2.23}$$

$$\Delta r = \frac{l_1}{l_2} mb \, \Delta t_0. \tag{7.2.24}$$

The reader should be able to recognize that all the above changes result from shifts of the IS curve to the right or left (depending on whether the parameters or exogenous variables in question increase or decrease in relation to their original levels). Notice that the changes of the equilibrium level of income and rate of interest associated with a change in transfer payments of the government are smaller in size than an equal change in any other variable or parameter, since the former changes are multiplied times the marginal propensity to consume.

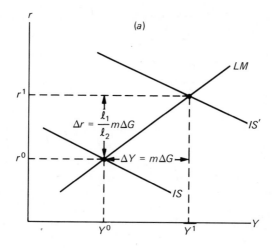

Figure 7.2.1a) *The Impact of a Change in Government Expenditures*

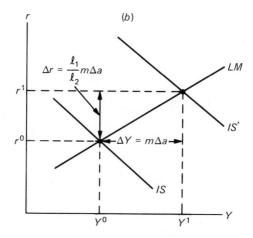

Figure 7.2.1b) *The Impact of a Change in Autonomous Consumption*

The effects of changes in the values of the exogenous variables can also be illustrated graphically. In panels (a) and (b) of figure 7.2.1, we have depicted the case of a change in government expenditures and autonomous consumption by using the relevant IS and LM schedules. First, consider the change in government expenditures from G^0 to G^1. As is shown in panel (a), this change (presume it is an increase) will cause the IS schedule to shift to the right. As this happens, the general equilibrium position moves from r^0, Y^0 to r^1, Y^1. This corresponding change in the equilibrium values of r and Y can be found by comparing the old and new equilibrium positions. In panel (b) we have illustrated the same principle for the alternative case involving positive changes in the parameter a.

Suppose that the government decides to change the tax rate from t_1 to t_1', $(t_1' > t_1)$. As we have seen from an earlier chapter, this change will result in reducing the magnitude of the multiplier and consequently the equilibrium level of income. To determine the resulting change in the equilibrium values of Y and r, we substitute t_1', along with the given values of M_s, P and G, in equations 7.2.11 and 7.2.12 and from the resulting form we subtract equations 7.2.13 and 7.2.14 to find:

$$\Delta Y = - \frac{\left[a + g_0 + bt_0 + G^0 - \frac{g_1}{l_2}\left(l_0 - \frac{M_s^0}{P^0}\right)\right]b(t_1' - t_1)}{\left[1 - b(1 - t_1) + g_1\frac{l_1}{l_2}\right]\left[1 - b(1 - t_1') + g_1\frac{l_1}{l_2}\right]}$$

and

$$\Delta r = \frac{-b(t_1' - t_1)l_1\left[a + g_0 + bt_0 + G^0 - \frac{g_1}{l_2}\left(l_0 - \frac{M_s^0}{P^0}\right)\right]}{l_2\left[1 - b(1 - t_1) + g_1\frac{l_1}{l_2}\right]\left[1 - b(1 - t_1') + g_1\frac{l_1}{l_2}\right]}.$$

But, given equation 7.2.13, the above equations can be further simplified to read:

$$\Delta Y = -bm'Y^0\,\Delta t_1 \tag{7.2.25}$$

and

$$\Delta r = -\frac{l_1}{l_2}bm'Y^0\,\Delta t_1 \tag{7.2.26}$$

where

$$m' = \frac{1}{1 - b(1 - t_1') + g_1\dfrac{l_1}{l_2}}.$$

From the above equations we see that the change in the equilibrium levels of income and rate of interest depend not only on the change in

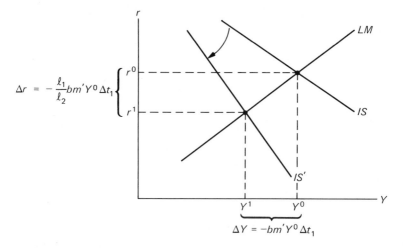

Figure 7.2.2 *The Impact of a Change in the Tax Rate*

the tax rate but also on the initial equilibrium level of income. The larger the initial equilibrium level of income, *ceteris paribus,* the larger the change in income and rate of interest will be.

Again, the point can be examined by the use of a graphical approach. In figure 7.2.2, we have illustrated the impact of a change in the tax rate from t_1 to t_1'. As the tax rate increases, the IS schedule rotates to the left, causing a decline in both the rate of interest and the level of income. Notice that if we were to measure the shift in the IS horizontally, the shift would increase directly with increases in the initial equilibrium level of income. On intuitive grounds, this should make sense. As the tax rate is increased, a "wedge" is driven between national income and disposable income. The larger the original level of national income, the larger the amount of this wedge becomes.

The above registered changes in Y and r are due, as mentioned above, to either a parallel shift or, in the case of tax rate, a rotation of the IS curve. However, the most interesting characteristic of these changes is not their direction but their magnitude. Indeed, comparison of the multiplier equations for income with the corresponding equations in chapter 5 (5.5.12, 5.5.13, 5.5.14 and 5.5.15) indicates that for an equal change in the level of a parameter or an exogenous variable, the implied change in the equilibrium values of income by the former equations is smaller than those implied by the equations in chapter 5. While in chapter 5 the expenditure sector produced a multiplier which was equal to ($k' \equiv (1/$

$1 - b(1 - t_1)))$, the introduction of the monetary sector resulted in a new multiplier which was found to be equal to:

$$m \equiv \frac{1}{1 - b(1 - t_1) + g_1 \dfrac{l_1}{l_2}}.$$

However, since the parameters l_1 and l_2 are assumed to be positive quantities, it follows that:

$$[1 - b(1 - t_1)] < \left[1 - b(1 - t_1) + g_1 \frac{l_1}{l_2}\right]$$

which implies that $k' > m$.

At this point the reader may wonder about the reasons for such a change in the magnitude of the multiplier. To begin with, notice that changes in income registered in chapter 5 were the result of shifts of the IS curve to the left or right *leaving the rate of interest unchanged.* From equations 7.2.14, 7.2.21, 7.2.23 and 7.2.25, however, we see that once the monetary sector is introduced, the changes in income due to changes of the various parameters and exogenous variables which were found in chapter 5 are in effect an overstatement of the actual changes which occur. To appreciate the difference, consider, for example, an increase in the level of government expenditures. This increase will result in an increase of the equilibrium level of income, which in turn will result immediately in an increase in the demand for transaction cash balances. As we know from the previous chapter, however, this increase in the demand for transaction balances will show as a shift to the right of the total demand for cash balances. In view of the fact that the supply of money remains constant, it follows that a reshuffling of the relation between the two components of the aggregate demand for money will be necessary so that the change in the demand of the transaction component will be satisfied. Thus the speculative demand has to decrease accordingly in order to accommodate the increase in the transaction component. However, we know that this can be done only if the rate of interest increases.

A bit more mechanically, consider the equilibrium of the monetary sector:

$$\frac{M_s^0}{P^0} = l_0 + l_1 Y - l_2 r$$

Since the nominal money supply M_s^0 and the price level P^0 are assumed to remain constant, any increase of Y will throw the above equation out of balance unless this increase in Y is accompanied by an increase in r.

In fact, the rate of interest will increase to the level at which the released speculative balances will be exactly equal to the increase in the demand for cash balances for transaction purposes. But, since the rate of interest increases, this will result in a decrease in the level of investment, which eventually will partially cancel the increase in the level of income.

Thus, we can now see that the difference in the magnitude of the multipliers in question can be traced to the fact that in chapter 5 our analysis assumed a constant rate of interest. However, the introduction of the monetary sector, and in particular the equation for the demand for cash balances, introduces a feedback mechanism between these two sectors with the result that any change in the level of income (provided that the real money supply remains constant) will require a corresponding change in the rate of interest. Therefore, although the changes in the parameters and exogenous variables will result in a shift of the IS curve by the same amount as shown in chapter 5, the equilibrium level of income will change by an amount less than the shift in question.

The described mechanism is quite general and applies to any change of the parameters and exogenous variables of the model we have examined so far. However, the behavior of fiscal authorities may put pressure on interest rates through another mechanism not specifically incorporated into our model. As an example, assume that the government increases the level of its expenditures on goods and services. Also suppose that this increase in expenditures is financed by selling government bonds. While the government may issue these bonds at the current market rate of interest, depending on the conditions in the financial markets, the likelihood that the marketing of this issue will require reduced offering prices implies a higher rate of interest. In other words, the competition of the government with the private sector in financial markets may also result in a higher rate of interest.[1]

The above analysis has shed some light on the reasons for the inequality of these two types of multipliers. It should be apparent by now, however, that the term which is responsible for this discrepancy between these multipliers is the product $g_1(l_1/l_2)$ which appears in the denominator of m. This term, like t_1, plays the role of an automatic stabilizer. Because it consists mainly of parameters which appear in the monetary sector, it is called a monetary stabilizer.

The above discussion is summarized in figure 7.2.3. There we see that a shift of the IS from IS_0 to IS_1 due to an increase in an exogenous

---

[1] Here it is assumed that this joint policy of an increase in government expenditures accompanied by debt financing can take place without any change in the money supply. For a formal exposition of the means of financing government expenditures, see the appendix to chapter 15.

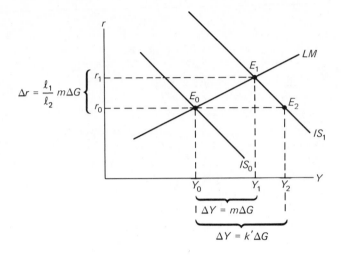

$$\Delta r = \frac{\ell_1}{\ell_2} m\Delta G$$

Figure 7.2.3   *The Effect of a Monetary Stabilizer*

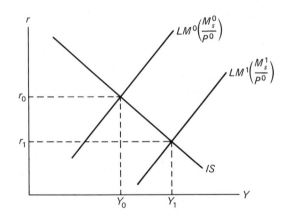

Figure 7.2.4   *The Impact of a Change in the Money Supply*

variable or parameter of the expenditure sector implies an increase in the equilibrium levels of the rate of interest and income from r_0 and Y_0 to r_1 and Y_1 respectively. The distance $Y_0 Y_1 = m\,\Delta G = m\,\Delta a = mb\,\Delta t_0 = m\,\Delta g_0$ whereas the distance $Y_0 Y_2 = k'\,\Delta G = k'\,\Delta a = k'b\,\Delta t_0 = k'\,\Delta g_0$ (see chapter 5 for the definition of k'). The latter change would take place if the rate of interest had not changed. As we can see, however, from equations 7.2.18, 7.2.20, 7.2.22, and 7.2.24, the rate of interest will not stay at its initial level r_0. Instead, it will increase to the level r_1, the change being equal to $\Delta r = (l_1/l_2)m\,\Delta G$, etc.

So far, we have focused on the impact of fiscal policies; but monetary policy, as exercised by the Federal Reserve, has also played an important role in the postwar experience of the United States. In general terms, expansionary monetary policy can be expected to increase income and decrease interest rates, whereas contractionary policy will have the opposite effects. In 1965, for instance, the Federal Reserve attempted to apply the brakes to a rapidly expanding economy by drastically slowing the growth of the money supply. To some extent, this may have alleviated some of the problems caused by the reluctance of fiscal authorities to show restraint. But the "credit crunch" was a severe step, and, by 1966, interest rates had climbed to their highest values since the 1920s. Eventually, by the end of 1966, the prospects of a recession induced the Fed to embark on a markedly more expansionary policy. The impact of monetary policy can also be demonstrated through the use of the LS-LM framework.

Suppose that the Federal Reserve increases the nominal money supply from M_s^0 to M_s^1 while all the other parameters and exogenous variables of the system remain constant. Substituting the new level of money supply into the reduced forms expressed by equations 7.2.11 and 7.2.12 and subtracting from the resultant quantities those given by equations 7.2.13 and 7.2.14 respectively, we obtain:

$$\Delta Y = \frac{g_1}{l_2} m \left(\frac{\Delta M_s}{P^0} \right) \tag{7.2.27}$$

and

$$\Delta r = - \frac{[1 - b(1 - t_1)]}{l_2} m \left(\frac{\Delta M_s}{P^0} \right). \tag{7.2.28}$$

Equations 7.2.17 and 7.2.28 establish that, *ceteris paribus,* an increase in the money supply will be accompanied by an increase in the equilibrium level of income and by a decrease in the rate of interest. This result should be expected since an increase in the stock of money will result in a decline of the rate of interest, which in turn will stimulate investment, giving an impetus for an increase in the equilibrium level of income.[2] This situation is depicted in figure 7.2.4 where Y_0 and r_0 are the initial and Y_1 and r_1 are the corresponding terminal values of income and rate of interest resulting from a shift of the LM curve from LM^0 to LM^1.

---

[2]Exercises: 1. By making use of the reduced forms for Y and r, determine the effect of a price change on the equilibrium values of these variables. Hint: In rationalizing your results consider first what happens to the demand for transaction cash balances.

   2. Show that a 100% increase in the nominal money supply implies the same change in the equilibrium levels of Y and r as a 50% decrease in the price level. Explain.

7.3 A Numerical Example

At this point it might be useful if we introduce a numerical example to help the reader secure the above ideas. Suppose that the system 7.2.1–7.2.7 of the previous section assume the following form:

$$Y = C + I + G \tag{7.3.1}$$

$$C = 30 + .8Y_d \tag{7.3.2}$$

$$I = 100 - 400r \tag{7.3.3}$$

$$Y_d \equiv Y - T \tag{7.3.4}$$

$$T = -50 + .25Y \tag{7.3.5}$$

$$\frac{M_d}{P} = 110 + .15Y - 500r \tag{7.3.6}$$

$$\frac{M_d}{P} = \frac{M_s}{P}. \tag{7.3.7}$$

We shall also assume that $P = 1$, $G = 250$ and $M_s/P = 235$.

To solve this system we may start from the expenditure sector, which can be condensed into the equation of the IS curve; i.e.:

$$.40Y + 400r = 420. \tag{7.3.8}$$

On the other hand, appropriate substitution of equation 7.3.6 and the value of the real money supply into 7.3.7 yields the algebraic expression for the LM curve; i.e.:

$$.15Y - 500r = 125. \tag{7.3.9}$$

Equations 7.3.8 and 7.3.9 can now be solved simultaneously to yield the solution values for Y and $r(Y = 1,000$ and $r = .05)$.

Having determined the equilibrium values of income and rate of interest, one may now substitute them in the equations of the system 7.3.1–7.3.7 to find the corresponding values of the rest of the endogenous variables. These are given by the first column of table 7.3.1.

Next, suppose that the government increases its expenditures on goods and services from 250 to 267.3 billion dollars. The resulting new equation of the IS curve is

$$.40Y + 400r = 437.3 \tag{7.3.10}$$

which can be combined once more with the expression of the LM curve, equation 7.3.9, to yield the corresponding new equilibrium values of

Table 7.3.1. *A Numerical Example*

Variables	Initial Equilibrium 1	$\Delta G = 17.3$ 2	$\Delta M = 26$ 3	$\Delta G = 17.3$ $\Delta M_s = 6.49$ 4
Y	1,000	1,033.3	1,040	1,043.25
T	200	208.3	210	210.8
Y_d	800	825	830	832.45
C	670	690	694	695.96
I	80	76	96	80
r	.05	.06	.01	.05
M_d	235	235	261	241.49
P	1	1	1	1
M_s	235	235	261	241.49
G	250	267.3	250	267.3
S	130	135	136	136.40
T − G	−50	−59.0	−40	−56.50

income and the rate of interest. These are $Y \cong 1033.33$ billion and $r \cong .06$. To appreciate this solution, consider again the demand for money. From the previous chapter we know that the total demand for real cash balances $(M_d/P = l_0 + l_1 Y - l_2 r)$ is equal to the sum of the demand for real transaction balances $(M_{t,d}/P = l_1 Y)$ and the demand for real speculative ones $(M_{s,d}/P = l_0 - l_2 r)$. In terms of our example, $l_0 = 110, l_1 = .15,$ and $l_2 = 500$. Thus, when the level of income is equal to 1,000 billion, the demand for transaction balances is equal to 150 billion (i.e., $M_{t,d}/P = .15 \times 1,000$). Since the real money supply is held constant at the level of 235 billion, the monetary sector will be at equilibrium if and only if the speculative demand for money is equal to the difference between total supply and demand for transaction balances. In other words $M_{s,d}/P$ has to be equal to $(235 - 150 = 85)$. By setting the equation of the demand for speculative balances equal to this amount (i.e., $M_{s,d}/P = 85 = 110 - 500r$), we find the rate of interest which will induce people to hold (demand) speculative cash balances amounting to $85 billion. This rate of interest is equal to 5%.

When the government increases the spending on goods and services from $250 to $267.3 billion, the level of income starts increasing. The transaction demand for money will also increase and consequently, since the money supply remains constant, this increase in the transaction balances has to be accommodated by an equal release from the speculative holdings. In particular, since income increases to 1,033.3 billion, the corresponding demand for transaction purposes will increase to 155 ($M_{t,d}/P$ = .15 × 1,033.3). Thus, at the new equilibrium, speculative balances can be only $80 billion. Setting the equation for speculative balances equal to 80 billion (80 = 110 − 500r) we now find that the rate of interest has to increase to 6% in order to induce the transfer of these $5 billion from speculative to transaction balances. As a result of this increase in the rate of interest, the level of investment will decrease and thus income will not eventually increase as much as it would have if the rate of interest had remained constant. This is shown in table 7.3.1 where the level of investment has decreased by $4 billion. Graphically, this example corresponds to diagram 7.2.1.

Let us now suppose that the Federal Reserve increases the nominal money supply from 235 to 261. The equation of the new LM curve becomes:

$$.15Y - 500r = 151. \qquad\qquad (7.3.11)$$

Combining the above equation with the initial expression for the IS curve (equation 7.3.8) and solving the resulting system, we find that the new equilibrium levels of income and rate of interest are equal to Y = 1040 and r = .01. Thus, given the postulated parameters and exogenous variables of the system 7.3.1–7.3.7, an increase in the money supply by $26 billion results in an increase in the level of income by $40 billion and in a decrease in the rate of interest by .04.

In relation to the above changes, it is interesting that the change in income was the result of a change in investment which in turn was the result of a change in the rate of interest. The order of reaction could be thought to be the following. First, the increase in money supply forces the rate of interest to decrease. As a result of this, investment increases and consequently income starts expanding. This eventual convergence to a new equilibrium will be the outcome of an increase in the demand for cash balances and, as we show, the rate of interest will settle at a level which will be somewhere in between its original level and the one resulting immediately from the increase in the money supply.

The reader should have already suspected that this is another result of the monetary stabilizer. In all the changes we have shown, the final equilibrium is achieved partly by changes in income and partly by changes in the rate of interest. Thus any change in the parameters or exogenous variables of the system is accompanied by an income and an interest effect. In fact, the greater the interest or monetary effect, the less the effects of the multiplier will be. We have already seen this result in the previous section and we shall study it again in the next one. What is important here is to appreciate that all the above described sequences show how the equations of the model are used simultaneously in order to determine the values of the variables involved. That is, at any point in time, income and the rate of interest must be such that the economic units (people as well as institutions) are willing to hold the existing stock of money, and at the same time income and the rate of interest must ensure that the flow of injections (I + G) absorbs the flow of leakages (S + T) produced by the economy.

7.4 Neutralization of the Interest Effects

So far, all the changes in parameters and exogenous variables we have described have resulted in corresponding changes of the equilibrium levels of income and the rate of interest. The outcome of this simultaneous change was that the usual multiplier we met in chapter 5 in connection with the derivation of the IS curve has been reduced.

The purpose of this section is to show an alternative way of exercising economic policy so that the interest effects are neutralized. Suppose that the government wishes to increase the level of income, and that to achieve this it decides to increase spending on goods and services. From the above analysis we know that if G increases this will result in an increase in both income and the rate of interest. Although the government could increase its spending by enough to attain its goal, it might be easier if the rate of interest were to be fixed at its current level. This can be done by a simultaneous increase in the money supply and government expenditures.

Consider figure 7.4.1 and let us assume that the economy is currently at E^0 characterized by the equilibrium values Y^0 and r^0. Suppose also that the authorities would like to increase income to Y^D. From the diagram, we see that this can be achieved either by shifting the IS curve from position IS^0 to IS^2, implying an enormous change of government expenditures, or by instituting a relatively moderate change in government expenditures, provided that the money supply is increased in such a way that the rate of interest remains constant. This simultaneous manipulation of monetary and fiscal policy which results in a constant rate of interest is shown by IS^1 and LM^1 of figure 7.4.1.

Suppose now that the government will increase the expenditures on goods and services by a certain amount. But by how much should the money supply change in order to obtain full multiplier effects (or, what is the same, in order to keep the rate of interest constant)? The answer

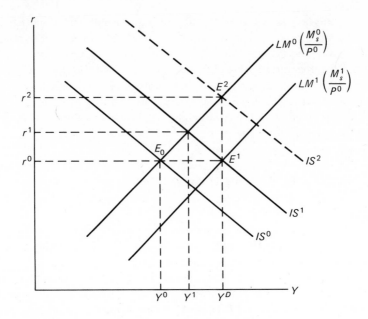

Figure 7.4.1 *Neutralization of the Interest Effect*

to this question is quite simple provided that we recall equations 7.2.11 and 7.2.12, which for convenience are reproduced here. We have found that the equilibrium values of Y and r were given by:

$$Y = \frac{a + g_0 + bt_0 + G - \dfrac{g_1}{l_2}l_0 + \dfrac{g_1}{l_2}\dfrac{M_s}{P}}{1 - b(1 - t_1) + g_1\dfrac{l_1}{l_2}}$$

and

$$r = \frac{l_1[a + g_0 + bt_0 + G] + [1 - b(1 - t_1)]\left(l_0 - \dfrac{M_s}{P}\right)}{l_2\left[1 - b(1 - t_1) + g_1\dfrac{l_1}{l_2}\right]}.$$

Suppose that currently government expenditures are set at G^0 and the nominal money supply and price level at M_S^0 and P^0 respectively. Let us also suppose that the government decides to increase its spending to G^1 and the money supply to M_s^1 while the price level remains constant at P^0. Substituting this set of values for the exogenous variables and subtracting Y^0 and r^0 from Y^1 and r^1, we find:

$$\Delta Y = m\left[\Delta G + \frac{g_1}{l_2}\Delta M_s\right] \tag{7.4.1}$$

and

$$\Delta r = m\{l_1\,\Delta G - [1 - b(1 - t_1)]\,\Delta M_s\}. \tag{7.4.2}$$

Now, how much should the money supply increase, given an increase in G, so that $\Delta r = 0$? Setting equation 7.4.2 equal to zero we obtain:

$$m\{l_1\,\Delta G - [1 - b(1 - t_1)]\,\Delta M_s\} = 0.$$

And solving for ΔM_s in terms of ΔG we find:

$$\Delta M_s = \frac{l_1}{1 - b(1 - t_1)}\,\Delta G. \tag{7.4.3}$$

Thus, if the change in the money supply assumes the value given by 7.4.3, the rate of interest will remain constant. Substituting now the value for the change in money supply from 7.4.3 into 7.4.1, we obtain:

$$\Delta Y = m\left[\Delta G + \frac{g_1}{l_2}\,\frac{l_1}{1 - b(1 - t_1)}\,\Delta G\right]$$

which can be simplified to read:

$$\Delta Y = m\,\Delta G\left\{\frac{l_2[1 - b(1 - t_1)] + g_1 l_1}{l_2[1 - b(1 - t_1)]}\right\}.$$

Dividing the numerator and denominator of the expression within the braces by l_2, we obtain:

$$\Delta Y = m\,\Delta G\left[\frac{1 - b(1 - t_1) + g_1\dfrac{l_1}{l_2}}{1 - b(1 - t_1)}\right].$$

But the numerator is the inverse of m. Consequently, the above expression can be rewritten as:

$$\Delta Y = \frac{1}{1 - b(1 - t_1)}\,\Delta G$$

or

$$\Delta Y = k'\,\Delta G \tag{7.3.17}$$

where

$$k' \equiv \frac{1}{1 - b(1 - t_1)}.$$

Obviously, equation 7.3.17 is exactly the same as equation 5.5.11 of chapter 5. In both instances the multiplier assumes its full value provided that the monetary policy is flexible enough to prevent any change in the rate of interest. This case is depicted in column 4 of table 7.3.1, where government expenditures have increased by the same amount as in column 2 ($17.3 billion), but where the nominal money supply has also risen.[3]

7.5 Summary

This chapter has shown how the product and money markets interact to determine equilibrium values for the endogenous variables they include. In addition, it was shown (provided that we exclude the extreme properties of the demand-for-money equation) that both fiscal and monetary

---

[3]Exercises: 1. Determine the IS and LM curves which underlie the solution values of column 4 of table 7.3.1. Compare the implied new value of the multiplier with the one which corresponds to the system 7.3.1–7.3.7.

2. Consider the structural equations 7.3.1 and 7.3.7 and suppose $P^0 = 1$, $G^0 = 250$ and $M_s^0/P^0 = 235$. Find the policy mix (i.e., the combination of fiscal and monetary policy) which will allow you to attain the target $Y = 1,050$ on the assumption that the change in the rate of interest will be equal to zero.

3. Suppose that the economy can be depicted by the following set of structural equations:

$$Y = C + I + G$$
$$C = 30 + .8Y_d$$
$$I = 100 - 400r + .10Y$$
$$Y_d \equiv Y - T$$
$$T = -50 + .25Y$$
$$\frac{M_d}{P} = 110 + .15Y - 500r$$
$$\frac{M_d}{P} = \frac{M_s}{P}$$

and suppose also that currently $P^0 = 1$; $G^0 = 150$; and $M_s^0/P^0 = 235$. (a) Determine the solution values of the endogenous variables; (b) Suppose now that $\Delta G = 14$; $\Delta M_s = 14$. Determine the corresponding equilibrium values of the endogenous variables on the assumption that each of the above changes take place separately; (c) Finally, suppose that $\Delta G = 14$. Determine the change in money supply so that $\Delta r = 0$.

policy are capable of exerting considerable influence on the equilibrium values of the system.

Although we shall have a further opportunity to elaborate on this, we have seen that an increase in government expenditures, given the real money supply, will be accompanied by an increase in the rate of interest and a simultaneous increase in the level of income. On the other hand, values of the exogenous variables of the expenditure sector, an increase in the real money supply will also result in an increase in the equilibrium level of income but it will be accompanied by a decrease in the rate of interest.

This suggests that while changes in both policies result in changes in the equilibrium level of income in the same direction, their impact on the equilibrium level of the rate of interest will be different.

Suggested Further Reading

Hansen, A. *A Guide to Keynes.* New York: McGraw-Hill, 1953.

Hicks, J. R. "Mr. Keynes and the Classics." *Econometrica* 5 (April 1937), 147–59. Reprinted in American Economic Association, *Readings in the Theory of Income Distribution.* Homewood, Ill.: R. D. Irwin, 1951, pp. 461–76.

Laidler, D. *The Demand for Money: Theories and Evidence.* Scranton, Pa: International Textbook Co., 1969, part 1, chap. 2.

Appendix 7A

The Effects of a Change in Price Expectations

Up to this point we have explicitly assumed that the price level is determined exogenously. Although on several occasions we allowed prices to change in order to investigate different properties of the system, these changes were considered to have no effect on the expectations of the individual economic actors regarding future behavior of prices. This, in turn, enabled us to equate the real with the market rate of interest and, therefore, our analysis evolved around "the" rate of interest. However, when economic actors expect that the price level will change, this equality is no longer legitimate and the analysis must be modified accordingly. In doing so, we shall make four assumptions.[1] First, the initial level of prices is still determined exogenously. Second, the change in the price level depends on the level of excess demand (measured in relation to full-employment income). In other words, regardless of what level of prices we start with, the change will depend on the difference between full-employment income and the equilibrium level of income (i.e., $Y_E - Y_F$). If Y_E is greater than Y_F then $\Delta P > 0$, and conversely. Third, we shall assume that price expectations are determined exogenously. This last assumption is necessary to enable us to investigate a dynamic problem with our present analytical tools. Finally, in the same spirit, we shall assume that when economic actors' expectations are satisfied they do not change them.

Let us begin by assuming that the prospective rate of return on investment and the rate of interest on, say, bonds are both equal to 2% and that there is no expectation of a price increase. Then, the lender who makes available $100 of funds for one year expects to receive after the expiration of the contract his principal of $100 plus $2 of interest. Since the price level is not expected to change, it follows that the purchasing power of $102 is also expected to remain the same.

Now consider what happens when the lender anticipates a 10% increase in the price level. Under these circumstances, if he continues to lend his funds at a 2% rate, then he must expect to incur a loss in the purchasing power of his principal and the interest he receives as well. In

---

[1] For a different use of price expectations and their effects on the price level, see chapter 18.

particular, the expected purchasing power of the principal and interest he will receive after one year will be $100 ÷ 1.10 = $90.91 and $2 ÷ 1.10 = $1.81 respectively. In other words, the expected purchasing power of his principal one year from now is equivalent to $90.91 at today's prices, and that of the interest he will receive, only $1.81. It follows, therefore, that if the lender is to be as well off as when prices were expected to remain unchanged, he must receive an interest rate well above 2% to compensate him for the anticipated reductions in purchasing power. More explicitly, he should ask a rate of interest which is equal to the real rate (i.e., the rate he demands when there is no expectation of a price increase) plus the expected loss in purchasing power of his principal and interest, namely:

$$i = r + (1 + r)\frac{\Delta P^e}{P} \tag{7.A.1}$$

where i denotes the market rate of interest, r, the real rate, and $(1 + r)(\Delta P^e/P)$, the compensation the lender will ask for the expected loss of purchasing power per dollar lent. In terms of our example, he would ask a rate of interest which would be equal to $i = .02 + (1 + .02) \times (.10) = .122$ or 12.2%.

According to this illustration, then, the lender should be indifferent if the market rate is 2% with no expected price increase or 12.2% with a 10% expected price increase. The reader can verify that at the end of the year the lender will receive $112.20 from which $100.00 will be for the repayment of his principal, $2.00 for interest and $10.20 for the expected loss of his purchasing power due to an anticipated 10% price increase. Indeed, under these circumstances his expected purchasing power remains the same, since $112.2 ÷ 1.10 = $102.00.

From the borrower's point of view the situation appears to be quite the same. If he expects higher prices he will be willing to pay a higher interest rate since he anticipates paying off his contractual obligation in dollars whose purchasing power is less than those he borrowed. This leads to the conclusion that if borrowers and lenders agreed on a 2% rate of interest when they both expect no price increase, then they will also agree to a 12.2% rate when they anticipate a 10% price increase. And since the reaction of both parties is the same, the market rate in each period will adjust to reflect the latest price expectations.

Our discussion suggests that what really counts for both borrowers and lenders is not the market rate of interest per se, but the difference between this rate and the expected change in the price level, i.e., the real rate of interest. Without loss in generality, therefore, we can express investment as a function of the real rate. Under the present circumstances, there is no basis to suppose that the risk or the expected rate of profit associated with any investment project will change along with the price level. Consider, for example, the case of a firm that uses equity capital for investments and suppose that all prices including wages rise in the same proportion. Under these circumstances profits as a level will rise by the same proportion but real profits as a percent are not affected. It follows that, disregarding the effects on cash balances, this firm does not have to change its investment strategy because it expects that prices will rise. Therefore, the willingness of the various economic units (be it consumers, firms or institutions of financial intermediation) to lend and borrow for investments, in our sense, should not change as expectations concerning prices change. Accordingly, our investment equation should be specified in terms of the real rate; namely,

$$I = g_0 - g_1 r. \tag{7.A.2}$$

Now, solving equation 7.A.1 for the real rate in terms of the nominal, we obtain:

$$r = \frac{i - \dfrac{\Delta P^e}{P}}{1 + \dfrac{\Delta P^e}{P}}. \tag{7.A.3}$$

Inserting the value of r from equation 7.A.3 into the investment function, we find:

$$I = g_0 - g_1 \left[\frac{i - \dfrac{\Delta P^e}{P}}{1 + \dfrac{\Delta P^e}{P}} \right]$$

which can be simplified to read:

$$I = g_0 + \left[\frac{g_1 \dfrac{\Delta P^e}{P}}{1 + \dfrac{\Delta P^e}{P}} \right] - \left[\frac{g_1}{1 + \dfrac{\Delta P^e}{P}} \right] i. \tag{7.A.4}$$

Equation 7.A.4 expresses the demand for investment as a function of the money rate of interest. The reader can observe that in the case in which prices are not expected to change (i.e., when $\Delta P^e / P = 0$), the premium

Table 7.A.1.   *The Demand for Investment Expressed in Terms of Real and Money Rates for* $\dfrac{\Delta P^e}{P} = .10$

r	$(1 + r)\dfrac{\Delta P^e}{P}$	i	$I_{(r)}$	$I_{(i)}$
.02	.102	.122	92	92
.03	.103	.133	88	88
.04	.104	.144	84	84
.05	.105	.155	80	80

which the economic actors are willing to pay over the real rate is zero and therefore i = r. This is also apparent from equation 7.A.4 which for i = r collapses into equation 7.A.2 as one would expect. By the same token, we can also verify that when the community anticipates price changes, equation 7.A.4 suggests that the initial investment schedule as expressed by equation 7.A.2 will shift in a nonparallel fashion since both its intercept and its slope change. Perhaps a quick numerical example will help to illustrate this point. Consider the following demand-for-investment equation

$$I = 100 - 400r \tag{7.A.5}$$

and suppose that the community expects a 10% price increase (i.e., $\Delta P^e/P = .10$). Given this price-change expectation, the market rate will climb above the real rate by an amount equal to $(1 + r) \times (.10)$. Expressing investment in terms of money rates (see equation 7.A.4), we immediately obtain:

$$I = 136.4 - 363.4\,i. \tag{7.A.6}$$

Clearly, the above two equations should show the same demand for investment provided that for each real rate we use the corresponding market rate, given the premium the community is willing to accept due to the expected price increase (see equation 7.A.1). Table 7.A.1 delineates this case by providing the numerical values which correspond to all variables for a series of real rates on the assumption that $\Delta P^e/P = .10$.

In table 7.A.1 $I_{(r)}$ and $I_{(i)}$ denote the demand for investment expressed in terms of real and market rates. The difference between these two rates appears in the second column and, as the reader can see, it changes in the same direction as the real rate. The reader should be able to figure

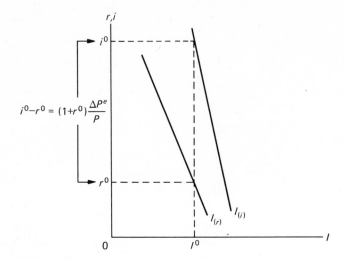

Figure 7.A.1   *Demand for Investment with Non-zero Price-change*
Expectations

out why it does so. Notice also that equations 7.A.4 and 7.A.5 provide
us with the same demand for investment as long as we substitute for
each real rate the corresponding money rate. Figure 7.1 depicts the case
of an expected price increase ($\Delta P^e/P > 0$).

In figure 7.A.1 the vertical axis measures both the real and the money
rate of interest whereas the horizontal measures the demand for investment. As we mentioned earlier, the vertical difference between the
schedules $I_{(i)}$ and $I_{(r)}$ depicts the premium over the real rate which will
be asked by lenders (and which borrowers are willing to pay) due to their
expectation concerning price behavior. This difference increases as the
real rate increases due to the compensation the lenders ask for the
anticipated loss in the purchasing power of the interest they receive.

So far, our analysis suggests that if the community anticipates changes
in the price level, this necessitates the recognition of two different rates
of interest, the difference being the premium the lenders will ask over the
real rate due to the expected price change. In turn, this implies that the
investment schedule drawn against the market rate will shift since the
introduction of price expectations into the model affects its intercept as
well as its slope. Therefore, *ceteris paribus,* these circumstances will trigger
a similar shift of the underlying IS curve as well. To see this disregard the
government activities and express the expenditures sector in terms of
the familiar system of equations:

$$Y = C + I \tag{7.A.7}$$

$$C = a + bY \tag{7.A.8}$$

$$I = g_0 + \left[\frac{g_1 \dfrac{\Delta P^e}{P}}{1 + \dfrac{\Delta P^e}{P}} \right] - \left[\frac{g_1}{1 + \dfrac{\Delta P^e}{P}} \right] i. \tag{7.A.9}$$

Substitution of equations 7.A.8 and 7.A.9 into 7.A.7 yields the equation of the IS curve, i.e.

$$Y = \left(\frac{1}{1-b} \right) \left[a + g_0 + \frac{g_1 \dfrac{\Delta P^e}{P}}{1 + \dfrac{\Delta P^e}{P}} \right] - \left(\frac{1}{1-b} \right) \left[\frac{g_1}{1 + \dfrac{\Delta P^e}{P}} \right] i.$$

$$\tag{7.A.10}$$

From equation 7.A.10 we see that the introduction of expected changes in prices results in a rotation of the IS curve similar to that of the demand-for-investment schedule (compare equation 7.A.10 with equation 5.4.4). This is illustrated in figure 7.A.2 on the assumption that $\Delta P^e/P > 0$.[2]

We see that the vertical displacement of the IS curve, under these circumstances, is equal to the compensation the lender will ask per dollar lent at each real rate of interest and for a given percent of expected price change.

But what happens to the LM curve when price expectations are introduced in the monetary sector? To answer this, consider first the demand for cash balances. In chapter 6 we argue that the decision of how much liquid cash balances the economic actor wants to hold depends upon his opportunity cost. The higher his opportunity cost, the smaller the amount of cash balances he will be willing to hold. But in the present case the opportunity cost to the individual holder of cash balance, and by extension to the community as a whole, is the money rate and not the real rate.[3] Therefore, the demand for cash balances is appropriately expressed as a function of the market rate of interest. We may then write:

---

[2] Prove that in figure 7.A.2 it is also true that $i^0 - r^0 = (1 + r^0)(\Delta P^e/P)$.

[3] The reader is reminded of our discussion concerning the rate of interest a lender would ask on the assumption of a change in the price level.

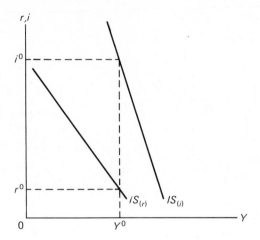

Figure 7.A.2 *The Equilibrium of the Expenditures Sector with Non-zero Price-change Expectations*

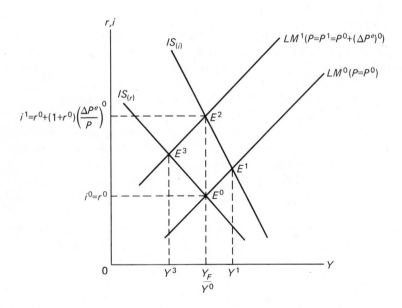

Figure 7.A.3 *General Equilibrium of the Expenditures and Monetary Sectors with Non-zero Price-change Expectations*

$$\frac{M_d}{P} = l_0 + l_1 Y - l_2 i \qquad\qquad (7.A.11)$$

which can be combined with the exogenously given money supply to yield:

$$\frac{M_s^0}{P} = l_0 + l_1 Y - l_2 i. \qquad\qquad (7.A.12)$$

We see therefore that changes in the market rate of interest due to expected price changes can be expressed in terms of movements along the LM curve. The intersection of the IS and LM curves will provide us once more with the solution value of the system.

Now suppose that the expected rate of price increase is equal to zero so that $i^0 = r^0$. In such a case the equilibrium of the system is depicted by point E^0 with the corresponding values $i = r = r^0$ and $Y = Y^0$ (see figure 7.A.3). Also suppose that these values happened to yield full-employment equilibrium. Now suppose that the community anticipates a positive rate of inflation equal to $(\Delta P^e/P)^0$. This implies that the IS curve will rotate to the right from $IS_{(r)}$ to $IS_{(i)}$. However, in view of the fact that the introduction of the expected price change does not affect the LM curve, the new equilibrium will occur at point E^1 associated with an income level equal to Y^1. Notice now that the new equilibrium level of income Y^1 is greater than the full-employment level and, therefore, this generates the need for a price increase to restore equilibrium at full employment. In turn, the rising price level will result in a shift of the LM curve to the left as the real money supply decreases. The price rise will continue until the LM curve intersects the IS curve once more at the full-employment level of income.

In figure 7.A.3 this is shown by point E^2 which is given by the intersection of $IS_{(i)}$ and LM. It is worth observing that while once more $Y^0 = Y_F$, the equilibrium interest has increased to $i = r^0 + (1 + r^0)(\Delta P^e/P)^0$. Notice also that the price level which corresponds to the new equilibrium E^2 is equal to P^1 which is higher than P^0 by the amount of the expected price change, i.e., $(\Delta P^e)^0$. Thus, one of the conditions of the new equilibrium is that prices increase at the same rate as expected. In other words, existing inflationary expectations result in a once-and-for-all increase in prices, but certainly not in a continuous inflation.

To be sure, if the expected rate of inflation remains at $(\Delta P^e/P)^0$, then equation 7.A.10 clearly shows that the IS curve will remain at the position $IS_{(i)}$ and, consequently, as long as the monetary authorities do not alter the money supply the economy will not be subjected to any further price increase. Suppose, for example, that prices do not change and now assume that the economic actors reverse their expectations and anticipate price stability, i.e., $(\Delta P^e/P)^1 = 0$. Then the IS curve will shift to the left (see point E^3) and as long as the monetary authorities do not interfere, a deflationary process will ensue, shifting thereby the LM^1 curve to the right until the economy comes once more to rest at the point E^0.

CHAPTER 8

The Effects of the Extreme Properties of the Demand-for-Money Function

8.1 Introduction

We now turn to an investigation of the extreme properties of the demand-for-money function. As we saw in the previous chapters, the basis for the derivation of an upward-sloping LM curve was the assumption that the demand for money is negatively related to the rate of interest. However, this view is not shared by all economists. There has been considerable debate both about the specification and the arguments to be included in the demand-for-money function, and the elasticity and the stability of this relationship.

The stakes involved in this debate, as we shall shortly see, are extremely high. The divergence of opinions has a very important bearing on the exercise of stabilization policies and the relative potency of the various stabilization tools. This chapter will present briefly the fundamentals of the two generic and competing theories, which traditionally are classified under the broad labels of classical and Keynesian views of the demand-for-money function.

8.2 The Quantity Theory Approach

Initially, economists of the classical tradition did not introduce the role of money in their model by casting it, as we did, in terms of its demand and supply. Instead, they introduced money by using the so-called equation of exchange. But in spite of its original rationale, the equation of exchange can be readily transformed into a legitimate theory of the demand for money capable of being subjected to empirical verification.

Irving Fisher, whose name is associated with this approach, started his analysis by using a simple identity. His view can best be illustrated by the means of an example.

Suppose that a vintner from Sonoma and a baker from San Francisco meet each other on their way to Los Angeles where they both plan to sell their products which they carry along with them in their buggies. Let us also suppose that only the baker carries money, say, $1, and that the value of the product each of them has for sale amounts to $50.

Let us now watch this couple during their trip. On the way, after the baker has exhausted his water supply, he asks for some wine from the vintner, who immediately agrees to sell him a dollar's worth to quench his thirst. Later, the vintner depletes his food provisions and asks for some bread from the baker, who proceeds to sell him a dollar's worth. These rounds go on until by the end of their journey to Los Angeles neither of them has anything to sell, but both have had a very good time.

Let us now try to see the economic implications of their action. The sum of the sales is equal to the value of wine and bread. So, if we designate by P_w and P_b the prices of wine and bread respectively and by T_w and T_b their corresponding quantities sold, then the total value of transactions can be written as:

$$P_w T_w + P_b T_b.$$

The above value of transactions ($100) was carried out by the means of $1, which changed hands several times (in our example, 100 times). Without any loss of generality and according to the definition we have used for the money supply, this $1 constitutes the money supply of this community of two, i.e., $M_s = 1$. If we write V_t for the velocity of circulation, the number of times this $1 changed hands during the process of transactions, we arrive at the following fundamental identity:

$$M_s V_t \equiv P_w T_w + P_b T_b. \tag{8.2.1}$$

Having derived identity 8.2.1, it takes only one step further to generalize its meaning to cover the economy as a whole. Suppose that we define T to designate the volume of transactions, in constant prices, which takes place within a period of time, say one year, in the economy, and P to be an implicit price deflator (an index number). Then the above identity can be rewritten as:

$$M_s V_t \equiv PT. \tag{8.2.2}$$

Notice that we have already emphasized the fact that both 8.2.1 and 8.2.2 are in effect identities. The meaning of this is that they are both always true—regardless of the supply of money (M_s), the velocity of circulation (V_t) will assume a value that will accommodate these expressions. In other words, one may very well argue that both expressions are only the *definition* of the velocity of circulation, i.e.,

$$V_t \equiv \frac{PT}{M_s}.$$

(8.2.3)

In terns of our example, since $M_s = \$1$ and $PT = \$100$, it follows that $V_t = 100$; should the money supply increase to $2, the velocity of circulation would automatically assume the value of 50 so that both sides of 8.2.2 would be equal.

Thus, expression 8.2.2 is not a theory and consequently it cannot tell us anything about behavior. To make any progress we need to introduce some assumptions about the variables involved. To this end, Fisher assumed first that the quantity of money in 8.2.2 is determined independently of any other variable; in other words, M_s, according to Fisher, is an exogenous variable. Furthermore, assuming full employment of the economy, T, the volume of transactions, is also considered as a constant. If now we also presume that at each point in time V_t can be taken as a constant, then we can readily establish the proposition that the level of prices is a function of the supply of money, i.e.:

$$P = f(M_s).$$

(8.2.4)

In particular, according to 8.2.2, the relation 8.2.4 should imply that the level of prices, P, is exclusively determined by and is proportional to the money supply. By assuming that V_t and T are constants, the equation of exchange becomes a theory, the so-called quantity theory of money, which attempts to explain the determination of the price level. Under these circumstances identity 8.2.2 can be rewritten as:

$$M_s V_t^0 = PT^0$$

(8.2.5)

where the superscripts have been added to indicate that the corresponding quantities are considered constants. The reader can now see how equation 8.2.4 can be derived via equation 8.2.5 to express P as a function of the money supply, i.e.,

$$P = \alpha M_s$$

(8.2.6)

where

$$\alpha \equiv \frac{V_t^0}{T^0}.$$

By introducing the above assumptions the expression 8.2.2 ceases to be a simple truism or identity defining the velocity of circulation and becomes instead a legitimate theory of the determination of the price level. That is, it claims that for any given value of M_s there is one and only one value of P which makes the statements 8.2.5 and 8.2.6 true; it further suggests that any change in the money supply will be accompanied by a proportionally equal change in the price level. From another point of view, given our assumptions, the price level will be adjusted in such a way that the supply of money will be equal to the demand for money. That is, if we start from an equilibrium and the supply of money increases, this increase will end up in the market place and, since the economy is already at full employment, the price level will have to increase proportionately so that the demand for money will increase by an amount equal to the increase in the money supply.

The reader familiar with the theory of prices will find that the quantity theory relation between P and M_s is not quite in agreement with the explanation advocated by price theory. Indeed, from price theory we know that the price of a commodity changes only as a result of a change in the relation between its demand and supply. The quantity theory of money, on the other hand, claims that the money supply as well as its changes are very important in the determination of the price level. But since we know that the price of a commodity will increase if there is an excess demand for it, and since the quantity theory claims a causal relation between the quantity of money and prices, it follows that to be valid it must also show how an increase in the quantity of money necessarily generates an excess demand in all markets, thereby leading to a general increase in the price level. It should be noticed that the existence of an excess of demand over supply in all commodities markets is only a *necessary* condition for a general rise in prices. For the establishment of the quantity theory of prices, we also need the assumption of full employment.

To appreciate this, suppose that the money supply increases. Assuming that V_t remains constant, the product PT will have to increase. But, since T is fixed at T^0 due to the assumption of full employment, the only way the product PT^0 can increase is via an increase in P. One explanation for this goes as follows: if the money supply increases, the economic units of the community will find that they have more cash balances than they need. As a result, they will attempt to exchange them with marketable debt claims. This will lead to an increase in the market value of these debt claims, which means that the rate of interest will fall, and consequently, provided that investment is sensitive to fluctuations of the rate of interest, the demand for investment will increase. If then the economy is fully employed, the competition for the available supply of the given output will result in an increase of prices, equal (in percentage terms) to the increase in the money supply.

If, on the other hand, there are available idle resources, the increase in the demand for investment will lead to an increase in output as well as in prices unless the supply of goods is perfectly price-inelastic. Therefore, a change in the money supply may or may not be associated with a proportional change in the price level, depending on whether the economy is fully employed or not. Thus, the effect of an increase in the money supply on the effective demand and consequently on prices depends entirely on the position of the economy when it accepts the injection of the money supply. This is all one needs to say in regard to the relation between changes in the stock of money and price level. Under these circumstances it would be more legitimate to drop the superscript from the volume of transactions and write equation 8.2.5 as:

$$M_s V_t^0 = PT \tag{8.2.7}$$

or

$$M_s = kPT \tag{8.2.8}$$

where

$$k \equiv \frac{1}{V_t^0}.$$

From equation 8.2.8 we see that the product (PT)—i.e., the value of the volume of transactions (T)—is proportional to the money supply. This is in agreement with what the above analysis has suggested. Notice, however, that these results depend on two crucial assertions; first, that a change in the money supply will force a change in the rate of interest and second, that a change in the rate of interest will induce a change in the demand for investment.

Although the version of the quantity theory of money we have presented so far may appear unconnected with any theory of the demand for money, it is nevertheless only one step removed from becoming one. Equation 8.2.8 could be considered the combination of a demand-for-money function in which the demand for money depends on (in fact is proportional to) the value of transactions (i.e., PT), and an equilibrium condition equating the demand for with the supply of money, namely:

$$M_d = kPT \tag{8.2.9}$$

and

$$M_d = M_s \tag{8.2.10}$$

where k is the factor of proportionality. Combination of 8.2.9 with 8.2.10 produces equation 8.2.8 above.

Now to the extent that in the short run the relation between NNP and total transactions (turnover) T remains stable, one may write that

$$M_d = l_1 PY \qquad (8.2.11)$$

which can be combined once more with the equilibrium condition 8.2.10 to give

$$M_s = l_1 PY \qquad (8.2.12)$$

where l_1 is defined to be the inverse of income velocity (i.e., $l_1 \equiv 1/V$) as opposed to the transaction velocity. In other words, V is defined as the number of times a unit of money changes hands in transactions involving only *final* goods and services.

Thus, from equation 8.2.11 we can see that the quantity theory can be cast in terms of the demand for and supply of money. However, regardless of the way one wants to cast the theory (through the velocity approach or through the demand for cash balances approach), the reader should keep in mind that the crucial assumption of the theory is that V_t, or V, are constant quantities. To what extent the assumption squares with the actual behavior of the economy is an empirical question which can be resolved only with reference to the data. Tests of this hypothesis will be reserved until chapter 15.

Recapitulating, the use of the transaction or quantity theory of money approach to monetary theory leads to the establishment of a causal relationship between the demand for money and the level of the money value of total transaction, PT. In addition, by assuming that the total volume of transaction bears, at least in the short run, a stable relationship with its corresponding level of value-added (NNP), the demand for money can be expressed as a function of NNP in current prices (PY). In fact, regardless of whether it is PT or PY on which we assume the demand for money depends, their relation with M_d appears to be one of proportionality.

It is also interesting to notice that equations 8.2.9 and 8.2.11 are not at variance with the concepts developed in chapter 6, since we can divide both equations by the price level and express the demand for real cash balances as a function of real income, Y, or the real volume of transactions, T, i.e.:

$$\frac{M_d}{P} = kT \qquad (8.2.13)$$

and

$$\frac{M_d}{P} = l_1 Y. \tag{8.2.14}$$

From the above two equations, one can see that what the quantity theory of money advocates is that the relation between real money and income is governed principally by the necessity of using money to effect transactions. In fact, this relation in some sense appears to be a technical one. As money income (PY) increases, more money (M_d) is required to facilitate the transactions which are implied by this higher level of money income.

The above version of the quantity theory of money is closely related to, but should not be confused with, another theory of the demand for money advocated and taught by a group of Cambridge University economists. In particular, Alfred Marshall, A. C. Pigou, Dennis Robertson, and Keynes himself, before the publication of his *General Theory*, were the primary proponents of a theory which came to be known as the "Cambridge" or the "cash balances" approach to monetary economics.

This group of economists did not start, like Fisher, by asking what determines the amount of money necessary to facilitate a given volume of transactions within a certain period, but rather by investigating the factors which determine the amount of money the individual economic units desire to hold. Thus, this school of thought addresses itself directly to the problem of the demand for money and avoids the roundabout method we developed earlier.

Although we shall postpone a more detailed discussion of this view and its modern version, it suffices to say that the proponents of this school argue that, *ceteris paribus,* the demand for money in nominal terms is proportional to money income. Thus, they write the demand for money as

$$M_d = l_1 PY$$

which, once more, if combined with the equilibrium condition of the money market:

$$M_d = M_s$$

results in:

$$M_s = l_1 PY$$

from which we can immediately derive that

$$M_s \frac{1}{l_1} = PY$$

or

$$M_s V = PY$$

which looks very much like Fisher's approach.

Thus, according to the above views, the demand for money does not depend on the rate of interest. Indeed, since quantity theorists argue that the only motive for holding money is to lubricate transactions, it follows that rational behavior would dictate that any residual amount of money not needed for transaction purposes should be converted into income-yielding marketable debt claims.

The above thoughts are colorfully summarized by Patinkin as follows:

> In its cash balance version—associated primarily with the names of Walras, Marshall, Wicksell and Pigou—neoclassical theory assumed that, for their convenience, individuals wish to hold a certain proportion, K, of the real volume of their transaction, T, in the form of real money balances. The demand for these balances thus equals KT. Correspondingly, the demand for nominal money balances is KPT, where P is the price level of commodities transacted. The equating of this demand to the supply of money, M, then produced the famous Cambridge equation $M = KPT$. In the transactions version—associated primarily with the names of Newcomb and Fisher—the velocity of circulation, V, replaced its reciprocal, K, to produce the equally famous equation of exchange, $MV = PT$. These equations were the parade-grounds on which neoclassical economists then put the classical quantity theory of money through its paces.[1]

From the above analysis, it follows that the demand for money implied by the quantity theory is at variance with the view presented in chapter 6, since it ignores not only the fact that there is a cost associated with the transaction of securities but also that economic units may choose to hold cash balances due to what we have called the speculative motive.

By following the reasoning of the quantity theory we have arrived in effect at a case in which speculative demand is always zero regardless of the value of the rate of interest, i.e.:

$$\frac{M_{s,d}}{P} = g(r) = 0 \qquad \text{for any } r > 0.$$

Thus, we may say that this includes one of the extreme values we mentioned in chapter 6, i.e.:

---

[1] See D. Patinkin, *Money, Interest and Prices,* 2d ed. (New York: Harper and Row, 1965), p. 163.

$$\frac{M_{s,d}}{P} = g(r) = 0 \qquad \text{if } r > r_u.$$

Before we proceed to analyze the effects of such a specification in the demand for money function it will be worth our while to summarize our analysis. To do this let us write the demand for money according to the classical theory as:

$$\frac{M_d}{P} = l_1 Y - 0 \cdot r. \tag{8.2.15}$$

Notice that in the above equation the coefficient of the rate of interest is equal to zero, to indicate the fact that according to this view fluctuations of the rate of interest per se will not change the desired amount of real cash balances. If we now define $E_{m_d,Y}$ and $E_{m_d,r}$ to be the elasticities of real cash balances with respect to real income and the rate of interest respectively, we find that we have made the assertion that $E_{m_d,Y} = 1$ and $E_{m_d,r} = 0.$[2]

8.3 The Classical Range of the Money-Demand Schedule

Consider again the model consisting of equations 7.2.1–7.2.7, rewritten here:

$$Y = C + I + G \tag{8.3.1}$$

$$C = a + bY_d \tag{8.3.2}$$

$$I = g_0 - g_1 r \tag{8.3.3}$$

$$Y_d \equiv Y - T \tag{8.3.4}$$

$$T = -t_0 + t_1 Y \tag{8.3.5}$$

$$\frac{M_d}{P} = l_0 + l_1 Y - l_2 r \tag{8.3.6}$$

$$\frac{M_s}{P} = \frac{M_d}{P}. \tag{8.3.7}$$

---

[2]The reader should notice that $E_{m_d,Y}$ and $E_{m_d,r}$ are defined as:

$$E_{m_d,Y} = \frac{\Delta m_d / m_d}{\Delta Y / Y} \quad \text{and} \quad E_{m_d,r} = \frac{\Delta m_d / m_d}{\Delta r / r}$$

where:

$$m_d \equiv M_d / P \text{ and } \Delta m_d \equiv \Delta M_d / P.$$

As before, we assume that $G = G^0$, $M_s = M_s^0$ and $P = P^0$. In addition, in the classical case both l_0 and l_2 are equal to zero.

Combining equations 8.3.1–8.3.5, we derive the equation of the IS curve, which appears to be the same as before, i.e.:

$$[1 - b(1 - t_1)]Y + g_1 r = a + g_0 + b t_0 + G^0. \qquad (8.3.8)$$

On the other hand, combination of equations 8.3.6–8.3.7 yields the equation of the LM curve, i.e.:

$$l_1 Y = \frac{M_s^0}{P^0}. \qquad (8.3.9)$$

Thus, although the insertion of the quantity theory of money leaves the equation of IS unchanged, the equation of the LM curve changes substantially.

We may next use equation 8.3.9 to solve for income in terms of exogenous variables and parameters:

$$Y^0 = \frac{1}{l_1} \cdot \frac{M_s^0}{P^0}. \qquad (8.3.10)$$

Substituting the value of income from 8.3.10 into 8.3.8 and solving for the rate of interest, we find that:

$$r^0 = \frac{a + g_0 + b t_0 + G^0}{g_1} - \frac{[1 - b(1 - t_1)]}{g_1 l_1} \cdot \frac{M_s^0}{P^0}. \qquad (8.3.11)$$

Equations 8.3.10 and 8.3.11 provide us with the equilibrium levels of income and the rate of interest.

The reader should observe that while the equilibrium value of the rate of interest is certainly affected by the exogenous variables and parameters which appear in both the expenditure and monetary sectors, the equilibrium level of income is affected only by the real money supply. To appreciate the meaning of this observation, examine the qualitative and quantitative implications of changes in the exogenous variables of the model.

Suppose that the government changes its own level of expenditures from G^0 to G^1 ($G^1 > G^0$). From equation 8.3.10 we see that the level of income will not change at all since G does not appear in this equation. Thus we can write that

$$\Delta Y = 0 \, \Delta G. \qquad (8.3.12)$$

On the other hand, substituting the new value of G into equation 8.3.11 and subtracting it from the original expression, we find that

$$\Delta r = \frac{1}{g_1} \Delta G. \tag{8.3.13}$$

Thus, under these circumstances while the change in government expenditures results in an increase in the rate of interest, it fails miserably in changing the level of income.

Next, suppose that the government changes the tax rate from t_1 to t_1' ($t_1' < t_1$). Going once more through the usual motions, we find that

$$\Delta Y = 0 \, \Delta t_1 \tag{8.3.14}$$

and

$$\Delta r = \left(\frac{b}{g_1 l_1}\right)\left(\frac{M_s^0}{P^0}\right) \Delta t_1 \tag{8.3.15}$$

which, given the value of income from 8.3.10, can be rewritten as

$$\Delta r = \frac{b}{l_1} Y^0 \, \Delta t_1. \tag{8.3.16}$$

Thus, once more we see that attempts of the government to increase the equilibrium level of income via a decrease in the tax rate would result only in an increase in the rate of interest, leaving the equilibrium level of income unchanged. Therefore, the exercise of fiscal policy under these circumstances will not result in a change in the equilibrium level of income, but only in a change in the corresponding rate of interest.

On the other hand, suppose that the government attempts to change the equilibrium values of the rate of interest and income via changes in the nominal supply of money. Assume that the nominal money supply changes from M_s^0 to M_s^1 ($M_s^1 > M_s^0$). Substituting this new value of M_s into equations 8.3.10 and 8.3.11 and subtracting them from the original expressions, we find:

$$\Delta Y = \frac{1}{l_1}\frac{\Delta M_s}{P^0} \tag{8.3.17}$$

and

$$\Delta r = -\frac{[1 - b(1 - t_1)]}{g_1 l_1} \cdot \frac{\Delta M_s}{P^0}. \tag{8.3.18}$$

Thus, an increase (decrease) in the nominal money supply results in an increase (decrease) in the equilibrium level of income and a decrease (increase) in the equilibrium rate of interest.

We now illustrate the above thoughts graphically. Notice first that the proposition that the demand for money is insensitive to fluctuations

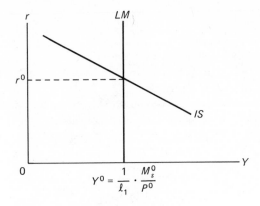

Figure 8.3.1   *The Classical View*

of the rate of interest results in a vertical LM curve, designating the fact that the equality of the demand for money with its supply can occur at only one level of income. This can be seen from the equation of the LM curve which assumes the form:

$$Y^0 = \frac{1}{l_1} \cdot \frac{M_s^0}{P^0}. \tag{8.3.19}$$

The graph of the above equation is depicted in figure 8.3.1. From this diagram we see that the monetary sector is at equilibrium at one and only one level of income regardless of what value the rate of interest assumes.[3] To find the solution values of Y and r, we combine the LM curve with the corresponding IS curve, which, as we have seen, remains the same as in the previous chapter.

The changes in government expenditures, autonomous consumption (a), investment (g_0) or government transfers (t_0) are depicted, as we know, by lateral shifts of the IS curve. For reasons of comparison, figure 8.3.2 depicts the results of a shift of the IS curve due to any of the above reasons under the two alternative assumptions regarding the interest elasticity of the demand for money. Panel (a) illustrates the general case (see figure 7.2.1) in which the demand for money is sensitive to fluctuations of the rate of interest; panel (b) depicts the case of the

---

[3]The careful reader will notice that the LM schedule is based on the presumption of a fixed price level. As the price level varies, the LM schedule drawn in figure 8.3.1 will shift. We have "frozen" the price level in order to simplify the present analysis as much as possible; however, we shall relax this unrealistic assumption in our discussion of the labor market (chapter 9).

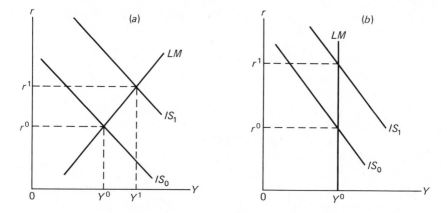

Figure 8.3.2 *The Effect of a Shift in the IS Schedule: The Classical View Contrasted to the Intermediate Case*

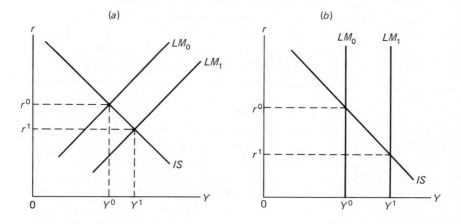

Figure 8.3.3 *The Effect of a Shift in the LM Schedule: The Classical View Contrasted to the Intermediate Case*

quantity theory of money, according to which the demand for money is insensitive to fluctuations of the rate of interest. These two diagrams repeat once more the story equations 8.3.12 snd 8.3.14 have already told us.[4] The effectiveness of monetary policy under the quantity-theory approach is examined in figure 8.3.3. When the monetary authorities

---

[4]Exercise: Use a diagrammatic approach to illustrate the effects of a change in the tax rate under the alternative assumptions with respect to the demand for money.

change the nominal money supply, this forces the LM curve to shift while the IS curve remains at the same position. In figure 8.3.3, panel (a) describes the case of the previous chapter, whereas panel (b) depicts the case of the quantity theory of money. Notice that in the latter case, income rises by an amount equal to the full shift in the LM schedule, whereas a smaller change occurs in the system described by panel (a).

Comparing panels (a) and (b) in figures 8.3.2 and 8.3.3, we can see the vast difference associated with these two views. According to the above analysis, the assumption that the parameters l_0 and l_2 of equation 8.3.6 are equal to zero, reflecting the view of the quantity theory of money, leaves fiscal policy with no teeth whatsoever. Economists who believe that the demand for money behaves according to the hypothesis of the quantity theory of money do not have much use for fiscal policy. Instead, the same economists would argue that the only potent stabilization tool to be used is monetary policy.

The reader may very well ask the reasons for the resulting differences in the effectiveness of these two stabilization policies. First, consider an expansionary monetary policy like the one shown in figure 8.3.3.[5] As the money supply increases, say, via an open market operation, the excess holdings of money are channeled into the government securities market, thus driving their prices up and interest rates down. The fall in interest rates, in turn, stimulates investment. And, finally, the rise in investment produces an expansion in the level of income. Equilibrium in the money market is reattained when money demand rises to equality with money supply. In the general case shown in panel (a) of figure 8.3.3, falling interest rates induce people to demand more cash balances for speculative purposes, and the rise in the level of income requires more money to be held for transaction balances. But in the quantity-theory version depicted by panel (b), there is no speculative demand for money. Thus, the whole burden of the adjustment falls on transaction demand. As long as the new money supply exceeds transaction demand, the rate of interest will keep falling, thereby causing investment to rise and income to grow. The new money-market equilibrium is reached only when income expands enough to absorb the increment in the money supply into transactions balances. Thus, the quantity theory leads to a greater potency for monetary policy than is implied by the case of panel (a).[6]

---

[5] Refer to the appendix to chapter 6 for a review of the instruments of monetary policy.

[6] For a broader interpretation of this mechanism, as put forth by the modern monetarist school of thought, see chapter 15 and appendix 15.A.

Notice that the effectiveness of monetary policy, as indicated by both panel (a) and panel (b), depends on two critical assumptions: first, that an increase in the money supply will force interest rates downward (i.e., that people will use the excess money to purchase interest-bearing assets); and second, that investment is sensitive to fluctuations in the rate of interest.

Fiscal policy, unlike its monetary counterpart, affects economic activity directly by altering the level of government expenditures on goods and services and/or the level of tax rates. However, despite this direct influence on the demand for goods and services, panel (b) of figure 8.3.2 shows that its value as a stabilization tool is nil. To illustrate, suppose that the government wishes to increase its spending on goods and services in an attempt to increase the level of income. If this increase in spending were financed by increasing the public debt, then the rate of interest would increase, thereby discouraging an equal amount of investment. The final result would be associated with a redistribution of total demand between the private sector and government, while the level of income would remain the same.[7] Thus, this increase in G would be associated with a higher rate of interest but not income. We assume here that the rate of interest will in effect rise at such a level that the resulting decrease in investment will be exactly equal to the increase in government spending.

In order to illustrate this point, suppose that the increase in the rate of interest is such that the decrease in investment is not equal to the increase in the governmental spending, i.e., ($|\Delta I| < |\Delta G|$). In this case total demand has increased and consequently the level of income will have to increase. Given the absence of speculative balances, this last increase will generate a proportional increase in the transactions demand for money. In view of the fact that the nominal money supply remains constant, this increase in the demand for cash balances will force the individual economic units to liquidate government securities.

---

[7] Economic literature contains a number of arguments concerning the adverse effect of government expenditures on private investment. One of the general terms used currently to describe this phenomenon is "the crowding-out effect." But "crowding out" connotes many things to many people. John Hicks (through his IS-LM analysis) shows some effect on investment even in the intermediate range of the LM. The classics hypothesized a complete cancellation of the expansionary effects of increased government expenditures. And, more recently, the monetarist school has argued that the impact of a change in government expenditures may be weakened through the effects of financing these expenditures on capital markets (see chapter 15 and appendix 15.A). In subsequent discussions, we shall use the term "crowding-out effect" to denote a completely offsetting change in private investment—that is, the special case where income does not rise as a result of expanded government expenditures.

The increase in the supply of securities, however, will press down their price, increasing the rate of interest. This last increase will result in a discouragement of investment. The above process will continue until the rate of interest rises enough to choke off an amount of investment equal to the increase in the governmental spending, for it is only then that transaction demand can fall back to its original level, thereby again equaling money supply.

Let us illustrate the above ideas with the help of a numerical example. Consider the following system.

$$Y = C + I + G \tag{8.3.20}$$

$$C = 30 + .8Y_d \tag{8.3.21}$$

$$I = 300 - 400r \tag{8.3.22}$$

$$Y_d \equiv Y - T \tag{8.3.23}$$

$$T = -50 + .25Y \tag{8.3.24}$$

$$M_d/P = .15Y \tag{8.3.25}$$

$$M_s/P = M_d/P. \tag{8.3.26}$$

Furthermore, assume that the exogenous variables take on the values:

$$G = 446, \ M_s = 300 \text{ and } P = 1.$$

From equations 8.3.25 and 8.3.26 we can determine immediately that $Y = \$2,000$ billion. Next, substituting for Y in equation 8.3.24, we find that the tax revenues of the government will be equal to $T = \$450$ and by using the definition of disposable income, 8.3.23, we can determine that $Y_d = \$1,550$. Having determined disposable income, one can solve for the level of consumption expenditures, which is $C = \$1,270$. Consequently, from the equilibrium condition, 8.3.20, we find that $I = \$284$. Substituting now the value of I into equation 8.3.22, we find that the equilibrium rate of interest is equal to 4%. Table 8.3.1 provides a summary of the solution of the system.

Column 1 gives the equilibrium values of the system described above. On the other hand, column 2 describes the new solution values of the system on the assumption that the government expenditures on goods and services have increased by $4 billion, i.e., $\Delta G = 4$. Following the procedure we just traced out, we find that the only differences to be observed are a decrease in the government surplus from $4 billion to zero, and an increase in the rate of interest from 4% to 5%. This last increase in the rate of interest produces a decrease in the level of investment which is equal to the change in the expenditures of the government, i.e., $4 billion.

Table 8.3.1. *A Numerical Example*

Variables	1	2 $\Delta G = 4$	3 $\Delta M_s = 3$
Y	2000	2000	2020
T	450	450	455
Y_d	1550	1550	1565
C	1270	1270	1282
I	284	280	292
r	.04	.05	.02
M_d	300	300	303
M_s	300	300	303
P	1	1	1
G	446	450	446
S	280	280	283
T − G	4	0	9

This result could be obtained immediately by considering once more equation 8.3.13, which describes the change in the rate of interest due to a small change in government expenditures, i.e.:

$$\Delta r = \frac{1}{g_1} \Delta G. \tag{8.3.27}$$

On the other hand, from the investment equation

$$I = g_0 - g_1 r$$

we can obtain that

$$\Delta I = -g_1 \, \Delta r. \tag{8.3.28}$$

Substituting now the value of Δr from 8.3.27 into 8.3.28, we find how much the investment will decrease due to an increase in government expenditures by ΔG, i.e.:

$$\Delta I = -\frac{g_1}{g_1}\Delta G$$

or

$$\Delta I = -\Delta G. \tag{8.3.29}$$

In other words, equation 8.3.27 gives us a change in the rate of interest which will generate a change in investment which will exactly counteract the increase of governmental expenditures in question.

Finally, column 3 of table 8.3.1 summarizes the solution values of the variables on the assumption that the nominal money supply, M_s, increases from \$300 billion to \$303 billion. The differences between the two views presented above can now be seen easily by comparing columns 2 and 3 with column 1.

In conclusion, if the quantity theory of money, as analyzed above, is an accurate description of the behavior of the demand for money, then, as the advocates of this view believe, the only effective stabilization policy is monetary policy. Fiscal policy is considered a sterile exercise in frustration, since it affects only the distribution but not the level of total demand.

8.4 The Liquidity Trap

We now turn to analyze the other extreme case of the demand for money, i.e., the case in which its speculative segment becomes infinitely elastic when the rate of interest assumes the lower value of its "normal" range.

In chapter 6 we argued that at this point the market does not have any bullish attitude left; instead, everybody has become a bear since there is a convergence of opinion that the next change in the rate of interest will be upwards. Thus, everybody is willing to hold cash; i.e., everyone would like to dispose of his bonds at this very price. Due to this convergence of opinion the demand for money becomes perfectly elastic with respect to the rate of interest. The result of this attitude is that the rate of interest cannot decline even if the monetary authorities manipulate the money supply. Suppose that the monetary authorities seek to increase the equilibrium level of income and for this they attempt to decrease the rate of interest by engaging in open market operations. Under normal circumstances, this increased demand for government securities would result in an increase in their price, producing immediately a lower rate of interest. However, due to prevailing market psychology everybody

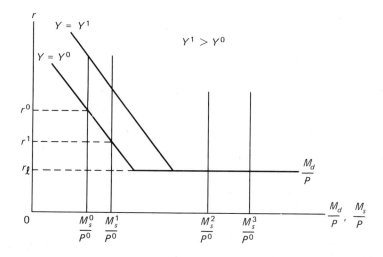

Figure 8.4.1 *The Liquidity Trap*

wants to sell; therefore, the supply of consols can very easily accommodate the increase in their demand caused by the monetary authorities. Thus, the urgency to sell is so high that the price of consols remains the same, implying that the rate of interest is pegged at that very level. And since the rate of interest remains constant, the level of investment does not change. The result is that the monetary authorities are completely unable to increase the equilibrium level of income. This case is illustrated in figure 8.4.1.

To be consistent with previous chapters, the schedules of the demand for money have been drawn linear with a kink at the rate r_l (for its definition see chapter 6). Notice that, given the price level, an increase in the real money supply from M_s^0/P^0 to M_s^1/P^0 results in a decrease in the rate of interest from r^0 to r^1. However, if the increase in the nominal money supply happens to correspond to the segment of the demand for cash balances which is characterized by an infinite interest elasticity, then this action by monetary authorities does not result in any change in the rate of interest. Depending on the sensitivity of investment to fluctuations of the rate of interest, the monetary authorities may succeed in the first case in their attempt to increase the level of income, but in the second case their policy is doomed to fail since their action cannot induce a decline in the rate of interest. In other words, the economy is trapped at whatever the level of income happens to be at that point in time. This rather startling result was first suggested by Keynes and it is known as the liquidity trap case.

Let us now see the implications of such a behavior of the demand for money on the properties of the system we have been using, namely:

$$Y = C + I + G \tag{8.4.1}$$

$$C = a + bY_d \tag{8.4.2}$$

$$I = g_0 - g_1 r \tag{8.4.3}$$

$$Y_d \equiv Y - T \tag{8.4.4}$$

$$T = -t_0 + t_1 Y \tag{8.4.5}$$

$$M_d/P = l_0 + l_1 Y - l_2 r \tag{8.4.6}$$

$$M_d/P = M_s/P. \tag{8.4.7}$$

The above system is the same as the one used in chapter 7 and needs no further explanation. In addition to our assumption about the values of G, M_s and P, we shall also assume that the coefficient of the rate of interest in equation 8.4.6 is very large. Thus, while in the previous section we assumed that $l_0 = l_2 = 0$, here we assume that $l_2 \to \infty$.

In chapter 7 we found that the equilibrium values for Y and r were (see equations 7.2.13 and 7.2.14):

$$Y^0 = \cfrac{1}{1 - b(1 - t_1) + g_1 \cfrac{l_1}{l_2}} \left[a + g_0 + bt_0 + G^0 - \frac{g_1}{l_2} \left(l_0 - \frac{M_s^0}{P^0} \right) \right] \tag{8.4.8}$$

and

$$r^0 = \cfrac{l_1 [a + g_0 + bt_0 + G^0] + [1 - b(1 - t_1)] \left[l_0 - \dfrac{M_s^0}{P^0} \right]}{l_2 \left[1 - b(1 - t_1) + g_1 \dfrac{l_1}{l_2} \right]}. \tag{8.4.9}$$

We also found that a change in the government expenditures from G^0 to G^1 ($G^1 > G^0$) was associated with the following changes in the equilibrium values of Y and r (see equations 7.2.17 and 7.2.18):

$$\Delta Y = \cfrac{1}{\left[1 - b(1 - t_1) + g_1 \dfrac{l_1}{l_2} \right]} \Delta G \tag{8.4.10}$$

and

$$\Delta r = \frac{l_1/l_2}{\left[1 - b(1 - t_1) + g_1 \dfrac{l_1}{l_2}\right]} \Delta G. \tag{8.4.11}$$

Notice, however, that our assumption in regard to l_2, i.e., $l_2 \to \infty$, implies that the ratio $l_1/l_2 \to 0$ and consequently the above expressions can be rewritten as:

$$\Delta Y = \frac{1}{1 - b(1 - t_1)} \Delta G$$

or

$$\Delta Y = k' \Delta G \tag{8.4.12}$$

and

$$\Delta r = \frac{l_1}{l_2} k' \ \Delta G$$

which is reduced to

$$\Delta r = 0 \ \Delta G. \tag{8.4.13}$$

Similarly we find that:

$$\Delta Y = k' \Delta a \tag{8.4.14}$$

$$\Delta r = 0 \ \Delta a \tag{8.4.15}$$

$$\Delta Y = k' \Delta g_0 \tag{8.4.16}$$

$$\Delta r = 0 \ \Delta g_0 \tag{8.4.17}$$

$$\Delta Y = k' b \ \Delta t_0 \tag{8.4.18}$$

$$\Delta r = 0 \ \Delta t_0 \tag{8.4.19}$$

$$\Delta Y = bk' \ \Delta t_1 \tag{8.4.20}$$

$$\Delta r = 0 \ \Delta t_1 \tag{8.4.21}$$

where

$$k' \equiv \frac{1}{1 - b(1 - t_1)}$$

is the same multiplier as we found in chapter 5 under the assumption that the rate of interest was exogenous.

Thus, the assumption of a demand for money which is infinitely elastic with respect to the rate of interest (i.e., the assumption that l_2 approaches infinity at the current rate of interest) leads directly to two interrelated conclusions. First, any shift in the IS schedule—including those induced by a change in fiscal policy—leaves the rate of interest unchanged. Second, the insensitivity of the rate of interest causes income to change by the amount of the shift in the IS schedule. Or, in terms of our multiplier analysis of chapter 5, the equilibrium level of income changes by the *full* multiplier amount (e.g., k' times the change in G). This finding is in direct opposition to the corresponding results of the previous section. There we saw that the introduction of the quantity theory as a behavioral assumption about the demand for money leads to the conclusion that fiscal policy is incapable of changing the equilibrium level of income. Now, we find that the existence of the Keynesian liquidity trap leads to the conclusion that fiscal policy is extremely potent.

On the other hand, we have also found that in general, a change in the nominal money supply (see equations 7.2.27 and 7.2.28) produces the following changes in the equilibrium values of Y and r:

$$\Delta Y = \frac{g_1}{l_2} \left[\frac{1}{1 - b(1 - t_1) + g_1 \frac{l_1}{l_2}} \right] \frac{\Delta M_s}{P^0} \tag{8.4.22}$$

and

$$\Delta r = - \frac{[1 - b(1 - t_1)]}{l_2 \left[1 - b(1 - t_1) + g_1 \frac{l_1}{l_2} \right]} \frac{\Delta M_s}{P^0}. \tag{8.4.23}$$

But in the liquidity trap case, these expressions become:

$$\Delta Y = 0 \cdot \frac{\Delta M_s}{P^0} \tag{8.4.24}$$

and

$$\Delta r = 0 \cdot \frac{\Delta M_s}{P^0} \tag{8.4.25}$$

since again $l_2 \to \infty$.

Thus, as hypothesized earlier, we see that the Keynesian liquidity trap assumption leads to the conclusion that monetary policy is incapable of changing either the rate of interest or (as a result) the leve of income.

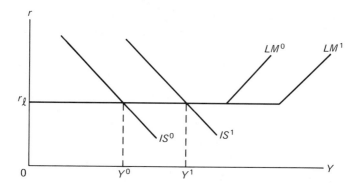

Figure 8.4.2   *The Impact of a Shift in the IS Schedule: The Liquidity Trap Case*

We may now illustrate the above ideas graphically. First, notice that once the liquidity trap is added to the demand for money schedule, the LM curve assumes a horizontal range at the interest rate r_l. This is shown in figure 8.4.2. To find the solution values of Y and r we combine the LM curve with the corresponding IS curve, which, as can be seen from the system 8.4.1–8.4.7, has not changed. Ignoring for the time being the upward-sloping part of LM, the solution of the problem is given in figure 8.4.2. A shift of the IS from IS^0 to IS^1 results in a change in income from Y^0 to Y^1 with no change in the corresponding rate of interest. On the other hand, a change in the nominal money supply leaves the horizontal part of the LM curve the same and consequently fails to change either of the two variables, Y or r.

8.5 Summary

Table 8.5.1 summarizes the above results. We consider three models, of which the so-called intermediate is the one used in chapter 7. Its main distinguishing characteristic is that the coefficient of the rate of interest in the equation of the demand for money is a positive but finite number (i.e., $0 < l_2 < \infty$).

The "Yes" or "No" listings denote the fact that a certain policy is or is not capable of having an impact on the equilibrium value of the variable in question. It is interesting to see how dramatic are the differences (in terms of the implied policies) between the classical and Keynesian models.

Table 8.5.1. *Summary View*

Model Variable → Policy ↓	Classical Model (The quantity theory) $l_0 = l_2 = 0$		Intermediate Model $0 < l_2 < \infty$		Keynesian Model $l_2 \to \infty$	
	ΔY	Δr	ΔY	Δr	ΔY	Δr
1. Monetary Policy	Yes Equation 8.3.17	Yes Equation 8.3.18	Yes Equation 7.2.27	Yes Equation 7.2.28	No Equation 8.4.24	No Equation 8.4.25
2. Fiscal Policy	No Equation 8.3.12	Yes Equation 8.3.13	Yes Equation 7.2.17	Yes Equation 7.2.18	Yes Equation 8.4.12	No Equation 8.4.13

Figure 8.5.1 combines all three models to correspond to the summary in table 8.5.1, depicting all the results of the analysis in this chapter. As can be seen, the LM curve has two kinks which separate in effect the main hypothesis about the behavior of the demand for money from its extreme cases. The liquidity-trap case holds at r_l, whereas the quantity theory is presumed to hold at values of the interest rate above r_u. The intermediate case is in effect for values of r between r_l and r_u.[8]

Consider LM^0 and its intersection with the various curves. In the case of the liquidity trap, since the rate of interest does not change, a shift in the IS curve has full multiplier effects. On the other hand, when IS intersects LM in its intermediate range, the result is that both income and the rate of interest increase. But since r increases, the change in income is tempered relative to the liquidity trap case. Finally, in the classical range, a shift in IS results only in an increase in the rate of interest, with no increase in the level of income. If now we increase the money supply, i.e., shift the LM from LM^0 to LM^1, we see that this does not affect the position of the liquidity trap. Thus, while such a shift results in an increase in income and a decrease in the rate of interest in both the classical and the intermediate ranges, it has no effect on either of these two variables in the liquidity trap case.

On this basis, therefore, a typical advocate of the classical school would prescribe only monetary policy while an extreme Keynesian

---

[8] Our explanation coincides with the quantity theory for $r > r_u$, and so we have drawn the LM schedule as a vertical line over the range. But keep in mind that the quantity theory, taken in its entirety, hypothesizes a vertical LM schedule at each and every interest rate.

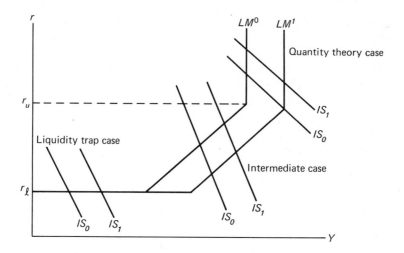

Figure 8.5.1 *The Impact of a Shift in the IS Schedule: The Three Alternative Cases*

economist would argue for fiscal policy in order to exert influence on the equilibrium level of income. Thus we see that the introduction of the rate of interest as a variable in the demand-for-money function by Keynes allowed fiscal policy to gain respectability along with monetary policy.

However, as was pointed out, the liquidity trap is not the only case in which monetary policy may fail to change the level of income. Indeed, even if the monetary authorities may succeed in lowering the rate of interest via an increase in the money stock of the community, income will not increase unless investment is sensitive to fluctuations in the rate of interest. In a schematic fashion the classical view can be summarized as follows.

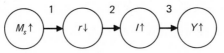

An increase in the money supply results in a decrease in the rate of interest which in turn is associated with an increase in the demand for investment which finally results in an increase in the equilibrium level of income.

To what extent this chain reaction will take place depends primarily on the strength of the various links. For example, the liquidity trap destroys the first link between M_s and r. Thus, a stimuli generated by an increase in M_s fails to reach the target variable Y. Now we see that if investment is not sensitive to fluctuations in the rate of interest, link 2 is destroyed with the same result.

In other words, if the interest elasticity of investment is equal to zero, then the IS curve is vertical and consequently any shift of the LM curve results in a change in the rate of interest, leaving the level of income the same. At this point we shall let the reader work through the graphical analysis of alternative policies in the context of an interest-inelastic investment schedule.

Suggested Further Reading

Ackley, G. *Macroeconomic Theory.* New York: Macmillan, 1961.

Fisher, I. *The Purchasing Power of Money.* 2d ed. New York: Macmillan, 1920.

Friedman, M. "The Quantity Theory of Money." *Encyclopedia of Social Sciences,* 1958.

Keynes, J. M. *The General Theory of Employment, Interest and Money.* New York: Harcourt, Brace, 1936, chaps. 13–15, 17.

———. *Tract on Monetary Reform.* London: Macmillan, 1923, chap. II.

Patinkin, D. "Price Flexibility and Full Employment." *American Economic Review* 38 (September 1948), 543–64. Reprinted in American Economic Association, *Readings in Monetary Theory.* Homewood, Ill.: R. D. Irwin, 1951, pp. 252–83.

Pigou, A. C. "The Value of Money." *Quarterly Journal of Economics* 32 (1917–18), 38–65. Reprinted in American Economic Association, *Readings in Monetary Theory.* Homewood, Ill.: R. D. Irwin, 1951, pp. 162–83.

Robertson, D. H. *Essays in Monetary Theory.* London: Staples Press Ltd., 1946.

Wicksell, K. *Lectures on Political Economy,* vol. II, *Money.* London: George Routledge and Sons Ltd., 1946.

CHAPTER 9

The Labor Market

9.1 Introduction

In the previous chapters, a two-sector model of the economy was developed and used to analyze the determination of general equilibrium. In the course of that analysis, we made the simplifying assumption that the price level was exogenous. This assumption—useful as it may have been for expositional purposes—was extremely unrealistic. Therefore, we shall now consider the price level as one of the endogenous variables of the economy. Once we do so, however, we are obligated to show the way in which the relationships in the economy interact to determine the general price level. In order to examine this interaction, we must introduce a third sector—the labor market—into our analysis.

There is also a more direct reason for examining the labor market: it allows us to consider the determination of the level of wages and employment. Up until this point, we have ignored wages almost completely, and have talked about employment only indirectly in our discussion of "full-employment" output. At that time, we did recognize some implicit relation between output and employment; however, the association was never specified explicitly. In this chapter, we shall begin by establishing a formal functional relation between output and employment under a set of simplifying assumptions. Then, with this relation as a "bridge" between the product market and the labor market, we shall be able to integrate the labor market into our model of the rest of the economy.

As one might expect, there are actually several views of the way in which the labor market operates. We shall examine some of the more familiar descriptions in this chapter and then incorporate each of these models into the general equilibrium model developed in the last chapter. This process will allow us to highlight an extremely important point:

the structure of the labor market is crucial in determining *all* of the values of the endogenous variables in the general model of the economy. That is, the characteristics of the labor market affect the way in which the economic system "settles" on equilibrium values of output, the general price level, and the amount of employment. Because of this phenomenon, the efficacy of alternative economic policies depends in part upon the structure of the labor market. In fact, it will be shown that many of the historical arguments concerning the need for overt economic policy and the shape this policy should take can be traced to disagreements over the workings of the labor market.

9.2 The Aggregate Production Function

In micro theory, a substantial amount of time is devoted to the discussion of the technological relation between inputs and output. This type of relation, traditionally called a production function, can be specified formally in mathematical terms as:

$$x = g(n, k) \tag{9.2.1}$$

where x = output of the firm;
n = the amount of labor used by the firm;
k = the amount of capital used by the firm.

The characteristics of the production function are usually examined for two production periods: the "short run" and the "long run." The short run is ordinarily defined to be some period in which the firm can vary *some* of its factors of production (e.g., labor) but in which it cannot vary others (e.g., capital).[1] The long run, on the other hand, is generally defined to be a period which is long enough for the amounts of *all* factors to be changed. Obviously, the specification of short- and long-run periods in terms of weeks, months, or years, depends upon the characteristics of the factors of production used by the individual firm. As an example, a firm which uses only shovels as capital could probably increase or decrease its capital stock within a very short period; thus, in this case, even the long run would be a matter of days. At the other extreme, the producer of turbines may have to place orders for heavy capital equipment far in advance of the desired date of delivery; conse-

---

[1] There is a problem here about the definition of capital as either capital "in use" or capital "in place." We shall ignore this issue for the time being, but will consider it later in this chapter.

quently, his long-run period may be several months at a minimum. At any rate, the conceptual distinction between these two production periods proves extremely useful for analytical purposes. If we restrict our treatment to the two-factor case involving labor and capital, we can envision a firm's short-run production function as a modified form of equation 9.2.1:

$$x = g(n, k^0). \tag{9.2.2}$$

In the above equation, the term k^0 denotes a fixed capital stock. The interpretation of 9.2.2 is that, given the size of the capital stock, output is a function of only the amount of labor used in production. The total product of labor is the amount of output the firm can produce with each possible quantity of labor. Of course, as labor is increased we expect output to expand (over the relevant range of production). The ratio of this change in output to the corresponding change in labor is referred to as labor's marginal product (call this MP_n). That is:

$$MP_n = \frac{\Delta x}{\Delta n} \quad \text{with} \quad k = k^0. \tag{9.2.3}$$

According to micro theory, we generally find that as labor is increased (holding the other factors of production constant), total product will eventually begin to increase at a decreasing rate.[2] This phenomenon is called the "law of diminishing returns."

Refer to figure 9.2.1 for a graphical depiction of the total product and the marginal product schedules for an individual firm. Notice that over some initial range of labor use (up to n_1) total product may increase at an increasing rate. This is reflected by the rising marginal product schedule over that range. However, the firm eventually confronts some

---

[2]This characteristic of the marginal product of labor can be stated quite simply in mathematical terms. Given the production:

$$x = g(n, k)$$

the marginal product of labor is defined as the partial derivative of g with respect to n.

$$MP_n = \frac{\partial g(n, k)}{\partial n}.$$

The law of diminishing returns simply states that, beyond some value of n (say, n_1), the second partial derivative with respect to n is negative. That is:

$$\frac{\partial^2 g(n, k)}{\partial n^2} < 0 \text{ for } n_1 < n < n_2$$

The value n_1 can be called the "point of diminishing returns," and n_2 is that level of employment which is associated with the maximum output.

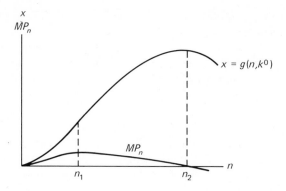

Figure 9.2.1   *Total and Marginal Product of Labor on
the Firm Level*

range of labor (n_1 to n_2) over which total product rises at a decreasing
rate. This means that between n_1 and n_2 marginal product is positive,
but declining. It is in this range that firms will operate (as we shall
illustrate later). Notice that the individual firm's short-run production
function (as characterized by the marginal- and total-product
schedules) relates output to the amount of labor used. As we have
interpreted the productivity schedules, knowledge of the amount of
labor used by the firm allows us to calculate the output which could be
generated. Conversely, if we know the output level at which the firm is
operating, we can determine the amount of labor needed to produce it.
It is this characteristic of the short-run production function which makes
it extremely useful for our analysis. We shall later make use of the
marginal-product relation to specify a demand-for-labor function.

In macroeconomic literature, economists often specify a production
function which pertains to the entire economy, rather than to an individual firm's production process. This aggregate production function
relates the amount of labor and capital used by the entire business
sector to the amount of final output the economy can generate. We can
denote the aggregate production function as:

$$Y = F(N, K) \tag{9.2.4}$$

where Y is aggregate output (i.e., aggregate real income), and N and K
are the aggregate amounts of labor and capital used in production. If we
now apply the short-run assumption of a fixed capital stock, the aggregate production function can be specified as:

$$Y = F(N, K^0) \tag{9.2.5}$$

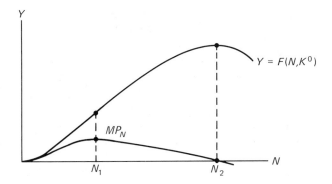

Figure 9.2.2 *Total and Marginal Product of Labor on the Aggregate level*

which formally states the proposition that, given the capital stock, aggregate output is a function of the employment of labor over the entire economy.[3] Ordinarily, we ascribe the same characteristics to the short-run relation between aggregate output and employment as are presumed for the corresponding micro relation. In particular, it is generally assumed that above some level of aggregate employment (N_1), increases in employment will induce successively smaller increments in output. In other words, we assume that the law of diminishing returns applies at the macro, as well as the micro, level. Given this assumption, the aggregate production function can be presented in figure 9.2.2. Notice that the general shapes of the output and marginal product schedules correspond to those for the firm in figure 9.2.1.

For an individual firm involved in the production of a single good, the production function should be reasonably well defined. However, as we attempt to aggregate this relationship over all firms in the economy, we run into rather serious conceptual difficulties. Although some of the

---

[3] See section 2 of chapter 5 in connection with the assumed constancy of the stock of capital. Essentially, we suggested there that "short-run" models of the economy generally suffer from an inconsistency in that they include an equation for net investment (i.e., the net change in the stock of capital) and at the same time make use of the assumption that the capital stock is constant. The impact of the procedure is that investment is considered an important element of aggregate demand, whereas its influence on productive capacity is treated as insignificant. Net investment is generally approximately 8% of aggregate demand, which makes it an extremely important component. However, net investment constitutes a much smaller percent of the existing capital stock; for example, quarterly net investment may add less than 1% to the productive capacity of the economy. Although internal inconsistencies of this sort are never completely justified, we can suggest that the resultant bias introduced into the model is fairly small.

objections to the analytical use of an aggregate production function are highly technical, we can still give the student a feeling for one of the major problems involved. Take any one level of aggregate employment between N_1 and N_2. Is it reasonable to suggest that there is a unique level of aggregate output associated with this amount of employment? Obviously not, for the labor could be distributed in any number of ways among industries; thus, aggregate output would depend upon the allocation of labor, as well as the amount of labor employed by the economy. Or we could look at the same objection in terms of marginal product. If the amount of labor increases, by how much does aggregate output increase? It depends, of course, on where the additional laborers are used. If they are employed by firms with high marginal productivity of labor, then the aggregate marginal product will appear to be high; if they are hired by firms in which marginal product of labor is low, the aggregate marginal product will appear to be correspondingly low. In defining an aggregate production function, we have to assume a given allocation of labor across firms for the whole economy. This, of course, is unrealistic in a situation where expansion of labor usage is generally an uneven process, to say the least.

There is also an objection which applies to both the individual and the aggregate versions of short-run production functions. The short-run production function is supposed to represent the relation between labor and output with a given stock of capital. However, it should be realized that the amount of capital "in stock" and the amount of capital "in use" may be extremely different quantities. Even over some very short period of time, producers often change the rate at which they utilize their capital. A producer with seven machines can choose to use fewer than seven if market conditions dictate this course of action. In fact, one of the foremost economic indicators is the capacity-utilization rate of manufacturing companies. The measure may vary from 60 to 70% in very slow periods to 90 or even 100% in brisk times. As this rate of capital usage changes, the marginal-product-of-labor schedule will shift, thus effecting a corresponding shift in the demand for labor. The point here is that even in the short run, when the capital *stock* is "fixed," the relation between labor and output will change as the capital utilization rate changes. Thus, in this sense, the concept of the short run is not quite so useful as it would otherwise be.

In the remaining analysis, we shall postulate a given short-run production relation between labor and output, even though we have enumerated some of the conceptual problems of this approach. There are two reasons for doing so. First, the short-run aggregate production function has been used in most of the theoretical macro models in economic literature; if we are to analyze and compare those models, it is necessary to examine each of their components. Second, the aggregate production function—despite its admitted limitations—does serve as a relatively reasonable and simple proxy for the relation between inputs and output on a national scale. A more exact specification of this relation would entail more complexity than allowed by the scope of our analysis. Still, throughout our discussion, the student should keep in mind the limitations of this and other equations which are used to describe aggregate economic behavior.

9.3 Theories of the Labor Market

Now that we have established a link between the labor market and the product market, we can begin to consider the mechanics of the labor market itself. There are several alternative theories of the labor market, each hinging on some notion about the interaction between supply and demand forces.

Equilibrium Under Perfect Competition in Labor and Product Markets

The perfectly competitive model of the labor market embodies many implicit assumptions. First, it presumes an extremely large number of buyers (firms) and sellers (laborers) acting independently in such a way as to maximize their individual well-being. It is generally assumed that firms attempt to maximize profits by choosing some optimum amount of labor at each and every possible wage rate, and that laborers act in such a way as to maximize their own statisfaction by choosing some optimum combination of income and leisure at each and every wage. It must also be assumed that wages are flexible, so that this "price" of labor can act to bring the market into equilibrium. In addition, labor must be treated as a homogeneous quantity. Making all of these simplifying assumptions, we can rather easily describe the resultant operation of the labor market. The model we shall derive and illustrate is often associated with the classical school of economics; thus, we shall sometimes refer to it as the classical model of the labor market.

In a perfectly competitive model, the derivation of the demand for labor is a straightforward process involving the use of a profit-maximization criterion and one of the short-run characteristics of production. To begin, we use the idea that a firm operating in perfect competition will, in the short run, produce at the point where price equals short-run marginal cost:

$$P = SRMC. \qquad\qquad (9.3.1)$$

Short-run marginal cost (SRMC) is simply the additional cost associated with the production of an extra unit of output, given some variable factors and some fixed factors. In our analysis, we have been considering a production process which involves only two factors of production: labor (the variable input) and capital (the fixed input). In this type of case, the short-run marginal cost is just the extra labor cost necessary to generate an extra unit of output. Given the definition of marginal cost we can write:

$$SRMC = \frac{\Delta(SRTC)}{\Delta x}$$

where SRTC is short-run total cost and x is the firm's output. But the change in total cost in the short-run is just the change in labor cost, so we can express SRMC as:

$$SRMC = \frac{\Delta(W \cdot n)}{\Delta x}$$

where W is the money wage rate and n is the firm's employment. Since W is considered constant by the individual firm,[4] the above equation becomes:

$$SRMC = W\frac{\Delta n}{\Delta x}$$

or:

$$SRMC = W / \frac{\Delta x}{\Delta n}.$$

And, remembering that $MP_n = \Delta x/\Delta n$, we have:

$$SRMC = \frac{W}{MP_n}. \qquad\qquad (9.3.2)$$

Hence, we see that short-run marginal cost is, in the two-factor case, nothing but the wage rate divided by the marginal product of labor. Plugging this expression into the profit-maximizing condition (9.3.1), we obtain:

---

[4]In a perfectly competitive labor market, there are many buyers and sellers of labor. Because of this, the individual firm is a "price-taker" in the sense that it considers the wage beyond its own control.

$$P = \frac{W}{MP_n}$$

or:

$$\frac{W}{P} = MP_n. \tag{9.3.3}$$

The above expression is the familiar condition that the firm in perfect competition will hire labor up to the point where labor's marginal product is equal to the real wage (W/P). Thus, if we plot the demand for labor against the real wage, this demand schedule will be the marginal product schedule itself. As a consequence, the equilibrium condition (9.3.3) is also considered the firm's labor-demand equation. And, for the same reason, the marginal-product-of-labor schedule is treated as the firm's labor-demand schedule.

Equation 9.3.3 can also be cast in a slightly different fashion in order to lend an intuitive flavor to its interpretation. If we multiply both sides of 9.3.3 by the price (P), we obtain:

$$W = P \cdot MP_n. \tag{9.3.3.'}$$

This condition can be interpreted as follows: firms will hire labor up to the point where the additional cost of an extra unit of labor (in this case, W) is just equal to the corresponding addition to the firm's receipts. The term on the right side of the equation ($P \cdot MP_n$) represents the value of the output generated by the extra unit of labor. It is thus called the value of the marginal product of labor.

With the same reservations as in our discussion of the aggregate production function, we can define a demand-for-labor function for the entire economy in an analogous fashion. Starting with the short-run aggregate production function (9.2.5), we can derive the marginal product of labor as:

$$MP_N \equiv \frac{\Delta Y}{\Delta N} = F'(N, K^0) \tag{9.3.4}$$

where $F'(N, K^0) \equiv \dfrac{\Delta F(N, K^0)}{\Delta N}$

and, given the existence of perfect competition in factor- and product-markets, we can consider the aggregate demand for labor to be determined by the equation of the real wage and the marginal product:

$$\frac{W}{P} = MP_N = F'(N, K^0). \tag{9.3.5}$$

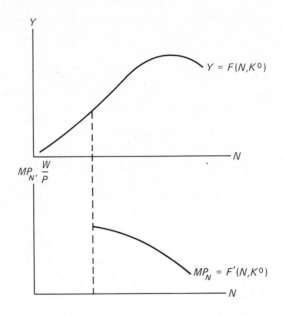

Figure 9.3.1   *The Aggregate Demand for Labor*

Again, the equilibrium condition (9.3.5) can be interpreted as an aggregate labor-demand equation. And, as was the case for the individual firm, the aggregate marginal-product schedule can be used as an aggregate labor-demand schedule. In figure 9.3.1, the short-run aggregate production schedule and the associated demand-for-labor schedule are plotted. (These are the same two schedules as in figure 9.2.2, but the second schedule now has an additional meaning; we thus present it again.) The reader will notice that only the downward-sloping portion of the marginal product schedule has been included as the labor-demand schedule. The reason for this is simple: the rule for profit-maximization (P = SRMC) applies only to that range of the marginal cost schedule which is upward-sloping. But for SRMC to have a positive slope, it is necessary in this case for the marginal product of labor to diminish as output increases. Thus, the downward-sloping portion of the MP_n schedule is the only portion relevant to the formulation of labor demand. Another point should be made here. We have drawn the marginal product schedules (for both the firm and the economy) on the presumption that the capital stock is given. However, the student should recognize the fact that any variation in the size of the capital stock (or, according to our earlier discussion, the utilization of capital) will cause a shift in the marginal product schedule.

The supply of labor is determined by the joint behavior of all laborers. If they act in such a way as to maximize their satisfaction from leisure and income, the amount of labor-hours they offer will be related to the wage they get for sacrificing an hour's worth of leisure. If workers do not suffer from money illusion, then they should consider the *real* wage when determining their individual supplies of labor. This means that workers should realize that an equal percentage increase in money wages (W) and prices (P) would leave them no better or worse off, and that an increase in prices at a greater (lesser) rate than the increase in money wages worsens (betters) their position. If workers are not subject to money illusion, the number of labor-hours offered will depend on the real wage. In order to facilitate our analysis, we can write this relationship in its aggregate form as:

$$\frac{W}{P} = S(N). \tag{9.3.6}$$

Equation 9.3.6 can be interpreted as follows: the real wage that workers require will depend upon the number of labor-units they are required to give up. In general, the higher the required amount of employment, the higher the corresponding real wage will have to be in order to induce that amount of labor to provide services. As the real wage increases, each hour of labor offered (and leisure sacrificed) brings higher compensation. This may induce two different responses on the part of the laborer: first, the extra compensation may tend to bring about a substitution of work for leisure, since the latter is now more expensive in the sense of opportunity costs; second, the additional hourly wage may tend to cause the worker to take *more* leisure hours, since it now takes fewer hours of work to earn the same total income as was earned before the wage increase. The first of these effects is called the substitution effect, and, by itself, would generate a positive association between the real wage and hours of labor supplies. The second effect is termed the income effect; it tends to encourage a negative relation between the real wage and house of labor supplied.

The relative strengths of these two effects will determine the shape of the individual's supply-of-labor schedule. It is ordinarily conceded that at relatively low values of the real wage, the substitution effect is dominant—thus causing an upward-sloping labor supply schedule over this range. It is possible that the income effect becomes dominant for some individuals at high real wages, thus causing the labor-supply schedule to "bend backwards." In the aggregate, one would probably not expect to find a backward-bending supply curve, at least over the relevant range of values of the real wage. So we shall depict the aggregate supply-of-labor schedule as being positively sloped, thus assuming

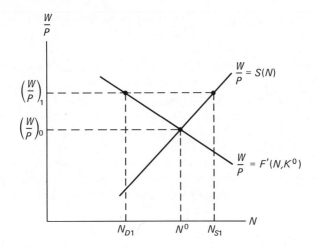

Figure 9.3.2   *Labor-Market Equilibrium with Flexible Real Wages*

that the relation embodied in our aggregate labor-supply function (9.3.6) is a positive one between N and W/P.

The aggregate supply-of-labor function is shown in graphical form in figure 9.3.2, with the aggregate demand-for-labor schedule from figure 9.3.1 superimposed on it. Notice that we can find a real wage rate at which the quantity of labor supplied equals the quantity demanded. This is the equilibrium value of the real wage, $(W/P)_0$. Any other value of the real wage would be accompanied by either excess supply or excess demand. As an example, the wage $(W/P)_1$ would generate a higher amount of labor supplied (N_{S1}) than firms would be willing to hire at that real wage (N_{D1}). If the real wage is flexible—i.e., if it is permitted to vary freely in both the upward and the downward directions—it will adjust to any discrepancies in the quantities of labor supplied and demanded.

To illustrate this process, suppose that the real wage were currently at $(W/P)_1$, where laborers are willing to offer more hours of work than firms are willing to purchase. In this case, the excess workers would compete against each other and against currently employed workers for the relatively scarce jobs. This competition would tend to drive money wages (W) down. Of course, the general price level might also be expected to fall under these circumstances, but we can assume for the sake of simplicity that prices would not fall as rapidly as money wages. Under this condition, a decrease in the money wage (W) would force the real wage (W/P) down and thus start to correct the deficiency between N_S and N_D. As W/P fell, the amount of labor offered would decrease and the amount of labor firms are willing to hire would increase. This process should continue until, eventually, the equilibrium position is attained. Keep in mind that the eventual convergence on this equilibrium position is contingent upon the flexibility of money wages and the relative insensitivity of prices to variations in money wages. These conditions will be proved to be very important when we look at the historical controversy between Keynes and the classics over the operation of the labor market.

We can now turn to an algebraic exposition of the attainment of equilibrium. The perfectly competitive labor market can be described by the two equations:

$$\frac{W}{P} = F'(N, K^0) \tag{9.3.7}$$

$$\frac{W}{P} = S(N). \tag{9.3.8}$$

The first equation is the labor-demand equation introduced earlier; the second equation is the labor-supply relation. We have implicitly assumed that the market yields an equilibrium, making no distinction between the real wage firms are willing to pay at a certain level of employment (the W/P in the demand function) and the real wage laborers require at each level of employment (the W/P in the supply equation). At the equilibrium, both of these real wages will be equated.[5] To find the equilibrium level of employment, we need only equate labor demand

---

[5] We could rewrite equations 9.3.7 and 9.3.8 respectively as:

$$\left(\frac{W}{P}\right)^D = F'(N, K^0) \tag{9.3.7'}$$

$$\left(\frac{W}{P}\right)^S = S(N) \tag{9.3.8'}$$

where $(W/P)^D$ is the "demand-price" of labor and $(W/P)^S$ is the "supply-price." The "demand-price" is defined as the real wage the business sector is willing to pay per unit of labor at each level of aggregate employment; the "supply-price" is the real wage required by laborers at each level of aggregate employment. In equilibrium, we would have the condition:

$$\left(\frac{W}{P}\right)^D = \left(\frac{W}{P}\right)^S \tag{9.3.9'}$$

This, along with 9.3.7' and 9.3.8', would give us a system of three equations in three unknowns, $(W/P)^D$, $(W/P)^S$ and N, which could be solved for the equilibrium values of the variables.

and labor supply by setting 9.3.7 equal to 9.3.8. Doing so, we obtain the equilibrium relation:

$$F'(N, K^0) = S(N) \tag{9.3.9}$$

which can be viewed as a single equation with only one unknown (N). Under normal circumstances, we can solve uniquely for the equilibrium value of employment, N^0. And once we know N^0, we can use either the labor-demand equation (9.3.7) or the labor-supply equation (9.3.8) to obtain the equilibrium value of the real wage, $(W/P)^0$.

As an illustration of the mechanics of equilibrium determination in perfect-competition market, consider a labor market described by the following set of equations:

$$\frac{W}{P} = 1.0 + .02N \qquad \text{(supply function)}$$

$$\frac{W}{P} = 4.0 - .01N \qquad \text{(demand function)}$$

where N denotes employment in thousands. Equating the two functions, we would have:

$$1.0 + .02N = 4.0 - .01N$$

and, solving for the value of N which satisfies this expression, we obtain:

$$N^0 = 100.$$

Given this value of employment, we can solve for the real wage which corresponds to it. We can use either the labor-supply or the labor-demand function, insofar as the equilibrium condition is met at N^0. Using the labor-demand equation, we obtain:

$$\left(\frac{W}{P}\right)^0 = 4.0 - .01(N^0)$$

$$\left(\frac{W}{P}\right)^0 = 4.0 - .01(100)$$

$$\left(\frac{W}{P}\right)^0 = 3.0$$

where $(W/P)^0$ is the equilibrium real wage rate. (The reader should verify the point that using the labor-supply equation would have given the same result and know why this is so.)

We have just illustrated that a perfectly competitive labor market with flexible wages and the absence of money illusion would result in the determination of an equilibrium value for both the real wage and the level of employment. Earlier, we postulated a short-run production relationship between employment and output. Thus, given the competitive structure analyzed in this section, the labor market mechanism would help to determine aggregate output (and less directly, the rate of interest and the level of prices) in the short run. To illustrate this point, we shall combine the labor-market equations 9.3.7, 9.3.8, and 9.3.9 with the production function and the equations of the product- and money-markets derived in the previous chapter. To simplify matters, we shall use the condensed forms of the product- and money-market equations (i.e., the equations of the IS and LM schedules). It will be remembered that the equality of aggregate demand for and aggregate supply of final product required:[6]

$$[1 - b(1 - t_1)]Y + g_1 r = a + g_0 + bt_0 + G^0 \qquad (7.2.11)$$

and that the equality of money demand and money supply necessitated:

$$\frac{M_s^0}{P} = l_0 + l_1 Y - l_2 r. \qquad (7.2.12)$$

Now, we add the short-run production function:

$$Y = F(N, K^0) \qquad (9.2.4)$$

and the labor-market equations:

$$\frac{W}{P} = F'(N, K^0) \qquad (9.3.7)$$

$$\frac{W}{P} = S(N) \qquad (9.3.8)$$

The system composed of equations 7.2.11, 7.2.12, 9.2.4, 9.3.7, and 9.3.8 consists of five equations and five endogenous variables (Y, r, P, W/P, and N), and will yield unique solution values for the endogenous variables under normal circumstances. As it turns out, the solution of the system is fairly simple. As an aid to examining the sequence of determination of the solution values, refer to figure 9.3.3. In that diagram, we have set up a flow chart showing the relationships in the system. First, we need to know the value of the capital stock (K^0) in

---

[6]The IS equation shown here corresponds to the model incorporating an income tax and induced investment, as developed in chapter 5 (see equation 5.5.6). Multiplying both sides of equation 5.5.6 by $[1 - b(1 - t_1)]$ and transferring the term associated with the variable rate of interest to the left-hand side of the equality sign, we derive equation 7.2.11.

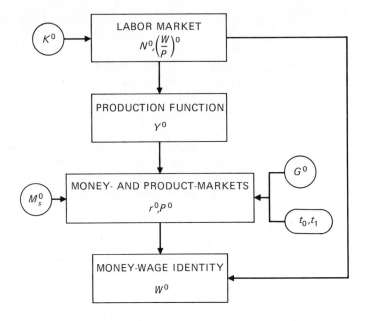

Figure 9.3.3   *A Flow-Chart of the Model when Labor Supply is a Function of Real Wages*

order to obtain the labor-demand equation; once we have this, the labor market relationships will determine the equilibrium values of employment and the real wage (N^0 and $(W/P)^0$). Knowing N^0 and K^0, we can use the production function to solve for the value of real output which can be generated (Y^0). Given the value of Y^0, and given the values of the exogenous variables and parameters of the money- and product-markets (M^0, G^0, t_0, t_1, etc.), we can solve equations 7.2.11 and 7.2.12 for the equilibrium values of the rate of interest and the price level (r^0 and P^0). Then, given the equilibrium values of the real wage and the price level, we can use the obvious implicit identity:

$$W^0 \equiv \left(\frac{W}{P}\right)^0 P^0$$

to obtain the equilibrium money wage.

Perhaps a quick numerical example will help to solidify the point. Assume the following values for the coefficients of the IS relation (7.2.11) and the LM equation (7.2.12): $a = 30$, $b = .8$, $t_0 = 50$, $t_1 = .25$, $g_0 = 100$, $g_1 = 400$, $l_0 = 110$, $l_1 = .15$, and $l_2 = 500$. Plugging these values into the appropriate slots, we obtain:

$$.40Y + 400r = 170 + G^0 \qquad\qquad\qquad \text{(IS)}$$

and

$$\frac{M_s^0}{P} = 110 + .15Y - 500r. \qquad\qquad\qquad \text{(LM)}$$

Now specify a numerical version of the short-run production function as:[7]

$$Y = 5N - .01N^2 + 2K^0. \qquad\qquad \text{(production function)}$$

Further, add to the system the labor-market equations:[8]

$$\frac{W}{P} = 5 - .02N \qquad\qquad\qquad \text{(demand for labor)}$$

$$\frac{W}{P} = 2 + .01N. \qquad\qquad\qquad \text{(supply of labor)}$$

Now, go through the determination of the equilibrium values of the endogenous variables. First, take the labor-market equations and equate them to each other to obtain:

$$5 - .02N = 2 + .01N.$$

Solving for N, we obtain:

$$N^0 = 100.$$

We can now use the labor-supply equation to obtain the equilibrium real wage:

$$\frac{W}{P} = 2 + .01N = 2 + .01(100)$$

$$\left(\frac{W}{P}\right)^0 = 3.$$

---

[7]Notice the shape of the schedule depicting this production function. Pick a numerical value for K^0 and plot the resultant relation between Y and N. Does it correspond to the expected "shape" for such a relation?

[8]Notice that the labor-demand equation can be derived explicitly from the production function as follows:

$$MP_N \equiv \frac{dY}{dN} = 5 - .02N$$

and, using the condition that firms hire workers until $MP_N = W/P$, we have:

$$\frac{W}{P} = 5 - .02N$$

Notice that we have found a unique pair of values for employment and the real wage. We can use the equilibrium level of employment to solve for the level of output. Substituting $N = 100$ into the production function, we get;

$$Y = 5(100) - .01(100)^2 + 2K^0$$

$$Y = 400 + 2K^0$$

which is the reduced-form equation for Y in terms of the exogenous capital stock. We shall assume that $K^0 = 300$; then:

$$Y^0 = 400 + 2(300)$$

$$Y^0 = 1000.$$

Now that we know the value of output, we can turn to the money-market and product-market equilibrium conditions to solve for the equilibrium values of the price level and the rate of interest. Restating those conditions and substituting $Y^0 = 1000$, we have:

$$.40(1000) + 400r = 170 + G^0 \tag{IS}$$

$$\frac{M_s^0}{P} = 110 + .15(1000) - 500r. \tag{LM}$$

This two-equation system contains four variables; however, two of them (G and M_s) are exogenous. For the sake of the example, assume that $G^0 = 250$ and $M_s^0 = 235$. Then we would have:

$$400 + 400r = 420 \tag{IS}$$

and

$$\frac{235}{P} = 110 + 150 - 500r. \tag{LM}$$

First, we can use the IS equation to solve for the rate of interest:

$$400r = 20$$

$$r^0 = .05.$$

And, once we know the equilibrium rate of interest, we can use the LM equation to find the price level:

$$\frac{235}{P} = 260 - 500(.05)$$

$$235 = (260 - 25)P$$

$$P^0 = 1.0.$$

Given the values of Y, r and P, the interested reader could go back to the original structural equations of the product- and money-markets (listed in chapter 7) to solve for the equilibrium values of the other variables of the system.

Full Employment. Now that we have analyzed the determination of wages and employment under perfectly competitive conditions in both the product market and the labor market, we can turn our attention to the concept of full employment. We shall define the full employment of labor as the situation in which jobs are available to everyone who would be willing to work at the perfectly competitive equilibrium wage. An important corollary of this type of definition is that the universal existence of perfect competition and the flexibility of real wages will ensure the achievement of a position of full employment of labor. If these market conditions were to hold in the real world, we would need no overt economic policy in order to combat unemployment.

One other concept now lends itself to a rigorous definition. In our treatment of the money and product markets, we referred to the "full-employment level of output"; however, we intentionally allowed that term to remain fairly ambiguous. We now define the full-employment level of output (Y^F) as that level of output which could be produced, given technology and the size of the capital stock, with the perfectly competitive equilibrium amount of labor. If we designate N^F as the equilibrium level of employment in a perfectly competitive situation and Y^F as the corresponding full-employment level of output, we could use the aggregate production function (9.2.4) to write:

$$Y^F = F(N^F, K^0).$$

Policy makers often designate the achievement of Y^F as a major economic goal. One reason for this fascination with full-employment output is that it indirectly implies full employment of labor. And, given our existing institutions—particularly the fact that wages constitute the major source of income for most people—it is obviously desirable for an economy to provide jobs for those who want to work. The economic cost of unemployment is obvious since it decreases the consumption possibilities of the society in question. But such economic losses are only part of the whole picture, for labor-market unemployment is also associated with other social evils. Unemployment (narrowly defined) is not randomly distributed; rather, it tends to fall most heavily on unskilled laborers. Consequently, those groups most vulnerable to joblessness lose the self-respect associated with engaging in productive endeavors. Furthermore, because the unskilled comprise a large portion of lower-income groups, unemployment tends to make the income distribution less uniform than it would be in times of prosperity. Given the rather broad appeal of egalitarianism, this is also considered a social evil.

This multidimensional character of unemployment was enunciated most succinctly by Heller, who noted:

> The term "full employment" stands as a proxy, as it were, for the fulfillment of the individual as a productive member of society, for the greater equality that grows out of giving every able-bodied worker access to a job, and for a nation's determination to demonstrate that a market economy, based on freedom of choice, *can* make full and productive use of its greater potential.[9]

The impact of government policy on the rate of unemployment became clear in the aftermath of the great depression of the 1930s. People sharpened their economic and social consciences when they realized that some of the widespread unemployment had been avoidable.

The acceptance of unemployment as a central responsibility of economic planners was formalized in the Employment Act of 1946, which committed both public and private sectors of the economy to the pursuit of maximum employment as a national goal. But the verbal commitment was not matched with a full-scale effort until late in 1960, when President Kennedy gave it "new life with his call to 'return the spirit as well as the letter of the Employment Act'."[10]

The Employment Act left the quantitative definition of "maximum" employment unspecified, partially as the result of the political compromises which allowed its passage. But each administration has adopted its own interpretation of the general goal, usually specifying it in terms of the unemployment rate. In the period immediately following passage of the act, 4% unemployment was commonly accepted as a working goal. As prosperity continued through the late 1940s and early 1950s, there were some who argued that even 3% might be a practical target. But by the middle of the 1950s, the most popular reference point had crept up to 5%. Then, during most of the Kennedy and Johnson administrations, official statements listed 4% as the "interim goal" of policy. The Nixon administration operated in the hopes of bringing the rate of unemployment down to approximately 5%, and policymakers in the Ford administration seem to be retaining this figure as a long-run goal.

---

[9] Walter Heller, *New Dimensions of Political Economy* (New York: W. W. Norton, 1970), pp. 59–60.

[10] Ibid., p. 61.

We have introduced the concept of full-employment output, not because we would suggest that it is *the* ultimate goal of economic policy, but rather because much of the controversy in macroeconomic literature revolves around the issue of whether or not the economy can be expected to generate such a level of output automatically and consequently without the exercise of economic policy. We shall turn our attention to that controversy in the next two chapters when we deal with the historical disagreement between Keynes and the classics.

The Impact of Rigidity of Real Wages

In our previous analysis, we assumed that any deviation from the full-employment equilibrium position in the labor market would be corrected by an adjustment in real wages. This adjustment was understood to be the product of a faster decrease in wages than in prices, implying a decrease in the real wage rate. Today, however, there is near consensus of opinion that wages are affected to a great extent by institutional factors. In addition, even in the face of some unemployment, union leaders seldom accede to absolute decreases in wage rates. To do so would generally invite the wrath of rank-and-file members. Furthermore, some wages are governed by legal provisions like minimum wage laws, and in some cases—notably government services and public utilities—there is little incentive, if any, for producers to attempt to decrease wages in time of moderate unemployment.

But what if real wages are not flexible in the downward direction? We shall find that rigidity in real wages may lead to a chronic underemployment position in the labor market. In fact, this potential rigidity was often cited by the classics as a prime reason why significant amounts of unemployment might persist from time to time. Aside from this one difference, we shall find that the basic overall structure of the economy (or, at least, the way in which the economy generates values for the endogenous variables) is unchanged by the rigidity of real wages.

For the sake of exposition, presume that laborers act in concert to prevent real wages from dropping below some set value, $(W/P)_m$. This policy could be the result of the exercise of union power, but it is unnecessary to stipulate the reasons for the establishment of such a minimum real wage. If we take this policy into account in sketching the labor-supply curve, we obtain a "kinked" schedule like the one shown in figure 9.3.4 as N_sN_s. For the sake of comparison, we have also plotted the labor-supply schedule which would correspond to the absence of real-wage rigidity; it is denoted by the line $N_s'N_s$.

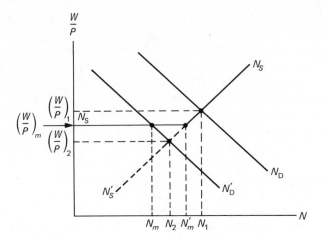

Figure 9.3.4   *Labor-Market Equilibrium with Rigid Real Wages*

Consider first the case in which the unrestricted interaction of labor supply and labor demand would result in a real wage which lies above $(W/P)_m$. In particular, suppose that the relevant aggregate labor-demand schedule is the one designated by N_D. If so, the intersection of N_D with the labor-supply schedule would establish an equilibrium real wage of $(W/P)_1$ and an equilibrium level of employment of N_1. Notice that the horizontal segment of the labor-supply function (representing the minimum real wage) does not come into play. At the perfectly competitive equilibrium real wage, everyone who wants to work at that wage will be hired—thus, the market generates full employment.

But now consider an alternative situation in which the labor-demand schedule (N_D') cuts the supply schedule on its horizontal segment. Had real wages been flexible, the equilibrium real wage would have been $(W/P)_2$ and the equilibrium level of employment would have been N_2 (which, according to our definition, would have been a full-employment position). But the existence of the wage rigidity prevents the real wage from falling below $(W/P)_m$; consequently, the business sector is willing to hire only N_m units of labor. Laborers are willing to offer a greater amount of labor; in particular, they are willing to offer N_m' units of labor at the minimum real wage. Had the real wage been allowed to take on its perfectly competitive equilibrium value, $(W/P)_2$, the quantity of labor supplied would have been N_2. Thus, the rigidity of real wages at $(W/P)_m$ creates involuntary unemployment of the amount $N_2 - N_m$.

It should be pointed out that in the last case, the point of intersection of N_D' with N_sN_s can be considered an "equilibrium" position in the sense that it does constitute a point from which there is no tendency for the market to move *given* the institutionalized rigid wage. If the rigidity is relaxed, then the position ceases to be an equilibrium point. It is interesting to note here that the full-employment position and the equilibrium position are not synonymous; discrepancies can exist under the type of model considered here.

Regardless of the way in which the labor-demand schedule intersects the labor-supply schedule (whether it be in the upward-sloping or the horizontal range), the equilibrium value of employment can still be used, along with the production function, to solve for the equilibrium level of real output. And, once we know this latter value, the equations of the product market and the money market can be used to find the equilibrium values of the rate of interest and the general price level. Thus, in terms of the mechanics of solution for the equilibrium values of the endogenous variables, little is changed by the introduction of rigid real wages into the labor market model.

From a policy standpoint, however, the modification of the labor market to include wage rigidities is crucial. In our first case (where wages fluctuated freely and the supply-of-labor schedule was upward-sloping throughout), the economy attained equilibrium at a level of full employment; thus, no overt economic policy was needed to expand employment and output. But in the rigid wage model, the economy could reach and maintain an equilibrium position involving unemployment of labor. In such an event, explicit policy measures would sometimes be necessary. Of course, theorists have differed on the appropriate policy to use in such a case; however, we shall postpone the discussion of alternative policies until the next chapter.

The Importance of Money Illusion

Throughout the preceding sections, we assumed that the quantity of labor supplied is a function of the *real* wage. However, this does not square with our actual experience. Indeed, Keynes has argued that ". . . ordinary experience tells us, beyond doubt, that a situation where labour stipulates (within limits) for a money-wage rather than a real wage, so far from being a mere possibility, is the normal case. Whilst workers will usually resist a reduction of money-wages, it is not their practice to withdraw their labour whenever there is a rise in the price of wage-goods."[11]

---

[11] J. M. Keynes, *The General Theory of Employment, Interest and Money* (New York: Harcourt, Brace, 1936), p. 9.

We shall now revise our hypothesis about the supply of labor and investigate the effects of introducing in the model the assumption that the laborers are subject to some degree of money illusion. The reader should remember that money illusion in this context is an attitude according to which workers respond differently to a change in real wages depending on the cause for the change. The presence of money illusion means that a 5% decrease in real wages due to a price rise (money wages constant) will not be viewed by workers as equivalent to the same decrease in real wages due to a fall in money wages (prices constant).

Actually, Keynes had two basic objections to the classical description of the labor market. First, he suggested that laborers do not respond as adversely to a rise in the general price level as they do to a fall in their money wages. If they did, he claimed, this would mean that workers currently unemployed (but willing to work at the going wage) would withdraw their services from the market if prices were to rise even a slight amount.[12] Second, Keynes argued that bargaining between business and labor does *not* directly determine the real wage; instead, the real wage is determined by "other forces" in the economy. We shall consider this point further in the following pages.

To examine the importance of money illusion, we shall first assume that the money wage is completely flexible. This assumption does not capture the flavor of the Keynesian argument, but it does allow us to sort out the effects of money illusion and wage rigidity. Our labor market model can now be revised formally to read:

$$\frac{W}{P} = F'(N, K^0) \qquad\qquad (9.3.10)$$

$$W = S(N). \qquad\qquad (9.3.11)$$

Equation 9.3.10 is the demand-for-labor equation (specified in the same way as it was in the classical analysis). Equation 9.3.11 is the supply-of-labor function incorporating an extreme type of money illusion; in particular, it embodies the assumption that laborers consider *only* money wages and ignore prices completely.

First, consider the properties of the labor market itself. Notice that the two equations (9.3.10 and 9.3.11) contain three distinct variables: the real wage (W/P), the nominal wage (W) and the level of employment (N).[13] Thus, under normal circumstances, we cannot solve uniquely

---

[12]Ibid.

[13]Alternatively, we could consider the variables of the system to be W, P and N. In either event, there are three distinct variables contained in only two equations.

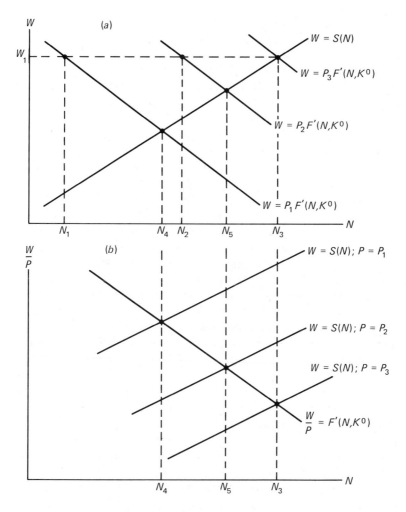

Figure 9.3.5   *Labor-Market Equilibrium with Money Illusion*

for the equilibrium values of these variables. This point can be illustrated graphically as well as mathematically. Refer first to figure 9.3.5, panel (a). Notice that we have placed the *nominal* wage on the vertical axis. This allows us to plot the labor-supply function as a single schedule relating the money wage rate (W) and the level of employment (N). However, when we attempt to depict the labor-demand relation, we have somewhat of a technical problem. The demand for labor, it will be remembered, is based on a comparison of labor's marginal product and the *real* wage. Thus, given a series of values of the money wage and a schedule of marginal products of labor at different amounts of employment, the demand for labor will depend upon the price level. In fact, we find that in order to plot the demand for labor against the money wage, we must presume some price level; thus, we obtain one demand schedule for each hypothetical value of the general price index.

In panel (a), we have sketched only three of the infinite number of hypothetical demand schedules. To further explain the multiplicity of demand schedules, consider the following illustration. Suppose that the money wage is currently at the value W_1 [see panel (a)] and that the price level is P_1. Given these values, we could compute the real wage as W_1/P_1. Corresponding to this real wage there will exist some amount of labor for which the marginal product falls to a level equal to W_1/P_1. Call this level of employment N_1. Now, suppose that the price level were $P_2(P_2 > P_1)$. The real wage corresponding to W_1 would be lower then in the previous case $(W_1/P_2 < W_1/P_1)$; thus, the business sector would demand more labor at W_1 than it did in the first example. In fact, it would be willing to hire N_2 units of labor at W_1. With an even higher price, P_3 $(P_3 > P_2 > P_1)$, the real wage corresponding to W_1 would be even lower; consequently, firms would be willing to hire an even greater amount of labor (N_3) at W_1. To generalize this point, we can say that plotting labor demand against the money wage results in an infinite number of labor-demand schedules—one for each possible value of the price level. Furthermore, we can observe that the relevant demand schedule shifts to the right as the price level increases. On more intuitive grounds, we are just saying that, given the money wage rate, firms will demand more labor the higher the price of their output.

The supply-of-labor schedule and the demand-for-labor schedules plotted in panel (a) trace out a whole series of equilibrium points (again, one for each possible price level). As a result, we cannot find a *unique* equilibrium in the labor market. Obviously, if we knew the price level we could choose the equilibrium money wage and level of employment; however, we have already emphasized the fact that the other markets of the economy do not uniquely determine the price level. We cannot assume a level we have not yet found.

The same point can be made with the use of a slightly different diagram like the one in panel (b) of figure 9.3.5. There, we have plotted the supply and demand schedules against the *real* wage. As a consequence, we now have only one labor-demand schedule (the same one as we drew earlier in figure 9.3.2); however, insofar as the labor-supply relation is written in terms of the *money* wage, there will be an infinite number of labor-supply schedules (one for each possible price level). The student should use a procedure analogous to that employed in panel (a) to rationalize the relative positions of the three supply schedules depicted. Again, we see that the system cannot yield a unique set of solution values for the three endogenous variables.

Although the labor market does not yield a unique set of equilibrium values for N, W/P, and W, it does provide some extra information with regard to the overall economic model. In fact, we find that the addition of the labor-market equations to the IS-LM model developed earlier will result in a determinate system (again, under normal circumstances). To illustrate this point, we can combine the labor-market equations with the product-market and money-market equilibrium equations and the production function. Doing so, we obtain the following system:

$$[1 - b(1 - t_1)]Y + g_1r = a + g_0 + bt_0 + G^0 \qquad (7.2.11)$$

$$\frac{M_s^0}{P} = l_0 + l_1Y - l_2r \qquad (7.2.12)$$

$$Y = F(N, K^0) \qquad (9.2.4)$$

$$\frac{W}{P} = F'(N, K^0) \qquad (9.3.7)$$

$$W = S(N) \qquad (9.3.11)$$

and the implicit identity:

$$W \equiv \left(\frac{W}{P}\right)P. \qquad (9.3.10)$$

The above set of six equations contains six unknowns: N, Y, r, P, W/P, and W; it can thus be solved for the equilibrium values of these six variables. Once we know these values, of course, we can go back to the structural equations of the product and money markets and obtain equilibrium values for all of the other endogenous variables of the model. The crucial point is this: the system of six equations depicted above is not subject to the type of market-by-market solution we used in the model assuming the absence of money illusion. Instead, these six equations must be solved simultaneously for the values of the variables involved. In intuitive terms, this means that *each* market affects the others; we cannot look at any one market in complete isolation from the others. The system can be depicted in terms of a flow chart like the one shown in figure 9.3.6. Given the values of the exogenous variables (K^0, M_s^0, and G^0) and the policy parameters (t_0 and t_1), the markets in the system must act interdependently to determine the values of the endogenous variables.

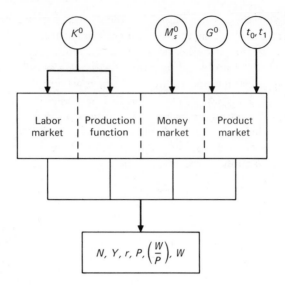

Figure 9.3.6   *A Flow-Chart of the Model with Money Illusion*

The reader will remember that in our first model including the labor market, the labor market affected the other markets, but was not directly affected *by* the others. Employment was determined at some particular level which depended only on the productivity of labor and labor's willingness to work. Variations in the values of the exogenous variables and parameters of the money and product markets (of most importance, the money supply, government expenditures, net transfers and the tax rate—all policy variables) had no effect on the level of employment. But in our new model in which money illusion is incorporated, this is no longer true. Variations in the value of any of the exogenous variables generally *will* have an effect on employment. Thus, when money illusion is present, we find that economic policy can be used to bring about desired changes in the level of employment. Our discussion in the next chapter will focus on this issue much more closely.

9.4 Summary

In introducing the labor market into our model of the economy, we first had to consider the concept of a short-run aggregate production function. We found that this function was, at best, a rather loose general relationship between aggregate employment and output. Nevertheless, it provided us with an extremely convenient bridge between the labor market and the rest of the economy.

We next turned to an investigation of the determination of wages and employment under several alternative sets of assumptions. Our first model reflected the existence of perfect competition in both the labor and the product markets and the absence of money illusion and wage rigidities. In this idealized framework, we found that both employment and the real wage were uniquely determined by the labor-supply and labor-demand relations. Furthermore, we discovered that full employment was automatically attained (in fact, it was identical with equilibrium). Thus, there was no need to worry about the use of economic policy to alleviate unemployment.

We next considered two modifications of the perfectly competitive model: namely, wage rigidity and money illusion. According to our analysis, wage rigidity was a potential cause of unemployment, in that it could result in the establishment of a "minimum" wage which was above the perfectly competitive wage. In the rigid-wage model, we found that the equilibrium values of wages and employment were still uniquely determined in the labor market (given the level of the minimum wage).

Our analysis of the influence of money illusion illustrated the fact that any number of equilibrium positions would be consistent with the labor-market relations. In order to determine a unique equilibrium for the labor market (and, for that matter, for the entire economy), we had to combine all of the equations of our general equilibrium model. In doing so, we found that the product, money, and labor markets could interact in such a way as to yield unique equilibrium values for all of the endogenous variables of the model. The importance of money illusion in the context of economic policy should become much clearer after our discussion of Keynes and the classics in the next chapter.

Suggested Further Reading

Brownlee, O. H. "The Theory of Employment and Stabilization Policy." *Journal of Political Economy* 58 (October 1950), 412–24.

Ferguson, C. E. *Microeconomics.* Homewood, Ill.: R. D. Irwin, 1972, chap. 13.

Hansen, A. *A Guide to Keynes.* New York: McGraw-Hill, 1953.

Keynes, J. M. *The General Theory of Employment, Interest and Money.* New York: Harcourt, Brace, 1936.

Rees, A. "Wage Determination and Involuntary Unemployment." *Journal of Political Economy* 59 (April 1951), 143–53.

Tobin, J. "Money Wage Rates and Employment." In *The New Economics,* edited by S. E. Harris. New York: Knopf, 1947, pp. 572–87.

PART
FOUR

Keynes and the Classics

CHAPTER 10

Classical Theory

10.1 Introduction

In this and the next chapter, we set out to examine the highly touted controversy between the classical school of thought and the Keynesian view of the economy. Much of the theory which has been outlined in chapters 3 through 9 has been essentially Keynesian; furthermore, we have referred to some of the underlying principles of classical thought in those chapters. As a result, very few new concepts need to be introduced, and the major purpose of these chapters is to organize the elements of Keynesian and classical theories into economic models, and to compare these models in a systematic fashion.

It would be misleading to think of all classical theory as a collection of universally held views. On the contrary, one could accurately describe the classical school as a heterogenous grouping of theorists, each of which held his own distinct beliefs about the structure of the economy. Fortunately, close scrutiny of the works of some of the foremost classical theorists uncovers a few principles which seem to have been almost universally accepted during the two centuries prior to the 1930s. By examining these principles, one can achieve a relatively good understanding of the spirit behind the classical attitude of laissez faire.

10.2 General Principles of the Classical Model

Two notions provide a common thread running through the thoughts of classical writers: Say's Law and the quantity theory of money. These principles are related, but distinct, tenets.

Say's Law suggests that supply creates its own demand. It guarantees that all goods produced in the economy will be purchased, that any increase (or decrease) in output will generate an equivalent increase (or decrease) in spending. One of the assumptions underlying this conclusion was that people hold money only for transactions purposes. And, as we noted in chapter 8, this assumption was in turn based on the argument that no one would be willing to forgo any interest payment in order to hold money in idle balances. Given this argument, the classics contended that the following chain of events would inevitably take place: production would be set at the full-employment level; the value of production would be distributed in the form of factor payments; and, finally, all income would be spent on the goods and services produced (i.e., none of the income would be used to add to money holdings). Of course, the classics recognized that a wide array of goods and services would be produced and that excess demand could occur temporarily in any market. But if this were to happen, it was assumed that relative prices would adjust in such a way as to bring about equilibrium in each and every market.

Associated with the notion of Say's Law was the quantity theory of money (see chapter 8). By assuming that the velocity of money was constant over the short run and that real income would take on its full-employment level (which would also be fixed in the short run), the quantity theory was used in effect by the classics as a theory of determination of the general price level. Indeed, as we saw earlier, any increase or decrease in the nominal money supply (M_s) would be translated into a proportional increase or decrease in prices.

Both Say's Law and the quantity theory of money illustrate the classical reliance on the flexibility of prices. In order for Say's Law to operate, relative prices had to adjust so as to "clear" all markets. And, in order for the quantity theory version of general price determination to be valid, the general price level had to adjust to accommodate any variation in the money supply. We shall find that the classics also had a great deal of faith in the flexibility of wages and interest rates. It is this faith which lay behind their general belief that the market mechanism would generate full employment.

The generalities presented above should give the student a feeling for the classical economic philosophy. However, a full appreciation of the classical position and the Keynesian revolution requires a more detailed analysis of a formal classical model of the economy. We shall present two such models. The first one is rather naive; the second is more realistic and, correspondingly, more complex. In the first description, we shall ignore the decomposition of production into consumer goods and investment goods. This simplification allows us to omit the product, or capital, market from consideration.[1] Then, in a second model, we shall include an explicit classical description of the product market.

10.3 The Classical Model without a Product Market

As a first approximation, the classical thinking can be conveniently summarized in terms of the following structural equations.

$$\frac{W}{P} = F'(N, K^0) \tag{10.3.1}$$

$$\frac{W}{P} = S(N) \tag{10.3.2}$$

$$Y = F(N, K^0) \tag{10.3.3}$$

$$P = \frac{V^0}{Y} M_s^0 \tag{10.3.4}$$

$$W \equiv \left(\frac{W}{P}\right) P. \tag{10.3.5}$$

In the above system, 10.3.1 is the demand-for-labor equation which incorporates the idea that firms operating in perfect competition will be willing to hire up to the point where the real wage is equal to the marginal product of labor, while 10.3.2 is the supply-of-labor equation based on the assumption of wage flexibility and the absence of money illusion. Insofar as the two labor-market equations contain only two variables (W/P and N), they can, under ordinary circumstances, be solved for unique values of the two variables. Or, to put this in less abstract terms, the classical description of the labor market was one in which the interaction of the supply of labor and the demand for labor would generate a unique equilibrium for the real wage and the level of employment. And, because of the presumption of wage flexibility, the equilibrium level of employment corresponded to a full-employment position.

---

[1] In our earlier discussions, the product market was viewed as having two roles: First, it helped to determine the total amount of output forthcoming in equilibrium; second, it was the mechanism which decomposed output into consumption and investment. In the classical model, the second of these roles was the only viable one; thus, they used the term *capital market* to characterize that process. When we use the term *product market*, then, we refer to the classical capital market.

Once the equilibrium level of employment was established, the corresponding level of real output was determined by the production function of the economy (10.3.3). And, since N was established at the full-employment level, the corresponding output would also be a full-employment amount. Whatever the value of aggregate output, Say's Law assured that aggregate demand would take on an identical value. Thus, the full-employment output would automatically be an equilibrium amount.

In the classical scheme, the price level would take on a value which would accommodate full-employment output, given the money supply and the income-velocity of circulation. This implication of the quantity theory was discussed above, and was captured in the behavioral relation 10.3.4. The equilibrium money wage would then be determined by the equilibrium price and the real wage identity 10.3.5. Thus, according to the above system the labor market is used to determine relative prices, W/P, while the quantity theory determines the absolute level of prices, P.

The classical version of the structure of the economy is depicted in diagrammatic form in figure 10.3.1, where we have presented the basic relationships outlined in equations 10.3.1–10.3.5. We can use these four panels to further illustrate the sequence of determination outlined above. First, consider panel (a), where the labor market relations are sketched. The equilibrium values of employment and the real wage, N^0 and $(W/P)^0$, are determined at the intersection of the labor-supply and labor-demand schedules. The production function is plotted in panel (b) under the assumption of a fixed capital stock. If we project the value N^0 up to panel (b), we can obtain the equilibrium level of output, Y^0. Given the value Y^0, we can next graph the quantity theory relation between the money supply and the general price level. Insofar as this relation is a proportional one, the relevant schedule is a ray from the origin with a slope of V^0/Y^0; this is shown in panel (c). Given the value of the nominal money supply, M_s^0, the equilibrium price level is found to be P^0. In panel (d), we have graphed the identity involving the price level, the money wage and the real wage. The equilibrium real wage determines the slope of the schedule; and, given P^0, the equilibrium money wage is established at W^0.

Perhaps a numerical example will help solidify the student's understanding of the simple classical model. Suppose that the economy is characterized by the following structural equations:

$$\frac{W}{P} = 20 - .02N \qquad \text{(demand for labor)}$$

$$\frac{W}{P} = 13 + .05N \qquad \text{(supply of labor)}$$

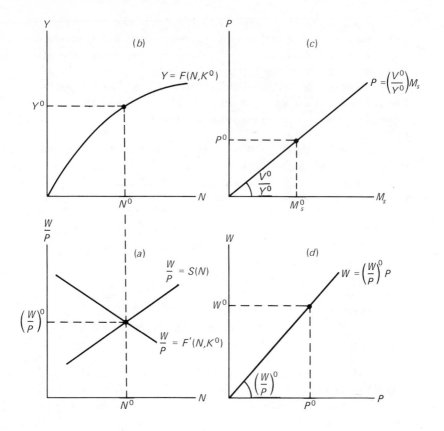

Figure 10.3.1   *A Simple Classical Model*

$$Y = 20N - .01N^2 \qquad \text{(production function)}$$

$$P = \left(\frac{5}{Y}\right)M_s \qquad \text{(quantity theory)}$$

$$W \equiv \left(\frac{W}{P}\right)P. \qquad \text{(money wage identity)}$$

We can begin by solving the labor-market equations for the equilibrium level of employment. Substituting for the real wage from the second equation into the first equation above and solving for N, we can obtain $N^0 = 100$. Substituting $N^0 = 100$ into either the labor-supply or labor-demand equation, we find that the corresponding real wage rate $(W/P)^0$ is equal to 18. Now, using the production function (10.3.5) to solve for the level of output, we find that $Y^0 = 1900$. The price level will depend on the velocity of money ($V^0 = 5$) and the money supply.

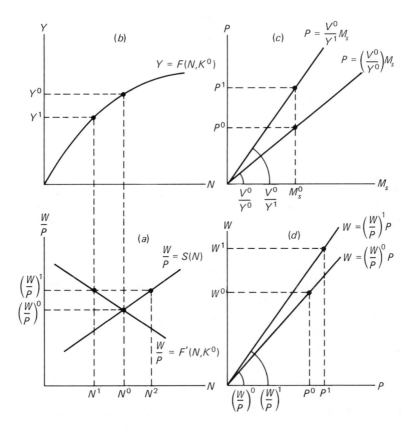

Figure 10.3.2 *Automatic Adjustment to Full-Employment in the Simple Classical Model*

Assume that the money supply is 456; then the price level is found to be equal to $P^0 = 1.2$. And, insofar as the real wage and the price level are known, we can proceed to use 10.3.5 to find the corresponding money wage, which is: $W^0 = 21.6$.

So far, we have shown that, in equilibrium, the classical model would generate full employment. However, it remains to be shown that an adjustment process would take place to restore the economy to that full-employment equilibrium in the event that some divergence should occur. As an example, suppose that the real wage takes on a value greater than its equilibrium level, say $(W/P)^1$. Is there an inherent mechanism in the economy which would cause the full-employment equilibrium to be established?

Figure 10.3.2 provides the answer. Examine panel (a). Insofar as $(W/P)^1$ is greater than the equilibrium real wage, the quantity of labor

demanded by the business sector (N^1) will be less than the quantity supplied (N^2). Employment will be determined by the lesser of these two
quantities; i.e., the actual level of employment will be N^1. The discrepancy between labor demand and labor supply will be reflected in a
positive level of involuntary unemployment.[2] And, due to the fact the
only N^1 units of labor are hired, output will be at Y^1, far below its full-
employment equilibrium value [See panel (b)]. Because output has
fallen from Y^0 to Y^1, the price level must rise to absorb the given money
supply. This is shown in panel (c). The schedule relating the price level
and the money supply rotates counterclockwise as Y falls. Thus, given the
value of the nominal money supply (M_s^0), the new price level will be
P^1. As we move to panel (d), we see two changes. First, the relation
between W and P changes due to the higher real wage, $(W/P)^1$. Second,
the price level [as established in panel (c)] takes on a higher value, P^1.
The joint effect of these two changes is that the money wage is considerably higher than it was initially, taking on a value of W^1. Notice,
of course, that the *ratio* of W^1 to P^1 is higher than was the ratio of W^0
to P^0—i.e., the real wage is, by our initial assumption, higher than it was
in equilibrium. In summary, if the real wage exceeds its equilibrium
value, employment and output will fall short of their respective equilibrium levels and prices and wages will be above their equilibrium values.

According to the classics, the existence of unemployment would set off
a round of adjustments which would induce the economy back to the
original full-employment equilibrium position. If unemployment
existed, laborers would drive down the money wage through their
competition for relatively scarce jobs. This process would continue—
given flexible wages—until all those who wanted to work were employed.
In terms of the labor-market diagram [panel (a) of figure 10.3.2], the
falling money wage rate would push the real wage back down to its full-
employment equilibrium value $(W/P)^0$ and employment would increase
from N^1 to N^0. This expansion of employment would generate an
increase in output from Y^1 to Y^0 [see panel (b)], the latter of which
would be a full-employment output. Given the expanded output and
the exogenously determined money supply, prices would fall until they
reached a level (P^0) compatible with the absorption of the extra output.

---

[2] According to our definition of full employment of the labor force, the level of unemployment here would be $N^0 - N^1$. If we were to use another definition of unemployment—
that which denotes it as the difference between labor supply and labor demand at the
going wage—its quantitative measure would be $N^2 - N^1$. The choice between two such
definitions is probably not all that important in the present context. In either case, some
involuntary unemployment exists at the real wage $(W/P)^1$.

Note that money wages would fall faster than prices, so that their movements would be consistent with the declining real wage. By referring to panel (d), we can see that the eventual equilibrium money wage would be W^0, the value derived from a real wage of $(W/P)^0$ and a price level of P^0.

It should be kept in mind that the adjustment process outlined above is contingent upon the assumption that wages and prices are flexible in the downward direction. In particular, it is necessary that laborers allow their money wage to fall when unemployment exists; it is also necessary that firms lower their prices whenever aggregate supply exceeds aggregate demand. We shall discuss these assumptions much more fully when we introduce Keynes' attack on the classical model.

10.4 A More Sophisticated Version of the Classical Model

The abbreviated model presented above captures some of the essential flavor of classical thought. However, the simplifications used in its specification give rise to two problems. First, it takes no account of the determination of the way in which expenditures (or output) would be allocated between consumption and investment. Instead, Say's Law was used to ensure that all output would be absorbed, regardless of the decomposition of that output between consumption and investment goods. Of course, the contention that output would reach equilibrium at its full-employment level made the investigation of the determination of consumption and investment less interesting. Insofar as the full-employment level of output was fixed in the short run, any variation in consumption would be offset by a change in investment in the opposite direction. This is not to say that the classics were completely uninterested in the determination of consumption and investment; on the contrary, they recognized that the percentage of output devoted to investment goods would be directly related to the rate of growth an economy would experience. But the distinction between *types* of expenditures on goods and services was thought to be relatively unimportant in the classical short-run environment.

The Wicksellian Capital Market

The second shortcoming of the simple classical model was that it did not fully explain the mechanism by which a change in the money supply will affect the general price and money wage levels. This aspect of the model was criticized by Knut Wicksell, one of the foremost classical theorists of his day. Wicksell maintained the traditional classical assumption that people will want to hold no money in idle balances; however, he explicitly took account of the fact that some percentage of income would be held in the form of saving. Due to the withdrawal of saving from the income stream, not all of factor income would be returned to the business sector in the form of consumption expenditures. But this recognition of saving did not constitute a departure from the basic spirit of classical thought. According to Wicksell, savings would *not* be held in the form of idle cash balances. Instead, the income devoted to saving would be used to purchase interest-bearing assets. Furthermore, the act of purchasing these assets would facilitate investment in plant and equipment by the sellers of the financial assets. In general terms, the saving withdrawn from the income stream would automatically be returned in the form of investment expenditures. The result of this process would be that the *sum* of consumption and investment expenditures would necessarily be equal to the actual level of income; thus, again, supply would create its own demand.

In our analysis of the Wicksellian view of the capital market (in which saving and investment were brought into equality), we shall make some simplifying assumptions. First, we shall assume that there are no financial intermediaries—i.e., that the sale and purchase of financial assets involves direct transactions between buyers and sellers with no middle man needed to handle the transactions. Second, we shall assume that there is no market for old securities, implying that all financial transactions involve only new security issues. It simplifies matters by allowing us to ignore financial transactions which are essentially pure transfers of debt, but add nothing to the pool of investable funds.

The initial question to be answered pertains to the determination of consumption and saving. The student should keep in mind the context of the Wicksellian argument. In the short run, income presumably did not vary (it was established at its full-employment level). Thus, one would not be inclined to use variations in income as an explanation of variations in consumption and saving. Instead Wicksell set out to explain the determination of the allocation of a *fixed* income between consumption and saving.[3]

---

[3]Actually, Wicksell's analysis was specified in nominal—rather than real—terms: "saving" referred to nominal income withheld from present consumption; "investment" referred to money purchases of capital goods. But our analysis will be presented in real terms, so that we may maintain a treatment comparable with that presented in previous chapters. This procedure does ignore one of the differences between the classical model (where saving and investment were often cast in nominal terms) and the Keynesian model (developed in real terms). But this difference is minor relative to others we shall investigate and we thus do little damage by ignoring it.

According to Wicksell, the amount of income saved by an individual depends upon the rate of interest. Insofar as all savings were presumed to be used to purchase interest-bearing assets, the rate of interest could be considered a reward for saving. *Ceteris paribus,* the higher this interest rate, the more future consumption could be effected with a dollar saved today, and consequently, the more willing an individual would be to defer consumption by saving. This rationale led Wicksell to postulate a positive relation between aggregate saving (S) and the market rate of interest (r):

$$S = S(r). \tag{10.4.1}$$

Wicksell also presumed investment to be related to the rate of interest. We have rationalized the negative association between I and r in a previous chapter,[4] and have captured it in the equation:

$$I = I(r). \tag{10.4.2}$$

Given the Wicksellian savings and investment relations, equilibrium in the capital market would occur at that interest rate at which saving equals investment. That condition is formally expressed as:

$$I = S. \tag{10.4.3}$$

Figure 10.4.1 depicts the Wicksellian capital market. In our diagram, the equilibrium interest rate would be r^0 and the equilibrium values of saving and investment would be S^0 and I^0 respectively. Notice that in the classical model the interest rate itself is determined in the capital market.

As the rate of interest increased, saving would increase and consumption would decrease by an equal amount. This notion can be captured diagrammatically through the use of the schema set forth in figure 10.4.1. The interest rate is measured along the vertical axis, while the horizontal axis is used to measure saving, consumption and income (all three, of course, are in the same units and can thus be plotted in this fashion). The vertical income schedule reflects the constancy of the full-employment income level. In particular, it denotes the fact that only the composition—rather than the aggregate amount—of income is affected by the interest rate. The equilibrium rate of interest is established by the intersection of the saving and investment schedules. Suppose that the investment schedule is give by $I = I(r)$; then the equilibrium interest rate will be r^0. At this interest rate, saving and investment take on the values S^0 and I^0 respectively. If we now use the identity:

---

[4]See chapter 5 for a heuristic motivation of this relation and chapter 13 for a full development.

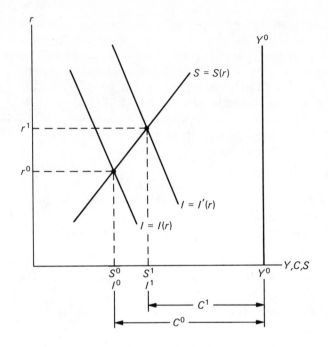

Figure 10.4.1   *The Wicksellian Capital Market*

$$C \equiv Y - S \qquad\qquad (10.4.4)$$

we can depict the level of consumption at r^0 as the distance from S^0 to Y^0. This distance is denoted in the diagram as the level of consumption C^0. If the investment function were different, say, $I = I'(r)$, the resultant equilibrium rate of interest would take on another value. For a higher rate, say, r^1, the equilibrium level of saving would be higher. If we denote this alternative saving level as S^1, we can again use this quantity along with the level of income to obtain the corresponding value of consumption (C^1). And, again, the components of income $(C^1$ and $S^1)$ would sum to the value of expenditures $(C^1$ plus $I^1)$.

The mechanism of the Wicksellian capital market was an extremely important building block in the classical model. It allowed for saving, but insured that these savings would be matched by an equal amount of investment expenditures. As a result, any level of income would generate an equal amount of expenditures. The analysis presumed that the interest rate would be flexible enough to bring saving and investment into equality. As long as this flexibility was maintained, the full-employment income level would also be an equilibrium level. Referring back to figure 10.4.1, the student will see that as long as investment and saving are equal, total income will be matched by an equal amount of expenditures. At our first equilibrium position (r^0, I^0, S^0, C^0), total income would be $Y^0 = C^0 + S^0$; total expenditures would be the sum of consumption expenditures and investment expenditures ($C^0 + I^0$). Insofar as S^0 and I^0 are equal, income and expenditures are equal. If the investment schedule lies further to the right, the equilibrium interest rate would be higher (say, at r^1). At this higher interest rate, both saving and investment would again be equated, this time at a higher level. Consumption would fall to C^1. But still, the sum of expenditures (C^1 plus I^1) would exhaust total output (C^1 plus S^1, which would be equal to Y^0).

Notice carefully that the capital market has a completely different function in the Wicksellian model than it had in the simple Keynesian model presented in chapter 3, where the equality of saving and investment determined the equilibrium level of income. In the Wicksellian model, income is determined *outside* of the capital market; the capital market simply generates values of saving and investment which will accommodate that predetermined level of income.

A Restatement of the Quantity Theory

Now, we return to a point raised earlier with regard to the relation between the nominal money supply and the general price level. According to the naive version of the quantity theory, the constancy of income (at the full-employment level) and the income velocity of money gave rise to a proportional association between M_s and P. But, as we claimed in our introduction to the more sophisticated version of the classical model, the naive theory offered a rather weak description of the type of behavior which would lead to this proportionality. We shall find that Wicksell's capital market can be used to provide a more adequate rationale for the quantity theory of prices.

It should be remembered that saving in the Wicksellian capital market was considered to be a flow of investable funds. In treating them as the *only* funds available for investment purposes, we implicitly assumed that the money supply remained at some constant level over the period of consideration. As long as the money supply is constant, according to the classics, individuals will reach some equilibrium position in which they hold money only for transactions purposes. The real amount people want to hold for transactions purposes will depend upon the level of *real* income (Y). In equilibrium (where everyone holds just the desired amount of cash balances), the only source of investable funds will be current saving. Furthermore, the only use of funds (other than for consumption) will be investment; no funds will be "hoarded." Thus the rate of interest would be determined strictly by the interaction of the saving and investment functions. But suppose that we take into account the possibility that the money supply increases. Insofar as transaction needs are intially met by existing cash balances (given the price level and the level of real income), the increment in the money supply constitutes excess funds in the hands of individuals. It is possible that some of this excess could be siphoned off in the form of "hoarding," but we shall ignore this possibility in order to simplify the analysis. Ruling out additional hoarding, the supply of loanable funds would consist of saving out of current income plus the increase in the money supply during the current period. In real terms, this gives us:

real loanable funds $= S + \Delta m_s$

where, as before,

$$\Delta m_s = \Delta\left(\frac{M_s}{P}\right).$$

In figure 10.4.2, we have sketched an investment schedule and two loanable funds schedules. The first loanable funds schedule (a) corresponds to the assumption that both the nominal money supply and the price level are constant at the levels M_s^0 and P^0 respectively. If these two variables (M_s and P) are held constant, the *real* money supply is also constant; thus, the only source of real loanable funds will be saving. Given this, the interest rate will take on a value, r^0, at which saving and investment will be equal. This value is often referred to as the natural rate of interest. The equality of saving and investment is consistent with the full-employment level of output, Y^0, and the economy is thus in equilibrium.

Now suppose that the authorities increase the nominal money supply from M_s^0 to M_s^1. Given the original price level, the real money supply will increase by an amount given by:

$$\Delta m_s = \frac{M_s^1}{P^0} - \frac{M_s^0}{P^0}.$$

Due to the increase in the real money supply, the loanable funds schedule shifts to (b). The interest rate falls to r^1, the level at which the supply of loanable funds is equal to the demand for loanable funds. But at this point, investment exceeds saving by the amount of the increment in the real money supply (i.e., $I^1 > S^1$; or $I^1 = S^1 + \Delta m_s$). The excess of investment over saving results in a corresponding excess of aggregate demand over aggregate supply. Presuming that output is already at its full-employment level, no expansion in real output will be forthcoming

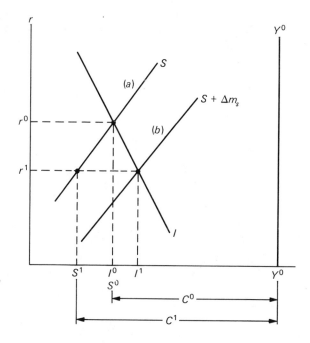

Figure 10.4.2 *The Quantity Theory in a Wicksellian Framework*

to absorb the excess demand. As a result, prices begin to rise. As prices rise, the real money supply starts to shrink back to its original level, and the loanable funds schedule shifts back toward (a). As long as there is any discrepancy between saving and investment, prices will continue to rise. The question is: How far will prices have to increase before the pressure of excess aggregate demand is alleviated? The answer is that prices will have to rise until the real money supply falls back to its original level, thus pushing the supply-of-funds schedule back to its original position at (a). In a sense, the price level must increase by enough to counteract the influence of the rise in the nominal money supply. In order for this to happen, though, prices must rise by the same percentage as did the nominal money supply. But this is exactly what the quantity theory of prices would suggest: an increase in the nominal money supply, under full-employment conditions, will induce a proportional increase in the general price level. From the above we see then that Wicksell provided a more sophisticated view of the process through which this reaction would take place, and thus lent additional substance to the quantity theory. Keep in mind, however, that the Wicksellian analysis held only under the assumption that full employment prevailed.

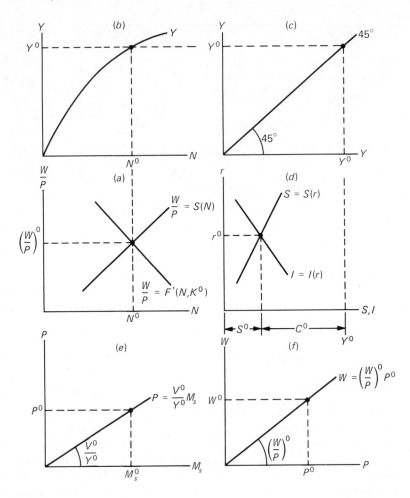

Figure 10.4.3   *An Expanded Classical Model*

The Classical Model Respecified

The inclusion of the Wicksellian capital market into the classical model
is illustrated by figure 10.4.3. Most of the basic elements of that scheme
are identical to those of the simple model presented earlier. Again, the
labor market (panel a) determines the real wage and the level of employment. The labor-market equilibrium is one in which the market is
"cleared"; that is, full employment of labor is attained at the point of
equilibrium. Given employment (N^0), total output (Y^0) can be derived

from the production function represented in panel (b). Panel (c) is used as a mechanical device to aid in the presentation of the model. We have sketched a 45-degree line there in order to cast the full-employment level of output (Y^0) from the vertical axis of panel (b) to the horizontal axis of panel (d). Given this level of income, the decomposition of income into consumption and saving and the corresponding decomposition of aggregate expenditures into consumption and investment is accomplished in the capital market. This is shown in panel (d). In the classical model, the interest rate is assumed to adjust to that value (r^0) at which saving (S^0) and investment (I^0) are equal. The determination of the level of income and the assumption of a given nominal money supply (M_S^0) allows solution for the corresponding price level (P^0) through the quantity-theory equation depicted in panel (e). Then, given the price level, the value of the money wage (W^0) is found through the real-wage identity shown in panel (f).

The Classical Dichotomy

The pattern of determination of the variables in the classical model results in what is often referred to as the classical dichotomy. The dichotomy refers to the fact that the classical model can be broken into two sectors: the real sector, in which the values of the real variables are determined; and the monetary sector, in which the values of the purely monetary variables are determined. Whereas changes in the real sector affect the monetary sector, changes occurring in the monetary sector do not affect the real sector. The endogenous real variables are income, employment, the real wage, saving, investment, consumption and the rate of interest. The endogenous monetary variables are the nominal wage and the price level.

We can illustrate the classical dichotomy fairly easily by referring back to figure 10.4.3. As we pointed out in our discussion of that set of diagrams, the values of all of the endogenous real variables were determined in the markets represented by panels (a), (b) and (d). More specifically, the level of employment and the real wage were determined in the labor market, the level of output was then determined by the production function, and the rate of interest and the levels of consumption, saving and investment were determined in the capital market. On the other hand, we used the quantity theory and the real wage identity [depicted by panels (e) and (f)] only to find the equilibrium values of the monetary variables, the money wage and the price level. Although the equilibrium values of the monetary variables depended on the values of the real variables (in particular, income and the real

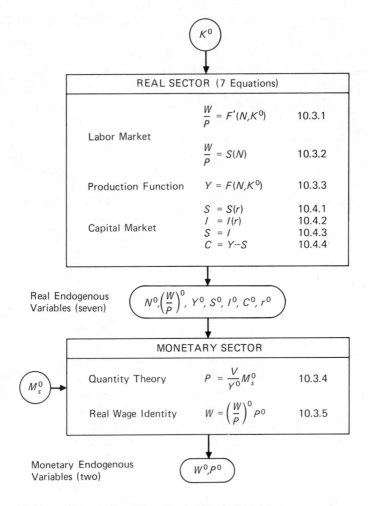

Figure 10.4.4 *A Flow-Chart for the Classical Model*

wage), the equilibrium values of the real variables were not contingent on the values of the monetary variables.

The classical dichotomy can be further illustrated by reference to the flow chart in figure 10.4.4 incorporating the equations of the classical model. As the reader can verify, the real sector is a self-contained system, i.e., the number of unknowns is equal to the number of equations. Therefore under normal circumstances this system can be solved to yield a unique solution for the variables involved. These values can then be injected into the monetary sector which, given the money supply and the velocity, can yield the corresponding equilibrium values of the price level and money wage rate, as the chart shows.

Notice, however, that while the values of the variables determined in the real sector do affect what happens in the monetary one, the reverse is not true. In particular, the conclusion that changes in the nominal money supply would leave the equilibrium values of the real variables unchanged led the classics to consider money as being *neutral*.

10.5 Wage Rigidity and Monetary Policy in the Classical Framework

In all of the previous analysis, we described the classical model under the assumption that wages, prices and interest rates were flexible. As a result of this assumption, the classical model indicated that the economy would generate full employment automatically. It would be a mistake to think that all classical writers exhibited this blind faith in the actual workings of the economy. They did observe rather high levels of unemployment from time to time, and were forced to explain the source of this malady within the general context of their view of the economy. With few exceptions, the classics blamed unemployment on the downward rigidity of money wages. According to our previous comments, unemployment in the labor market should set off a chain of adjustments throughout the economy. The first link in this chain consisted of a decrease in the money wage, which would induce the business sector to expand employment and output. But the classics recognized that workers might resist this cut in money wages, regardless of the level of unemployment. Should this be the case, the economy could be stranded at a position of less than full employment.

The classical "cure" for the unfortunate circumstances described above was extremely straightforward. Insofar as an increase in employment required a drop in *real* wages (and not necessarily money wages), the labor-market rigidity could be bypassed by using overt economic policy to raise prices. A sufficient increase in the general price level, the classics contended, would bring about the necessary decline in real wages. In order to increase prices, the classics called on monetary policy: they thought that an increase in the money supply could force prices up to a level which would leave the real wage at its full-employment equilibrium level. Some caution should be exercised here, though. The quantity theory would not strictly hold in underemployment situations; thus, the increase in the money supply would cause prices to rise less than proportionally. The additional supply of money would be absorbed

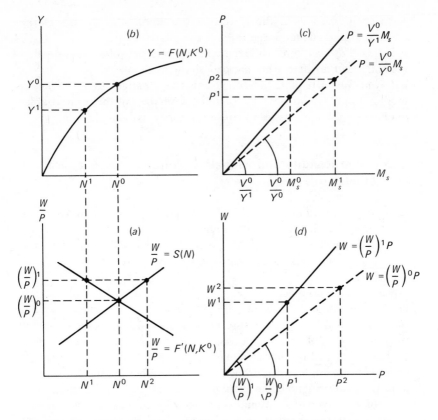

Figure 10.5.1   *Monetary Policy: the Classical Cure for Rigid Wages*

partly by an increase in prices and partly by an increase in output. The
end result would be a lower real wage, higher prices, higher employment
and a higher level of output (presumably, a full-employment level).

   The mechanics of the classical monetary policy can be presented more
simply if we restrict our analysis to the simple classical model. Ignoring
the capital market, the economy can be described by figure 10.5.1.
Suppose the real wage is currently at $(W/P)^1$, which is above the equilibrium real wage, $(W/P)^0$. Due to the relatively high real wage, employment is at N^1—the amount of labor the business sector is willing to hire
at the going real wage. Unemployment exists, and can be measured as
the discrepancy between the quantity of labor supplied at the classical
equilibrium position (N^0) and the quantity demanded (N^1). Given
employment at N^1, output is equal to Y^1 (again, a value below the
full-employment amount, Y^0). Moving to panel (c), we find that the
price level takes on a value, P^1, which is consistent with the given money

supply (M_s^0) and the level of output (Y^1). The money wage, according to panel (d), would be W^1, the value consistent with the current real wage, $(W/P)^1$, and the price level P^1.

As the student should note, the values of all the variables are the same as those described in figure 10.3.2 under the conditions of disequilibrium. In that prior analysis, we illustrated how the money wage would adjust to market forces in such a way as to bring the economy back to the full-employment position. But we no longer assume a flexible money wage; thus, the initial catalyst to adjustment is absent. In the absence of overt policy, the economy could maintain operation at the underemployment position described above.

Monetary expansion, according to classical thought, would be an efficient instrument for the reattainment of full employment. It is difficult to trace through the impact of this increase in the money supply in very accurate terms, insofar as adjustments are assumed to occur simultaneously in all markets. But we can give the student a feeling for the eventual qualitative repercussions which were supposed to follow. First, refer to panel (c). Suppose that the authorities increase the money supply from M_s^0 to M_s^1. If output were already at the full-employment level, the price level would rise in proportion to the changes in the money supply, along the solid price line given by $P = (V^0/Y^1)M_s$. But Y_1 is below full employment; hence, as prices start to rise, a series of events occur: the real wage falls, employment increases and output expands. Because of the expanding output, the price schedule rotates in a clockwise fashion; part of the increase in M_s is used to facilitate more transactions. Thus, prices rise along a shifting price line, eventually reaching a new equilibrium at P^2. As prices rise, money wages also rise, but by a smaller percentage. This is shown in panel (d). Notice that the original money wage line (shown as a solid line) depended upon a given real wage. But as prices rise, the real wage is assumed to fall;[5] thus, the money wage line rotates clockwise. The money wage eventually increases to W^2, the value consistent with the new price level (P^2) and the equilibrium real wage, $(W/P)^0$. In other words, the eventual money wage will satisfy the condition that:

$$\frac{W^2}{P^2} = \left(\frac{W}{P}\right)^0$$

---

[5] It should be recognized that an assumption is needed here. Conceivably, a rising price level *could* induce a *more* rapidly rising money wage. And, if this were the case, the economy would move further away from equilibrium and into a never-ending inflationary spiral. But this is really a problem in dynamics, rather than statics. The classics implicitly assumed that wages would rise less rapidly than prices under the circumstances, and thus that the real wage would fall.

As the real wage falls toward $(W/P)^0$, employment expands toward N^0 [see panel (b)], eventually ending at that equilibrium level. Concurrently, output rises toward Y^0 [panel (a)], the original full-employment level of output.

The process of adjustment described above is based on the assumption, of course, that the increase in the money supply was the appropriate one. In a sense, we assumed that the appropriate monetary policy was taken, then proceeded to describe the classical hypothesis as to the effects of that policy. The major point of this analysis should be clear: in the event that rigid wages exist, monetary policy can be used in order to move the economy back to a full-employment equilibrium.

10.6 Summary

The classical model embodied the optimism of the economists of the time. Chronic unemployment was deemed an unlikely occurrence, something which would be prevented by the unfettered workings of the economic system. Government interference in the economic sphere would be unnecessary under normal circumstances. If unemployment did exist, it was blamed on an artificiality in the economic system; in particular, rigid wages were presumed to be the culprit. Even with wage rigidity, though, unemployment could be cured fairly simply by a discrete manipulation of the money supply. Fiscal policy was completely unnecessary in the classical view of the economy.

Suggested Further Reading

Brunner, K. "Inconsistency and Indeterminancy in Classical Economics." *Econometrica* 19 (April 1951), 152–73.

Fisher, I. *The Purchasing Power of Money* 2d ed. New York: Macmillan, 1920.

Hickman, W. B. "The Determinancy of Absolute Prices in Classical Economic Theory." *Econometrica* 18, (January 1950), 9–20.

Keynes, J. M. *Tract on Monetary Reforms.* London: Macmillan, 1923, chap. 2.

Lange, O. "Say's Law: A Restatement and Criticism." In *Studies in Mathematical Economics and Econometrics,* edited by O. Lange et al. Chicago: University of Chicago Press, 1942.

Leontief, W. "The Consistency of the Classical Theory of Money and Prices." *Econometrica* 18 (January 1950), 21–24.

Patinkin, D. "The Indeterminancy of Absolute Prices in Classical Economic Theory." *Econometrica* 17 (January 1949), 1–27.

————. "The Invalidity of Classical Monetary Theory." *Econometrica* 19 (April 1951), 134–51.

————. "Relative Prices, Say's Law and the Demand for Money." *Econometrica* 16 (April 1948), 135–54.

Pigou, A. C. "The Value of Money." In American Economic Association, *Readings in Monetary Theory.* Homewood, Ill.: R. D. Irwin, 1951.

Robertson, D. H. *Essays in Monetary Theory.* (Lansing: Staple Press, Ltd., 1946.

Wicksell, K. *Lectures on Political Economy.* Vols. 1 and 2. London: Routledge and Kegan Paul, 1934 and 1935.

The Keynesian Revolution

11.1 Introduction

Any comparison of the classical and Keynesian models is, unfortunately, bound to oversimplify the differences of opinion between the two schools of thought. A full and accurate comparison would entail the specification of a whole range of classical models (one for each of the views taken by some classical writers) and a long series of Keynesian models (one for each stage of development through which the original Keynesian model has passed). Such a comprehensive treatment would take up far more space than we care to devote to this issue. We have chosen instead to consider reasonably representative versions of the models as the easiest (if not the best) way of highlighting the most important differences between classical and Keynesian thought.

First, we shall contrast the structural equations of the classical and Keynesian models; then we shall analyze the properties of the full Keynesian model in considerable detail; finally, we shall investigate the impact of economic policy in a Keynesian world.

11.2 A Summary and Comparison of the Classical and Keynesian Models

In order to summarize the difference between the complete classical and Keynesian models, we reproduce in table 11.2.1 the equations comprising these two theoretical constructions. To simplify matters, the models are specified under the assumption of no government expendi-

Table 11.2.1. *A Comparison of the Classical and Keynesian Models*

	Classical Model		Keynesian Model	
labor market	$\dfrac{W}{P} = F'(N, K^0)$	(10.3.1)	$\dfrac{W}{P} = F'(N, K^0)$	(11.2.1)
	$\dfrac{W}{P} = S(N)$	(10.3.2)	$W = S(N)$	(11.2.2)
			$W = W_0$ for $N < N_1$	(11.2.3)
production function	$Y = F(N, K^0)$	(10.3.3)	$Y = F(N, K^0)$	(11.2.4)
product, or capital market	$S = S(r)$	(10.4.1)	$S = S(Y)$	(11.2.5)
	$I = I(r)$	(10.4.2)	$I = I(r)$	(11.2.6)
	$I = S$	(10.4.3)	$I = S$	(11.2.7)
	$C \equiv Y - S$	(10.4.4)	$C \equiv Y - S$	(11.2.8)
money market	$P = \dfrac{V^0}{Y} M_s^0$	(10.3.4)	$\dfrac{M_d}{P} = l_1 Y + g(r)$	(11.2.9)
			$\dfrac{M_s^0}{P} = \dfrac{M_d}{P}$	(11.2.10)
wage identity	$W \equiv \left(\dfrac{W}{P}\right) P$	(10.3.5)	$W \equiv \left(\dfrac{W}{P}\right) P$	(11.2.11)

tures and no taxes. A comparison of these models market by market will reveal the differences between them.

The labor markets of the two models differ substantially from each other. In the classical model, there is no money illusion and, in this formal statement, no wage rigidity. The former assumption allows the labor market to determine uniquely the equilibrium values of the real wage and the level of employment. The latter assumption guarantees that labor-market equilibrium will yield full employment. In the Keynesian model, laborers suffer from money illusion. This assumption, embodied in the labor-supply function, makes the labor market incapable of yielding unique equilibrium values for employment and the real wage. In addition, wages are presumed to be rigid over some range of values of employment. As a result, some of the labor-market equilibrium positions (those occurring in the range of rigid wages) are characterized by unemployment (see chapter 9).

The production function is the same across the two models, but plays a distinctly different role in each. In the classical framework, the production function is the mechanism via which the inevitable full-employment position in the labor market is translated into a full-employment level of output. According to the Keynesian point of view, the production function merely links each of the potential equilibrium levels of employment with a consistent amount of output.

The product, or capital, market plays a subsidiary role in the short-run classical model. Given the full-employment level of output, this market merely allocates output between consumption and investment. The interest rate—the opportunity cost of investable funds and return on saving—brings saving and investment into equality. In the process, the equilibrium rate of interest is itself uniquely determined. The product market plays a critical role in the Keynesian model (although perhaps not so critical as Keynes thought). It establishes the series of combinations of income and the rate of interest at which investment and saving are equal. This equilibrium relationship between Y and r is used as one of the legs in determining the equilibrium values of all of the endogenous variables of the model.[1]

The money market of the classical model is typically written in condensed form as the quantity theory equation (10.3.4). Simple as it may seem, it occupied a key role in the classical scheme. Given the level of income (at full-employment), the money supply determined the absolute price level. The Keynesian money market exhibits recognition of a speculative, as well as a transaction, motive for holding money. It thus allows the demand for money to be related to both income and the rate of interest. Like the other markets of the Keynesian model, the money market cannot by itself yield unique equilibrium values for all the endogenous variables it contains. But it does generate a relationship between Y, r and P which is instrumental in determining the equilibrium values of income, employment and the other variables of the full model.[2]

In most of our earlier analysis, we presumed that the price level was exogenously determined. Under that assumption, the Keynesian money and product markets would jointly determine the equilibrium values of Y and r. But our discussion of the labor market (chapter 9) proceeded

---

[1] The role of the classical capital market was investigated in chapter 10; this version of the Keynesian product market was analyzed in chapters 5 through 8.

[2] The money wage identities are presented only to show how the solution of the two models can be attained; they are implicit in everything we have said so far in this chapter, but their importance in the models is mechanical rather than conceptual.

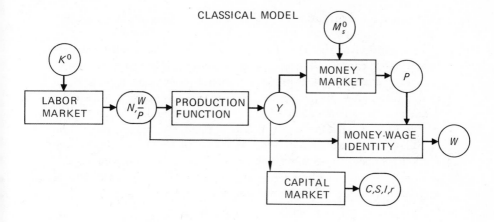

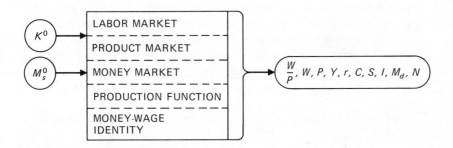

Figure 11.2.1 *The Classical and Keynesian Models: Flow-Chart Comparison*

under the more realistic assumption that the price level is determined within the system. We argued there that the price level, the level of income and the rate of interest are the results of the interaction of all three markets of the economy.

In figure 11.2.1, the interaction of the three markets is described with the use of flow charts for both models. Notice the step-by-step solution of the classical system. First, the labor market generates values for employment and the real wage (given the size of the capital stock). Then, the technological relation as expressed by the aggregate production function is used to determine the level of output. Given the nominal money supply, the quantity-theory equation establishes the price level, and the money wage identity translates the real wage and the price level into the corresponding money wage. Finally, the capital market determines the distribution of output between consumption and investment.

The solution of the Keynesian model, unlike that of its classical counterpart, cannot be decomposed so neatly into successive steps. Instead, the labor market, product market, money market, production function and money wage identity are used to determine simultaneously, given the exogenous values of the capital stock and nominal money supply (and, over some range of employment, the money wage), the equilibrium values of all the endogenous variables. The outcome in each market is dependent in some way on what happens in the others. The following section will investigate the interdependent behavior of the three markets in a fully specified Keynesian model.

11.3 The Full Keynesian Model

In analyzing the full Keynesian model, it is desirable to reiterate Keynes' hypotheses about the product, money, and labor markets. As we have seen, each market is characterized by an equilibrium condition and a set of behavioral relations describing the actions of economic actors. We shall reexamine each of these market descriptions briefly, then tie them together to illustrate the joint determination of the endogenous variables of the model. In doing so we shall assume, once more, a closed economy.

We begin by recasting the Keynesian product market in terms of the following equations:

$$Y = C + I + G \tag{11.3.1}$$

$$C = a + bY_d \tag{11.3.2}$$

$$I = g_0 - g_1 r \tag{11.3.3}$$

$$Y_d \equiv Y - T \tag{11.3.4}$$

$$T = -t_0 + t_1 Y. \tag{11.3.5}$$

As the reader will recognize, equations 11.3.1–11.3.5 correspond to the relations used in earlier chapters. In particular, we explicitly take account of the role of the government in economic transactions.[3] Since the above five equations contain six endogenous variables (Y, Y_d, C, I, T and r) and one exogenous variable (G) none of the values of the endog-

---

[3]Government expenditures and taxes were ignored in the previous section in order to make the Keynesian model more closely comparable to the classical construct.

enous variables can be uniquely determined, even for a given value of G. In chapter 7, we confronted this problem and our discussion led us to the IS schedule showing all of the combinations of Y and r which would leave this market in equilibrium. Combination of the above equations yields the expression for the IS schedule:

$$[1 - b(1 - t_1)]Y + g_1r = a + g_0 + bt_0 + G^0 \qquad (11.3.6)$$

where G^0 is the given value of government expenditures.

The Keynesian money market can be characterized in linear form by the relations:

$$\frac{M_d}{P} = l_0 + l_1Y - l_2r \qquad (11.3.7)$$

$$\frac{M_s^0}{P} = \frac{M_d}{P}. \qquad (11.3.8)$$

These, too, should be familiar relations. The first one (11.3.7) is the demand-for-money-function. The liquidity trap would entail an infinitely large value for l_2, whereas the classical range would be given by $l_0 = l_2 = 0$. Our linear specification is made for algebraic simplicity. Equation 11.3.8 indicates the money-market equilibrium condition and formalizes the assumption that the nominal supply of money is exogenous. In chapters 6–8, we made the simplifying assumption that the real money supply was exogenous. We now drop that assumption and replace it with the more realistic one given above.

Notice that we now have to treat the price level as a distinct endogenous variable in our treatment of the money market; thus, the equations of the model must now be used in some way to show how the price level is determined. The money-market equations contain five variables (M_d, Y, r, M_s and P), of which only one (M_s) is exogenous. Obviously, we cannot expect this system to yield a unique solution for the values of the endogenous variables. We faced a similar problem in chapter 6, even when the real money supply was assumed exogenous. We found then that we could trace out an infinite number of combinations of values for income and the rate of interest which would leave the money market in equilibrium. We called the locus of these combinations the LM schedule. But our problem is now further complicated by the fact that we have an additional endogenous variable (P) to be considered. Each time the price level changes, the real money supply will vary, thus altering the combinations of Y and r which satisfy the equilibrium condition. We analyzed this problem briefly at the beginning of chapter 7 (see figure 7.1.1 and associated text). There we pointed out that there will be a different LM schedule for each alternative price level. As the price level increases, the real money supply contracts, thus causing the LM schedule to shift to the left. Consequently, the Keynesian money market can be described graphically by a *family* of LM schedules, each one showing the values of Y and r which would bring the money market into equilibrium at a particular price level. This family of curves is shown by equation 11.3.9, which combines the equations of the monetary sector:

$$\frac{M_s^0}{P} = l_0 + l_1 Y - l_2 r. \qquad (11.3.9)$$

Figure 11.3.1 depicts the diagrammatic solution, incorporating the comments raised above about the endogenous character of the price level. Product-market equilibrium is satisfied at any point along the IS schedule. We have drawn three LM schedules, one for each of the three specified price levels: P_0, P_1 and $P_2 (P_0 < P_1 < P_2)$. Given a price level, any point on the corresponding LM schedule would yield a money-market equilibrium. Combining the two markets in this fashion, we find that we can obtain one combination of equilibrium values for Y and r at each price level. That is, even the joint operation of these two markets does not determine uniquely the values for these variables. To make this point even more explicit, we have drawn a schedule depicting the equilibrium levels of income associated with alternative price levels and have presented it in panel (b) as an ISLM schedule. The label ISLM denotes that any point on the schedule can yield *both* product-market *and* money-market equilibrium. Although the interest rate is not shown explicitly in panel (b), the schedule is drawn on the presumption that the interest rate takes on its equilibrium value at each income level. For example, at the point P_2, Y_2, the interest rate would be r_2 [as determined by the intersection of the IS and LM in panel (a)].

The shape of the ISLM schedule (given the linear structure of the product- and money-market) can be derived from the IS and LM equations. Solving for r from the LM equation (11.3.9) we obtain:

$$r = \frac{l_0}{l_2} + \frac{l_1}{l_2} Y - \frac{1}{l_2} \frac{M_s^0}{P}. \qquad (11.3.10)$$

Now, substituting this expression into the IS equation (11.3.6), we can solve for Y in terms of P:

$$Y = \frac{a + g_0 + bt_0 + G^0 - g_1 \dfrac{l_0}{l_2} + \dfrac{g_1}{l_2} \dfrac{M_s^0}{P}}{1 - b(1 - t_1) + g_1 \dfrac{l_1}{l_2}}$$

or: $Y = A + B\dfrac{M_s^0}{P}$ (11.3.11)

where:

$$A \equiv \frac{a + g_0 + bt_0 + G^0 - g_1\dfrac{l_0}{l_2}}{1 - b(1 - t_1) + g_1\dfrac{l_1}{l_2}}$$

and

$$B \equiv \frac{g_1/l_2}{1 - b(1 - t_1) + g_1\dfrac{l_1}{l_2}}.$$

Notice that equation 11.3.11 suggests a hyperbolic relation between income and prices.

The ISLM schedule is often referred to as the aggregate demand schedule, although the student should not confuse it with the aggregate demand schedule analyzed in chapter 4. That schedule showed a relationship between income and demand, whereas the relation involved here is between the price level and demand. In particular, panel (b) of figure 11.3.1 shows the level of real aggregate demand corresponding to each possible price level. The inverse relationship is based on the following series of events: As P increases, the real money supply falls; as the real money supply declines, interest rates are forced upward; and, as interest rates rise, the level of investment falls; as investment declines, income decreases, causing the amount of consumption to decrease. And, finally, the joint decrease in consumption and investment constitutes a lowering of the value of aggregate demand. In this and subsequent chapters, the term *aggregate demand schedule* will refer to the relation in figure 11.3.1.

The Keynesian labor market is comprised of the behavioral relations:

$$\frac{W}{P} = F'(N, K^0)$$ (11.3.12)

and

$$W = S(N)$$ (11.3.13)

where

$$W = W_0 \qquad \text{for} \qquad N \leq N_1.$$ (11.3.14)

The first of these (11.3.12) is the demand-for-labor equation; whereas,

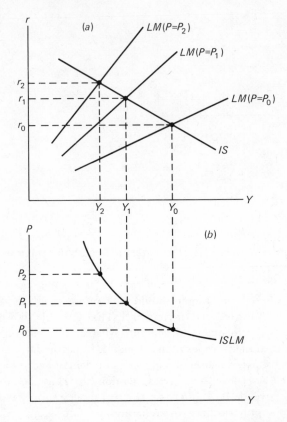

Figure 11.3.1   *The Keynesian Aggregate Demand Schedule*

the second (11.3.13) is the supply-of-labor function. The supply side of the market is characterized by money illusion and the rigidity of money wages over some level of employment ($N < N_1$). As pointed out in chapter 9, an equilibrium condition is also incorporated implicitly into the model in that the supply and demand equations are written in terms of the same money wage variable.[4] If we ignore the range of rigid wages, the two equations of the market contain three endogenous variables: N, W/P, and W (or, if you prefer, N, W and P). Again, if we restrict our analysis to the rigid-wage range, we have only the demand

---

[4]See chapter 9 for a review of this. We suggested there that the equilibrium condition in the Keynesian labor market calls for the equality of the supply price and demand price of labor. In that we do not distinguish between these two variables in writing the supply and demand relations, we implicitly assume equilibrium to take place.

equation to use in finding the values of the endogenous variables N and W/P (or N and P). Under either condition, we have more endogenous variables than equations; consequently, the labor market does not determine uniquely the equilibrium values of the endogenous variables it contains. All of these points were treated extensively in chapter 9, but we can now offer a new twist to the analysis. In panel (a) of figure 11.3.2, we have sketched a supply-of-labor schedule and three labor-demand schedules. Notice that each demand schedule is drawn on the presumption of a specific price level. Observe also that the demand schedule shifts to the right as the price level increases. For convenience, we have chosen the same three price levels considered in our discussion of money- and product-market equilibrium. For each price we find an equilibrium level of employment; thus, this market also fails to offer a determinant solution for the endogenous variables it incorporates.

We can link the labor market to the other markets of the economy by noting that in the short run the level of employment determines the amount of output producers will produce. This relation between employment and output is given by the production function:

$$Y = F(N, K^0). \qquad (11.3.15)$$

If each price level yields a distinct equilibrium value for employment, then it is also true that each price level will be accompanied by a level of output which is consistent with labor-market equilibrium. This phenomenon is shown graphically in the four panels of figure 11.3.2. First, choose a price (say, P_1) and refer to the corresponding labor-demand schedule; then find the equilibrium level of employment at that price (e.g., N_1) from panel (a). Now, trace down to panel (b) and find the level of output corresponding to the specified equilibrium level of employment (e.g., Y_1). In order to show the relation between the assumed price level and the resultant level of output, use panels (c) and (d) to graph Y against P. The resultant schedule is labeled labor-market equilibrium. Notice carefully that this schedule is upward-sloping. This shape is the result of the following scheme: as price increases, the labor-demand schedule shifts to the right; this causes the equilibrium level of employment to rise; as employment rises, the level of output will rise as well.

The labor-market equilibrium schedule is based on labor-supply conditions, technology, and the profit-maximizing behavior of producers. It depicts a relationship between the price level and the amount of output the business sector is *willing* to produce. Because of its nature, it is called the aggregate supply schedule. It can be shown that, given the shapes of the labor-supply schedule and the production function, the aggregate supply schedule becomes steeper as the price level becomes higher.[5] The intuitive rationalization for this shape combines two interrelated concepts: first, successive increments in the price level will bring smaller and smaller increases in employment; second, successive increases in labor will induce smaller and smaller increases in output (due to the law of diminishing returns to the variable factor). We shall thus maintain this hypothesized shape of the aggregate supply schedule throughout our remaining analysis.

We are left so far with two equilibrium relations between output (real income) and the aggregate price level: one stemming from the combined equations of the product- and money-markets and the other derived from the labor-market relations. Neither of these relations determines uniquely the equilibrium values of these two variables. Instead, the equilibrium levels of income and prices are determined jointly by *all three* markets. This can be shown quite simply by combining figures 11.3.1 and 11.3.2 in such a way as to depict the two price-output relations in the same diagram. This is done in figure 11.3.3.

Focus attention on panel (b), where we have presented the ISLM and the labor-market equilibrium schedules. First, consider only the solid schedules in that diagram. As can be seen, there is only one combination of price and output which would satisfy both relations: P_1 and Y_1. This point is marked as E, denoting that it is the general equilibrium position for the economy. At any other combination of values, at least one of the markets of the economy would be in disequilibrium.

---

[5] Suppose that the labor-market equations are given by:

$$\frac{W}{P} = u_0 - u_1 N \qquad\qquad \text{labor-demand}$$

$$W = u_2 + u_3 N \qquad \text{for } N > N_0 \qquad \text{labor supply}$$

$$W = W_0 \qquad\qquad\quad \text{for } N \leq N_0$$

and that the production function is:

$$Y = u_0 N - \frac{1}{2} u_1 N^2.$$

The system can be used to solve for Y in terms of P. First, presume that the relevant range of the labor-supply schedule lies below N_0. In this case, the equation of the aggregate supply schedule is:

$$Y = u_0 [(u_0 - W^0/P)/u_1] - \frac{1}{2} u_1 [(u_0 - W^0/P)/u_1]^2$$

which suggests that increases in P bring successively smaller increments in Y as P takes on higher and higher values. The student should work through the alternative case where $N > N_0$.

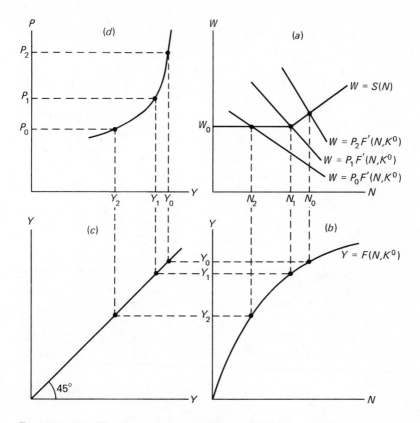

Figure 11.3.2   *The Keynesian Aggregate Supply Schedule*

Once we have found the equilibrium values of P and Y, we can trace backward through the system to find the corresponding levels for all of the other endogenous variables.

Much of the controversy between Keynes and the classics was over the automaticity of full employment. If P_1, Y_1 are the equilibrium values of price and output, the associated equilibrium level of employment will be N_1 and the corresponding money wage will be W_0. According to the labor-market diagram shown in panel (c), the equilibrium will be associated with full employment. That is, N_1 is a level of employment which absorbs all those who want to work at the competitively determined wage. But, as should be apparent from the construction of figure 11.3.3, full employment is only a special case rather than an automatic result of the structure of the economy. If aggregate demand were lower, unemployment would result. To verify this, suppose that

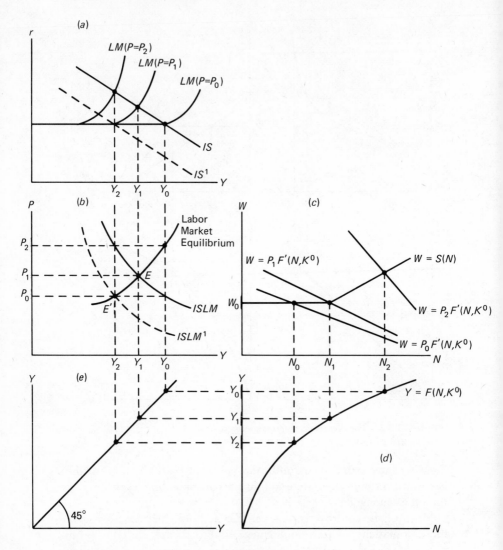

Figure 11.3.3 *The Full Keynesian Model*

(due perhaps to a decline in autonomous investment) product-market equilibrium is give by IS^1 rather than IS [see panel (a)]. If the IS schedule shifts to the left, the ISLM schedule of panel (b) will shift correspondingly to $ISLM^1$. For example, as we have shown, the price level P_0 is now consistent with Y_2 in the product- and money-markets. The new general equilibrium point is represented by E' in panel (b) and this entails a lower price (P_0) and a lower level of output (Y_2). As we trace backward through the labor-market diagrams to panel (c), we find that the equilibrium level of employment is now N_0. But although N_0 is an equilibrium value, it is *not* a full-employment value. Instead, the new general equilibrium of the economy entails unemployment of labor.

This is one of the crucial points of the Keynesian revolution: equilibrium does not necessarily entail full employment. As a consequence of this conclusion, overt economic policy may be necessary for the attainment of full employment.

11.4 Fiscal and Monetary Policy in the Full Keynesian Framework

Although we have already dealt with alternative policy prescriptions, it would be interesting to work out once more the implications of overt economic policies in the context of the full Keynesian model. Let's consider a case in which the economy is operating at point E_0 of figure 11.4.1, with $Y = Y_0$, $P = P_0$ and $r = r_0$. Suppose that this equilibrium position entails unemployment, and that the authorities choose to use fiscal policy to alleviate the problem. In particular, presume that an increase in government expenditures is chosen as the appropriate policy. This policy action will cause the IS schedule to shift to the right by some multiple of the change in G.[6] If prices were to remain unchanged, the economy would move to E_2 (along the original LM schedule) and the level of income would increase to Y_2.[7] This is reflected by the fact that the aggregate demand schedule shifts by the amount $Y_2 - Y_0$ at the original price level. But the shift in the aggregate demand schedule puts pressure on prices, forcing the general price level up to P_1. The rise in prices induces a movement along the aggregate supply schedule (from E_0 to E_1), reflecting the willingness of producers to expand output as prices rise. But the rise in prices also forces interest rates upward (as the LM shifts to the left) and this tends to dampen the expansionary effect of the fiscal policy. In our IS-LM model of chapters 7 and 8 the policy would have left us at E_2, with $Y = Y_2$, $r = r_2$ and prices unchanged at P_0. But the inclusion of the price level as an endogenous

---

[6]In terms of our earlier analysis of chapter 5, the shift would be given by k' ΔG.

[7]The increase in income from Y_0 to Y_2 would be given by m ΔG, where the multiplier, m, is the one used in chapter 7.

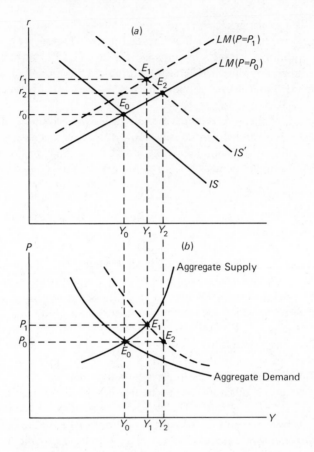

Figure 11.4.1   *Fiscal Policy in the Full Keynesian Model*

variable creates another feedback into the system. Increases in aggregate demand stimulate price rises, which, due to their effect on interest rates, cause investment to fall.[8] Fiscal policy can generally still be used to stimulate the economy, but the effectiveness of such policy is ordinarily less dramatic than one would think from the relatively simple analyses of chapter 7.

The prospects for expansion through monetary policy are also dimmed somewhat by the recognition of the price level as an endogenous variable. Begin with the same equilibrium position and the same prob-

---

[8] We concentrate here on the income effects of policy; we shall treat the inflationary effects of such policies in more detail in a later chapter.

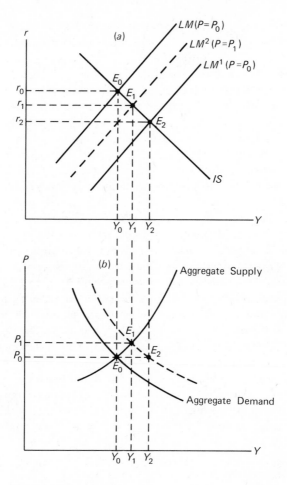

Figure 11.4.2 *Monetary Policy in the Full Keynesian Model*

lem of unemployment, and analyze the impact of monetary policy in the expanded model. Refer to figure 11.4.2. Given the existence of some unemployment, the appropriate monetary policy would entail an expansion of the money supply. In terms of panel (a), this would cause a rightward shift of the LM schedule at each and every level of prices. Ignoring any price rises momentarily, suppose that the LM schedule shifts from LM to LM^1, with P = P$_0$. As we saw in chapter 7, this would prompt a decrease in the interest rate, which would stimulate investment and cause the level of income to rise (in this case, to Y_2).[9] This is mirrored in panel (b), where the aggregate demand schedule shifts by the amount $Y_2 - Y_0$ at the price P_0. But the movement of aggregate demand creates a temporary condition of excess demand, and the price level begins to rise. As prices rise, the real money supply shrinks and the LM schedule starts shifting to the left. Equilibrium is eventually reached at point E_1, where $P = P_1$, $Y = Y_1$ and $r = r_1$. The price rise partially counteracts the rise in the money supply. As long as the aggregate supply schedule is not vertical, *some* increase in output will occur. Prices will not rise in the same proportion as the nominal money supply, so the net result is an effective increase in the real money supply. That is, the price rise will cause the LM schedule to shift only part of the way back to its original position at $LM(P = P_0)$. But, again, we find that policy effectiveness is generally diminished by the sensitivity of prices to changes in economic conditions. Again, the analysis in chapter 7 turns out to be an overly optimistic account of the exercise of policy.

This joint impact of monetary and fiscal policy on both income and prices lies at the roots of a dilemma sometimes faced by policymakers. When the economy faces the dual problems of unemployment and inflation, as has been the case recently, expansionary policy may lead to unacceptable increases in prices. And attempts to lower prices (or the rate of their increase) through contractionary policy may generate damaging increases in unemployment. We shall discuss this problem at some length in chapter 18. For now, remember that policy making in an economy even more complex than the model described in this chapter may at times be as much a matter of values as of mechanics.

11.5 Summary

In this chapter, we contrasted the classical and Keynesian models by comparing their descriptions of the labor, product, and money markets. Based upon the differences we found there, it was to be expected that they would offer different policy prescriptions. To find the policy implications of the full Keynesian model, we first analyzed the effect of making the price level endogenous. As we found, short-run equilibrium can be viewed in the context of the interaction of the aggregate demand and aggregate supply, where each of these relations links output with the price level. The position of the aggregate demand schedule is contingent upon the values of the exogenous variables of the money and

---

[9]See chapter 7 for the multiplier for monetary policy in the case where prices are exogenously determined.

product markets: government expenditures, the tax rate, the level of transfer payments, and the nominal money supply. Monetary and fiscal policy operate through changes in the values of these variables and the consequent shift in the aggregate demand schedule. But, in general, each shift of aggregate demand is accompanied by a price change as well as an output change. In a later chapter, we shall find that this phenomenon lies at the core of the trade-off between full employment and inflation.

Suggested Further Reading

Hicks, J. R. *Critical Essays in Monetary Theory.* Oxford: Clarendon Press, 1967, chap. 4.

Johnson, H. G. "Inside Money, Outside Money, Income, Wealth and Welfare in Monetary Theory." *Journal of Money, Credit and Banking* 1 (February 1969), 39–61.

Klein, L. R. *The Keynesian Revolution.* New York: Macmillan, 1947.

Lange, O. *Price Flexibility and Employment.* Bloomington, Ind.: Principia Press, 1944.

Leijonhufvud, A. *On Keynesian Economics and the Economics of Keynes.* New York: Oxford University Press, 1968.

Meltzer, L. A. "Wealth, Saving and the Rate of Interest." *Journal of Political Economy* 59 (April 1951), 93–116.

Modigliani, F. "Liquidity Preference and the Theory of Interest and Money." In American Economic Association, *Readings in Monetary Theory.* Homewood, Ill.: R. D. Irwin, 1951, pp. 186–240.

Patinkin, D. *Money, Interest, and Prices.* 2d ed. New York: Harper and Row, 1965.

————. "Keynesian Economics and Quantity Theory." In *Post-Keynesian Economics,* edited by K. K. Kurihara. New Brunswick, N.J.: Rutgers University Press, 1954, pp. 123–52.

————. "Price Flexibility and Full Employment." In American Economic Association, *Readings in Monetary Theory.* Homewood, Ill.: R. D. Irwin, 1951, pp. 252–83.

Smith, W. L. "Graphical Exposition of Complete Keynesian System." *Southern Economic Journal* 23 (September 1956), 115–25. Reprinted in W. L. Smith and R. L. Teigen, *Readings in Money, National Income and Stabilization Policy.* Homewood, Ill.: R. D. Irwin, 1965, pp. 104–12.

Appendix 11.A

The Real-Balance Effect

As we saw in chapter 10, the classics had great faith in the workings of the private market. In particular, they relied on the flexibility of wages, prices, and the rate of interest in order to ensure the automatic attainment of full employment. One of the criticisms made by Keynes was known as the "inconsistency argument." According to Keynes, there was nothing to guarantee that the rate of interest which equated full-employment saving and investment could be attained. In particular, Keynes argued that both saving and investment were quite interest-inelastic, and that the required rate of interest could well be negative. If this were the case, the economy could be doomed to operate at an underemployment position.

This Keynesian suggestion resulted in one of the most elegant statements in economics, made by A. C. Pigou in defense of the classical theory:

> As money wage-rates fall money income must fall also and go on falling. Employment, and so real income, being maintained, this entails that prices fall and go on falling; which is another way of saying that the stock of money, as valued in terms of real income, correspondingly rises. But the extent to which the representative man desires to make savings otherwise than for the sake of their future income yield depends in part on the size, in terms of real income, of his existing possessions. As this increases, the amount that he so desires to save out of any assigned real income diminishes and ultimately vanishes; so that we are back in the situation . . . where a negative rate of interest is impossible.[1]

To appreciate Pigou's statement, let us assume that the nominal cash balances of the community are fixed at the level M^0 (where M^0 is defined to be the amount of money in circulation—i.e., it includes cash outside of the commercial banks plus demand deposits). Then assuming that P denotes as usual the general price index, the real cash balances will be equal to M^0/P.[2]

---

[1] A. C. Pigou, "The Classical Stationary State," *Economic Journal* 53 (1943), 343–51.

[2] The reader should notice that according to the definition of the cash balances, they are equal to the money supply.

With the above definitions in mind we can see that Pigou does not argue that the representative individual will consume more simply because the falling price level implies an increase in his wealth. He rather argues that the increase in the value of the real cash balances will satisfy in effect, at least partially, their motives for saving out of a certain level of income.[3]

Thus, the saving function he postulates can be reasonably written as:

$$S = f\left(Y, r, \frac{M^0}{P}\right). \tag{11.A.1}$$

In the above functional relation, it is assumed, as usual, that the level of savings moves directly with the level of income and the rate of interest and inversely with the real value of cash balances, i.e.,

$$\frac{\Delta S}{\Delta Y} > 0; \quad \frac{\Delta S}{\Delta r} > 0; \quad \frac{\Delta S}{\Delta\left(\frac{M^0}{P}\right)} < 0.$$

A plausible linear representation of the above relation is:

$$S = -a + (1 - b)Y + cr - e\left(\frac{M^0}{P}\right). \tag{11.A.2}$$

Now, to drive the argument home, we may rewrite the above function as

$$r = \frac{a}{c} - \frac{(1 - b)}{c}Y + \frac{e}{c}\left(\frac{M^0}{P}\right) + \frac{1}{c}S. \tag{11.A.3}$$

The tenet of the argument then is that if the price level decreases from P^0 to P^1, real cash balances will increase from (M^0/P^0) to (M^0/P^1). The outcome of such an increase will be a shift of the saving schedule from S^0 $(Y^0; M^0/P^0)$ to S^1 $(Y^0; M^0/P^1)$.

Thus, one may argue that there exists a sufficiently low price level for which the saving function attains a positive intercept. Then regardless of the interest sensitivity of the investment schedule, its intersection with

---

[3]Actually, Pigou is referring also to the real value of physical assets (possessions) held by the representative individual. We may, however, assume that this component of the wealth remains constant for the purpose of our discussion and consequently concentrate explicitly only on the issue of cash balance. On this see D. Patinkin, "Keynesian Economics and the Quantity Theory," in *Post-Keynesian Economics,* ed. K. K. Kurihara (New Brunswick, N.J.: Rutgers University Press, 1954), p. 126. In general, the Pigou effect requires only the existence of some class of assets held by the public which are not also claims against the public. Claims against the government, claims against foreigners, and physical assets would thus qualify as bases for the effect.

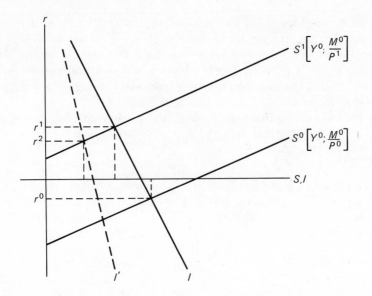

Figure 11.A.1   *The Real Balance Effect*

the saving function will indeed take place at a positive rate of interest. In addition, this intersection, given a sufficient level of deflation, could occur at the full-employment level of income.

Figure 11.A.1 illustrates the argument. We have drawn the graphs of equation 11.A.3 which correspond to the full-employment level of income, Y^0, and two different price levels, P^0 and P^1 ($P^1 < P^0$), i.e.,

$$r = \left[\frac{a}{c} - \frac{(1-b)}{c}Y^0 + \frac{e}{c}\left(\frac{M^0}{P^0}\right)\right] + \frac{1}{c}S$$

and

$$r = \left(\frac{a}{c} - \frac{(1-b)}{c}Y^0 + \frac{e}{c}\left(\frac{M^0}{P^1}\right)\right] + \frac{1}{c}S.$$

As the reader can verify, the change of the price level (for a given level of nominal cash balances and real income) implies a vertical displacement of the savings function. Consider, for example, S^0 and I. Their intersection occurs at r^0, which is negative. Therefore, the full-employment level of income, Y^0, is inconsistent with economic reality, i.e., a positive rate of interest. However, if the behavioral assumption of Pigou is correct, then a deflationary process will shift the saving schedule upward and to the left so that its intersection will occur at an r which is positive. Such a case is depicted by the rate r^1 which is obtained by the intersection of S^1 [Y; M^0/P^1] and I.

The diagram also shows that this argument is on *a priori* grounds independent of the interest sensitivity of the investment schedule. Indeed, schedule I' is by far less sensitive than I. Nevertheless, the intersection occurs at r^2 which is once more positive.

Notice that the argument is based not on a change of prices relative to money wages (as was the argument in chapter 9), but rather on a decrease in the absolute level of prices. Thus, although the real wage rate W/P may not fall because both W as well as P decrease at the same rate, nevertheless the falling price level by itself will ignite the mechanism implied by Pigou, the real balance effect or Pigou effect.

Although the above analysis should be sufficient for the appreciation of the Pigou effect, the reader may obtain a bit more insight by looking at this concept from another angle.

Suppose that we make use of equation 11.A.2 to find the corresponding consumption function, i.e.,

$$C \equiv Y - S = Y - \left[-a + (1 - b)Y + cr - e\frac{M^0}{P} \right]$$

from which we can obtain

$$C = a + bY - cr + e\frac{M^0}{P}. \tag{11.A.4}$$

From equation 11.A.4 we can see clearly that the level of real consumption expenditures depends upon the level of real cash balances held by the private sector. In particular the above equation asserts that a change in the real cash balances through, for example, a decrease in the price level will result in an increase in the level of real consumption.

If we also assume, as usual, that the level of investment depends on the rate of interest, as well as no governmental activity, the expenditure sector of the economy can be written as:

$$Y = C + I$$

$$C = a + bY - cr + e\frac{M^0}{P}$$

$$I = g_0 - g_1 r.$$

From the above set of equations we can derive the IS curve which, assuming that the price level is equal to P^0, is

$$Y = \left[\frac{1}{1 - b} \right]\left[a + g_0 + e\frac{M^0}{P^0} \right] - \left[\frac{c + g_1}{1 - b} \right]r. \tag{11.A.5}$$

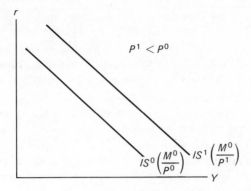

Figure 11.A.2   *Product Market Equilibrium when Real Balances Enter the Saving Function*

From the above equation we see that the relation between Y and r, or the equilibrium of the expenditure sector, can no longer be represented by a simple schedule. Instead we have a family of schedules, one for each postulated price level. Figure 11.A.2 illustrates the case.

Now, recalling also that the LM curve shifts to the right because of either an increase in the nominal money supply or a decrease in the price level (see equations 6.7.18 and 6.7.19 and figure 6.7.4), let us cast Pigou's argument in terms of the IS and LM curve. This is done in figure 11.A.3.

In figure 11.A.3 the vertical line Y_f denotes the full-employment level of income and IS^0 and LM^0 the initial state of affairs at price level P^0. The equilibrium level of income is equal to Y_0.

Notice that IS^0 intersects the Y-axis at a level of income which is smaller than the full-employment level even at zero rate of interest. Obviously, full employment can be achieved only at points A and B. Equilibrium at point A, however, is excluded since this could only occur via a shift of the IS curve, say due to fiscal policy (remember, the classics argued that $\Delta Y / \Delta G = 0$). Thus, according to Keynes, only point B is relevant in this case.

Now, increases in the nominal money supply or a considerable deflation would result in a parallel shift of the LM curve to the right. But even so, as long as the IS curve remained fixed, this would not be enough since r_f is still negative. But the Pigou effect consists of a decrease in savings and a concurrent rightward shift of the IS schedule as prices fall. This eventually will result in a full-employment equilibrium at a positive rate of interest.

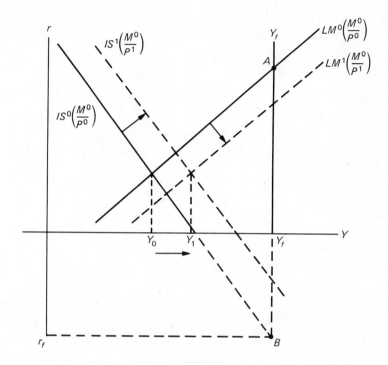

Figure 11.A.3 *The Real Balance Effect in an IS-LM Context*

Thus, the real balance effect, although it is not established as a logical certainty, nevertheless offers a conceivable way out of the Keynesian hold. This is why some economists have called it a last-ditch defense of the classical views.

To be sure, the Pigou effect has been the subject of several attacks on both theoretical and empirical grounds. Indeed, regardless of any redistributional effects implied by the deflationary process, it is very questionable if the existing structural and institutional characteristics of our economies are compatible with the concept of deflation, particularly the extent of the deflationary process which may be required to attain full employment.

Appendix Suggested Further Reading

Lloyd, C. "Real Balance Effect, Sine Qua What?" *Oxford Economic Papers* 14 (October 1962), 267–74.

————. "The Real Balance Effect and the Slutsky Equation." *Journal of Political Economy* 72 (June 1964), 295–99.

————. "Two Classical Monetary Models." In *Value Capital and Growth*, edited by J. N. Wolfe. London: Aberdeen University Press, 1968, pp. 305–17.

Patinkin, D. *Money, Interest and Prices*. 2d ed. New York: Harper and Row, 1965, chaps. 1, 2 and Appendix 2.

————. "Price Flexibility and Full Employment." In American Economic Association, *Readings in Monetary Theory*. Homewood, Ill.: R. D. Irwin, 1951, pp. 252–85.

Advanced Theories of Economic Behavior

CHAPTER 12

Consumption Theories

12.1 Introduction

In an earlier chapter we found that Keynes' consumption function was a significant departure from the tenets of the classical school of thought. Given the intuitive plausibility of the consumption function, one is tempted to wonder why this basic relation between consumption and income had not been recognized before.[1] The explanation for this apparent oversight lies in the general view of the economy held by the classical theorists. Since the classical school maintained that the economy automatically gravitated toward a full-employment equilibrium, the only question pertinent to the classics was the determination of the allocation of a fixed level of income among alternative dispositions. Therefore, the choice of the interest rate as a major determinant of the allocation of income between present consumption and the provision for future consumption (savings) was not totally unfounded.

Keynes, in recognizing that chronic discrepancies could exist between the actual level of income and the full-employment level, was able to raise questions which had previously been considered irrelevant. Insofar as he contended that it was the level of aggregate demand that determined equilibrium income, it became necessary for him to specify the determinants of its level. Indeed, the Keynesian consumption function is the product of such an effort.

In chapter 3 we developed the Keynesian speculations about the behavior of consumption expenditures. In particular, we asserted four basic propositions: first, that the real expenditures on consumption can be expressed as a stable function of real income; second, that the MPC

---

[1] Actually, the idea was not completely new with Keynes. However, he was the first to make the relation explicit and use it in revamping the classical model of the economy.

obeys the double restriction $0 < MPC < 1$; third, that $MPC < APC$, which implies that the relation of consumption expenditures and income is nonproportional; and fourth, that the MPC decreases as income increases.[2] Because of the focus on observed income as the driving force behind consumption, we refer to the Keynesian consumption relation as the absolute income hypothesis.

The propositions about the consumption function and the associated characteristics of the relation between MPC and APC gave rise to the stagnation thesis which became fashionable in the era of the 40s. The proponents of this idea reasoned that, since consumption expenditures do not increase proportionally with income, the gap between income and expenditures on consumption would become increasingly wider as a percentage of income. And, in view of the capricious nature of investment, it would be left to government expenditures to fill this gap. Therefore, the latter component of aggregate demand should be growing at a faster pace than GNP itself.

The stagnation doctrine, however, ignored both the feedback effects which changes in income may have upon the behavior of investment (see chapter 13), and the point that consumption expenditures depend not only on income but on other variables as well.

12.2 Empirical Evidence on the Consumption Function

Two types of data were used to test the Keynesian absolute income hypothesis: cross-section data and time-series data. Cross-section data reflect the relative behavior of a group of individuals at some point of time; time-series data capture the pattern of aggregate behavior over a time span.

In particular, budget or cross-section data would be used to test the relation:

$$c_j = c_j(y_j, x_{1j}, x_{2j}, \ldots, x_{nj}) \tag{12.2.1}$$

where c_j is the consumption expenditures of the j-th economic actor in the sample group, y_j is that individual's level of income and the x_{ij}'s are variables representing n attributes or characteristics of each of the individuals. The latter variables would be included in the statistical test in order to standardize for the differences in these characteristics among the individuals in the study. For example, in such a cross-

---

[2]Actually, in chapter 3 we ignored this alleged property and we assumed that MPC was constant.

section analysis we would probably want to standardize for such attributes as family size, age of the head of household, educational level, and so on. In doing so, we would be recognizing the fact that these characteristics might well vary significantly from one family to another, and that this variation would probably tend to affect the relative levels of consumption expenditures.

On the other hand, time-series data could be used in testing an alternative specification of the consumption function:

$$C_t = C(Y_t, X_{1t}, X_{2t}, X_{3t}, \ldots, X_{mt}) \qquad (12.2.2)$$

where C_t is the sum of real consumption expenditures of some group of individuals (ordinarily, all consumers) at time t, Y_t is the combined income of that group, and the X_{it}'s are characteristics of the group taken as a whole. In this case, the X_{it}'s are included to standardize for the variation of the values of these characteristics *over time* and the consequent effect of their variation on the time path of consumption expenditures. The identity of these latter variables would generally, although not necessarily, differ from the identity of the x_{ij}'s in equation 12.2.1. For example, average age, educational level and family size of the group studied in the time series analysis might not vary substantially over the time period, and thus might not be included in the time-series test of the consumption function. Instead, we might include variables such as the interest rate and the level of prices (both of which would have identical values over the cross section at some point in time).

With these general methodological comments in mind, we now turn to the results of some of the empirical analyses of the consumption function.[3]

Department of Commerce Data

The efforts of the U.S. Department of Commerce to provide complete data on national income and product accounts for use in World War II mobilization planning culminated, in 1942, in the generation of consumption data for the entire United States back to 1929. It was inevitable that this new body of information be applied in testing the absolute income hypothesis.

The Department of Commerce time-series data generally reveal that aggregate consumption and aggregate income are nonproportionally related to each other over relatively short spans of time (say, ten-twenty

---

[3] See Gardner Ackley, *Macroeconomic Theory* (New York: Macmillan, 1961), for a more detailed analysis of empirical evidence on the shape of the consumption relation.

years). That is, they suggest that, over such periods, the APC varies as income changes. Furthermore, they are consistent with the notion that the MPC is fairly constant over the short run. However, the immutability of the relation is brought into question by what appears to be a tendency for the short-run consumption schedule to shift over long periods of time.

Budget Studies

The first data used to study the relation between levels of income and its disposition were those generated by studies of the behavior of cross sections of consumers. These studies were based on data reflecting both income and consumption expenditures for some specified time period, so they could be used to infer approximations of the relation between those two variables for the economic actors included in the cross section. Budget studies generally indicate a nonproportional relationship between family income and family consumption. That is, they show that, at some point in time, the average propensity to consume declines as income increases. In addition, most such studies find that the consumption relation is nonlinear, with the marginal propensity to consume declining somewhat at higher levels of income. These findings are consistent with Keynes' hypothesis. However, successive budget studies (applied to the same group of individuals) often suggest that the family consumption schedule drifts upward with generally expanding income levels. This last result does cast further doubt on the hypothesis that the absolute level of income is the main determinant of consumption.

Kuznets' Study

In order to test the characteristics of the consumption function over the long run, Simon Kuznets compiled and published in 1946 estimates of aggregate consumption and income for overlapping decades over the period 1869–1938.[4] His estimates suggest that, over a relatively long period of time, consumption and income tend to be proportionally related. This, of course, is not necessarily inconsistent with the evidence discussed above; but it did suggest that long-run behavior of consumers differed somewhat from their short-run consumption patterns. It appeared that, in view of Kuznet's study, any theory designed to explain the movement of consumption expenditures should provide an explana-

---

[4]Simon Kuznets, *National Product since 1869* (New York: National Bureau of Economic Research, 1946).

tion of the differences between the apparent short-run and long-run consumption relations.

Much of the research in the analysis of consumer behavior was subsequently (and understandably) directed to the reconciliation of the apparently conflicting sets of evidence. The result of this attempted reconciliation was a series of new theories on consumer behavior, each replacing absolute income with another variant of income. In the following section, we present three examples of these innovations: the relative income, the permanent income and the life-cycle hypotheses.

12.3 The Relative Income Hypothesis

In 1949, James Duesenberry presented his relative income hypothesis.[5] In doing so, he took issue with two of the implicit assumptions underlying the Keynesian consumption function. First, he argued that Keynes had mistakenly presumed that the consumption expenditures of one family were independent of the expenditures of all other families. If we were to apply the absolute income hypothesis to the behavior of a cross section of families, it would imply that each potential level of income would be related to a particular level of consumption expenditures. Thus, if the entire income distribution shifted upward, those families earning some specific level of income (say $5,000) would spend the same amount on consumption as those who had previously earned that amount. As a consequence, the average propensity to consume would depend only on the absolute level of income. It is this characteristic which, argued Duesenberry, implies independence of consumer behavior.

Duesenberry suggested that there is a strong "demonstration effect" in the consumption decision. That is, the behavior of one consumer would depend upon the behavior of those consumers with whom he associates. Thus, to refer back to the example given above, the family making $5,000 *before* the increase in the overall level of incomes would spend a *lower* percentage of income on consumption than would the family earning $5,000 *after* the increase. Had all incomes doubled, the family now making $10,000 would occupy the same position on the income distribution as it occupied when earning $5,000; thus, it would spend the same percent of income as it had previously spent.

---

[5] J. S. Duesenberry, *Income, Saving and the Theory of Consumer Behavior* (Harvard University Press, 1949).

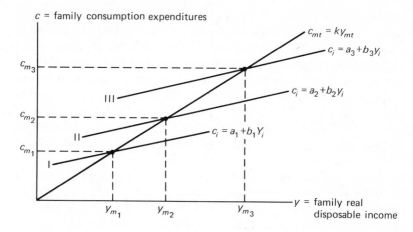

c = family consumption expenditures

$c_{mt} = ky_{mt}$

$c_i = a_3 + b_3 y_i$

$c_i = a_2 + b_2 y_i$

$c_i = a_1 + b_1 Y_i$

c_{m_3}

c_{m_2}

c_{m_1}

III

II

I

y_{m_1} y_{m_2} y_{m_3}

y = family real disposable income

Figure 12.3.1   *Duesenberry's Reconciliation of Budget Studies and Kuznets' Study*

As can be demonstrated, this hypothesis focused on the conceptual difference between a cross-section consumption function and an aggregate time-series consumption function. Consequently, it allowed Duesenberry to reconcile the results obtained through budget studies and those generated by Kuznet's study. Since this point is far from obvious, the diagrammatic exposition in figure 12.3.1 will help to illustrate it. First, consider schedule I, which depicts the relationship between family income (y_i) and family consumption (c_i) at time t = 1. Notice that the shape of this family consumption schedule corresponds to that observed in the budget studies cited earlier. More specifically, *within a distribution of income,* the average propensity to consume declines as we move from low to high family incomes. This characteristic is consistent with both the absolute income hypothesis and Duesenberry's relative income hypothesis. But suppose that all families receive proportional increases in income in period t = 2, thus leaving the income distribution unchanged. According to Keynes, this would be reflected by a movement *along* schedule I, since, as he claimed, the level of consumption depends only on the absolute level of income. However, the Duesenberry hypothesis suggests that the consumption schedule would shift from I to II.

To illustrate this point, presume that in the initial period (t = 1), mean family income is y_{m_1} and the corresponding level of consumption is c_{m_1}. Given the proportional change in all incomes, the family originally earning y_{m_1} in period 1 will maintain its position in the income distribution by earning y_{m_2} in period 2. And, since its position in the distribution of income is unchanged, its average propensity to consume will remain constant, resulting in a level of consumption at c_{m_2}. If we were to apply this same principle to each of the families (each of which maintains its position in the income distribution and thereby maintains its APC), we would derive the consumption schedule labeled II in figure 12.3.1. Thus, in the context of the Duesenberry relative income hypothesis, a general (and proportional) rise in the levels of income would cause successive cross-section studies to reveal shifts in family consumption schedule.

As the consumption schedule shifts over long periods of time (as income rises secularly in such a way as to preserve the income distribution) we could expect long-run time-series studies to expose a *proportional* relationship between aggregate consumption and aggregate income. This conclusion can be derived quite easily from figure 12.3.1. Consider the relationship between mean income (y_m) and mean consumption (c_m) over time. Since both would increase proportionally over the long run, the locus of combinations of y_m and c_m would be a straight line from the origin. That is, over time we would find that:

$$c_{m_t} = ky_{m_t}. \tag{12.3.1}$$

This can be translated into a secular aggregate consumption function by noting that:

$$c_{m_t} = \frac{C_t}{F_t} \tag{12.3.2}$$

and

$$y_{m_t} = \frac{Y_t}{F_t} \tag{12.3.3}$$

where C_t = aggregate consumption at time t;
$\quad\quad Y_t$ = aggregate income at time t;
$\quad\quad F_t$ = number of families at time t.

Thus, equation 12.3.2 can be rewritten as:

$$\frac{C_t}{F_t} = k\frac{Y_t}{F_t}$$

or:

$$C_t = kY_t. \tag{12.3.4}$$

As should be apparent, equation 12.3.4 indicates a proportional relation between C_t and Y_t; in other words, the average propensity to consume (k) is a constant in the long run. Again, Duesenberry's theoretical analysis seemed to fit prior empirical results. In this case, his proportional long-run aggregate consumption function corresponds to the findings of Kuznets' study reviewed earlier. Thus, he was able to reconcile the seemingly contradictory results of the budget studies and Kuznets' study.

Duesenberry further objected to another of Keynes' implicit assumptions. More specifically, he argued that Keynes' unique relationship between aggregate consumption and income embodied the unrealistic assumption that, during short-term cyclical fluctuations, the reaction of consumption to increases (decreases) in income is symmetric. To replace this assumption, Duesenberry offered the following hypothesis:

> Over time, the relation between aggregate consumption and aggregate income is not completely reversible. As income increases secularly, consumption will grow proportionally; but over the cycle, as income falls from its peak, consumers will attempt to maintain consumption standards set previously.[6]

Duesenberry suggested, then, that over the business cycle, aggregate consumption would depend not only on current disposable income, but also on the ratio of current income to the previous peak level of income. He formalized this proposition in the relation:

$$\frac{C_t}{Y_t} = a - b\frac{Y_t}{Y_0} \tag{12.3.5}$$

where Y_0 = previous peak income.

Notice that the consumption function is stated in terms of the average propensity to consume (C_t/Y_t). According to Duesenberry, secular growth in income results in a constant long-run average propensity. This can be verified by noting that if income grows over the long-run at an average rate of r percent per year, the long-run ratio of current imcome (Y_t) to previous peak income (Y_0) would be $(1 + r)$ i.e., $Y_t/Y_0 = (1 + r)$, and the average propensity to consume would be given by:

$$\frac{C_t}{Y_t} = a - b(1 + r) = k \qquad \text{where } a > 0 \qquad (12.3.6)$$
$$b > 0$$

[6]Ibid., p. 7.

where k is a constant. But, as the economy moves through a business cycle, the ratio Y_t/Y_0 will vary, thus bringing about cyclical variations in the APC.

Duesenberry's estimated form of equation 12.3.5 was:

$$C_t/Y_t = 1.066 - .166\, Y_t/Y_0. \tag{12.3.7}$$

Thus, given a secular rate of growth of 3%, $Y_t = 1.03Y_0$ and:

$$C_t/Y_t = 1.066 - .166(1.03) = .895.$$

This computed value of the secular APC corresponds very closely to that obtained by Kuznets in the study mentioned earlier. Over a cycle, of course, the ratio Y_t/Y_0 departs from the secular pattern. Suppose, for instance, that income temporarily declines by 5%. If so, the APC would be given by:

$$C_t/Y_t = 1.066 - .166(.95) = .908.$$

The average propensity to consume is higher than the secular propensity because, given the decline in income, consumers spend a greater percent of their income in order to maintain some of their previous buying habits. On the other hand, as the economy comes out of the recession, the rate of growth of income may be higher than the secular rate. As an example, presume that income grows temporarily at 15% per year. The APC would now be:

$$C_t/Y_t = 1.066 - .166(1.15) = .875.$$

This relatively low value reflects the fact that consumers may be slow to change their standard of living as quickly as income rises over the expansionary stage of the cycle. (This may indicate the general tendency for consumers to react slowly to income changes; we are all, after all, creatures of habit.)

Again, a graphic analysis (see figure 12.3.2) will undoubtedly help to clarify the point. Suppose that we begin at point A, and that income increases smoothly over time. According to Duesenberry, consumption would increase proportionally (i.e., according to a constant APC); hence, the economy would move to a point like B. Suppose now the income decreases. Rather than decreasing consumption proportionally, consumers will try to protect the standard of living obtained while at B. As a result, consumption will be decreased *less than* proportionally, moving the economy to point C. Now, as income starts to increase again, consumers will eventually move back toward point B. If income increases more rapidly than the secular rate of growth, consumers may not adjust their spending habits fully; thus, they may move toward point D, where

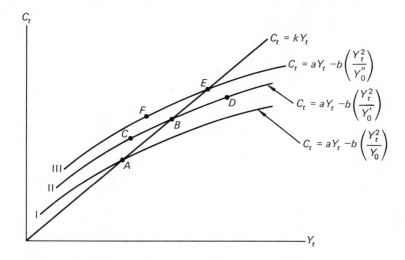

Figure 12.3.2 *Duesenberry's Reconciliation of Time-Series Results*

the average propensity to consume is below its long-term value (k). However, if income resumes its long-term growth rate (r), consumers will adjust along the long-run consumption function—say, from B to E. Then, if the economy enters another downturn, consumers move toward F (rather than B) in an attempt to protect the consumption habits developed at E.

Over very long periods of time, this overall pattern repeats itself as the economy moves through a time path consisting of both secular and cyclical movements. If we employ data from the whole period, we would observe a scatter points around a line like that given by $C_t = kY_t$. However, if we were to collect data for a shorter interval of time, the observations might be dominated by the influence of cyclical variation; thus, we might find a relationship similar to those described by schedules I, II and III in figure 12.3.2.

12.4 A Note on the Intertemporal Aspects of Consumer Behavior

The first author to make use of the preference maps in the study of intertemporal consumer choice was Irving Fisher.[7] He suggested in effect that

---

[7] I. Fisher, *The Rate of Interest* (New York: Macmillan, 1907).

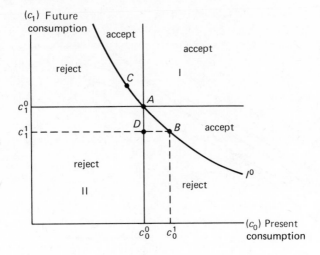

Figure 12.4.1   *The Individual's Tradeoff between Present and Future Consumption*

the prerequisite for such a choice is the possibility of substituting a portion of one year's income with that of another. This idea, twisted a bit, was used by both Friedman and Modigliani, Brumberg and Ando (hereafter referred to as MBA) in their attempt to theorize on consumer behavior. Indeed, their basic premise is that the consumer allocates over time his consumption expenditures in order to maximize his overall level of satisfaction. They postulate therefore a utility function which for a two-period planning horizon assumes the form:

$$u = u(c_0, c_1) \tag{12.4.1}$$

where c_0 and c_1 denote the consumption expenditures associated with periods 0 and 1 respectively.

From the above utility function, we can derive the corresponding indifference curves. Refer to figure 12.4.1 and suppose that our economic actor is at position A, which combines c_0^0 of present consumption and c_1^0 of next period's consumption. Now assume that the consumer prefers more goods to less,[8] and we offer him a combination of goods which is located in quadrant I. Such a combination will include a greater quantity of at least one of the consumption levels. Then by virtue of our assumption the consumer will certainly prefer any combination of c_0 and c_1 which is located in quadrant I. On the other hand, it is quite obvious

---

[8] This is the so-called strong dominance axiom, otherwise known as the piggy axiom.

that the consumer will reject any combination associated with quadrant II.

From the combinations of c_0 and c_1 associated with the remaining two quadrants we have three possibilities. Some combinations will clearly be rejected by the consumer because he feels that he is worse off than at position A. Other points will be accepted for the opposite reason and in between he may be indifferent. Suppose we take away from him a quantity of $c_1^0 - c_1^1$ from future consumption. Now his new position is at point D and clearly he is worse off. Next, suppose that we try to compensate him by increasing the quantity of c_0, and assume that by increasing c_0 to c_0^1 the consumer is just compensated for the loss of c_1. The new position of the consumer is point B, characterized by (c_0^1, c_1^1). By construction, however, points A and B provide the consumer with the same level of satisfaction. The locus of all such points (or combinations of c_0 and c_1 which provide the consumer with the same level of satisfaction) are called indifference loci or curves. The diagram shows that the indifference curve is given by the boundary line between the accepted and rejected regions. Clearly, indifference curves which are located northeast of I^0 are associated with higher levels of satisfaction, whereas those located southwest of I^0 are associated with lower levels of satisfaction.

Therefore, maximization of satisfaction means that the consumer attempts to reach as high an indifference curve as possible. In this maximizing scheme certain constraints are imposed. Assuming that the consumer has no other assets and that he does not plan to accumulate any savings in the interim period, the two-period model would require that all debts contracted in one period should be repaid in the next, and that all saving accumulated in one period should be used to finance consumption in the next. In other words, this analytical scheme precludes perpetual borrowing or lending. It follows therefore that the consumer operates under the constraint that the present value of his consumption expenditures is equal to the present value of his income (see appendix 6.A for a discussion of the present value concept).

His constraint therefore can be written as

$$y_0 + \frac{y_1}{(1 + r)} = c_0 + \frac{c_1}{(1 + r)} \tag{12.4.2}$$

where y_0, y_1 are the consumer's income at periods 0 and 1 and r denotes the discounting factor. This constraint is depicted in figure 12.4.2, where line AB indicates all the options the consumer has in disposing of his total resources. For example, should he decide to consume everything during this period, then he should borrow against his future income. If the rate of interest is r, then the maximum he can borrow is

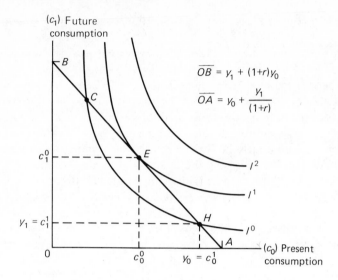

Figure 12.4.2   *Optimum Allocation of Income between Present and Future Consumption*

the present value of his future income, i.e., $y_1/(1 + r)$. Therefore the total available resources are equal to $y_0 + y_1/(1 + r)$ and this is the most he can spend on present consumption. This is shown at point A. On the other hand, should he decide to postpone all consumption expenditures in period 0 in favor of spending in period 1, then the most he could spend would be the sum of his future and present income plus the interest he would earn by lending y_0 for one year:

$$y_1 + y_0 + y_0 r = y_1 + y_0(1 + r).$$

This is indicated by point B in figure 12.4.2. Needless, to say, any point along AB would also show a feasible allocation of his total income.[9]

From 12.4.2 we can see that the level of satisfaction indicated by I^2 is not attainable since any combination of c_0 and c_1 associated with this indifference curve is beyond the means of our economic actor. The best he can do is to allocate his income intertemporally to obtain the quantities c_0^0 and c_1^0. In other words, the maximum satisfaction is derived at point E, where the slope of his indifference curve is equal to the slope of his budget line. Suppose that his income is y_0 and y_1 and that he spends accordingly so that $y_0 = c_0^1$ and $y_1 = c_1^1$. This is given by point H. Obviously, by reducing his present consumption and increasing his

---

[9]Exercise: Find the slope of the budget constraint (AB) and rationalize its meaning.

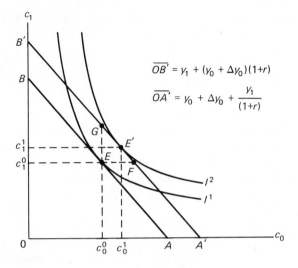

The equations shown in the figure:

$$\overline{OB}' = y_1 + (y_0 + \Delta y_0)(1+r)$$

$$\overline{OA}' = y_0 + \Delta y_0 + \frac{y_1}{(1+r)}$$

Figure 12.4.3 *The Impact of a Change in Income*

future consumption, he will be better off since he can reach a higher indifference curve. In terms of our example, if he saves (lends) a quantity $s = c_0^1 - c_0^0$ and uses it in the next period, he will achieve optimum satisfaction.

Now, suppose that his present income increases by Δy_0.[10] Under these circumstances, assuming that the rate of interest does not change, the budget constraint will shift to the right of point A by an amount Δy_0, as figure 12.4.3 indicates.

Figure 12.4.3 shows that the new intertemporal equilibrium of the economic actor in question is designated with point E', which is associated with increased levels of consumption expenditures in both periods. Actually, this solution excludes two cases. The increase of income could result in a decrease in future consumption and in an increase in present consumption. In such a case point E' would be found along $A'B'$ but it would be lower than point F. Alternatively, if this increase in income were accompanied by a decrease in the level of present consumption and an increase in the future, point E' would be on the $A'B'$ line but above G. These possibilities, however, are excluded since they both imply that consumption of one period or the other is an inferior good.

---

[10]Exercise: work out the case in which his future income increases by Δy_1. Incidentally, why is an increase in present or future income depicted by a parallel shift of the intertemporal budget constraint?

Next consider points F and G themselves. At point F, for example, the increase in income has resulted in an equal increase in consumption. This, however, would imply that $\Delta c_0/\Delta y_0 = 1$, which is a very unlikely case. Thus, we are left with the possibility depicted in figure 12.4.3 which suggests that an increase in the present value of income, whether it is due to an increase of the first- or second-period income, will result in an increase of every component of the consumption stream. For example, if we consider a span covering thirty years, such an increase in the present value of income would result in a corresponding increase of the consumption expenditures for each year.

The above analysis can be conveniently formalized by writing:

$$c_{jt} = f(PW_{jt}) \tag{12.4.3}$$

where c_{jt} denotes the expenditures of the j-th economic actor at time t and (PW_{jt}) is his corresponding present worth. In addition, our comments about telescoping the impact of present worth on consumption expenditures imply that equation 12.4.3 must also satisfy the condition

$$0 < \frac{\Delta c_{j\tau}}{\Delta(PW_{jt})} < 1 \qquad \tau = t, t+1, \ldots t+n.$$

In other words, an increase (decrease) in the level of present worth will be accompanied by an increase (decrease) in consumption expenditures of *all* subsequent periods.

Both Friedman's as well as MBA's hypotheses are anchored more or less on the above analysis. The points of departure of both models share the following basic characteristics. First, the standard of living, or to use Friedman's terminology, the permanent level of consumption of an individual, is determined by his perception of the value of current and prospective net worth. Second, the observed level of consumption expenditures of an economic actor over some time interval will tend to fluctuate randomly around the level of his permanent consumption. Third, the observed income of the economic actor over some time interval will reflect directly the overall level of net worth on which his permanent level of consumption depends.

12.5 The Permanent Income Hypothesis

Friedman's first major point is that both consumption and income include "permanent" and "transitory" components.[11] Thus, observed

---

[11] M. Friedman, *The Consumption Function* (Princeton University Press, 1957).

values of consumption (c) and income (y) from cross-section data could be decomposed as follows:

$$c = c_P + c_T \qquad\qquad (12.5.1)$$

$$y = y_P + y_T \qquad\qquad (12.5.2)$$

where c_P and y_P are the "permanent" components of consumption and income, and c_T and y_T are the respective "transitory" components. The distinction between permanent and transitory consumption was made on two grounds. First, Friedman argued that *observed* consumption expenditures do not always reflect real consumption. As an example, the *use* of a consumer's durable (such as an auto, a washing machine, etc.) is spread over the lifetime of that good, whereas the expenditure itself may be "lumped" into one period. He maintained that consumption—if it is to reflect basic consumer behavior—should be defined in terms of the use of consumer goods rather than the purchase of these items. Second, Friedman contended that consumers may deviate from "normal" behavior in response to exceptional circumstances, and that the consumption purchases resulting from this deviation should not be considered a reflection of the basic consumption-income relation. As an example, families incurring extraordinary medical costs during some period may exhibit a much higher than usual average propensity to consume, due to transitory consumption expenditures.

The difference between permanent and transitory income was founded on the existence of "windfall" gains or losses made by consuming units. According to Friedman, each family has an implicit notion of its permanent income, based on an evaluation of its total wealth (both human and nonhuman). A person makes an investment in human wealth (i.e., obtains skills), and expects a stream of returns on that investment (i.e., wage and salary receipts). Correspondingly, a person with financial assets expects some stream of returns on this type of investment. If we evaluated the present discounted value of these two series of expected returns, we could obtain a measure of a person's current human and nonhuman wealth. Given this present worth, PW, permanent income could be defined as:[12]

$$y_{Pj} = r(PW_j) \qquad \text{for the } j^{th} \text{ individual} \qquad (12.5.3)$$

where, in particular, PW_j is defined to be:

$$PW_j = \sum_{\tau=1}^{\infty} \frac{y_{\tau j}}{(1 + r)^{\tau-1}}$$

---

[12]It is assumed here that the stream of returns accrues to the individual over a long period of time.

where $y_{\tau j}$ is the flow of expected income to the j-th person during the τ-th future period. On the other hand, transitory income would include temporary or "one-shot" gains and losses (e.g., inheritances, unexpected capital gains or losses, loss of income due to injury or temporary over- or underemployment, etc.).

Friedman hypothesized that the basic long-run relation between permanent consumption and permanent income was one of proportionality. This notion could be formalized in terms of both cross-section and aggregate time-series analysis by the two equations:

$$c_{Pj} = k(r, u, w)y_{Pj} \tag{12.5.4}$$

and

$$C_{Pt} = k(r, u, w)Y_{Pt} \tag{12.5.5}$$

for C_P = aggregate permanent consumption

Y_P = aggregate permanent income

and where r is the rate of interest, u is a generic variable representing the tastes and habits of the consumer(s) in question, and w is the ratio of human to nonhuman wealth. The function $k(r, u, w)$ was considered to be roughly constant over the long run; but it was admittedly subject to short-run variations over time and individual variations in a cross section of consumers. In order to translate this theoretical relationship into a hypothesis concerning the relation between observed consumption and observed income, Friedman used three assumptions:

1. permanent income and transitory income are independent;

2. permanent consumption and transitory consumption are independent;

3. transitory consumption and transitory income are independent.

Most criticisms of the permanent income hypothesis have centered on these three assumptions (especially the last one).

Given these assumptions, Friedman (like Duesenberry) was able to reconcile the results of the early empirical studies of the consumption function. To illustrate this point, refer to figure 12.5.1, which represents the cross-section relationship between individual consumption and individual income. The ray from the origin represents the long-run proportional relationship between consumption and income on an individual basis. Over the long run, transitory components of both variables will cancel out; thus, the *observed* relation corresponds to the proportional relation between the *permanent* components. However, at

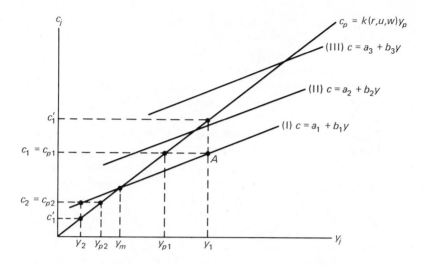

Figure 12.5.1 *Friedman's Reconciliation of Budget Studies and Kuznets' Study*

some point in time, a cross-section study will generally reflect a *non-proportional* consumption schedule like the one labeled I in figure 12.5.1. In a cross section, measured income includes both permanent and transitory components. Those who fall at the upper range of the income distribution (i.e., those with measured income above the mean, y_m) would tend to have positive transitory income (e.g., windfall gains), whereas those at the lower end of the income distribution (i.e., those below y_m) would tend to have negative transitory income (e.g., windfall losses). Since transitory consumption is unrelated to transitory income (by Friedman's assumption), families with observed income y_1 (part of which is transitory) would spend less than c_1' on consumption. On the average, they would be expected to spend only a fraction (k) of their permanent income. Suppose that only y_{P1} of y_1 is permanent income; then, according to the relation between c_P and y_P, these families would spend, on the average, only c_{P1} on permanent consumption. And, since transitory consumption and transitory income are unrelated, transitory consumption could be expected to average out to zero. Thus, a measured income of y_1 would result in an average family consumption level of c_1. This is depicted by point A in the diagram.

Now, suppose that we pick a level of measured income from the bottom range of the income distribution (y_2). Since this would generally include some *negative* transitory income, the permanent component (y_{P2}) would be higher than y_2. Permanent consumption would be some fraction k of y_{P2}—that is, c_{P2}. And given the assumed independence of transitory consumption and transitory income, transitory consumption would average out to zero; hence, observed consumption would have an average value of $c_2 = c_{P2}$.

Schedule I would explain the nonproportional relationship between measured income and measured consumption found in the budget studies. And, given the "averaging out" of transitory income and consumption over the long run, the basic proportional relationship between c_P and y_P would dominate. Without loss of generality, let the relationship $c_P = ky_P$ be applied to mean family income. If we were to assume secular growth in income (leaving the distribution of income unchanged), we could aggregate over families to obtain a proportional aggregate long-run consumption function. Multiplying mean family income (y_{Pt}) and mean family consumption (c_{Pt}) by the number of families at time t, we could obtain:

$$F_t c_{Pt} = k(r, u, w) \cdot (F_t y_{Pt}). \tag{12.5.6}$$

And, assuming that, for each family, transitory income and consumption average out to zero over the long run,

$$C_t = F_t c_{Pt} \quad \text{and} \quad Y_t = F_t y_{Pt}. \tag{12.5.7}$$

Hence, we would have the long-run aggregate consumption function:

$$C_t = k(r, u, w)Y_t \tag{12.5.8}$$

which, if r, u and w are constant, yields a proportional relationship.

The permanent income hypothesis could also be used to reconcile the different shapes of the Kuznets (long-run) and Commerce Department (short-run) consumption functions. Looking at aggregate consumption and income, we could decompose observed consumption into:

$$C_t = C_{Pt} + C_{Tt} \tag{12.5.9}$$

which upon substitution for permanent consumption yields:

$$C_t = kY_{Pt} + C_{Tt}. \tag{12.5.10}$$

This last equation simply denotes that observed consumption will depend on permanent income and random transitory consumption. A person's permanent income, as suggested earlier, depends upon the present discounted value of his wealth (both human and nonhuman). But, given the interest rate, this value of wealth is determined by the stream of returns it generates. Further, this stream of returns would be best evidenced by income receipts of the consumer in question. Wages and salaries would constitute the appropriate return on human wealth; interest receipts, dividends, etc., would be the returns on nonhuman wealth. Thus, the sum of these two types of returns would give permanent income.

But because of the inclusion of transitory income in observed income, the task of defining the concept of permanent income, an inherently nonmeasurable variable, appears to be far easier than translating it into operational terms for use in empirical testing. In accordance, Friedman's suggestion was that permanent income may be approximated by a weighted sum of current and past values of observed income. The simplest weighting system which has been used extensively in empirical work is that of a converging geometric series, according to which permanent income is approximated by:

$$Y_{P,t} = \lambda[Y_t + (1 - \lambda)Y_{t-1} + (1 - \lambda)^2 Y_{t-2} + \ldots$$
$$+ (1 - \lambda)^n Y_{t-n} + \ldots]. \qquad (12.5.11)$$

The main characteristic of this weighting system is that λ is assumed to obey the double restriction $0 < \lambda < 1$. If $\lambda > 1$ then this would imply that measured income has an oscillating effect on permanent income; whereas, if $\lambda < 0$, then $Y_{P,t}$ would assume negative values. Neither of these alternatives appears to be particularly attractive. It is also interesting that the use of a converging geometric series as a weighting system implies that the memory of the economic actor fades gradually and therefore recent values of measured income assume more of an important role in the approximation of his permanent income.[13]

On the other hand, one of the most useful features of approximating permanent income with the aid of a geometric series is the ease of manipulation of the model. Suppose that we use equation 12.5.11 for period $t - 1$ instead of t and multiply the resulting expression by $(1 - \lambda)$ to obtain:

---

[13]Exercises:

1. Prove that for $0 < \lambda < 1$; $\Sigma_{j=1}^{\infty}\lambda(1 - \lambda)^j = 1$

2. Consider the sequence of numbers 200, 190, 185, 182, 181, 175, 176, 174, 172, 173, 174, 170, 168, 165, 160, 159, 155, 156, 157, 154, 152, and suppose that they denote the values of measured income from period t to period $t - 19$. Determine the value of permanent income of period t, assuming that $\lambda = .3$.

3. Given the approximation of permanent income as depicted by equation 12.5.11, find the corresponding approximation of the transitory component. Hint: Use the information given by equation 12.5.2.

4. In view of your approximation of the transitory component of income in Exercise 3 above, could you make an argument for or against the first assumption of Friedman: namely, that permanent and transitory income are independent of each other?

5. Prove that if measured income grows at a constant rate r, so does permanent income.

$$(1 - \lambda)Y_{P,t-1} = \lambda[(1 - \lambda)Y_{t-1} + (1 - \lambda)^2 Y_{t-2} + \ldots$$
$$+ (1 - \lambda)^{n+1} Y_{t-n-1} + \ldots]. \qquad (12.5.12)$$

Subtracting equation 12.5.12 from 12.5.11 we find that:

$$Y_{P,t} - (1 - \lambda)Y_{P,t-1} = \lambda Y_t$$

or

$$Y_{P,t} = \lambda Y_t + (1 - \lambda)Y_{P,t-1}. \qquad (12.5.13)$$

From the above expression we see that permanent income appears to be a linear combination of the measured income of the same period and the permanent income of the previous period. Now suppose that we want to measure the effect (on permanent income) of a small once-and-for-all change in current income. From equation 12.5.13 we see that:

$$\Delta Y_{P,t} = \lambda \Delta Y_t + (1 - \lambda) \Delta Y_{P,t-1}.$$

Assume that $\Delta Y_t = \$1$. Since $\Delta Y_{P,t-1} = 0$, (i.e., the permanent income of the previous period is not affected by the change in the current measured income), it follows that $\Delta Y_{P,t} = \lambda$. However, this is not the whole story; equation 12.5.13 holds not only for period t but for all periods. Therefore we can write:

$$\Delta Y_{P,t+1} = \lambda \Delta Y_{t+1} + (1 - \lambda) \Delta Y_{P,t}$$

The important thing to notice now is that since the change in measured income occurred only in period t, it follows that $\Delta Y_{t+1} = 0$ and therefore $\Delta Y_{P,t+1} = (1 - \lambda) \Delta Y_{P,t}$. But we already know that $\Delta Y_{P,t} = \lambda$. It follows then that $\Delta Y_{P,t+1} = \lambda(1 - \lambda)$. Similarly, we can also find that $\Delta Y_{P,t+2} = \lambda(1 - \lambda)^2$ and more in general $\Delta Y_{P,t+j} = \lambda(1 - \lambda)^j$ for $j = 1, 2, 3, \ldots n, \ldots$

Figure 12.5.2 provides the per-period change in the permanent income due to an once-and-for-all increase in the current measured income by \$1. Notice the declining impact of this change as time passes. We can now make use of the approximation of permanent income given by equation 12.5.11 to substitute for Y_{Pt} in equation 12.5.10. Ignoring the transitory component of measured consumption we find[14]

$$C_t = k[\lambda Y_t + \lambda(1 - \lambda)Y_{t-1} + \lambda(1 - \lambda)^2 Y_{t-2} + \ldots].$$

Lagging the above equation one period and multiplying the resulting expression by $(1 - \lambda)$ we obtain

---

[14] We assume that the transitory consumption is included in the stochastic term which here is ignored since our model is strictly deterministic.

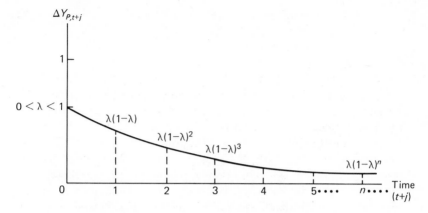

Figure 12.5.2 *The Impact of a Change in Measured Income*

$$(1 - \lambda)C_{t-1} = k[\lambda(1 - \lambda)Y_{t-1} + \lambda(1 - \lambda)^2 Y_{t-2} + \ldots].$$

Comparison of the above two equations reveals that

$$C_t - (1 - \lambda)C_{t-1} = \lambda k Y_t$$

which can be rewritten as[15]

$$C_t = \lambda k Y_t + (1 - \lambda)C_{t-1}. \tag{12.5.14}$$

From equation 12.5.14 we can see therefore that when permanent income is approximated by the weighting system of equation 12.5.11, then this amounts to expressing consumption expenditures as a function of current measured income and measured consumption expenditures of the previous period.

We now return to the main theme of reconciliation and see the implications of using permanent income as an explanatory variable in the consumption function. Consider the basic consumption relation implied by the permanent income hypothesis:

$$C_t = k Y_{P,t} \tag{12.5.15}$$

---

[15] Exercises:

1. Suppose that current income changes once and for all by $1. Estimate the corresponding change in: (a) permanent income; (b) consumption expenditures.

2. Estimate once more the total changes in permanent income and consumption expenditures on the assumption that income changes continually by $1.

By using the expression for current permanent income in terms of measured income and the previous period's permanent income (from equation 12.5.13), we can obtain:[16]

$$C_t = k(1 - \lambda)Y_{P,t-1} + k\lambda Y_t. \qquad (12.5.16)$$

Both of these equations represent the same fundamental hypothesis; however, one can interpret the second one as the short-run version of the first.[17] Since for any given period t the previous period's value of permanent income $(Y_{P,t-1})$ is a predetermined quantity, it follows that the expression $k(1 - \lambda)Y_{P,t-1}$ is a constant for that period. In this respect, the second equation closely resembles the absolute-income hypothesis, in that it has a nonzero intercept.[18] The difference between these two versions is that the short-run schedule will shift over time when income varies, due to the fact that last period's measured income affects last period's permanent income. When the economy attains a long-run equilibrium and measured income exhibits no tendency for change, then eventually $Y_{P,t-1}$ will become equal to Y_t (and hence both will be equal to $Y_{P,t}$) and the second equation will collapse into the first. Thus, the above two versions will intersect each other at a point where $Y_{P,t} = Y_{P,t-1} = Y_t$.

Figure 12.5.3 depicts a long-run consumption schedule and two short-run schedules. Notice that each of the short-run schedules is based upon a given value for $Y_{P,t-1}$. For each of these values (say, $Y_{P,t-1}^0$), only one point on the associated short-run schedule satisfies the long-run consumption equation (e.g., at $Y_t^0 = Y_{P,t}^0$). This point would represent the position of the economy in a long-run equilibrium. As the economy moves from one long-run equilibrium to the next, it moves around the

---

[16]Notice that equation 12.5.15 given the approximation of $Y_{P,t}$ by equation 12.5.11, can be reduced to either equation 12.5.14 or equation 12.5.16. Exercise: Use equation 12.5.16 to derive equation 12.5.14. Hint: Use equation 12.5.11.

[17]Exercise: Suppose that one suggests that the estimated version of equation 12.5.16 for the economy is

$$C_t = .08Y_{P,t-1} + .72Y_t$$

Find the long-run marginal propensity to consume as well as the base used for the approximation of permanent income (i.e., $\lambda = ?$). Given the above estimated form of equation 12.5.16, can you estimate the coefficients of equation 12.5.14 on the assumption that these equations hold exactly?

[18]Notice that the coefficient of measured income, the short-run marginal propensity to consume, is smaller than the long-run MPC. The reason for this is that the contribution of current measured income to permanent income is only λY_t.

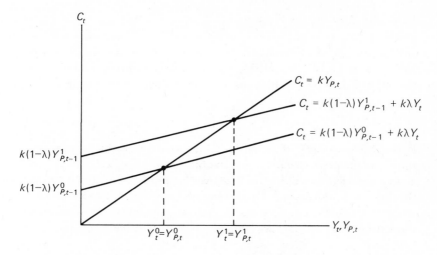

Figure 12.5.3 *Friedman's Reconciliation of Time Series Results*

long-run consumption schedule, and thus long-run data would tend to trace out a proportional relation between income and consumption. But studies in which relatively short periods of observation are used (thus dominated by oscillations of income around a long-run equilibrium path) would generally reveal a nonproportional relationship between observed income and observed consumption. That is, the former type of study would be based on periods long enough so that transitory income roughly cancels out, whereas the latter type would emphasize the effect of the positive and negative levels of transitory income associated with the business cycle.[19]

In summary, Friedman's permanent income hypothesis provided a means of explaining the conflicting results of early empirical studies. Like the relative income hypothesis, it distinguished between a short-run and a long-run consumption function. The latter, according to Friedman, was essentially a proportional relation; the former, nonproportional.

---

[19]Exercise: Assume that k = .8 and λ = .9. Find the expression for the short-run and long-run consumption equations. Then assume that income takes on the following values for periods t − 4 through t + 5: 980, 1000, 1050, 1075, 1100, 1150, 1150, 1150, 1150, 1150. Determine the values of permanent income for periods t through t + 5, and find the associated values of consumption implied by the two versions of the consumption function.

12.6 The Life-Cycle Hypothesis

The starting point of the MBA hypothesis is the assumption that the individual actor of age t attempts to maximize utility,[20] which is expressed as a function of his consumption stream over the span of his life; i.e.:

$$u_j = u_j(c_t, c_{t+1}, \ldots c_L). \tag{12.6.1}$$

It is further assumed that the individual maximizes his satisfaction subject to the present value or worth of the total resources, current and expected, which he will accumulate over his productive life (i.e., up to the time of his retirement). These resources can be identified as the sum of the individual's present assets, α_{jt}, plus the present value of his non-property (labor) income, w_{jt}, minus the present value of his planned bequests, q_{jt}; i.e.:

$$(PW_{jt}) = \alpha_{jt} + w_{jt} - q_{jt}. \tag{12.6.2}$$

Assuming now that $y^e_{j\tau}$ denotes his expected labor income at some future date τ, q_{jL} the terminal value of his bequests, N and L his planned retirement age and actual lifetime respectively, and r a measure of the rate of return on his assets, we may write:

$$w_{jt} \equiv \sum_{\tau=t}^{N} \frac{y^e_\tau}{(1 + r)^{\tau-t}}$$

and

$$q_{jt} \equiv \frac{q_{jL}}{(1 + r)^{L+1-t}}.$$

In view of the above definitions, equation 12.6.2 can be rewritten as:

$$(PW_{jt}) = \alpha_{jt} + \sum_{\tau=t}^{N} \frac{y^e_\tau}{(1 + r)^{\tau-t}} - \frac{q_{jL}}{(1 + r)^{L+1-t}}. \tag{12.6.3}$$

---

[20]See F. Modigliani and R. Brumberg, "Utility Analysis and Consumption Function: An Interpretation of Cross-section Data," in *Post-Keynesian Economics,* ed. K. K. Kurihara (New Brunswick, N.J.: Rutgers University Press, 1954), pp. 388–436; also F. Modigliani and A. Ando, "The 'Permanent Income' and the 'Life-Cycle' Hypothesis of Saving Behavior: Comparison and Tests," *Proceedings of the Conference on Consumption and Saving,* eds. I. Friend and R. Jones (University of Pennsylvania, 1960). Vol. II, pp. 49–175; and F. Modigliani and A. Ando, "The 'Life-Cycle' Hypothesis of Saving: Aggregate Implications and Tests," *American Economic Review* 53 (March 1963), 55–84.

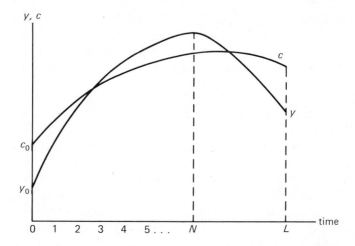

Figure 12.6.1 *Consumption and Income over an Individual's Lifetime*

Therefore, the problem now becomes: Maximize the intertemporal utility, equation 12.6.1, subject to the constraint of the present value of resources as expressed by equation 12.6.3. The solution of this problem yields a functional relation between the level of consumption and the corresponding present value of resources of the individual actor:[21]

$$c_{jt} = \gamma(PW_{jt}) \qquad 0 < \gamma < 1 \tag{12.6.4}$$

Equation 12.6.4 suggests that the consumption expenditures of the j-th individual at time t depend on his estimate (perception) of the present value of his worth. To appreciate the meaning and implications of this functional relationship consider figure 12.6.1.

Let us assume that an individual begins his "productive" life at age 21. Accordingly, figure 12.6.1 marks the horizontal axis with 0 at this age. As the person proceeds through his life his productivity, and as a result his income, increases up to the point of his retirement, N. From this point on, his income declines, but not his consumption, as figure 12.6.1 indicates. In other words, this hypothesis suggests that the consumer takes into consideration the profile of the stream of income during his whole productive life and paces his consumption expenditures

---

[21]Actually the establishment of the behavioral equation 12.6.4 requires also that any increase (decrease) of the present worth is allocated over present and future consumption expenditures in the same proportion as the total present worth. On this see section 12.4.

accordingly. At the beginning of his career and between retirement and death he accumulates negative savings. These are balanced by his positive accumulation in the middle of his working life. Typically, the difference, if any, between these two opposite accumulations is positive and equals the economic actor's planned bequests.

The MBA hypothesis implies that cross-section studies should exhibit a falling APC as income increases; therefore MPC $<$ APC. Suppose that we select a random cross section of the population and classify the individuals in the sample according to their incomes. According then to the MBA hypothesis the likelihood is that the high-income groups contain more persons which belong there only because they are in their middle ages; therefore their APC should be relatively low. Conversely, the low-income groups probably contain people who belong there only because they are young and at the early steps of their careers, and therefore their APC should be relatively high.

To make the hypothesis operational and capable of being subjected to empirical testing, we need to obtain an estimate of the present value of worth. For this assume that the j-th individual does not plan to leave any bequests. We assume therefore that $q_{jL} = 0$, and consequently equation 12.6.2 is simplified to

$$(PW_{jt}) = \alpha_{jt} + w_{jt}.$$

From the definition of w_{jt} we can see that it can be expressed as the sum of the present labor income and the discounted values of expected future income up to the time of his retirement; i.e.:

$$w_{jt} = y_{jt} + \sum_{\tau=t+1}^{N} \frac{y_{j\tau}^e}{(1 + r)^{\tau-t}}.$$

Now we need an approximation of the second term of the above expression. For this, suppose that we define the average expected income to be:

$$\bar{y}_{jt}^e = \left(\frac{1}{N - t}\right)\left[\sum_{\tau=t+1}^{N} \frac{y_{j\tau}^e}{(1 + r)^{\tau-t}}\right]$$

where $(N - t)$ denotes the remaining productive years of the economic actor (i.e., the years up to his retirement). From the above expression then we can obtain

$$\sum_{\tau=t+1}^{N} \frac{y_{j\tau}^e}{(1 + r)^{\tau-t}} = (N - t)\bar{y}_{jt}^e. \tag{12.6.5}$$

Therefore w_{jt} can be expressed as

$$w_{jt} = y_{jt} + (N - t)\bar{y}^e_{jt}$$

and consequently the present value of the individual's worth can assume the form

$$(PW_{jt}) = \alpha_{jt} + (N - t)\bar{y}^e_{jt}.$$

Now we need only worry about $\bar{y}^e_{jt}$. What we really have to do is to express $\bar{y}^e_{jt}$ in terms of observable variables. For example, one could postulate that the average future expected labor income $(\bar{y}^e_{jt})$ of the j-th individual is a function of (is determined by) his level of education, his profession, etc. One of the simplest assumptions one can make is that $\bar{y}^e_{jt}$ is related to the present income, i.e., y_{jt}. For example one can write

$$\bar{y}^e_{jt} = \beta y_{jt} \qquad \text{where } \beta > 0. \tag{12.6.6}$$

Such an assumption presumes that people revise or form their expectations about their future earnings in such a way that if current labor income increases by, say, \$1, then they expect that the future income will increase by β.

Alternatively, one could assume that people, in expressing their expectations about future earnings, consider not only the level of their current income, but also the recent history of its evolution as well. In such a case we could write

$$\bar{y}^e_{jt} = \sum_{i=0}^{m} a_i y_{j,t-i} \qquad \text{where } a_k < a_l \qquad \text{if } l < k.$$

The last assumption, it should be obvious, leads to a formulation of expected income which is very similar to the notion of permanent income. However, regardless of what approximation of $\bar{y}^e_{jt}$ one adopts, the test of the pudding is in the eating; and in the present context the choice among the various alternatives depends on their performance against actual data.

Although MBA tested several hypotheses in regard to $\bar{y}^e_{jt}$, here we shall use only that incorporated in equation 12.6.6. Substituting then the value of $\bar{y}^e_{jt}$ from 12.6.6 into the consumption function, equation 12.6.4, we obtain:

$$c_{jt} = \gamma\alpha_{jt} + \gamma[1 + \beta(N - t)]y_{jt}. \tag{12.6.7}$$

This is the consumption function of the j-th individual expressed in terms of his assets and labor income. From this, assuming any aggregation problem away, we can derive the aggregate consumption function of the economy by summing up all the individual consumption functions; i.e. (letting T denote time):

$$C_T = \gamma A_T + \gamma_1 Y_T^l \qquad (12.6.8)$$

for

$$C_T \equiv \sum_{j=1}^{M} c_{jt}; \qquad A_T \equiv \sum_{j=1}^{M} \alpha_{jt}; \qquad Y_T^l = \sum_{j=1}^{M} y_{jt}$$

and $\gamma_1 \equiv \gamma[1 + \beta(N - t)]$ and where M denotes the number of households or individual economic actors in the community. Notice that since we are aggregating over individuals, t can now be interpreted as the *average* age of the population.

Ando and Modigliani have provided us with several tests of equation 12.6.8. A typical product of their effort for the American economy is[22]

$$C_T = .06A_T + .7Y_T^l. \qquad (12.6.9)$$

From the coefficients of equation 12.6.9 we can identify all the parameters of equation 12.6.8. Indeed, comparing these two equations we see that

$$\gamma = .06 \text{ and } \gamma_1 = .06[1 + \beta(N - t)] = .7.$$

Assuming now that the average age of retirement is at sixty-five and that a person starts his productive life at twenty-one, it follows that the total number of productive years is forty-four, i.e., $N = 44$. Furthermore, assuming also that the average age of the population is, say, 39 ($t = 14$), the above expression becomes $.06[1 + 30\beta] = .7$ from which we can immediately find that β is approximately equal to .36. In other words, for each \$1 increase in current labor income, the average expected income, $\bar{y}_{jt}^e$, increases by 36 cents.

Now we may see the implication of the MBA hypothesis in regard to cyclical and secular variations of APC. First, notice that at any given point of time γA_T can be considered as a constant and therefore the aggregate consumption function can be drawn as a straight line with a slope γ_1, the coefficient of Y_T^l, and intercept γA_T. This is shown in figure 12.6.2. We can see then that during short-run income fluctuation, when assets remain fairly constant, the MBA hypothesis suggests the consumption function looks exactly like the Keynesian version. The difference, however, is that its intercept will change as a result of accumulation of assets through the process of savings, and therefore this process will cause the consumption function to drift upward over time.

It follows therefore that in the long run as income grows we observe points like those along the kY line. To see this consider once more equation 12.6.8 and divide both sides by Y to obtain:

---

[22]See Modigliani and Ando, "The 'Life-Cycle' Hypothesis," section II.

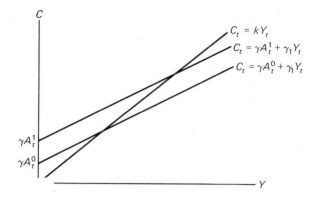

Figure 12.6.2   *The MBA Reconciliation of the Short and Long-Run Time-Series Results*

$$\frac{C_T}{Y_T} = \gamma \frac{A_T}{Y_T} + \gamma_1 \frac{Y_T^l}{Y_T}. \tag{12.6.10}$$

Then the question of constancy of APC pegs on the question of the constancy of the ratios A_T/Y_T and Y_T^l/Y_T, i.e., the ratio of current assets and wage bill to output. Indeed, the long-run behavior of these two ratios for the American economy has been one of constancy.

Therefore we may write

$$\frac{C_T}{Y_T} = k \tag{12.6.11}$$

where

$$k \equiv \gamma \frac{A_T}{Y_T} + \gamma_1 \frac{Y_T^l}{Y_T}.$$

From the above analysis we can see therefore that the MBA hypothesis is capable of providing an explanation of the constancy of the APC in the long run, and of the change in the APC as income varies over the business cycle in the short run.

12.7 Summary and Some Policy Implications

So far, we have focused on the efforts of various theorists to reconcile what appeared to be conflicting evidence of the nature of the consumption function. In the process, we have found that each theory draws a distinction between the short- and long-run behavior of consumption expenditures. Furthermore, each theory implies that we should expect

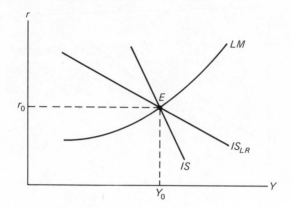

Figure 12.7.1   *Short and Long-Run Equilibrium*

the short-run MPC to be lower than the long-run MPC. But, as we observed in earlier chapters, the value of the MPC is an important ingredient in determining the response of the economy to changes in the values of the policy variables. We cannot avoid the preliminary observation, then, that the effectiveness of alternative policies will not be the same in the long run as in the short run. In this section, we offer a generalized view of the policy implications of the three theories.[23]

Our analysis will be based on the relatively simple IS-LM model developed in chapter 7. Hence, we shall ignore variations in the general price level. Figure 12.7.1 depicts an initial equilibrium position at point E, where the LM schedule intersects two IS schedules. The schedule labelled IS_{LR} indicates alternative long-run product-market equilibrium positions; it is based on a proportional long-run relationship between consumption and income. The other IS schedule (designated simply as IS) is the short-run product-market equilibrium relation, and is derived from a short-run consumption function. First notice that the short-run IS is steeper than its long-run counterpart. The reason for this is that the MPC (and hence the multiplier) is larger in the long run than it is in the short run; hence, a decline in the rate of interest, by stimulating an increase in investment, would have a larger impact on income in the long run than it would in the short run. The second point to consider is that the short-run IS schedule will shift as the short-run consump-

---

[23] Each of the three theories postulates a different type of behavior for aggregate consumption, so their policy implications will differ somewhat; nevertheless, we shall attempt to look at only the general implications shared by the three hypotheses.

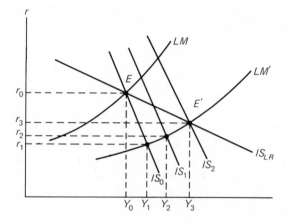

Figure 12.7.2 *Impact of Monetary Policy: Short and Long-Run Effects*

tion schedule shifts. In the context of the relative income hypothesis, any change in previous peak income would cause such a shift. In the permanent income hypothesis, the position of the short-run IS would depend upon the last period's permanent income. And, according to the MBA hypothesis, a shift would be caused by a change in consumer assets. None of these factors, however, would affect the position of the long-run IS schedule, though, since the corresponding long-run consumption relations already take them into account.

With these comments as a basis, let's consider the impact of a typical public policy. Suppose that, in an attempt to expand income, the Fed increases the money supply, thus forcing the LM schedule to the right. As is illustrated in figure 12.7.2, the short-run effect of the policy would be an increase in income to Y_1 and a decrease in the interest rate to r_1. But this increase in income, according to the theories presented in this chapter, will not terminate the long-run tendency for change. Friedman would argue that the change in measured income in this period would cause an increase in permanent income (indeed, this is the only reason why consumption would increase at all); thus, as we enter the *next* period, consumers would exhibit consumption behavior based upon the higher level of the previous period's permanent income. Or, in terms of our earlier analysis (see equation 12.5.16), the short-run consumption schedule would shift upward. But as this happens, the short-run IS schedule would shift to the right, say to IS_1. This movement would cause another increase in measured income, from Y_1 to Y_2; and, correspondingly, permanent income would rise. In the next period, the consumption schedule would rise again (due to the previous period's increase in permanent income), and another shift in the short-run IS would occur. This progression will continue until some new *long-run* equilibrium is reached. In terms of figure 12.7.2, this will happen when the economy finds itself at point E', with a short-run IS schedule at IS_2.[24] What are the basic characteristics of this point? In order to have both short- and long-run equilibrium, measured income and permanent income would be equal. So the income adjustments would have to get progressively smaller, until eventually measured and permanent income would converge on a value (like Y_3) and maintain it.

The relative income hypothesis would imply the same type of adjustment. The increase in the money supply would stimulate an increase in income in the short run. Then, in the next period, consumers would observe a higher "previous peak income." This, in turn, would cause a shift in the short-run consumption schedule, since its position is determined partially by previous peak income; thus, the short-run IS would move to the right. But this movement would stimulate a new higher level of income, and would lead to another adjustment in the next period. Eventually, income will converge on a new long-run equilibrium position (like E') where there is no inherent tendency for further adjustments. Insofar as this would require a constant value for previous peak income, the long-run equilibrium point would entail its equality with current income.

The life-cycle hypothesis gives analogous results. The first increase in income generates additional saving, and this adds to the rise of the consumers' stock of wealth. And, as we saw earlier, an increase in wealth theoretically causes a shift in the short-run consumption schedule (and, hence, the short-run IS). Again, the adjustment process covers several periods.[25]

The common characteristic of these three theories is their recognition of the influence of the past on current behavior. It is this feature which leads to the conclusion that our monetary policy would stimulate a series

---

[24]Exercise: Rationalize the fact that the increase in money supply implied in figure 12.7.2 results in a large, apparently short-run, decrease in the rate of interest which after the initial impact starts climbing until the economy reaches once more full long-run equilibrium.

[25]The diagrammatic model doesn't accommodate the life-cycle hypothesis as well as we might seem to be suggesting. At any level of income beyond the break-even point, some net saving occurs, thus causing a change in the stock of wealth. Thus, not even E' could be considered a true long-run equilibrium. But, aside from this problem, the analogy serves its purpose.

of steps in a long-run adjustment process.[26] It is also for this reason that ignoring the power of inertia (which exerts influence on the behavior of various economic variables) can lead to misleading results.

Policymakers must be concerned not only about the eventual equilibrium point associated with a policy, but also about the path the economy will follow over time and the speed of its adjustment toward its new resting point. Each theory, of course, provides its own claims about policy implications.

A recent example is provided by the 10% income tax surcharge imposed in the middle of 1968 and eventually extended through the end of 1969. This income-tax increase was advertised as temporary and it was aimed at combating the problem of inflation generated by sharply increased government expenditures for goods and services at a time when the economy was at or near full employment. Now even if we assume that government spending on goods and services did not increase, what would one expect in view of the permanent-income hypothesis from such a temporary income-tax increase? The answer is nothing much. Indeed, such a countercyclical measure, being advertised as only temporary, could have little effect on permanent income and therefore generate as little an effect on current consumption.

Several facts concerning the behavior of consumption expenditures follow pretty closely the scenario provided by the hypotheses developed in this chapter. The average ratio of personal savings to personal income for the six quarters before the increase in the tax rate was .073. The same average ratio for six quarters after the imposition came down to .06. In particular, it is quite revealing that between the second and third quarter of 1968 the ratio fell from .072 to .056. How did consumption fare during this period? From the second half of 1968, it grew at an annual rate of .105. However, between the first and second half of 1968, the rate of growth was reduced to .085, and it continued to decrease to .072 and .06 subsequently in the first and second half of 1969.[27] Thus, we see that consumers sharply decreased their savings to protect their level of consumption. As a result, fiscal policy grossly missed the target at which it was aimed. In general, the relatively minor short-run effects of many policies could probably be partially explained by the types of theories we have analyzed here.

---

[26]Exercise: In the context of these three models, analyze the impact of a rise in government expenditures by making your own assumptions concerning the attitude of economic actors in regard to their permanency. Hint: As G increases, both short- and long-run IS schedules will shift to the right initially.

[27]For a fascinating analysis on this see: Robert Eisner, "What Went Wrong?", *Journal of Political Economy* 70 (May–June 1971), 629–41.

Suggested Further Reading

Ackley, G. *Macroeconomic Theory.* New York: Macmillan, 1961.

Arena, J. J. "The Wealth Effect and Consumption: A Statistical Inquiry." *Yale Economic Essays* 3 (Fall 1963), 251–303.

Ball, R. J. and Drake, P. S. "The Relationship between Aggregate Consumption and Wealth." *International Economic Review* 5 (January 1964), 63–81.

Bodkin, R. G. "Windfall Income and Consumption." *American Economic Review* 49 (September 1959), 602–14.

Brown, T. M. "Habit Persistence and Lags in Consumer Behavior." *Econometrica* 20 (July 1952), 355–71.

Evans, M. K. "The Importance of Wealth in the Consumption Function." *Journal of Political Economy* 75 (August 1967), 335–51.

———. *Macroeconomic Activity: Theory, Forecasting and Control.* New York: Harper and Row, 1969, chaps. 2–3, pp. 13–72.

Fisher, M. R. "Exploration in Savings Behavior." *Bulletin of the Oxford Institute of Statistics* 18 (August 1956), 201–77.

Goldsmith, R. *A Study of Savings in the United States.* Princeton, N.J.: Princeton University Press, 1955.

Griliches, Z., Maddala, G. S; Lucas, R; and Wallace, N. "Notes on Estimated Aggregated Quarterly Consumption Functions." *Econometrica* 30 (July 1962), 491–500.

Keynes, J. M. *General Theory of Employment, Interest and Money.* New York: Harcourt, Brace, 1936, chaps. 8, 9 and 10.

Koyck, L. M. *Distributed Lags and Investment Analysis.* Amsterdam: North Holland, 1954.

Mayer, T. "The Propensity to Consume Permanent Income." *American Economic Review* 56 (December 1966), 1158–77.

Modigliani, F. "Monetary Policy and Consumption: Linkages via Interest Rates and Wealth Effects in the FMP Model." In *Consumer Spending and Monetary Policy: The Linkages.* Monetary Conferences Series no. 5. Boston: Federal Reserve Bank of Boston, 1971, pp. 9–84.

Spiro, A. "Wealth and the Consumption Function." *Journal of Political Economy* 70 (August 1962), 339–54.

Suits, D. B. "The Determinants of Consumer Expenditures: A Review of Present Knowledge." In Commission on Money and Credit, *Impacts of Monetary Policy.* Englewood Cliffs, N.J., Prentice-Hall, 1963, pp. 1–53.

Tobin, J. and Dolde, W. "Wealth, Liquidity and Consumption." In *Consumer Spending and Monetary Policy: The Linkages.* Monetary Conferences Series no. 5. Boston: Federal Reserve Bank of Boston, 1971, pp. 99–146.

Zellner, A. "The Short-Run Consumption Functions." *Econometrica* 25 (October 1957), 552–67.

Appendix 12.A

Distributed Lag Models of the Consumption Function

We have already seen that the response of a variable to changes in another often comes with some delay in time. This lapse of time between a cause and its effect is called a time lag. This lag in response may be of a certain length of time, in which case we refer to it as a specific lag; or it may not concentrate on a point in time but instead be spread over time, in which case we have a distributed lag. To be more explicit, suppose we postulate that current consumption expenditures depend upon the level of income of the previous period, i.e.:

$$C_t = a + bY_{t-1}. \tag{12.A.1}$$

In this case we see that, *ceteris paribus,* any change in C_t will reflect a corresponding change in the income of the previous period or alternatively any change in Y_{t-1} is concentrated on changing the consumption expenditures of the current period. This is the case of a specific lag of one period.

On the other hand, in section 12.5 we saw that the presence of permanent income in the consumption function implies that

$$C_t = \lambda k Y_t + (1 - \lambda)C_{t-1}.$$

Now suppose that current measured income changes by \$1. We have already seen that the corresponding change in current consumption expenditures amounts to $\Delta C_t = \lambda k$. It was also pointed out that $\Delta C_{t+1} = (1 - \lambda)\lambda k$ and that, after n periods, $\Delta C_{t+n} = (1 - \lambda)^n \lambda k$. Table 12.A.1 summarizes the resulting chain reaction.

From table 12.A.1 we see therefore that the process goes on continually, from period to period, until the impetus for further changes dissipates. We may now turn to the task of estimating the total change in C due to a given change in Y. This change (ΔC) will be equal to the sum of changes which are distributed over time like the estimates depicted in table 12.A.1, i.e.:

$$\Delta C = \Delta C_t + \Delta C_{t+1} + \Delta C_{t+2} + \ldots + \Delta C_{t+n} + \ldots \tag{12.A.2}$$

Substituting the corresponding values of these changes from table 12.A.1 and factoring out the quantity λk we find

Table 12.A.1.

Period	Change in Consumption by Each Period
t	$\Delta C_t = \lambda k \, \Delta Y_t = \lambda k$
t + 1	$\Delta C_{t+1} = (1 - \lambda) \, \Delta C_t = (1 - \lambda)\lambda k$
t + 2	$\Delta C_{t+2} = (1 - \lambda) \, \Delta C_{t+1} = (1 - \lambda)^2 \lambda k$
t + 3	$\Delta C_{t+3} = (1 - \lambda) \, \Delta C_{t+2} = (1 - \lambda)^3 \lambda k$
$\vdots$	$\vdots$
t + n	$\Delta C_{t+n} = (1 - \lambda) \, \Delta C_{t+n-1} = (1 - \lambda)^n \lambda k$
$\vdots$	$\vdots$

$$\Delta C = \lambda k[1 + (1 - \lambda) + (1 - \lambda)^2 + \ldots + (1 - \lambda)^n + \ldots] \, \Delta Y_t$$

But notice that as long as $0 < \lambda < 1$ the expression in brackets is a converging geometric series and therefore a little algebraic manipulation yields immediately:[1]

$$\Delta C = \lambda k\left(\frac{1}{\lambda}\right) = k \, \Delta Y_t \qquad (12.A.3)$$

In other words, we find that the total change in consumption expenditures is equal to k, which is the long-run MPC of Friedman's consumption function (see equations 12.5.10 and 12.5.11). This change, however, is distributed over a number of periods.[2] From the above analysis it becomes apparent that the study of distributed lag models falls well

---

[1]As a matter of fact this could also be found by realizing that when the impact of change in Y on C ceases then $C_t = C_{t-1}$ for all t's and therefore

$$C = \lambda kY + (1 - \lambda)C$$

from which we may derive

$$C - (1 - \lambda)C = \lambda kY$$
or
$$C = kY.$$

Therefore

$$\Delta C/\Delta Y = k.$$

[2]Compare equation 12.A.3 with your solution of exercises 1 and 2 in footnote 15, section 12.5.

within the realm of dynamic analysis, since it not only provides us with information concerning successive equilibrium positions, but also traces the particular path along which a variable travels in the process of attaining them.

At this point the reader may ask why economic responses may produce a distributed lag pattern. The main reason may be the existence of various frictions which prevent the response from materializing immediately, thus forcing it to be spread over several periods.

This friction usually appears in the form of psychological, technological, or institutional rigidities; or it is due to the general uncertainty which characterizes the evolution of various economic phenomena.[3] Depending on whether we refer to the first or the second set of reasons, the emerging model is called a rigidity (or partial adjustment) or expectations (or adaptive expectations) model respectively.

Distributed Lags Due to Technological and Institutional Rigidities

The theory of consumer behavior is that the consumer tries to maximize his satisfaction given a set of prices and his income. However, in the process of this maximization he is supposed to make decisions about demanded quantities of goods ranging from perishables to stocks of durables. The existence of the stock of durable goods is one of the reasons for distributed lag responses. The adjustment of a variable from its present level to the desired one may be difficult not only for reasons of liquidity or inertia but also because it may imply the purchase of complementary commodities, which requires time. Consider the case in which frozen perishable commodities are introduced in the market. The demand for such commodities may not be substantial at the beginning unless the manufacturers of refrigerators provide adequate storage space in refrigerators. Thus the demand for frozen commodities will increase over time as the production of refrigerators with larger freezers increases. Again, the purchase of a car may await the building of additional garage space or a substantial depreciation of cars presently in the possession of the individual. In addition, one could suggest that the short-run response of a variable may not be the same as in the long run because of frictions due to the imperfect knowledge which characterizes the various markets.

All these considerations lead to the conclusion that in each period only a fraction of the desired adjustment takes place; this notion can be

---

[3] For an extensive development of these ideas the reader is referred to M. Nerlove, *Distributed Lags and Demand Analysis for Agricultural and Other Commodities,* Agriculture Handbook 141, U.S. Department of Agriculture, June 1958.

expressed easily enough. Suppose, for example, that C_t^* denotes the desired purchases of durable goods at time t. Then the expression $(C_t^* - C_{t-1})$ is the corresponding desired change of this flow. Furthermore, if the actual change of the purchases of the goods in question is expressed by $(C_t - C_{t-1})$, then according to the above notions the actual change in flow will be only a fraction of the desired one. This allows us to write

$$C_t - C_{t-1} = \lambda[C_t^* - C_{t-1}] \qquad 0 < \lambda < 1 \qquad (12.A.4)$$

where λ is the so-called coefficient of adjustment.

Notice now that the quantity C_t^* is a variable which is never observed, since some change will always occur before the consumer has time to fully adjust his consumption to this level. However, this quantity is very crucial because it is the only quantity which in effect depends, *ceteris paribus* all other variables, upon the level of income. Despite the fact that C_t^* is never observed, nevertheless equation 12.A.4 can still be made operational by assuming that

$$C_t^* = kY_t. \qquad (12.A.5)$$

Substituting now equation 12.A.5 into 12.A.4, we obtain

$$C_t - C_{t-1} = \lambda kY_t - \lambda C_{t-1}$$

which can be written as

$$C_t = \lambda kY_t + (1 - \lambda)C_{t-1}.$$

Thus we may conclude that, as Nerlove has shown (see footnote 3), the recognition of various rigidities can justify equation 12.5.14 directly without any appeal to Friedman's permanent income hypothesis.[4]

Distributed Lags Due to Uncertainty

The above ideas were developed on the assumption that no uncertainty concerning the future exists. This section analyzes briefly the case in which uncertainty is the main cause for distributed lag behavior. An example may help the reader to appreciate the concept. Suppose that the government reduces the tax rate as a result of a countercyclical policy. This, we already know, implies that, *ceteris paribus,* the disposable

---

[4]Our example here was cast in terms of flows of durable commodities. This should not, however, be taken to imply that it cannot be used for the case of nondurables. In a very important recent contribution Houthakker and Taylor have expanded the above notions to apply in the case of both durable and nondurable commodities. See H. S. Houthakker and L. D. Taylor, *Consumer Demand in the United States: Analyses and Projections,* 2d ed. (Cambridge: Harvard University Press, 1970).

income of the individual will increase. The question now is if and to what extent the reduction in the tax rate will result in an increase of his consumption expenditures. This would depend upon the way our subject looks upon the tax decrease. If, for example, he thinks that this decrease is going to last for a very short period of time, then he may not increase his consumption at all. His behavior, however, will change gradually the longer this tax reduction lasts. Now compare the above case with the case in which tax rates do not decrease but instead the consumer receives an increase in his income which makes his disposable income equal to that of the previous example. But now assume that he considers this increase as a permanent one.[5] Under these circumstances consumption will probably increase immediately and assume its equilibrium value. Even though the consumption expenditures of the economic actor might eventually be equal in the two cases, nevertheless the paths they follow over time will be substantially different from each other. Thus, we see that once we introduce uncertainty into the system, a distributed lag behavior of the various variables involved appears to be quite plausible.

The above discussion suggests in effect that consumption expenditures depend on some measure of "normal" expected income. It is therefore legitimate to ask how the individual generates measures of such a variable. To formalize these ideas suppose that the measured income for period t is equal to Y_t and that the corresponding expected income is Y_t^*. Usually such an individual has based his decision on, and consequently has formed expectations for, such a variable in the past. Also his predictions about expected (normal) income have been partially successful in the past. To compensate for such a partial success, therefore, he expects that his normal income would be somewhere in between what he expected it to be in the previous period and what it turned out to be in the current one. One way of representing such behavior in view of these facts is to express his prediction of the expected income at period t as a weighted average of expected income at $t - 1$ and actual income at t, i.e.:

$$Y_t^* = \lambda Y_t + (1 - \lambda)Y_{t-1}^*. \tag{12.A.6}$$

Notice that since the weights in 12.A.6 add up to one, it follows that Y_t^* will be somewhere in between Y_t and Y_{t-1}^*. Another way of writing

---

[5] It should be noted, however, that with the exception of some very obvious and trivial cases, what is permanent and what is transitory depends crucially on the length of the individual actor's time horizon. In the myopic case in which the consumer's horizon is short, say, one month, then every change in current income could be considered to be permanent; on the other hand, if his horizon is very long, then almost every change could be considered as transitory. Normally, the horizon is of such a length that one finds both concepts present.

equation 12.A.6 would be

$$Y_t^* - Y_{t-1}^* = \lambda[Y_t - Y_{t-1}^*]. \tag{12.A.7}$$

The above equation suggests that only a fraction of the deviation between his current income and normal income of the previous period, i.e. $(Y_t - Y_{t-1}^*)$, is recognized as a change in the normal expected income by the individual.

To express Y_t^* in terms of observed variables we may lag equation 12.A.6 one period to find:

$$Y_{t-1}^* = \lambda Y_{t-1} + (1 - \lambda)Y_{t-2}^* \tag{12.A.8}$$

and substitute the above expression into equation 12.A.6 to obtain:

$$\begin{aligned} Y_t^* &= \lambda Y_t + (1 - \lambda)[\lambda Y_{t-1} + (1 - \lambda)Y_{t-2}^*] \\ &= \lambda Y_t + \lambda(1 - \lambda)Y_{t-1} + (1 - \lambda)^2 Y_{t-2}^*. \end{aligned} \tag{12.A.9}$$

Similarly, we can proceed to substitute Y_{t-2}^* into 12.A.9 and then Y_{t-3}^* and so on for as many periods as we care. After, say, n substitutions the resulting expression will be

$$\begin{aligned} Y_t^* &= \lambda Y_t + \lambda(1 - \lambda)Y_{t-1} + \lambda(1 - \lambda)^2 Y_{t-2} + \ldots \\ &\quad + \lambda(1 - \lambda)^n Y_{t-n} + \lambda(1 - \lambda)^n Y_{t-n}^*. \end{aligned}$$

Now assuming that n is a very large number and in view of the fact that $(1 - \lambda)$ is a positive fraction, it follows that $(1 - \lambda)^n$ can become and remain as small a quantity as we care to make it. Thus, under normal circumstances, the term $(1 - \lambda)^n Y_{t-n}^*$ becomes altogether negligible and Y_t^* no longer depends on its initial values. Therefore we may write

$$\begin{aligned} Y_t^* &= \lambda[Y_t + (1 - \lambda)Y_{t-1} + (1 - \lambda)^2 Y_{t-2} + \ldots \\ &\quad + (1 - \lambda)^n Y_{t-n} + \ldots]. \end{aligned} \tag{12.A.10}$$

If we now assume that the consumption expenditures depend on Y_t^*, i.e.:

$$C_t = kY_t^*,$$

substitution of Y_t^* from 12.A.10 into the above expression will lead to:[6]

$$C_t = \lambda k Y_t + (1 - \lambda)C_{t-1}. \tag{12.A.11}$$

Thus, Nerlove was able to show that the introduction of friction due to either rigidities or uncertainty can justify directly equation 12.A.14, which is implied by Friedman's hypothesis.

---

[6]For this derivation see once more the derivation of equation 12.5.14.

C H A P T E R 13

Investment Theories

13.1 Introduction

The current state of the theory of investment is, to say the very least, unsettled. No reputable economist would suggest that the level of desired investment is solely determined by any one factor; nevertheless, economists do disagree on the relative importance of alternative factors affecting investment. As was the case for our analysis of post-Keynesian consumption theories, it would be impossible for us to present an exhaustive treatment of all the contributions to investment theory.[1] Nevertheless, we can examine some of the most important and most basic theories of investment: the Keynesian marginal-efficiency-of-capital approach, the simple accelerator principle, the capital-stock adjustment principle, the internal funds hypothesis and neoclassical theory. After presenting an analysis of the bare bones of these theories, we shall review one of the empirical studies aimed at testing their importance.

Our investigation will sometimes take us into the realm of dynamic analysis. Traditional investment analysis has been concerned not only with relationships among variables at some equilibrium position, but also with the time-pattern of adjustment of those variables to their equilibrium values. Because of the limited goals of our present analysis, we shall not pursue all of the dynamic properties of alternative theories; such an exposition will be presented in simplified form in our later chapter on growth models.

As a start, one should first establish the basic motive for investment. To the extent that investment is carried out by firms (and this is true for

---

[1] A much more comprehensive review of investment literature can be found in R. Eisner and R. H. Strotz, "Determinants of Business Investments," in *Impacts of Monetary Policy,* ed. Commission on Money and Credit (Englewood Cliffs, N.J.: Prentice-Hall, 1963), pp. 60–333.

the types of investment with which we are dealing here), we might expect that the profit motive underlies expenditures on capital goods. Although some economists have suggested that firms have goals other than the attainment of profits,[2] it is generally felt that these other goals are of secondary importance to most firms. If firms generally act in such a way as to attempt to maximize profits, then it seems plausible to presume that they also base their investment plans on the profitability of the capital goods being considered. Given this, the businessman must consider both the cost of the capital good and the revenues generated by it.

Obviously, firms will not have an exact measure of the profitability of a piece of machinery; to do so, they would have to know exactly what stream of returns they would receive from the use of that machine over its entire lifetime. Since the returns on capital accrue over a long period of time, the businessman must try to estimate the future stream of returns as best he can. Then, he must somehow compare this stream of returns to the cost of the capital good.

There are several conceptual questions involved in this comparison. First, what constitutes the stream of returns accruing to a piece of capital? This can be answered fairly simply if we keep in mind that capital, being a factor of production, contributes to the output the firm can produce and sell. Thus, the returns on a piece of capital will be the extra firm revenue generated through its use. Of course, if the use of an extra piece of capital entails the use of more labor and materials, the extra cost of these other factors of production should be subtracted from the extra gross revenue the firm obtains through its expanded output. Thus, from the standpoint of the firm, the returns on capital would be the stream of extra net revenues (gross revenues minus the extra costs of *other* factors) attributable to the use of the capital.

The second question involves the actual way in which the series of returns can be compared with the price of the piece of capital. Although the cost of purchasing a capital good is incurred by the firm upon delivery, the returns are experienced over the entire lifetime of the capital. How can we compare a present expense with future income? Obviously, it would not be legitimate to just sum the returns and to compare this sum with the price of capital. A dollar earned today has a higher value than a dollar to be earned in some future period; and, conversely, a dollar's return next year has a lower value than a dollar's return today.

---

[2] See, for example: W. J. Baumol, *Business Behavior, Value, and Growth* (New York: Harcourt, Brace and World, 1967); and O. E. Williamson, *The Economics of Discretionary Behavior: Managerial Objectives in the Theory of the Firm* (Englewood Cliffs, N.J.: Prentice-Hall, 1964).

In order to compare present outlays with future income, we must find the present value of that future income.

The present value of a dollar received n periods from now is defined as the amount of money one would have to put into a risk-free interest-bearing asset (e.g., a savings account or a "safe" bond) in order to generate a dollar n periods from now. Since those returns are experienced over a long period of time, we can apply the discounting procedure outlined in appendix A of chapter 6 to find the present value of that stream of returns. We shall denote the returns from the use of capital by the series:

$$R_1, R_2, R_3, \ldots R_n$$

where the subscript denotes the period in which the return takes place. Suppose, for instance, that a piece of machinery is expected to yield net returns of $100 per year for 5 years and $50 for another 5 years; then the stream in question would be:

$$100, 100, 100, 100, 100, 50, 50, 50, 50, 50.$$

In order to find the present value of any such stream of returns, we must discount each element by the market rate of interest. As we saw before (see equation 6.A.6), this discounting process involves dividing the return of the tth period (R_t) by $(1 + r)^t$. Taking account of the whole stream of returns coming from capital, the present value of a piece of capital (V_0) is given by:

$$V_0 = \frac{R_1}{(1 + r)} + \frac{R_2}{(1 + r)^2} + \frac{R_3}{(1 + r)^3} + \ldots + \frac{R_n}{(1 + r)^n}.$$

$$(13.1.1)$$

The reader might wonder why we have discounted the stream of returns on physical capital by the market rate of interest rather than by the percentage return on capital. The reason is fairly simple: it is *one* of the ways of viewing the firm's choice between the purchase of interest-bearing assets (e.g., bonds) and the purchase of physical capital. The use of the market rate of interest in the discounting formula takes into account the cost of using a dollar for physical investment. This cost can be either a direct cost (if the firm borrows money at the current market rate of interest in order to carry out investment) or an opportunity cost (if the firm uses internal funds to purchase capital). Hence, the present value of the stream of returns on capital, computed by discounting by the market rate of interest, does denote the amount of money the firm would have to have in order to generate the *same* stream of income by buying interest-bearing assets.

Given this characterization of the present value of capital, it should be a simple matter to devise a decision rule to be used by firms in the determination of whether or not to buy a particular piece of capital. If the present value of the returns from a capital good is greater than the price of that good, the firm should buy the capital good; if the present value is less than the price, the firm should not buy the capital good. In the first case, the firm would have to spend more on interest-bearing assets than it would have to spend on the capital good in order to generate the same stream of returns.

As an illustration, suppose that a machine yields a series of returns with a present value of $100, and that the price of that machine is $90. In this case, the same stream of returns could be obtained by buying *either* $90 worth of capital *or* $100 worth of interest-bearing assets. Obviously, the former alternative ($90 worth of capital) would be the logical choice. On the other hand, if the same capital good had a present value of only $80, the firm should not purchase it, since $80 worth of interest-bearing assets would yield the same returns on $90 worth of capital. Denoting the supply price of a capital good as C and its present value as V_0, the decision rule pertaining to each unit of capital would be:

If $V_0 > C$, buy that unit of capital.

If $V_0 < C$, don't buy that unit of capital.

13.2 The Marginal-Efficiency-of-Capital Approach

In the preceding section, we illustrated one way in which firms could evaluate investment opportunities, by estimating the future returns on capital and deriving their present value by discounting by the market rate of interest. This present value was then compared to the supply price of capital. An alternative, but similar, approach to the evaluation of investment decisions was developed by Keynes in his *General Theory*. In essence, Keynes considered the same characteristics of capital (the returns and the supply price) and used them to derive a measure of the rate of return generated by investment. This rate of return was called the marginal efficiency of capital.

In order to explain the concept of marginal efficiency of capital, let's go back to our discussion of bond prices, where we saw that the market rate of interest can be used to translate the present price of a bond into its value at some future date. It should also be obvious that knowledge of the current price of a bond and its value at some future date would allow us to solve for the implied rate of interest. Suppose that you were

offered a bond for the price of $100 and that the bond was to be re-
deemed in one year for $110. What would be the implicit annual
percentage return on that bond? We could use the formulation of
equation 6.A.4 to find that this percentage return would be 10%. That
is, if $P_0 = 100$ and $P_1 = 110$, then

$$(1 + r) = \frac{P_1}{P_0} = \frac{110}{100} = 1.10$$

$$r = 1.10 - 1 = .10.$$

And the same procedure could be used for a bond of any maturity.

Given this brief discussion concerning the yield on bonds, it would
appear that we could follow the same procedure to find a rate of return
on physical investment. Insofar as the rate of interest does *not* generally
constitute the percentage yield on physical capital, we need to define
this yield in such a way as to distinguish it from the market rate of
interest. Using Keynesian terminology, we shall define the marginal
efficiency of capital as that discount rate, which, if applied to the stream
of returns on capital, would equate the present value of those returns to
the supply price of capital. More mechanically, the marginal efficiency
of capital (MEC) is the discount rate which satisfies the equation:

$$C = \frac{R_1}{(1 + MEC)} + \frac{R_2}{(1 + MEC)^2} + \frac{R_3}{(1 + MEC)^3} + \cdots$$

$$+ \frac{R_n}{(1 + MEC)^n}. \tag{13.2.1}$$

According to the Keynesian approach, the MEC could be compared
to the market rate of interest and the comparison would yield a decision
rule for firms considering the purchase of capital goods. The appropriate decision rule would be: if the marginal efficiency of capital
exceeds the market rate of interest, the firm should buy the capital good;
if the marginal efficiency of capital is less than the market rate of interest,
the firm should forgo the purchase of the capital good. That is, for each
unit of capital:

if $MEC > r$, buy the capital good

if $MEC < r$, do not buy the capital good.

The foregoing cursory analysis of the investment behavior of an individual firm should allow us to formulate a theory of the way in which
aggregate investment is determined. We should first attempt to show
how the business sector—as a whole—determines the desired level of its
capital stock.

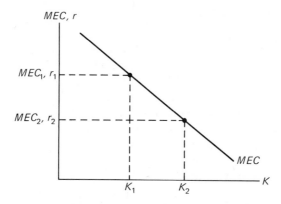

Figure 13.2.1 *The Marginal Efficiency of Capital*

In the process we shall assume that, given the state of technology and the general level of demand for the products of the business sector, the marginal efficiency of capital declines as the stock of capital increases. One might wonder why, since any piece of capital could be exactly duplicated. Remember, however, that the returns from capital (and therefore capital's marginal efficiency) are not solely determined by the physical attributes of capital. These returns also depend on the productivity of capital when used in conjunction with the other factors of production, and on the market conditions surrounding the sale of final goods and the hiring of the other factors of production.

First turn to the concept of productivity. If the labor force is already fully employed, the increased use of capital would eventually bring about diminishing marginal productivity of capital. In other words, if no more labor is available to be used in conjunction with additional units of capital, each additional unit of capital would yield a smaller increase in output than the last. Thus, the physical returns on capital would decline as the capital stock increased. In the case where some additional labor could be secured, it is possible that it could be obtained only through the incentive of higher wages. If so, the net returns to capital would be reduced by the higher labor cost associated with the increased use of both capital and labor. Even if neither of these influences were present, the expanded use of capital stock would (through its influence on output) tend to lower product prices. This in itself would tend to diminish the marginal efficiency of capital. These factors, taken together, allow us to specify a marginal-efficiency-of-capital schedule like the one shown in figure 13.2.1.

In figure 13.2.1, we have represented the capital stock as K, and have measured it along the horizontal axis. Both the marginal efficiency of capital (MEC) and the rate of interest (r) are measured along the vertical axis. Corresponding to our previous comments, the schedule represents the inverse relationship between the stock of capital and the marginal efficiency of capital. Given the rate of interest, r_1, the business sector would desire to have a capital stock of K_1. Each unit of capital up to K_1 would have an MEC (or a rate of return) greater than the rate of interest; but any additional units of capital would yield an MEC below the rate of interest. As the interest rate falls to r_2, the desired capital stock increases to K_2. The intuitive explanation for this phenomenon is that the fall in the interest rate has made all of those units of capital with MEC's between MEC_1 and MEC_2 profitable. It should be noted that the MEC schedule is drawn under the assumption of a *given supply price* of capital (C), and thus abstracts from the supply side of the capital goods market. Thus, the MEC reflects the rate of return on capital at some general price level of capital. For purposes which should become apparent very soon, assume that the given supply price of capital is the one which would prevail if total production of capital goods were just high enough to replace worn-out capital.

The marginal-efficiency-of-capital approach is not, in itself, a theory of investment. Instead, it is a framework for analyzing the business sector's determination of the optimal capital stock. In order to translate this framework into a theory of investment, we must also know the current actual level of the capital stock. In general terms, discrepancies between the actual stock and the desired stock of capital will generate the need for net investment. However, the level of net investment the business sector is actually willing to carry out during any period will be affected by variations in the price of capital. The MEC schedule is drawn for a given level of capital-goods prices; nevertheless, it should be obvious that as the demand for new capital goods increases, the prices of those goods may be driven upward.

In figure 13.2.2, we have presented a typical supply curve for new capital goods. Suppose that the amount of new capital produced for replacement purposes is 50, and that the price of capital is 10 at that level of production. As production expands beyond that point (i.e., as net investment takes place) the supply price increases. For a level of production at 100 (net investment of 50) the supply price is 15; as production goes to 150, the price of capital rises to 21. Rising capital goods prices will lower the rates of return on successive purchases of capital goods, and will thus diminish the amount of investment the business sector will be willing to carry out during any period. Thus, in general, net investment during any period will be less than the discrepancy between the profit-maximizing capital stock (defined at a particular supply price) and the actual capital stock.

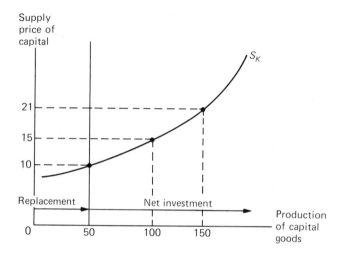

Figure 13.2.2 *Capital-Goods Supply Schedule*

For a diagrammatic explanation of the relationship between the interest rate and the level of net investment, refer to figure 13.2.3. Suppose that the rate of interest is current 7%, and that the economy has adjusted its capital stock to the corresponding optimum level of 1,000. Now, suppose that the interest rate falls to 5%. According to the marginal-efficiency-of-capital schedule, the business sector would want 1,050 units of capital at the *current* price of capital. Referring to panel (b), the desired *eventual* change in the capital stock (again, at the current price of capital) would be 50. However, as net investment is made, the price of capital rises and causes the rate of return on successive units of capital to fall. Consequently, the business sector does not find it profitable to add all 50 units of capital to its stock during the current period. Instead, net investment would be somewhat lower (say, 25). Now, suppose that the interest rate had fallen to .03, rather than to .05. If so, the desired capital stock would be 1,100. Given the assumed actual capital stock of 1,000, the desired eventual change would be 100. This is shown in panel (b). Again, however, the rise in capital prices due to the enlarged demand for capital goods would cause businesses to increase their capital stock by less than 100 (say, 40). If we were to do the same thing for several rates of interest, we could trace out a schedule showing the levels of net investment which would accompany alternative interest rates, given the original stock of capital. This schedule is called the marginal-efficiency-of-investment (MEI) schedule.

The student should keep in mind that there are two basic conceptual differences between the MEC schedule and the MEI schedule. First,

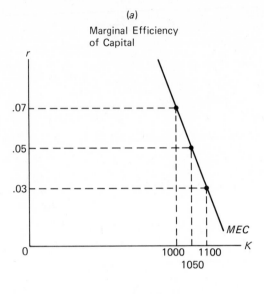

(a)

Marginal Efficiency
of Capital

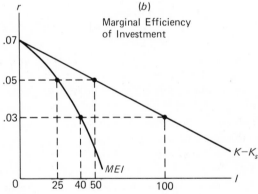

(b)

Marginal Efficiency
of Investment

Figure 13.2.3   *Marginal Efficiency of Investment*

the MEC is based on a given supply price for capital, whereas the MEI takes into account induced changes in this price. Second, the MEC represents the rate of return on all successive units of capital without regard to the existing capital stock, whereas the MEI shows the rate of return on just those units of capital over and above the existing capital stock.

Notice that the MEI schedule will *shift* as the existing capital stock changes; figure 13.2.4 illustrates this point. As a starting point, presume

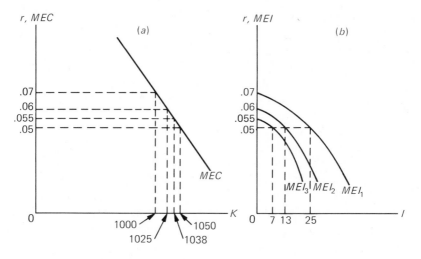

Figure 13.2.4 *Shifts in the MEI Due to Changes in the Capital Stock*

that the initial period finds the economy with a capital stock of 1,000 and an interest rate of 7%. Because capital has already been purchased up to the point where the MEC equals the rate of interest, there is no incentive for net investment. But now suppose that the interest rate falls to 5%, thus creating a discrepancy between the desired and existing capital stocks. We can trace out the path of adjustment as the business sector moves toward the new desired level of capital. In the first period, the relevant *MEI* schedule (MEI_1) is the one based on the existing stock of capital (1,000). According to our previous analysis, a 5% rate of interest would induce a net investment of only 25 in the current period. As the next period begins, the new existing stock of capital is 1,025 (the original stock plus the net investment of the previous period). The new MEI schedule is MEI_2, which lies below MEI_1. The downward shift in the MEI schedule is attributable to the increase of capital during the last period. Given the new capital stock (1,025), the rate of return resulting from the addition of one more unit of capital will be 6%; and, as the purchase of capital expands, the economy travels along MEI_2 until the marginal efficiency of investment reaches .05 (assuming that the interest rate remains at 5%). Presume that this occurs at a net investment of 13, as is shown in panel (b). As we begin the next period, the capital stock has reached a level of 1,038 (1,025 plus 13). According to panel (a), the MEC is approximately .055 at that amount of capital; thus, the new MEI schedule (MEI_3) starts at .055. According to panel (b), the net investment taking place in this period would be approximately 7—thus raising the stock of capital of 1,045.

By now it should be apparent that *some* adjustment in the capital stock (i.e., some net investment) will continue until the stock of capital rises to equality with the desired stock. This adjustment may take several periods; in fact, the number of periods required for the complete adjustment depends on the sensitivity of the price of capital to variations in the demand for capital.

The general points of our discussion of the MEI are these: first, given the size of the existing capital stock, net investment is inversely related to the rate of interest (i.e., the MEI schedule is downward sloping); second, the MEI schedule shifts as the capital stock changes. Thus, the level of net investment is related to both the rate of interest and the size of the existing capital stock. Writing this relation in function form we have:

$$I = I(r, K). \tag{13.2.2}$$

13.3 The Simple Accelerator

The Keynesian analysis highlighted the importance of market rate of interest as a direct cost or an opportunity cost of investable funds. However, Keynes did not completely ignore the influence of other variables on investment. In fact, he emphasized the importance of shifts in the MEC schedule due to variations in the factors affecting the expected stream of returns. Although the relationship between investment and the rate of interest is conceptually well founded, it is generally agreed that the strength of the relationship is rather weak over the normal range of interest rates. Thus, in terms of the Keynesian analysis, the major movements in investment are due to shifts of the investment demand schedule. But what factors are responsible for shifts in the schedule? One of the most direct lines of reasoning would be that, since investment demand is a *derived* demand, like the demand for other factors of production, variations in demand for final goods and services should be the major responsible factor. The technological relationship between final output and capital was used by J. M. Clark in specifying his accelerator principle of investment.[3]

Suppose we begin with an aggregate production function specified in general terms as:

---

[3] See J. M. Clark, "Business Acceleration and the Law of Demand," *Journal of Political Economy* 25 (March 1917), 217–35.

$$Y^P = F(K,N) \qquad (13.3.1)$$

where Y^P = potential aggregate production;
K = amount of capital in existence;
N = amount of labor in existence.

Potential aggregate production is the amount of output which could be produced if all the existing capital were used to its fullest extent. In other words, it is the amount of output the economy could produce if all firms were operating at full-capacity utilization. Now, make two critical assumptions. First, assume that, as production expands, the ratio of capital (K) to potential output (Y^P) is approximately constant; and let that constant be denoted by the letter β. This allows us to write for some time period t:

$$K_t = \beta Y_t^P. \qquad (13.3.2)$$

Also, assume that, at time t, all existing capital is being used; that is, presume that firms are operating at full-capacity levels of output. If this is true, then actual output (which we shall designated as Y) will be equal to potential output, and our relationship becomes:

$$K_t = \beta Y_t. \qquad (13.3.3)$$

Now, if this relation holds for time t, and if β is roughly constant over time, then we can also specify that, in period $t - 1$:

$$K_{t-1} = \beta Y_{t-1}. \qquad (13.3.4)$$

Subtracting equation 13.3.4 from equation 13.3.3, we obtain:

$$K_t - K_{t-1} = \beta(Y_t - Y_{t-1}). \qquad (13.3.5)$$

But net investment is defined as the change in capital stock; therefore, we can write:[4]

---

[4]The student might find the following treatment useful. If we were to attempt to relate the present capital stock to the capital stock of the previous period, we could write:

$$K_t = K_{t-1} - D_t + I_t^g$$

where D_t is the depreciation of capital taking place between the previous and the present period and I_t^g is the total amount of capital purchased over that interval. Now, noting that net investment is just the difference between the total purchases of capital (I_t^g) and the amount of capital which "wore out" (D_t), we have:

$$I_t \equiv I_t^g - D_t$$

Consequently, the relation between past and current capital stock becomes:

$$K_t \equiv K_{t-1} + I_t$$
$$\text{or:} \quad I_t \equiv K_t - K_{t-1}$$

$$I_t \equiv K_t - K_{t-1}. \tag{13.3.6}$$

In view of 13.3.6, equation 13.3.5 can be rewritten as

$$I_t = \beta(Y_t - Y_{t-1}). \tag{13.3.7}$$

This formulation relating the change in output to the level of investment is known as the accelerator equation.

A numerical example will be useful to illustrate the nature of the accelerator equation. Presume that we begin in period 1, and that in this period all firms are operating at full capacity. Instead of looking at the aggregate relationships we've mentioned, we'll look at the behavior of an individual firm planning its investment according to the accelerator principle. This procedure allows us to ignore the feedback effects of investment on the level of demand.[5]

Using this simplifying procedure, assume that we have an individual firm whose output (in constant dollars) is $500 million and whose capital stock is $750 million. This implies that the firm's capital-output ratio, β, is equal to 1.5. Assuming that this capital-output ratio does not change over time, consider the effects of a rise in the demand for its products over time. Refer to table 13.3.1. Notice that, as the demand for the firm's output increases by $50 million in period 2, its net investment is set at a level equal to $75 million(1.5 × 50 million) in order to allow the production of the extra output. Now, as long as demand keeps increasing, net investment will remain positive (as the firm expands the capital stock in such a way as to just satisfy the extra demand through increases in output). But notice the pattern traced out by net investment. At first, over periods 2, 3, and 4, net investment *increases* as a result of larger and larger *increments* in output. Then, however, over periods 5 through 8, investment declines; this is due to the fact that output is increasing at a successively slower rate. As output is increasing, some net investment is necessary; but the smaller the increase in output, the lower the level of investment. When output finally stabilizes at a level of 900 million, the level of net investment falls to zero. Naturally, the capital stock will be much higher in period 10 than it was in period 1 (the student should check this and prove that the new level of capital stock would be $1,350 million); however, there is no need for further increases in capital.

---

[5] If we were to consider the entire economy, the feedback effects would generate what is called a multiplier-accelerator model. See chapter 16 for a full description of this type of model.

Table 13.3.1. *A Numerical Example of the Accelerator Principle*

t time period	Firm's output (in millions of dollars)	Change in firm's output (in millions of dollars)	Firm's capital-output ratio	Firm's net investment (in millions of dollars)
1	500	—	1.5	—
2	550	50	1.5	75.0
3	625	75	1.5	112.5
4	725	100	1.5	150.0
5	800	75	1.5	112.5
6	850	50	1.5	75.0
7	875	25	1.5	37.5
8	900	25	1.5	37.5
9	900	0	1.5	0.0
10	900	0	1.5	0.0

13.4 The Capital-Stock Adjustment Principle

Hollis Chenery took issue with the simple accelerator model proposed by Clark.[6] As we pointed out in the previous section, the simple accelerator is based on the technological relationship between capital and output as reflected in the capital-output ratio, β. Chenery questioned the adequacy of this relation in explaining the behavior of firms operating under conditions of uncertainty. He first suggested that movements in demand are not always viewed as permanent. More generally, firms may require a sustained movement in demand before fully adjusting their capital stock to the level necessary to accommodate the new demand conditions. Operationally, this means that firms will follow a partial adjustment process, in which they satisfy some of the extra demand through increased production (which requires more capital) and some of it through the depletion of inventories. If the new level of demand is sustained, then a series of partial adjustments will be made, eventually closing the gap between the original level of capital and its new desired level.

In addition, Chenery pointed out that even the initial step in the partial adjustment process could not be taken immediately. Even after

---

[6]See H. Chenery, "Overcapacity and the Acceleration Principle," *Econometrica* 20 (January 1952), 1–28.

the decision to purchase capital is made, a gestation period must elapse before the capital can actually be purchased and delivered. If the firm produces its own capital, its production time would have to be taken into account; if the firm buys its capital from another firm, time will be needed for the order to be filled.

To take account of these two modifications of the accelerator, Chenery suggested that the investment equation should be rewritten as a lagged, partial adjustment relationship:

$$I_{t+j} = b\beta(Y_t - Y_{t-1}) \tag{13.4.1}$$

where j denotes the length of the gestation period and b is a reaction coefficient. The reaction coefficient, b, represents the fraction of the desired change in the capital stock of period t which would be put into effect (through the purchase of new plant and equipment) in period $t + j$. According to the partial adjustment principle, we would expect b to fall between zero and one. As an illustration, suppose that $b = .5$. This would mean that one-half of the desired change in capital stock would be accomplished in the jth period after the initial change in demand.

Chenery went on to argue for another modification in the accelerator theory. He pointed out (as had Clark himself) that the simple accelerator mechanism would operate only under the assumption that firms were operating under conditions of optimal capacity utilization. If this were not true, then changes in demand might be met through changes in capacity utilization, rather than changes in the amount of capital. As an example, suppose that a firm is operating far below its normal rate of capacity utilization, and that demand suddenly increases. This would certainly lead to a higher rate of utilization of existing capacity, but would not necessarily induce any change in the capital stock at all. Thus, if we want to allow for the existence of excess capacity, the change in demand will not be a very good indicator of the desired change in the capital stock.

In an attempt to modify the accelerator equation, to accommodate the existence of excess demand, Chenery suggested that the change in demand be replaced by the deviation of demand from its normal level. The normal level (Y^N) was defined as the output which could be produced with the existing level of capital by using that capital at the desired rate of utilization. The implicit assumption behind this modification is that producers will have already adjusted their capital stock to what they consider the normal level of output. This, of course, differs from (and is more realistic than) the implicit Clark assumption that the last period's output entailed operation at the optimal rate of utilization.

Using the notion of normal output, the investment equation can be rewritten as:

$$I_{t+j} \equiv \Delta K_{t+j} = b\beta(Y_t - Y_t^N) \qquad (13.4.2)$$

where β is now interpreted as the capital output ratio at the optimal rate of capacity utilization. And, since:

$$Y_t^N \equiv \frac{K_t}{\beta} \qquad (13.4.3)$$

we could rewrite 13.4.2 as:

$$I_{t+j} \equiv \Delta K_{t+j} = b(\beta Y_t - K_t). \qquad (13.4.4)$$

The term βY_t could be interpreted as the present desired stock of capital, insofar as β is the capital-output ratio at the optimal rate of utilization. If we were to specify:

$$K_t^* \equiv \text{desired stock of capital} = \beta Y_t \qquad (13.4.5)$$

then we could write the investment equation as:

$$I_{t+j} = b(K_t^* - K_t) \qquad (13.4.6)$$

which embodies the rather plausible assumption that investment of period $t + j$ will be some fraction b of the discrepancy between the actual and desired capital stocks.

It should be emphasized that the Chenery capital-stock adjustment model is more flexible than the simple accelerator, in the sense that it allows for a time lag in firms' response and a partial adjustment to changes in demand conditions. In fact, the Chenery principle is often referred to as the "flexible accelerator." Another numerical example will illustrate some of the characteristics of the flexible accelerator. Again, we shall use an analysis of a single firm (rather than the entire business community) to avoid the influence of aggregate investment on aggregate demand.

Suppose that the hypothetical firm in question is now producing $500 million worth of output and that it has a capital stock equal to $750 million (both in constant dollars). In addition, presume that the firm is operating at its desired level of capacity utilization, and that its capital-output ratio at that level of utilization is 1.5. We have made the situation the same as in our previous example of the simple accelerator only so we could focus on one of the most important implications of the capital-stock adjustment principle: namely, the nature of partial adjustments to changes in the level of demand. Let's assume that there is a lag of one period between any change in demand and the resultant change in

Table 13.4.1. *A Numerical Illustration of the Capital-Stock Adjustment Principle*

t time period	Firm's output (in millions of dollars)	Demand for firm's product (in millions of dollars)	Change in the firm's inventory stock	Capital-output ratio	Actual stock of capital (in millions of dollars)	Desired stock of capital (in millions of dollars)	Net investment
1	500	500	0	1.5	750	750	0
2	500	700	−200	1.5	750	1050	0
3	600	700	−100	1.5	900	1050	150
4				1.5			
5				1.5			
6				1.5			
7				1.5			
8				1.5			
9				1.5			
10				1.5			

purchases of new plant and equipment (i.e., $j = 1$). Furthermore, presume that the partial adjustment coefficient, b, is equal to .5. This means that the firm will close one-half of the gap between actual and desired capital stock in each period (allowing, of course, for the one-period gestation time). Now, just to simplify matters even further, presume that the demand for the firm's product increases to $700 million in the second period and remains there for the succeeding periods. Since we are allowing a lag in investment and only partial adjustment to changes in demand, we must also allow for a discrepancy between the firm's demand and its output. To do so, we introduce changes in inventories into the analysis. We shall consider such inventory changes undesired, and thus shall not have to include them in net investment.

Refer to table 13.4.1 for the discussion. In period 1, the firm is producing just enough to satisfy demand; thus, there is no change in inventories. Furthermore, the desired and actual stocks of capital are equal; assuming that this has been true for several periods, the firm undertakes no net investment. Now, suppose that, in period 2, demand increases to $700 million. If the firm considers this new level of demand to be a permanent one, it would revise its desired capital stock to $1,050 million (i.e., 1.5 × 700 million); however, since it takes one period to complete the purchase of any new plant and equipment, net investment remains at zero and the actual capital stock thus remains unchanged. Since the actual capital stock is still $750 million, output cannot be expanded;[7] thus, the extra sales ($200 million) must be made out of inventories. In period 3, the firm will be able to make an adjustment in its capital stock (the one-period gestation period has now lapsed). If its partial adjustment coefficient (b) is equal to .5, this implies that it will buy some amount of new plant and equipment equal to one-half of the difference between its actual capital stock (750 million) and its desired capital stock ($1,050 million) of the previous period. In this case, their net investment would be $150 million and their new actual capital stock would be $900 million. With this new, higher, amount of capital, the firm could produce $600 million worth of output. The new level of output can be found by using the definition of the capital output ratio:

$$\beta = \frac{\text{actual stock of capital}}{\text{potential output}} = 1.5$$

which implies that:

$$\text{Potential output} = \frac{1}{\beta}(\text{actual stock of capital})$$

$$\frac{1}{1.5}(\$900 \text{ million}) = \$600 \text{ million}.$$

The adjustment process will continue until the firm's actual capital stock grows to equality with its desired capital stock.[8]

13.5 Financial Considerations in the Investment Decision

The accelerator hypothesis (in either its naive form or its modified form) clearly emphasizes the physical, or technological, side of the investment decision. It focuses on the relationship between changes in demand and the consequent alterations in the desire of firms to buy new plant and equipment. In doing so, it largely ignores the conditions surrounding the financing of investment projects. Obviously, the exclusion of financial considerations limits the usefulness of the accelerator hypotheses. In fact, in order for the simple accelerator relation to provide a very good explanation of movements in investment over time, two assumptions (in addition to the ones already mentioned earlier) would be necessary.

---

[7] Assume here that the firm does not overutilize capital in order to increase output.

[8] As an exercise, the student should attempt to complete the columns of table 13.4.1 under the assumption that there are no further changes in the demand for the firm's output.

First, the desired amount of capital per unit of output would have to be independent of the cost of raising funds for investment; second, the cost of raising funds would have to be independent of the amount needed by firms.[9]

The first assumption would be necessary in order for one to hypothesize a constant capital-output ratio (β). If this ratio of desired capital to output is related to the rate of interest, then the value of β would change over the business cycle (as the rate of interest changed). Given the importance of this assumption, how likely is it that it conforms to the actual behavior of businessmen? Some theorists argue that this likelihood is rather small. They point out that firms will try to choose the least-cost method of production, and that this choice will be based upon the relative prices (as well as the relative productivities) of the factors of production. Since the interest rate is a rough measure of the cost of using funds to buy capital, variations in interest rates should be expected to affect the combination of factors used at each level of output. As interest rates rise, we might expect the capital-output ratio to fall (since, *ceteris paribus,* capital would have become more expensive relative to the other factors of production); as interest rates fall, we would think that the capital-output ratio would rise (as capital becomes cheaper relative to the other factors).

As we saw earlier, Keynes emphasized the importance of the rate of interest in his marginal efficiency of capital approach. Nevertheless, most subsequent empirical studies have suggested that investment and the rate of interest do not seem to be very highly correlated over time. These negative empirical findings were used as a rationale for minimizing the importance of the rate of interest in theories of investment.

The second implicit assumption underlying a purely physical relationship between changes in output and levels of investment—that the cost of raising investable funds is unaffected by the amount raised—is challenged by a group of economists we shall call the residual funds theorists. In much of investment theory, it is assumed that the supply of investable funds is perfectly elastic with respect to the rate of interest. That is, it is presumed that the cost of raising funds stays the same, no matter how large a sum is needed.

As we pointed out in the beginning of this chapter, there are two ways of viewing the cost of investable funds. In the case of funds already in the coffers of firms (internal funds), there is an opportunity cost of using these funds for investment purposes, which is the yield the firm could

---

[9] J. Duesenberry, *Business Cycles and Economic Growth* (New York: McGraw-Hill, 1958), p. 38.

obtain by using the funds to buy interest-bearing assets. If firms need to borrow funds from an outside source (external funds), there is a direct cost. If the cost of using external funds exceeds the opportunity cost of using internal funds, then it would be logical to presume that firms would prefer internal financing to external financing. And, if this preference is exhibited (as it seems to be), then the *amount* of available internal funds should be a partial determinant of the amount of investment firms are willing to carry out. In fact, if the cost of external financing substantially exceeds the opportunity cost of internal financing, some firms may limit their investment expenditures to the amount of their internal funds. Two issues need to be discussed in this context: first, what should we include in "internal funds"; second, why should the cost of investable funds increase as firms begin to use external funds?

The answer to the first question is fairly simple. If we are speaking about the internal funds available for *gross* investment, then the relevant measure would include retained earnings plus the pool of depreciation allowances made by the firm.[10] If we are referring to the funds available for net investment (gross investment minus replacement investment, where the latter is theoretically financed from depreciation allowances), then retained earnings would be the appropriate figure.

If internal funds remained at a relatively constant level over the business cycle, we wouldn't expect them to have much of an effect on the level of investment. However, this is not the case. Instead, retained earnings tend to fluctuate a great deal as the general level of business activity changes. The reason for this rather intense variability lies in the definition of retained earnings: the difference between net (after-tax) profits and dividend payments. Net profits tend to move rather dramatically (as compared to income, consumption, etc.) over the business cycle; however, dividends tend to stay relatively constant, due to firms' reluctance to establish an erratic dividend policy. Thus, retained earnings will vary substantially as the level of business activity varies. If managers consider the amount of internal funds to be somewhat of a constraint on investment expenditures, we might expect the variations in retained earnings to be an important determinant of investment. Obviously, no one would suggest that there is a rigid tie between internal funds and investment expenditures. It is recognized that investors will often invest *less* than is available in the form of retained earnings (for example, in the case where few profitable invest-

---

[10]Obviously, firms may also have some funds left over from previous years; however, we shall ignore these (except in the case of depreciation reserves) in order to simplify the analysis.

ment opportunities are foreseen). And, it is obvious that, if prospective investments yield a high enough return, investors will debt-finance some of these expenditures. Nevertheless, there is still thought to be a *tendency* for investment to be related to the level of available internal funds.

It still remains to be shown why external financing might entail a higher cost of funds than internal financing. The rising cost of funds is partially due to the real characteristics of the financial markets and partially due to the psychological makeup of entrepreneurs. Our earlier treatment of the marginal efficiency of investment was simplified by assuming that the MEI is compared against "the" market rate of interest. As any novice knows, there is no such thing as "the" rate of interest. Instead, financial markets are characterized by a complex structure of interest rates, where differences among these interest rates are based partially on risk differentials and varying maturities. A "perfect" financial market—one in which there is full knowledge and perfect competition—would generate a structure of interest rates which fully reflected some consensus about risk and maturity differentials, but real-world markets do not generally do so. Imperfections often distort the interest-rate structure. For example, lending institutions are ordinarily able (and willing) to take advantage of their preferred position in the financial arena to drive a wedge between their borrowing and lending rates. As a result, the rates at which firms would lend funds (their internal cost) is often lower than the rates they must pay in order to secure funds through external financing.

Even aside from any real differences between the costs of internal and external financing, there seems to be an aversion on the part of firms toward debt-financing. It may be that managers simply desire to avoid the appearance of overextension in their handling of investment programs; or, managers may consider the costs of keeping dividends relatively modest (thereby freeing internal funds) to be lower than the costs of external financing. At any rate, empirical studies do seem to confirm that firms have a general preference for internal financing.[11]

To extend the ideas presented above, the cost of obtaining external funds may increase (for both the individual firm and the business sector as a whole) as the amount raised increases. First, consider the individual firm. As it successively raises more and more funds from lending institutions, its debt position worsens. As this happens, the firm becomes a less-favored customer and consequently faces higher borrowing rates. One

---

[11] For example, see J. R. Meyer and E. Kuh, *The Investment Decision* (Harvard University Press, 1957).

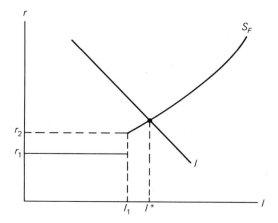

Figure 13.5.1 *The Residual-Funds Approach*

could also hypothesize that the firm's psychological costs of external financing increase as the amount borrowed increases.[12] If we look at the business sector as a whole, the rationale for a rising cost of external funds is slightly different. In this case, increasing demands for investable funds may prompt rationing procedures on the part of lenders. Banks may refuse credit to some of their less desirable customers (e.g., smaller firms with already relatively high amounts of debt) and may raise interest rates across the board for those who are granted loans. Even the casual observer of economic conditions has undoubtedly witnessed the lemming-like rush of individual banks toward higher "prime" rates when loan demand increases.[13]

Let us quickly recapitulate our preliminary comments concerning the residual funds theory of investment. First, we saw that, for either real or psychological reasons, external financing may be associated with higher interest costs than internal financing. Second, we observed that the cost of external funds rises as the amount to be raised increases. Using both of these notions, we can sketch a cost-of-funds schedule like the one shown in figure 13.5.1. Since the cost-of-funds schedule can be viewed as a supply schedule for investable funds, we have labeled it S_F, with the cost of funds constant at the level r_1. This corresponds to the range of

---

[12]This is the general approach taken by James Duesenberry in *Business Cycles and Economic Growth* (McGraw-Hill, 1958).

[13]The prime rate is that interest rate charged to banks' most-favored customers. According to rumor, some borrowers may actually qualify for it; obviously, most do not.

investment which could be financed through the use of residual funds, or retained earnings. At I_1, we have shown the discontinuity in the cost of funds corresponding to the switchover from internal to external funds. The cost of using external financing originates at r_2 and increases as more and more of these funds are secured. Since we have both a supply-of-investable-funds schedule (S_F) and a demand-for-investable-funds schedule (I), we can use a traditional supply and demand analysis to analyze the determination of an equilibrium level of investment. Given the positions of both S_F and I, the equilibrium level of investment will occur at their point of intersection (I^* in figure 13.5.1).

The theoretical model advanced by residual funds theorists can be used in conjunction with the accelerator and MEI models to analyze the movement of investment over time. First, however, we need to integrate these three theories into one general (although eclectic) model of investment behavior. Suppose that we consider a hypothetical firm which considers both movements in demand and financing costs when making investment plans. We could characterize its investment demand function in general as:

$$I = f(r, \Delta Y). \tag{13.5.1}$$

Equation 13.5.1 expresses investment demand as a function of two variables: "the" rate of interest (r) and the change in the level of demand (ΔY).

In order to plot this relation graphically, we can use a device employed in earlier chapters (see chapter 5) and explicitly depict the relationship between investment and the rate of interest for alternative values of the change in demand. Setting the change in demand equal to ΔY_1 and $\Delta Y_2 (\Delta Y_1 < \Delta Y_2)$, respectively, we can sketch the two corresponding investment demand schedules as I_1 and I_2 in panel (a) of figure 13.5.2. For simplicity, assume that the supply-of-funds schedule remains fixed over the relevant periods. For each of the investment demand schedules (I_1, I_2) there corresponds an equilibrium amount of investment (I_1^* and I_2^*). First, consider a time period which is characterized by a change in demand equal to ΔY_1, and the existence of internal funds sufficient to carry out investment plans. Let I_1^* denote the equilibrium level of investment during this period. Now, suppose that the change in demand increases in the next period to ΔY_2, thus moving the investment demand schedule to I_2. If internal funds are still sufficient to carry out the higher level of investment, and if the market rate of interest (r_1) remains unchanged, investment will increase to I_2^*. Notice that, in this case, investment increases by the full shift in the investment demand schedule. If one were to observe this event in the real world, he would be tempted to

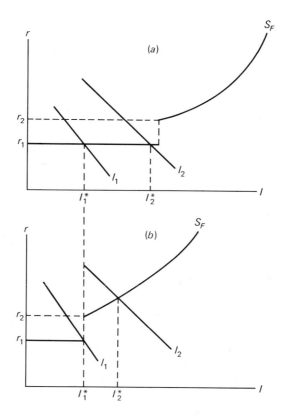

Figure 13.5.2   *Shifts of the Investment-Demand Schedule
in a Residual-Funds Framework*

conclude that the effect of an increase in the growth of demand is rather strong—i.e., that the generalized accelerator relation between I and ΔY is substantial.

However, suppose instead that internal funds had been insufficient to finance the new, higher, level of investment. Consider panel (b) of figure 13.5.2, in which we have sketched a supply-of-funds schedule reflecting a much lower level of retained earnings (i.e., the horizontal segment of S_F is much shorter). Assume that the growth of income again changes from ΔY_1 to ΔY_2, and that the investment demand schedule shifts accordingly from I_1 and I_2. Notice that the increase in the equilibrium value of investment is far smaller in this example than it was in the previous case. In this case, the relation between ΔY and I was weakened by the lack of available internal funds. Thus, the increase in the growth of demand had a relatively weak effect on the level of investment. Because of the existence of interest-rate differentials and the hypothesized importance of internal funds, the residual funds hypothesis and the accelerator theory might be combined in the investment equation:

$$I = f(r_1, r_2, L, \Delta y) \qquad (13.5.2)$$

where L represents residual funds.

During periods of plentiful internal funds, we might expect the accelerator hypothesis to provide a fairly adequate explanation of movements in investment; on the other hand, during periods of relatively scarce internal funds, the accelerator concept is likely to be a less satisfactory description of investment behavior. This general conclusion has been substantiated by Meyer and Kuh in their analysis of investment during the period 1946–50. After investigating a cross section of 700 firms in 12 manufacturing industries, they concluded that the accelerator "worked very well in 1946 and 1947 when almost every industry faced a seller's market, had good prospects, and ample liquidity—the presence of the latter being particularly important."[14] On the other hand, the accelerator was much less important in the other year's studies, which were characterized by relatively low levels of liquidity.

13.6 The Neoclassical Model

The foregoing theories of investment are extremely specialized, in that they focus on only selected key aspects of the investment decision. One could also argue that they lack sufficient foundation in the theory of individual firm behavior. At the least, they imply rather oversimplified views of the motivation and behavior of individual firms. Because of their simplistic nature, they tend to abstract from the effects on investment of several key policy variables. For example, none of these theories is designed to explain the role of federal corporate tax policy in capital markets.

In this section, we present an overview of the neoclassical theory of investment.[15] Unlike many of its predecessors, the neoclassical investment model is derived from explicit assumptions about firm motivation

---

[14] Meyer and Kuh, *The Investment Decision,* pp. 190–91.

[15] For an excellent exposition of neoclassical investment theory, see R. E. Hall and D. W. Jorgenson, "Tax Policy and Investment Behavior," *American Economic Review* 57 (June 1967), 391–414.

and behavior. It is based on the assumption that a firm attempts to maximize the present value of its net profits, subject to a variety of market and nonmarket constraints. Given the constraints, the optimization procedure leads to the choice of an optimal stock of capital and an associated decision rule for investment. In our presentation, we first introduce the notion of the user cost of capital; second, we consider the determination of the optimal capital stock in a neoclassical context; third, we discuss the translation of changes in the optimal capital stock into desired levels of net investment.

The User Cost of Capital

In chapter 9, we considered the demand for labor. We argued there that a profit-maximizing firm operating in perfect competition would hire labor up to the point where the value of labor's marginal product fell into equality with the money wage. With a few adaptations, an analogous treatment can be devised for the demand for capital. As we pointed out earlier, capital differs conceptually from labor in one very important respect. Labor services are purchased period by period and thus the wage (the payment per period per unit of labor services) is directly measurable and directly comparable to the value of labor's marginal product. But capital is usually purchased in one period and used over a number of periods; consequently, the value of capital's current marginal product cannot be legitimately compared to its supply price. Conceptually, though, we should be able to view a firm as buying units of capital *service*, either by renting capital from another firm, or from itself. If a producer rents capital, the rental payment would constitute the cost per period of using the capital. The rental payment could thus be termed a user cost, and the profit-maximizing firm would hire capital services up to the point where the value of capital's marginal product equaled rental cost. Of course, firms generally buy, rather than rent, capital. But even in this case, one could deduce the implied cost per period of using the services from a piece of capital.[16] Thus, at least conceptually, we could find an implied user cost for capital services.

This user cost would depend on several factors. First, it would be affected by the supply price of a unit of capital (C), and the rate of interest (r).[17] The importance of these variables was discussed earlier

---

[16] As in the analogous case of labor, the appropriate figure would be the implied cost of a unit of capital service of some given quality.

[17] Actually, we should make a distinction here among alternative rates of interest in order to take account of the differential rates applying to the sources of financing of capital expenditures. But this refinement is not crucial to the basic neoclassical model, and is thus ignored.

when we analyzed the MEC and MEI approaches. Second, it would be dependent upon the real rate of depreciation of capital (δ). The faster a piece of capital depreciates, the more rapidly its services diminish. Or, looking at it from a slightly different perspective, the higher the rate of depreciation, the higher the maintenance and replacement cost per unit of equal-quality capital service. Third, the user cost would be contingent upon the way in which capital usage is treated in the framework of tax policy.

For simplicity, let's focus on the behavior of the corporate sector of the economy. The corporate income tax could be considered either a deduction from the value of capital's marginal product (in that it diminishes the net return from use of capital) or an extra cost of using capital (because it increases the firm's outlays at a given level of capital usage). Using the latter connotation, it should be apparent that a rise in the corporate tax rate (t_c) will cause an increase in the user cost of capital. On the other hand, the corporate income tax structure allows for a depreciation deduction in arriving at taxable corporate income. The more rapidly firms are allowed to depreciate capital, the higher the present value of the depreciation deduction, and thus the lower the user cost of capital. We shall represent the allowable speed of depreciation by the symbol d. One more tax provision deserves mention. During certain periods in the United States, firms have been permitted to deduct a certain percentage of their current investment expenditures from their tax liabilities. This provision is known as the investment tax credit. The higher the percentage (k) of investment expenditures allowed as a tax credit, the lower the user cost of capital.

The above comments can be condensed by specifying the user cost of capital as a function of the variables mentioned. Using c to denote user cost, we have:

$$c = c(C,r, \delta,t_c,d,k) \tag{13.6.1}$$

where

$$\frac{\Delta c}{\Delta C}, \frac{\Delta c}{\Delta r}, \frac{\Delta c}{\Delta \delta}, \frac{\Delta c}{\Delta t_c} > 0$$

and

$$\frac{\Delta c}{\Delta d}, \frac{\Delta c}{\Delta k} < 0.$$

The Optimal, or Desired, Capital Stock

The firm's problem in choosing an optimal capital stock is to find the profit-maximizing (cost-minimizing) combination of labor and capital services at each level of output. As we saw in chapter 9, labor will be hired up to the point where its wage equals the value of its marginal product. Correspondingly, capital (or the services of one equal-quality unit of capital for one period) will be demanded up to the point where the user cost of capital equals capital's marginal product. Traversing this latter relation for the entire economy, we would thus have the desired capital stock defined by the condition:

$$c = P \cdot MP_K \qquad\qquad (13.6.2)$$

where MP_K denotes the marginal product of capital and P represents the overall price level.

In order to simplify our exposition, we assume that capital's marginal product is proportional to its average product, the ratio of output to capital.[18] Thus, we have:

$$c = P \cdot \alpha \frac{Y}{K} \qquad\qquad (13.6.3)$$

where α is the factor of proportionality. Since equation 13.6.3 describes a profit-maximizing relation, we can use it to solve for the desired capital stock, which we shall denote by K^*:

$$K^* = \alpha \frac{PY}{c}. \qquad\qquad (13.6.4)$$

This last equation suggests (rather plausibly) that the desired capital stock is positively related to aggregate income and the general price level and inversely related to the user cost of capital.

Net Investment: The Response to Changes in the Desired Capital Stock

As we have seen in our treatment of the flexible accelerator, producers respond to changes in the desired capital stock only with a reasonable

---

[18] Neoclassical theorists generally derive such a relation by assuming a Cobb-Douglas production function:

$$Y = AK^\alpha N^\beta.$$

The marginal product of capital would thus be:

$$MP_K \equiv \frac{\partial Y}{\partial K} = \alpha A K^{\alpha-1} N^\beta$$

or

$$MP_K \equiv \frac{\partial Y}{\partial K} = \alpha \frac{Y}{K}$$

where α is the elasticity of output with respect to capital.

lag; furthermore, the adjustment process is likely to be spread over a number of periods. Hall and Jorgenson, working within the context of a neoclassical model, assume the following type of relation between net investment and the desired capital stock:

$$I_t = \sum_{j=0}^{\infty} \mu_j \, \Delta K_{t-j}^*. \tag{13.6.5}$$

Equation 13.6.5 is analogous to the Chenery version of the flexible accelerator, except that it uses changes in the desired capital stock, rather than the difference between the desired and actual stocks of capital, as the driving force behind investment.[19] Because of the cumulative effects of past movements in K^*, net investment is specified as a weighted average of all past changes.

Substituting our expression for K^* from equation 13.6.4, the investment equation can be written as:

$$I_t = \alpha \sum_{j=0}^{\infty} \mu_j \, \Delta\left(\frac{PY}{c}\right)_{t-j}. \tag{13.6.6}$$

Using the hypothesis contained in equation 13.6.6, Hall and Jorgenson estimated the effects of alternative tax policies.[20] The neoclassical investment model offers a very direct path for the influence of such policies. In general, a change in the provisions of the corporate income tax will affect the user cost of capital, c, and this in turn will cause a change in the time path of net investment according to the scheme set forth in 13.6.6. The conclusions of Hall and Jorgenson were dramatic, but not completely unexpected. In capsule form, they found that:[21]

1. In 1955, anywhere from 17.5 to 70.8% of net investment (depending on the type of business sector and the type of investment considered) was attributable to the legalization of accelerated depreciation in 1954.

2. In 1963, over 14% of the observed net investment in equipment could be traced to the shortening of depreciable capital lifetimes first allowed in 1962.

---

[19]The student should recognize this as a type of distributed lag relation. Refer to appendix 12.A for a discussion of this point.

[20]Hall and Jorgenson, "Tax Policy and Investment Behavior."

[21]Hall and Jorgenson also considered the impact of alternative policies on replacement investment. But we do not think we do an injustice to their outstanding work by ignoring this and other conclusions they were able to reach.

3. Over 40% of the actual net investment in equipment in 1963 was the result of the 1962 investment tax credit.

We have given considerable emphasis in this text to the importance of fluctuations in net investment and the multifaceted impact of fiscal policy. The neoclassical model allows a marriage of these two phenomena.

Evidence

How reliable is the neoclassical model in comparison to the others we have discussed? Partial evidence is provided by Jorgenson and Siebert.[22] These investigators compared the ability of some of the theories to explain observed movements in the investment of a sample of firms selected from the *Fortune* Directory. Looking at the data for the postwar period 1946–63, they concluded that the neoclassical model was superior to both the flexible accelerator and the internal funds (liquidity) theories according to every criterion used.[23] This finding does not per se detract from the contributions embodied in the other investment models; each theory has its own purpose and its own use. Nevertheless, it does help to establish the neoclassical model as one of the most viable descriptions of the investment process.

13.7 Summary

In this chapter, we considered several of the alternative theories of investment. Although our analysis was anything but exhaustive, it should serve to illustrate the complexity of the problem of describing investor behavior. Indeed, most of the theories we analyzed were deliberate attempts to focus on one dimension of the investment decision. But the efficient application of policy requires that we have a reasonably comprehensive and accurate hypothesis about investment, so we can forecast problems in the economy associated with movements in investment, and can determine within relatively narrow bounds the impact on investment of alternative policies.

---

[22] D. W. Jorgenson and C. D. Siebert, "A Comparison of Alternative Theories of Corporate Investment Behavior," *American Economic Review* 58 (September 1968), 681–712.

[23] Jorgenson and Siebert considered two forms of the neoclassical model based on the alternative assumption that capital gains don't enter the investment function; they also evaluated the "expected profits" model. We ignored these results in order to restrict our attention to the theories we have had time and space to cover.

Of the theories investigated here, the neoclassical theory seems to enjoy the most acceptance at the present. But there is much work to be done in this area before we have an adequate theory of investment. For instance, the impact of alternative types of technological change (ignored in our presentation) must be researched in more depth. Furthermore, the quantification and analysis of producer expectations must be developed to a much greater degree. We have yet to answer Keynes' classic observation that:

> . . . there is the instability due to the characteristic of human nature that a large proportion of our positive activities depend on spontaneous optimism rather than on a mathematical expectation, whether moral or hedonistic or economic. Most . . . of our decisions to do something positive, the full consequences of which will be drawn out over many days to come, can only be taken as a result of animal spirits—of a spontaneous urge to action rather than inaction, and not as the outcome of a weighted average of quantitative benefits multiplied by quantitative probabilities. . . . Thus, if the animal spirits are dimmed and the spontaneous optimism falters, leaving us to depend upon nothing but a mathematical expectation, enterprise will fade and die. . . .[24]

Suggested Further Reading

Ackley, G. *Macroeconomic Theory.* New York: Macmillan, 1961, chap. 17, pp. 460–504.

Alchian, A. A. "The Rate of Interest, Fisher's Rate of Return over Cost, and Keynes, Internal Rate of Return." *American Economic Review* 45 (December 1955), 938–43.

Almon, S. "The Distributed Lag between Capital Appropriations and Expenditures." *Econometrica* 33 (January 1965), pp. 178–96.

Bailey, M. "Formal Criteria for Investment Decisions." *Journal of Political Economy* 67 (October 1959), 476–88.

Dhrymes, P. J., and Kurtz, U. "Investment, Dividend, and External Finance Behavior of Firms." In *Determinants of Investment Behavior.* New York: Columbia University Press for NBER, 1967, pp. 427–67.

---

[24] J. M. Keynes, *The General Theory of Employment, Interest and Money* (New York: Harcourt, Brace, 1936), pp. 161–62.

Eisner, R. "A Permanent Income Theory for Investment: Some Empirical Explorations." *American Economic Review* 57 (June 1967), pp. 363–90.

Evans, M. K. *Macroeconomic Activity, Theory, Forecasting and Control.* New York, Harper & Row, 1969, chap. 4–5, pp. 73–149.

Grumfeld, Y. "The Determinants of Corporate Investment." In *The Demand for Durable Goods,* edited by A. C. Harberger. Chicago: University of Chicago Press, 1960, pp. 211–66.

Hirshleifer, J. "On the Theory of Optimal Investment Decision." *Journal of Political Economy* 66 (August 1958), pp. 329–52.

Jorgenson, D. W. "The Theory of Investment Behavior." In *Determinants of Investment Behavior,* edited by R. Ferber. New York: Columbia University Press, 1967.

Keynes, J. M. *The General Theory of Employment, Interest and Money.* New York: Harcourt, Brace, 1936, chap. 11–12.

Koyck, L. M. *Distributed Lags and Investment Analysis.* Amsterdam: North-Holland 1954.

Modigliani, F. and Miller, M. "The Cost of Capital, Corporation Finance and the Theory of Investment." *American Economic Review* 48 (June 1958), pp. 261–97.

Stockfisch, J. "The Relationships between Money Cost, Investment, and the Rate of Return." *Quarterly Journal of Economics* 70 (May 1956), pp. 295–302.

Witte, J. "The Micro Foundations of the Social Investment Function." *Journal of Political Economy* 71 (October 1963), 441–56.

CHAPTER 14

Alternative Theories of Money

14.1 Introduction

This chapter will present briefly some alternative theories of the demand for money in order to expose the interested reader to some modern developments in this important area of investigation.

These theories either have been the intellectual foundations of some modern views or have sprung out of the generic theories we have already presented in chapter 8. For instance, the Cambridge approach to the demand for money falls in the first category since the work of the Chicago school under the leadership of Milton Friedman appears to be its sophisticated modern version. Moreover, the views of William Baumol and James Tobin could be considered as theories of the demand for money characterized by their Keynesian flavor.

14.2 The Cambridge Approach

Fisher's equation of exchange was presented in chapter 8; we also showed that, by making use of certain assumptions, the exchange equation can be readily transformed into a highly testable behavioral equation for the demand for money: the so-called quantity theory of money. However, as was argued there, this view of the demand for money was a specialized theory of demand characterized by its macro-economic flavor.

In contrast to the above approach, the Cambridge school of thought, under the leadership of Marshall and Pigou, advanced another view.

Although the main lines of its argument are based on more traditional ground as far as demand theory is concerned, nevertheless its conclusions are quite close to those advanced by Fisher.

To be sure, as early as 1917 Pigou's arguments about the reasons for the demand for money were based on the utility money provides, rather than on the necessity to effect transactions at a given point in time. The following paragraph from Pigou's article on the value of money is quite revealing not only because of the reasoning involved but also because it helps to place the views of Keynes (another Cambridge economist) on the subject in their appropriate historical perspective. ". . . Everybody is anxious to hold enough of his resources in the form of title to legal tender [money] both to enable him to effect the ordinary transactions of life without trouble, and to secure him against unexpected demands, due to a sudden need or to a rise in the price of something he cannot easily dispense with."[1]

From the above excerpt we can see that Pigou had anticipated at least two of the Keynesian motives: the transaction and the precautionary motives. However, even more significantly, since he attributes utility to holding cash balances, the demand for money can be derived exclusively within a microeconomic framework of reference. Under these circumstances the rational economic actor will choose (desire) to hold that amount of cash balances which will allow him to maximize his utility or satisfaction. But if this is so, then according to Pigou's analysis the demand for money should depend on a set of variables entirely different than the macroeconomic ones proposed by Fisher.

Therefore this microeconomic framework of analysis lends itself to the suggestion that the demand for money should depend upon the opportunity cost of holding money, the prices of other alternative assets, a budget-type constraint, and the tastes and preferences of the individual economic actor. The microeconomic theory of consumer behavior recognizes that regardless of the individual's desires his market behavior is indeed constrained by the level of his income. In other words, the consumer behaves in such a way that he attains the maximum level of satisfaction his level of income will allow. By the same token, according to the Cambridge approach, the demand for money can be derived by using the constraint of the stock of wealth possessed by the consumer.

To be more explicit, regardless of the amount of cash balances an individual wants to hold (demand), he is undoubtedly constrained by the total amount of his possessions (wealth). In addition, although his

---

[1]A. C. Pigou, "The Value of Money," *The Quarterly Journal of Economics* 32 (November 1917), 41.

wealth is the upper bound of the amount of cash balances he may wish to hold, it is quite doubtful that he would have only cash in his portfolio. Financial markets offer a whole constellation of other assets one may wish to hold; and although they are not as liquid as money, they exhibit other advantages money does not possess. All financial instruments as well as stocks fall in this category. Therefore, above a certain amount of cash balances, the individual would be willing to exchange some of the advantages of cash balances for some provided by other assets.

Recapitulating, according to the Cambridge approach in general and Pigou in particular, the demand for money should depend upon the volume of transactions anticipated by the individual, his stock of wealth, the opportunity cost of holding money and, finally, upon his tastes and preferences.[2] Although the Cambridge approach to the theory of the demand for money is rich with implications (and, in fact, anticipates many later developments in the field), its usefulness is limited when it comes to specifying the appropriate relationships, defining variables, and establishing the relative importance of the determinants of money demand.

In fact, by assuming that in the short run the volume of transactions, level of income and stock of wealth are all constant proportions of each other, the Cambridge approach leads to the conclusion that, given the values of all the other variables, (including opportunity costs) the demand for money in nominal terms is proportional to the money level of income. This macroeconomic relation aggregated over all individuals (assuming of course that their individual demands are independent of each other) yields the now famous equation:

$$M_d = kPY. \tag{14.2.1}$$

On the other hand, the equilibrium condition of the monetary sector is as usual:

$$\frac{M_d}{P} = \frac{M_s}{P}. \tag{14.2.2}$$

Combination of the above two equations yields the familiar expression:

$$M_s = kPY. \tag{14.2.3}$$

---

[2]In addition to the above variables, it is worth noticing that both Marshall and Pigou also suggested that uncertainty in regard to the future should be expected to influence the demand for money. Following this line of argument, Keynes specified economic uncertainty in a narrower fashion by identifying it with future fluctuations of the rate of interest. This is the speculative motive, which we have already met in a previous chapter.

The last equation looks very similar indeed to the Fisherian one (see equation 8.2.12).

From the above analysis we can see that the Cambridge approach to the demand for money is cast well within the general framework of demand theory, unlike the Fisherian version. As a result the flexibility provided by this approach has lent more viability to monetary theory than the rather rigid Fisherian one. However, the most important contribution of the Cambridge school of thought in this regard has been the fact that it paved a new, more promising, path of inquiry than the one provided by Fisher's model. This approach has led modern economists to consider explicitly the derivation of the demand for money through a utility analysis and to view money as one asset within the framework of a multi-asset portfolio.

14.3 The Modern Version of the Quantity Theory of Money

Although the Cambridge approach and in particular the work of Pigou and Marshall placed the problem of demand for money within a microeconomic framework, it was the Chicago school under Friedman's leadership which gave the final push in this direction and produced a more explicit and comprehensive statement on this subject.

Indeed, Friedman's version of the quantity theory of money is by far more complete than the ones produced by Fisher or the Cambridge economists. His claim is that the demand-for-money function is stable over time, and that it plays a considerable role in the determination of other important variables, like the levels of money income and prices. Furthermore, because of the alleged stability of this function, it becomes one of the most important tools available in the economists' analytical kit; as a result, both predictions and policy based on it should be more fruitful than the ones yielded by the application of the Keynesian analysis.[3]

---

[3]The reader should recall that the transformation of the equation of exchange into a theory of demand for money is based on the assumption of constant velocity. Friedman now relaxes this restrictive assumption and substitutes for it the claim that the velocity is stable. As the reader should recall, the Keynesian attack against the quantity theory was framed in terms of the famous liquidity trap. This view argued that during high levels of unemployment the demand for money is infinitely elastic at a low positive rate of interest. At this rate and under these circumstances, changes in the real supply of money regardless of their origin—i.e., changes in the nominal level of supply given prices or changes in prices given the nominal money supply—have no effect on the level of income. So the role of the demand for and supply of money was restricted in determining only the rate of interest.

One of the main characteristics of Friedman's work is that it makes no distinction between transaction and speculative balances, i.e., between active and idle balances. His interest is directed toward the identification of the factors which determine the quantity of money economic actors desire to hold. In relation to this, he views money as being one type of asset which yields a flow of services to its holders according to the function it performs. In his own words, ". . . The most fruitful approach is to regard money as one of a sequence of assets, on a par with bonds, equities, houses, consumer durables and the like."[4]

Thus, Friedman's approach is to cast the problem of the demand for money in the same analytical framework as the demand for consumer durables. Indeed, he argues that "to the ultimate wealth-owning units in the economy, money is one kind of asset, one way of holding wealth. To the productive enterprise, money is a capital good, a source of productive services that are combined with other productive services to yield the products that the enterprise sells."[5]

From the above it becomes then quite clear that his analysis is based in effect on the theory of a consumption service. Thus, following the usual approach to the theory of consumer choice, he identifies three major factors on which the demand for money should depend. The first of these factors is the financial constraint, which he specifies as the stock of total wealth of the economic actor. The second is of course the various prices, which for the problem at hand assume the form of returns on money and on other alternative assets; and the third is the set of tastes and preferences of the individual. Furthermore, to square his analysis with that of the theory of choice, he also assumes a decreasing marginal rate of substitution between money and alternative assets. Thus, in general terms, his demand-for-money function can be written as:

$$\frac{M_d}{P} = f\left(i_b, i_e, \frac{1}{P} \cdot \frac{dP}{dt}, w, W, u\right)$$

where i_b is the yield of bonds, i_e is the rate of return of stocks, $1/P \cdot dP/dt$ is the rate of price change over time (which could be considered a rate of return on holding physical goods), w is the ratio of nonhuman to human wealth, W is the wealth of the economic actor, and u denotes the tastes and preferences of the individual.

---

[4]M. Friedman, "The Demand for Money: Some Theoretical and Empirical Results," *The Journal of Political Economy* 67 (August 1959), 349.

[5]M. Friedman, "The Quantity Theory of Money—A Restatement," in *Studies in the Quantity Theory of Money,* ed. M. Friedman (Chicago: University of Chicago Press, 1956).

In the above specification, the first three terms are included in order to capture the direct as well as opportunity cost of holding cash balances. Opportunity cost has been defined to be the income which could have been earned had the individual actor allocated his cash balances to alternative forms of wealth. Since money is not considered an inferior good, an increase in any one of these rates (which implies an increase in the cost of holding cash balances) causes a decrease in the demand for money. Thus, the relation of the demand for money with the rate of returns in question is an inverse one.

The efficacy of using wealth as a constraint in the demand for money has been successfully argued already by the Cambridge economists. However, what was lacking in their work was an explicit measure of wealth to be used for empirical purposes. On this subject Friedman expends considerable effort. To begin with, the wealth of an individual could be considered as the difference between his assets and liabilities (in other words, that amount of cash balances which he can obtain by liquidating all his assets—durable goods, bonds, equities, etc.—minus his liabilities). However, Friedman argues that this definition of wealth is very narrow since it excludes the stream of income which can be earned from the individual's labor. He suggests that "From the broadest and most general point of view, total wealth includes all sources of income or consumable services. One such source is the productive capacity of human beings, and accordingly this is one form in which wealth can be held."[6]

To be sure, one could very well argue that the annual income of the individual is only the return to his human capital engaged in the productive process. In this sense and from an economic point of view, this stream of income, generated by his productive activities, is no different from that of a long-term bond or equity and therefore one could easily estimate its worth by calculating its present value according to the formulas we presented in chapter 13 and appendix 6.A.

According to this line of argument, the rate of interest expresses the relationship between the stock of wealth and the flow of income. Therefore one may use the relation

$$W = \frac{Y}{r}\left[1 - \frac{1}{(1 + r)^t}\right]$$

to associate these variables. But in view of the fact that the productive span, t, of the person is large, the above equation can be approximated by

---

[6] Friedman, "The Quantity Theory of Money."

$$W = \frac{Y}{r}.$$

However, in interpreting the above approximation of wealth a word of caution is in order. Indeed, income used in such a broad sense should not be confused or identified with measured income. There are two reasons for this: first, because measured income includes an amount necessary to maintain the human productive capacity; and second, because it contains transitory components. We see then that Friedman generalizes the concept of wealth to include both human and nonhuman capital.

One problem which arises from such a definition of wealth has to do with the potential substitutability between its various components. Although one may readily substitute alternative nonhuman forms of wealth with each other, this substitutability becomes difficult when we consider the human component. True, one may accept that a certain degree of substitutability exists between human and nonhuman capital. For instance, an economic actor may choose to improve the productivity of his human capital (and consequently his earning capacity) by selling some nonhuman capital to finance his college education. Alternatively he could decide to increase the nonhuman component of his wealth at the expense of his human component (say, education). However, despite some limited substitutability between the above two components of wealth, human capital, in the absence of human labor markets, cannot be purchased or sold.

In view of the above, one may wonder if in considering the demand for cash balances it would be better to use as a relevant constraint only the nonhuman element of wealth. Friedman's solution is to use an inclusive definition of wealth, and to compensate by including the ratio of nonhuman to human wealth in his demand-for-money function. This last ratio is closely related to the ratio of wealth to income, which in effect plays the role of human wealth in his model.

In regard to this last ratio, the theoretical expectation is that the larger the human component of an individual actor's total stock of wealth, the larger his demand for cash balances will be. The rationale of such a relationship is that the holding of a larger stock of money is one way of counterbalancing the illiquidity or lack of marketability of human capital. Thus, the above discussion suggests that *ceteris paribus* an increase (decrease) of the stock of total wealth or the ratio of human to nonhuman wealth will be accompanied by an increase (decrease) in the demand for money.

Finally, the reaction of the demand for cash balances to changes in the rate of change in prices will be the same as the one which corresponds to the rates of interest. In other words, an increase (decrease) in the rate of change in prices, *ceteris paribus,* will be accompanied by a decrease (increase) in the demand for money.

Therefore, Friedman specifies both the variables deemed important in the decision making of individual economic actors in regard to the demand for money, as well as their qualitative impact on money demand. However, although he is explicit about the signs associated with each argument in the demand-for-money function, he does not make much of a commitment concerning their relative importance.

Thus, any evaluation of his interpretation of the quantity theory of money must rest on its empirical verification, as it should. After all, the traditional theory of consumer behavior does not make any commitment about the relative importance of the variables involved in the demand function either, and one should not expect Friedman's theory to go any further than this point.

From the above presentation, we may see clearly the direction which empirical analysis should follow. In particular, it should first resolve the issue of the relative, as well as absolute, importance of the various rates of interest in the demand-for-money function. Second, it should decide on the issue of the appropriate constraint—i.e., income vs. wealth—to be used in the demand-for-money function. Finally, it should provide some evidence about the claim that this function—and consequently the velocity—is stable over time.

The importance of this research cannot be exaggerated. Indeed, these questions are the kernels of modern monetary theory, since the effectiveness of the various policy instruments depends, as we saw in chapter 8, on the answers to these questions.

14.4 Baumol's Approach

In chapter 6 we argued that the primary factor which determines the level of the demand for transaction cash balances was the level of income. However, this view was based on the implicit assumption that the rate of interest fluctuates around a "normal" value. Otherwise, as both Keynes and Alvin Hansen argued, a relatively high rate of interest could conceivably result in an economization of the demand for transaction balances.[7]

Therefore, we see that under some circumstances the transaction component of the demand for cash balances can become a function of

---

[7] A. Hansen, *Monetary Theory and Fiscal Policy* (New York: McGraw-Hill, 1949).

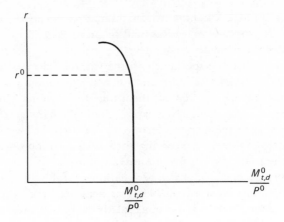

Figure 14.4.1   *The   Relation   between   Transaction
Demand and the Interest Rate*

the rate of interest as well as the level of income. Figure 14.4.1 depicts the
relation of the demand for real cash balances with the rate of interest on
the assumption that the level of real income is constant. From figure
14.4.1 we can see that above a certain critical rate of interest, r^0, the
demand for real transaction cash balances becomes sensitive to changes
in the rate of interest.

Although the specification of such a relation between the demand
for real cash balances and the rate of interest has been advanced on a
more or less ad hoc basis, Baumol and Tobin developed the above ideas
in an explicit and rigorous fashion.[8] We shall develop Baumol's
approach.

This approach is a successful adaptation in economic theory of a well-
known theorem in elementary operations research concerning the
management of inventory investments. To keep the analogy, Baumol
assumes in general that the stock of cash balances held by the individual
can be considered as his inventory of the medium of exchange. Now,
as in the case of the firm, the individual may choose to hold a high or a
low level of inventories in relation to his needs. The problem then is
determining the optimum level of inventories (in our case cash balances)
which, given the needs (transactions), minimizes the cost. The cost in
the case of the individual is an opportunity cost, the return which could

---

[8]W. Baumol, "The Transactions Demand for Cash: An Inventory Theoretic Approach,"
Quarterly Journal of Economics 66 (November 1952), 545–56; and J. Tobin, "The Interest
Elasticity of the Transactions Demand for Cash," *Review of Economics and Statistics* 38
(August 1956), 241–47.

have been earned if the individual had used the excess balance to purchase various financial instruments. These instruments obviously should satisfy the requirement of high marketability so that the consumer or firm would be able to choose the period over which he would like to hold them.

Suppose that an individual (be it a consumer or a firm) receives a payment of real income equal to, say, Y dollars which he anticipates dispersing within a certain time at a constant rate. In addition, suppose that he receives this income in terms of a number of bonds which he sells in equal lots of size, S. Further assume that there is absolute certainty not only about the income received and his spending, but also about the rate of interest (which will be taken as being constant throughout the period of consideration at r^0). Finally, assume that each sale is associated with a brokerage fee which is equal to b dollars.[9]

From the above assumptions it follows that since each lot size is equal to S dollars, the number of bond sales will be equal to Y/S and consequently the corresponding total expenditures on brokerage fees will amount to $b(Y/S)$ dollars. The interesting thing to observe now is that since each lot size is equal to S dollars, the average cash balances carried in each of the time intervals will be equal to $S/2$ dollars. To put it in another way, since he starts at the beginning of each cash period with S amount of dollars and he ends up with zero, then, in view of the uniform rate of his expenditures, on the average he holds $(S + 0)/2$. Thus, the opportunity cost which corresponds to his average holdings $(S/2)$ is equal to $r(S/2)$.

Adding up the direct cost of brokerage fees and the opportunity cost, we find that his total cost amounts to

$$C = b\frac{Y}{S} + \frac{S}{2}r \qquad (14.4.1)$$

The problem the rational economic actor faces is to determine the value of S (i.e., the amount of dollars withdrawn in each period) so that the cost will be at a minimum. If he decides to withdraw small amounts each time then the opportunity cost decreases; but at the same time, since the number of withdrawals (Y/S) necessarily increases, the total brokerage fees will increase. Conversely, if he decreases the number of withdrawals by increasing the lot sizes, he will save brokerage fees but will also increase his opportunity cost.

Notice that equation 14.4.1 expresses the cost, C, as a function of the lot sizes, S, since everything else is assumed to be constant. Consequently,

---

[9]Notice that since his expenditures during this period amount to Y, it follows that his income is equal to the volume of his transactions.

to determine the minimum value of C we differentiate 14.4.1 with respect to the variable S and we set this derivative equal to zero, i.e.:

$$\frac{dC}{dS} = -\frac{bY}{S^2} + \frac{1}{2}r = 0. \tag{14.4.2}$$

The above equation can be solved now for S in terms of the parameters to find the optimum value.[10] Thus we find:

$$S = \sqrt{\frac{2bY}{r}}. \tag{14.4.3}$$

From equation 14.4.3 we clearly see that, given our assumptions, the rational economic actor will demand to hold (the size of each lot will be) an amount which is proportional to the square root of the value of his transactions or income (Y).

To drive the argument home in terms of familiar notation, since the average amount of cash holdings is equal to $S/2$, it follows that the demand for money for transaction purposes according to Baumol's approach can be written as:

$$\frac{M_{t,d}}{\cdot P} = \frac{S}{2} = \frac{1}{2}\sqrt{\frac{2bY}{r}}. \tag{14.4.4}$$

The above expression can be further simplified by using the definition:

$$l \equiv \frac{1}{2}\sqrt{2b}$$

to obtain:

$$\frac{M_{t,d}}{P} = lY^{.5}r^{-.5}. \tag{14.4.5}$$

We can now use equation 14.4.5 to derive a number of important conclusions. First, the above expression suggests that the transaction demand for cash balances does not vary in proportion with the level of total expenditures or income. This lack of proportionality seems to be in direct opposition with the results of the Fisherian or Cambridge approach. In addition, equation 14.4.5 also indicates that as income or transactions increase the corresponding demand for transaction cash balances does not increase proportionally. This last observation implies that there are some economies of scale in the management of cash

---

[10]The reader should be able to verify that the second-order conditions are satisfied since $d^2C/dS^2 > 0$.

balances.[11] If we now carry this result one step further we see that this segment of the demand for money is not independent of the distribution of income or volume of transactions among the various economic actors. More explicitly, a redistribution of income or transactions resulting in larger firms, for instance, would immediately imply a reduction in the demand for money.

Second, we can also see from equation 14.4.5 that the transaction demand for money varies inversely with respect to the rate of interest; and finally, we see that the reason for holding cash balances for transaction purposes is in effect the existence of a nonzero brokerage cost. Indeed, if the brokerage fee b assumes the value zero, then the above equation indicates that $M_{t,d}/P = 0$. The last finding implies that if there were no cost associated with the sales of financial instruments, there would be no need to hold cash balances for transaction purposes, since the switch from bonds, say, to cash would be free of any cost.

From the above analysis it appears that the existence of brokerage fees constitutes an important reason for holding cash for transaction purposes. In view of this it would be interesting to take a second look at this concept. The identification of b with brokerage fees appears to be a rather narrow and, for that matter, misleading interpretation. A more general one would be to identify b with any cost involved in the process of disposing instruments of financial intermediation regardless of their particular nature. In other words, one should consider not only the out-of-pocket material cost but also all the psychological or physical costs. Such an interpretation of b would be more consistent with reality than the one used by the model itself.

Finally, it is clear that the derivation of the square-root formula, as it came to be known, does not necessitate the use of any assertion about the alleged association of utility with holding cash balances.

14.5 The Liquidity-Preference Theory Revisited

In chapter 6, section 3, it was assumed that each economic actor formed his own expectations about the future level of the rate of interest. In addition, it was assumed that this expectation was held with a considerable amount of confidence. On this basis, it was argued that once this

---

[11]This would indicate, of course, that in effect the management of cash balances, in particular on the part of firms, has reached a rather interesting level of sophistication. However, empirical studies have not yet confirmed this in a satisfactory and unambiguous fashion.

expectation materialized, the individual would switch his portfolio from bonds (cash) into cash (bonds) depending on whether he was a bull or a bear.

The purpose of this section is to relax the assumption about the degree of confidence which characterizes the expectations of individuals. We shall introduce uncertainty into our line of argument and see if and to what extent this new element results in a modification of our previous conclusions. For this, our previous treatment of liquidity-preference theory is not very helpful. To appreciate the new line of argument, we shall recast the theory in slightly different terms so that the difference between the views will become more obvious.

Assume that the economic actor is confronted with the choice of holding his idle cash balances in terms of cash or consols (maintaining the assumption of an unchanged price level). Suppose also that the current rate of interest is r_c and that he is *certain* that at the end of a period (which we shall take as a unit) this rate will be r_e. It follows then that according to equation 6.3.4 the current price of consols is $V^c = C/r_c$ whereas by the same token the corresponding expected price will be $V^e = C/r_e$. Thus, the holder of consols will realize a capital gain or loss which will be equal to[12]

$$G = V^e - V^c. \tag{14.5.1}$$

But since $C = V^c r_c$ and $V^e = C/r_e$, it follows that the above expression can be written as:

$$G = \frac{V^c r_c}{r_e} - V^c$$

from which we further obtain:

$$G = V^c \left(\frac{r_c}{r_e} - 1 \right).$$

Dividing both sides by V^c, the above expression becomes:

$$g \equiv \frac{G}{V^c} = \left(\frac{r_c}{r_e} - 1 \right) \tag{14.5.2}$$

where g denotes the capital gain or loss in percent terms.

However, the total expected return (p) of the asset-holder will be equal to the sum of expected capital gain or loss and the interest he stands to earn for holding this consol for the period in question, i.e.:

---

[12]The reader should appreciate that G will be greater than, equal to or less than zero depending on whether r_c is greater, equal to, or less than r_e.

$$p = g + r_c.$$

Substitution of g from 14.5.2 yields

$$p = \frac{r_c}{r_e} - 1 + r_c. \tag{14.5.3}$$

The above expression can be greater than, equal to, or less than zero. Therefore, we can say that given the economic actor's "stubbornness" concerning his expectations about the future rate (i.e., r_e), there will always exist a current rate of interest (say, r_c^*) which will yield a zero rate of return to his investment (i.e., $p = 0$). To find this rate we may substitute r_c^* into equation 14.5.3 and set p equal to zero, i.e.:

$$\frac{r_c^*}{r_e} - 1 + r_c^* = 0$$

which can be solved for r_c^* in terms of r_e to obtain:

$$r_c^* = \frac{r_e}{1 + r_e}. \tag{14.5.4}$$

Equation 14.5.4 tells us the current interest rate which the individual would associate with a zero rate of return. We may therefore call r_c^* the critical or break-even rate.[13]

Now, suppose that we consider an individual whose break-even rate (r_c^*) is equal to the current rate r_c. If this is the case, then it is clear that his expected net return will be equal to zero; therefore he would be indifferent to the form in which he holds his idle cash balances. Should the current rate exceed his break-even rate, though, his return would be positive (i.e., $p > 0$), and therefore he would invest all his idle cash balances into bonds. Conversely, if $r_c < r_c^*$, this would imply that any investment in bonds would give a negative return and therefore he would hold his speculative balances in terms of cash. Thus, according to this model we find once more that holding cash and holding bonds are two mutually exclusive events. Furthermore, we also see that as the current rate of interest declines, more and more people find that their critical rate is greater than the current rate and therefore larger and larger amounts of idle cash balances are held. This indeed establishes the negative relation between the rate of interest and the demand for speculative cash balances. Figure 14.5.1 summarizes this relationship. Notice that current as well as break-even rates are measured along the

---

[13] At this juncture, it is important to notice that since each actor has his own expected rate, it follows that each of them would expect to break even at different rates as well.

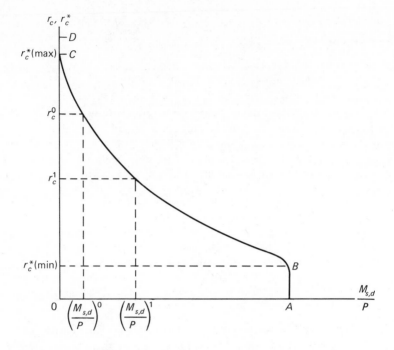

Figure 14.5.1   *Demand for Speculative Cash Balances*

vertical axis, whereas the horizontal axis denotes quantities of demanded speculative cash balances.

To interpret figure 14.5.1, it is important to observe first that since
there exists a one-to-one correspondence between expected rates and
break-even rates, it follows that, given the distribution of the community's expected rates, there will be a corresponding distribution of
the break-even rates as well. We may then pick the maximum and
minimum break-even rates of the community and mark them. These are
denoted by r_c^* (max) and r_c^* (min) along the vertical axis. Let us now
suppose that the current rate (r_c) is greater than the community's maximum break-even rate [i.e., $r_c > r_c^*$ (max)]. This means that every member of the community expects positive net returns and therefore all idle
cash balances are invested in consols. The demand for speculative cash
balances is equal to zero. As the current rate declines, however, some
members of the community find that their break-even rate is higher than
the current rate and therefore demand cash (since investing in consols
would imply a negative expected return). The lower the current rate of
interest, the larger the number of people who find themselves in this

predicament and therefore the larger the demand for speculative cash balances. This will continue down to the point r_c^* (min) in which case if $r_c < r_c^*$ (min) every member of the community will expect negative returns and therefore everyone holds his speculative balances in terms of cash. It can be said that OA indicates the community's total idle cash balances which would be available for purchasing consols.

One of the major criticisms of the liquidity-preference theory is directed against its assumption concerning the confidence with which economic actors hold their expectations. To make any progress in explaining the behavior of the demand for speculative balances, it is therefore necessary to relax this assumption of certainty. This was accomplished successfully by Tobin, who recast liquidity preference as a behavior toward risk.[14]

Tobin's Theory of Liquidity Preference

We just saw that the Keynesian assumption of certainty implies that for each current rate of interest economic actor has a definite expectation about its future level; therefore we were able to express his total expected returns as

$$p = g + r_c$$

where g denotes the capital gain or loss in percentage terms and r_c the current rate of interest. It was further argued that the individual would keep his balances in terms of either cash or consols depending on whether $r_c < r_c^*$ or $r_c > r_c^*$. These two alternatives appeared to be mutually exclusive.

Contrary to the above treatment, Tobin envisions a world in which portfolios consist of cash or bonds or both and where each economic actor is *uncertain* about the future rate of interest. If this is the case, then it follows that the individual will also be uncertain about g. Tobin proposes then that g is a random variable and that the economic actor makes his decisions on this basis.[15] He also assumes that, according to the subjective assessment of the individual economic actor, the average value of g ($\bar{g}$) is equal to zero. Therefore, this implies that the average return ($\bar{p}$) antici-

---

[14]This theory was developed in Tobin's famous article, "Liquidity Preference as Behavior Toward Risk," *Review of Economic Studies* 25 (February 1958), 65–86.

[15]In fact, he assumes that g is a random variable independent of r, i.e., ". . . The investor considers a doubling of the rate just as likely when the rate is 5% as when it is 2% and a halving of the rate just as likely when it is 6%." Tobin, ibid. Exercise: In what respect are these assumptions different from those of Keynes? Explain in as much detail as possible.

pated by the individual is equal to r_c, which of course is a constant at any given time, i.e.

$$\bar{p} = r_c \quad (\text{for } \bar{g} = 0)$$

This average return expected by the individual was derived on the assumption that all balances are invested in consols. However, now suppose that a person's portfolio consists of A_1 proportion of cash and A_2 proportion of consols. Therefore

$$A_1 + A_2 = 1 \quad \text{and} \quad 0 \le A_2 \le 1. \tag{14.5.5}$$

Clearly, if $A_1 = 0$ then $A_2 = 1$, suggesting that everything is invested in consols. Under these circumstances the return will assume its largest value as well. If on the other hand $A_1 = 1$, then the portfolio consists of cash only and therefore there is no return whatsoever. Between these two extreme values we find various returns depending on the proportion of cash invested in consols. Thus, we may write in general that[16]

$$\bar{p} = A_2 r_c. \tag{14.5.6}$$

In other words, according to equation 14.5.6, the average return expected by the individual depends on the proportion of portfolio represented by consols and increases as A_2 becomes larger.

On the other hand, the dispersion of the expected return around its average value indicates how large or small the likelihood is that this portfolio will be associated with capital gains or losses. More explicitly, a low degree of dispersion of expected returns around its average value would imply a high probability that the portfolio yield would be very close to r_c. Conversely, a large dispersion would indicate that the investor may experience large capital gains or losses.

It seems reasonable therefore to express the risk associated with a portfolio in terms of the dispersion around its average expected yield. Assuming then that an A_2 proportion of portfolio is invested in consols, we can write

$$R = A_2 S \qquad 0 < S < 1 \tag{14.5.7}$$

where R denotes the risk associated with the portfolio and S, a fixed

---

[16]As an example, suppose that the individual has $10,000 for investment. Assume also that he can purchase, at par value of $1,000 at 5%, 10 consols. If he invests everything in consols (i.e., $A_2 = 1$) then his return will be $(50 \times 10)/10,000 = 5\%$. Now suppose that he invests only $6,000 by purchasing 6 consols of $1,000 at 5%. The return to his portfolio, which now consits of $6,000 consols and $4,000 cash will be $(50 \times 6)/10,000 = 3\%$. This can be found also as $\bar{p} = 6000/10,000 \times .05$ where $A_2 = 6000/10,000$.

constant, stands for the risk coefficient. From 14.5.7, we see that since S is a constant, the risk (R) varies directly with the proportion of consols included in the portfolio. If $A_2 = 0$, then $R = 0$, since there is no risk for holding cash. On the other hand, the maximum value of risk (i.e., S) will be obtained for $A_2 = 1$, or when the portfolio includes only consols.

From equations 14.5.6 and 14.5.7, we see therefore that the individual can increase his return by increasing the proportion of consols in his portfolio, but as he does this his risk also increases. He cannot have his cake and eat it too.

To find the direct relation between the risk and the average return expected by the individual associated with his portfolio, we solve equation 14.5.7 for A_2, i.e.

$$A_2 = \frac{R}{S} \tag{14.5.8}$$

and substitute this value for A_2 into equation 14.5.6 to obtain

$$\bar{p} = \frac{r_c}{S} R. \tag{14.5.9}$$

Equation 14.5.9 indicates how the individual can exchange risk for return given his subjective estimate of the risk coefficient and the market conditions (r_c). Indeed, we can immediately verify that for each additional degree of risk he is willing to undertake his average expected return will increase by the ratio r_c/S, i.e.

$$\frac{\Delta \bar{p}}{\Delta R} = \frac{r_c}{S}. \tag{14.5.10}$$

We may now summarize the argument. If the individual wishes an average return to his portfolio equal to $\bar{p}^0$ then we see from 14.5.9 that, given the market conditions and his estimate of risk coefficient, he will have to accept a risk equal to R^0. On the other hand, from equation 14.5.7 we also see that this level of risk corresponds to an investment in consols which is equal to a proportion A_2^0 of his portfolio. Therefore, under these conditions, cash will be represented in this portfolio by the proportion A_1^0, which is equal to $(1 - A_2^0)$.

Figure 14.5.2 depicts these relationships graphically. The ray OB^0 in figure 14.5.2 or its equation 14.5.9 provides us with the alternatives of the individual as they are given by the market. Suppose, for example, that the current rate of interest is at r_c^0, and that the individual sets a target of average return at $\bar{p}^0$. Then according to the ray OB^0 he is supposed to assume risk equal to R^0 and from the lower part of the

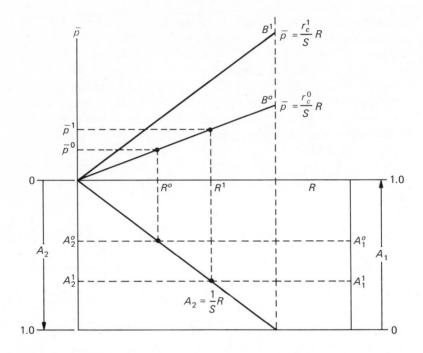

Figure 14.5.2   *Exchange of Risk and Return Imposed upon the Individual*

diagram we see that this will imply A_2^0 proportion of his portfolio invested in consols. Thus, the distance from point A_2^0 to 1 at the lower left-hand side of the diagram gives us the proportion of cash involved in this portfolio. This can also be read in the right-hand side of the lower diagram, where the proportion of cash is represented by the distance OA_1^0. Also, notice that as the current rate of interest increases (decreases) OB^0 will rotate upward (downward) from point zero.

So far, we have indicated what the market will allow the individual to do given his subjective evaluations. However, from this information we cannot derive what the individual would consider as the optimal mix of his portfolio. For this we need to know his attitude toward risk and return. In other words, once he is given the ratio according to which the market allows him to exchange risk for return, his problem is to find the combination which is most satisfactory to him.

Assume that return as an addition to his wealth is considered desirable whereas risk is supposed to be undesirable. And also postulate that his utility function depends upon these two variables, i.e.

$$U = U(\bar{p}, R). \tag{14.5.11}$$

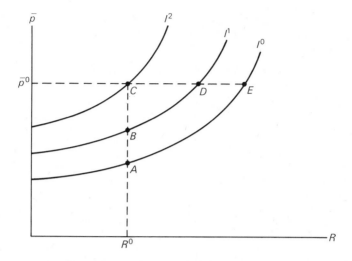

Figure 14.5.3 *Subjective Tradeoff between Risk and Return*

From the above utility function, we can derive the corresponding indifference curves of the individual (see chapter 12.4 for another derivation of indifference curves).

In figure 14.5.3, we have drawn a family of indifference curves. As in chapter 12, we shall define them here as providing us with all combinations of risk and return for which the individual is indifferent. But unlike the indifference curves we found in chapter 12, those in figure 14.5.3 slope upward and indicate higher levels of satisfaction as we move toward the northwest. In other words, the satisfaction associated with I^0 is smaller than that associated with I^1, which in turn is smaller than that associated with I^2. This can be seen by considering a level of risk, say, R^0. According to figure 14.5.3, the corresponding return associated with I^0 is R^0A, with I^1 is R^0B and with I^3 is R^0C. Since, however, for the same risk the return R^0C is greater than R^0B it follows that the combination of risk and return associated with point C is preferred to that associated with point B and therefore the level of satisfaction associated with I^2 is greater than that associated with I^1. A similar argument holds for I^1 and I^0.[17]

Note that the indifference curves are convex toward the risk axis and denote the preference of an economic actor called a *diversifier*. According to these indifference curves, this individual demands, as risk increases by

---

[17]Exercise: Make a similar argument by using a constant return $\bar{p}^0$.

equal amounts, increasingly higher corresponding increments of return.

To recapitulate, figure 14.5.2 tells us how the market allows the individual to exchange risk for return. On the other hand, figure 14.5.3 tells us how he would like to exchange them. To find the combination which will maximize his satisfaction, we combine these two figures. Obviously, the individual will attempt to reach as high an indifference curve as possible given the constraint imposed by the market. This is shown in figure 14.5.4.

Suppose that the economic actor is at point A. It should be clear that at this point, although he exchanges according to what the market dictates, he does not maximize his satisfaction. Maximum satisfaction occurs at point E where the risk he has to undertake according to the market conditions is equal to the risk he is willing to undertake according to his preferences. In other words, the individual will maximize his satisfaction at the point where OB (his constraint) is tangent to an indifference curve. This is the highest indifference curve he can reach. Now we are in the position to determine the optimum mix of his portfolio. This is done in figure 14.5.5.

We see that E^0 is characterized by a risk equal to R^0 and therefore we can immediately obtain the associate optimum structure of portfolio from the lower part of figure 14.5.5; i.e., A_1^0 proportion will be devoted to consols and $A_1^0 = 1 - A_2^0$ will be kept in cash.

Now suppose that the current rate of interest increases from r_c^0 to r_c^1. This results in a new constraint OB^1, and the new equilibrium of the actor is dislocated to E^1. From figure 14.5.5, we see that the corresponding optimum allocation of portfolio consists of A_2^1 proportion in consols and $A_1^1 = 1 - A_2^1$ proportion in cash.

This analysis suggests that as the interest rate increases, given S, the proportion of a portfolio held in cash decreases, and so it follows that Tobin was able to derive once more a negative relationship between the demand for speculative cash balances and the rate of interest without using the strong assumption of certainty about future rates as Keynes did. Furthermore, we see that his relationship between the rate of interest and speculative cash balances does not imply the all-or-nothing behavior which characterized the Keynesian liquidity preference theory.

14.6 Conclusions

The only way to resolve the issues we have raised about the demand for money is to subject these various hypotheses to empirical verification. In the last fifteen years, our knowledge about the properties of the demand

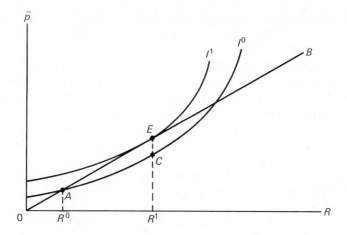

Figure 14.5.4 *Optimum Combination of Risk and Return*

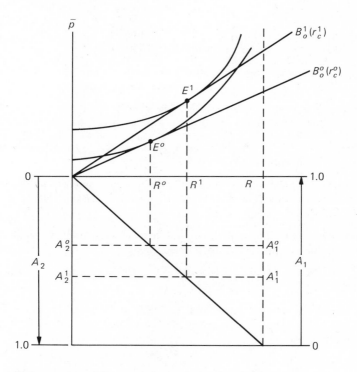

Figure 14.5.5 *Effect of an Increase in the Current Rate of Interest on the Optimum Portfolio Mix*

for money has increased considerably, chiefly through the work of Tobin, Latané, Friedman, Bronfenbrenner-Mayer, and, more recently, Brunner-Meltzer, Lee, Tiegen and Laidler.[18] The evidence accumulated so far suggests strongly that money-demand responds positively to changes in income and negatively to changes in rates of interest. Moreover, the use of empirical techniques has failed to confirm the existence of a liquidity trap. However, there is some evidence that the interest-elasticity of money-demand is higher at low rates of interest than it is at high rates. In addition, most empirical investigations have found that the demand for money appears to be a stable function of income and interest rates, and that it is therefore an important structural relation from the standpoint of the exercise of economic policy.

Suggested Further Reading

Bronfenbrenner, M. and Mayer, T. "Liquidity Functions in the American Economy." *Econometrica* 28 (October 1960), 810–34.

Brunner, K. and Meltzer, A. H. "Predicting Velocity: Implications for Theory and Policy." *Journal of Finance* 18 (May 1963), 318–54.

———. "The Uses of Money: Money in the Theory of an Exchange Economy." *American Economic Review* 61 (December 1971), 784–805.

Chow, G. C. "On the Long-run and Short-run Demands for Money." *Journal of Political Economy* 74 (April 1966), 111–31.

Christ, C. F. "Interest Rates and 'Portfolio Selections' Among Liquid Assets in the U.S." In Christ et al., *Measurements in Economics*. Palo Alto, Calif.: Stanford University Press, 1963, pp. 201–18.

Duesenberry, J. "The Portfolio Approach to the Demand for Money and Other Assets." *Review of Economics and Statistics* 45 (February 1963, 9–24.

Feige, E. *The Demand for Liquid Assets: A Temporal Cross-section Analysis.* Englewood Cliffs, N.J.: Prentice-Hall, 1964.

Friedman, M. "Interest Rates and the Demand for Money." Reprinted in Friedman, *The Optimum Quantity of Money and Other Essays*. Chicago: Aldine, 1969, pp. 141–56.

---

[18]For a more comprehensive list of names and full bibliographic references, see any standard money and banking text.

Hicks, J. R. "A Suggestion for Simplifying the Theory of Money." *Economica* 2 (February 1935), 1–19. Reprinted in J. R. Hicks. *Critical Essays in Monetary Theory.* Oxford: The Clarendon Press, 1967, chap. 4.

Hirshleifer, J. "Investment Decision under Uncertainty." *Quarterly Journal of Economics* 79 (November 1965), 509–36.

Johnson, H. G. *Essays in Monetary Economics.* London: George Allen and Unwin, 1967, chap. 5.

Khusro, A. M. "An Investigation of Liquidity Preference." *Yorkshire Bulletin of Economic and Social Research* 4 (January 1952), 1–20.

Laidler, D. "Some Evidence on the Demand for Money." *Journal of Political Economy* 74 (February 1966), pp. 55–68.

Markowitz, H. *Portfolio Selection.* New York: Wiley, 1959.

Meltzer, A. "The Demand for Money: The Evidence from Time Series." *Journal of Political Economy* 71 (June 1963), 219–46.

————. "The Demand for Money: A Cross-Section Study of Business Firms." *Quarterly Journal of Economics* 77 (August 1965), 405–22. See also: R. C. Vogel and G. S. Maddala. "The Demand for Money: A Cross-Section Study of Business Firms: Comment." *Quarterly Journal of Economics* 79, 153–59; and A. Meltzer. "Reply." *Quarterly Journal of Economics* 79, 162–65.

Sharpe, W. F. "Capital Asset Prices: A Theory of Market Equilibrium under Conditions of Risk." *Journal of Finance* 19 (September 1964), 435–42.

Tiegen, R. L. "Demand and Supply Functions for Money in the United States: Some Structural Estimates." *Econometrica* 32 (October 1964), 476–509.

CHAPTER 15

The Monetaristic Debate

15.1 Introduction

As the previous chapters have suggested, the issue of how and to what extent money influences economic activity has been long-debated and controversial. Since the publication of Keynes's *General Theory* in the mid-1930s the views advanced have ranged from saying money does not matter at all, to saying money is all that matters. Today, after more than thirty years of debate, the opposing camps are not significantly closer, although the sophistication of the argument has evolved and the emphasis has shifted as our understanding of economic relations has increased. Perhaps, in some measure, this schism may be attributed to the fact that beneath the various arguments one can clearly identify strong and opposing ideological views concerning the relative positions of government and individual economic actors within the framework of the socioeconomic complex.

During the evolution of this debate, the late forties and early fifties witnessed an almost complete dominance of the Keynesian views in the academic community. This was basically due to the fact that the empirical evidence provided during that period suggested that changes in the money supply, although affecting interest rates, nevertheless exerted little influence on aggregate demand. Therefore, a large number of economists rejected monetary policy as a stabilization instrument and emphasized instead the use of fiscal policy.[1] However, these views

---

[1] It was conceded, however, that Pigou's real cash balance effect on consumption served to reconcile the deep cleavage between the neoclassical theory and Keynesian economics. On this see P. A. Samuelson, "Reflection on the Merits and Demerits of Monetarism," in *Issues in Fiscal and Monetary Policy: The Eclectic Economist Views the Controversy*, ed. James J. Diamond (Chicago: DePaul University, 1971), pp. 7–21.

were not shared by the political establishment of that era, and, as a result, were not reflected in the exercise of stabilization policies.

With the assumption of the presidency by John F. Kennedy in 1961, a new intellectual regime dominated Washington. The suites of the presidential counselors were filled by Keynesian economists. The outcome of such a change was that the material which was taught in advanced macroeconomic seminars became the conventional wisdom of the presidential conference rooms. Keynesian theory assumed the role of the pillar of stabilization policies of the day. Indeed, the apparent success of the investment tax credit of 1962 and the tax cut of 1964 appeared to suggest that the exercise of fiscal policy by an enlightened government could resolve a great deal of time-honored economic problems and, consequently, the new economics carried the day.

In recent years, however, the success of modern Keynesian theory has been questioned while the advocates of the modern quantity theory of money, otherwise known as the monetarist school of thought, have experienced a remarkable swelling of their ranks. (To be sure, the popularity of the monetarist doctrine has traced such a meteoric arc that some of its proponents have begun talking about a monetarist counterrevolution.) The eclipse of the Keynesian school is related, at least in part, to the apparent failure of the Keynesian prescriptions to maintain economic stability during the buildup of U.S. involvement in Vietnam. The action which was specifically called to task was the income tax surcharge of June 1968, which allegedly failed to contain aggregate demand in terms of both timing and magnitude.[2]

---

[2]It should be noted that this view is certainly not shared by all economists. For example, Arthur Okun, one of the principal architects of this policy, has recently argued that the fiscal measure in question resulted in the curtailment of some components of aggregate demand. In particular, he suggests that the spending on nondurable goods and services appeared to have been reduced considerably, while other categories (most notably new automobiles) did not exhibit the same sensitivity, if any at all. See A. Okun, "The Personal Tax Surcharge and Consumer Demand, 1968–1970," *Brookings Papers on Economic Activity* No. 1, (Washington, D.C.: The Brookings Institution, 1971), pp. 167–204.

It is also worth mentioning that the expectation of a reduction in expenditures due to the increase in the "effective" tax rate is fairly naive since it is based only on *ceteris paribus* analysis. To be sure, the final outcome will also depend on the behavior of government expenditures, which at that time were on the increase. Furthermore, in chapter 12 we saw that according to the permanent income hypothesis, for example, such a result should be anticipated in view of the fact that the surcharge in question was levied for only one year and the government went out of its way to make this clear (see chap. 12). For an interesting discussion of these points see R. Eisner, "Fiscal and Monetary Policy Reconsidered," *American Economic Review* 50 (December 1969), 897–905; also his "What Went Wrong," *Journal of Political Economy* 79 (May–June 1971), 629–41.

Another reason which has not been investigated adequately in the literature is that conceivably we may not have been using the appropriate budget constraint in our effort to

Even more significantly, however, the rise of the new quantity theory of money is due to the intellectual efforts of a small dedicated number of scholars who seem never to have been convinced about the relative merits of a large part of Keynesianism. In particular, the work of Karl Brunner, Milton Friedman and Allan Meltzer has been the hard core of the theoretical foundation of monetarism and recently has been augmented by a substantial amount of empirical evidence provided by a team of economists working at the Federal Reserve Bank of Saint Louis.

Before we embark on our analysis of monetarism, it might be instructive to dismiss one extreme view which is often misconstrued as a modern monetarist view. In chapter 8 it was shown that, given a demand-for-money function exhibiting zero elasticity with respect to the interest rate, only monetary policy could be used to affect the levels of output and employment. Under these strict circumstances, fiscal policy affects only the rate of interest, with no attendant impact on the real measures of economic activity. Instead, changes in fiscal activities simply produced a completely counteracting change in investment spending, thus leaving the level of aggregate demand (and, hence, the equilibrium level of income) unchanged.[3] However this view is a direct carry-over from the naive quantity theory of money; Friedman as well as others have taken the opportunity to reject it on more than one occasion.[4]

To be sure, a large number of empirical studies have established that the demand for cash balances depends on the rate of interest and therefore the hypothesis of zero interest-elasticity has become quite incompatible with accumulated empirical evidence.[5] These findings have

---

[2]*(continued)*   explain the behavior of the economic actor. More explicitly, unlike the expenditures on nondurable goods and the majority of services, the expenditures on durables ("big-ticket" items) can be purchased through installment credit. An increase, therefore, in the number of installments or monthly payments may very well be viewed either as an increase in the disposable income or alternatively as a decrease in the price of the commodity in question. Given certain realistic assumptions concerning the time horizon considered by the economic actor during his planning period, such an increase in the number of installment payments could easily outweigh the effect of an income tax surcharge on disposable income.

[3]This is the so-called crowding-out effect; i.e., fiscal actions, through their effects on the rate of interest, crowd out expenditures of the private sector. For the extreme case of this effect see our analysis in chapter 8.3, particularly equation 8.3.29, and appendix 15.A.

[4]See, for example, M. Friedman, "Interest Rates and the Demand for Money," *Journal of Law and Economics* 9 (Octover 1966), 71–86; also his "The Quantity Theory of Money—A Restatement," in *Studies in the Quantity Theory of Money*, ed. M. Friedman (Chicago: University of Chicago Press, 1956); also "A Theoretical Framework for Monetary Analysis," *Journal of Political Economy* 78 (March–April 1970), 193–238.

[5]For a summary of the evidence accumulated during the 1960s see D. Laidler, *The Demand for Money: Theories and Evidence* (Scranton, Pa.: International Textbook Co., 1969).

certainly influenced both the tone and the course of subsequent discussions of the subject to the extent that a recent account of the state of the debate has referred to the zero interest-elasticity of the demand for cash balances as an exceptional case indeed.[6] It is also worth mentioning that if one relaxes the exogeneity assumption on the money supply and instead accepts the empirically supported hypothesis that it is a function of the rate of interest, then the whole discussion of zero interest-elasticity of the demand for cash balance becomes altogether irrelevant, since the last relation between interest and money supply breaks the exclusive relation between income and money stock.[7]

The above discussion suggests that both views agree that the interest elasticity of the demand-for-cash-balance is not equal to zero. However, they do disagree on the size of this elasticity or, to put it in another way, on the magnitude of the slope of the LM curve. The Keynesian position is said to advocate a high interest-elasticity whereas monetarism is said to advocate a low one. By implication, the Keynesian view can be translated as suggesting that the money velocity is unstable. And this is contrary to the monetaristic view, which accepts a fairly stable velocity and therefore emphasizes its use as an instrument to predict changes in the money income. More specifically, monetarists have argued that ". . . although marginal and average velocities differ, the velocity function is sufficiently stable to provide a relation between changes in money and changes in money income."[8] In this sense, it appears that the kernel of the difference between these two schools of thought can be summarized in their contrasting views with regard to the demand for money and velocity. In particular, Fand writes: "The post-Keynesian

---

[6] See D. Fand, "Monetarism and Fiscalism," *Banca Nazionale del Lavoro Quarterly Review* 94 (September 1970), 276–307.

[7] To see this, let us assume, in terms of our model, that the money supply is an increasing function of the rate of interest and write: $M_s/P = n_0 + n_1 r$. Let, in addition, the demand for money be a function of the level of income, i.e.,

$$\frac{M_d}{P} = l_1 Y.$$

The above two equations can now be combined by using the equilibrium condition

$$\frac{M_s}{P} = \frac{M_d}{P} \qquad \text{to yield:} \qquad n_0 + n_1 r = l_1 Y,$$

which, of course, is the equation of the LM curve expressing the level of income or rate of interest as an increasing function of the other variable.

[8] See D. Fand, "Keynesian Monetary Theories, Stabilization Policy and Recent Inflation," *Journal of Money, Credit and Banking* 1 (August 1969), 556–87.

quantity and income theories thus differ sharply in their analysis of the money demand function. In the modern quantity theory it serves as a velocity function relating either money and money income or marginal changes in money and money income . . . ; in the income theory, it serves as a liquidity preference theory of interest rates, or of changes in interest rates (if the price level is given and determined independently of the monetary sector)."[9]

Having dismissed the case of zero interest-elasticity of the demand for money as the main characteristic of monetarism, we may now proceed to examine in a more detailed fashion its basic premises. Fortunately, we have available a fair number of accounts and summary statements which depict the current state of monetaristic thought. In particular, Brunner has recently provided us with a small number of propositions which are "defining characteristics of monetaristic position":[10]

Proposition 1. The dominant factors which influence economic activity are monetary impulses. This proposition claims that the rate of monetary expansion is the principal determining factor of total spending and, therefore, output, employment and the general price level.

Proposition 2. The transmission mechanism of monetary impulses has, in general, a microeconomic character and consists of a large-scale reshuffling of asset portfolios of economic units (firms or individual economic actors) due to a change in asset prices and yields. This reshuffling involves not only financial but also real assets.

Proposition 3. The majority of the destabilizing shocks experienced by the economy are the outcome of governmental interference as expressed by fiscal policy or the result of discretionary actions taken by the monetary authorities. This proposition claims that the economy is basically stable and does not generate by itself continuous fluctuations ranging from a state of massive unemployment to a state of inflation. If, in fact, these maladies occur, it is primarily due to shocks imposed by forces outside the system expressed primarily in terms of severe reversals of monetary and fiscal policy.

---

[9] See D. Fand, "Some Issues in Monetary Economics," *Banca Nazionale del Lavoro Quarterly Review* 90 (September 1969), 228.

[10] See K. Brunner, "The 'Monetarist Revolution' Monetary Theory," *Weltwirtschaftliches Archiv* 105 (1970), 1–30, section II. For other sources, the reader may also consult K. Brunner, "The Role of Money and Monetary Policy," *Federal Reserve Bank of St. Louis Review* 50 (July 1968), 9–24; D. Fand, "Some Issues in Monetary Economics," *Federal Reserve Bank of St. Louis Review* 52 (January 1970), 10–27; and D. Fand, "A Monetarist Model of the Monetary Process," *Journal of Finance* 25 (May 1970), 275–89. Also see L. Andersen and K. Carlson, "A Monetarist Model of Economic Stabilization," *Federal Reserve Bank of St. Louis Review* 52 (April 1970), 7–25.

Proposition 4. The use of small-scale models, expressed even in terms of a single equation, is indeed capable of capturing the main thrust of the relation between target variables and policy instruments.

In what follows, we shall present and analyze empirical evidence advanced in support of monetarism and comment, whenever it is deemed necessary, on the theoretical underpinning of the relevant hypothesis.

The monetary counterrevolution found its original stimulus largely in the controversy surrounding the results of two studies labored by Friedman and his coworkers. The first examined the historical evidence provided by the U.S. economy for the period 1867–1960, and the second consisted of an econometric study which assessed the relative stability of the monetary velocity and the expenditures multiplier. Both studies were used to derive inferences concerning the relative explanatory power of monetary and fiscal actions in determining the level of economic activity, specifically GNP.

15.2 The Friedman-Schwartz Study

In this seminal work, Friedman and Ann Schwartz (hereafter FS) set out to study the behavior of the money supply vis-à-vis the behavior of economic activity in the United States.[11] Their effort was aimed at establishing a causal relationship between changes in the levels of these two variables. One of the main observations of the study was that the money supply tended to be on the increase during the economic cycles included in the time period (1867–1948) with the notable exception of the periods listed in table 15.2. In view of the above evidence, one may very legitimately wonder if the relation between major business recessions and absolute decreases in the money supply is merely coincidental or casual. The FS claim was that such evidence could support two important generalizations:

> [1] There is a one-to-one relation between monetary changes and changes in money income and prices. Changes in money income and prices have, in every case, been accompanied by a change in the rate of growth of the money stock, in the same direction and of appreciable magnitude and there are no comparable disturbances in the rate of growth of the money

---

[11] See M. Friedman and A. J. Schwartz, *A Monetary History of the United States 1867–1960*, (Princeton, N.J.: Princeton University Press, 1963). Also see M. Friedman and A. J. Schwartz, "Money and Business Cycles," *Review of Economics and Statistics* 45, Supplement, (February 1963), 32–64.

Table 15.2.   *Selected Time Intervals and Corresponding Percentage Changes In the U.S. Money Supply*

Time Interval	% Change in the U.S. Money Supply*
1873–79	−4.9
1892–94	−5.8
1907–08	−3.7
1920–21	−5.1
1929–33	−35.2
1937–38	−2.4

*Money is defined to include time deposits as well as currency and demand deposits.

Source: Friedman and Schwartz, "Money and Business Cycles," p. 34.

stock unaccompanied by changes in money income and prices. [2] The changes in the stock of money cannot consistently be explained by the contemporary changes in money income and prices. The changes in the stock of money can generally be attributed to specific historical circumstances that are not in turn attributable to contemporary changes in money income and prices. Hence, if the consistent relation between money and income is not pure coincidence, it must reflect an influence running from money to business.[12]

Consider as an example the case of the 1920–21 episode. Due to the 1918 demobilization, economic activity had fallen and the inflation which had characterized the period during World War I had resumed. Under these circumstances, gold reserves started declining fairly rapidly and the Treasury urged the Federal Reserve to act decidedly to stop inflation. The reaction of the Fed (in January 1920) was to increase the rediscount rate by 1.25% from 4.75 to 6.00 (which has the dubious honor of being the largest single rise of this rate in the entire monetary history of the country). However, despite such a large increase in the rediscount rate, prices did not react as quickly as anticipated and the Federal Reserve of New York pushed the rate upward to the level of 7% in June 1920. These increases resulted in sharp contractions in the Federal Reserve credit outstanding and consequently in the supply of money by 5.1%. And this in turn yielded a reduction in the index of industrial production of 24 points from 124 in 1920 to 100 in 1921.

Or consider the 1929–33 period of the Great Depression. The stock market crash took place in October 1929. Before that traumatic incident

---

[12]See Friedman and Schwartz, "Money and Business Cycles," p. 50.

the Federal Reserve had taken steps to reduce the money supply in an attempt to curb what was considered excessive speculation in the stock market. But this initial small decrease in the money supply from 1929 to 1930 developed into a sharp declire due to a wave of bank failures beginning in late 1930. Between October 1930 and January 1931 there were more than 700 bank failures as the number of depositors who attempted to convert their deposits into currency increased. The outcome of such an attempt was first, the decline in the deposit-currency ratio and second, a scramble for liquidity by the banks and hence a decline in the deposit-reserve ratio.

FS argue that all these problems could have been avoided had the Federal Reserve shown an adequate measure of leadership. Indeed, the commercial banks had assumed all along that the Federal Reserve would not allow the money supply to decline and that it would have to come to their aid. However, this did not happen, and in fact when Europeans went off the gold standard in September 1931, the Federal Reserve reacted by raising the rediscount rate in October on the premise that this would protect the country from an outflow of gold. The outcome of this was a considerable further decline in the money supply, which resulted in another wave of bank failures. In fact, during the second part of 1931, there were more than 1,850 bank failures. During this period the stock of money declined at an annual rate of 35.2%. Concurrently, during the period 1929–33 the United States experienced a dramatic drop in economic activity. The industrial production index registered an 88-point decline, from 188 to 100. This last change in the level of economic activity was attributed by FS to the change in the level of the money stock.

15.3 The Friedman-Meiselman Study

The other empirical evidence provided in favor of the monetarist doctrine was an econometric comparison of the impact of monetary and fiscal policy by Friedman and David Meiselman (FM) in a now well-known study.[13] Their complaint was that the increase in the popularity of Keynesianism during the 1950s was unfounded, insofar as there was no empirical evidence supporting explicitly the superiority of the new doctrine over the old one. They argued that theories should be

---

[13] See M. Friedman and D. Meiselman, "The Relative Stability of Monetary Velocity and the Investment Multiplier in the United States," in Commission on Money and Credit, *Stabilization Policies* (Englewood Cliffs, N.J. Prentice-Hall, 1963), pp. 168–268.

accepted or rejected only on the basis of their relation to actual experience. In particular, they suggested that:

> . . . the view that the quantity of money matters little is typically held for either of two reasons: one, because the quantity of money is regarded as adapting to the "needs of trade," and hence is regarded as a passive element in the economic system, determined by and responsive to other economic and uneconomic factors, but incapable of being a source of disturbance; the other, because the ratio of money to other assets is regarded as variable and pliable, and hence the economic effects of changes in the quantity of money are regarded as highly unpredictable.
>
> The alternative view holds that the quantity of money does matter, and for three reasons: one, because the quantity of money is capable of being controlled fairly accurately by deliberate policy; two, because changes in the quantity of money can produce substantial changes in the flow of income, prices and other important variables; three, because the relationships between stock of money and other assets are relatively, stable, and dependable.[14]

In their attempt to assess and compare the explanatory power of the two theories, FM faced an initial problem of choice between a sophisticated analysis, which necessarily would involve the use of large numbers of variables, and a simplified approach which would lend itself to a wide range of evidence and circumstances. They chose the second alternative and reduced the problem to measuring the relative degree of correlation between the stock of money and autonomous expenditures with the level of income.

The quantity theory, in its simple form, advocates that the relation between total demand and stock of money should be stable and, consequently, predictable. Therefore, the theory would suggest that:

$$Y = f(M) \tag{15.3.1}$$

which, expressed in linear form, may be written:

$$Y = v_0 + v_1 M. \tag{15.3.2}$$

In the above equation v_1 denotes the marginal income velocity (i.e.,

[14]Ibid., pp. 167–68. Incidentally, compare this statement with that of A. Okun, assessing in 1968 the effectiveness of the 1964 revenue tax cut: ". . . monetary policies made a major contribution to the advance, *but that contribution can be appropriately viewed as permissive, rather than causal* [italics added]. The monetary authorities supplied a good set of tires to roll on, but they did not contrive the engine. That came from fiscal policies." See A. Okun, "Measuring the Impact of the 1964 Tax Reduction" in *Perspectives on Economic Growth*, ed. W. Heller (New York: Vintage Books, 1968), p. 44.

$\Delta Y/\Delta M = v_1$) and v_0 is another constant,[15] whereas M stands for the community's stock of money and is defined to include currency in public circulation plus adjusted demand deposits plus time deposits in the hands of commercial banks.

On the other hand, the Keynesian theory claims that the major sources of changes in demand are shifts in autonomous expenditures. In its simplest form this latter relationship may be written:

$$Y = \alpha + kA \qquad\qquad (15.3.3)$$

where A denotes autonomous expenditures (defined to include net private domestic investment, plus the government deficit on income and product accounts, plus the net foreign balance).[16] Equation 15.3.3 is nothing else but the reduced form of the endogenous variable income, as the reader will recall from chapter 3.[17]

Therefore, the coefficients α and k are uniquely related to the coefficients of the consumption function: namely, autonomous consumption (a) and the MPC (b). Furthermore, we can also see that the slope of equation 15.3.3 is the multiplier itself.

However, for various statistical reasons, when FM tested the two hypotheses by using actual data, it was deemed desirable to use the reduced form of consumption expenditures, i.e.,

$$C = a + k'A \qquad\qquad (15.3.4)$$

---

[15] Notice that according to our discussion in chapter 8, the marginal and average income velocity appeared to be the same since the relationship between income and money was one of proportionality. However, the assumption of identical marginal and average income velocities is not required by the theory per se and Friedman and Meiselman decided to allow the data to settle the issue. See also Fand, "Keynesian Monetary Theories, Stabilization Policy and Recent Inflation."

[16] See Friedman and Meiselman, "Relative Stability," p. 184.

[17] Indeed, assuming that A is an exogenous variable, the simple version of Keynesian expenditures sector may be written:

$$Y = C + A$$
$$C = a' + bY,$$

from which we can immediately obtain:

$$Y = \frac{a'}{1 - b} + \frac{1}{1 - b}A.$$

The above equation can be rewritten as:

$$Y = \alpha + kA$$

$$\text{where} \quad \alpha \equiv \frac{a'}{1 - b} \quad \text{and} \quad k = \frac{1}{1 - b}.$$

and for reasons of comparison the quantity theory was written:

$$C = v_0' + v_1'M. \tag{15.3.5}$$

where v_0', v_1' and k' are suitably-defined constants.

Using the above two equations for statistical tests, it was found that the exogenous variable M in equation 15.3.5 outperformed decidedly the corresponding variable A in equation 15.3.4 in terms of explaining the behavior of the variable C. Indeed, according to this test the balance was tipped in favor of the quantity theory and it appeared that the velocity of money was consistently more stable than the multiplier. The only exception to this conclusion seemed to be the period of the Great Depression during the 1930s. Therefore, the conclusion was inevitable; the simple Keynesian equation was "almost completely useless as a description of stable empirical relationships, as judged by six decades of experience in the United States."[18]

Therefore, this empirical evidence, according to FM, indicated that money not only matters, but in addition, it is the dominant factor which influences economic activity. In particular, they concluded that their findings supported the conclusion ". . . that control over the stock of money is a far more useful tool for affecting the level of aggregate demand than control over autonomous expenditures. Changes in autonomous expenditures may have important effects on income, but these effects are far more variable from year to year than the effects of changes in the stock of money."[19] It is clear then, that according to FM the use of monetary policy to influence the course of economic activity is more efficient and powerful than policies which change autonomous expenditures. They argue that the stock of money is also easier to control and in practice can be determined by the monetary authorities within fairly narrow margins.

The views expressed by Friedman and Meiselman were considered by Keynesian economists rather extreme, and in some measure, unjustified. Indeed, one may say that with the exception of a few hard-core Keynesians,[20] the profession in general has neither ignored nor underestimated the importance of money as an influential factor in the determination of the level of economic activity. This should have been clear from chapter 7. At any rate, Friedman and Meiselman left them-

---

[18]Friedman and Meiselman, "Relative Stability," p. 187.

[19]Ibid., p. 213.

[20]See for example N. Kaldor, "The New Monetarism," *Lloyds Bank Review* (July 1970), 1–18.

selves open to several objections which could be raised against their study, and indeed, Keynesian economists were quick to point them out.

To begin with, it has been argued that, contrary to the quantity theory, the simple two-equation system used as a representative of "the" Keynesian theory is a simplified version to be used only in the classroom for expository purposes. To test the theory the only choice is to use a larger system of equations which would depict more adequately both the spirit and the letter of Keynesianism. Therefore, because of the misspecification in question, the FM model renders results which for all practical purposes should be considered worthless.[21]

Furthermore, although the method used by Friedman and Meiselman (regression analysis) to draw their inference is capable of establishing the existence of a systematic relationship between variables, it cannot be used to conclude causality. What can be said unequivocally is that money income and the stock of money are related very highly to each other. But this does not determine if the stock of money affects income, or alternatively, if income affects the stock of money, or even if other variables affect both simultaneously. Therefore the causality issue should have been settled and established independently of any statistical analysis. Suppose that we find that the length of skirts varies directly with the price of stocks in the stock market and that this relation is characterized by a high correlation coefficient. What can we conclude from this concerning causality?

It can be shown that changes in money income can indeed have feedback effects on the money supply (defined as the sum of currency and demand deposits). Suppose that we witness an increase in the level of income due to an increase in the autonomous segment of aggregate demand (e.g., government expenditures, or investments which are due exclusively to the introduction of new technology) and assume also that the monetary authorities do not accommodate this increase in income by initiating a corresponding increase in the money supply. Such an increase in income most likely will affect the money supply for three distinct reasons.[22] First, since income will increase, it follows that the demand for transaction cash balances will increase and this in turn will result in higher rates of interest. Provided now that the Federal Reserve

[21]On this point see A. Ando and F. Modigliani, "The Relative Stability of Monetary Velocity and the Investment Multiplier," *American Economic Review* 55 (September 1965), 695.

[22]On this point see W. L. Smith, "Time Deposits, Free Reserves and Monetary Policy," in *Issues in Banking and Monetary Analysis,* ed. G. Pontocorno, R. P. Shay, and A. G. Hart (New York: Holt, Rinehart and Winston, 1967), pp. 79–113.

does not change its rediscount rate, the increased spread between the market and rediscount rates will result in increased borrowing by commercial banks from the Federal Reserve System. In addition to this, an increase in the rate of interest will most likely be accompanied by an effort to economize on excess reserves and an increase in the demand for federal funds, implying a more efficient use of the available reserves by the whole commercial banking system.

Second, the increase in the rate of interest in question will also result in a reshuffling of bank portfolios. More explicitly, such an increase in the rate of interest will spring a switch from time deposits to securities, provided that the banking system does not increase the interest paid on these deposits, or alternatively, that increases in the rates of interest are accompanied by additional minimum time requirements (the time period during which the depositor cannot withdraw his deposits, e.g., six months or one year or five years). Such a shift from time deposits to securities would mean an increase in demand deposits due to the fact that purchasers of securities withdraw funds from time deposits to pay the sellers of securities who deposit these monies in current accounts.

Third, if the rate of interest on time deposits increases then some holders of demand deposits will shift into time deposits. At this point, the money supply (the sum of currency and demand deposits) has decreased by the full amount of the shift. However, this shift from demand to time deposits generates at the same time excess reserves by an amount which is equal to the difference between the legal reserve requirements for demand and time deposits. Disregarding any drains of the system, the demand deposits can now be expanded due to the existence of excess reserves. This last expansion, however, is by necessity less than the initial withdrawal of demand deposits.

From the above analysis we can see clearly that the first two reactions will contribute positively to the money supply, whereas the third reaction will cause a decline in it. Experience, however, suggests that the sum of the first two reasons most likely outweighs the negative effect of the third reason, and therefore the net outcome will be an increase in the stock of money. This conclusion will hold *a fortiori* if the Federal Reserve refuses to adjust the interest rate ceiling imposed by regulation Q or is slow in doing so.[23] Indeed, in this event the third effect does not materialize while the second one is maximized.

Finally, another reason why the line of causation may be opposite to the one suggested by Friedman and Meiselman is one they themselves mention but do not accept; namely, the "leaning against the wind"

---

[23] Regulation Q imposes ceilings on the rates commercial banks may pay on time deposits.

attitude, or "meeting the needs of the trade." For example, the Federal Reserve Bank may want to adjust the stock of money now and then in order to accommodate seasonal variations in the demand for money which occur because of changes in income. Such behavior can be observed during the Christmas period when the demand for currency increases.

The above arguments and examples point out one thing: that it is very difficult to assess the various positions and that it is even more difficult (and for that matter hazardous) to infer conclusively the line of causation (even if one introduces lagged variables to test it as FM did).[24] As the reader can see, the issue is far from settled. Recent studies have shown that business expansion and consequently business demand for loans encourages banks to decrease the magnitude of excess reserves. This supports the argument that the supply of money, contrary to the original monetarist position, may exhibit an endogenous character.[25] Although this last finding has not been denied by the monetarists it has, nevertheless, been suggested that its effects are too small to be capable of reversing the main conclusion concerning the line of causation.[26]

Above and beyond the issue of the direction of causation, the FM study has been criticized because of the operational definitions it used for both autonomous expenditures and money. It has been shown that the use of different definitions for these two variables can yield results which are no longer as one-sided as FM have claimed.[27]

---

[24]On this issue see J. Tobin, "Money and Income: *Post Hoc Ergo Propter Hoc?*", *Quarterly Journal of Economics* 84 (May 1970), 301–317; M. Friedman, "Comment," 318–27 and J. Tobin, "Rejoinder," 328–29.

[25]On this see P. Hendershott, *The Neutralized Money Stock* (Honewood, Ill.: R. D. Irwin, 1968).

[26]See R. G. Davis, "Does Money Matter? A Look at Some Recent Evidence," *Federal Reserve Bank of New York Monthly Review* 51 (June 1969), 119–31, and also L. C. Andersen, "Additional Evidence on the Reverse-Causation Argument," *Federal Reserve Bank of St. Louis Review* 51 (August 1969), 19–23. See also K. Brunner and A. H. Meltzer, "Friedman's Monetary Theory," *Journal of Political Economy* 80 (September–October 1972), 837–51.

[27]On this issue there are several studies. For example, see A. Ando and F. Modigliani, "The Relative Stability of Monetary Velocity and the Investment Multiplier," *American Economic Review* 55 (September 1965), 693–728; also M. Deprano and T. Mayer, "Autonomous Expenditures and Money," ibid., 729–52; M. Friedman and D. Meiselman, "Reply," ibid., 753–85; A. Ando and F. Modigliani, "Rejoinder," ibid., 786–90; and M. Deprano and T. Mayer, "Rejoinder," ibid., 791–92. Also in an interesting article D. D. Hester showed that the correlation coefficient Friedman and Meiselman found can be expressed as a function of the definitions they used for the variables in question; see D. D. Hester, "Keynes and the Quantity Theory: A Comment on Friedman-Meiselman CMC Paper," *Review of Economics and Statistics* 46 (November 1964); and M. Friedman and D. Meiselman, "Reply," and D. D. Hester, "Rejoinder," ibid.

15.4 The Federal Reserve of St. Louis Study

As was pointed out in the introduction to this chapter, much of the empirical evidence in support of monetarism has been provided by a dedicated group of economists working for the Federal Reserve Bank of St. Louis.[28] One of the most important empirical contributions provided is that associated with the names of Leonall C. Andersen and Jerry L. Jordan, who developed a model which is much of the same character as that of Friedman and Meiselman. The purpose of building the model was to study the relative importance of monetary and fiscal actions as explanatory factors for aggregate demand. In particular, they set out to test a three-fold proposition: "The response of economic activity to fiscal relative to that of monetary actions (I) is greater, (II) is more predictable, and (III) is faster."[29]

To analyze these three propositions Andersen and Jordan established some empirical relationships between total spending and various measures of monetary and fiscal actions. These relationships are not unlike those used by FM in that they are characterized by their laconic simplicity. In particular, they postulated that total spending depends on government actions (measured in terms of a concept of government deficit), monetary actions (measured in terms of the level of money stocks) and a generic variable summarizing all other forces which conceivably have an impact on total spending. More explicitly they argued that:

$$Y = F(E,R,M,Z) \qquad\qquad (15.4.1)$$

where:

$Y \equiv$ Total spending (i.e., GNP in current prices)
$E \equiv$ High-employment government expenditures
$R \equiv$ High-employment government receipts
$(R - E) \equiv$ High-employment budget surplus
$M \equiv$ Money supply (defined as the sum of currency and demand deposits)
$Z \equiv$ A generic variable summarizing all other forces that influence total spending.

Equation 15.4.1 can be expressed in terms of first differences to obtain

---

[28] See L. C. Andersen and J. L. Jordan, "Monetary and Fiscal Actions: A Test of Their Relative Importance in Economic Stabilization," *Federal Reserve Bank of St. Louis Review* 50 (November 1968), 11–23.

[29] Ibid., p. 11.

$$\Delta Y = F(\Delta E, \Delta R, \Delta M, \Delta Z).$$

To make the hypothesis more easily testable, it was further assumed that the above equation is linear in its arguments:

$$\Delta Y = a_1 \Delta E + a_2 \Delta R + a_3 \Delta M + a_4 \Delta Z. \tag{15.4.2}$$

In equation 15.4.2, the term ΔZ denotes the indirect influence that monetary and fiscal actions may exert on the dependent variable and therefore it can be expressed itself as a function of the same arguments, i.e.:

$$\Delta Z = b_0 + b_1 \Delta E + b_2 \Delta R + b_3 \Delta M. \tag{15.4.3}$$

Substituting now 15.4.3 into equation 15.4.2 we obtain

$$\Delta Y = b_0 a_4 + (a_1 + b_1 a_4) \Delta E + (a_2 + b_2 a_4) \Delta R$$
$$+ (a_3 + b_3 a_4) \Delta M \tag{15.4.4}$$

where, by construction, the coefficients of the various arguments in equation 15.4.4 embody both the direct as well as the indirect impact of fiscal and monetary actions. With respect to the signs of the various coefficients, the a priori expectations are that changes in GNP should be positively related to changes in the money stock (M) and changes in high-employment expenditures (E), whereas changes in high-employment receipts (R) are expected to have a negative influence. By the same token, the high-employment surplus (i.e., receipts minus expenditures) is expected to have a negative influence on GNP. Equations 15.4.5, 15.4.6 and 15.4.7 provide us with a typical sample of the empirical findings based on equation 15.4.4.[30]

$$\Delta Y = 2.10 + 1.51^*\Delta M_t + 1.59^*\Delta M_{t-1} + 1.47^*\Delta M_{t-2}$$
$$\quad\;(1.88)\;\;(2.03)\qquad\;(2.85)\qquad\qquad(2.69)$$

$$+ 1.27\,\Delta M_{t-3} + .36\,\Delta E_t + .53^*\Delta E_{t-1} - .05\,\Delta E_{t-2}$$
$$\quad\;(1.82)\qquad\quad(1.15)\qquad(2.15)\qquad\quad(.19)$$

$$- .78^*\Delta E_{t-3} + .16\,\Delta R_t - .01\,\Delta R_{t-1} - .10\,\Delta R_{t-2}$$
$$\quad(2.82)\qquad\quad(.53)\qquad\;(.03)\qquad\qquad(15.4.5)$$

$$\Delta Y = 2.28^* + 1.54^*\Delta M_t + 1.56^*\Delta M_{t-1} + 1.44^*\Delta M_{t-2}$$
$$\quad\;(2.76)\;\;(2.47)\qquad\;(3.43)\qquad\qquad(3.18)$$

$$+ 1.29^*\Delta M_{t-3} + .40\,\Delta E_t + .54^*\Delta E_{t-1} - .03\,\Delta E_{t-2}$$
$$\quad\;(2.00)\qquad\quad(1.48)\qquad(2.68)\qquad\quad(.13)$$

---

[30] The numbers in parentheses directly below each coefficient denote "t" values associated with them. The regression coefficients marked by an asterisk (*) are statistically significant at the 5% level.

$$- .74^*\Delta E_{t-3}$$
$$(2.85) \tag{15.4.6}$$

$$\Delta Y = 1.99^* + 1.57^*\Delta M_t + 1.94^*\Delta M_{t-1} + 1.80^*\Delta M_{t-2}$$
$$(2.16)\quad (2.17)\qquad (3.60)\qquad (3.37)$$

$$+ 1.28\,\Delta M_{t-3} - .15\,\Delta(R - E)_t - .20\,\Delta(R - E)_{t-1}$$
$$(1.88)\qquad\quad (.65)\qquad\qquad (1.08)$$

$$+ .10\,\Delta(R - E)_{t-2} + .47^*\,\Delta(R - E)_{t-3} \tag{15.4.7}$$
$$(.55)\qquad\qquad (1.95)$$

From the above equations we can see several things. First, the total response of GNP to changes in money supply complies with the hypothesis. All coefficients associated with M are positive and statistically significant. On the other hand, the coefficients associated with the various expressions of fiscal actions do not appear to be consistent with the a priori expectations concerning their signs and, in large measure, they are not statistically different from zero. Consider, for example, equation 15.4.6. In there we see that while all coefficients associated with ΔM are statistically significant and positive, from the coefficients associated with high-employment government expenditures only those of ΔE_{t-1} and ΔE_{t-3} appear to be significant, but two out of these four coefficients (i.e., ΔE_{t-2} and ΔE_{t-3}) have a negative sign, indicating that an increase in this variable will have adverse effects on the change of GNP. Furthermore, the coefficients associated with each policy action may be summed to provide an indication of the overall response of the GNP to the use of this instrument. From this point of view we see once more that monetary policy appears to be, according to the St. Louis model, far more potent than fiscal policy. Consider once more equation 15.4.6. It appears that a $1 increase in the money supply will result after four quarters in $5.83/4 = \$1.46$ increase in GNP, while a $1 increase in high-employment expenditures most likely would not result in any increase in GNP.[31]

The equation as well as the results Andersen and Jordan have derived have somewhat puzzled economists associated with the Keynesian tradition. Indeed, the equation they have used has been subject to different interpretations and the confusion is due, to some extent, to the authors themselves. In their work they suggest that:

---

[31]The reason we divide the total response of 5.83 by 4 is that GNP is expressed in annual and not quarterly rates. On the other hand, the fiscal reaction should be equal to $.17/4 = .04$, but, unfortunately, this number is not statistically different than zero.

This article does not attempt to test rival economic theories of the mechanism by which monetary and fiscal actions influence economic activity. Neither is it intended to develop evidence bearing directly on any causal relationships implied by such theories. More elaborate procedures than those used here would be required in order to test any theories underlying the familiar statements regarding results expected from monetary and fiscal actions. However, empirical relationships are developed between frequently used measured of stabilization actions and economic activity. These relationships are consistent with the implications of some theories of stabilization policy and inconsistent with others . . .[32]

However, in a later publication it is claimed that ". . . this general specification represents the reduced form for that class of structures [models] which has ΔM and ΔE [i.e., changes in the stock of money and changes in the high-employment federal expenditures] as exogenous variables. In this form the total spending equation remains uncommitted as to the structure; it is potentially consistent with both Keynesian and the quantity theory models."[33] This view has not been accepted as yet by the profession.[34]

The results and the forecasting record of the St. Louis equations are still a fascinating puzzle for all nonmonetarist economists who are used to large econometric models, so much more since other econometric models in the Keynesian tradition have yielded results which are diametrically opposite to those of St. Louis. To be sure, the St. Louis model has been subjected to numerous attacks ranging from issues associated with the choice of their explanatory variables to problems having to do with statistical biases in their estimation.[35]

In relation to the last criticism, the reverse-causation argument contends that the econometric evidence provided by monetarists in support of the hypothesis that changes in the money stock dominate (i.e.,

---

[32] See Andersen and Jordan, "Monetary and Fiscal Actions," p. 11.

[33] See L. C. Andersen and Keith M. Carlson, "A Monetarist Model for Economic Stabilization," *Federal Reserve Bank of St. Louis Review* 52 (April 1970), 9.

[34] See for example R. M. Rasche, "Comments on a Monetaristic Approach to Demand Management," *Federal Reserve Bank of St. Louis Review* 54 (January 1972), 26–32. In there, he argues that the St. Louis equation is not a "reduced form" of an unspecified system but instead just one component of a structural system.

[35] On this see, for example, F. de Leeuw and J. Kalchbrenner, "Monetary and Fiscal Actions: A Test of Their Relative Importance in Economic Stabilization—Comment," *Federal Reserve Bank of St. Louis Review* 51 (April 1969), 6–11; and E. M. Gramlich, "The Usefulness of Monetary and Fiscal Policy as Discretionary Stabilization Tools," *Journal of Money, Credit and Banking*, 3 (May 1971), 506–32.

explain) changes in the level of economic activity is compromised by the possible reverse influence of the economic activity on the money supply. In particular, Tobin argues,

> . . . The Fed has been supplying money on demand from the economy instead of using the money supply to control the economy. . . . As a result, the Fed has allowed the supply of money to creep up when the demand for money rose as a result of expansion in business activity, and to fall when business activity has slacked off. This criticism implies that the supply of money has, in fact, not been an exogenously controlled variable over the period of observation. It has been an endogenous variable, responding to changes in economic conditions and credit market indicator. . . .
>
> The evidence of association between money and income reflects to a large degree, this response mechanism of the Federal Reserve . . . It cannot be used simultaneously to support the reverse conclusion: namely that what they have done is the cause of the changes in income and GNP.[36]

Despite all these attacks, one could argue that the St. Louis equation had taken the weather quite well. However, a recently published study by Carl Christ casts serious doubts on the findings of the St. Louis econometric model—so much more since his model appears to be quite similar to that of St. Louis. Its distinctive feature is that it also incorporates what is known as the "federal government budget restraint." In his study, Christ investigates the period spanned between 1891–1970 and finds that increases in both federal spending and money supply (defined as the sum of currency in the hands of the public and reserves of the commercial banks) have had substantial stimulative effects on the level of economic activity. In addition, upon breaking his sample period into subperiods, he also finds that the quantitative effects are stable throughout the various subperiods.

Furthermore, the speed of response of economic activity to government expenditures is high, which would not be established, at least to a similar extent, in the case of monetary policy. Such a result directly contradicts the claim advanced by Andersen and Jordan that the effects of money supply changes relative to changes in fiscal policy were "large," "predictable" and "fast."[37]

---

[36]See J. Tobin, "The Role of Money in National Economic Policy—A Panel Discussion," in *Controlling Monetary Aggregates* (Boston: Federal Reserve Bank of Boston, 1969), pp. 21–24.

[37]On this see C. Christ, "Monetary and Fiscal Influences on U.S. Money Income, 1891–1970," *Journal of Money, Credit and Banking* 5 (February 1973), 279–300.

On the basis of the above comments, therefore, it is not surprising that a large segment of the profession is not prepared as yet to adopt the rather impressionistic world portrayed by the St. Louis team. However, it can also be said that the St. Louis efforts have introduced a more reasonable and less assertive tone to the discussion, so that one can afford the luxury of being optimistic that the debate will eventually produce some common grounds of resolution. One of them may be channels of transmission, which we deal with in the next section.

15.5 The Transmission Channels of Monetary Impulses

In the previous section we discussed the monetarist contention that the dominant factors which influence economic activity are changes in the stock of money. The reader should be careful to notice that the word used was *dominant*, for monetarists do not maintain that money is the exlusive force which exerts influence on either real or nominal levels of economic activity. Other factors which can be influential include those which can generate changes in the demand for money, productivity, or factor endowment, or even those which are included in the generic Keynesian term "animal spirit." This much is not denied by monetarists.[38] The proposition is not that all these factors do not play any role, but rather that the leading role is performed by monetary impulses. It is therefore necessary to ask what are the channels via which these monetary impulses, expressed in terms of changes in the stock of money, reach the real sector and yield changes in income, prices and other variables.[39] To be sure, this question appears to be quite independent of any empirical evidence concerning the influence (or lack thereof) of money on the level of economic activity.

The major recent development in monetary theory has been the explicit introduction of a generalized version of the theory of asset choice, including both financial and real assets. The kernel of this approach

---

[38]See, for example, L. C. Andersen, "The State of the Monetarist Debate," *Federal Reserve Bank of St. Louis Review* 55 (September 1973), p. 3.

[39]On this subject the reader may consult the Friedman and Meiselman study, pp. 217–222, and pp. 59–63; also H. Johnson, "Monetary Theory and Policy," *American Economic Review* 52 (June 1962), 335–84; K. Brunner, "The Report of the Commission on Money and Credit," *The Journal of Political Economy* 69 (December 1961), 605–20; K. Brunner, "Some Major Problems of Monetary Theory," *Proceedings of the American Economic Association* 51 (May 1961), 47–56; K. Brunner and A. H. Meltzer, "The Role of Financial Institutions in the Transmission Mechanism," *Proceedings of the American Economic Association* 53 (May 1963), 372–82.

is to consider changes in the stock of money as altering the optimum (desired) structure of the portfolios of the economic unit (individuals or firms) and thereby inducing various adjustments designed to restore the structure of the portfolios (including both assets and liabilities) at desired levels corresponding to the new altered rates of interest and imputed yields. In the process of such reshuffling the monetary impulses are transmitted (spilled over) into the expenditure sector through changes in the demand for various financial and real assets which, in turn, affect the level of output and prices. The main characteristic of this approach is its microeconomic flavor. In the final analysis this mechanism is not different from the one we use to derive the demand of a certain commodity, given the preference relations of the economic actor as well as the prices of all commodities. In fact, its general nature has been described as evolving from the various writings of Knut Wicksell, Irving Fisher and John Maynard Keynes.

Actually, a rudimentary version of the portfolio adjustment approach was included in *General Theory*. According to the Keynesian analysis, the way the public allocated its financial wealth between bonds and speculative cash balances depended on "the" rate of interest. In turn, the rate of interest induced changes in the demand for investment, which, through the multiplier, resulted in changes in the current output.

On the other hand, the neo-Keynesian approach broadens considerably the spectrum of assets to include not only government bonds, but also open market commercial paper, industrial bonds, equities, savings and loans shares, mortgages and the like. Given this type of portfolio, the adjustment mechanism may be described briefly as follows: suppose that the monetary authorities engage in open market operations and purchase, say, treasury bills. This will directly lower the yield on bills and will generate a sympathetic movement of the rates of interest in general through the process of arbitrage involving a chain of portfolio substitutions. More explicitly, the holders of, say, bills sell them to the Federal Reserve because they are offered a good price for them. But now they find their portfolios with more cash balances than they desire to hold. As a result, they attempt to adjust the structure of their portfolios by reducing the amount of cash balances and purchasing interest-yielding financial assets. This increase in the demand of this type of asset, however, results in an increase of their market price, thereby reducing their current yield.

In addition, the reserves of commercial banks will increase either because they themselves liquidate a part of their portfolio by selling bills to the Fed, or alternatively, because the individual economic actors who sell bills to the Fed deposit the proceeds of the sale in their checking accounts. Such an increase in deposits, given our fractional reserve system, will add to the reserves of the banks relative to their deposits. The banks in turn will use the bulk of the additional reserves to advance loans on more favorable terms and conceivably to purchase other financial securities, thereby exerting further downward pressure on current yields. Now, with the expected marginal return of real capital at least temporarily unchanged, the decline in the yields on financial assets encourages the issue of new debts which will be used to finance newly created assets (investment), thereby increasing once more the level of current output. This is the result of a new wave of adjustment processes which takes place in the portfolio of the firms. Since the market rate declines relative to the yield of real capital, this in turn generates a gap between the desired and actual stock of capital, which in time leads to the production of new capital goods.

In addition to the above effects, however, we will also observe some wealth effects. This appears at first glance as inconceivable since monetary policy operates through the swapping of one asset (bills) for another (cash balances) and therefore there is seemingly no change in wealth. This is not quite so, however, since the reduction of the market rates does imply an increase in the present value of the future stream of income (which is equivalent, as we already know from chapter 6, to an increase in the market value of outstanding bonds). This increase in wealth in turn will stimulate economic activity through increases in aggregate demand.

The mechanism just described operates through a well but narrowly defined spectrum of financial assets and markets. On the other hand, monetarists have argued in favor of a transmission mechanism which appears to be of a broader range, including financial as well as real assets. They argue that the adjustment process takes place through the portfolios of all economic units, both individual households and firms. Such a treatment is consistent with Friedman's view concerning the behavior of consumption expenditures and the demand for money (see chapters 12 and 14). According to his view, an individual's portfolio should include not only cash balances and other financial assets of various kinds but also ". . . a host of other assets, even going so far as to include consumer durables, consumer inventories of clothing and the like and, maybe also, such human capital as skills acquired through training, and the like.[40]

In some sense, then, the consumer may be thought of as an agent who produces and consumes simultaneously all the services produced by these goods. Therefore, the division of economic units into households

---

[40]See Friedman and Schwartz, "Money and Business Cycles," p. 61.

and firms is arbitrary and one can argue that the same adjustment process should be taking place in their portfolios. But if this is the case, it is necessary to extend the concept of yields to include the implicit or imputed rates which correspond to this broader spectrum of assets. Therefore, the portfolios of households are at equilibrium or disequilibrium, and subject to the adjustment process, under the same circumstances as those of firms. It follows that monetary policy, by altering the various interest rates, opens the same type of gap between the desired and actual levels of stocks in the portfolios of households and therefore triggers the same adjustment process which results in changes in the level of aggregate demand and prices.

To recapitulate, the monetarist position concerning the transmission mechanism is that monetary impulses change interest rates and relative prices of both real and financial assets. These changes necessitate a reallocation of asset holdings, which imply changes in the demand for real assets. In addition, these portfolio adjustments include changes in the demand for consumables. This approximate mechanism has been characterized by Brunner as the "weak monetarist thesis."[41]

It seems, however, that this mechanism is by now widely accepted by monetary economists regardless of their persuasion. The evolution of Tobin's writings suggests the existence of a mechanism which is quite similar with the above.[42] Andersen admits that he would consider this transmission mechanism as ". . . close to the Tobin view, except that it takes into consideration many more rates of return and market prices of goods and services.[43]

A corollary which can be derived from our discussion concerning the transmission mechanism is associated with the appropriate conduct of monetary policy. The neo-Keynesian view would suggest that monetary policy should be gauged via its influence on a well-defined set of interest rates, since this is in effect the trigger of the mechanism itself. Therefore, not only should targets be expressed in terms of interest levels, but also

---

[41] See K. Brunner, "The Role of Money and Monetary Policy," *Federal Reserve of St. Louis Review* 50 (July 1968), 18–19.

[42] See for example J. Tobin, "Money, Capital and Other Stores of Value," *American Economic Review Proceedings* 51 (May 1961), 26–37; also his "An Essay on Principles of Debt Management," in Commission on Money and Credit, *Fiscal and Debt Management Policies* (Englewood Cliffs, N.J.: Prentice-Hall, 1963), pp. 143–218; and also, "A General Equilibrium Approach to Monetary Theory," *Journal of Money, Credit and Banking* 1 (February 1969), 15–29; also Warren L. Smith, "A Neo-Keynesian View of Monetary Policy," in *Controlling Monetary Aggregates,* (Boston: Federal Reserve Bank of Boston, 1969), pp. 105–36.

[43] See L. C. Andersen, The State of the Monetarist Debate," p. 3.

market rates can be viewed as indicators of the looseness or tightness of the policy, given the profile of the economy at that time.

On the other hand, the monetaristic position is that monetary policy should be conducted in terms of controlling the growth of monetary aggregates rather than aiming at target interest rates or money market conditions. This position is indeed consistent with the monetarists' view of the range of portfolio effects considered and the fact that a large number of yields imputed to various assets is not observable. However, since the adjustment process involves reshuffling of the whole portfolio, they hold that the neo-Keynesian view is too narrow to capture these movements. Furthermore, it is quite conceivable that the use of the level of market rates may give the decision makers the wrong impression of what really happens in the economy. In chapter 7 we saw that when there are expectations of future inflation, a premium is driven like a wedge between the real and the market rates of interest. It is possible therefore to see at periods of changing expectations concerning future inflation a crossing of signals; i.e., the monetary authorities may base their policy on current nominal rates while the correct variable to observe for policy would be the *ex-ante* real rates. Under these circumstances, increases in the money supply may be accompanied by increases in the market rates of interest, and conversely.

In addition, recent work in investment theory associated primarily with the research of D. Jorgensen has shown that the rate of interest is only one component of the user cost of new capital which, in turn, appears to be an important explanatory variable of the behavior of the demand for investments. Other components of this variable are associated with the various tax policies and in particular the investment tax credit. (See chapter 13 for a review of this hypothesis.) Therefore, the extent of influence an interest-rate change will exert on the demand for investment depends on the influence such a change has on the user cost. For example, suppose that the market rates increase. This would imply an increase in the level of the user cost of new capital and thus a decrease in the demand for new investment. But now let us assume that within the framework of fiscal policy the government increases the investment tax credit. This last action amounts to a decrease in the user cost and therefore, *ceteris paribus,* one would expect that the demand for investment would increase. The question then is what happens to the demand for investment. Obviously, the answer depends on the relative strength of these two opposing forces, the interest-rate level and the investment tax credit. If, for example, the net effect is a decrease of the user cost, then the demand for investment will increase in spite of the fact that interest rates went up. This discussion suggests that the rele-

vant explanatory variable in the determination of the demand for investment is not the interest rate or the investment tax credit rate alone, but
instead their joint values.[44] It follows therefore that concentrating only
on the appropriate rate of interest and designing a policy to achieve
certain goals on the basis of market rates may not be so proper as might
have been thought, and in fact, may be downright misleading due to the
multiplicity of factors affecting investment.

The general monetarist criticism of using interest-rate levels as a
signal for monetary policy is well founded. However, the monetarist
alternative of aiming policy at the goal of a particular growth rate of
the money supply is subject to the same shortcoming. To be sure, the
monetarists' suggestion is based on their assumption that the money
supply is an exogenous variable. However, to the extent that this is not
the case any policy which is based on the rate of change of this variable
will be equally misleading.

15.6 The Question of Stability of the Market Economy

In addition to the above presentation, we have suggested that monetarists contend that the economy is inherently stable, that it is capable of
absorbing various disturbing shocks (e.g., a change in the growth of
money) so that the level of output will naturally resume, after some
time, its long-run growth path.[45] In fact, they would argue that the
system itself does not have a tendency to produce such disturbances, and
that fluctuations are due to the interference of the government and its
associated, misguided policies. For example, they argue that to a large
extent the cause of the Great Depression of the thirties was inappropriate
monetary policies. In fact, the government interfered to solve economic
problems which were originally generated by its previous interference.
The analogy which is used very often is that the government's actions
were similar to attempting to treat the shaking hands of an alcoholic by
giving him a pitcher of martinis.

The issue here may be given several interpretations. If monetarists
suggest that post-Keynesians generally believe that the economy is
inherently unstable, this is not correct. To be sure, Keynesians have
argued that the system is oscillatory or subject to fluctuations and

---

[44]On this point see R. H. Rasche, "Comments on a Monetarist Approach to Demand
Management."

[45]See for example L. C. Andersen, "The State of the Monetarist Debate," p. 7.

that also it has the tendency to move around an equilibrium position which is below that of full employment. But this position cannot be translated to mean that they perceive an inherently unstable economy. On the other hand, if they mean to question the Keynesian postulate that economic policies stabilize (or at least do not destabilize) the economy, then there is a problem. Concerning the first interpretation of stability, we have empirical evidence that the economy oscillates but is fundamentally stable. In regard to the second issue, we have to admit that the evidence, if there is any, is too meager to support any position.

15.7 Conclusions

The major result of the monetarist counterrevolution has been that the majority of economists now agree that money matters. Money has received a great deal of attention in theory, econometric model building and stabilization policies. This notwithstanding, neither has the rule of the stable growth of monetary aggregates been accepted nor is it likely to be accepted on the basis of the current evidence in any foreseeable future.

On the other hand, if this debate is to be resolved, it would be desirable if monetarists would spell out, more explicitly than they have done so far, the channels via which money influences GNP in current prices.

Suggested Further Reading

Brunner, K. "The Report of the Commission on Money and Credit." *The Journal of Political Economy* 69 (December 1961), 605–20.

Brunner, K. and Meltzer, A. H. "The Place of Financial Intermediaries in the Transmission of Monetary Policy." *The American Economic Review* 53 (May 1963), 372–82.

———. "The Uses of Money: Money in the Theory of an Exchange Economy." *The American Economic Review* 61 (December 1971), 784–805.

———. "Friedman's Monetary Theory." *The Journal of Political Economy* 80 (September/October 1972), 837–51.

Cagan, P. *The Channels of Monetary Effects on Interest Rates.* New York: National Bureau of Economic Research, 1972.

———. "Why Do We Use Money in Open Market Operations?" *The Journal of Political Economy* 66 (February 1958), 34–46.

Christ, C. F. "Econometric Models of the Financial Sector." *Journal of Money, Credit and Banking* 3 (May 1971), 419–49.

———. "A Model of Monetary and Fiscal Policy Effects on Money Stock, Price Level, and Real Output." *Journal of Money, Credit and Banking* 1 (November 1969), 683–705.

Davis, R. G. "The Role of the Money Supply in Business Cycles." *Federal Reserve Bank of New York Monthly Review* 50 (April 1968), 63–73.

DeLeeuw, F. and Gramlich, E. M. "The Channels of Monetary Policy." *Federal Reserve Bulletin* 55 (June 1969), 472–91.

Eisner, R. "Factors Affecting the Level of Interest Rates: Part II." United States Savings and Loan League. *Savings and Residential Financing: 1968 Conference Proceedings,* 1968.

Fisher, L. *The Purchasing Power of Money: The Determination and Relation to Credit Interest and Crises.* rev. ed. New York: Reprints of Economic Classics, 1963.

Friedman, M. "Comments on the Critics." *The Journal of Political Economy* 80 (September/October 1972), 906–50.

———. "A Monetary and Fiscal Framework for Economic Stability." *The American Economic Review* 38 (June 1948), 245–64.

———. "A Monetary Theory of Nominal Income." *The Journal of Political Economy* 79 (March/April 1971), 323–37.

Gramlich, E. M. and Chase, S. B. Jr. "Time Deposits in Monetary Analysis." *Federal Reserve Bulletin* 51 (October 1965), 1380–1406.

Gurley, J. G. and Shaw, E. S. *Money in a Theory of Finance.* Washington, D.C.: The Brookings Institution, 1960.

Hicks, J. R. *Critical Essays in Monetary Theory.* Oxford: The Clarendon Press, 1967.

Laidler, D. "Expectations, Adjustment, and the Dynamic Response of Income to Policy Changes." *Journal of Money, Credit and Banking* 5 (February 1973), 157–72.

Leijonhufvud, A. *On Keynesian Economics and the Economics of Keynes: A Study in Monetary Theory.* New York: Oxford University Press, 1968.

Modigliani, F. "The Monetary Mechanism and its Interaction with Real Phenomena." *The Review of Economics and Statistics* 45 (February 1963), 79–107.

————. "Monetary Policy and Consumption: Linkages via Interest Rates and Wealth Effects in the FMP Model." In *Consumer Spending and Monetary Policy: The Linkages.* Monetary Conferences Series no. 5. Boston: Federal Reserve Bank of Boston, 1971.

Patinkin, D., *Money, Interest and Prices: An Integration of Monetary and Value Theory.* 2d ed. New York: Harper and Row, 1965.

Samuelson, P. A. "Money, Interest Rates and Economic Activity: Their Interrelationship in a Market Economy." The American Bankers Association, *A Symposium on Money, Interest Rates and Economic Activity.* 1967.

Silber, W. L. "The St. Louis Equation: 'Democratic' and 'Republican' Version and Other Experiments." *The Review of Economics and Statistics* 53 (November 1971), 362–67.

Smith, P. E. "Lags in the Effects of Monetary Policy: Comment." *The American Economic Review* 62 (March 1972), 230–33.

Tobin, J. "Commercial Banks as Creators of 'Money.'" In *Banking and Monetary Studies,* edited by D. Carson. Homewood, Ill. R. D. Irwin, 1963.

————. "An Essay on Principles of Debt Management." In *Commission on Money and Credit, Fiscal and Debt Management Policies.* Englewood Cliffs, N.J.: Prentice-Hall, 1963.

————. "A General Equilibrium Approach to Monetary Theory." *Journal of Money, Credit and Banking* 1 (February 1969), 15–29.

————. "Monetary Semantics." *Targest and Indicators of Monetary Policy,* edited by K. Brunner. San Francisco: Chandler, 1969.

————. "Money, Capital, and Other Stores of Value." *The American Economic Review* 51 (May 1961), 26–37.

———— and Brainard, W. C. "Pitfalls in Financial Model Building." *The American Economic Review* 58 (May 1968), 99–122.

Tucker, D. P. "Dynamic Income Adjustments to Money-Supply Changes." *The American Economic Review* 56 (June 1966), 433–49.

Wicksell, K. *Lectures on Political Economy: Money.* vol. 2, edited by L. Robbins. London: Routledge and Kegan Paul, 1950.

Appendix 15.A

Wealth Effects and the Impact
of Financing a Deficit

The purpose of this appendix is to take up the problem of financing governmental economic activity and investigate the impact of such a change on the properties of our model.[1] Chapters 7 and 8 dealt with the effects of a change in government expenditures given the various assumptions concerning the shape of the LM curve. However, the issue of how these expenditures are to be financed was postponed until now — not only because the required model is more complicated, but also because the problem at hand is closely related to the monetaristic position. Recently there has been considerable concern regarding the size of the government deficit. Such concern is not because of a vague general disapproval of unbalanced budgets, but is rather related to a hypothesis known as "crowding out" or "the crowding-out effect."

More specifically, in chapter 7 it was argued that an increase (decrease) in government spending will shift the IS curve to the right (left) and, provided that the money supply remains constant, will result in an increase (decrease) of the equilibrium level of income and rate of interest (see figure 7.2.1.A and equations 7.2.17–7.2.18). Furthermore, this increase in the rate of interest was rationalized as the necessary incentive to reduce the demand for speculative cash balances so that the increase in the transaction demand for money (due to the increase in the level of income) would be accommodated, given the unchanged money supply. Our assumption was that such an increase in government expenditures was to be financed by the issuance of new public debt. And, although this was mentioned briefly (see chapter 7.2), we did not pursue the implications of such a line of thinking since this argument could not be accommodated within the framework of our model.

---

[1] In relation to this topic, the reader is referred also to W. L. Silber, "Fiscal Policy in IS-LM Analysis: A Correction," *Journal of Money, Credit and Banking* 2 (November 1970), 461–72; R. W. Spencer and W. P. Yohe, "The Crowding Out of Private Expenditures by Fiscal Policy Actions," *Federal Reserve Bank of St. Louis Review* 52 (October 1970), 12–24; also R. W. Spencer and W. P. Yohe, "A Historical Analysis of the 'Crowding Out' of Private Expenditures by Fiscal Policy Actions," Federal Reserve Bank of St. Louis, *Paper* No. 13 (January 31, 1971); and A. S. Blinder and R. M. Solow, "Analytical Foundations of Fiscal Policy," in *The Economics of Public Finance* (Washington, D.C.: The Brookings Institution, 1974).

The means of financing a deficit is actually a crucial consideration, principally because of its impact on the wealth of the private sector. If the government finances a deficit by expanding the money supply, private wealth (in money form) is directly increased. Alternatively, if a deficit is accommodated by the creation of public debt (the sale of bonds to the public), the public's wealth will be expanded in the form of the extra bonds it holds.[2] These changes in wealth, it will be demonstrated, may well affect economic behavior. In keeping with recent literature, we shall hypothesize that both consumption and money demand are sensitive to changes in the overall level of wealth. Moreover, we shall see that the two alternative means of financing a deficit, through their different effects on the *composition* of wealth (most importantly, the relative holdings of bonds and money) will have differential effects on the equilibrium position of the economy.

The omission of the consideration of the means of financing deficits and the subsequent feedback effects operating through changes in the level and composition of wealth renders the IS-LM analysis somewhat incomplete; as a result, there is a cause to question some of the general conclusions drawn from that model. To appreciate the shortcomings in question, let us assume that the level of taxes, T, is determined exogenously and that there is an increase in government spending financed by the issuance of new bonds. Such an increase in the outstanding public debt will result, *ceteris paribus,* in a rise of the market rate of interest since the public will have to be induced to increase its bond holdings relative to its cash balances. But notice that this last pressure on the rate of interest is, at least as a first approximation, independent of and in addition to that due to the increase in the transaction demand for cash balances mentioned earlier. Therefore, it is argued that the increase in the rate of interest may choke off some amount of the demand for private investment which may be equal to or more than the increase in government expenditures, resulting thereby in no change in, or even a net decrease of, the equilibrium level of income. However, let us assume that the economy reacts typically. Consider figure 15.A.1.

Suppose that this increase in G is a permanent one. Since the tax level is assumed to be fixed at, say, $T = T^0$, it follows that the government will run a continuous deficit on the order of $(G^1 - T^0)$. But as the public's bond holdings increase, period after period, this expansion in wealth may cause an alteration in the behavior of consumption and

---

[2]Note here that the money supply is presumed to stay constant in that the proceeds from the sale of bonds will be reinjected into the economy in the form of extra government expenditures and/or tax reductions.

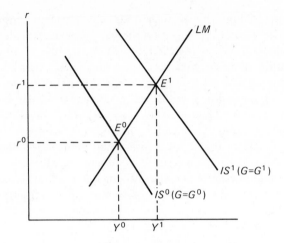

Figure 15.A.1   *Equilibrium and Quasi-equilibrium of the Expenditures and Monetary Sector*

money demand. And any such changes will have subsequent effects on the equilibrium levels of income and the rate of interest. If such changes occur, positions like E^1 cannot be considered as true equilibrium positions.

On the other hand, let us assume that government spending increases by ΔG only for one period and then it returns to its initial level. In this case, according to figure 15.A.1 the economy will follow a path which will take it from E^0 to E^1 and then back to E^0. But if this change in G is financed by an equal change in public debt, then it is not clear at all that the economy will come to rest finally at E^0. To be sure, since the money supply is assumed to be constant, it follows that the economic actors will have to accommodate this increase in public debt by increasing their holdings of government bonds relative to cash balances. However, we know that such a reshuffling of portfolios can take place only by a change (in this case an increase) in the rate of interest.

From the above examples we can clearly see that the analytical scheme of IS-LM has to be modified to take into consideration the issue of financing public expenditures. This amounts to introducing one more equation into our system which suggests that the difference between government expenditures and tax revenues (i.e., the deficit or surplus) must be equal to the sum of changes in government bonds outstanding and money supply, i.e.:

$$G - T = \Delta B + \Delta M_s \tag{15.A.1}$$

(where ΔB denotes the change in government bonds outstanding). Since equation 15.A.1 has to be satisfied simultaneously with the other relations of the system and since it depicts clearly the behavior of the government, it is sometimes called the government budget constraint. Furthermore, by definition, in the long run all changes in stocks and flows must be equal to zero; therefore in a true long-run equilibrium, the government budget would be balanced, implying that $G = T$. However, since our basic concern is the implementation of fiscal policy with a relatively short-run perspective, we shall not treat the implications of such a long-run equilibrium. Instead we shall assume that there is a deficit (surplus) which is financed by changes in money supply or public debt outstanding or both. Under these conditions we shall see how the conclusions drawn in chapter 7 have to be altered. Consider the following system of structural equations.[3]

$$Y = C + I + G \tag{15.A.2}$$

$$C = a + bY_d + cW \tag{15.A.3}$$

$$I = g_0 - g_1 r \tag{15.A.4}$$

$$Y_d \equiv Y - T \tag{15.A.5}$$

$$M_d = l_0 + l_1 Y + l_2 W - l_3 r \tag{15.A.6}$$

$$M_d = M_s \tag{15.A.7}$$

$$W \equiv K + M_s + B \tag{15.A.8}$$

$$G = T + \Delta M_s + \Delta B. \tag{15.A.9}$$

In the above system, all variables are expressed in real terms. In addition we assume that government expenditures (G), tax revenues (T), money supply (M_s) and capital stock (K) are all exogenous and fixed at G^0, T^0, M_s^0 and K^0 respectively.[4] Moreover, we assume that the general price level is exogenous and takes on the value $P = 1$. These

---

[3] See Silber, "Fiscal Policy in IS-LM Analysis," pp. 464–65.

[4] Notice that the assumption of $K = K^0$ introduces a bias since a change in the rate of interest will result in a change in the level of investment which will change the level of the stock of capital. But since K appears in both the consumption function and the demand for real cash balances it follows that both the IS and LM curves would have to shift. Our reason for maintaining this assumption is that while we keep the analysis on a relative simple level the bias introduced is not considered to be serious given the magnitude of I in relation to that of K. Furthermore, we also assume that the level of tax revenues is constant and not a function of the level of income. This assumption also will make some difference in our analysis but this difference will be one of degree and not of nature.

assumptions, taken together, give the model the same general character as one treated earlier in chapters 7 and 8.[5]

Notice that equations 15.A.2–15.A.5 make up the expenditures sector, 15.A.6–15.A.7 comprise the monetary sector, and 15.A.8 and 15.A.9 stand for the definition of wealth (including the stock of capital) and the government budget constraint respectively. The reader should notice that consumption expenditures as well as the demand for real cash balances are expressed as a function of the level of wealth. The rationale for the inclusion of such an explanatory variable in these two behavioral equations has been adequately provided in chapters 12 and 14. Furthermore, we assume that the impact of wealth on consumption expenditures is positive and satisfies the restriction that $0 < c < 1$ (see figure 12.4.3, equation 12.A.3 and associated comments).

In addition, we assume that $0 < l_2 < 1$. This assumption (which, incidentally, has been adequately established by empirical evidence) suggests that an increase in wealth will not be accompanied by an equal increase in the demand for real cash balances. Therefore, if, for example, such an increase in wealth is the outcome of a corresponding increase in the money supply (i.e., $\Delta W = \Delta M_s$; see equation 15.A.8), then this will result in an excess money supply which, in turn, will exert, *ceteris paribus,* a downward pressure on the rate of interest. Figure 15.A.2 makes this point clear.

In figure 15.A.2 we see that if $l_2 \geq 1$ then the new demand for real cash balances (associated with Y^0 and W^1) would have cut the supply curve. M_s^1, at a point at or above B, implying that at the rate of interest r^0 there is an excess demand for real cash balances and that the interest rate would have to increase. But this result would be nonsense. However, for $l_2 < 1$ we observe that at $r = r^0$ there is an excess supply of money equal to AB and this will necessitate the downward slide of the interest rate to $r = r^1$. This case, as we shall shortly see, implies a shift of the LM curve itself to the right.[6]

On the other hand, if the increase in wealth is the result of the issuance of new public debt (i.e., $\Delta W = \Delta B$), then this will generate an excess demand for money which, in turn, will result, *ceteris paribus,* in an increase in the rate of interest. Figure 15.A.3 illustrates this case.

In figure 15.A.3 we see that at $r = r^0$ an increase in wealth due to the issuance of new government bonds generates an excess demand for real

---

[5]The assumption of a lump-sum tax is not particularly crucial here, at least as far as the general conclusions are concerned.

[6]Notice, however, that if $l_2 = 1$ then the LM curve will not shift at all. This can also be seen from equation 15.A.13.

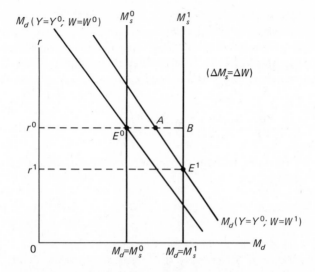

Figure 15.A.2 *The Effects of a Change in Money Supply When the Demand for Money Depends on the Level of Wealth*

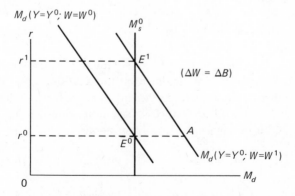

Figure 15.A.3 *The Effects of a Change in the Outstanding Level of Government Debt When the Demand for Money Depends on the Level of Wealth*

cash balances (since the money supply remains constant) which amounts to the distance E^0A. Such a development will result in an upward movement of the rate of interest to $r = r^1$. In this case, as we shall also see momentarily, the LM curve itself will shift to the left.

Indeed, combination of equations 15.A.6 and 15.A.7 yields the LM curve, i.e.:

$$r = \frac{l_0 - M_s^0 + l_2 W^0}{l_3} + \frac{l_1}{l_3} Y. \qquad (15.A.10)$$

From 15.A.10 we see that the corresponding value of the rate of interest for $Y = Y^0$ is r^0, i.e.:

$$r^0 = \frac{l_0 - M_s^0 + l_2 W^0}{l_3} + \frac{l_1}{l_3} Y^0. \qquad (15.A.11)$$

Suppose now that the money supply changes to $(M_s^1 > M_s^0)$. It is clear that such a change affects only the intercept of 15.A.11, and the corresponding value of r at a given income level becomes:

$$r^1 = \frac{l_0 - M_s^1 + l_2 W^1}{l_3} + \frac{l_1}{l_3} Y^0. \qquad (15.A.12)$$

Subtracting equation 15.A.11 from 15.A.12, we obtain

$$\Delta r = \frac{-\Delta M_s + l_2 \Delta W}{l_3}.$$

However, from equation 15.A.8 we see that $\Delta M_s = \Delta W$. Therefore, the above expression can be written

$$\Delta r = - \left(\frac{1 - l_2}{l_3} \right) \Delta M_s. \qquad (15.A.13)$$

Since $0 < l_2 < 1$, the change in the rate of interest is negative, implying that the LM curve itself shifts downward and to the right.

On the other hand, suppose that wealth changes because the government issues new bonds to finance its spending. Substituting the new value of wealth in equation 15.A.11, we obtain:

$$r^2 = \frac{l_0 - M_s^0 + l_2 W^1}{l_3} + \frac{l_1}{l_1} Y^0. \qquad (15.A.14)$$

Subtracting equation 15.A.11 from 15.A.14, we find that, at a given level of income,

$$\Delta r = \frac{l_2}{l_3} \Delta W$$

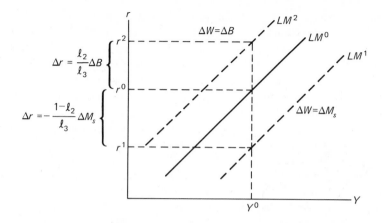

Figure 15.A.4 *The Effects of an Increase in Money Supply or an Increase in the Level of Government Debt on the LM Curve When the Demand for Money Depends on the Level of Wealth*

or

$$\Delta r = \frac{l_2}{l_3} \Delta B. \tag{15.A.15}$$

Therefore we see that the change in wealth stemming from the bond financing of the deficit results in a shift of the LM curve upward and to the left since this time the rate of interest increases. Figure 15.A.4 summarizes these two cases.

The above analysis suggests that the direction of the shift of the LM curve depends on the way the government chooses to finance the change in its spending. Therefore, we see that, given a shift of the IS curve due to an increase in G and any initial induced effects of the change in wealth on the level of consumption expenditures, the level of income will increase unequivocally if the government chooses to finance this increase by allowing the money supply to expand.[7] However, the same cannot be said, a priori, for the case in which the government chooses to finance its spending by issuing new public debt, since in the latter case the rightward shift of the IS curve is accompanied by a left-ward shift in the LM curve. Indeed, the final outcome in this case will depend on the magnitude of the relative shifts which, in turn, depends

---

[7]As an exercise, the student can compute the quantitative shift in the IS schedule for a given change in government expenditures under the assumption that consumption is related to wealth.

on the relation of the various slopes with each other. Figure 15.A.5 can be used to delineate these cases.

In figure 15.A.5a the initial equilibrium (assuming that we start with $G^0 = T^0$) is at Y^0 and r^0. An increase in G shifts IS^0 and LM^0 to IS^1 and LM^1 (since this increase in G is financed by an equal increase in M_s). On the other hand, figures 15.A.5b and c depict the case in which the increase in government expenditures is financed by the issuance of new public debt. As the reader can see, Y^1 may lie either to the right (figure 15.A.5b) or to the left (15.A.5c) of Y^0. Notice that the crowding-out effect would require that either $Y^1 = Y^0$ or $Y^1 < Y^0$. However, as we mentioned before, all E^1 points are only quasi-equilibriums. If the change in G is a permanent one, say, from G^0 to G^1 ($G^1 > G^0$), then the government budget will show a deficit which will have to be financed period after period (since T is fixed at T^0) either by increasing the money supply or by expanding the level of the outstanding public debt—i.e., $\Delta B = G^1 - T^0$ or $\Delta M_s = G^1 - T^0$ or $k \, \Delta B + (1 - k) \, \Delta M_s = G^1 - T^0$ for $0 < k < 1$. But these changes necessitate, in turn, continuous shifts of both the IS (through the effects of wealth on consumption) and the LM (through the effects of wealth on the demand for real cash balances or the effects of changes in money supply or both).

To determine algebraically the conditions under which each particular outcome will occur we may use the structural equations 15.A.2–15.8.9 to solve for the variable income. In particular, the IS and LM equations can be derived by combining equations 15.A.2–15.A.5 and 15.A.6–15.A.7 respectively, i.e.:

$$Y = \frac{1}{1 - b}[a + g_0 - bT + cW + G] - \frac{g_1}{1 - b}r \quad (15.A.16)$$

and

$$r = \frac{l_0 - M_s + l_2 W}{l_3} + \frac{l_1}{l_3}Y. \quad (15.A.17)$$

Substituting r from equation 15.A.17 into 15.A.16, we find the equilibrium value of Y. (Notice that since we assume initially that $G^0 = T^0$, this solution value for income is a genuine equilibrium):

$$Y^0 = \left[\frac{1}{1 - b + g_1 \dfrac{l_1}{l_3}} \right]$$

$$\left[a + g_0 - g_1 \frac{l_0}{l_3} - bT^0 + G^0 + \left(c - g_1 \frac{l_2}{l_3} \right) W^0 + \frac{g_1}{l_3} M_s^0 \right].$$

$$(15.A.18)$$

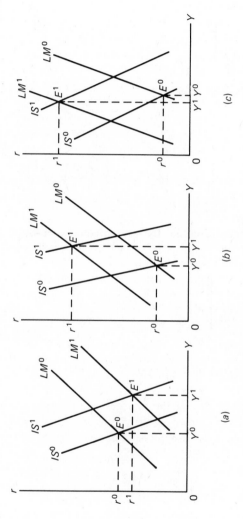

Figure 15.A.5 *Equilibrium and Quasi-Equilibrium of the Monetary and Expenditure Sectors When Con-*
(a, b & c) *sumption Expenditures and the Demand for Money Depend on the Level of Wealth (given the means of financing the public debt)*

We are now interested in ascertaining the impact of an increase in government expenditures on the assumption that such an increase is financed by a corresponding increase in the money supply. Suppose that G^0 increases to G^1 and therefore W^0 increases to W^1 and M_s^0 to M_s^1 so that $\Delta G = \Delta W = \Delta M_s$. Substituting the new values for these variables into equation 15.A.16, we find:

$$Y^1 = \left[\frac{1}{1 - b + g_1 \dfrac{l_1}{l_3}}\right]$$

$$\left[a + g_0 - g_1 \frac{l_0}{l_3} - bT^0 + G^1 + \left(c - g_1 \frac{l_2}{l_3}\right)W^1 + \frac{g_1}{l_3}M_s^1\right].$$

$$(15.A.19)$$

Subtracting 15.A.18 from 15.A.19, we obtain:

$$\Delta Y = \left[\frac{1}{1 - b + g_1 \dfrac{l_1}{l_3}}\right]\left[\Delta G + \left(c - g_1 \frac{l_2}{l_3}\right)\Delta W + \frac{g_1}{l_3}\Delta M_s\right]$$

from which we can determine that the government expenditures multiplier is equal to:

$$\frac{\Delta Y}{\Delta G} = \left[\frac{1}{1 - b + g_1 \dfrac{l_1}{l_3}}\right]\left[1 + \left(c - g_1 \frac{l_2}{l_3}\right)\frac{\Delta W}{\Delta G} + \frac{g_1}{l_3}\frac{\Delta M_s}{\Delta G}\right].$$

$$(15.A.20)$$

Notice that the government expenditures multiplier depends on the impact the change in G has upon W and M_s (i.e., $\Delta W/\Delta G$ and $\Delta M_s/\Delta G$). Therefore, to evaluate $\Delta Y/\Delta G$ we must evaluate $\Delta W/\Delta G$ and $\Delta M_s/\Delta G$. However, during the first period we have $\Delta W = \Delta M_s = \Delta G$. Therefore, the government multiplier for the first period (assuming that the income changes are exhausted in each period) will be equal to:

$$\left(\frac{\Delta Y}{\Delta G}\right)_{\substack{\text{at the end} \\ \text{of 1 period}}} = \mu\left[1 + \left(c - g_1 \frac{l_2}{l_3}\right) + \frac{g_1}{l_3}\right]$$

where

$$\mu \equiv \left[1 - b + g_1 \frac{l_1}{l_3}\right]^{-1}.$$

Since we have assumed that the government expenditures changed permanently, and since the deficit $(G^1 - T^0)$ will be maintained period after period and has to be financed, in our example, by changes in money supply, it follows that the cumulative change in the money supply by the end of the second period due to the change in government expenditures is twice as large as the deficit of the first period. Therefore, we can conclude that after two periods $\Delta W/\Delta G = \Delta M_s/\Delta G = 2$ and the multiplier expressed by equation 15.A.20 becomes

$$\left(\frac{\Delta Y}{\Delta G}\right)_{\substack{\text{at the end} \\ \text{of 2 periods}}} = \mu\left[1 + 2\left(c - g_1\frac{l_2}{l_3}\right) + 2\frac{g_1}{l_3}\right].$$

In general, if the budget deficit persists for n periods, $\Delta W/\Delta G = \Delta M_s/\Delta G = n$ and the government expenditures multiplier will be:

$$\left(\frac{\Delta Y}{\Delta G}\right)_{\substack{\text{at the end} \\ \text{of n periods}}} = \mu\left[1 + n\left(c - g_1\frac{l_2}{l_3}\right) + n\frac{g_1}{l_3}\right]. \qquad (15.A.21)$$

We now want to see if $\Delta Y/\Delta G$ is positive (i.e., if income increases) given our assumptions. For this it is sufficient to show that the factor $[1 + n(c - g_1 l_2/l_3) + n(g_1/l_3)] > 0$, since we already know that $\mu > 0$. With a little algebraic manipulation, we find:

$$1 + n\left(c - g_1\frac{l_2}{l_3}\right) + n\frac{g_1}{l_3} = 1 + nc + (1 - l_2)\frac{ng_1}{l_3}$$

which appears to be greater than zero since $0 < l_2 < 1$, and also keeps increasing as n increases. Therefore, given our assumptions, an increase in government spending financed by an expansion in the money supply will result in a continuous expansion of the level of income until full employment is reached (beyond that, presumably, inflation will ensue).

Next, suppose that the increase in government spending is financed by an increase in the outstanding level of public debt, i.e., $\Delta B = G^1 - T^0$. Then, since $\Delta M_s/\Delta G = 0$, equation 15.A.20 becomes

$$\frac{\Delta Y}{\Delta G} = \mu\left[1 + \left(c - g_1\frac{l_2}{l_3}\right)\frac{\Delta W}{\Delta G}\right].$$

After n periods we see that:

$$\left(\frac{\Delta Y}{\Delta G}\right)_{\substack{\text{at the end} \\ \text{of n periods}}} = \mu\left[1 + n\left(c - g_1\frac{l_2}{l_3}\right)\right]. \qquad (15.A.22)$$

Therefore, the question of whether the effect of debt-financed government expenditures is expansionary or contractionary depends on the sign of the expression in brackets:

$$\left(\frac{\Delta Y}{\Delta G}\right)_{\substack{\text{at the end} \\ \text{of n periods}}} \gtreqless 0 \qquad \text{if } 1 + n\left(c - g_1\frac{l_2}{l_3}\right) \gtreqless 0.$$

Dividing through by n (for $n > 0$), we find that this condition reduces to

$$\frac{1}{n} + c \gtreqless g_1\frac{l_2}{l_3}.$$

For $n \to \infty$ the above expression becomes

$$c \gtreqless g_1\frac{l_2}{l_3}$$

or what is the same[8]

$$\frac{\Delta C}{\Delta W} \gtreqless \frac{\Delta I}{\Delta r} \cdot \frac{\dfrac{\Delta M_d}{\Delta W}}{\dfrac{\Delta M_d}{\Delta r}}. \tag{15.A.23}$$

Condition 15.A.23 then suggests that the debt-financed increase in government expenditures will be expansionary (i.e., $\Delta Y/\Delta G > 0$) as long as the impact of an increase in wealth on consumption is greater than the corresponding effect of such an increase in wealth on the demand for investment. Furthermore, we can see that the validity of the "crowding out" allegation cannot be determined unequivocally by theoretical considerations alone. Such a question can be answered only with reference to empirical evidence. Notice, however, that the kernel of the issue is in effect the relative effects of wealth on consumption and interest rates (which, in turn, affect investment demand). To take advantage of the empirical work done in this area we may cast 15.A.23 in terms of the relevant elasticities, i.e.:

$$\frac{\Delta C}{\Delta W} \gtreqless \epsilon_{I,r} \cdot \frac{\epsilon_{M_d,W}}{\epsilon_{M_d,r}} \cdot \frac{I}{W} \tag{15.A.24}$$

where $\epsilon_{I,r}$, $\epsilon_{M_d,W}$ and $\epsilon_{M_d,r}$ denote the elasticity of investment with

---

[8] See Silber, "Fiscal Policy in IS-LM Analysis," p. 64.

respect to the rate of interest, the elasticity of the demand for real cash balances with respect to wealth and the elasticity of the demand for cash balances with respect to rate of interest respectively.

According to the existing empirical evidence, it seems that this condition is indeed satisfied. Modigliani estimates that $\Delta C/\Delta W = .053$, Bischoff has estimated that $\epsilon_{I,r} = -.23$ and Chow has found that $\epsilon_{M_d,w} = .64$ and $\epsilon_{M_d,r} = -.64$ respectively.[9] Substituting these values into 15.A.24 we obtain

$$.053 > .23 \times \frac{.64}{.64} \times \frac{I}{W}$$

from which we see that

$$.23 > \frac{I}{W}.$$

That is, given our assumptions, the change in government expenditures will be expansionary if the above inequality is satisfied. In particular, if the ratio of investment to wealth is less than 23%, then $\Delta Y/\Delta G > 0$.[10] To be sure, this condition is satisfied since the ratio I/W is a far smaller number than 23% for the time frame of the analysis. To see this more clearly, rewrite I/W as[11]

$$\frac{I}{W} = \frac{I}{K} \cdot \frac{K}{W}.$$

Now I/K under the most favorable circumstances is not more than .05 and clearly K/W is less than one (see identity 15.A.8). Therefore I/W is for all practical purposes less than .05.

---

[9] See F. Modigliani, "Monetary Policy and Consumption: Linkages via Interest Rates and Wealth Effects in the FMP Model," in *Consumer Spending and Monetary Policy: The Linkages* (Boston: Federal Reserve Bank of Boston, 1971), p. 14; C. W. Bischoff, "The Effects of Alternative Lag Distributions," in *Tax Incentives and Capital Spending*, ed. G. Fromm (Washington, D.C.: The Brookings Institution, 1971); and G. C. Chow, "On the Long-Run and Short-Run Demand for Money," *Journal of Political Economy* 74 (April 1966), 119, Table 1.

[10] Notice that if this inequality is satisfied then *a fortiori* the inequality

$$\frac{1}{n} + c > g_1 \frac{l_2}{l_3}$$

for $n = 1$ will be satisfied as well. This, of course, means that an increase in government expenditures financed by issuance of new bonds will never result in a reduction in the level of income (the intersection of the IS and LM curves lies to the left of the initial equilibrium) during the first period. This comment should be carefully contrasted with figure 15.A.5.

[11] On this see Blinder and Solow, "Analytical Foundations of Fiscal Policy," p. 54.

In this appendix we attempted to spotlight briefly the problem of financing government expenditures and to investigate some of the effects of the policy-induced changes in wealth on the other endogenous variables of the model. The analysis suggested explicitly that the effects of wealth on income and, by extension, on all other variables are too important to be ignored. At the same time, however, we also found that, given the model used, the likelihood of full crowding out appears to be fairly small. Our interest focused on the cases in which $\Delta Y/\Delta G \leq 0$, which was the meaning we gave to the crowding or full crowding-out effect. Otherwise, we would be bringing coal to Cardiff if we simply admitted that the government expenditures multiplier is less than the one proposed for pedagogical reasons in chapter 5. This is trivially true and has been known since Hicks' writings in the thirties. Therefore, although crowding out is intrinsically a matter of degree, the new thoughts concerning this problem are focused on the hypothesized case in which fiscal policy has zero or perverse effects on the level of income.

In some sense, the crowding-out argument can be interpreted as saying also that the financial market is just "so large" and therefore only "so much" demand for loanable funds can be satisfied. Consistency, of course, requires one to define the mechanism of crowding out with reference to a certain financial market. The broader geographically the market definition, the smaller the likelihood of full crowding out. Developed countries like the United States or Germany have access to international capital markets, and the implementation of fiscal policies in these countries should be based on the recognition of access to foreign funds. Given the expanded communications network which characterizes international capital markets and the vast amounts of funds existing in them, the possibility of full crowding out becomes somewhat less plausible on intuitive grounds.

Given this, one cannot escape the thought that behind this issue there may be a more fundamental problem than the assessment of the net impact of debt-financed government spending on the level of income. This may concern the potential shift in the use of resources from the private to the public sector that results from any crowding out, the effect of this shift on the profile of the product mix and the relation of government to the individual economic actor.

Appendix Suggested Further Reading

Brunner, K. and Meltzer, A. "Money, Debt and Economic Activity." *Journal of Political Economy* 80 (September/October 1972), 951–77.

Christ, C. "A Short-run Aggregate Demand Model of the Interdependence and Effects of Monetary and Fiscal Policies with Keynesian and Classical Interest Elasticities." *American Economic Review* 57 (May 1967), 434–43.

———. "A Simple Macroeconomic Model with a Government Budget Restraint." *Journal of Political Economy* 76 (January 1968), 53–67.

Hansen, B. "On the Effects of Monetary and Fiscal Policy: A Taxonomic Discussion." *American Economic Review* 63 (September 1973), 546–71.

Ott, D. J. and Ott, A. "Budget Balance and Equilibrium Income," *Journal of Finance* 20 (March 1965), 71–77.

Ritter, L. S. "Some Monetary Aspects of Multiplier Theory and Fiscal Policy." *Review of Economic Studies* 23 (1955–1956), 126–31.

Tobin, J. "An Essay on Principles of Debt Management," In Commission on Money and Credit, *Fiscal and Debt Management Policies.* (Englewood Cliffs, N.J.: Prentice-Hall, 1963).

PART SIX

International Economic Activity

Macroeconomic Theory in an International Environment

16.1 Introduction

The theoretical model we developed in earlier chapters described the economic structure of a country characterized by economic isolation. But isolationism of this type is rare among modern economies. In fact, international economic relations play so important a role in some countries that these economies might be more meaningfully described as subsystems of broader international economic systems. This chapter will map, in rather impressionistic terms, the implications of projecting a national economy on an international canvas. In the process, we shall be able to draw a number of important theorems which can be derived by applying macroeconomic theory in such an environment.

We shall first lay the necessary groundwork by introducing some new concepts and terminology. In particular, we shall start by considering the balance of international payments and its individual entries, and then turn to an explanation of the meaning and mechanics of international exchange rates. Next, we shall introduce the foreign sector into our model and focus on the behavior of an economy involved in international transactions.

16.2 The Balance of International Payments

The balance of international payments is a comprehensive summary statement of the international relations of a country for a certain period of time (traditionally a calendar year). More specifically, the balance of payments registers not only the flow of goods between the national borders as expressed by imports and exports, but also all other contractual agreements which give rise to financial claims between one country and the rest of the world.

Table 16.2.1 provides a fairly condensed version of the recent evolution of the U.S. balance of payments by highlighting its most strategic items. As the reader can see, the various components are classified, first according to their nature, and second according to the direction of their flow.

According to the first distinction, the various entries of the balance of payments are grouped into three classes. The first includes only the flow of goods and services, the second registers the flow of capital, and the third consists of reconciliatory items which play the role of balancing (settling) any difference generated by the previous two categories. On the other hand, all items in the balance of payments, regardless of their classification by nature, appear either with a plus sign if they give rise to an inflow of dollars (credits) or with a negative sign if they result in an outflow of dollars (debits).

Merchandise flow has usually been responsible for approximately two-thirds of the balance of goods and services. The remainder of this account consists of various services, of which the most important components are travel and transportation and income receipts from capital investments. The first component of table 16.2.1 summarizes the result of private transactions in commodities. It is the algebraic sum of merchandise exports (inflow of dollars) and merchandise imports (outflow of dollars). For the year 1973, for example, the outcome of this type of international transactions favored U.S. residents since the inflow of dollars (value of exports) exceeded the corresponding outflow (value of imports) by $.5 billion. Although "military transactions, net" (item 4) also represent transactions in commodities, because of their special nature they are not included in the previous component. In 1973, as in every other year since World War II, this item has contributed to the balance of payments negatively, signifying that the outflow of dollars due to payments of the U.S. military to other countries has offset the corresponding inflows from military sales by the United States to other countries. The next major item is made up of expenditures on any kind of transportation and tourism. Both items have regularly registered negative amounts. The component "investment income, net" (item 6) represents the difference between inflows of dollars due to earnings of American investments abroad and outflows that result from earnings of foreign investments in the United States. While the bulk of American investments consists of investment in plant and equipment, foreign

Table 16.2.1 *U.S. Balance of Payments, 1970–73**
(in billions of dollars)

Line	Item, Credits (+) and Debits (−)	1970	1971	1972	1973
	FLOWS OF GOODS AND SERVICES				
1.	Merchandise Trade Balance (2 + 3)	2.1	−2.7	−7.0	0.5
2.	exports (+)	42.0	42.8	48.8	70.3
3.	imports (−)	−39.9	−45.5	−55.8	−69.8
4.	Military Transactions, net	−3.4	−2.9	−3.6	−2.2
5.	Travel and Transportation, net	−2.0	−2.3	−3.0	−2.7
6.	Investment Income, net	6.2	5.0	4.5	5.3
7.	Other Services, net	0.6	2.8	3.1	3.5
8.	BALANCE ON GOODS AND SERVICES (1 + 4 + 5 + 6 + 7)	3.6	−0.2	−6.0	4.4
9.	Remittances, Pensions, and Other Transfers	−1.4	−1.6	−1.6	−1.9
10.	BALANCE ON GOODS, SERVICES AND REMITTANCES (8 + 9)	2.2	−1.8	−7.6	2.4
11.	U.S. Government Grants (excluding military)	−1.7	−2.0	−2.2	−1.9
12.	BALANCE ON CURRENT ACCOUNT (10 + 11)	0.4	−3.8	−9.8	0.5
	LONG-TERM FLOW OF CAPITAL				
13.	Long-Term Private Capital Flows, net	−1.5	−4.4	−0.1	0.1
14.	U.S. Government Capital Flows, net	−2.0	−2.4	−1.3	−1.5
15.	BALANCE ON LONG-TERM CAPITAL FLOWS, NET (13 + 14)	−3.5	−6.8	−1.4	−1.4
16.	BALANCE ON CURRENT ACCOUNT AND LONG-TERM CAPITAL ACCOUNT (12 + 15)	−3.0	−10.6	−11.2	−0.9
	SHORT-TERM FLOW OF CAPITAL				
17.	Non-liquid Short-Term Private Flows, net	−0.5	−2.3	−1.5	−4.3
18.	Allocation of Special Drawing Rights	0.9	0.7	0.7	0.0
19.	Errors and Omissions, net	−1.1	−9.8	−1.8	−2.6
20.	BALANCE ON SHORT-TERM CAPITAL FLOWS, NET (17 + 18 + 19)	−0.7	−11.4	−2.6	−6.9
21.	NET LIQUIDITY BALANCE (12 + 15 + 20, or 16 + 20)	−3.8	−22.0	−13.8	−7.8
	ACCOMMODATING ITEMS				
22.	Liquid Private Capital Flows, net	−6.0	−7.8	3.5	2.5
23.	OFFICIAL RESERVE TRANSACTION BALANCE (21 + 22)	−9.8	−29.8	−10.3	−5.3
24.	Liquid Liabilities To Foreign Official Agencies	7.6	27.6	9.7	4.5
25.	Other Liabilities to Foreign Official Agencies	−0.3	−0.2	0.6	0.7
26.	Change in U.S. Official Reserve Assets, net	2.5	2.4	0.0	0.2
27.	Gold Transfers, net (included in 26)	0.8	0.9	0.5	0.0
28.	TOTAL FINANCING OF OFFICIAL RESERVE TRANSACTION BALANCE (24 + 25 + 26)	9.8	29.8	10.3	5.3

Source: *Federal Reserve Bulletin*, December 1974, Table A60.

*Individual items may not add up to totals due to rounding.

investments represent mainly portfolio investments. For reasons which will become apparent shortly, this item has contributed positively to the U.S. balance of payments for a long time. The algebraic sum of components 1, 4, 5, 6, and 7, gives us the "balance on goods and services" (item 8). In 1973, this balance turned in favor of the United States by $4.4 billion.

"Remittances, pensions, etc." is the next component that enters in the balance of payments. It represents gifts sent by American residents to friends and relatives in other countries as well as pensions paid to Americans living abroad. Due to the large number of immigrants this country has accepted over the years, this item has traditionally shown a debit balance. The algebraic sum of items 8, 9 and 11 gives the "Balance on current account" (item 12). All items below this component are classified as not current and include short- and long-term capital movements as well as official reserve transactions.

The distinction of capital movements into short and long term is quite arbitrary. It depends on whether they are expected to persist for more or less than a period of a year. On this basis, investments in plant and equipment are considered, for example, to be long-term capital investments. On the other hand, the purchase of various foreign instruments of financial intermediation, such as bonds, may be classified either way depending on the time left to maturity. By the same token, since time to maturity is used as the demarcation line, corporate stock transactions are considered to be long-term movements because these stocks have no maturity date.

According to this definition the next two component are classified as long-term capital flows. From them, "U.S. government capital flows, net" (item 14) represents mainly loans advanced by the U.S. government to foreign official agencies. In recent years, this item appears regularly with a debit balance since repayments of earlier loans are usually offset by larger amounts of new loans advanced by the U.S. government. One of the most important items which appears in the balance of payments is the "long-term private capital flows, net" (item 13). Since World War II, the majority of years have shown considerable outflows associated with this component. As was mentioned earlier, the bulk of U.S. private long-term capital outflow represents direct investment in plant and equipment undertaken by American firms in foreign lands. There are three main reasons for the net outflow on this account. First, American firms want to expand their activities in rich and heavily populated markets which conceivably would have been denied to them because of high tariffs. This is the case, for example, of the European Common Market area where American investments have in effect circumvented the existing tariff walls and therefore are capable of competing with European firms or within the whole Common Market territory on the same terms. Second, such investments may secure an uninterrupted flow of raw materials for which there is a shortage at home. And, finally such investments abroad may result in cost cutting due to the special characteristics of the labor market in these countries or even because their location implies savings in transportation costs.

Combining the balance on the current account with the long-term capital movements (private and public) we obtain the "balance on current account and long-term capital" (item 16). This balance, depending on whether it is negative or positive, is better known as the "basic" deficit or surplus.

The next entry (item 17) represents short-term loans advanced by banks and other nonbanking firms to foreigners. This item has for some years now shown a debit balance. The "allocations of special drawing rights" (SDRs), otherwise known as "paper gold," are a new international reserve asset administered by the International Monetary Fund (IMF) and generated by common agreement of the nations which are members of this international institution.[1] This asset, like gold or a country's holdings of foreign currencies, can be used to settle international payments. Since any allocation of special drawing rights from IMF is considered to be an inflow of dollars, it follows that when this item appears in the balance of payments it enters as a credit. In 1973 there were no allocations; but, as the reader can verify from table 16.2.1, the other three years registered positive amounts. The components "errors and omissions, net" represents unrecorded transactions and statistical discrepancies. Since it is conceded that the bulk of such errors occurs in the area of the nonliquid short-term private capital flows, it is customary to record it at this stage of the statement.

The algebraic sum of the current account and the short- and long-term capital accounts provides us with what is considered perhaps the most important balance of the statement: the "net liquidity balance" (item 21). Since this balance is the culmination of all previous balances it can be used by itself as an indication of what happens to the international reserves of the country. More explicitly, a credit in the balance shows that the economic units of this country (individual economic actors and firms) have liquid claims against the rest of the world which exceed their corresponding liquid liabilities. Conversely, if the liquid liabilities of this country exceed its corresponding liquid claims, then we

---

[1] The International Monetary Fund is an organization established in 1946 in order to iron out problems arising from international economic transactions.

say that the country experiences a net liquid deficit which (if it persists) will call sooner or later for some corrective action.

Any deficit or surplus in the balance of payments must be settled. Thus, the components which absorb or finance the surplus or deficit generated by the various transactions recorded in the previous amounts are called "accommodating items." This term is used in contradistinction to the previous components, which sometimes are called "autonomous." The reader should not get confused at this juncture by the use of the term *autonomous*. In this connection it means that given the values all these components assumed, the accommodating items, as a sum, will have to offset whatever value appears as a net liquidity balance. Therefore, accommodating items should not be considered as exogenous variables. In fact, the majority of them will be treated later in this chapter as endogenous variables. Thus, to recapitulate, the outcome of all transactions which gave rise to a flow of dollars across the borders is summarized in terms of a deficit or surplus expressed by the "net liquid balance." All items below this balance are considered accommodating in the sense that they play the role of settling the financial differences of this country with the rest of the world.

The first of the accommodating components, according to table 16.2.1, is the "liquid private capital flows, net." This item represents short-term movements of capital which facilitate to a large extent the process of international trade. They cover mostly changes in the commercial bank deposits and short-term government securities. For example, suppose that we import a Volkswagen from Germany. If the German exporter chooses to increase his demand deposits by the value of the automobile he sold, then this will be considered an accommodating transaction. Indeed, the imports have increased by the value of the imported VW; but notice that this increase was financed by an equal increase in the short-term capital flow from Germany to the United States. In other words, as long as foreigners are willing to let their deposits or other liquid assets in the United States grow, then this accommodating item could by itself take care of the deficits of the balance of payments. However, it appears that the extent of changes in these liquid assets which the foreigners will be willing to accept depends on the existing interest differential between the U.S. and other important financial centers of the world.

The algebraic sum of the net liquid balance and the net amount of liquid private capital flows (item 22) provides us with the "official reserve transaction balance." This balance for the year 1973 was $-5.3 billion and it is the amount which is called for settlement by the U.S. agencies. The official means of settlement are usually dollars which the foreign central banks are willing to hold, special drawing rights, other convertible currencies and gold. Foreign central banks can absorb dollars by purchasing them in terms of their own currency. Furthermore, the Federal Reserve and the U.S. Treasury Department can also absorb deficits in the balance of payments by providing official reserves. Indeed, during the sixties considerable amounts of the balance of payments deficits were absorbed by outflows of gold from the United States. Therefore, the foreign central banks did not increase their holdings of U.S. dollars via purchases in their own currency, but instead increased their holdings of gold. Continuous depletion of the U.S. holding of gold, however, led to an understanding among central banks in the late sixties that they would not continue to demand gold in exchange for their holding of dollars, until in August 1971 the convertibility into gold of U.S. dollars held by official foreign agencies was ended by President Nixon.

Although we have classified the various items of the balance of payments in accordance with their nature and direction of flow, nevertheless all components are more or less interdependent. For example, the balance of goods and services has always been influenced favorably by the direct investment undertaken by American firms abroad since these investments often take the form of subsidiaries of domestic firms which apparently—by using American-produced equipment and products—generate an increase of exports. In addition, the balance of goods and services is influenced by such investments since it includes all the income receipts from these investments. To be sure, if a country is capital importing, it would be expected to exhibit deficits in the current account while at the same time the capital account would show surpluses. In fact, one could argue that the capital imports play the role of financing the deficit of the current account or even that it is the importation of capital that causes the deficit in the current account. Such interrelations among the various components, therefore, lead to the conclusion that public policy, at least under normal circumstances, ought to aim its efforts at the overall position of the balance of payments and not at any particular components or even group of components.

It should be quite clear that no country can maintain continuously a deficit in the balance of payments. Such a situation calls for corrective action. The remainder of the chapter will analyze some of the alternatives open to a government under one set of conditions. But first we should take a look at the concept of exchange rates.

16.3 The Demand for and Supply of Foreign Exchange

The concept of money—at least in the terms in which we defined it in chapter 6—does not extend to assume an international scope. French francs are not considered to be money in the United States; dollars are not money in France. Thus, one may very well argue that for all practical purposes, international economic transactions resemble the characteristics of barter for one of the trading partners. More explicitly, suppose that an American automobile producer sells cars in France for francs. We can argue that from his point of view he is engaging in barter, i.e., a sale of cars and a purchase of francs (or, if we prefer, a short-run claim on France). Provided that the American automobile seller is not interested in purchasing French commodities with the proceeds of his own sale, then it will be necessary for him to sell francs for dollars in what is called the foreign exchange market.

In general, it can be argued that every international economic transaction is matched by a complementary sale in the foreign exchange market where one currency is sold for another. Therefore foreign exchange, which is defined to be every foreign currency from the point of view of every national currency, is nothing else but one more commodity, the price of which could be determined by the interaction of its supply and demand. However, in reality the foreign exchange market has generally not been free (at least until recently) to determine the price of a national currency in terms of another. To see this point, let us start from the fundamentals of the demand for and supply of foreign exchange.

In most of what follows in this section, we'll abstract from the capital accounts and concentrate on the use of exchange to facilitate transactions involving the exchange of goods and services across international borders. In this context, the demand for a country's exports, like the demand for any set of goods, depends partially on the prices charged to the rest of the world. But, insofar as goods are typically purchased with the currency of the exporting country, there are two factors which determine the prices charged to foreigners. First, the price of the goods in terms of the exporter's currency determines the number of units of that currency importers will have to buy for each unit of the good in question. And, second, the exchange rate determines the price of the exporter's currency in terms of the importer's. Ignoring changes in the first factor, we can then use standard demand theory to postulate a relationship between the demand for a country's exports and the exchange rate at which its currency can be translated into others.

Consider a two-country world, in which the trading partners are France and the United States. The relevant exchange rate can be considered a dollar-price of francs, or, equivalently, the franc-price of dollars. If the exchange rate rises, this means that francs will be more expensive in terms of dollars—i.e., that it will take more dollars to buy a franc. If this happens, then, the dollar-price of a French good will increase from the standpoint of Americans. And, according to traditional

Dollar price of francs

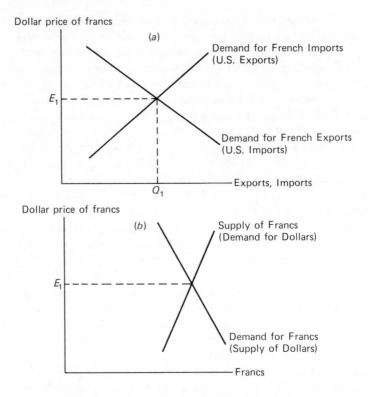

Figure 16.3.1   *Supply of and Demand for Foreign Currency*

demand theory, we can expect the quantity demanded of French exports to fall. This relation is shown in panel (a) of figure 16.3.1, where we have sketched a downward-sloping demand schedule for French exports. Notice that, in the two-country model, this also gives us the U.S. demand for imports.[2]

As the demand for French goods varies, there will also be a change in the demand for francs. If, as the exchange rate falls, the quantity of French exports increases by a greater percentage, then the demand for francs will also increase. Or, in alternative terms, if the demand for French exports is *elastic* with respect to their price, we will have a negative association between the dollar-price of francs and the quantity of

[2]Also, keep in mind that this demand schedule is based on a set of *ceteris paribus* assumptions. Perhaps most important is the fact that income of the importing country is held constant.

francs demanded.[3] Because dollars are offered in exchange for francs in our two-country analysis, the demand for francs also indicates the supply of dollars in the exchange market.

By definition, any increase in the dollar-price of francs translates into a decrease in the franc-price of dollars. And, since French importers pay for U.S. goods with dollars, such a decrease in the exchange rate will make U.S. goods more attractive to the French. We would thus expect increases in the exchange rate to induce increases in the foreign demand for U.S. exports (French imports). This is the reasoning behind the upward-sloping schedule in panel (a) of our figure. Furthermore, as long as the foreign demand for U.S. goods is elastic with respect to price, the demand for dollars (the supply of francs) will be positively associated with the exchange rate, as shown in panel (b).

If exchange rates are flexible — free to vary in response to international money-market conditions — then they will be determined by an equilibrating process. That is, the equilibrium value of each exchange rate will be determined by the supply of and the demand for one currency in terms of another. In our simplified case, abstracting again from transactions on the capital accounts, the equilibrium exchange rate would be E_1, the "price" at which the demand for and supply of francs (dollars) would be equated. Since we based our analysis on the need for foreign currency for current-account transactions, it should also be apparent that E_1 would leave each country's current account with neither a deficit nor a surplus. If we were to broaden our analysis to include the need for exchange to lubricate capital transactions, then we would include them in the demand for and supply of francs (dollars), and would obtain some equilibrium exchange rate which would leave each country's balance of payments in equilibrium. Thus, as long as the market for foreign exchange is "cleared" through the operation of flexible exchange rates, there is no need for the use of accommodating items (e.g., gold transfers). These items would be used only to accommodate temporary deviations from equilibrium. But such is not typically the case; exchange rates have normally been "fixed," rather than "flexible."

The present international monetary system operates under the auspices of the International Monetary Fund (IMF). The IMF is an organization established in 1946, in a pact referred to as the Bretton Woods Agreement, in order to iron out problems arising from international economic transactions. The membership of the organization consists of over 100 countries outside the Communist bloc. Until re-

---

[3]It is generally agreed that the demand for foreign goods is typically elastic; thus, it is not unreasonable to ignore alternative cases.

cently, under the charter of the IMF, the par values of currencies were defined in terms of gold. The relative values of two currencies (in terms of gold) yielded an exchange rate via which one currency was exchanged for the other. For instance, until 1971 the U.S. dollar was defined as .88807 grams of gold and a British pound was given a value of 2.1378 grams. Thus, one British pound was considered worth $2.40(2.1378/ .88807) in international exchange.[4]

Exchange rates were maintained through the actions of member countries. More explicitly, the monetary authorities of each country (except the United States) were obligated to maintain the value of their currency vis à vis foreign currencies within a margin of 1% of parity by purchasing or selling U.S. dollars at the agreed-upon exchange rate in exchange for their own currency. Furthermore, the United States maintained the dollar-value of gold (or the gold-value of the dollar) by purchasing or selling gold in a free fashion at the official price of $35 per ounce. Thus, according to the Bretton Woods pact, the dollar was tied to gold and all the other currencies were, in turn, tied to the dollar. One result of the arrangement was that the majority of IMF member countries maintained their international reserves in terms of both gold and dollars.

Despite the delicate political environment, the Bretton Woods agreement, as described in general above, served the immediate needs of international economic transactions. However, this should not be interpreted as implying that there were no problems. The system was subjected from time to time to various pressures; but there was always enough flexibility for reforms within its fundamental framework. These pressures were therefore absorbed, at least in terms of short-term solutions, but such temporary solutions did not make the problems disappear. Eventually, the continuous accumulation of the U.S. balance of payments deficit hastened the collapse of the system.

Due to the continuous weakness of its balance of payments and the resultant massive movement of dollars into foreign currencies (for example, during the period 1960–69 the net liquid balance registered a deficit of $13.2 billion), the United States was finally forced in August 1971 to suspend the convertibility of the dollar into gold and other reserve currencies. This action culminated in a realignment of the ex-

---

[4]It may be more familiar to quote the old currency prices in terms of troy ounces (a troy ounce contains 31.10348 grams). The corresponding values of the two currencies given in terms of the respective prices of gold were $35.00 in U.S. currency and 14.90 in pounds.

change rates of the ten major industrial economies, an action which took place at the Smithsonian Institution in Washington in December 1971 and became known as the Smithsonian agreement.

According to this agreement, the gold content of the dollar was reduced by approximately 8%, so the official price of gold (albeit ineffective since the Treasury was not redeeming dollars with gold) rose to $38. However, despite this dollar devaluation, the U.S. international economic performance remained quite poor (see table 16.2.1) during 1972; and, as a result, it was recognized by all parties that the Smithsonian agreement had not gone far enough. Therefore, a second realignment was proposed and took place on February 12, 1973. In contrast to the Smithsonian agreement, according to which virtually all countries established new par values for their currencies, this time Italy and Japan chose to float their currencies, thus joining Canada, Switzerland and Great Britain, who had already done so.

The anomaly that prevailed in foreign exchange markets during the period resulted in another floating among major currencies. Six members of the European community—West Germany, France, the Netherlands, Belgium, Luxemburg and Denmark—decided to maintain fixed rates among themselves (within a 2.25% margin), but to float as a bloc vis à vis dollars and other currencies. Subsequently, these countries were joined by Norway and Sweden.

For a period of several months after the decision of these countries to float their currencies, the U.S. dollar held its own and no substantial change in the exchange rates was observed. However, the subsequent few months witnessed a rapid deterioration of the dollar vis à vis this group. By July 1973 the dollar was devalued by approximately 20% against the German mark and 15% against the French franc. From July on, however, the dollar staged a remarkable comeback; by the end of the year its value had, for all practical purposes, been restored to its previous level. This recovery was due to various reasons, among which the skyrocketed price of oil was paramount. Western Europe and Japan are more dependent on oil than is the United States. Therefore, relatively speaking, their position deteriorated faster than that of the United States, with the result that the dollar was strengthened considerably.[5]

---

[5]For a fuller description of the events of the early 1970s, see the statement by Arthur F. Burns before the Subcommittee on International Economics of the Joint Economic Committee, June 27, 1973, as published in the *Federal Reserve Bulletin*, July, 1973, pp. 508–12.

Ever since the 1973 developments, floating exchange rates have been the international economic order. And, in view of the present degree of uncertainty which prevails in the international economic scene, any suggestion that countries will return to fixed exchange rates may appear premature. But, in the meantime, there is a strong tendency for countries to move back slowly toward regional fixed-rate systems revolving around currencies such as the German mark, the Japanese yen, and the American dollar. Signs of dissatisfaction with the floating system have appeared in many places, and it is conceded that central bank officials often tend to seize any opportunity to peg their currencies to any other currency which for some reason seems to be able to remain stable for a little while. To be sure, the adoption of floating rates resulted in the prevention of severe international chaos following the quadrupling of oil prices. However, in many other ways their alleged benefits have not materialized. It is true that the expectation that floating rates would result in a reduction of the massive flows of "hot" money from one country to another did largely materialize; but, unfortunately, this development has not led to the anticipated dampening of volatility of various currencies.

The outcome of such a behavior of currencies is clearly reflected in the cost of hedging, which has increased tenfold during the last decade, thus hampering the growth of international trade. The change in currency values can more than offset a company's normal profit margin. And although it can be argued that a company may insulate its profits by hedging in the forward exchange markets, such insurance has become prohibitively expensive. Furthermore, not all companies can use the forward markets. For example, firms which produce on order and whose delivery or sales will consummate in the future (say, a year or more) may find themselves incapable of using forward markets either because they do not exist or, if they do, because they are very thin indeed.

In addition, floating rates have not measured up in terms of their anticipated automatic equilibrating role in the balance of payments. Neither have they been successful in insulating the economy in such a way that governments are able to set an independent fiscal and monetary policy. Indeed, it appears that the anticipated high correlation between surpluses (or deficits) and exchange rates has not been borne out by the actual behavior of these variables.

The above comments do not purport to make the case against the floating exchange rates. This falls beyond the scope of this book. Our intention is rather to suggest that given the present form of the institutional international environment, the textbook case of floating exchange rates is rather unattainable. The next section will analyze the case of fixed exchange rates. Our only justification is our value judgment (and we would submit that the efficacy of value judgments, like beauty, is in the eyes of the beholder) that this system is closer to the "normal" institutional environment.

16.4 The Foreign Sector in a Macro Model

In this section, we shall consider the modifications involved in incorporating the foreign sector into the model employed to describe the operations of the economy. Our first step is to revise the notion of the product-market equilibrium condition. The most basic version of this condition is that aggregate supply and aggregate demand must be equal; this much remains unchanged. But the assumption of an open economy introduces international flows of goods and services in the form of imports and exports, and these flows must be incorporated in our definitions of aggregate supply and aggregate demand.

Aggregate demand now contains a domestic component $(C + I + G)$ and a foreign element, exports (Ex). Thus, we now write:

$$AD \equiv C + I + G + Ex. \tag{16.4.1}$$

On the other hand, the source of satisfying this demand is not only domestically produced final goods, but imports (Im) as well. In other words, our aggregate supply is equal to the sum of Y and Im:

$$AS \equiv Y + Im. \tag{16.4.2}$$

It follows then that equilibrium will be achieved only if aggregate demand is equal to aggregate supply:

$$Y + Im = C + I + G + Ex$$

which can be rewritten as

$$Y = C + I + G + Ex - Im. \tag{16.4.3}$$

Thus, the new equilibrium condition includes the trade account of the balance of payments as expressed by the magnitudes of Ex and Im.

We could also express the equilibrium condition in terms of leakages and injections, as we have done in previous chapters. Suppose that we transfer the variables C and Im in the left-hand side of equation 16.4.3 to get:

$$Y - C + Im = I + G + Ex.$$

Recalling now that $Y - C \equiv S + T$ and substituting accordingly in the above expression, we further obtain:

$$S + T + Im = I + G + Ex. \qquad (16.4.4)$$

The left-hand side of equation 16.4.4 gives us the total amount of leakages from the flow of income. Unless they are equal to the total amount of injections (depicted by the right-hand side), the level of income will not be at equilibrium.

We must now incorporate in our model some behavioral relations to summarize our speculations about the new variables. We start with the variable imports (Im) which we shall assume to be endogenous and to depend mainly on the general conditions of the domestic economy. More specifically, imports reflect a demand for (foreign) goods, and therefore should be associated directly with the level of income and inversely with the level of their prices, or more accurately, the relative level of prices (i.e., the relation of foreign prices to domestic ones). Disregarding the influence of relative prices, our assumption with respect to income can be written algebraically as:

$$Im = f(Y).$$

We shall also assume that the relation is a linear one, and write accordingly:

$$Im = m_0 + m_1 Y \qquad (16.4.5)$$

where m_0 stands for the autonomous part of imports and $m_1 = \Delta(Im)/\Delta Y$ denotes the marginal propensity to import. In addition, we shall assume that the marginal propensity to import obeys the double restriction

$$0 < m_1 < 1.$$

Equation 16.4.5 is in all aspects similar to our consumption function and consequently we shall not dwell upon it any further.

Since a country's exports constitute part of the imports of the rest of the world, symmetry would require that they be specified as a function of the income of foreign economies. But, insofar as we shall attempt to describe the behavior of the national economy, we shall assume that foreign income is exogenously determined; consequently exports will also be treated as an exogenous variable.

If we are to use our newly specified model to analyze balance of payments problems and the general effect of financial flows across countries, we must also consider the capital account. In this regard, we shall argue that net flows of capital into a country (F) depend upon relative rates of interest across economies. In formal terms, we specify:

$$F = -f_0' + f_1(r - r_f) \tag{16.4.6}$$

where r is the domestic rate of interest, r_f is the rate of interest in the rest of the world, and f_0' and f_1 are positive constants. Obviously, both r and r_f vary over time in response to domestic and international conditions, but to force our model to maintain manageable proportions, we shall assume that the foreign rate of interest is exogenously determined (i.e., that it is determined outside the confines of our model of the domestic economy). This allows us to write:

$$F = -f_0 + f_1 r \tag{16.4.7}$$

where $f_0 \equiv f_0' + f_1 r_f$ is treated as a constant from the standpoint of our analysis. Equation 16.4.7 will be used subsequently, but the reader should understand that this relation is derived for a certain value of the foreign rate of interest.

It might be worthwhile to point out that the net flow of capital can be positive or negative, depending on the value of the interest rate. The demarcation point is the rate of interest:

$$r = \frac{f_0}{f_1}$$

for which the net flow of capital is equal to zero. Thus, for any rate of interest in the range $0 < r < f_0/f_1$, the net flow of capital will be negative (indicating a deficit in the domestic economy's capital account), and the net flow will be positive (resulting in a surplus in the capital account) for $r > f_0/f_1$.

16.5 Equilibrium and Adjustments in an Open Economy, without Predetermined Targets

In the previous sections we introduced the various concepts and variables associated with the foreign sector. We are now prepared to augment the model we have used so far with these relationships in order to investigate how its properties are modified once we recognize that the economy is engaged in economic transactions with the rest of the world.

In studying the results of such an augmentation we shall deliberately ignore the labor market as well as the extreme properties of the monetary sector as they were developed in chapter 8. Thus, the international sector will be added to the IS-LM model we studied in chapter 7. This decision leaves us with no other alternative but to assume once more that the price level is exogenously determined. In addition, we shall maintain the assumption that the money supply is exogenous. This latter assumption, as we shall see later, is crucial in the examination of the adjustments made by an economy in the face of a balance of payments disequilibrium.

With these qualifications in mind, let us consider the following system of equations:

$$Y = C + I + G + Ex - Im \qquad (16.5.1)$$

$$C = a + bY_d \qquad (16.5.2)$$

$$I = g_0 - g_1 r \qquad (16.5.3)$$

$$Y_d \equiv Y - T \qquad (16.5.4)$$

$$T = -t_0 + t_1 Y \qquad (16.5.5)$$

$$M_d/P = l_0 + l_1 Y - l_2 r \qquad (16.5.6)$$

$$M_d/P = M_s/P \qquad (16.5.7)$$

$$Im = m_0 + m_1 Y \qquad (16.5.8)$$

$$F = -f_0 + f_1 r \qquad (16.5.9)$$

$$B \equiv F + Ex - Im. \qquad (16.5.10)$$

From the above system, equations 16.5.1 and 16.5.7 depict the equilibrium conditions of the expenditure and monetary sector. On the other hand, identities 16.5.4 and 16.5.10 are the definitions of disposable income and balance of payments, respectively. In particular, according to 16.5.10 the balance of payments of the country in question is defined to be the algebraic sum of the net flows of capital (F), and the trade balance $(Ex - Im)$. Finally, equations 16.5.2, 16.5.3, 16.5.5, 16.5.6, 16.5.8 and 16.5.9 are the behavioral equations depicting the various hypotheses in regard to the endogenous variables of the model. From these, equation 16.5.8 links imports to income, whereas equation 16.5.9 posits that the net flow of capital (i.e., the net result of the capital account) is a function of the domestic rate of interest.

The above system contains fourteen variables: Y, C, I, G, Ex, Im, Y_d, T, r, M_d, M_s, P, F, and B, cast into ten equations. From these variables we shall assume that G, M_s, Ex and P are determined exogenously, whereas all the rest are assumed to be endogenous. It follows then that under normal circumstances and for any assumed or given value of the exogenously determined variables, the system should be capable of providing a unique solution for the endogenous variables involved. For reasons of simplicity we shall finally assume that $P = 1$.

To determine the solution values of the endogenous variables, we first derive the reduced form of the system. Here we shall focus our attention on the reduced form of only the variables Y, r and B.

As usual, equations 16.5.1, 16.5.2, 16.5.3 and 16.5.8 can be combined to obtain the expression for the IS curve, which in this case can be found to be:

$$[1 - b(1 - t_1) + m_1]Y + g_1 r = a + g_0 + bt_0 - m_0 + G + Ex. \tag{16.5.11}$$

Equation 16.5.11 is similar to 7.2.11, modified appropriately to take into account the trade activity of the domestic economy with the rest of the world. It depicts the equilibrium of the expenditure sector in the case of a open economy. To distinguish it from our original IS equation (which pertained to a closed economy), we shall refer to it as the ISMX equation.

On the other hand, equations 16.5.6 and 16.5.7 yield the following expression of the LM curve:

$$l_1 Y - l_2 r = \frac{M_s}{P} - l_0. \tag{16.5.12}$$

Finally, substituting the right-hand side of equations 16.5.8 and 16.5.9 for the variables Im and F into the definition of the balance of payments (i.e., equation 16.5.10), we obtain:

$$B = -f_0 + f_1 r + Ex - m_0 - m_1 Y. \tag{16.5.13}$$

Thus, we see that the system 16.5.1–16.5.10 collapses into a system of three equations, 16.5.11, 16.5.12, and 16.5.13, in three endogenous variables, Y, r and B. By using the first two equations of the above system, we can derive the reduced form of Y and r. This should not be an unfamiliar task, since this system is very similar to that of chapter 7.

To this end we use equation 16.5.12 to solve for r in terms of Y to find:

$$r = - \frac{\left[\dfrac{M_s}{P} - l_0\right]}{l_2} + \frac{l_1}{l_2}Y. \tag{16.5.14}$$

Substituting this expression for r into 16.5.11, we obtain:

$$[1 - b(1 - t_1) + m_1]Y + g_1\left[-\frac{\left(\dfrac{M_s}{P} - l_0\right)}{l_2} + \frac{l_1}{l_2}Y\right]$$

$$= a + g_0 + bt_0 - m_0 + G + Ex.$$

Finally, solving the above equation for Y, we find:

$$Y = \left[\cfrac{1}{1 - b(1 - t_1) + m_1 + g_1\cfrac{l_1}{l_2}}\right] \cdot$$

$$\left[a + g_0 + bt_0 - m_0 + G + Ex - \frac{g_1}{l_2}l_0 + \frac{g_1}{l_2}\frac{M_s}{P}\right].$$

$$(16.5.15)$$

Equation 16.5.15 is the reduced form of the variable income. Substituting now this expression into 16.5.14, we obtain the reduced form of r:

$$r = \cfrac{l_1[a + g_0 + bt_0 - m_0 + G + Ex] + [1 - b(1 - t_1) + m_1]\left[l_0 - \cfrac{M_s}{P}\right]}{l_2\left[1 - b(1 - t_1) + m_1 + g_1\cfrac{l_1}{l_2}\right]} \cdot$$

$$(16.5.16)$$

If we now define for simplicity

$$n \equiv \left[\cfrac{1}{1 - b(1 - t_1) + m_1 + g_1\cfrac{l_1}{l_2}}\right]$$

then n is the new multiplier, and the above expressions can be further simplified to read

$$Y = n[a + g_0 + bt_0 - m_0 + G + Ex] + n\frac{g_1}{l_2}\left[\frac{M_s}{P} - l_0\right]$$

and

$$r = \frac{l_1}{l_2}n[a + g_0 + bt_0 - m_0 + G + Ex]$$

$$+ \frac{1}{l_2}n[1 - b(1 - t_1) + m_1]\left[l_0 - \frac{M_s}{P}\right].$$

Having obtained the reduced forms of Y and r, one could proceed to substitute them in the third equation of the system (16.5.13) to obtain the corresponding reduced form for the variable B. The result of such an attempt would be an aesthetically unappealing expression. Instead, we shall follow a short-cut method which will become apparent shortly.

In the meantime, let us assume that the exogenous variables, G, Ex, and M_s are all fixed at G^0, Ex^0, and M_s^0 respectively. Substituting those values into the reduced forms of Y and r and recalling that $P = 1$, we obtain the solution (equilibrium) values of these variables; namely,

$$Y^0 = n[a + g_0 + bt_0 - m_0 + G^0 + Ex^0] + n\frac{g_1}{l_2}[M_s^0 - l_0]$$

$$(16.5.17)$$

$$r^0 = \frac{l_1}{l_2}n[a + g_0 + bt_0 - m_0 + G^0 + Ex^0]$$

$$+ \frac{1}{l_2}n[1 - b(1 - t_1) + m_1][l_0 - M_s^0]. \qquad (16.5.18)$$

The determination of the equilibrium values of income and rate of interest allows us to identify the impact which changes of the various parameters and exogenous variables have upon the solution values of these variables.

We start with changes in factors which imply a shift of the *ISMX* curve. Suppose then that the government changes its own level of expenditures on goods and services from G^0 to G^1 ($G^1 > G^0$) while everything else remains constant. Substituting this new value for G in the reduced form for Y and r (16.5.15 and 16.5.16), and subtracting from the resulting equations the values Y^0 and r^0 as given by 16.5.17 and 16.5.18, we obtain:

$$\Delta Y = n \Delta G \qquad (16.5.19)$$

$$\Delta r = \frac{l_1}{l_2}n \Delta G \qquad (16.5.20)$$

where n was defined to be the multiplier. Since the marginal propensity to import is a positive quantity, its presence in the denominator of the multiplier expression results in a reduction of its value compared with the one we found in chapter 7. Thus, for an equal change in the government expenditures, income will change by a smaller amount if the country is engaged in international economic transactions than if it is not. The reason for this new result can be attributed to the fact that since imports are a leakage and a function of income, an increase in the latter results in an increase in the former and thus part of the generated expenditures spill abroad via international trade. In other words, we see that international trade is the vehicle which transfers various economic stimuli from one country to another.

Similar effects are obtained when we change the autonomous parts of consumption (a), investment (g_0), transfer payments (t_0), and exports (Ex). The reader can easily verify that the impact of changes in the parameters and exogenous variables in question upon Y and r are given by the following equations:

$$\Delta Y = n\,\Delta a \tag{16.5.21}$$

$$\Delta r = \frac{l_1}{l_2} n\,\Delta a \tag{16.5.22}$$

$$\Delta Y = n\,\Delta g_0 \tag{16.5.23}$$

$$\Delta r = \frac{l_1}{l_2} n\,\Delta g_0 \tag{16.5.24}$$

$$\Delta Y = nb\,\Delta t_0 \tag{16.5.25}$$

$$\Delta r = \frac{l_1}{l_2} nb\,\Delta t_0 \tag{16.5.26}$$

$$\Delta Y = n\,\Delta Ex \tag{16.5.27}$$

$$\Delta r = \frac{l_1}{l_2} n\,\Delta Ex \tag{16.5.28}$$

$$\Delta Y = -n\,\Delta m_0 \tag{16.5.29}$$

$$\Delta r = -\frac{l_1}{l_2} n\,\Delta m_0. \tag{16.5.30}$$

The above equations, 16.5.21–16.5.30, are similar to the ones we found in chapter 7 and consequently require little elaboration. However, the reader may ask why an increase in exports results in an increase in the rate of interest. The answer to this is that as income increases so does the demand for cash balances for transaction purposes. However, in view of the fact that the nominal money supply is constant and assuming that the increase in exports is satisfied by an increase in real income without any change in the price level, an increase in the rate of interest is necessary in order to induce the release of the required funds from the speculative balances. Notice that this result is based on the assumption that the real money supply does not change. However, should the increase in exports be associated with changes in the money supply, obviously this result would not be valid anymore. The opposite holds for the case of equations 16.5.29 and 16.5.30, where an increase in the

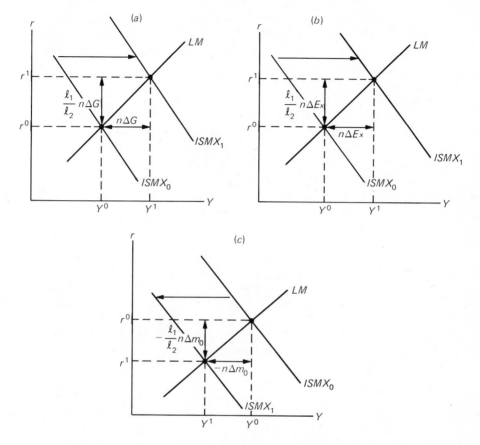

Figure 16.5.1   *The Effects of Shifts in the ISMX Schedule*

autonomous part of imports, implying a shift of the ISMX (downward and to the left), results in a decrease in the rate of interest.[6]

   Panels (a), (b), and (c) of figure 16.5.1 show explicitly the implied changes in the endogenous variables Y and r due to a shift of ISMX generated by a change in the various parameters and/or exogenous variables of the model. Notice that in panel (c) of figure 16.5.1 the

---

[6]Here we find one of the shortcomings of the model we use. Indeed, the increase in exports, provided that the Fed does not interfere, will in effect have an expansionary influence on the money supply. The result obtained in the text would prevail if the Fed were to neutralize the effect of the increase in exports by selling securities in the open market so that the money supply would remain at the same level. We shall discuss this point later in the chapter.

increase in the autonomous level of imports results in a shift of ISMX to the left with the outcome that the equilibrium level of both income and the rate of interest decrease, as equations 16.5.29 and 16.5.30 have already suggested.

Now, let us consider the case in which the LM shifts. For this we assume that the monetary authorities increase the nominal money supply from M_s^0 to M_s^1 while all other parameters and exogenous variables of the model remain the same. Substituting the new level of nominal supply into the reduced forms of Y and r and subtracting from the resulting quantities the initial equilibrium values for income and rate of interest given by equations 16.5.17 and 16.5.18, we obtain:

$$\Delta Y = \frac{g_1}{l_2} n \, \Delta M_s \qquad (16.5.31)$$

$$\Delta r = - \frac{[1 - b(1 - t_1) + m_1]}{l_2} n \, \Delta M_s. \qquad (16.5.32)$$

From equations 16.5.31 and 16.5.32, it becomes evident that an increase in the nominal money supply, *ceteris paribus,* will result in an increase in the level of income and at the same time, a decrease in the rate of interest.[7] Of course, the magnitude of change is now different from that implied by our analysis in chapter 7, since the associated multiplier has decreased; but the direction of change remains the same. Figure 16.5.2 depicts these results.

The above analysis has now paved the way toward the investigation of the impact of changes in the exogenous variables and parameters on the balance of payments. To this end consider once more equation 16.5.13:

$$B = -f_0 + f_1 r + Ex - m_0 - m_1 Y. \qquad (16.5.13)$$

Assuming now that the exogenous variables are set at G^0, Ex^0, M_s^0, and $P^0 = 1$, the solution values of income and the rate of interest which correspond to the above values of exogenous variables are Y^0 and r^0. Substituting these values for Y and r into 16.5.13, we find that the corresponding balance of payments is:

$$B^0 = -f_0 + f_1 r^0 + Ex^0 - m_0 - m_1 Y^0. \qquad (16.5.33)$$

Thus, the solution set of the system 16.5.1–16.5.10 includes the values Y^0, r^0, and B^0. Substitution of these values in the model will determine

---

[7]This is in effect the result we would obtain in the case of an increase of exports provided that the Federal Reserve let the automatic mechanism work.

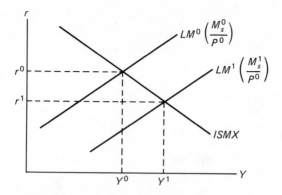

Figure 16.5.2   *The Effects of a Shift in the LM Schedule*

the corresponding solution values of the rest of the endogenous variables.

Let us now suppose that because of a change in government expenditures from G^0 to G^1 ($G^1 > G^0$) the equilibrium values of income and the rate of interest become Y^1 and r^1 respectively. Substitution of the new equilibrium values for Y and r into 16.5.13 results in

$$B^1 = -f_0 + f_1 r^1 + Ex^0 - m_0 - m_1 Y^1. \qquad (16.5.34)$$

Comparison of equations 16.5.33 and 16.5.34 reveals that

$$\Delta B = f_1 \, \Delta r - m_1 \, \Delta Y. \qquad (16.5.35)$$

Equation 16.5.35 gives us the impact of a change in government expenditures on the balance of payments. Its meaning should not be difficult to understand. Suppose that the nominal money supply remains constant (since the price level is assumed to be constant as well, it follows that the real money supply is assumed to be constant). Then an increase in government expenditures will result in an increase in the equilibrium levels of income and rate of interest. But since income increases by ΔY, it follows that this will be accompanied by an increase in the level of imports by $\Delta Im = m_1 \, \Delta Y$ (see equation 16.5.8). Similarly, the increase in the rate of interest by Δr will make the domestic financial markets more attractive, resulting in an algebraic change in the flow of capital by $\Delta F = f_1 \, \Delta r$ (see equation 16.5.9). In other words, if F is negative, signifying a net outflow of capital from the domestic financial markets to foreign ones, the increase in the rate of interest will decrease the deficit in the capital account. If, on the other hand, F is positive, indicating that capital flows from abroad into the domestic markets, then the increase of the rate of interest in question will further increase the surplus.

But since exports remain constant, it follows that the sum of the change in capital flows and imports will be equal to the change in B. This result could, after all, be obtained directly from the definition of B given by identity 16.5.10.

To put it in a less technical way, an increase in the equilibrium level of income will result in an increase in imports and thereby, given the exogenously determined level of exports, will contribute to the deterioration of the trade account. On the other hand, given the initial relation between the rates of interest at home and those abroad, an increase in the former will make the domestic financial market more attractive than before, which will result in an increase in the inflow or a decrease in the outflow of capital. This is exactly what equation 16.5.35 shows; that is, the algebraic sum of these two forces will determine the final outcome in regard to B.

Now, to determine the amount of change in the value of B due to a change in G, we substitute the values of ΔY and Δr from equations 16.5.19 and 16.5.20 into 16.5.35 to obtain:

$$\Delta B = f_1 \frac{l_1}{l_2} n\, \Delta G - m_1 n\, \Delta G.$$

Factoring out $n\, \Delta G$, the above expression can be further simplified to read

$$\Delta B = \left[f_1 \frac{l_1}{l_2} - m_1 \right] n\, \Delta G. \tag{16.5.36}$$

From 16.5.36, we see that in view of the fact that $n > 0$, the sign of ΔB depends on the expression $[f_1 l_1/l_2 - m_1]$. Normally, this expression is negative, implying that an increase in government expenditures will have adverse effects on the outcome of international economic transactions. More explicitly, if there is a balance of payments deficit the increase in government expenditures will increase it, whereas if there is a surplus it will decrease it. The opposite but rather unlikely results would be obtained if $[f_1 l_1/l_2 - m_1]$ were positive.[8] Finally, if this ex-

---

[8] This was the case of Canada during the 1950s. Indeed, for the expression $[f_1 l_1/l_2 - m_1]$ to be greater than zero it is sufficient that $f_1 > l_2 m_1/l_1$. In other words, the responsiveness of capital movements to interest fluctuations (f_1) has to be greater than the product of the amount by which the community desires to reduce its holdings of idle cash balances in response to a 1% increase in the rate of interest (l_2) and the ratio of the marginal propensity to import (m_1) to the inverse income velocity of transactions cash balances (l_1). In terms of annual data of the Canadian economy, the ratio m_1/l_1 was approximately equal to one whereas f_1 was larger than l_2 by a factor of 2–4. More explicitly, a 1%

pression is equal to zero, then $\Delta B = 0$, which means that the increase in the inflow of capital due to the increase in the rate of interest is exactly equal to the increase of imports due to the increase in the equilibrium level of income. Should this be the case, a change in government expenditures leaves the outcome of international economic transactions unaffected.

The same results would hold if instead of a change in government expenditures the economy experienced a change in autonomous consumption (a) or investment (g_0). Had we chosen to change the transfer payments or the tax rate, the magnitude of change in B would have been different. We shall leave these cases as an exercise for the interested student.

Next, suppose that exports increase autonomously from Ex^0 to Ex^1. In this case equation 16.5.33 becomes:

$$B^1 = -f_0 + f_1 r^1 + Ex^1 - m_0 - m_1 Y^1. \qquad (16.5.37)$$

Subtracting 16.5.33 from 16.5.37, we obtain

$$\Delta B = \Delta Ex + f_1 \Delta r - m_1 \Delta Y. \qquad (16.5.38)$$

From 16.5.38 we see that the change in the level of exports acts upon B not only directly but also indirectly via changes in the equilibrium level of income and rate of interest. The interpretation of 16.5.38 is quite similar to that of 16.5.35: the change in exports has a direct effect and an indirect effect operating through changes in Y and r.

Substituting the values of ΔY and Δr from equations 16.5.27 and 16.5.28 into 16.5.38, we find

$$\Delta B = \Delta Ex + f_1 \frac{l_1}{l_2} n \, \Delta Ex - m_1 n \, \Delta Ex$$

which can be rewritten as

$$\Delta B = \left[(1 - nm_1) + nf_1 \frac{l_1}{l_2} \right] \Delta Ex. \qquad (16.5.39)$$

---

[8](*continued*)   increase in the rate of interest would attract, say, $500–$1,000 million while the corresponding desired reduction of idle cash balances amounted to $200–$300 million.

Under these circumstances, the amount of capital attracted as a result of budgetary expansion ($\Delta G > 0$), with a constant money supply, will exceed the induced increase in imports and therefore the outcome of this policy will be an improvement rather than a deterioration of the balance of payments. On this point see R. Rhomberg, "A Model of the Canadian Economy under Fixed and Fluctuating Exchange Rates," *The Journal of Political Economy* 72 (February 1964), 3.

From equation 16.5.39, we see that the sign of ΔB depends on the coefficient of ΔEx, namely,

$$\left[(1 - nm_1) + nf_1\frac{l_1}{l_2}\right].$$

This expression, we assert, is for all practical purposes positive. In particular, it is fair to assume that the marginal propensity to import, m_1, is no larger than .10. Thus, unless the multiplier, n, is very large indeed, the coefficient of ΔEx cannot be negative. As a matter of fact one could determine the range of the multiplier for which this expression would be negative.[9]

Thus, our conclusion is that an increase (decrease) in exports, *ceteris paribus*, always results in an improvement (deterioration) of the outcome of the balance of payments.

Finally, we may study the impact of a change in the nominal money supply on B assuming that the price level, P, remains constant. For this purpose we consider once more equation 16.5.35:

$$\Delta B = f_1 \Delta r - m_1 \Delta Y \qquad (16.5.35)$$

Substituting the value of ΔY and Δr from 16.5.31 and 16.5.32 into 16.5.35, we obtain:

$$\Delta B = -f_1\frac{[1 - b(1 - t_1) + m_1]}{l_2}n \Delta M_s - m_1\frac{g_1}{l_2}n \Delta M_s.$$

Factoring out $-(1/l_2)n \Delta M_s$, the above expression becomes

$$\Delta B = -\frac{1}{l_2}\{f_1[1 - b(1 - t_1) + m_1] + m_1g_1\}n \Delta M_s.$$

$$(16.5.40)$$

---

[9]Indeed, let us suppose that

$$1 - nm_1 + nf_1 l_1/l_2 < 0.$$

This implies that

$$n[f_1 l_1/l_2 - m_1] < 1.$$

Recalling now that $[f_1 l_1/l_2 - m_1]$ is usually a negative quantity, we obtain that

$$n[m_1 - f_1 l_1/l_2] > 1$$

from which we find immediately that $n > 1/[m_1 - f_1 l_1/l_2]$. In other words, the coefficient of ΔEx in equation 16.5.39 will be negative if the multiplier exceeds the value $1/[m_1 - f_1 l_1/l_2]$, which is a very large quantity indeed. Consequently, this case can be excluded for all practical purposes.

Equation 16.5.41 suggests that an increase in the money supply has adverse effects on the outcome of international economic transactions. In other words, an increase in the nominal money supply, *ceteris paribus*, will result in an increase in a deficit or a decrease in a surplus. The reason for this is that both the trade and the capital account deteriorate simultaneously. The increase in income will generate more imports, and given the exogenously determined level of exports, the trade account will deteriorate. On the other hand, since the rate of interest decreases, this implies that, given the rates of interest prevailing abroad, the domestic financial markets become less attractive for foreign capital so that the inflow of capital decreases or, alternatively, its outflow increases. In either case, the capital account will deteriorate as well. Thus the combination of these two effects will reinforce each other, resulting in an unfavorable change in the outcome of the balance of payments.[10]

16.6 The Automatic Adjustment Mechanism in Theory and Practice

The preceding analysis was based on two particularly critical assumptions: first, that the level of income and rate of interest in the rest of the world were fixed, and therefore insensitive to the behavior of the domestic economy; and second, that the nominal money supply of the domestic economy was exogenous. The relaxation of these assumptions would complicate the algebraic model to the point that it would no longer be very useful as a tool for learning. However, the importance of the assumptions compels us to depart temporarily from an algebraic treatment in order to investigate the impact of induced changes in

---

[10]Exercise:

Consider an economy characterized by the following structural equations:

$Y = C + I + G + Ex - Im$
$C = 30 + .8Y_d$
$I = 95.6 - 400r$
$Y_d \equiv Y - T$
$T = -50 + .25Y$
$M_d/P = 110 + .15Y - 500r$
$M_d/P = M_s/P$
$F = -2.4 + 60r$
$Im = 5 + .02Y$
$B = F + Ex - Im.$

Also assume that: $G = 155$, $M_s = 235$, $Ex = 24.4$, and $P = 1.0$. Find the effect on B of a change in G by 10; find the effect on B of a change in M_s by 20.

foreign income and interest rates and the domestic supply of money.

First, assume that the economy in question plays an important enough role in the international scheme to have an impact on the level of economic activity in the rest of the world. An alteration in the behavior of the domestic economy will have international repercussions, and these effects, in turn, have a feedback effect on the position of the domestic country. We shall concentrate on the direct feedback effects on the balance of payments, ignoring for the most part any second and subsequent rounds in the international adjustment process.

Suppose that the exports of the domestic economy decrease for some reason. The initial result will be that the balance of payments of this country will worsen and the domestic income will decrease, as we saw in the previous section. But since our exports constitute part of the imports of foreign nations, a decline in our exports induces an increase in the income of our trading partners. The rise in income in the rest of the world will, in turn, cause an expansion in their demand for imports (our exports), and this will tend to partially counteract the worsening of the domestic economy's balance of payments. Or, suppose that a change in tastes causes our economy's citizens to increase their demand for imports. The immediate effect is to expand any deficit in our current account (or diminish a surplus), but the rise in imports also stimulates a rise in foreign income. And this latter impact will, in general, cause an increase in the demand for our exports. The effect of changes in imports or exports on the foreign income level and the consequent feedback effect on economic transactions is known as the income effect. It is an adjustment mechanism which tends to cushion the extent of change in a country's balance of payments, and thus lends a stability of sorts to international markets.

We also find that the mere existence of surpluses and deficits in the balance of payments of trading partners tends to ignite monetary effects. Presume that the domestic economy experiences a deficit in its balance of payments. As we pointed out in section 16.3, this implies that the demand for American dollars falls short of their supply. Or, looking at this from another perspective, it implies that Americans have an excess demand for foreign currency. It follows, then, that the price of dollars (in terms of foreign currencies) will be pressured to fall in the absence of policy intervention. But in view of the fact that the monetary authorities are committed to maintain the value of the currency within a certain margin of parity, it follows that they will have to accommodate the situation. In particular, the Fed will be forced to provide commercial banks with enough foreign currency to make up the difference between the inflow and outflow of that currency. In doing so, the Fed will charge the commercial banks by deducting from their reserves.[11] But, as we found in chapter 6, this reduction in bank reserves will force a contraction in the domestic money supply unless the monetary authorities take other actions to resist this decrease. And, as was illustrated in the previous section of this chapter, the reduction in the money supply will cause an improvement in the country's balance of payments.

On the other hand, a surplus in the balance of payments enjoyed by the domestic economy will generate diametrically opposite experiences. This surplus implies that the supply of foreign exchange exceeds the demand. Consequently, the price of dollars in terms of the foreign currency will increase unless the Federal Reserve will step in and absorb the amount which is equal to the surplus in the balance of payments. However, the Federal Reserve in doing so will increase the reserves of the commercial banks, and as a result the money supply will increase by a multiple of this amount.[12] But since the domestic money supply increases, this will lead to a decrease in the rate of interest and consequently the domestic demand for investment will increase. This last increase will cause a further increase in the level of income, which in turn will result in an increase in imports. Thus, we see that the balance of payments of the rest of the world will improve once more because of the monetary effects on the income of the domestic economy.

The above analysis suggests that a disequilibrium in the balance of payments ignites an automatic feedback mechanism which propels the balance of payments back toward equilibrium. However, the monetary effects do not affect the balance of payments only because of their impact on the level of income. Since the changes in the money supply have driven a wedge between the prevailing rates of interest in these two economic regions, this will generate profit opportunities for the interest-sensitive capital. Indeed, the high rate of interest of the rest of the world

---

[11] If a U.S. importer pays for foreign goods with a check drawn on the commercial banking system, the check will be deposited in a foreign bank and will require a transfer of funds from the domestic bank to the foreign bank. If the latter institution accepts U.S. currency, the decrease in the domestic money supply is direct; if the transaction requires foreign exchange, the domestic commercial bank may have to go through the Fed, thus setting off the mechanism described in the text.

[12] American exporters may settle their accounts with the rest of the world either in terms of dollars or in terms of the currency of the rest of the world. If they settle in terms of dollars, deposits of the commercial banks will increase directly, whereas if they settle in terms of foreign currency the Federal Reserve will absorb it for dollars. In either case, the result will be an expansion of the domestic money supply.

may very well induce a reshuffling of the domestic portfolios in favor of foreign securities.[13]

We see then that the rate of interest plays a dual role in the corrective process. In other words, it not only affects indirectly the balance of trade through its impact on income, but it also acts directly via its effects on the capital account.

The above mechanism will continue to be in motion as long as there is a disequilibrium in the balance of payments of these two trading partners. Thus, in principle at least, one may argue that the automatic mechanism through its income and monetary effects is capable of restoring equilibrium in the foreign sector.

Although, as we pointed out above, the automatic mechanism in principle should be sufficient to correct short-run problems of the balance of payments, in practice it usually does not. This is not due to any disguised internal inconsistency in the analysis of the mechanism, but rather the result of the exercise of the sovereign rights and powers of the national governments. National governments insist on being able to determine their priorities autonomously and to have a free hand in using their instruments to reach their goals. For example, if a country has a considerable amount of unemployment and at the same time has a balance of payments deficit, the automatic mechanism, operating through a reduction in the money supply, would lead to further domestic unemployment. Such a development might prove to be disastrous from a social point of view. In such a case, given the reserve position of the country as well as its relation with its international partners, the policymaker could neutralize the effects of the deficit on the rate of interest in order to avoid an undesirable deflationary process. For example, the monetary authorities could increase the money supply by purchasing government securities in the market. Needless to say, painful as it may be, the deficit country eventually will have to go through the process of deflation once the tolerance of the creditors has been exhausted.

On the other hand, for a country experiencing a surplus in the balance of payments the choices are relatively easy. Indeed, there is no reason why the policymaker, for example, should accept an induced expansion in the money supply if he considers such a development undesirable. This would be avoided altogether by a contractionary

---

[13]For example, the market price of bonds in the rest of the world, due to the increase in the rates, has now decreased. Consequently, domestic capital may be exported not only to seek the higher yields but also the expected considerable capital gains which will be realized should the equilibrium in the balance of payments be restored.

policy in the money supply so that the surplus of the foreign sector would be effectively neutralized.

Thus, we see that although in all other respects the automatic mechanism at work produces exactly symmetrical results, the intervention of governments results in a fundamental assymmetry, negating the potential restoration of equilibrium in the balance of payments. To be sure, a country with a surplus is under no pressure whatsoever. However, it should be quite obvious that there is an upper limit to the sum of deficits a country is capable of accumulating. Unless there is a willingness on the part of foreign partners to loan the country foreign exchange or other international reserves (for example, gold), it will be limited by its own international reserve position. This is exactly the reason that deficit countries are usually asked to clean their house by subjecting themselves to the painful process of deflation. And this is also the reason why there is always a bias in favor of deflation characterizing the international economic scene.

In the following sections we shall present a model which will account for the adjustment process of an economy opened to foreign repercussions, where the balance of payments is an important target variable. Again, for the sake of simplicity, but not accuracy, we shall assume that the money supply remains exogenous and is controlled exclusively by the monetary authorities. As was pointed out above, under normal circumstances the money supply in reality is affected by various developments in the balance of payments. Nevertheless, in essence, we are assuming that the monetary authorities of the domestic economy automatically act in such a way as to neutralize the induced changes in the money supply.

16.7 Income Adjustments in an Open Economy, with Predetermined Targets

The previous section introduced the reader to the concept of interdependence among the various sections of the economy on the assumption that the country was engaged in economic relations with the rest of the world. In doing so, we deliberately left open questions of policy attempting to achieve predetermined targets. For example, although the outcome of the international economic transactions turned occasionally against the domestic economy by indicating a deficit, we showed no concern whatsoever for this problem.

To be sure, in the short run and under normal conditions, running a deficit in the foreign account may not be the source of serious concern. But this is certainly not so when long-run considerations are taken into account. In other words, a country may run a deficit in the trade account and may also cover this deficit by attracting (borrowing) an inflow of foreign capital from abroad. But this solution, although acceptable temporarily, is not feasible permanently since frequent use of it may have a bearing on the credit rating of the country as lenders eventually become restless and ask the repayment of these loans.

Thus, the question becomes if and to what extent a country is able to seek deliberate ways of influencing the results of its international economic transactions. The previous section paved the way for answering this question since it showed that at least some of the components of the balance of payments can be subjected to policy manipulations. For example, we saw that an increase in government expenditures or the nominal money supply results in general in a deterioration of a country's balance of payments. Thus, we concluded that if a country wishes to improve the results of its economic transactions with the rest of the world the opposite prescription would be the correct one. So far, so good. But let us now suppose that the country runs a deficit in the balance of payments, while at the same time its equilibrium level of income is far below the full-employment level. Under these circumstances, the policymaker is confronted with a serious economic dilemma. As the reader can see, each problem demands a use of policy instruments diametrically opposite to those required for the solution of the other problem. Reduction of the deficit in the balance of payments calls for a contractionary policy, whereas an increase in the level of employment would require an expansionary one. Thus, it appears that, superficially at least, there is a basic incompatibility in the use of policy instruments to accommodate these two problems. It would also seem that the policymaker may have to resolve this policy dilemma by making a value judgment as to which of these two evils is the worse.

Although this may appear to be a partical solution since one of the problems may have to go unsolved, the policymaker, due to restrictions imposed by social and political institutions, may not be able to entertain any value judgment whatsoever. Thus, the relevant question is: do we have the ability to cope with such a problem? The answer to this question is in the affirmative, but the student will have to bear with us for a little while.

Let us begin by reproducing the system of the previous section:

$$Y = C + I + G + Ex - Im \qquad (16.7.1)$$

$$C = a + bY_d \tag{16.7.2}$$

$$I = g_0 - g_1 r \tag{16.7.3}$$

$$Y_d \equiv Y - T \tag{16.7.4}$$

$$T = -t_0 + t_1 Y \tag{16.7.5}$$

$$\frac{M_d}{P} = l_0 + l_1 Y - l_2 r \tag{16.7.6}$$

$$\frac{M_d}{P} = \frac{M_s}{P} \tag{16.7.7}$$

$$Im = m_0 + m_1 Y \tag{16.7.8}$$

$$F = -f_0 + f_1 r \tag{16.7.9}$$

$$B = F + Ex - Im. \tag{16.7.10}$$

Our assumptions about the variables involved are that G, M_s, Ex and P are considered exogenous while the other are endogenous. Again, the meaning of the above equations is the same as in the previous section. From the previous section we saw that, given the exogenous variables, the above system collapses into three equations with three unknowns, i.e.:

$$[1 - b(1 - t_1) + m_1]Y + g_1 r = a + g_0 + bt_0 - m_0 + G + Ex \tag{16.7.11}$$

$$l_1 Y - l_2 r = \frac{M_s}{P} - l_0 \tag{16.7.12}$$

$$m_1 Y - f_1 r + B = -m_0 - f_0 + Ex. \tag{16.7.13}$$

Now suppose that the policymaker, for reasons of his own, decides that it would be desirable to achieve a value for B which is equal to B^0. Then, substituting this value into equation 16.7.13, we obtain

$$m_1 Y - f_1 r + B^0 = -m_0 - f_0 + Ex. \tag{16.7.14}$$

Since now B is no longer a variable but a fixed quantity, equation 16.7.14 can be rewritten

$$m_1 Y - f_1 r = -m_0 - f_0 + Ex - B^0. \tag{16.7.15}$$

This substitution of B with its target value B^0 changes the profile of the whole problem. Our system now consists of equations 16.7.11, 16.7.12, and 16.7.15, which contain only two unknowns, Y and r. Under normal circumstances such a system does not possess any solution whatsoever. Indeed, we seek a pair of values for Y and r which will satisfy the following: first, equation 16.7.11 so that the expenditure sector will be at equilibrium; second, equation 16.7.12 for the equilibrium of the monetary sector; and finally, equation 16.7.15, which reflects the target value of B set by the policymaker. In short, we ask too much from this system. Now, as we know, under normal circumstances equations 16.7.11 and 16.7.12 can be solved uniquely to give us the values of Y and r for which the domestic economy will be at equilibrium. However, these solution values of Y and r may or may not satisfy the third equation; and since the policymaker is determined to accept only a value of B equal to B^0, this solution may not be acceptable at all. In other words, the third equation of the system, 16.7.15, plays the role of a *constraint* in regard to the solution values for Y and r which we are prepared to accept. Thus, any attempt to solve the system the way it stands would take us to an intellectual *cul-de-sac*.

To appreciate a bit better the nature of problem at hand, let us assume for a moment that exports are fixed at the level Ex^0. Solving equation 16.7.14 for r in terms of Y, we obtain

$$r = \frac{[m_0 + f_0 + B^0 - Ex^0]}{f_1} + \frac{m_1}{f_1}Y. \qquad (16.7.16)$$

By construction, equation 16.7.16 provides us with all pairs of income and the rate of interest which satisfy the requirement $B = B^0$. For the sake of concreteness let us assume that the policymaker chooses the target $B^0 = 0$. Under these circumstances, figure 16.7.1 depicts the graph of equation 16.7.16 on the assumption that $Ex = Ex^0$ and $B = B^0 = 0$.

From equation 16.7.16 as well as its accompanying graph, we see that the FF curve slopes upward to indicate the fact that as long as B is to maintain a value equal to $B^0 = 0$, any increase in the level of income should be associated with an increase in the rate of interest. The reason for this relationship is that since an increase in income will induce an increase in imports, it follows that, given the level of exports, B will assume negative values unless the rate of interest increases, thereby making the domestic financial markets attract an increased inflow of foreign capital.

More concretely, an increase in income by ΔY will induce an increase in imports which will be equal to $m_1 \Delta Y$. On the other hand, an increase in the rate of interest by Δr will result in an algebraic increase of the inflow of foreign capital by an amount which is equal to $f_1 \Delta r$. But since B is supposed to maintain the value zero, it is necessary that:

$$m_1 \Delta Y = f_1 \Delta r$$

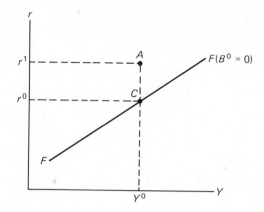

Figure 16.7.1 *The Balance-of-Payments Policy Constraint*

from which we can derive:

$$\frac{\Delta r}{\Delta Y} = \frac{m_1}{f_1}.$$

The last expression is the slope of the FF curve as depicted by equation 16.7.16.

It follows then that the slope of FF, m_1/f_1, shows the change in the level of the interest rate which corresponds to a small change in the level of income so that $B = 0$. Thus, point C as well as any other point along the FF curve will have the property that $B = 0$. Now let us consider some point off the FF curve, say, A. At this point imports are the same as those associated with point C, since in both cases the corresponding level of income is equal to Y^0. However, at point A the inflow of capital will be greater than the one associated with point C (since $r^1 > r^0$), implying that, given the exogenously determined level of exports, point A (and for the same reason any point above FF curve) will be associated with a surplus in the foreign sector account, namely, $B > 0$. This could be easily seen by observing equation 16.7.16 in which B is a component of the intercept. Thus, if B assumes positive values the result will be that FF curve will shift upward and to the left. Figure 16.7.2 depicts three different positions of the FF curve associated with three different targets for the foreign sector.

Now to return to our problem, the requirement is to seek a pair of values for Y and r which satisfies simultaneously all three sectors: the expenditure, the monetary and the international sectors. Figure 16.7.3 shows graphically the nature of our problem.

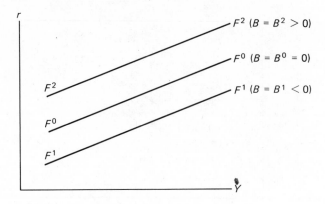

Figure 16.7.2   *Balance-of-Payments Constraint with Alternative Values of the Surplus (Deficit)*

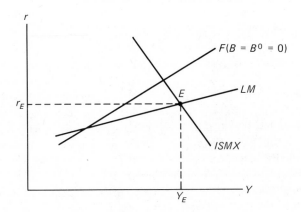

Figure 16.7.3   *General Equilibrium and the Balance-of-Payments*

From this figure, we see that the solution of equations 16.7.11 and 16.7.12, which indicates the equilibrium of the domestic economy, occurs at point E, the intersection of the ISMX and the LM curve. Notice, however, that since E lies below the FF curve this means that the country runs a deficit in the foreign account ($B < 0$). It follows then that this equilibrium point is not acceptable to the policymaker, since B is not equal to zero. The only equilibrium points which could be acceptable to the policymaker are those which lie on the FF curve. Thus,

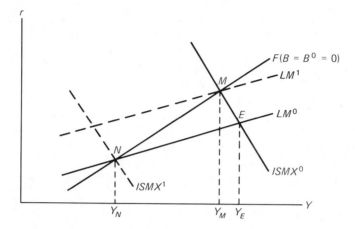

Figure 16.7.4 *Policies for Achieving the Desired Balance-of-Payments*

we can now appreciate what we meant by saying that equation 16.7.15, as represented by the FF curve, plays the role of a constraint on the solution values of equations 16.7.11 and 16.7.12 (i.e., the intersection of the ISMX and LM curves).

Thus, to summarize, the requirement that B = 0 restricts the equilibrium of the domestic economy to a position on the FF curve. This, however, can be only the result of sheer luck and we may ask what can be done to ensure that the domestic equilibrium is consistent with the desired balance of payments. The solution to this problem generally requires the intervention of the policymaker, who can commit either fiscal or monetary policy or both to achieve his targets. For example, if he decides to use fiscal policy, he could decrease government expenditures so that by shifting the ISMX curve to the left its intersection with the LM would occur at point N, as figure 16.7.4 shows. At point N the domestic economy is at equilibrium and the same time the target $B^0 = 0$ is also satisfied. Alternatively, one could also attempt to obtain the same result by using monetary policy. In this case, the monetary authorities should decrease the nominal money supply (given the price level) so that by shifting the LM curve to the left its intersection with ISMX would occur at point M.

Let us now try to solve the problem algebraically. For this purpose we reproduce once more the system 16.7.11, 16.7.12 and 16.7.13.

$$[1 - b(1 - t_1) + m_1]Y + g_1 r = a + g_0 + bt_0 - m_0 + G + Ex^0$$
$$(16.7.11)$$

$$l_1 Y - l_2 r = \frac{M_s}{P} - l_0 \tag{16.7.12}$$

$$m_1 Y - f_1 r = -m_0 - f_0 + Ex^0 - B. \tag{16.7.13}$$

As the reader can observe, in the above system we have already substituted the assumed value of exports, $Ex = Ex^0$.

Suppose now that the policymaker decides to use government expenditures in order to attain the predetermined target. The problem involves finding that value of G which will be consistent with $B = B^0$. From a previous section, we know that solution of equations 16.7.11 and 16.7.12 yields the following values for Y and r:

$$Y = n[a + g_0 + bt_0 - m_0 + G + Ex^0] + n\frac{g_1}{l_2}\left[\frac{M_s^0}{P^0} - l_0\right]$$

and

$$r = \frac{l_1}{l_2} n[a + g_0 + bt_0 - m_0 + G + Ex^0]$$

$$+ \frac{1}{l_2} n[1 - b(1 - t_1) + m_1]\left[l_0 - \frac{M_s^0}{P^0}\right]$$

where:

$$n \equiv \left[\frac{1}{1 - b(1 - t_1) + m_1 + g_1\frac{l_1}{l_2}}\right].$$

Regardless of the value we substitute for G, the above values of Y and r satisfy both the expenditure and monetary sectors. The reader should also notice that since we have not as yet determined the value of G, neither are the values of Y and r determined.

We may substitute the above expressions for Y and r into the constraint, equation 16.7.15, to obtain:

$$m_1 n\left\{[a + g_0 + bt_0 - m_0 + G + Ex^0] + \frac{g_1}{l_2}[M_s^0 - l_0]\right\}$$

$$-f_1 n\left\{\frac{l_1}{l_2}[a + g_0 + bt_0 - m_0 + G^0 + Ex^0]\right.$$

$$\left. + \frac{1}{l_2}[1 - b(1 - t_1) + m_1][l_0 - M_s^0]\right\}$$

$$= -m_0 - f_0 + Ex^0 - B^0. \tag{16.7.17}$$

Notice that in the above expression we have also substituted $P^0 = 1$.

The important thing now is that equation 16.7.17 contains only one unknown, G, since all the other parameters and exogenous variables are given. Thus, solving this equation for G we find that value of the government expenditures which satisfies the condition B = 0. In other words, we essentially force the ISMX and LM schedules to intersect each other on the FF curve, thus allowing the coincidence of equilibrium of the product and money markets and a zero balance of payments. This solution value for G can be found to be:

$$G^0 = -[a + g_0 + bt_0 - m_0 + Ex^0] + \left[\cfrac{n}{m_1 n - \cfrac{f_1 l_1}{l_2}} \right]$$

$$\left\{ \frac{f_1}{l_2}[1 - b(1 - t_1) + m_1] - m_1 \frac{g_1}{l_2} \right\} [M_s^0 - l_0]$$

$$- \left[\cfrac{1}{m_1 n - \cfrac{f_1 l_1}{l_2}} \right] [m_0 + f_0 - Ex^0 + B^0]. \qquad (16.7.18)$$

It goes without saying, of course, that the reader is not expected to tax his memory by attempting to remember this awkward expression. His understanding of it is all that is required.[14]

---

[14]Exercise: Suppose that the economy is characterized by the system of structural equations:

Y = C + I + G + Ex − Im

C = 30 + .8Y_d

I = 95.6 − 400r

$Y_d \equiv Y - T$

T = −50 + .25Y

$\dfrac{M_d}{P} = 110 + .15Y - 500r$

$\dfrac{M_d}{P} = \dfrac{M_s}{P}$

F = −2.4 + 60r

Im = 5 + .02Y

B = F + Ex − Im

In addition, assume that the government spends on goods and services $117 billion and that nominal money supply, the exports and the price level are fixed at the levels $235, $24.4 billion and 1 respectively. Find the initial equilibrium values of Y and r, and solve for the balance of payments position. Then, find the level of government expenditures which would yield a zero value for B. At this new value of G, also find the resultant equilibrium for the domestic economy.

There is one lesson to be learned from the above analysis: if the policymaker sets one target, in our case a certain value on the outcome of the balance of payments, then attainment of this goal will require the commitment of *one* policy instrument. Although in our analysis we used government expenditures as a policy instrument, the policymaker could have used either the tax rate or the money supply. We shall ask the reader to go through these cases as an exercise.

Let us now complicate the picture a bit by assuming that the deficit in the foreign sector is accompanied by a considerable degree of unemployment. As we saw at the beginning of this section, neither monetary nor fiscal policy alone will be sufficient to solve this problem.[15] To appreciate this, look at figure 16.7.5.

The initial equilibrium levels of income and the rate of interest are given by the combination Y_E and r_E at point E, where ISMX^0 intersects LM^0. Since, however, point E lies below the FF curve, it follows that the foreign sector runs a deficit. If the problem were only to close the gap of the international sector, then the policymaker could solve it easily either by decreasing, say, government expenditures so that the ISMX^0 would shift to the left to point A, or alternatively by decreasing the money supply in such a way that the LM^0 curve would shift to the left to pass through point B. In both cases, the intersection of ISMX and LM would occur along the FF line and thus the target would be attained. This solution would be acceptable as long as the policymaker was not concerned with the equilibrium values of income and employment. But we now assume that he is concerned, and that he explicitly sets as a second target a full-employment level of income, Y_F.

In such a case, a glance at figure 16.7.5 reveals immediately that one-instrument prescriptions won't do. The use of any one policy tool can be used to satisfy one objective, but only at the expense of the other. However, this problem can be solved if the authorities are willing to commit monetary and fiscal policy instruments simultaneously. More explicitly, since the requirement of the policymaker is to reach point

---

[15]This has been termed by R. A. Mundell as *the assignment problem*. This terminology is due to the fact that the government usually assigns responsibility for the pursuit of various policy targets to different government agencies which can exert control on the various policy instruments. For example, the Board of Governors of the Federal Reserve System, which controls the money supply, is given the responsibility of the external equilibrium, whereas the Treasury, which controls the fiscal policy, is given the responsibility of internal equilibrium. In a more general sense the assignment problem refers to the delegation of responsibilities to the various government agencies so that the operation will be carried out in the most efficient fashion. See R. A. Mundell, "The Appropriate Use of Monetary and Fiscal Policy for Internal and External Stability," *International Monetary Fund Staff Papers* 9 (March 1962), 70–79.

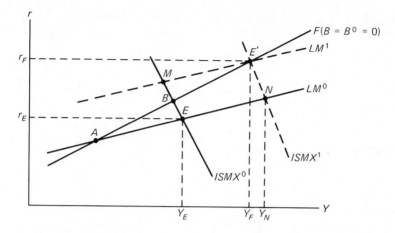

Figure 16.7.5 *Joint Use of Monetary and Fiscal Policy: The Case of Two Policy Goals*

E', this can be done by increasing government expenditures so that the ISMX shifts to $ISMX^1$, while at the same time reducing the nominal money supply in such a way that the LM schedule shifts to LM^1.

Thus, we have arrived in an interesting conclusion: if there are two targets to be achieved, it will be necessary for the policymaker to commit the same number of policy instruments.[16]

Let us now solve this problem algebraically. For this, we shall assume that the policymaker intends to manipulate government expenditures and the nominal money supply to achieve his joint objectives. We shall also assume that the price level is equal to one and that the level of exports is settled at Ex^0. (In reality, the level of exports is not known; neither can it be controlled by the policymaker. Thus, realistically, before one solves the problem at hand it is necessary to predict the value exports most likely will assume.)

Consider once more the system 16.7.11–16.7.13:

$$[1 - b(1 - t_1) + m_1]Y + g_1r = a + g_0 + bt_0 - m_0 + G + Ex$$

$$l_1Y - l_2r = \frac{M_s}{P} - l_0$$

$$m_1Y - f_1r + B = -m_0 - f_0 + Ex^0.$$

---

[16]In a linear system like ours, in general, the attainment of n targets requires the commitment of n independent policy instruments.

We know that using the first two equations we can obtain

$$Y = n[a + g_0 + bt_0 - m_0 + G + Ex^0] + n\frac{g_1}{l_2}\left[\frac{M_s}{P^0} - l_0\right]$$

and

$$r = \frac{l_1}{l_2}n[a + g_0 + bt_0 - m_0 + G + Ex^0]$$

$$+ \frac{1}{l_2}n[1 - b(1 - t_1) + m_1]\left[l_0 - \frac{M_s}{P^0}\right].$$

To simplify the above expressions let us further define

$$A \equiv n[a + g_0 + bt_0 - m_0 + Ex^0] - n\frac{g_1}{l_2}l_0$$

$$H \equiv \frac{l_1}{l_2}n[a + g_0 + bt_0 - m_0 + Ex^0] + \frac{1}{l_2}n[1 - b(1 - t_1) + m_1]l_0$$

and

$$D \equiv \frac{1}{l_2}n[1 - b(1 - t_1) + m_1].$$

Using the above definitions in the expressions for Y and r and again letting $P^0 = 1$, we obtain:

$$Y = A + nG + n\frac{g_1}{l_2}M_s \qquad (16.7.19)$$

and

$$r = H + \frac{l_1}{l_2}nG - DM_s. \qquad (16.7.20)$$

Substituting equation 16.7.19 and 16.7.20 into the constraint (equation 16.7.13) we find:

$$m_1\left[A + nG + n\frac{g_1}{l_2}M_s\right] - f_1\left[H + \frac{l_1}{l_2}nG - DM_s\right]$$

$$= -m_0 - f_0 + Ex^0 - B.$$

Factoring out G and M_s, the above expression can be rewritten

$$n\left[m_1 - f_1\frac{l_1}{l_2}\right]G + \left[m_1 n\frac{g_1}{l_2} + f_1 D\right]M_s = -m_0 - f_0 + Ex^0 - B$$

$$- m_1 A + f_1 H.$$

$$(16.7.21)$$

At this point we may recall that the targets in regard to the values of Y and B set by the policymaker are $Y = Y_F$ and $B = 0$ respectively. Thus, the problem becomes to find the values of G and M_s which will allow us to attain the targets of full employment and zero deficit in the balance of payments. If we substitute Y_F (a known quantity) for Y in equation 16.7.19 and separate the knowns from the unknowns we find:

$$nG + n\frac{g_1}{l_2}M_s = Y_F - A. \tag{16.7.22}$$

Furthermore, substituting the value $B = B^0 = 0$ in equation 16.7.21, we find:

$$n\left[m_1 - f_1\frac{l_1}{l_2}\right]G + \left[m_1 n\frac{g_1}{l_2} + f_1 D\right]M_s$$

$$= -m_0 - f_0 + Ex^0 - m_1 A + f_1 H. \tag{16.7.23}$$

We have then generated a system of two equations which contain two variables, i.e., the policy instruments to be used. The solution of this system will yield the values of G and M_s for which the targets Y_F and $B^0 = 0$ will be attained.[17]

---

[17] Exercise: Suppose that the economy can be depicted by the following system of structural equations:

$$Y = C + I + G + Ex - Im$$

$$C = 30 + .8Y_d$$

$$I = 95.6 - 400r + .10Y$$

$$Y_d \equiv Y - T$$

$$T = -50 + .25Y$$

$$\frac{M_d}{P} = 110 + .15Y - 500r$$

$$\frac{M_d}{P} = \frac{M_s}{P}$$

$$F = -2.4 + 60r$$

$$Im = 5 + .02Y$$

$$B = F + Ex - Im$$

Suppose also that presently the exogenous variables assume the following values: $G = 155$, $M_s = 248.75$, $Ex = 24.40$, and $P = 1$.

As the reader can verify, under these circumstances the equilibrium level of income is $1,025 billion and the corresponding balance of payments is a deficit of $1.7 billion. At this point, let us assume that the policymaker decides to pursue a full-employment policy while at the same time he requires $B = 0$. For the sake of concreteness we shall assume the full-employment output is estimated to be $1,050 billion. Determine the values of G and M_s for which $Y = Y_F = 1,050$ and $B = 0$.

A very interesting conclusion from the above analysis is that for the first time the instruments of monetary and fiscal policy, as exemplified by changes in G and M_s, appear to be complements of, rather than substitutes for, each other. This means, contrary to our experience thus far, not only that they have to be combined in a certain way, but also that their roles can no longer be considered interchangeable. In the conditions outlined above, appropriate use of these instruments would imply that we reserve the use of fiscal policy for adjustments in internal equilibrium, and use monetary policy for external problems.

Before we conclude this section, some qualifications are in order about the behavioral assumptions embodied in the model. It was argued that the appropriate instrument to be used for attaining external equilibrium is monetary policy. The rationale of such a conclusion was that, in the case of a deficit, a deflationary policy generated by a reduction in the nominal money supply would affect not only the trade account but also the capital account. Earlier in this chapter we saw that two of the principal components of the capital account were direct investments and portfolio investments consisting of stocks as well as other instruments of financial intermediation.

In the case of direct investment, we have to recognize that the evidence is rather meager as to what motivates such capital to cross the national borders. It could be argued, however, that, *prima facie,* direct investments are responsive to relative profit opportunities at home and in the rest of the world. But to the extent that the expected returns on investments are associated directly with prosperity and brisk economic activity, one could argue that deflationary policies do not create the most conducive environment for attracting foreign capital intended for direct investment. Therefore, unless other more particular reasons exist, e.g., location advantages in regard to raw materials and/or penetration of larger markets, the likelihood is rather small that a deflationary policy will attract direct investment capital.

On the other hand, although portfolio investment, in particular its short-term components, appears to be sensitive to the interest differentials between the various financial centers, there is a significant controversy about the importance of their magnitude. According to one view, reflected in equation 16.7.9, the existence of a differential in the interest rate between various financial centers would induce a continuous flow of funds which will not stop until and unless *this* differential is eliminated. Contrary to this view, it has been also argued that the existence of such a differential will induce mainly a once-and-for-all reshuffling of investment portfolios. The owners of such portfolios may be attracted by the interest differential and change their portfolio diversification in favor of securities of the higher-interest country. But this readjustment takes place once and does not continue over a time span. True, marginal additions to the portfolio may favor the high-interest markets as long as this differential exists, but these additions, although continuous, do not constitute a significant amount of capital transfers.

Thus, equation 16.7.9 could be pronounced erroneous on several counts: first, because it does not differentiate between the various types of capital investments; and second, because, according to the portfolio approach, it indicates a continuous flow as long as the interest differential exists.

16.8 Summary

This chapter has analyzed the workings of an economy engaged in international economic transactions. We first took a cursory look at the balance of payments account, noting that it can be sorted into the current account (dealing with the flow of goods and services) and the capital account (referring to the flow of financial capital). Then, we considered the way in which exchange rates are determined. Furthermore we restricted our subsequent analysis to a world in which exchange rates are fixed, rather than flexible.

Next, we revised our description of the economic system to include international transactions. In doing so, we hypothesized that capital flows would be a function of the domestic rate of interest (given international rates), imports would be related to domestic income, and exports would be exogenously determined. Several major effects of this modification were observed: first, the multipliers associated with policy variables would decrease, due to the existence of a marginal propensity to import (another leakage in the system); second, changes in foreign conditions would affect the domestic economy through their impact on our exports; third, the balance of payments would be affected—either directly or indirectly or both—by a change in any one of the exogenous variables of the system. But this latter conclusion hinted at a potential problem: if policies designed to cure domestic problems also have an effect on the balance of payments (a target variable), policymakers may be forced to make trade-offs between domestic goals and a favorable international payments status.

In analyzing the exercise of policy with dual policy goals, we found that monetary and fiscal policy should be viewed as complementary, rather than substitute, policies. In more general terms, we pointed out that the more goals an economy has, the more policy instruments it will need to achieve those goals. Given the existence of a limited number of instruments, we came back to the basic economic problem: we continually face trade-offs among a wide variety of objectives.

Suggested Further Reading

Branson, W. H. "Stock and Flows in International Monetary Analysis." In *International Aspects of Stabilization Policies,* edited by A. Ando, R. Herring and R. Marston. Boston: Federal Reserve Bank of Boston, 1974.

Caves, R. E. "Flexible Exchange Rates." *American Economic Review* 53 (May 1963), 120–29.

Johnson, H. G. "Equilibrium Under Fixed Exchange Rates." *American Economic Review* 53 (May 1963), 112–19.

Kenen, P. B. "Short-term Capital Movements and the U.S. Balance of Payments." In *The United States Balance of Payments. Hearings Before the Joint Economic Committee.* Washington: U.S. Government Printing Office, 1963.

Kindleberger, C. P. *International Economics.* 4th ed. Homewood, Ill.: R. D. Irwin, 1968.

Meltzer, L. "Underemployment Equilibrium in International Trade." *Econometrica* 10 (April 1942), 97–112.

Mundell, R. A. "Capital Mobility and Stabilization Policy Under Fixed and Flexible Exchange Rates." *Canadian Journal of Economics and Political Science* 29 (November 1963), 475–85.

Rhomberg, R. R. "A Model of the Canadian Economy Under Fixed and Fluctuating Exchange Rates." *Journal of Political Economy* 72 (February 1964), 1–31.

——— and Boissonneault, L. "Effects of Income and Price Changes on the U.S. Balance of Payments." International Monetary Fund *Staff Papers* 11 (March 1964), 59–124.

Robinson, R. "A Graphical Analysis of the Foreign Trade Multiplier." *Economic Journal* 62 (September 1952), 546–64.

Salant, W. S., et al. *The United States Balance of Payments in 1968.* Washington: The Brookings Institution, 1963.

PART
SEVEN

Dynamics

CHAPTER 17

Economic Growth

17.1 Introduction

One of the most readily observable characteristics of almost any advanced economy is that—at least according to traditional measures—economic activity tends to grow over time. Regardless of interruptions in the expansion of an economy, data compiled over a period of 50 or 100 years would illustrate the general upward movement in production, income, consumption and other similar aggregate measures of activity. There are two basic issues involved in the study of growth. First, there is the normative judgment concerning the desirability of alternative growth rates. We shall contend later that the choice of a desired pattern of growth depends largely on the measure of growth under consideration. Second, given some definition of growth, there is a theoretical and empirical problem of pinpointing the determinants of growth and advocating alternative policies which can be used to regulate it.

17.2 Measures of Growth

Ideally, one could define growth in terms of the change in the total "well-being" generated by an economy over time. If one adopts this abstract definition, the efficacy of high rates of growth would be rather clear. Unfortunately, no one has yet devised a way to quantify well-being (or the change in it) directly; thus, we are forced to resort to indirect measures. Due to the set of ethics ingrained in many of our social, political and economic institutions, policymakers have historically clung to the use of some variant of income or output as an indirect but easily quantifiable proxy for well-being. This approach is generally rationalized on the grounds that aggregate income represents the total market value of the goods and services produced in the economy over some specified period of time. To the extent that the market system correctly evaluates these goods and services by generating prices which reflect their social values, income could be defended as a reasonable proxy for social welfare.

However, there are many cases in which the market price of a good or service misrepresents its social value. As an example, one could make the case that the market price of oil should be adjusted to reflect the ecological damage resulting from the refinement and use of oil; or, one could argue that the price of admission to a public beach understates the social value of access to such a recreational area. The general point here is that private markets do not always capture all of the benefits and costs of production and consumption. If benefits accrue to anyone other than the purchaser of a product, or if costs are incurred by anyone other than the producer, the market mechanism does not generate prices which reflect the social worths of the array of products in question. Under these conditions, the total market value of goods and services falls short as a measure of the social value of economic activity.

Another objection to the use of aggregate income as a proxy for social welfare involves the question of distribution. Movements in national income reveal nothing about the way in which products are distributed among individuals. Rapid growth in income could be associated with an increasing degree of inequality in the income distribution; or, alternatively, relatively low rates of growth of income could be accompanied by equalization of relative incomes. One cannot assume away the importance of distributional considerations; they are inextricably involved in the determination of social welfare.

Because of the various imperfections in the use of income growth as an indicator of the change in a society's well-being, the efficacy of rapid growth (of income) is, at best, unclear. Many social scientists—including both those considering themselves radical and those generally not so inclined—maintain that the policy of fostering rapid growth of output is a critical misdirection in our structure of economic goals. Others, choosing to minimize the importance of the imperfections discussed above, retain rapid income growth as a high-priority goal of economic policy.

Once we admit to the imperfections involved in defining growth in terms of changes in income, we can at least conceptually improve on that practice. One way to do this would be to attempt to adjust aggregate income to correct for the inadequacies of the market pricing system and the social loss or gain resulting from redistribution of income. (As an example of the first type of adjustment, we might subtract from income the cost of additional pollution generated over the period.) Alternatively, we could maintain the practice of defining economic growth in terms of the change in income, but abandon the illusion that our measure mirrors the growth of social welfare. If we take the latter approach (which seems more practical for the purposes of this text), we can no longer presume high rates of income growth to be good and low or even negative rates to be bad. Instead, we should balance the benefits of income growth against its social costs and choose what seems to be an optimal growth rate as *one* of our economic goals. Fortunately, current economic thought appears to be drifting in this direction.

Regardless of the merits of income growth, we still need to study the causes of such economic expansion and the ways in which economic policy can be used to regulate it. Thus, the study of growth theory should be considered important even by those who prefer a zero rate of growth of income. The remainder of this chapter is designed to introduce the student to some of the alternative views of the growth process.

17.3 General Causes of Growth

As we have seen in previous chapters, total output in the short run is determined by a rather complex set of supply and demand relationships. Although it is possible for the equilibrium level of output to fall below the full-employment level, it is, in general, difficult for the economy to maintain production beyond the full-employment level.[1] In other words, the full-employment level of output constitutes a barrier to the expansion of output. But, as we suggested in chapter 9, the productive capacity of an economy depends upon the availability of the factors of production. This notion was captured in the aggregate production function, in which we specified total output as a function of labor and capital. In that economic growth requires an expansion of productive capacity (in a sense, the relaxation of the full-employment barrier over time), we should be able to introduce the theory of growth by referring back to a modified form of the production function specified in chapter 9.

In particular, suppose that the economy's aggregate production function is given by:

$$Y = F(N, K, T) \tag{17.3.1}$$

where T represents the state of technology and N and K represent, as before, labor and capital usage respectively. Equation 17.3.1 differs

---

[1] Production above the full-employment level is conceivable, given the possibility of the extensive use of overtime and multiple shifts not ordinarily found in the business sector; however, we would not expect this situation to be maintained over a long period.

from our short-run production function (9.2.4) in two very important ways. First, we have included some measure of technology to take account of the fact that the productivity of the factors of production (and thus, the amount of output a given set of inputs is capable of producing) depends on the state of technology incorporated in the production process. Whereas one can reasonably ignore this phenomenon in a short-run analysis, it would be foolish to do so in an analysis of the process of long-run growth. Consequently, we shall spend a considerable amount of time investigating the different ways in which changes in technology can influence the growth path of an economy.

The second conceptual difference between our long-run production function and the short-run version used in the labor chapter is that the capital stock must be treated as an endogenous variable in our new equation. The student will remember that the formal macro models discussed in previous chapters were based on the assumption of a fixed capital stock. As we pointed out earlier, this assumption was inconsistent with the specification of an investment equation in which *net* investment (the net change in the capital stock) was allowed to take on positive or negative values. We rationalized the use of such an inconsistent pair of notions on the grounds that it allowed us to develop and compare more easily several macro models without significantly distorting the short-run descriptions of the economy we were attempting to set out. However, now that we have turned our attention to long-run problems (in particular, the issue of secular growth), it is no longer reasonable to assume the capital stock to be constant. Instead, we must recognize that changes in the economy's stock of capital will be a major source of economic growth.

We discussed the short-run relation between labor input and the level of production when we integrated the labor market into our overall description of the economy. We noted then that as the amount of employment increases, production will increase. However, that discussion was concerned with the determination of employment (and output) *given* the conditions of supply of and demand for labor. In the short run, the size and composition of the population is given; thus, variations in employment will be made possible only by changes in the *percentage* of the population actually employed. In an analysis of long-run growth, however, we must take explicit recognition of the fact that the population changes over time (both in size and in composition). Consequently, the supply-of-labor schedule should be viewed as shifting over time (as the demographic characteristics of the economy change). In short, growth in population (and hence in the labor force) must be considered as another potential source of growth. But one must exercise caution on this point. Growth in the labor force should (*ceteris paribus*) prompt an increase in aggregate output; however, that larger output would have to be distributed over a larger population. If we are concerned with the time path of total output, population growth will generally contribute in a positive way. However, if we were to define growth in terms of per capita output (which may be more meaningful from a welfare standpoint), growth in population may either add or detract from economic growth.

To summarize our introduction to growth theory, we can say that actual long-run economic growth depends upon the movement of all three arguments of the aggregate production function: technology, capital and labor. As these factors change over time, they will not only cause changes in output, but will also, in general, cause changes in the ways in which factors are combined in the production process. For example, a change in technology could cause the economy to use either more or less capital in the production of each unit of output; or, a change in the capital stock may affect the amount of labor used per unit of output. In general, improvement in technology and growth in the factors of production generate both expansion in output and alterations in the methods of production. We shall discuss both of these effects in the course of our analysis.

Growth models come in various degrees of complexity. In general, the degree of complexity involved in any particular theory of growth is inversely related to the number of simplifying assumptions one makes about the pattern of growth of the factors of production and the resultant potential changes in the methods of production. It would be impossible for us to examine all of the theories of growth proposed over the last 200 years. First, there are far too many such theories to allow us to compress them into the few pages allocated to this topic; second, some of the more recent theories can be presented fairly and accurately only through the use of rather sophisticated mathematical techniques. Our procedure will involve the explanation of some of the more familiar and tractable growth models and a brief exposition of some of the issues involved in the specification of more complex models.

17.4   Simple Capital-Accumulation Models: Domar and Harrod

Several growth theories fall into the general category of "simple" capital-accumulation models. Perhaps the most famous examples of this body of thought are the models presented by Sir Roy Harrod and Evsey Domar. These were among the first and most important attempts to describe economic growth formally as an internal process in which the behavior of economic units, rather than the influence of outside forces, determined the patterns of growth. The Harrod and Domar models are based on the notion that investment plays a dual role in any economy. As we have emphasized in previous chapters, investment constitutes an extremely important component of aggregate demand for output. But net investment is also important from another standpoint: in that it constitutes a change in the capital stock available to the business sector, it alters the *potential* output of the economy. The fact that investment affects the product market from both the demand side *and* the supply side makes it a crucial variable in the analysis of growth.

In order to simplify the presentation of growth theory, we shall make the assumption that the state of technology remains unchanged during the period of our consideration. Although this is an unrealistic assumption, it will allow us to focus on some of the basic characteristics of the models we analyze. In a later section, we shall drop this assumption and investigate the influence on growth stemming from alternative types of technological change.

The simple capital-accumulation models of the Harrod-Domar variety are based on the assumption that, in the absence of technological change, factors of production (capital and labor) tend to be combined in some fixed proportion over time. That is, the analysis presumes that the capital-labor ratio will not change as output expands. This assumption is used to justify the specification of an extremely simple relationship between total potential output (Y^P) and the capital stock (K). This association constitutes a special case of the aggregate production function introduced in the previous case. As we shall see, the assumption of fixed factor proportions is an integral part of the Harrod-Domar models; it distinguishes those models from an alternative view of growth propounded by neoclassical growth theorists.

One of the most important questions involved in the analysis of growth revolves around the conditions under which an economy can experience balanced growth. Although there are several ways in which balanced growth can be defined, we can begin with the general idea that it is some process whereby an economy experiences both growth of productive capacity and full utilization of the expanding capacity through time.[2] In order for such a situation to be maintained, aggregate demand must expand at some rate just sufficient to keep actual output growing at the same rate as potential output. If the conditions for balanced growth are satisfied, then growth can be accomplished without being accompanied by either unemployment or excess inflation. But

---

[2] We shall provide a more formal definition of balanced growth in the next section. By then, the student should have a better feeling for the nature of growth.

what are the conditions for balanced growth? One of the first theorists to attempt to answer this question was Domar.[3]

Domar's model of growth is exceptionally simple, yet it has formed the basis for several more complicated theories. Essentially, it is based on the idea we mentioned before: that investment affects both actual output (through its influence on aggregate demand) and potential output. But positive levels of net investment may not be enough to allow balanced growth. The effect of net investment on the demand side is only temporary, in the sense that increases and decreases in net investment will cause corresponding increases and decreases in aggregate demand. But the effect of net investment on potential output is cumulative. Any positive level of net investment adds to the productive capacity of the economy. If investment declines, but remains positive, potential output still increases (although by a smaller amount than it would have increased had investment not declined at all). To illustrate the point, consider a series of five periods in which net investment takes on the following values: 100, 75, 45, 30, 20. Over these five periods, aggregate demand (at each level of income) would decrease. Between the first and second periods, aggregate demand would fall by 25; between the second and third periods, by 30; between the third and fourth periods, by 15; and so on. However, potential output would increase over the whole time interval. Each period's net investment would constitute a net increase in the economy's capital stock, and thus would allow an expansion in output. In order to have balanced growth, it is necessary that aggregate demand expand as rapidly as potential output. And this, of course, means that investment itself must *increase* over time. The requirement for steady growth reminds one of the following passage from Lewis Carroll's *Alice in Wonderland:*

> Alice looked around in great surprise. "Why, I do believe we've been under this tree all the time! Everything's just as it was."
>
> "Of course it is," said the Queen; "what would you have it?"
>
> "Well, in our country," said Alice, "you'd generally get to somewhere else if you ran very fast for a long time, as we've been doing."
>
> "A slow sort of country!" said the Queen. "Now here, you see, it takes all the running you can do to keep in the same place. If you want to get somewhere else, you must run at least twice as fast as that."
>
> Lewis Carroll, *Through the Looking-Glass*

---

[3] Evsey Domar, "Expansion and Employment," *American Economic Review* 37 (March 1947), 34–55.

If we keep in mind that the equilibrium level of income is determined by the position of aggregate demand, we can describe balanced growth as a situation in which the equilibrium level of output corresponds to the potential output of the economy. Thus, the maintenance of balanced growth requires that investment grow at some rate just sufficient to keep equilibrium and potential output expanding at the same rates. By using the simple model presented by Domar, we can find such a required rate of growth of investment.

First, one needs to establish the effects of investment on productive capacity. To do so, Domar used the convenient assumption that labor and capital are combined in a fixed proportion. In addition, he assumed that the economy experienced constant returns to scale in production. These two assumptions, taken together, allow the specification of a proportional relation between potential output and the capital stock:

$$Y_t^P = \sigma K_t. \tag{17.4.1}$$

The term σ can be referred to as the *output-capital ratio,* or the factor of proportionality between output and capital. It can also be identified as the average product of capital. The production function can also be used to derive the impact on potential output of a change in the capital stock. Taking the first difference of both sides of equation 17.4.1, we find:

$$\Delta Y_t^P = \sigma \, \Delta K_t. \tag{17.4.2}$$

In this context, the term σ is called the *marginal output-capital ratio,* and can be interpreted as the change in potential output due to a one-unit change in the capital stock. As an example, suppose that $\sigma = .5$. This would mean that the addition of one more unit of capital to the available stock would make possible the production of an extra one-half unit of output per period. We can also make use of the definition of net investment:

$$I_t \equiv \Delta K_t \tag{17.4.3}$$

to rewrite equation 17.4.2 as:

$$\Delta Y_t^P = \sigma I_t. \tag{17.4.4}$$

Equation 17.4.4 suggests that the change in potential output in the current period is proportionally related to the current *level* of net investment.

Domar's next step is to establish a relationship between investment and the change in *actual* income. He uses a model of the economy very similar to the simple one introduced earlier in chapter 3. In particular,

he assumes away government economic activity, international trade
and undistributed corporate profits to obtain a simple multiplier model
in which the change in income is equal to the multiplier times the
change in the (exogenous) level of net investment:[4]

$$\Delta Y_t = \frac{1}{1 - b} \Delta I_t. \qquad (17.4.5)$$

The term $(1 - b)$ is just the marginal propensity to save, as designated
in our earlier chapters. Notice that according to equation 17.4.5 the
change in *actual* income is related to the *change* in (rather than the level
of) net investment.

Assuming that the economy starts out in a full-employment situation
$(Y^P = Y)$, the maintenance of balanced growth requires that the
change in potential output be equal to the change in actual output in
each period:

$$\Delta Y_t^P = \Delta Y_t. \qquad (17.4.6)$$

Substituting expressions 17.4.4 and 17.4.5 into 17.4.6 we obtain:

$$\sigma I_t = \frac{1}{1 - b} \Delta I_t$$

or, multiplying both sides by $(1 - b)$ and dividing by I_t, this becomes:

---

[4] The student can derive the expression for the change in actual income by using the system:

$C_t = b Y_t$ (consumption function)

$Y_t = C_t + I_t.$ (equilibrium condition)

The alert student will note that the specification of the consumption function above differs from the one used throughout most of the chapters of the text. Domar's specification of his savings function is based on a *proportional* consumption function of the type:

$C_t = b Y_t$

whereas we used a nonproportional relation:

$C_t = a + b Y_t.$

The Domar formulation implies that $a = 0$ which means that the consumption schedule (and the savings schedule) would pass through the origin. At a zero level of income, both savings and consumption would be equal to zero. Furthermore, Domar's consumption and savings equations embody the idea that the marginal propensity to consume (MPC) is equal to the average propensity to consume (APC) and, correspondingly, that the marginal propensity to save (MPS) is equal to the average propensity to save (APS). The proportionality of the consumption and savings functions was discussed earlier in our chapter on consumption. The student might want to go back to that analysis for a quick review of the point.

$$\frac{\Delta I_t}{I_t} = \sigma(1 - b).$$ (17.4.7)

According to equation 17.4.7, it is required that investment grow at a percentage rate equal to $\sigma(1 - b)$ in order for balanced growth to result. For this reason, $\sigma(1 - b)$ is often called Domar's "required rate of growth." According to Domar, it can also be shown that if investment grows at the required rate, output will expand at an equal rate. To see this, we can use an additional assumption of the Domar model—that savings (S_t) is proportional to the level of income:[5]

$$S_t = (1 - b)Y_t.$$ (17.4.8)

We also know that in the simple static model in which international trade and governmental economic activity are ignored the equilibrium position of the economy is given by the equality of desired saving and investment; thus equation 17.4.8 can be rewritten as:

$$I_t = (1 - b)Y_t.$$ (17.4.9)

Substituting for I_t from 17.4.9 into 17.4.7, we obtain:

$$\frac{(1 - b)\,\Delta Y_t}{(1 - b)Y_t} = \sigma(1 - b)$$

or:

$$\frac{\Delta Y_t}{Y_t} = \sigma(1 - b).$$ (17.4.10)

In a sense, then, the required rate of growth is also that rate at which income should grow in order to maintain balanced growth.

To further illustrate the implications of the Domar model, we can resort to a brief numerical example. Suppose that the propensity to save $(1 - b)$ is equal to .10 and that the output-capital ratio (σ) is .5. The required rate of growth would be given by:

$$\frac{\Delta I_t}{I_t} = \frac{\Delta Y_t}{Y_t} = (.5)(.10) = .05;$$

---

[5]This form of the savings function can be derived in a straightforward fashion from the proportional consumption function:

$$C_t = bY_t$$

and the definition of savings as a residual:

$$S_t = Y_t - C_t.$$

that is, investment and income would have to grow at a 5% rate in order that actual and potential output maintain equality with each other. Suppose that the propensity to save increased from .10 to .20; then the required rate of growth would double to 10%. The intuitive meaning of this repercussion would be as follows: since as saving increases at each level of income, a higher amount of investment will be needed to satisfy the equilibrium condition ($S_t = I_t$); because of the higher levels of investment, output would have to grow more rapidly to accommodate the larger increases in the capital stock. Or, if the output-capital ratio were higher a similar adjustment in the required rate of growth would be made. Assuming that the propensity to save stays at .10 and the output-capital ratio takes on a value of .6, the required rate of growth would be .06. This result is also subject to a rationalization. Because capital is now more productive with the higher value of σ, an increase in the capital stock will generate a larger increase in potential output than before; consequently, to maintain full utilization of this extra capacity, actual output or income will have to increase correspondingly; but this higher increase in income will induce a larger increase in savings, which necessitates a larger increase in investment (in order to maintain equilibrium), which produces a larger change in the capital stock . . . and so on, as the cycle repeats itself.

The student should exercise caution in interpreting Domar's purpose and conclusions. Keep in mind that he did *not* attempt to derive a rate at which the economy *would* grow under a certain set of circumstances. In fact, he makes no explicit attempt to explain the determination of net desired investment, the crucial variable in his model. Instead, he finds only that rate at which net investment and income *should* grow in order to maintain full utilization of the growing productive capacity at each point along the economy's growth path. Thus, we are left with a *requirement* for balanced growth but with no assurance that the economy will tend toward such a pattern.

Harrod set out to analyze the process of growth with a more ambitious goal in mind.[6] In particular, he attempted to find some growth rate which, once reached, would sustain itself. This purpose required that Harrod somehow include in his model some notion of the type of behavior which underlies the growth process. Harrod used a simple capital-accumulation model in the sense that he focused major attention on the growth of the capital stock as a determinant of income growth.

---

[6]Roy Harrod, "An Essay in Dynamic Theory," *Economic Journal* 49, (March 1939), 14–33.

Thus, his basic problem in describing the impetus behind growth centered on the specification of the behavior underlying net investment.[7]

Harrod's investment equation can be derived from the relationship between the capital stock and potential output during some time period. Assuming that the output capital ratio (σ) is constant, we can specify the proportional relation:

$$\Delta Y_t^P = \sigma \, \Delta K_t. \tag{17.4.11}$$

As the student will undoubtedly remember, this is the same equation as that included in our description of the Domar growth model. If we use the identity $I_t \equiv \Delta K_t$, we can rewrite equation 17.4.11 as:

$$\Delta Y_t^P = \sigma I_t$$

or, solving for investment explicitly:

$$I_t = \frac{1}{\sigma} \Delta Y_t^P. \tag{17.4.12}$$

The term $1/\sigma$ is the marginal capital-output ratio. (Remember that σ in the Domar model was defined as the marginal output-capital ratio; we retain that notation in this discussion.) Equation 17.4.12, as it stands, is still a technological relation between capital and potential output; it does not necessarily imply anything about the *behavior* of investors. However, as we saw in chapter 13, under a certain set of assumptions, this technological equation can be transformed into the accelerator theory of investment. Two assumptions are most critical here. First, in order that σ be treated as a behavioral constant, it is necessary that the marginal capital-output ratio remain constant. Second, it is necessary to assume that existing capacity is fully utilized—i.e., that producers have no excess capital stock which they could use to step up production. By making these assumptions, we can theorize that investors will behave in correspondence with the simple accelerator relation:

---

[7] Before beginning our analysis, one point should be made clear. Harrod was somewhat vague about some of the relations included in his model. In particular, he avoided a full description of the behavior of investors. Although he did suggest an accelerator relationship between investment and the change in income, he recognized that the simple accelerator is a reasonably good investment equation only under the condition that capacity is fully utilized (see chapter 13). Unfortunately, Harrod offered no formal hypothesis to explain the behavior of investors under conditions of excess capacity. As we shall see later in this analysis, this omission makes it difficult to fully interpret some of the points made in Harrod's analysis of growth.

$$I_t = \frac{1}{\sigma}\Delta Y_t. \tag{17.4.13}$$

Given the important assumptions outlined above, the transition between equations 17.4.12 and 17.4.13 can be rationalized quite easily. The change in potential output (ΔY_t^P) can be replaced by the change in actual output (ΔY_t) due to the assumption that capacity is fully utilized in periods t and t − 1. Under this assumption, any increase in actual production will have to be accomplished by a corresponding increase in potential output (through the appropriate change in the capital stock). It is also important to keep in mind that, because equation 17.4.13 describes investor behavior, I_t refers to *desired* investment. It is the amount of investment producers would want to accomplish given the change in output they wish to put into effect.

According to equation 17.4.13, a change in output induces a certain amount of net investment. But, as we have seen many times before, investment has a feedback effect on the equilibrium level of output. We have characterized this phenomenon several times before as the multiplier effect. For simplicity, assume that there is no governmental economic activity, no undistributed corporate profits and no international trade. Under these simplifying assumptions, the multiplier can be derived from the savings (or consumption) function. We shall follow Harrod in assuming that real saving is proportional to the level of real income:[8]

$$S_t = (1 - b)Y_t \tag{17.4.14}$$

where, again, b is the propensity to consume, and $(1 - b)$ is the propensity to save. In equilibrium, saving and desired investment must be equal—i.e., investment must be just large enough to offset saving at the equilibrium level of income. Using this equilibrium condition, we can equate the level of saving given by equation 17.4.14 with the desired level of investment to get the multiplier equation:

$$I_t = (1 - b)Y_t \tag{17.4.15}$$

or, in more familiar terms:

$$Y_t = \frac{1}{1 - b}I_t. \tag{17.4.16}$$

---

[8] We follow the same procedure here as we have used in our other simple descriptions of the economy by using *real income* and *output* interchangeably.

Equation 17.4.16 expresses the equilibrium level of income in terms of the desired level of investment; the coefficient $1/(1 - b)$ is the familiar multiplier coefficient from chapter 3.

So far, we have specified two relations between investment and income: the simple accelerator equation linking current net investment and the current change in income (17.4.13) and the multiplier relation between current income and current investment (formalized in either 17.4.15 or 17.4.16). In Harrod's analysis, the growth process will be generated by the interaction of these two relationships. An increase in investment will bring about an increase in income through the multiplier effect; but the increase in income determines the level of investment through the accelerator. Given this crucial interrelation between the accelerator and the multiplier, income must be constantly growing in order to satisfy these two equations. In order to find the rate of growth of income which would result from the multiplier-accelerator interaction, we can combine equations 17.4.16 and 17.4.13 to get:

$$Y_t = \frac{1}{1 - b}\left[\frac{1}{\sigma}\Delta Y_t\right]. \tag{17.4.17}$$

With some algebraic manipulation, equation 17.4.17 can be rewritten to yield what Harrod calls the "warranted rate of growth" (signified by the term G_w):

$$\frac{\Delta Y_t}{Y_t} = \sigma(1 - b) = G_w. \tag{17.4.18}$$

In order to understand the connotation of the term *warranted,* we need only recognize that equation 17.4.18 satisfies all of the equations on which it is based. It is derived in part from the equilibrium condition that saving equals investment; it also reflects the accelerator behavior of investors. If we begin with a period in which capacity is fully utilized $(Y = Y^P)$, the behavior of investors will generate a path of income which leaves the product market in equilibrium $(I = S)$. Thus, investors will be satisfied with the amount they have invested in each period. The rate of growth of income is "warranted" in the sense that, once it is attained, there will be no tendency for investors to move away from it. In fact, the behavior of investors embodied in the acceleration principle will tend to sustain growth at the warranted rate.

The expression for the warranted growth rate, as given by equation 17.4.18, is the same as that derived for Domar's required rate of growth (17.4.10). The equivalence of these expressions should not be misconstrued to mean that the Harrod and Domar analyses are identical. Although there are obvious similarities between the two theoretical models, the interpretation of Domar's "required" rate and Harrod's "warranted" rate differ significantly. As we pointed out earlier, Domar was concerned only with growth *requirements;* he found the rate at which investment (and income) would have to grow in order that expanding productive capacity be fully absorbed. He did not suggest any particular brand of investor behavior, and thus could not comment on any tendency of the economy to grow at the required rate. On the other hand, Harrod *did* incorporate a theory of investment behavior in his model. He concluded that, if investors behave according to the simple accelerator hypothesis, there would be a tendency for the economy to grow along the warranted growth path.

But if Domar had no investment theory and Harrod did have one, why are the warranted and required rates of growth identical? The answer lies in the assumptions behind the simple accelerator theory of investment. In order that the accelerator be operative, full-capacity utilization must be maintained and the output-capital ratio must be constant. But these are the same conditions as those that lie behind Domar's required rate of growth. The crux of the issue is that Harrod's assumptions allowed him to translate the technological relation between capital and output underlying the Domar model into the theory of investment on which his growth model is based. It is thus no accident that the expressions for the required and warranted rates of growth are identical.

In order to solidify the student's understanding of the interaction of the multiplier and accelerator in Harrod's model, we have presented a numerical example in table 17.4.1. In columns 2–7, we have listed the values of the critical variables of the system. In column 1, we have designated the period under consideration. Column 7 lists the rate of growth of income generated by the system in each period. For the illustration, we have assumed that $1 - b = .25$ and that $\sigma = .40$. We have further assumed that the economy starts out in period 1 in an equilibrium position entailing full utilization of capacity—i.e., that $I_1 = S_1$ and $Y_1 = Y_1^p$. With these conditions in mind, we can trace out the time path of the variables of the system under warranted growth.

Given the values of $(1 - b)$ and σ, the warranted growth rate will be.[9]

$$G_w = (1 - b)\sigma = .25(.40) = .10. \tag{17.4.19}$$

---

[9]The student should be careful to note that the rate of growth referred to in the Harrod model is the change in output as a percentage of *current* output, not past output.

Table 17.4.1. *Harrod's Warranted Growth Path*

(1)	(2)	(3)	(4)	(5)	(6)	(7)
Period	Y_t	Y_t^P	I_t	K_t	S_t	$G_W = \Delta Y_t / Y_t$
1	99.00	99.00	24.75	247.50	24.75	—
2	110.00	110.00	27.50	275.00	27.50	.10
3	122.22	122.22	30.55	305.55	30.55	.10
4	135.80	135.80	33.95	339.50	33.95	.10
5	150.78	150.78	37.70	377.20	37.70	.10

According to the analysis we've presented above, a 10% rate of growth of income will be sustained by the economy once it is reached. Our numerical example should illustrate this point. We begin by starting the system off with a 10% increase in output. Insofar as this output decision is made initially by producers, it might be most revealing to begin with the behavior of the business sector.

Suppose that producers anticipate a 10% rise in aggregate demand from 99 to 110 in period 2. In order to accommodate this expected increase in demand, producers would have to expand their output by an equal amount. Given the assumption that capacity is fully utilized in period 1, this requires that the capital stock increase to $275 (K_2 = Y_2^P/\sigma = 110/.4 = 275)$ in the second period. Given the assumptions behind the accelerator relation, investors will *want* to set net investment equal to 27.5 in order to accommodate the increase in output. Substituting the appropriate values into 17.4.13, we have:

$$I_2 = \Delta K_2 = \frac{1}{\sigma}(Y_2 - Y_1) = \frac{1}{.4}(110 - 99) = 27.5.$$

Thus, the capital stock will increase by 27.5, from 247.5 to 275.0 and output will expand from 99 to 110—all of this resulting from the fact that producers anticipated a 10% rise in aggregate demand. But what actually happens to aggregate demand? This can be determined by tracing further through the system. Given the new level of investment (27.5), we can find the corresponding equilibrium level of output from the multiplier equation (17.4.16). Substituting the value of net investment, we find the equilibrium level of income to be:

$$Y_2 = \frac{1}{1 - b}I_2 = \frac{1}{.25}(27.5) = 110.$$

This value is consistent with the level of output actually produced by the business sector. Thus, the behavior of producers has generated a level of income which is consistent with their expectations. In the new equilibrium, the condition that saving equals investment is, of course, met. This can be verified by using equation 17.4.14 to solve for the new level of saving:

$$S_2 = (1 - b)Y_2 = .25(110) = 27.5.$$

Thus, saving and net desired investment are brought into equality at the new level of income.

We can start period 3 by looking again at the investment decision. Producers note that a 10% rise in output during the previous period was completely absorbed by aggregate demand; thus, it is reasonable to assume that they would anticipate another 10% rise in demand during period 3. If so, they will plan to set output equal to 122.22. But, again, capacity was fully utilized in the previous period; thus, an expansion of output to 122.22 requires an increase in the capital stock. Acting according to the accelerator equation, producers set investment equal to 30.55:

$$I_3 = \Delta K_3 = \frac{1}{\sigma}(Y_3 - Y_2) = 2.5(122.22 - 110) = 30.55.$$

The capital stock is thus increased from 275 to 305.55 and, with this larger capital stock, output is set equal to 122.22. Again, we must verify that this level of output will satisfy the equilibrium condition. First, we look at the equilibrium level of income corresponding to a level of net investment of 30.55:

$$Y_3 = \frac{1}{1 - b}(I_3) = \frac{1}{.25}(30.55) = 122.22.$$

This equilibrium level of income is equal to the actual output produced by the business sector. At this level, saving will be equal to desired investment:

$$S_3 = (1 - b)Y_3 = .25(122.22) = 30.55$$

and, again, producers will be satisfied with the investment plans they have followed. Subsequent periods should reveal the same process described above: producers base investment plans on the expected change in demand, and, with the new capital stock, expand output by an amount equal to the expected rise in demand; then, because of the multiplier effect, the equilibrium level of income rises into equality with the new actual level of income. Investors are "satisfied" in the sense that their output is absorbed by aggregate demand. No undesired investment (discrepancy between aggregate supply and aggregate demand) results from their behavior.

"Knife-edge Instability" in the Harrod Model

The analysis presented above describes the movement of output along some warranted growth path. According to our analysis, once the economy reaches this path, it will continue moving along it due to the interaction of the multiplier and accelerator. But the discussion presumed that, as long as businessmen are satisfied with the previous period's investment, they will increase output at the same rate as it was increased in the previous period and will expand production by securing the necessary new capital equipment. This behavior may sound eminently reasonable on intuitive grounds, but it is not legitimate for us to ignore the possibility that departures from this behavior may occur.

As an example, suppose that output has been growing at a warranted rate of 10% for several periods, but that businessmen abruptly become pessimistic about the expected increase in aggregate demand for the current period. If they exhibit this pessimism by increasing output at a rate *lower* than 10% in the current period (and buy a proportionally smaller amount of new capital than they would have to accommodate a 10% increase in output), the economy will move away from the warranted growth path. According to Harrod, such a temporary divergence from the warranted growth path would *not* be self-correcting. In fact, once the increase in output falls below the warranted rate, there will be forces in the economy which will push it even further away from that rate. The same type of repercussion supposedly occurs if the rate of growth of output exceeds the warranted rate—i.e., a movement above the warranted path will stimulate a further upward divergence. Because of the lack of self-correcting forces in the Harrod model of the economy, his warranted growth path is said to be characterized by "knife-edge instability." We now turn to an investigation of this property of the multiplier-accelerator model used by Harrod.

First, suppose that the actual rate of growth of output *exceeds* the warranted rate. If so, then we would have the inequality:

$$\frac{\Delta Y_t}{Y_t} > \sigma(1 - b). \tag{17.4.20}$$

We can rephrase 17.4.20 by tracing backward to the implied relationship between saving and desired investment. First, multiply both sides of 17.4.20 by Y_t and divide both sides by σ. This procedure yields:

$$\frac{1}{\sigma} \Delta Y_t > (1 - b)Y_t. \qquad (17.4.21)$$

Notice that the term on the left of the inequality sign is the expression for desired investment from equation 17.4.13; furthermore, the term on the right is the expression for saving from equation 17.4.14. Hence, 17.4.21 can be rewritten as:

$$I_t > S_t. \qquad (17.4.22)$$

That is, desired investment will exceed the level of saving. As a consequence, aggregate demand will *exceed* aggregate output, and producers will have an incentive to increase output even more rapidly. The inequality depicted by 16.4.20 and 16.4.22 presents us with a rather unexpected conclusion: if output grows at a rate above the warranted rate, investors will consider the actual increase in output too low and will thus expand output at an even greater rate in the next period!

The alternative situation is given by the case in which the actual growth rate dips *below* the warranted rate. Under this circumstance, the economy would be characterized by the inequality:

$$\frac{\Delta Y_t}{Y_t} < \sigma(1 - b). \qquad (17.4.23)$$

Again, we can manipulate the inequality (17.4.23) in such a way as to find the implied relation between saving and desired investment. Multiplying both sides of 17.4.23 by Y_t and dividing by σ, we obtain:

$$\frac{1}{\sigma} \Delta Y_t < (1 - b)Y_t. \qquad (17.4.24)$$

But, again, the left side of 17.4.24 represents desired investment and the right side reflects saving; thus, the inequality can be expressed as:

$$I_t < S_t. \qquad (17.4.25)$$

According to equations 17.4.23–25, any drop of the actual growth rate below the warranted rate will be accompanied by an excess of saving over desired investment. But this situation would be a signal to producers that they have produced too much. As long as saving exceeds desired investment, inventories will be piling up; or stated differently, aggregate supply will exceed aggregate demand. Producers are bound to respond to this situation by increasing output by an even smaller amount in the next period than they did in the current period. Consequently, the actual growth rate will fall even further below the warranted rate. Each successive period will bring smaller increases (and, eventually, even

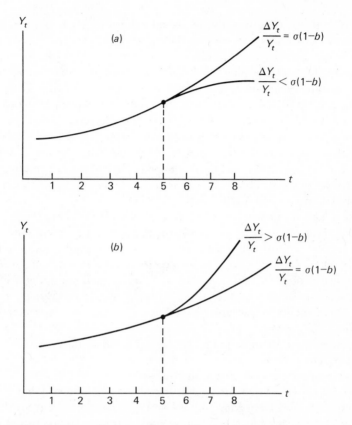

Figure 17.4.1 *Deviations from the Warranted Growth Path*

decreases) in the growth of output; and, as the change in output falls, there will be a stimulus for further contraction.

We can further illustrate the nature of the Harrod model in disequilibrium (i.e., in the case where actual growth deviates from the warranted rate) by referring to figure 17.4.1, panel (a). On the vertical axis, we have plotted income; on the horizontal axis, time. Suppose that actual growth of income follows the warranted path up through period 5, then falls below it in period 6. Due to the explosive feedback process outlined earlier, income moves successively further away from its warranted path, eventually even declining in absolute terms. In panel (b), we have depicted the opposite case. In period 6, income rises above the warranted path; thus, subsequent periods exhibit successively larger deviations.

The instability of the Harrod warranted growth path takes on additional importance once we recognize that deviations away from that path are not necessarily pure happenstance. Under some circumstances, an economy may not be able to maintain growth at the warranted rate. Furthermore, movement along the warranted growth path may not entail balanced growth if we define balanced growth more formally and meaningfully than we have done so far. In the beginning of this section, we suggested utilization of capital is a requirement of balanced growth. But this does not tell the whole story. Balanced growth (as the term is ordinarily defined) also entails full employment of the labor force. Thus, we can now offer the following formal definition: balanced growth is a situation in which output grows at some rate just sufficient to absorb all existing capital and labor into the production process. In a sense, balanced growth requires that the economy be on a path of full-employment, full-capacity equilibrium positions. Harrod's warranted rate of growth corresponds necessarily only to two of these conditions (full utilization of capital and satisfaction of the equilibrium condition that $I = S$). It may or may not correspond to full employment of the labor force, and thus may or may not depict balanced growth.

Explanation of these points requires that we introduce yet another Harrodian concept: the natural rate of growth. The natural rate of growth of output is the maximum rate which would be allowed by the expansion of the labor force. Until now, we have ignored labor almost completely and have concentrated on the expansion of output due to capital stock growth. But if, as we have assumed, factor proportions remain fixed and technology remains constant, then the labor force will have to grow at least as fast as the capital stock in order for any warranted rate of growth of output to be maintained. If the output-capital ratio is constant, and if the capital-labor ratio is constant, then production also entails a constant ratio of output to labor. But if firms maintain such a constant output-labor ratio, this means that the availability of labor becomes an important consideration. If we start out at some full-employment position (all available laborers are working), then output can grow no faster than the labor force grows.[10] Thus, under the assumptions we've built into the analysis, the natural rate of growth of output would be the rate of growth of the labor force. That is:

$$G_n = \eta \qquad\qquad (17.4.26)$$

---

[10]This result will not generally hold if technological change takes place, but we shall reserve that discussion until later.

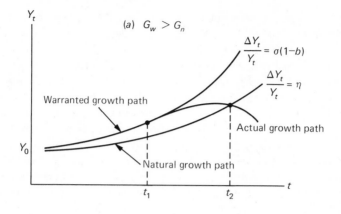

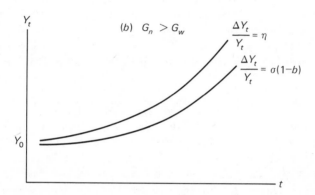

Figure 17.4.2 *Implications of Alternative Natural Rates of Growth*

where G_n is the natural rate of growth and η is the rate of growth of the labor force.

What happens if the warranted rate differs from the natural rate? For Harrod's answer to this extremely important question, turn to figure 17.4.2, panels (a) and (b). In panel (a), we have depicted the situation in which the warranted rate of growth exceeds the natural rate:

$$G_w > G_n. \tag{17.4.27}$$

In the original period, income takes on a value of Y_0; presume that this level of income entails full employment of labor and capital. As we go through time, the levels of income corresponding to the natural growth path lie below those dictated by the warranted path. Presume that the economy stays on the warranted path temporarily by using workers very intensively (e.g., through the use of overtime). Eventually, maintaining warranted growth will become impossible due to the shortage of labor; thus, the actual rate of growth will fall from the warranted rate. According to panel (a), this initial movement away from the warranted path occurs in period t_1. But, according to our earlier comments, any divergence away from the warranted path is self-reinforcing. As a result, the actual growth rate falls continuously, eventually (in period t_2) causing the actual growth path to fall below the natural path. As this happens, labor shortage is no longer a problem; in fact, unemployment starts to develop as time passes. The divergence of income away from its warranted growth path does not necessarily stop when labor shortage disappears. Instead, the behavior of investors (being disappointed in actual income growth, revising expected growth downward, and because of their own collective actions, being disappointed again in the subsequent period) would tend to promote further movement away from the warranted growth path.

An alternative case is presented in panel (b). There we have shown the situation where the natural rate of growth is higher than the warranted rate, or:

$$G_n > G_w \qquad\qquad (17.4.28)$$

This situation is relatively easy to describe. If the economy begins at Y_0, where full employment takes place, and moves through time, it is possible in the Harrod model for warranted growth to be maintained. But, in this case, unemployment is a chronic problem. Insofar as the economy is expanding too slowly to absorb the growing labor force, the level of unemployment grows over time.

In looking at these two alternative situations as reflected by panels (a) and (b), we find a rather pessimistic outlook being advanced, to say the least. Balanced growth (a correspondence between G_w and G_n) seems to be a highly unlikely prospect for any economy. As we shall see when we investigate the neoclassical arguments, this pessimistic view may not be fully justified. It is primarily the result of the rigidities of the Harrod model; if some of those rigidities are relaxed, the picture tends to brighten considerably.

17.5 The Role of Economic Policy in the Growth Process

So far, we have analyzed the mechanics of the Harrod and Domar models in order to get some insight into the process of growth. We have said nothing about the role of policymakers in the area of growth. Within the confines of the Harrod model, there is little room for overt economic policy. Since the warranted growth rate was determined by the output-capital ratio (σ) and the propensity to save $(1 - b)$, the only policy prescriptions one could make would involve changes in one of these two parameters. If, for instance, the warranted rate of growth exceeded the natural rate, it should be apparent that policymakers should attempt to lower σ or $(1 - b)$ or both. We can probably ignore the possibility that σ could be substantially affected, but it is possible that the propensity to save could be subject to some manipulation. The propensity to save probably varies across income groups, taking relatively high values for wealthier classes and relatively low values for poorer groups. According to this notion, the aggregate propensity to save could be decreased through a direct transfer of income from high-income to low-income groups. This "Robin Hood" policy would cause the warranted rate of growth to fall provided that the income transfers had no side effects on investors' behavior. Alternatively, the authorities could pursue a "consume for the sake of the economy" policy in an attempt to lower the value of $(1 - b)$.

If the warranted rate of growth happened to be too low relative to the natural rate, the opposite policies would be prescribed. In particular, income transfers from the poor to the rich could be used to increase the aggregate propensity to save. Or, policymakers could preach the doctrine of thrift in an attempt to increase growth. Interestingly, the classical economists *did* contend that thrift was the prime characteristic involved in the maintenance of high rates of growth. Only if saving was high, they suggested, could the economy devote a large amount of its resources to creation of capital. We shall pursue this point later in the chapter when we analyze the neoclassical view of growth.

The policy dicta described above would hardly fill a handbook on the appropriate exercise of policy tools. But this should be expected, in that we are attempting to draw policies from a model which was intended for other purposes. The Harrod model was meant to be only a first look at the internal process of growth under highly restrictive assumptions. It is the dynamic counterpart of the simple static model we investigated in chapter 3. In order to derive any meaningful rules of policy making, we should expand the model to include some of the policy tools introduced earlier. We shall now respecify a model similar to Harrod's, and include in it government expenditures and taxes. We shall find that, under the assumptions of the model, the manipulation of these fiscal tools can have some impact on the growth of the economy.

In general terms, the model presented below (like Harrod's) is based on a multiplier-accelerator interaction. The multiplier is derived, as usual, from the equilibrium condition that aggregate demand and aggregate supply be equal. This condition is specified as:

$$Y_t = C_t + I_t + G_t \qquad (17.5.1)$$

where G_t represents current government expenditures. Derivation of the investment multiplier requires that we make some assumptions concerning the determination of the components of aggregate demand. We shall use a consumption relation in which aggregate consumption is proportionally related to disposable income:

$$C_t = b(Y_t - T_t) \qquad (17.5.2)$$

where T_t represents total taxes and b is the propensity to consume out of disposable income. We shall further assume that the fiscal authorities generate tax revenues through the use of a proportional income tax, and that government expenditures are set equal to total tax revenues in each period (i.e., a balanced-budget policy is followed). These last two assumptions permit us to write:

$$G_t = T_t = vY_t \qquad (17.5.3)$$

where v is the tax rate. Using equations 17.5.2 and 17.5.3, the equilibrium condition (17.5.1) can be rewritten as:

$$Y_t = b(Y_t - vY_t) + I_t + vY_t. \qquad (17.5.4)$$

Notice that expression 17.5.4 involves two variables, Y_t and I_t. Although we cannot solve the equation for a unique pair of values for these variables, we can follow our familiar procedure of solving for income in terms of investment. Factoring out Y_t from the right side of the equation, we get:

$$Y_t = (b - vb + v)Y_t + I_t$$

or:

$$(1 - b + vb - v)Y_t = I_t$$

or finally:

$$Y_t = \frac{I_t}{1 - b + vb - v}. \qquad (17.5.5)$$

Equation 17.5.5 is the multiplier equation which results from our set of assumptions about the determination of government expenditures, taxes and consumption.[11] It relates the level of (or change in) income to the level of (or the change in) investment.

---

[11] As an exercise, the student might prove to himself that the multiplier given by 17.5.5 is larger than the multiplier of the Harrod and Domar models as long as b < 1.

Our next step involves the determination of investment expenditures. In order to maintain comparability with the Harrod model, we shall hypothesize an accelerator relationship between investment and the change in output. However, the simple accelerator of the Harrod framework is not satisfactory in the context of the present model, and will thus have to be modified somewhat for our use. To be more specific, the simple Harrodian accelerator equation was based on the presumption that the capital stock is increased only through *private* investment. But we have included government expenditures in our present model, and should consequently allow for the possibility that some of these public expenditures are used to create capital. As an example, the construction of a highway or the erection of a dam should be recognized as public investment rather than pure public consumption. Social capital (roads, dams, government office buildings, etc.) does play an important part in determining the productive capacity of the economy. We shall assume that some percentage (γ) of total government expenditures takes the form of net public investment.

As we have seen before, the accelerator is founded on the physical relation between potential output and the economy's capital stock. To begin the specification of our investment equation, then, we assume the following technological relationship:

$$\Delta Y_t^P = \sigma(I_t + \gamma G_t). \qquad (17.5.6)$$

The interpretation of 17.5.6 is this: the change in potential output is equal to the output-capital ratio (σ) times the net change in the aggregate capital stock; but the change in the capital stock is just total (private and public) net investment; and, as we assumed previously, public investment will be γ times total government expenditures.[12]

In order to transform 17.5.6 into a behavioral investment equation, we must assume that capital is fully utilized in periods t and t $-$ 1. This allows us to replace Y^P with Y, thus obtaining:

$$\Delta Y_t = \sigma(I_t + \gamma G_t). \qquad (17.5.7)$$

Now substituting for G_t from equation 17.5.3, we have:

---

[12]Equation 17.5.6 is based on the implicit presumption that the output-capital ratios for private and public investments will be equal. Although this may not be a very realistic assumption, it simplifies the presentation of the model with the following equation:

$$\Delta Y_t^P = \sigma_1 I_t + \sigma_2 \gamma G_t \qquad (17.5.6')$$

where σ_1 and σ_2 represent the output-capital ratios for private and public investment respectively.

$$\Delta Y_t = \sigma(I_t + \gamma v Y_t). \tag{17.5.8}$$

And this expression can be used to solve for net investment as:

$$I_t = \frac{1}{\sigma} \Delta Y_t - \gamma v Y_t. \tag{17.5.9}$$

Equation 16.5.9 can now be viewed as a modified accelerator equation. In that it differs in appearance from previous versions of the accelerator, it should be interpreted here on an intuitive level. It suggests that private investors change their capital stock in accordance with the prospective change in *their* output. The first part of the expression $[(1/\sigma) \Delta Y_t]$ represents the increase in the total (private and public) capital stock necessary to accommodate the increase in aggregate output. But part of this new capital requirement will be met through government expenditures, and this part should thus be subtracted from the total new capital requirement in order to find the desired level of private investment. But the second term in the expression $(\gamma v Y_t)$ is just the amount of government investment which will be forthcoming at the new level of output; consequently, it is subtracted from the total required increase in the capital stock. In short, 17.5.9 suggests that private investors will establish their investment needs as a residual between the total new capital requirement and the part satisfied through public investment.

We now have the two major ingredients necessary for our multiplier-accelerator growth model. The equilibrium level of income depends upon the level of investment (17.5.5), but the level of investment depends upon the change in the level of income (17.5.9). We can combine these two relations to find the warranted rate of growth of output. Toward this end, substitute for I_t from 17.5.9 into 17.5.5 to obtain:

$$Y_t = \left(\frac{1}{1 - b + vb - v}\right)\left(\frac{1}{\sigma} \Delta Y_t - \gamma v Y_t\right).$$

Now, multiply both sides of the equation by the multiplier:

$$(1 - b + vb - v)Y_t = \frac{1}{\sigma} \Delta Y_t - \gamma v Y_t$$

and add $\gamma v Y_t$ to both sides:

$$(1 - b + vb - v + \gamma v)Y_t = \frac{1}{\sigma} \Delta Y_t.$$

We can solve for the percentage change in income by multiplying both sides of the equation by σ and dividing by Y_t to get:

$$\frac{\Delta Y_t}{Y_t} = \sigma(1 - b + vb - v + \gamma v).$$

Finally, we can simplify the expression within parentheses by factoring v out of the last three terms. This yields a relatively uncomplicated expression for the warranted rate of growth:

$$\frac{\Delta Y_t}{Y_t} = \sigma(1 - b) - \sigma v(1 - b - \gamma). \qquad (17.5.10)$$

Given the behavior of consumers, investors and public authorities, the above rate of growth will tend to be maintained once it is reached. Notice that we have broken this new expression for warranted rate of growth into two terms. The first of these terms, $\sigma(1 - b)$, is identical to the Harrodian warranted rate. The inclusion of government expenditures and taxes in the model modifies the warranted rate by way of the second term, $\sigma v(1 - b - \gamma)$. The effects of public economic activity will depend on the values of the parameters contained in that second term. To begin our comparison with the Harrod model, note that if $v = 0$ (i.e., if the government is withdrawn from the model), the entire expression in 17.5.10 collapses into Harrod's warranted rate. If $v > 0$ (i.e., if government economic activity does take place) the warranted growth rate could be larger or smaller than the "no-government" rate, depending on the sign of the second term. In order for the warranted growth rate to be larger with government activity, the following inequality would be necessary:

$$-\sigma v(1 - b - \gamma) > 0. \qquad (17.5.11)$$

We should be able to interpret the meaning of this inequality, but a few mechanical procedures are first necessary. As long as σ and v are positive, we can divide both sides of 17.5.11 by σv without affecting the inequality; hence, we have:

$$-(1 - b - \gamma) > 0 \qquad (17.5.12)$$

as a shortened form of condition 17.5.11. To go one step further, add $(1 - b)$ to both sides of 17.5.12 to get:

$$\gamma > 1 - b. \qquad (17.5.13)$$

This inequality should yield some insight into the growth effects of government expenditures and taxes. According to 17.5.13, the proportion of government expenditures going to public investment (γ) must be larger than the propensity to save $(1 - b)$ in order for governmental activity of the kind described above to have a positive effect on the warranted growth rate. This condition becomes extremely plausible if we recall that the derivation of the warranted rate of growth included a stipulation that G = T; this, in turn, means that equilibrium requires the equality of savings and desired investment. If the propensity to save depicts the portion of disposable income going to savings, and if savings and investment are equated along the warranted growth path, then $(1 - b)$ also reflects the percentage of disposable income going toward private investment. By similar reasoning, γ represents the percentage of tax revenues devoted to the provision of public capital.

Thus, 17.5.13 suggests that if the percentage of tax revenues going to public investment is greater than the percentage of after-tax income going to private investment, then governmental economic activity will raise the warranted growth rate. Suppose, for instance, that the propensity to save is .10 and the percentage of taxes devoted to public investment is .20. If so, the expansion of the capital stock is increased by the process of public economic activity. If income is equal to $500 billion in some period, and if the tax rate is equal to .20, total tax receipts would be $100 billion. Out of this latter amount, $10 billion would have been invested through the private market system; but, out of the same amount, the authorities invest $20 billion. This has the effect of expanding the capital stock (and potential income) more rapidly than would have been the case in the absence of taxes and government expenditures. Thus, the warranted growth rate would be higher in our new model than it would be in a pure Harrodian model. Similar reasoning suggests, of couse, that if γ is smaller than $(1 - b)$, the inclusion of the public sector will decrease the growth rate. The proof of this proposition will be left to the student.

The point made above is not a trivial one. It leads us to the related conclusion that fiscal policy can be used to regulate growth. If $\gamma >$ $(1 - b)$, an increase in the value of v will increase the warranted growth rate and a decrease in the value of v will decrease that rate; alternatively, if $\gamma < (1 - b)$, an increase in the value of v will decrease the warranted growth rate and a decrease in v will cause the warranted growth rate to increase. In fact, the authorities themselves are free to choose the values of both v and γ in such a way as to reach a desired rate of growth. A change in v is a straightforward process; it involves an equal change in government expenditures and taxes (a balanced-budget policy of the type explained in chapter 4). A change in γ involves a decision to devote a smaller or larger share of public expenditures to the creation of capital. To the extent that fiscal policy can be used to affect the warranted rate of growth, discrepancies between the warranted and the natural rate need not automatically damn the economy to the fates described by Harrod. If the natural rate of growth is greater than the warranted rate, policy can be aimed at increasing the warranted rate. Assuming that $\gamma < (1 - b)$, an increase in v would be an appropriate policy in such a situation. Alternatively, if the warranted rate is greater than the natural rate, policymakers could attempt to decrease the former rate. In this case, again assuming that $\gamma > (1 - b)$, the value of v could be decreased toward this end. It thus becomes apparent that economic policy can be used to help promote balanced growth.

17.6 Neoclassical Growth Theory

The simple Harrod-Domar type of capital-accumulation growth models constituted a major step in the evolution of growth theory, in spite of the fact that they had several deficiencies.[13] One of their most important shortcomings was that they were based on the presumption of a constant capital-output (or output-capital) ratio. Ignoring the impact of technological change, such an assumption implies a lack of substitutability between the factors of production. And, as we shall see later in the analysis, the constancy of the capital-output ratio also restricts the types of technological change admissible within the confines of the model. Neoclassical growth theory is—at least in part—a reaction to the rigidities implied by the Domar and Harrod models. This section offers a very basic introduction to some of the concepts interwoven in neoclassical growth theory.

The student should recall from elementary micro theory that factors of production are generally substitutable for each other. That is, a given level of output can be produced in the long run with several alternative combinations of the factors of production. With an eye toward profit maximization, the individual firm chooses that combination of the factors which would be the least-cost combination able to produce a certain output. In loose terms, the process of cost minimization at each level of output entails an evaluation of the relative prices of the factors and their relative marginal products. If either their relative prices or their relative marginal products change, the firm will substitute one factor for the other(s). The use of a constant capital-output ratio tends

---

[13]All growth models must, by nature, treat the problem of capital accumulation. When we refer subsequently to "capital-accumulation growth models" we shall be referring to the Harrod-Domar type of exposition.

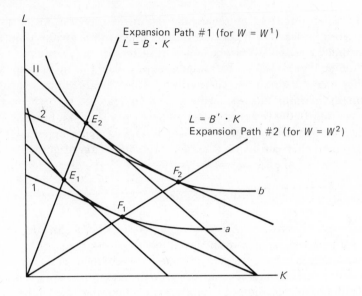

Figure 17.6.1 *The Firm's Expansion Paths with Alternative Wage Rates*

to ignore the possibility that such substitution takes place in the economy over time.

Figure 17.6.1 can be used to illustrate the point raised above. In that diagram, we have represented a set of isoquants and two alternative sets of isocosts.[14] Each of the isoquants (*a* and *b*) reflects the combinations of labor and capital that could be used to produce a specific level of output, given technology. Suppose that the prices of capital and labor are r^1 and W^1 respectively, thus allowing us to sketch a series of isocost schedules like I and II. The firm can minimize its total cost of production at each level of output by choosing that combination of labor and capital for which the following condition holds:

$$\frac{MP_n}{MP_k} = \frac{W^1}{r^1}. \tag{17.6.1}$$

Equation 17.6.1 is the (hopefully) familiar tangency condition for cost minimization. The schedule connecting all equilibrium points

---

[14] Students not familiar with isoquant-isocost analysis should consult a micro theory text. Although there are several excellent ones from which to choose, we might recommend one of the following: C. E. Ferguson, *Microeconomic Theory* (Homewood, Ill.: R. D. Irwin, 1972); R. A. Bilas, *Microeconomic Theory: A Graphical Approach* (New York: McGraw-Hill, 1972).

(i.e., those which satisfy 17.6.1) is called the firm's *expansion path*. For simplicity, let us assume that the expansion path in question (E_1, E_2, E_3 . . .) is linear. If so, it reflects a constant ratio of capital to labor over all scales of output. But the expansion path is contingent upon a particular ratio of factor prices. If the ratio W/r changes, the expansion path will shift. For example, suppose that the wage rate increases from W^1 to W^2. As a result of this change, the whole family of isocost schedules will become steeper. Under the factor-market conditions embodied in the new set of isocosts, (1,2, . . .) the firm will minimize total costs at each level of output by choosing that combination of labor and capital for which:[15]

$$\frac{MP_n}{MP_k} = \frac{W^2}{r^1}.$$

Insofar as labor is now relatively more expensive than it was initially, one would expect the firm to substitute capital for labor. This is reflected by the new expansion path (F_1, F_2, . . .): in particular, take note of the fact that the capital-labor ratio is uniformly higher along the new expansion path than it was along the original one. The general point is this: changes in relative factor prices will induce changes in the capital-labor ratio. But we shouldn't really stop here. It also be shown that, given technology, a change in the capital-labor ratio will ordinarily cause a corresponding change in the capital-output (or output-capital) ratio. If, at each level of output, the firm uses more capital and less labor than it did originally, then the ratio of output to capital will fall at each output. For example, if an output of 20 units originally entailed the use of 10 units of labor and 50 units of capital, the capital-labor ratio would be 5.0 and the capital-output ratio would be 2.5 (50 divided by 20). But suppose that a rise in the wage rate induces the firm to use 9 units of labor and 54 units of capital in order to produce the same level of output. If so, the capital-labor ratio would

---

[15]The student should remember that the slope of an isocost schedule is given by $-W/r$; thus, as W increases, each isocost takes on a more strongly negative slope.

It is not possible to offer a conclusive proof here that a change in the capital-labor ratio will *always* cause a corresponding change in the capital-output ratio when the level of output changes itself. Whether or not this is true depends on the particular properties of the production function. All that we can verify at this point is that a change in the capital-labor ratio will cause a corresponding change in the capital-output ratio *at some given level of output*. Nevertheless, it turns out that for most reasonable production functions, the same can be shown for the case where output varies due to a change in one of the factor prices. It is true that if we assume a Cobb-Douglas production function, an increase (decrease) in the capital-labor ratio will cause a corresponding increase (decrease) in the capital-output ratio.

rise from 5.0 to 6.0; correspondingly, the capital-output ratio would increase from 2.5 to 2.7 (54 divided by 20).

The general point to be understood from this exercise in micro theory is that, under general conditions, labor and capital will be substitutable to some degree. Changes in the relative prices of these factors will induce firms to alter the factor intensity of their production processes. But, if factors are substitutable, how realistic is the Harrod-Domar assumption of a fixed capital-output ratio? Isn't it possible that the capital-output ratio changes over time as the general level of factor intensity fluctuates? An investigation of these points allows us to focus on some of the basic differences between the capital-accumulation theories and the neoclassical approach.

In the Harrod model, allowance is made for differences in the rates of growth of factor supplies. According to Harrod, discrepancies between G_n and G_w would have rather serious consequences. As we noted earlier, if the rate of growth of the labor force exceeded the warranted rate of growth, serious unemployment would be a chronic problem. This notion has a Keynesian flavor in the sense that it is implicitly assumed that the market mechanism will fail to reestablish a full-employment equilibrium in the labor market. Regardless of the fact that the labor force is growing more rapidly than labor is being absorbed into production, wage adjustments either fail to occur or, if they do happen, have no effect on the rate at which labor is absorbed. In the alternative case, where the rate of growth of the labor force is below the warranted rate of growth, the economy is unable to maintain growth at the warranted rate. Again, the Harrod model exhibits a high degree of rigidity. The relatively slow expansion of the labor force precludes a more rapid growth of output. The relative scarcity of labor prompts no adjustments in the relative prices of the factors of production—or, if such an adjustment occurs, it has no effect on the relationship between the rate of growth of labor and the potential rate of growth of output.

The matter can be put in slightly different terms. If labor and capital grow at different rates, one would expect some change in their relative prices. And, given any change in the factor-price ratio, factor substitution should take place. To go one step further, the change in the capital-labor ratio effected by substitution would, in the case of our constant-returns-to-scale production function, induce a change in the desired capital-output ratio (an increase or a decrease, depending on the change in the capital-labor ratio). This series of arguments describes one of the basic lines of thought underlying neoclassical growth theory. In what follows, we shall pursue the point from the view of the neoclassical theorists and attempt to use it to contrast capital-accumulation and neoclassical growth models.

Simple capital-accumulation growth theories tend to emphasize the demand side of the growth process. As was the case in the Harrod model, both the investment function and the consumption (savings) function are key ingredients. The supply side tends to be deemphasized. In fact, the full specification of a production function is replaced with a relatively naive special case of a proportional relation between the capital stock and the level of aggregate output. Full-employment equilibrium seems to have been considered a happy—but unlikely—occurrence.

By contrast, neoclassical growth theorists tend to be significantly more optimistic. They place a great deal of faith in the operation of factor markets by assuming—either explicitly or implicitly—that factor markets will act in such a way as to ensure full-employment equilibrium. As we shall see, they presume that investment will adjust to the level of full-employment saving and that the labor force will be absorbed into production. Since the neoclassical theorists generally assume that the economy will tend toward full-employment equilibrium over time, their attention is focused on the determination of the time path of that full-employment level of output. Although this reliance on the efficiency of factor markets obscures the demand-side problems pointed out by Keynes, the neoclassical growth models do offer a much more sophisticated view of the supply side of aggregate economic activity than that presented by the capital-accumulation theorists.

In order to capture the spirit of the neoclassical approach to growth theory, let's return to the statement of the warranted and natural rates of growth. As will be remembered, the warranted rate of growth was the rate of growth of output and the capital stock which would equate desired savings and investment. Using the notation established earlier, the warranted growth rate is given by:

$$G_w = (1 - b)\sigma \qquad (17.6.2)$$

where $(1 - b)$ is the marginal (average) propensity to save and σ is the output-capital ratio. The natural rate of growth (the rate of growth of the labor force) is denoted by:

$$G_n = \eta. \qquad (17.6.3)$$

According to the neoclassical theorists, the economy will tend toward a balanced growth path which entails full employment of labor over time. In order for this to be true, however, it is necessary that the natural rate of growth be equal to the warranted rate. That is, the neoclassical connotation of balanced growth could be characterized by the condition:

$$G_w = G_n \qquad (17.6.4)$$

or:

$$(1 - b)\sigma = \eta. \tag{17.6.5}$$

In the Harrod model, b, σ and η were all treated as constants; thus, the equality of the natural and warranted growth rates would be, at best, unlikely. But the neoclassical school contended that the desired output-capital ratio (σ) should be specified as a variable. The rationale for this contention was that the desired output-capital ratio will depend upon the relative rates of growth of capital and labor. If σ is treated as a variable, then it is possible to find a value for it which would satisfy the conditions for balanced growth. In particular, the appropriate value for σ could be derived from equation 17.6.5 as:

$$\sigma = \frac{\eta}{(1 - b)}. \tag{17.6.6}$$

Given the rate of growth of the labor force and the propensity to save, the output-capital ratio would have to take on the value given by equation 17.6.6 in order to have both "warranted" (equilibrium) growth and full employment. The important contention of the neoclassical school is that this adjustment to the appropriate output-capital ratio will be accomplished through the factor-market mechanisms. This is the point to which we turn now.

Two basic ingredients are needed for our illustration of the neoclassical argument. First, we need a production function to characterize the actual aggregate technical relationship between inputs and output. For simplicity, we choose a Cobb-Douglas production function:

$$Y = AK^\beta N^{1-\beta}. \tag{17.6.7}$$

Since we intend to depict this function later in a two-dimensional diagram, we would like to express it in terms of two variables. Therefore, we divide both sides of 17.6.7 by N to obtain:

$$\frac{Y}{N} = A\left(\frac{K}{N}\right)^\beta. \tag{17.6.8}$$

The interpretation of 17.6.8 is that output per person (or per unit of labor) is directly related to the amount of capital per person. The second relation to be used is a restatement of the balanced-growth condition (17.6.6). Using the definition of σ as the output-capital ratio, we can write:

$$\frac{Y}{K} = \frac{\eta}{1 - b}$$

or:

$$Y = \frac{\eta}{1 - b} K. \tag{17.6.9}$$

And, to facilitate our diagrammatic analysis, we divide both sides of equation 17.6.9 by N to obtain:

$$\frac{Y}{N} = \frac{\eta}{1 - b} \cdot \frac{K}{N}. \tag{17.6.10}$$

Equation 17.6.10 can be interpreted intuitively as representing the relationship between output per person and the capital-labor ratio which must hold in order that equilibrium be maintained and the labor force be fully employed.

Notice that we've established two relationships between the output-labor ratio and the capital-labor ratio: one representing the actual production function (17.6.8) and the other characterizing the balanced-growth condition (17.6.10). In figure 17.6.2, we have depicted both of these relations. The shape of the production function exhibits the assumption of diminishing returns to capital (for our Cobb-Douglas function, this is expressed by the constraint that $0 < \beta < 1$). The balanced-growth condition is specified as a straight line, which follows from the assumption that η and b are both constant. The economy must operate somewhere along the schedule of the production function, inasmuch as it is a locus of feasible points of production for different factor mixes. As one can see from figure 17.6.2, there is only one value of the capital-labor ratio which would permit the economy to trace out a balanced-growth path. In particular, this value, $(K/N)_1$, is determined at the intersection of the production schedule and the balanced-growth line at point E. Corresponding to this capital-labor ratio will be an optimum value for the output-labor and the output-capital ratios. According to figure 17.6.2, the output per person associated with balanced growth is $(Y/N)_1$; furthermore, it should be apparent that the balanced-growth output-capital ratio could be found algebraically as:

$$\left(\frac{Y}{K}\right)_1 = \frac{\left(\frac{Y}{N}\right)_1}{\left(\frac{K}{N}\right)_1}.$$

It is interesting to note here that, in the absence of technological change, the neoclassical conditions for balanced growth call for output, capital and labor to grow at the same rate. This interpretation follows from the fact that, in the state of balanced growth defined by point E, the output-labor ratio is constant (which means that output and labor must grow at identical rates) and the capital-labor ratio is constant

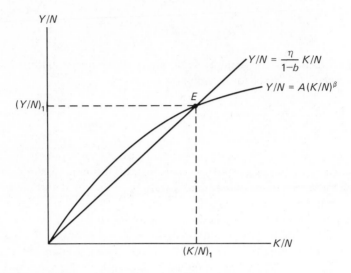

Figure 17.6.2   *Achievement of Balanced Growth in the Neoclassical Model*

(which implies that capital and labor must grow at equal rates). The balanced growth rate will be η, the natural rate of growth of labor.

The establishment of the conditions for balanced growth does not constitute a theory of growth per se. In order to have a meaningful theory in this respect, it is necessary to offer some hypothesis concerning the growth tendencies of the economy. The neoclassics do offer such a hypothesis: they contend that, in general, market forces will tend to push the economy toward the balanced-growth path.[16] In terms of figure 17.6.2, this can be translated as a hypothesis that any divergence from the balanced-growth condition (i.e., operation at E) will tend to be self-correcting. If this is true, then we say that the balanced-growth equilibrium is *stable*. In order to illustrate the stability of the system, we shall choose initial capital-labor ratios other than $(K/N)_1$ and shall explain why the economy would move back to $(K/N)_1$.

See figure 17.6.3 for our exposition. Suppose that the economy is currently operating at point H, where the capital-labor ratio is $(K/N)_2$ and the corresponding output per man is $(Y/N)_2$. Notice that point H lies above the balanced-growth line. Because of this, we have the following inequality:

---

[16]The self-correcting nature of the system depends on the characteristics of the production function. Given certain shapes for the production-function schedule, the balanced-growth equilibrium may not be stable. As an exercise, the student might try drawing the schedule of the production function so that it crosses the balanced-growth line from below and then check the stability of the equilibrium.

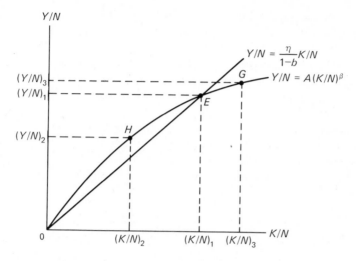

Figure 17.6.3 *Stability of Balanced-Growth Point*

$$\frac{Y}{N} > \frac{\eta}{1-b}\frac{K}{N}. \tag{17.6.11}$$

If we divide both sides of 17.6.11 by $[1/(1-b)]\,(K/N)$, we obtain:

$$(1-b)\frac{Y}{K} > \eta$$

or, expressing the output-capital ratio as σ:

$$(1-b)\sigma > \eta. \tag{17.6.12}$$

But notice that 17.6.12 just suggests that the warranted rate of growth of output and capital exceeds the rate of growth of the labor force. Under these circumstances, a condition of excess labor demand will initially develop at the going factor prices. This will cause an increase in the wage rate, and, as a consequence, encourage substitution of capital for labor. But, as capital is substituted for labor, the capital-labor ratio increases.[17] As long as there is any excess demand for labor, wages rise and the capital-labor ratio increases. In other terms, as long as the warranted rate of growth of capital and output exceeds that of labor, the

---

[17]To see this more directly, one could construct a series of rays from the origin to the schedule of the production function, and could compute the output-capital ratio at each value of K/N as the slope of the ray from the origin to the corresponding point on the production schedule. Doing so, it could be shown directly that the slope of the ray from 0 to H is higher than that of the ray from 0 to E. As we move along the production schedule from H to E, the slope of the ray (or, in other words, the output-capital ratio) declines.

capital-labor ratio will tend toward its balanced growth level, $(K/N)_1$; and, as this happens, output per person moves toward $(Y/N)_1$. Accordingly, it should be apparent that the output-capital ratio (which was assumed to be constant in the Harrod analysis) goes back toward its balanced-growth level, $(Y/K)_1$. Insofar as output is becoming more capital-intensive, the output-capital ratio decreases as the economy moves from H to E.

The alternative type of discrepancy from neoclassical balanced-growth would occur if the capital-labor ratio exceeds the value $(K/N)_1$. Suppose that the capital-labor ratio is currently at $(K/N)_3$. If so, then the economy will initially operate at G and the following inequality will hold:

$$\frac{Y}{N} < \frac{\eta}{1-b}\frac{K}{N} \tag{17.6.13}$$

or:

$$\frac{Y}{K} < \frac{\eta}{1-b}$$

which can be translated into:

$$(1-b)\sigma < \eta. \tag{17.6.14}$$

According to equation 17.6.14, the warranted rate of growth which would correspond to $(K/N)_3$ would be lower than the natural rate of growth. According to Harrod's analysis, this condition would result in chronic unemployment of labor. But in the neoclassical framework, unemployment (excess supply) in the labor market induces a fall in labor's wage. And, inasmuch as labor and capital are substitutable, this would induce an increase in the labor intensity of production. Or, in terms of the diagrammatic treatment, the capital-labor ratio would move from $(K/N)_3$ toward $(K/N)_1$ and the output-labor ratio from $(Y/N)_3$ to $(Y/N)_1$. In addition the output-capital ratio would rise as reflected in the steepening of the ray from the origin as it goes from OG to OE. Balanced-growth conditions would thus be reattained through the operation of the factor markets.

We saw that in the Harrod framework the economy's warranted rate of growth could be increased (decreased) by increasing (decreasing) the savings ratio. This conclusion does not hold for the neoclassical model; that is, a change in the savings ratio will not affect the balanced-growth rate itself. This can be illustrated by reference to the neoclassical balanced-growth condition:

$$(1 - b)\sigma = \eta. \qquad\qquad\qquad (17.6.15)$$

If $(1 - b)$ increases, balanced growth would necessitate a decrease in σ in order that the condition 17.6.15 would still hold. In other words, as long as the natural rate of growth, η, is constant, the output-capital ratio will have to vary in such a way as to offset any change in $(1 - b)$. In intuitive terms, an increase in the savings ratio would require that investment be higher at each level of income; in order for this to be accomplished, the capital intensity of production would have to increase (i.e., the output-capital ratio would have to fall). The process through which all of this would supposedly occur depends on one's notion of the characteristics of the capital market.

What we have presented in this section does not constitute a full neoclassical growth model. Instead, we have simply pointed out some of the common tendencies involved in almost all neoclassical descriptions of the growth process. We found that neoclassical models tend to emphasize the supply side, rather than the demand side, of the determination of aggregate output. We also noted that these models are based on a strong reliance on market mechanisms, especially in the labor and capital markets. Due to the presumed substitutability of factors of production, the *method* of production adapts to accommodate the natural rate of growth of labor. In particular, the output-capital ratio is flexible enough to bring the warranted rate of growth of the economy into equality with the natural rate of growth. In the state of balanced growth, labor, capital and output grow at equal rates.

If we were to analyze any particular neoclassical growth model, we would have to include a description of the market relationships of the economy. For example, we would have to define an explicit savings function, an investment function, a supply of labor function, and so forth. In addition we would have to take some notice of the existence of technological change—something we have ignored so far. Although we shall not examine any specific neoclassical models (and thus shall not consider specific sets of market relationships), we shall offer a brief introduction to the nature of technological change. This analysis is warranted by the unquestionable importance of technological change in the economic history of any developed country.

16.7 Technological Change

Although several classifications of technological change into "types" are possible, we can begin by suggesting two broad categories: innovations in the design of goods and services, and innovations in the modes of production. The first type pertains to the introduction of new (improved?) goods and services which are designed to meet new needs or satisfy old ones. Several examples of product innovation come to mind: the automobile at the turn of the century, television in the 1940s, and the hula hoop of the 1960s. The second type of technological change involves improvements in the quality of the factors of production and/or in the organization of the production process. A very diverse set of examples could fit this definition: the introduction of the Bessemer process, the provision of improved training of the labor force, the creation of improved transportation facilities, the use of the steam engine, and so on ad infinitum.

Obviously, the two broad classes of innovation are not mutually exclusive. To the contrary, the introduction of a new product often entails the use of new production technology. However, we can at least make a conceptual distinction along the lines suggested above. Although both types of technological change are important in the study of economic growth, we shall restrict our attention to the second class: improvements in the production process. The essential reason for this narrow approach is that the latter type of technological progress entails changes in productivity and thus directly allows expansion in the growth of production.

Neutral vs. Nonneutral Technological Change

The introduction of any technological change in production processes is designed to increase the productivity of at least one of the factors of production—to allow a larger level of output with a given amount of inputs, or, stated a bit differently, to allow the use of fewer inputs in the production of a given amount of output. The type of technological change occurring in an economy will help to determine the ways in which labor and capital are combined in production over time. Because factor productivities are changed, it is possible that technological change will bring about a revision of the optimal factor proportions used in the economy. As a result, the time path of technology will be an extremely important factor in the process of economic growth.

Technological change is often sorted into two general classes: neutral and nonneutral. In most general terms, neutral technological change refers to the constancy of the marginal product of one or more of the factors of production. Because technological change involves changes in the production function itself (as exemplified by shifts of the isoquants analyzed earlier), the constancy of the marginal product(s) in question must be specified with some point of reference. For example, neutrality can be defined in terms of what happens to marginal productivities at some capital-labor ratio, capital-output ratio, or output-labor ratio as technology changes. Because of the difficulty involved in characterizing neutral and nonneutral technological change in general terms, it is necessary to look at three distinct types of classification. Our discussion will touch on the definitions of neutrality offered by three growth theorists: John Hicks, Roy Harrod and Robert Solow.

Hicks-neutral and Nonneutral Change

Hicks categorizes technological change according to its effects on the *ratio* of the marginal products of capital and labor at some given factor proportion. First, he considers an innovation neutral if it raises the marginal products of all factors by the same proportion, and hence leaves relative marginal products unchanged, at a given capital-labor ratio. Given relative factor prices and given the existence of constant returns to scale, such a neutral technological change will leave factor proportions unchanged. The second possibility is that an innovation may be nonneutral; that is, it may cause a nonproportional change in the marginal products of the factors at the given capital-labor ratio. In this event, we can expect factor substitution to take place.

In the Hicksian framework, nonneutral technological change can be either relatively labor-saving or relatively capital-saving (labor-using). If an innovation increases the marginal product of capital relative to the marginal product of labor, he designates it as relatively labor-saving because it induces a substitution of capital for labor at each level of output. Alternatively, any innovation which increases the marginal product of labor relative to the marginal product of capital is considered relatively capital-saving since it encourages the substitution of labor for capital.

Hicks-neutral technological change constitutes a uniform improvement in the quality of *both* labor and capital. Consequently, it does not, in itself, encourage substitution between factors of production. We can use our concept of an aggregate production function in order to further analyze the nature of this type of innovation. In general terms, technology can be introduced into the production function as an argument. Let T_t represent the state of technology at time t. Then aggregate output would be given by:

$$Y_t = F(K_t, N_t, T_t). \tag{17.7.1}$$

If technological change is Hicks-neutral, then we can use the special form:

$$Y_t = a_t F(K_t, N_t) \qquad (17.7.2)$$

in order to describe the production process. The term a_t is defined as any positive function of T_t (i.e., as T_t increases, a_t increases). Notice that a_t has the effect of increasing the output an economy is able to produce at each combination of K_t and N_t (i.e., we define a_t so that $a_t > 0$).

Harrod-neutral and Nonneutral Change

Harrod defines neutral and nonneutral technological change in a different fashion than does Hicks. In particular, Harrod-neutrality involves a change in technology which leaves the marginal product of capital unchanged at a given capital-output ratio. It can be characterized as a uniform improvement in the quality or efficiency of the labor force. This type of technical progress is ordinarily attributed to increased educational opportunities for workers, but is assumed to apply to *all* workers (those recently hired as well as those in the working force for a long period of time).

More formally, Harrod-neutral technical progress implies that the aggregate production function can be written as:[18]

$$Y = F(K, a'N) \qquad (17.7.3)$$

where a′ is an index of the state of technology, or stated differently, a′ is an index of the efficiency per unit of labor at time t. Because of the way in which technology enters the production process in this case, Harrod-neutral technological change is said to be *labor-augmenting*. In terms of efficiency, a 10% increase in a′ would have the same effect as a 10% increase in the labor force. Or, as Hahn and Matthews put it: "Population growth causes there to be two men where there was previously one; Harrod-neutral technical progress causes one man to be able to do twice what he could have done previously."[19]

Because of this close analogy between Harrod-neutral progress and the growth of the labor force, we could consider the expression a′N as a measure of the labor force in "efficiency units." This definitional trick would allow us to recast the neoclassical model developed earlier by substituting labor measured in terms of efficiency for labor measured

---

[18]For notational simplicity, the time subscript will be dropped in subsequent equations.

[19]F. H. Hahn and R. C. O. Matthews, "The Theory of Economic Growth: A Survey," in *Surveys of Economic Theory: Growth and Development* (New York: St. Martin's Press, 1967), p. 50.

in man-hours. The conclusions we could draw from such an analysis would parallel those derived from the original specification in which changes in technology were assumed absent. In particular, we could find an output-capital ratio which would equate the warranted and natural rates of growth. Steady growth would be possible in the sense that output, capital and labor measured in efficiency units would be growing at equal rates. The balanced-growth condition would be reformulated as:

$$(1 - b)\sigma = \eta' \tag{17.7.4}$$

where η' is the rate of growth of labor measured in efficiency units, and $(1 - b)\sigma$ is the warranted rate of growth of output and capital. This condition could be restated as:

$$(1 - b)\frac{Y}{K} = \eta'$$

or: $$Y = \frac{\eta'}{1 - b}K$$

or, finally:

$$\frac{Y}{N} = \frac{\eta'}{1 - b}\frac{K}{N}. \tag{17.7.5}$$

The Cobb-Douglas production function, specified to include Harrod-neutral technical progress, would be:

$$Y = AK^\beta(a'N)^{1-\beta}$$

which could be rewritten as:

$$\frac{Y}{N} = A\left(\frac{K}{a'N}\right)^\beta. \tag{17.7.6}$$

Depicting equations 17.7.5 and 17.7.6 diagrammatically, we would obtain the schedules shown in figure 17.7.1. Notice that the axes now represent "output per efficiency unit of labor" and "capital per efficiency unit of labor." Balanced growth would occur at E, where the actual production process satisfies the balanced-growth condition. In the absence of any change in the parameters, the ratios established at E would be maintained throughout the process of growth. Let's analyze the balanced-growth values of each of these ratios. First, the ratio of K to a'N would be set at $(K/a'N)_1$. This means that, as technological progress occurs (i.e., as a' increases over time), the actual capital-labor

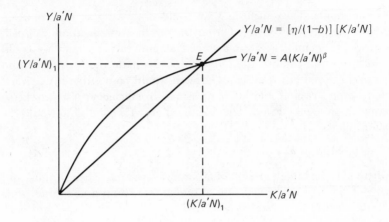

Figure 17.7.1   *Harrod-Neutral Technological Change*

ratio (K/N) would have to increase. In other words, although the balance between capital and efficiency units of labor would remain constant, this would imply fewer workers per unit of capital as technology improves. This characteristic is also reflected in the output-labor ratio. The ratio of output to efficiency units of labor would remain at $(Y/a'N)_1$ over time; however, as a' increases, this requires the actual output-labor ratio to increase. But this just means that output per person will increase as labor-augmenting technological growth takes place. This conclusion should appear plausible on intuitive grounds.

The third ratio to be considered is the output-capital ratio. As before, we can find its equilibrium value $(Y/K)_1$ by dividing the equilibrium values of the other two relevant ratios. In particular, we now have:

$$\left(\frac{Y}{K}\right)_1 = \frac{\left(\dfrac{Y}{a'N}\right)_1}{\left(\dfrac{K}{a'N}\right)_1}.$$

An interesting conclusion can be derived here. Notice that the output-capital ratio remains constant as Harrod-neutral progress happens. This, in fact, is why Harrod made the assumption that technological change was labor-augmenting when he specified the growth model we analyzed in section 17.4. This assumption allowed him to ignore the impact of technological change on the output-capital ratio.

Solow-neutral Technological Change

Robert Solow uses yet another approach in dividing technological change into neutral and nonneutral varieties. He defines neutral technical progress as any change in technology which leaves the marginal product of labor constant at a given output-labor ratio. Notice that this definition is analogous to that used by Harrod, with the term *labor* replacing *capital.* Whereas Harrod-neutral progress was labor-augmenting, Solow-neutral change is capital-augmenting. It is characterized by a uniform improvement in the efficiency of the existing (old and new) capital stock.[20] Using a general production function analogous to the old ones presented in the two previous sections, we can include Solow-neutral progress as follows:

$$Y = F(a''K,N) \tag{17.7.7}$$

where a'' is an index of the state of technology in period t. Note that a'' "modifies" K, rather than N. The meaning of this specification is that a change in technology of this type would have the same effect as a corresponding percentage change in the size of the capital stock.

We saw before that Harrod-neutral technological change allowed balanced growth in the sense that some capital-output ratio could be found which would equate the warranted and natural rates of growth. The same cannot be said for Solow-neutral change. With capital-augmenting progress, we would expect the output-capital ratio to rise as technology improves; furthermore, it can be shown that, given the proportional saving function, a constant equilibrium output-capital ratio is a prerequisite for steady growth at some constant rate. To verify this, we can again specify the warranted rate of growth of output from the Harrod model as:

$$G_w = (1 - b)\sigma$$

If the output-capital ratio (σ) falls over time, the warranted growth rate must also continually fall (unless, of course, the propensity to save rises as σ falls—but it is unlikely that this eventuality offers much of a solution).[21]

---

[20]It is especially important here to keep in mind that the technological change in question is presumed to apply uniformly to capital stock of all ages. We shall take up this point in the next section.

[21]The interested student might try to show that the same point is true for Hicks-neutral technological change.

Disembodied vs. Embodied Technological Change

Up until now, we have offered no explanation of the way in which technological change is incorporated into the production process. Implicitly, we presumed that improvements in the quality of labor and/or capital somehow applied equally to both old and new units of the factor(s) in question. In the case of labor-augmenting change, the quality of each member of the labor force was assumed to improve uniformly over time; in the instance of capital-augmenting innovation, each piece of capital equipment supposedly "improved" as technology changed. Progress of this description is referred to as *disembodied* technological change to capture the notion that the improvement in technology need not be embodied in new units of the factor(s) in question. In a sense, disembodied technological change occurs independently of the purchase of new capital and the hiring of new laborers.

Alternatively, we could consider what is perhaps a more relevant case: *embodied* technological change. Essentially, this concept covers any technical improvement which is embodied only in newly produced capital or newly trained laborers. In order to capture the benefits of such progress, the business sector must hire or purchase the new, improved units of these factors. Thus, change must be actively introduced into the production process through the procurement of those factors which "embody" the new technology.

In the event that innovations are of the embodied variety, the specification of the aggregate production function is considerably more complex than the simple specifications offered in the previous section. If, for instance, we were to assume an embodied variety of capital-augmenting change, we would have to distinguish between units of capital of different ages, or "vintages." Those purchased most recently would embody the latest technology, whereas those purchased in the relatively distant past would reflect an inferior state of technology. The aggregate production function in this case might be specified as:

$$Y = F(N, K^1, K^2, K^3, \ldots K^T) \qquad (17.7.8)$$

where the superscripts on K refer to the vintage of the units of capital in question. That is, we could use the definition that:

K^1 = current capital stock with an age of one period;
K^2 = current capital stock with an age of two periods;
K^T = current capital stock with an age of T periods.

Due to the complexity of the treatment of embodied technological change, we shall pursue the issue no further. Let it suffice to suggest to the student that our analysis can barely scrape the surface of some topics; growth theory is one such area.

16.8 Summary

This chapter should be considered nothing more than a brief introduction to the analysis of growth; as a result, there are relatively few explicit policy conclusions to be drawn from it. The general process of growth rests on several factors: changes in the capital stock, the labor force and the state of technology. This much is uncontested by theorists of different persuasions. Nevertheless, the prospects for balanced growth differ widely according to the implications of alternative models. In a Harrod-Domar world, where the capital-output ratio is fixed over time, the economy walks a tightrope. Any deviation from the balanced-growth path feeds on itself, causing prolonged problems of unemployment or inflation. On the other hand, in the context of a neoclassical model, the capital-output ratio adjusts smoothly and automatically to correct any movement away from balanced growth. One could argue, it seems, that the truth lies between these two extreme views. Factor markets are not completely insensitive to changes in demand and supply conditions; nor are they generally as responsive as we might like them to be. Thus, it would appear that neither the pessimism of the simple capital-accumulation models nor the optimism of the neoclassical approach is warranted. But these frameworks do serve the purpose of highlighting the critical issues involved in the generation of balanced growth.

Suggested Further Reading

Cass, D. "Optimum Growth in an Aggregate Model of Capital Accumulation." *Review of Economic Studies* 32 (July 1965), 233–42.

Denison, E. *The Sources of Economic Growth in the U.S.* New York: Committee for Economic Development, 1962, chaps. 4 and 12.

Diamond, P. A. "Disembodied Technical Change in a Two-Sector Model." *Review of Economic Studies* 32 (April 1965), 161–68.

Drandakis, E. M. and Phelps, E. "A Model of Induced Invention, Growth, and Distribution." *Economic Journal* 76 (December 1966), 823–40.

Hahn, F. H. and Matthews, R. C. O. "The Theory of Economic Growth: A Survey." *Economic Journal* 74 (December 1964), 779–902.

Johnson, H. G. "The NeoClassical One-Sector Growth Model: A Geometrical Exposition and Extension to a Monetary Economy." *Economica* 33 (August 1966), 265–87.

Jorgensen, D. W. and Griliches, Z. "The Explanation of Productivity Change." *Review of Economic Studies* 34 (July 1967), 249–84.

Kaldor, N. and Mirlees, J. A. "A New Model of Economic Growth." *Review of Economic Studies* 29 (June 1962), 174–92.

Kennedy, C. M. "The Character of Improvements and of Technical Progress." *Economic Journal* 72 (December 1962), 899–911.

Phelps, E. S. "The Golden Rule of Accumulation." *American Economic Review* 51 (September 1961), 638–42.

Robinson, J. *The Accumulation of Capital* (Homewood, Ill.: R. D. Irwin, 1956).

Solow, R. M. "A Contribution to the Theory of Economic Growth." *Quarterly Journal of Economics* 70 (February 1956), 65–94.

———. "Technical Change and the Aggregate Production Function." *Review of Economics and Statistics* 39 (August 1957), 312–20.

Swan, T. "Economic Growth and Capital Accumulation." *Economic Record* 32 (November 1956), 334–61.

C H A P T E R   18

Inflation

18.1 Introduction

Until now, our concern with problems of inflation has been only peripheral. We mentioned the concept in our discussion of inflationary and deflationary gaps in chapter 4, but made no rigorous attempt to investigate the meaning, causes or cures of inflationary conditions. Indeed, we ignored the determination of the price level until chapters 9 through 11—and even there our main concern was with treating the static equilibrium of income, prices, and the other variables of our economic system. We now turn to what should be considered an introduction to the complex body of thought comprising the theory of inflation. Our analysis will proceed in three steps: first, we shall define some of the terms associated with inflation and discuss alternative measures of it; second, we shall use the comparative-static approach developed in chapter 11 to focus on some of the ingredients of an inflationary process; third, we shall consider some assumptions about the dynamic behavior of the economy in order to more adequately describe inflation as a dynamic phenomenon.

If we are to deal with the "problem" of inflation, we obviously need a workable definition of the term in question. Any number of definitions are available in the literature—some specified in such vague terms as to be almost meaningless, and others riddled with such specific references as to connote something about the causes and effects, as well as the basic nature, of the phenomenon. We shall adopt a middle-ground approach by defining inflation as a sustained tendency for the general level of prices to rise over time.

The definition depends on three important terms characterizing inflation. First, we make an implicit distinction between *actual* price increases and a *tendency* for such increases. This distinction is important, in that it focuses on the fact that prices are not always free to fluctuate in response to market conditions. In the United States, we have seen periods in which artificial controls have been placed on wages and prices, restraining them from following the course they would have taken otherwise. The imposition of such controls took place in World War II and the Korean War, and again when President Nixon used the Economic Stabilization Act of 1970 to institute his "New Economic Policy." Periods in which the tendency for price rises is muffled through artificial controls are often referred to as times of *repressed inflation*. On the other hand, when tendencies are reflected in actual price increases, we say that we have a condition of *open inflation*. We shall avoid any attempt to analyze the former variant; instead, we shall concentrate on the latter. But it should be kept in mind that the absence of observed increases in the general price level does not necessarily imply the lack of inflationary pressures.

The second key term in our definition of inflation is the word *sustained*. Obviously, minor fluctuations in economic activity are likely to bring about sporadic increases and decreases in prices. A severe winter, a prolonged strike in a major industry, or any number of other factors could cause a small change in the level of prices. But these price movements, if they are random and roughly self-cancelling over relatively short periods of time, do not constitute inflation the way we have defined it. Obviously, there is no way to escape the ambiguity in the use of words like *sustained*. Certainly, a one-quarter spurt of prices would not necessarily constitute an inflationary period, whereas a three-year upward swing in prices almost surely would. But where should one place the dividing line? The only reasonable answer is that there is no unambiguous cutoff point. But this conceptual problem is unlikely to be very important from a policy standpoint.

We often make use of certain adjectives to denote the duration and the intensity of an inflationary period. Thus, the economist's vocabulary is laden with terms like *creeping inflation, galloping inflation* and *hyperinflation*. Again, one will find no specific definitions of these brands of inflation, only a general ranking. Creeping inflation is generally regarded as a tendency for prices to rise at a slow rate—say, 1 or 2% per year. At some point, we reach an area of galloping inflation, in which prices rise by substantially higher percentages, perhaps 7 or 8% per year. The most critical inflationary disease is hyperinflation, where prices rise so rapidly that confidence in the country's currency is severely shaken. The situation in Germany immediately after World War I, where prices rose at an annual rate of over 20%, stands as an example of this type of inflationary crisis. The reader will undoubtedly notice that there are substantial gray areas between these types. The lack of neatly divided "ranges" of inflation should be of little concern to us here. If inflation is a problem, the seriousness of the problem can be viewed as increasing fairly systematically as the rate of inflation increases. Inflation at a 5% rate is no less damaging if it is called creeping inflation than if it is called galloping inflation; a jump in the inflation rate from 2% to 8% should be viewed with concern, regardless of the adjectives applied to the two rates.

The third element of our definition of inflation is the reference to the "general level of prices." Obviously, individual prices will rise or fall over time as conditions in individual markets change, and these price adjustments are the mechanism via which resource allocation is altered. But inflation refers to upward movements in the overall level of prices. To measure it, we need some indicator which aggregates the prices of individual commodities and reflects their general movements. For this purpose, we use price indices, which are generally computed as the ratio of weighted prices of the current and base periods, where the weights are quantities of individual items purchased in the base year.[1]

Although several price indices could be used as measures of the general price level, three indices are most commonly used in reference to inflation: the consumer price index (CPI), the wholesale price index (WPI) and the implicit GNP deflator. Table 18.1.1 displays the recent history of the general price level as reflected by these three indicators. Careful inspection of the data in that table reveals a general similarity in the movement of the three price series since World War II. Each index shows a dramatic increase in prices in the immediate postwar period (1946–48) and in the periods 1951, 1967–71, and 1972–4. And, in general, relatively minor movements in the three indices tend to be coordinated over time. But, because each index measures the composite price of a different basket of goods,[2] some differences among their time paths can be discerned. For instance, the WPI declined from 1952 to 1953 and from 1960 to 1961, whereas both the CPI and the implicit GNP deflator rose during these intervals. In that the GNP deflator is the closest to a "general" price index, it seems plausible in practice to use

---

[1] See chapter 2 for a review of the construction of price indices. Implicit deflators are computed in a slightly different manner. In particular, the value of transactions at current market prices is divided by the value of those transactions valued at a set of base period prices.

[2] The consumer price index covers a "typical" basket of goods purchased by consumers; the wholesale price index pertains to prices received by wholesalers; and the GNP deflator applies to all those transactions recorded in GNP.

Table 18.1.1.   *Selected Price Indices*

Year	Consumer Price Index (1957–59 = 100)	Wholesale Price Index (1957–59 = 100)	Implicit GNP Deflator (1958 = 100)
1947	77.8	81.2	74.6
1948	83.8	87.9	79.6
1949	83.0	83.5	79.1
1950	83.8	86.8	80.2
1951	90.5	96.7	85.6
1952	92.5	94.0	87.5
1953	93.2	92.7	88.3
1954	93.6	92.9	89.6
1955	93.3	93.2	90.9
1956	94.7	96.2	94.0
1957	98.0	99.0	97.5
1958	100.7	100.4	100.0
1959	101.5	100.6	101.6
1960	103.1	100.7	103.3
1961	104.2	100.3	104.6
1962	105.4	100.6	105.7
1963	106.7	100.3	107.1
1964	108.1	100.5	108.8
1965	109.9	102.5	110.9
1966	113.1	105.9	113.8
1967	116.3	106.1	117.3
1968	121.2	108.7	122.3
1969	128.3	113.0	128.2
1970	135.3	117.1	135.2
1971	141.1	120.8	141.6
1972	145.7	126.4	146.1
1973	154.8	142.9	154.3
1974	171.8	169.9	170.2

Source: *Survey of Current Business*

changes in it as the major indicator of inflation. But this, of course, does not preclude the usefulness of the other indices in the study of price movements.

The mere fact that so much theoretical and empirical attention is paid to inflation suggests that it is considered an extremely important economic problem. The most extreme type of price rise—hyperinflation—has the rather obvious effect of ruining confidence in the monetary unit. As prices rise at exorbitant rates, money ceases to perform well as a store of value, and thus it becomes less acceptable as a payment for goods and services. Even milder forms of inflation generally lead to a worsening of the competitive position of domestic products in the world market. Furthermore, inflation tends to lead to a more unfavorable distribution of real income, in that it discriminates against individuals with relatively fixed incomes (e.g., social security recipients). Walter Heller spoke to these latter characteristics when he suggested that price stability is "our proxy for equity between fixed and variable income recipients and, in today's outward-looking economy, a vital condition for maintaining our competitive position in world markets without trade restrictions."[3]

Needless to say, the exercise of public policy designed to alleviate inflationary pressures requires some knowledge about the causes of such pressures. Noting the failure of economists to diagnose the root causes of inflation in many cases, Paul Samuelson and Robert Solow comment that: "Just as generals are said to be always fighting the wrong war, economists have been accused of fighting the wrong inflation."[4] One might add that, even after the fight has subsided, economists are often still uncertain that they engaged the right enemy or that they used the appropriate artillery. In the following section, we shall investigate two of the major theories of inflation: demand-pull and cost-push.

18.2 Demand-Pull vs. Cost-Push Theories of Inflation: A Comparative-Static Approach

Inflation is clearly a dynamic problem; nonetheless, we can gain considerable insight into alternative views of inflation by referring to the general static Keynesian model developed in chapter 11. As we illustrated there, the structural equations of a Keynesian economy can be reduced to obtain aggregate supply and aggregate demand relations which relate real income and prices. The simultaneous equilibrium of the money and product markets at alternative price levels gave us what we called the aggregate demand schedule. The aggregate demand schedule depicted a negative relation between real income (output) and the general level of prices. The interpretation of this schedule was that, given the values of the exogenous variables of the product and money

[3]W. Heller, *New Dimensions of Political Economy* (New York: W. W. Norton, 1970), p. 60.

[4]P. Samuelson and R. Solow, "Analytical Aspects of Anti-Inflation Policy," *American Economic Review* 50 (May 1960), p. 177.

markets, price decreases would expand the real money supply, thus reducing interest rates and raising the level of investment. And this rise in investment would induce an increase in the level of aggregate demand.

The behavior of firms and the labor force was summarized in an aggregate supply schedule. It was based on the following series of relations: the higher the price level, the higher the value of labor's marginal product, and thus the higher the amount of labor firms are willing to hire; the higher the demand for labor, the higher the level of employment; and, given the shape of the aggregate production function, the higher the amount of output firms will be willing to produce. The equilibrium price level and output of the economy were shown to be determined by the interaction of the aggregate supply and aggregate demand schedules.

In that the equilibrium general price level was derived from a set of assumptions about the exogenous variables of all three markets—the labor, money and product markets—it stands to reason that changes in the values of these exogenous variables will prompt changes in the general level of prices. To the extent that these price movements continue over time, they constitute a process of inflation; thus, the framework can be used as a background against which alternative theories of inflation can be presented. In what follows, we shall depart from our former reliance on algebraic treatment. We do so because the model has become too cumbersome at this point to warrant the use of an algebraic approach. Instead, we shall employ a diagrammatic presentation hinging on the aggregate supply and aggregate demand schedules mentioned above.[5]

Demand-Pull Inflation

In colloquial terms, demand-pull inflation is often defined as "too much money chasing too few goods." In more technical terms, it is the tendency for prices to rise in the face of the excess demand created by an autonomous shift in the aggregate demand schedule. Suppose that the economy's initial equilibrium occurs at point a in figure 18.2.1, indicating a price level, P_a, and income level, Y_a. Presume now that one of the exogenous components of aggregate demand (e.g., the autonomous part

---

[5]For an algebraic solution to a model similar to ours, see: Robert Holbrook, "The Interest Rate, the Price Level, and Aggregate Output," in *Readings in Money, Income and Stabilization Policy*, ed. W. L. Smith and R. L. Teigen (Homewood, Ill.: R. D. Irwin, 1970), pp. 43–65.

of investment) increases. In terms of panel (a), the exogenous "shock" causes the IS schedule to shift to the right by some multiple of the exogenous change. At each price level, the level of income increases and the rate of interest rises.[6] Thus, the aggregate demand schedule also shifts to the right, from AD to AD'. The movement of the aggregate demand schedule sets up the stimulus for a price rise. At the original level of prices, P_a, aggregate demand exceeds aggregate supply by the amount $c - a$. Because of this excess demand condition, prices begin to rise. A new equilibrium is reached by a process in which aggregate demand contracts along AD' and aggregate supply expands along AS.

On the demand side, rising prices cause a contraction of the real money supply, forcing individuals to liquidate interest-bearing assets in an attempt to fulfill transactions needs. As this happens, the rate of interest is forced up (bond prices are pushed down); the rise in the interest rate discourages induced investment, and the fall in investment continues until the original stimulus (the rise in prices) is stopped. Looking at the adjustment process from the supply side, we find that rising prices increase the value of labor's marginal product at each amount of employment; i.e., the labor demand schedule shifts to the right. If the economy is operating in a range of employment over which money wages are rigid, employment rises without a corresponding increase in wages; if the labor-supply schedule is upward-sloping, a simultaneous increase in employment and wages occurs. In either event, rising employment brings with it an expansion of aggregate supply along AS.

Assuming away any further shifts in the aggregate supply and aggregate demand schedules, the joint effect of rising aggregate supply and falling aggregate demand will eventually close the gap between the two, and a new equilibrium will be attained. Under the assumptions of the formal model underlying figure 18.2.1, then, an increase in one of the exogenous components of aggregate demand will bring an increase in the economy's equilibrium price level. But a one-shot change in prices doesn't strictly qualify under our definition of inflation, since it is not a "substained tendency" for prices to rise. In the context of the formal static Keynesian model used here, inflation of the demand-pull variety would result only from a succession of rises in the level of the autonomous portion of aggregate demand. For instance, a growing level of autonomous investment would shift the aggregate demand schedule to the right relative to the aggregate supply schedule from period to period,

---

[6]We ignore the possibility of a horizontal or a vertical LM schedule and assume instead that the economy is operating in the intermediate range of the LM.

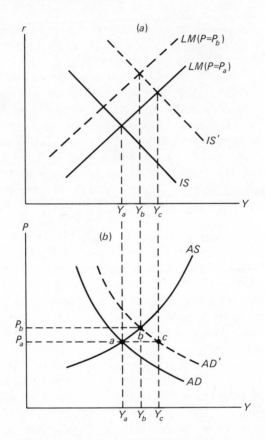

Figure 18.2.1   *Demand-Pull Inflation*

thus eliciting continual rises in the general price level. But, as we shall
see later, there are certainly more promising explanations of the inflationary process, each of which relies on a dynamic, rather than a static,
description of the economy. The analysis of this and the next section
can best be viewed as an introduction to the initiation of an inflation
through a shift in aggregate demand and supply.

Cost-Push Inflation

In the past twenty years, increased emphasis has been placed upon
another explanation of price movements: cost-push inflation. The cost-
push explanation of inflation has relied, in general, on the impact of
changes in money wages on the general price level.

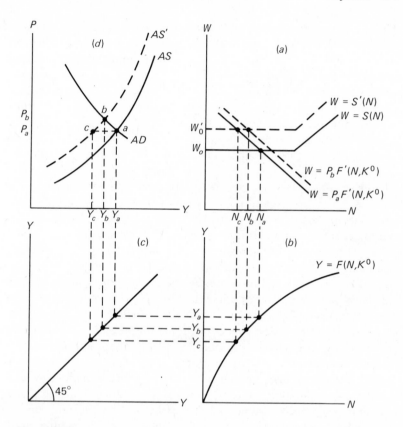

Figure 18.2.2 *Cost-Push Inflation*

In order to facilitate our analysis (and to allow it to be accomplished through comparative statics), let's assume that the level of money wages is exogenous over the relevant range of employment. Figure 18.2.2 illustrates the effects of a rise in money wages. Begin in panel (a). A change in W from W_0 to W'_0 causes the labor-supply schedule to shift upward. Along the new labor-supply schedule, each price level is associated with a lower level of employment than was originally the case. Or, looking at this from another angle, a higher wage forces producers to require a higher price level at each level of employment. In that employment and output are positively related through the production function, shown in panel (b), this can be translated to mean that each level of output will require a higher price level. Thus, the aggregate supply schedule shifts upward from AS to AS'. If we recall that producers hire to the point where the real wage is equal to the marginal product of labor, and that the marginal product is uniquely related to the level of employment (and output) in the short run, we can be more specific about the shift in aggregate supply. At each output along the aggregate supply schedule, the price level will rise by the same proportion as did the money wage, thus keeping the real wage constant. Thus, if wages rise by 5%, the aggregate supply schedule would shift upward by 5%.

The inflationary effect of the rise in autonomous money wages is given in panel (d). As the aggregate supply schedule shifts, a temporary disequilibrium is created at the initial price level, P_a. The excess of aggregate demand over aggregate supply exerts pressure on prices, and a price rise ensues. Again, the economy moves back along the aggregate demand schedule (from a to b) as rising prices cause the real money supply to contract, interest rates to rise, and induced investment to fall. A movement along the aggregate supply schedule (from c to b) can also be traced out. Point c would correspond to the amount of output producers would be willing to produce with the new money wage and the *initial* price level. But as prices start to rise (with money wages held at their new, but higher, value), the real wage falls. This induces the business sector to expand employment and output, but not all the way back to their original levels at point a. The net result of this process is the attainment of a new equilibrium (at b) where the price level is higher and output lower than they were before the rise in money wages.

Again, our analysis illustrates only a one-shot change in prices, rather than a process of inflation. But one can easily envision an economy in which wages keep rising over time in spite of current economic conditions. As long as wages keep rising more rapidly than labor's marginal product (at each level of employment), the aggregate supply schedule will trace out a series of upward shifts. Each rise in the aggregate supply schedule will bring with it a rise in prices and a fall in both employment and income. Eventually, though, the expanding level of unemployment should slow down the ascent of wages. Labor negotiators will eventually reach some point at which their trade-off between employment and the money wage favors the former at the expense of the latter. Then, according to the theory of cost-push inflation, the inflationary pressure should dissipate.

Although most of the literature on cost-push inflation has focused on autonomous increases in wages, recent developments have indicated that other costs can be responsible for this kind of impetus. The recent energy crisis, through its impact on the energy costs of firms, has undoubtedly contributed to the current inflation. Indeed, pressure on the prices of a variety of raw materials can be expected to have this general effect.

Moreover, increased ᴗmonopoly power (or increased recognition of this power by firms) can lead to something known as "profit-push" inflation. One would be hard pressed to attribute the rise in sugar prices during 1974, for instance, to a sharp increase in wage demands. As we go through the subsequent analysis, the student should recognize that the model could be modified to incorporate the influence of nonwage costs on prices, and that the general implications of this expanded analysis would parallel the ones we have drawn so far with reference to wages.

18.3 An Introduction to Dynamic Analysis of Inflation

Our preceding analysis was restricted to a comparative-static approach to inflation. But such descriptions of the process contribute little to the explanation of systematic and sustained movements of prices over time. The heart of inflation is the dependence of this year's general price increase on those taking place in the recent past. This dependence over time can be analyzed only within the confines of a dynamic model. There are many hypotheses about the economy's dynamic behavior, and some of these views add considerably to our understanding of inflation. We attempt to consider only two of these notions; and we do so aided by the use of highly simplifying assumptions. Each dynamic model is characterized, in fact, by only one path via which today's economic activity affects tomorrow's.

The Wage-Price Spiral

One aspect of the dynamic nature of the inflationary process is connoted by the frequent reference to the term *wage-price spiral*. Indeed, the notion underlying this phrase is that wages affect prices and that prices, in turn, affect wages. The interdependence of wages and prices generates a series of adjustments in these two variables over time—adjustments which reinforce each other and promote the type of sustained rise in prices (and wages) we have characterized as true inflation.

We have already investigated part of the mechanism entailed by the wage-price spiral. In particular, we have noted that an increase in autonomous money wages will force the aggregate supply schedule upward and stimulate a rise in the general price level. But because money wages *were* treated as completely exogenous, no further rises in W were necessarily forthcoming. In order to have a "spiral," we must introduce a feedback mechanism via which changes in prices induce shifts in the labor-supply shcedule (i.e., changes in W stemming from supply-side considerations).[7] In other words, we must specify money wages as an endogenous variable dependent in some way on the level of prices.

In order to make the model dynamic, we must also introduce time into the analysis by taking account of the lags involved in the relations among variables. Although many hypotheses could be advanced with regard to lags in various relationships, we shall concentrate on the adjustment time needed for the response of money wages to changes in the price level. More explicitly, we shall assume that an increase in prices will, after one period, induce an increase in money-wage demands. Or, in equivalent terms, we shall postulate that this period's rise in prices will cause an upward shift in next period's labor-supply schedule.

Our assumption about the effect of prices on money wages is hardly unrealistic. Labor unions often justify their wage demands on the basis of past increases in the cost of living, and their negotiating position is obviously enhanced by sympathetic public opinion. Furthermore, the dependence of wages on prices is often institutionalized in contractual agreements through the stipulation of escalator clauses.

Our analysis will ignore one important feature of an economy moving through time. In particular, we shall assume away increases in labor's productivity. This assumption in essence allows us to abstract from shifts in the production function and labor's marginal product schedule and confine our analysis to the bare bones of the wage-price spiral. Actually, the assumption is not a crucial one. An increase in productivity has the impact of shifting the aggregate supply schedule downward, whereas an increase in money wages causes an upward shift in the aggregate supply schedule. Since the wage-price spiral is based partially on continued upward movements in the aggregate supply schedule, our results could be obtained by assuming that money-wage demands rise more rapidly than productivity increases. We choose the abstraction only to simplify the diagrammatic presentation.

Suppose that the economy has been operating in the past, and is currently operating in period 1, at a level of income Y_1 and a level of prices P_1, as shown in panel (a) of figure 18.3.1. Tracing back through panels (b) and (c) to panel (d), we find the labor market in equilibrium at an amount of employment N_1 and a money wage W_1. Now, let's allow an exogenous shock to occur, starting the economy on a series of adjustments. Suppose that autonomous investment increases in period 2,

---

[7]Changes in W stemming from excess demand for labor do not qualify for the wage-price spiral, in that they constitute movements along the aggregate supply schedule rather than shifts in it.

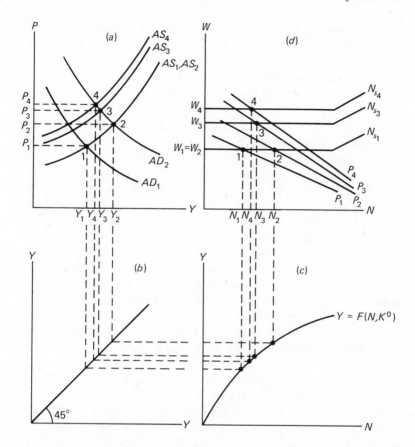

Figure 18.3.1 *The Wage-Price Spiral*

driving the aggregate demand schedule up to AD_2. The increase in aggregate demand moves the economy to point 2, where $P = P_2$ and $Y = Y_2$; and these changes are accompanied by an increase in employment to N_2. Because of the one-period adjustment time involved in the response of wages to changes in the price level, the labor supply schedule maintains its previous position. And, because the economy is operating along the horizontal segment of the labor supply schedule—where wages are insensitive to employment—the money wage stays at $W_2 = W_1$.

As we open up the third period, the feedback begins. Workers, noting the previous period's increase in the price level, step up their demands for wage increases. As a result, the labor supply schedule shifts upward, reflected by the fact that the "minimum acceptable" wage level rises from W_2 to W_3. This change causes the aggregate supply schedule to rise, indicating that producers now require a higher price level at each and every level of output. As is depicted in panel (a), the shift in the aggregate supply schedule moves the equilibrium to point 3, characterized by a lower level of output (Y_3) and a still higher level of prices (P_3).

In the fourth period, there is pressure for additional wage hikes. This arises from the fact that prices rose in the previous (third) period, thus affecting labor's cost of living. Suppose that new contractual arrangements force the labor-supply schedule up to N_{s4}, where wage rigidity occurs at W_4. Again, the aggregate supply schedule is driven upward, and the economy moves to point 4 in panel (a), causing the price level to rise to P_4 and the level of income to fall to Y_4. These rounds of adjustments continue through time, from period to period, inducing a continual rise in wages and the price level and a contraction in output and employment.

The process described above is a simplified dynamic description of inflation. But regardless of its simplistic nature, it focuses on the essence of one type of dynamic behavior. It also serves as an introduction to one of the problems associated with any dynamic view of inflation: given that inflation is a dynamic process, will this tendency for price increases intensify over time or will it eventually subside even in the absence of economic policy? In this context, we say that the system is stable if the price level eventually converges to a new equilibrium position, to be maintained over time, and unstable if the price level continues indefinitely its upward course away from the original equilibrium. In the simple wage-price spiral model presented here, it should be clear that the stability of the system hinges on two factors: first, the sensitivity of wages to prices; and, second, the sensitivity of prices to shifts in the labor supply schedule. The weaker these links in the chain of response, the more likely it is that prices will converge to some new (higher) level and maintain that position in the absence of further exogenous shocks.

Inflationary Expectations

The feedback effect of a change in the price level need not operate through the labor market; it can also stem from the effect of this period's price change on the level of next period's level of aggregate demand. In our static model, we assumed away money illusion in the product market which is expressed in real terms. Because of this, the level of aggregate demand was invariant to the level of prices (i.e., the IS schedule did not shift as prices changed). But in a dynamic context, where we recognize the relation between past, present and future events, it is not at all un-reasonable to hypothesize a relationship between price changes and shifts in aggregate demand. Both consumers and investors are concerned with the allocation of their expenditures over time. Consumers use some of their disposable income for current consumption, and use the rest to finance future consumption (through saving). Investors generally pay great attention to the timing of their purchases of plant and equipment. In both cases, one could argue that price expectations play a significant role in determining the timing of expenditures.[8]

Consider the consumer, for instance, who enters the current period planning to spend a certain amount on goods and services. Suppose that something happens to convince him that prices will rise much more substantially than he originally expected over the next several periods. As a rule, we would expect the consumer to adjust to this change in his expectations by speeding up his expenditures through a shift from saving to current consumption. The investor faced with the same expectations of a price increase would be likely to react in an analogous fashion, buying capital goods now at relatively low prices and hoping to sell his expanded final product later at higher prices.[9]

The question remains: how do price expectations introduce a dependence of the present on the past? The answer is that individuals tend to form expectations for the present partially on the basis of what has happened in the past. In the absence of foreseen changes in circumstances (e.g., the policy to be followed by fiscal and monetary authorities), consumers and investors generally form their expectations of this period's price increase by looking at the price increases of recent periods. If prices have risen in the recent past, individuals will normally expect this trend to continue. The strength of this relationship is captured in the elasticity of price expectations, which can be defined as the ratio of the expected percentage change in prices in the current period to the observed percentage change in price:

$$\epsilon = \left(\frac{\Delta P_t}{P_{t-1}}\right)^e \bigg/ \left(\frac{\Delta P_t}{P_{t-1}}\right)$$

where P_t is the general price level at the end of the current period, P_{t-1}

---

[8]For another discussion of the impact of price expectations, see appendix 7.A. Note that the earlier treatment ignored the way in which expectations are formed, whereas this section treats the issue, at least in an informal sense.

[9]See chapter 13 for a discussion of this point. Also note that our comments about the behavior of consumers and investors may not be true under conditions of hyperinflation, when confidence in the general state of the economy may be depressed.

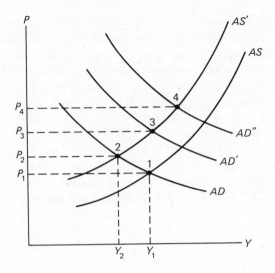

Figure 18.3.2   *Inflationary Expectations*

is the price level of the past period, and the superscript e denotes the "expected" price change. Our discussion above indicates that the elasticity of expectations is positive.

To illustrate the impact of price expectations, let us set up an analysis similar to the ones covered in previous sections. In particular, assume that the economy has been at a particular equilibrium position for the past several periods, and let that position be represented in period 1 by point 1 in figure 18.3.2. Suppose now that in period 2 an exogenous shock occurs, thus disturbing the system. For the illustration, presume that the labor-supply schedule shifts upward due to the negotiation of a higher level of money wages. The immediate repercussion of this event is that the aggregate supply schedule shifts upward, determining a new equilibrium at point 2, where the price level takes on a higher value, P_2. Given the rise in the price level from P_1 to P_2 over the second period, consumers or investors or both revise their expectations of the change in prices to transpire in the third period.

In that the aggregate demand schedule of periods 1 and 2 was based upon a given set of price expectations, the upward revision can be expected to cause a reallocation of current consumption or investment or both, with the net result being a rightward shift in the aggregate demand schedule. But as this happens, the price level is forced up further, reaching P_3 by the end of the period. As the fourth period opens, the rise in prices from P_2 to P_3 in the previous period makes its influence felt; consumers and/or investors revise their expectations again, based upon their most recent experience. If the price rise from P_2 and P_3 was greater than that from P_1 to P_2, then we can expect price expectations to be pushed upward even further, causing another rightward movement of the aggregate demand schedule, and a movement to a new price level P_4. If the price rise of the third period was less than that of the second, the effect on price expectations will be ambiguous. The expected change in prices may fall or rise (relative to its third-period value), depending upon the exact way in which expectations are formed. In either event, the economy will go through a series of adjustments before it eventually settles down (in the absence of any other exogenous shocks) to a price level which can be maintained over subsequent periods.

We can again analyze the stability of the system by looking at the chain of events which characterize the economy's path over time. The movement of prices from period 1 and on will depend upon four factors:

1. the initial change in the price level

2. the effect of a given change in prices on the expectations of future price changes (i.e., the elasticity of expectations)

3. the effect of a change in price expectations on the level of aggregate demand

4. the effect of a shift in aggregate demand on the current price level (as determined by the slope of the aggregate supply schedule).

The stronger the last three of these factors, the more likely the system is to be explosive; the weaker they are, the stronger the possibility of eventual convergence (again, in the absence of any further change in the value of any exogenous variable).

18.4 Monetary and Fiscal Counterinflationary Policies

Since inflation is considered an economic malady, we find that policy authorities often direct massive programs at its eradication. The Employment Act of 1946, one of the keystones of formal economic policy statements, seemed to be reflecting the newfound concern with inflation when it cited the need to foster "maximum purchasing power" in the economy. The policy instruments to be used include those monetary and fiscal policies we've dealt with at considerable length throughout this text.

The existence of demand-pull inflation in its purest form would call for measures restricting the expansion of aggregate demand. As we have seen in earlier chapters, this could be accomplished through the use of contractionary fiscal and/or monetary policies. Naturally, those who believe that changes in the money supply are chiefly responsible for expansions in aggregate demand would favor slowing down the increase in the money supply in order to stem inflation. And, those placing more reliance on fiscal measures would undoubtedly emphasize decreases in the growth of government expenditures and/or increases in the expansion of tax revenues. Naturally, restrictive monetary and fiscal policies, by slowing down the growth of aggregate demand, also dampen the expansion of income and employment. But, given that this type of inflation is generally associated with low rates of unemployment, the side effects are not considered too serious to accept.

In the case of cost-push inflation, the problem of inflation could be handled in the same fashion; however, the exercise of restrictive policies is likely to generate rather serious—and sometimes unacceptable— repercussions. As we saw in our analysis of wage-push inflation, increases in the money wage (relative to productivity) may persist over time, in spite of the presence of fairly high levels of unemployment. Indeed, these wage hikes, through their impact on the aggregate supply schedule, cause contractions in income and employment, thereby presenting an economy with the dual problem of inflation and growing levels of unemployment. A pure cost-push inflation is likely to be terminated (as we argued above) when unemployment grows to a high enough level to check demands for inflationary wage increases. The use of monetary and fiscal policies in this context reduces the growth of aggregate demand (or even its absolute level), thus essentially quickening the attainment of sufficiently high levels of unemployment to erase the cost-push pressure. But the avoidance of inflation and the maintenance of low unemployment rates are *both* important policy objectives; thus, economic planners are faced with a trade-off between these goals. Suppose that unemployment is at 4% and that prices are increasing at a rate of 3.5% per year. In order to slow the rate of inflation to 2%, it may be necessary to allow (or, indeed, induce) an unemployment rate of 6%. Or, to bring unemployment down to a lower level (say, 3%), which would call for *expansionary* policy, policymakers may have to accept an increase in the rate of inflation to 5%.

The inevitable trade-off between objectives in periods of wage-push inflation has been formalized by A. W. Phillips, who conducted an empirical investigation of this phenomenon for the United Kingdom.[10]

---

[10]See A. W. Phillips, "The Relation Between Unemployment and the Rate of Change in Money Wage Rates in the United Kingdom, 1862–1957," *Economica* 25 (November 1958), 283–99.

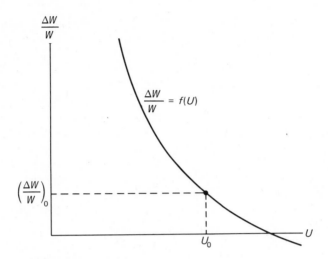

Figure 18.4.1 *The Phillips Curve*

Using the notion that the rise of money wage rates (in percentage terms) persists even in periods of positive unemployment, but that it diminishes as unemployment takes on successively larger levels, the relationship now known as the Phillips curve is attributed the shape depicted in figure 18.4.1. In that diagram, U denotes the rate of unemployment as a percentage of the labor force, and $\Delta W/W$ represents the proportional change in wages. The slope of the schedule represents the rate at which the economy can trade off between unemployment and wage rises, or the marginal effect on $\Delta W/W$ of a one-point change in the unemployment rate.

Although we have largely ignored changes in productivity until now, we did point out that it is not wage changes per se, but rather changes in wages relative to labor's marginal product, which contribute to inflation. Thus, we can, for some given rate of productivity increase, define a proportional rise in wages which would leave prices unchanged. Let us call this change $(\Delta W/W)_0$, as it is labeled in figure 18.4.1, and assume that it is associated with an unemployment rate of U_0. Given this point of reference, we can see that levels of unemployment below U_0 will give rise to inflationary pressures from the supply side, and that these pressures will be aggravated by policies directed at lowering unemployment below that level. From another perspective, any attempt to drive $\Delta W/W$ down toward $(\Delta W/W)_0$ will expand the value of U.

Since our direct concern is with sustained price increases (rather than with wage increases in themselves), the information embodied in

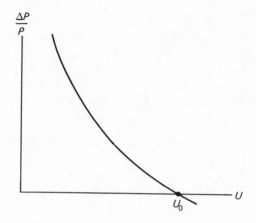

Figure 18.4.2 *The Trade-Off between Inflation
and Unemployment*

the Phillips curve of figure 18.4.1 can be recast in terms of the corresponding association between the rate of unemployment and the
percentage rise in the general price index. This variation is shown in
figure 18.4.2, where $\Delta P/P$ stands for the rate of inflation. Notice that the
rate of unemployment U_0 is associated with complete price stability,
because this is the value of U for which wages and productivity increase
at the same speed, and that prices tend to rise when U takes on a lower
value.

The Phillips curve of any particular economy acts as a constraint on
that country's achievement of the economic goals of price stability and
full employment. Although it is generally difficult to estimate the
shape and position of a country's Phillips curve at any point in time
(for reasons we shall cite later), rough estimates of its nature are
ordinarily available to guide policy. In 1960, for instance, Samuelson
and Solow ventured the "guess" that price stability would entail "something like 5 to 6% of the civilian labor forces being unemployed," and
that achievement of a 3% rate of unemployment would require a rate
of inflation between 4 and 5% per year.[11] But conditions change, and
there is strong belief that the Phillips curve has been shifting to the
right in recent years. In 1971, before the wage-price freeze of the Nixon
administration's Phase I, the GNP deflator was rising at a 6% annual
rate, even though the unemployment rate was around 6%. Thus, the
relation between unemployment and inflation is not an immutable

---

[11]Samuelson and Solow, "Anti-Inflation Policy," p. 192.

boundary precluding the attainment of more optimistic goals; nor is it an insurance policy against even less favorable conditions. Like almost any other "simple" economic relation, it is based on a litany of *ceteris paribus* assumptions. In this case, the assumptions pertain to the source of inflation and the mechanism through which it is promulgated, the structure of the labor and product markets, the state of expectations (especially those of workers) and a host of other conditions.

We can obtain at least a general understanding of the instability of the Phillips curve by sketching out one of the many algebraic models which could generate such a relationship. To do so, we need to make some hypotheses about the way in which prices and wages—two key variables—are related to the structure of the economy. One reasonable (and fairly general) hypothesis is that the rate of change of nominal wages is affected by the rate of unemployment at time t (U_t), the expected rate of growth of prices, and a variable, Z_t, representing a host of other conditions affecting the labor market. That is,

$$\frac{\Delta W_t}{W_{t-1}} = a + b\frac{1}{U_t} + c\frac{\Delta P_t^e}{P_{t-1}^e} + dZ_t. \qquad (18.4.1)$$

A similar formulation has been suggested by George Perry,[12] and variations have been used by a number of other economic analysts.[13] The general notion underlying the equation is that wage rates are set in a collective bargaining setting in which wage demands are inversely related to the unemployment rate, positively associated with the rate of change in the cost of living expected by workers, and somehow related to those other variables which influence the relative bargaining strength of labor and management.

Let us also assume that prices are determined through the following relation:

$$\frac{\Delta P_t}{P_{t-1}} = \frac{\Delta W_t}{W_{t-1}} - \frac{\Delta MP_t}{MP_{t-1}} \qquad (18.4.2)$$

---

[12] George Perry, *Unemployment, Money Wage Rates and Inflation* (Cambridge: Massachusetts Institute of Technology Press, 1966). The Perry formulation can be derived from ours by assuming that the expected rate of change of prices is dependent upon observed price changes and that the profit rate of firms is one of the variables represented by our Z_t.

[13] See, for example, P. Samuelson and R. Solow, "Anti-Inflation Policy," 192; O. Eckstein and T. A. Wilson, "The Determinant of Money Wages in American Industry," *Quarterly Journal of Economics* 76 (August 1962), 379–414; and W. G. Bowen and R. A. Berry, "Unemployment Conditions and Movements of the Money Wage Level," *Review of Economics and Statistics* 45 (May 1963), 167–72.

where MP represents the marginal product of labor. The above equation suggests that firms set prices on the basis of short-run marginal cost, which is determined by money wages and labor's marginal product.[14] Given this, the rate of change of prices would be determined by the rates of change of these variables.

The interaction of wages and prices is captured by equations 18.4.1 and 18.4.2, but they do not constitute a full self-contained model of the economy. To be consistent with the general Keynesian model we have developed at length in this and earlier chapters, we would have to recognize that these equations contain endogenous variables other than wages and prices. In particular, the unemployment rate is affected by all those variables which influence employment and output, price expectations are formed on the basis of economic conditions, and the marginal productivity of labor depends upon the level of employment. Nonetheless, equations 18.4.1 and 18.4.2 do introduce a dynamic price-wage mechanism into the analysis. Combining these two relations by substituting the wage equation into the price equation, we obtain:

$$\frac{\Delta P_t}{P_{t-1}} = a + b\frac{1}{U_t} + c\frac{\Delta P_t^e}{P_{t-1}^e} + dZ_t - \frac{\Delta MP_t}{MP_t}. \tag{18.4.3}$$

If we assume that the expected rate of inflation, the level of Z_t, and the rate of change of productivity are constant, then the above equation yields the Phillips relationship between the actual percentage rise in prices and the rate of unemployment. Under this *ceteris paribus* assumption with respect to the other variables in the equation, then, the economy faces a given trade-off between inflation and unemployment. But notice that, as the value of any of the other variables changes, the Phillips relation will shift.

Potentially, some of the root causes of the unfavorable combinations of inflation and unemployment of the late 1960s and early 1970s could be traced to such changes. For example it has been estimated that the

---

[14] We have seen one of the static counterparts previously when we characterized the labor demand equation with the relationship:

$$W_t/P_t = MP_t.$$

For small percentage changes, this relation could be written as:

$$\Delta P_t/P_{t-1} = \Delta W_t/W_{t-1} - \Delta MP_t/MP_{t-1}.$$

The same dynamic equation could be derived from the more general notion that firms set prices by applying some markup, k, to marginal cost; that is:

$$P_t = k(W_t/MP_t).$$

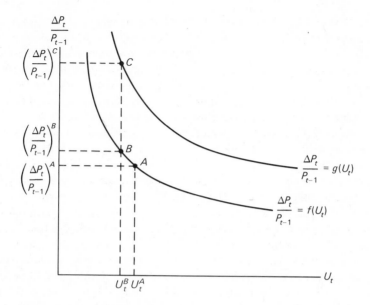

Figure 18.4.3 *Policy-Induced Shift in the Phillips Curve*

rate of growth of productivity declined from 2.5 to 1.9 between the periods 1955–65 and 1965–71.[15] This tendency would shift the Phillips curve upward by the full decline in productivity growth. Or, a change in workers' expectations about price changes could be affected by a number of factors, thereby causing a movement of the Phillips relation. Indeed, to the extent that expectations are based on past experience, one could argue that the position of this year's Phillips relation is partially dependent upon last year's rate of inflation. That is, the higher last year's inflation rate, the higher wage demands will be at a given unemployment rate and, consequently, the worse the trade-off will be between inflation and unemployment. To be sure, this phenomenon has some relevance to the current inflationary state.

To go a step further, the influence of price expectations can be crucial to the exercise of policy. Assume that the economy occupies position A in figure 18.4.3, where the unemployment rate is U^A and the rate of inflation is $(\Delta P/P)^A$. Suppose that the policymakers decide to use expansionary fiscal or monetary policy to decrease unemployment

---

[15] See W. D. Nordhaus, "The Recent Productivity Slowdown," *Brookings Papers on Economic Activity*, No. 3 (Washington, D.C.: Brookings Institution, 1972).

from U^A to U^B, and that they are willing to accept the increase in inflation indicated by the given Phillips relation, from $(\Delta P/P)^A$ to $(\Delta P/P)^B$. The mere announcement of this expansionary attitude may cause laborers to revise their price-change expectations upward, thus shifting the Phillips curve upward. Unemployment may fall (let us say by the desired amount), but only at the expense of a greater increase in inflation than policymakers anticipated (e.g., to $(\Delta P/P)^C$).

The catch-all variable, Z, can take on one or more of several identities. Several analysts have argued that firm profitability has a direct bearing on wage settlements (and hence on the position of the Phillips curve).[16] Consequently, periods of high profits may be expected to yield relatively adverse combinations of inflation and unemployment. Furthermore, the distribution of unemployment across occupations may play a role in overall wage settlements. This point is far from obvious, and thus needs some elaboration. The wage equation (18.4.1) is the result of an attempt to establish a relation between the aggregate unemployment rate and the rate of change of the overall level of wages. But wages are typically set in an occupational context, and each wage settlement is thus largely determined by the conditions in the occupation in question. Given the fact that workers in different occupations may respond differently to given rates of unemployment, a change in the distribution of occupational unemployment, with the aggregate rate of unemployment constant, may well alter the aggregate percentage change in wages.

This tendency may also help to explain the adverse economic conditions of the post–Vietnam War period. As the U.S. involvement in the war dwindled, the pattern of demand for goods and services changed; and, correspondingly, the distribution of labor demand was also affected. The demand for engineers, technicians, and some other occupational groups fell relative to the labor demand in some consumer goods industries. As a consequence, unemployment rates were very high in some occupations and relatively low in others. But wages tend to be rigid in the downward direction, and wages in high-unemployment industries did not decrease (or increase slowly enough) to counteract the strong pressure for wage hikes in low-unemployment occupations. The result, according to this line of thinking, was that the general rate of change of wages was higher than would normally be associated with the same aggregate rate of unemployment. This distortion in the distribu-

---

[16]See, for example, R. J. Bhatia, "Profits and the Rate of Change in Money Earnings in the U.S.: 1935–59," *Economica* 29 (August 1962), 255–63; and O. Eckstein and T. A. Wilson, "The Determination of Money Wages in American Industry," *Quarterly Journal of Economics* 76 (August 1962), 379–414.

tion of unemployment is a structural problem which is likely to accompany any drastic redistribution of the demand for final goods and services. When this type of distortion occurs, it calls for a broad policy of manpower training designed to shift workers from depressed occupations and into those of a greater national need.

The notion of structural adjustment need not be restricted to labor markets. In fact, we find that markets for goods and services are also subject to substantial periods of adjustment in the distribution of demand. If excess demand exists in some industries, prices (as well as wages) can be expected to rise at a relatively rapid pace there; but if a corresponding degree of excess supply occurs in other sectors of the economy, it is unlikely to induce offsetting price (and wage) decreases. This phenomenon can be incorporated into our simple model of wages and prices by adding a term X_t, which denotes the degree of structural distortion in product markets, to the price equation (18.4.2) to get:

$$\frac{\Delta P_t}{P_{t-1}} = \frac{\Delta W_t}{W_{t-1}} - \frac{\Delta MP_t}{MP_{t-1}} + hX_t$$

where, by hypothesis, $h > 0$. Combining this equation with the wage equation (18.4.1), we obtain a new Phillips relation:

$$\frac{\Delta P_t}{P_{t-1}} = a + b\frac{1}{U_t} + c\frac{\Delta P_t^e}{P_{t-1}^e} + dZ_t - \frac{\Delta MP_t}{MP_{t-1}} + hX_t. \quad (18.4.4)$$

As the degree of distortion in product markets increases, the Phillips relation between inflation and unemployment shifts outward. The effects of structural change on prices and wages is sometimes referred to as the demand-shift inflation. Although this type of inflation presumably lasts for relatively short periods of time—some period long enough for the adjustment to the new structure of demand or a reversion of the structure to its original state—it can be responsible for a significant displacement of the Phillips curve. Charles Schultze argues, for instance, that the problems of 1955–57, when prices rose at $3\frac{1}{2}\%$ (a rate higher than would "normally" be associated with unemployment in excess of 4%), could be attributed to the shift in demand into capital goods and away from housing and autos.[17]

The usefulness of the Phillips relation for policymaking is generally based upon two assumptions: first, some degree of money illusion in labor markets; and, second, a lack of full anticipation of future inflation.

---

[17]Charles Schultze, "Recent Inflation in the United States," *Study of Employment, Growth, and Price Levels,* Study Paper No. 1; Joint Economic Committee (Washington, D.C.: Government Printing Office, 1959), pp. 4–16.

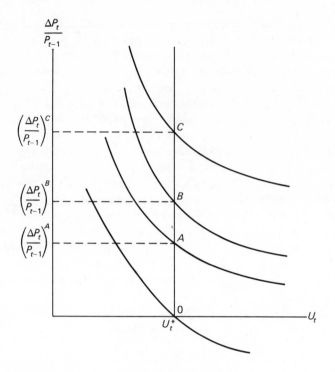

Figure 18.4.4   *The Long-Run Phillips Curve*

According to one school of thought, within which Milton Friedman is a prominent figure,[18] these two assumptions lose their validity in the long run. If this is true, they contend, we can achieve no long-run exchange of unemployment for inflation. Refer to figure 18.4.4 for the analysis. Suppose that the price level is constant ($\Delta P_t / P_{t-1} = 0$); then, as we saw earlier, in the absence of money illusion, the labor market yields a unique equilibrium level of employment. And given the positions of the labor supply and demand schedules, this can be translated into what Friedman calls a "natural" level of unemployment, U^*. The "natural" level of unemployment differs from the full-employment level discussed in earlier chapters in that it allows for some frictional unemployment (primarily people in the process of changing jobs). Now, suppose that inflationary pressures begin to develop (for example, through overt expansionary policy designed to reduce unemployment

---

[18]See, for example, Milton Friedman, "The Role of Monetary Policy," *American Economic Review* 58 (March 1968), 1–17.

below U_t^*). In the *long run,* workers will supposedly anticipate the rate of inflation (say, $(P_t/P_{t-1})^A$) and, given the lack of money illusion, will demand wage increases sufficient to keep their real wage constant at a particular level of employment (unemployment).[19] But as this happens, the short-run Phillips curve shifts upward and the economy moves to point A. The rate of unemployment is unchanged due to the fact that the real wage (and hence the equilibrium level of employment) has remained constant. If inflationary pressures intensify, with prices rising at the rate $(P_t/P_{t-1})^B$, workers will again (in the long run) anticipate this development and demand an equivalent rise in wages. Again, the real wage will remain at the same level and the economy will move to point B. In general, then, the economy maintains the "natural" rate of unemployment *regardless* of the rate of inflation; thus the long-run equilibrium combinations of inflation and unemployment form a vertical long-run Phillips curve. The validity of this line of argument is not clear. Certainly, short-run rates of unemployment are important, and, as we have seen throughout this text, can be affected by policy action. Whether or not these policies have any effect on the long-run rate of employment, they are still important means of affecting economic welfare.

18.5 The Role of Manpower Programs

The exclusive use of monetary and fiscal policies to achieve a reasonable combination of inflation and unemployment would ignore one of the more obvious facts of economic life: labor markets do not operate as smoothly and efficiently as we would like. The existence of unemployment does not necessarily indicate a corresponding lack of jobs, and consequently alleviating unemployment is not solely a question of expanding demand to create new jobs. Nor is inflation uniquely related to the rate of unemployment in the overall economy. There are many frictions in labor markets which prevent available workers from finding available jobs: high information costs, substantial retraining and relocation costs, and a variety of other factors leading to a tendency toward inertia. And these frictions help to aggravate the trade-off between inflation and unemployment faced by policymakers. To get an appreciation of the nature of the problem, consider the figures in table 18.5.1. Notice that the high rates of unemployment experienced in

---

[19]For simplicity, ignore productivity changes here.

Table 18.5.1.   *Vacancy and Unemployment Rates*

Year	Vacancy Rate	Unemployment Rate (Total Civilian Labor Force)
1969	1.3	3.5
1970	0.7	4.9
1971	0.5	5.9
1972	0.7	5.6
1973	0.9	4.9
1974	1.0	5.6

Source: *Survey of Current Business*

recent years coexisted with substantial vacancy rates.[20] This suggests that labor's mobility across occupational or geographical lines is low enough to generate a substantial degree of "mismatching" between jobs and workers. And, according to a growing number of economists, this malady gives rise to a strong national commitment to manpower programs.

The case of manpower training can be illustrated through the use of a simple algebraic model of the labor market. The model consists of four basic relationships: a behavioral relation between unemployment and vacancies; a hypothesized link between monetary/fiscal policy and the observed combination of unemployment and vacancies; a wage equation; and a price equation.

Vacancies generally occur when workers abandon jobs to seek more rewarding employment. The decision by an individual worker to leave a job depends on a number of factors, each having to do with the estimated prospects of finding better employment elsewhere. During periods of high unemployment, these prospects are relatively dim; as a result, relatively few workers will choose to give up the security of employment. On the other hand, the condition of low unemployment may encourage workers to seek better opportunities. As a result, we can hypothesize an inverse relationship between the vacancy rate and the unemployment rate. And, for simplicity, we can state this relation in linear form as:

$$V = a' - bU \qquad\qquad (18.5.1)$$

---

[20]For our purposes, the vacancy rate is defined as the number of job openings (vacancies) as a percentage of the labor force.

where V represents the vacancy rate and U, as before, is the unemployment rate.

But it should be recognized that this relation is valid only for a given set of labor market conditions. The combination of vacancy and unemployment rates observed at any point in time will depend upon the smoothness of the operation of the labor market. Our rationale for the inverse relation between vacancies and unemployment was concerned with the *flow* of workers out of jobs and into the search for new employment. But the number of vacancies existing at some point in time is a *stock*, and depends upon the speed with which vacancies can be filled. And this, in turn, depends upon a number of factors, including the degree of compatibility between the skills of the unemployed and the types of vacancies, the geographical matchup between vacancies and jobseekers, and the degree of (and cost of) job information available in labor markets. As any of these conditions is improved, the stock of both vacancies and unemployment can be expected to decrease. To capture this point, we can respecify the vacancy-unemployment relation as:

$$V = a - bU - cE \qquad (18.5.2)$$

where E is an index of the efficiency with which vacancies are filled by unemployed workers.

Equation 18.5.2 depicts the relation between vacancies and unemployment at each level of labor-market efficiency. But it does not tell us which combination of V and U will be attained at any time. To complete this part of the story, we need to know something about the overall relationship between the labor force and the total number of jobs available. First, suppose that aggregate labor supply and labor demand are equal. If so, the vacancy rate would equal the unemployment rate (each job vacancy would be matched by an unemployed worker). But as labor demand expands (relative to the labor force) job opportunities increase and the vacancy rate rises above the unemployment rate. Conversely, as labor demand contracts, vacancies fall below the unemployment rate. To generalize this relationship, we can write:

$$V - U = d + fQ \qquad (18.5.3)$$

where Q represents those policies which affect the ratio of the aggregate demand for labor to the labor force. For instance, changes in monetary and fiscal policies would be characterized as changes in the value of Q.

Our next assumption is that wage settlements, as represented by the rate of change of wages, depend on the ratio of vacancies to unemployment. That is:

$$\frac{\Delta W}{W} = g\frac{V}{U}.\tag{18.5.4}$$

The general notion underlying this equation is that wage changes are very sensitive to the employment prospects faced by workers. And, the higher the vacancy rate relative to the unemployment rate, the better these prospects will be. (Note that this specification of the wage equation abstracts from some of the other factors considered in the previous section.) To complete the system, we need to link prices to wages. To do this, we can use one of the relationships of the previous section:

$$\frac{\Delta P}{P} = \frac{\Delta W}{W} - \frac{\Delta MP}{MP}.\tag{18.5.5}$$

The system contained in 18.5.2–18.5.5 could be solved for its endogenous variables ($\Delta P/P$, $\Delta W/W$, U and V) in terms of the exogenous variables (Q and $\Delta MP/MP$); however, the purpose of our analysis is to derive a Phillips curve from the structural equations. To accomplish this objective, we can substitute 18.5.2 into 18.5.4 and the resulting equation into 18.5.5 to get:

$$\frac{\Delta P}{P} = g\left(\frac{a}{U} - b - c\frac{E}{U}\right) - \frac{\Delta MP}{MP}.\tag{18.5.6}$$

In analyzing 18.5.6, notice first that it is a Phillips relation, in that it relates the rate of inflation to the rate of unemployment. Notice also that the variable representing fiscal and monetary policy (Q) doesn't enter the equation. The reason for this is that, in the context of this model, these policies cause a movement *along* the curve, rather than a shift in its position. The most pertinent implication of the relationship is the role of the efficiency of job markets, as represented by the variable E. The model employed here suggests that any policy which would improve the degree of efficiency of channeling the unemployed into vacant job positions would shift the Phillips curve to the left (i.e., would decrease the rate of inflation at each rate of unemployment).

The policies designed to improve labor-market efficiency are relatively straightforward. Retraining programs designed to give the unemployed the kinds of skills required by industry are crucial. This is particularly true in times when the composition of final demand—and hence the makeup of labor demand—is undergoing rapid change. Furthermore, improved dissemination of employment information, through private or government efforts, can play a significant role by both facilitating "matchups" between jobseekers and jobs and by aiding the unemployed to form realistic expectations about job opportunities. As production becomes more highly specialized and employment skills become increasingly sophisticated, the need for such programs intensifies. It is not unreasonable to suggest then, that manpower programs will play an increasingly important role in the policy arena.

18.6 Wage-Price Guideposts and Controls

In the previous section, we considered the use of monetary and fiscal policy to combat inflation. During certain periods of U.S. experience, concern over inflation has run so high that these traditional tools have been considered insufficient. To put it another way, policymakers have, at times, decided that *no* point on the economy's Phillips curve could be considered a satisfactory state of affairs. During these critical periods, the authorities have resorted to the use of wage-price guideposts and wage-price controls.

The Kennedy and Johnson administrations employed essentially voluntary guidelines on wage and price increases. In 1962, the Council of Economic Advisors recommended that wage increases be kept at a level consistent with gains in labor productivity. If this type of guideline is observed, the limited rise of wages will allow price stability. For example, if wages and productivity both rise by 3% per year, there will be no wage-push pressure on the general level of prices. In terms of our earlier analysis, the labor-supply and labor-demand schedules would rise by an equal amount, thus inducing no shift in the aggregate supply schedule. Since labor productivity varies over the business cycle, guideposts are generally based on some estimate of the long-run trend of productivity. The Kennedy policy was vague, however, in that it enunciated no explicit productivity figure. This was due partially to the inherent problem in computing such a trend for an economy which had undergone two recent recessions (1957–58 and 1960–61). Equally vague was the companion stipulation that price increases should be forthcoming only in those industries in which wages rose more rapidly than labor's productivity in that particular industry. The Johnson administration eventually extended the guidelines by formalizing the trend-productivity estimate as 3.2% per year. The guideposts remained in effect until 1967, when they were abandoned with little fanfare.

The effectiveness of voluntary guideposts is a matter of considerable debate. It is true that prices in the United States rose at very low rates during the first four years of the Kennedy-Johnson guideposts, from 1962 through 1965. But it is also interesting to note that prices climbed rapidly in 1966, when labor and product markets started to tighten up.

Indeed, the inability of the guidelines to stop price rises was a prime factor in their being dropped in 1967. It was deemed unrealistic to expect labor to follow the productivity criterion in light of the large increase in prices of the previous year.

Obviously, an evaluation of the impact of this (or any) policy involves an effort to standardize for those other factors which might have played a role in the movement of prices during the years in question. Those studies which have followed this procedure generally conclude that the increase of wages and prices were slowed somewhat by the guidelines.[21] Yet many observers dispute the effectiveness with which controls were placed on the experiments. Samuelson, for instance, argues that two phenomena not considered by these studies may have been partially responsible for the apparent (but temporary) success of the guideposts.[22] First, he suggests that the sluggish conditions of the 1950s and early 1960s could have made the economy less prone to inflation in the guidepost years than it would have been otherwise. Second, he points out that the increasing importance of imports in key industries (e.g., steel) could have altered the price-setting behavior of the business sector.

It is unlikely that any definite conclusions will be reached with regard to the impact of voluntary guidelines over this period. Yet, the basic notion of establishing a norm for wage and price increases is likely to be used—implicitly or explicitly—in future years.

A more extreme type of direct counterinflationary policy involves the imposition of binding wage and price controls. Until recently, rigid legal limits on wage and price increases were reserved for wartime emergency conditions. They were used in the United States during World War II and the Korean War, when war mobilization exerted pressure on the economy's productive capacity. Under conditions like these, contractionary monetary and fiscal policies would be hazardous, given the policy goal of maintaining reasonably high levels of production of war materials and consumer goods. It is not surprising to find a variety of artificial controls during periods of declared war. It is undoubtedly easier to instill a spirit of national sacrifice and cooperation under these conditions.

---

[21] See, for instance, testimony given by Gary Fromm and George L. Perry in Joint Economic Committee, *The Wage-Price Issue: The Need for Guideposts,* Hearings (Washington, D.C.: Government Printing Office, 1968); and J. Sheahan, *The Wage-Price Guideposts* (Washington, D.C.: Brookings Institution, 1967).

[22] P. Samuelson and A. Burns, "Wage-Price Guideposts and the Need for Informal Controls in a Mixed Economy," in *Full Employment, Guideposts, and Economic Stability: Rational Debate Seminars* (Washington, D.C.: American Enterprise Institute for Public Policy Research, 1967), pp. 46–66.

When President Nixon first took office, it was expected that he would avoid tampering with the private market mechanism. But the substantial price increases of 1969, 1970 and the first two quarters of 1971 coincided with substantial unemployment rates, and this condition gave rise to mounting criticism of the administration's economic posture. Clearly, the situation was serious enough to warrant concern on both economic and political grounds. Many economists, perhaps the most outspoken of which was John Kenneth Galbraith, saw the problem as one which could not be treated with the traditional tools of monetary and fiscal policy. They argued that it was time to revert to the regulation of prices and wages by public authority. President Nixon reversed his earlier stands and announced a ninety-day moratorium on most wages and prices in August 1971, referring to the freeze as part of Phase I of his New Economic Policy. In November, three months later, Phase II was initiated. It involved a limit of 5.5% on wage increases, and a ceiling on price rises for most commodities. The elements of Phase II were designed to slow the rate of observed inflation to somewhere between 2 and 3% by the end of 1972. Even though the goal was not reached,[23] the legal restrictions of Phase II were replaced with the less stringent stipulations of Phases III and IV.

It is too early to appraise adequately the success of the New Economic Policy. If we were to judge its success in relation to the initial goals of the Nixon administration, we would have to conclude that it was far from completely successful. Of course, we should probably apply a more reasonable criterion. If we maintain our view of inflation as a *tendency* for rising price levels, actual data taken from the period of controls (August 1971 to January 1973) would not reflect the extent of success of those policies. Rather, the New Economic Policy will not receive its real test until the movement of prices in the next few quarters can, through econometric methods, be compared to those which would have ensued in the absence of controls.[24]

18.7 Summary and Conclusions

In this chapter, we've offered a glimpse of some of the predominant views of inflation. Using a comparative static approach, we investi-

---

[23] Indeed, the consumer price index (all items) increased by 3.5% from November 1971 to November 1972. Moreover, the price index for foodstuffs increased by 11.3% for the same period, while its wholesale counterpart increased by 13.8%.

[24] The student reading this passage may well already know more of the success or failure of the controls than did the authors at the time of writing.

gated the basic concepts of demand-pull and cost-push inflation. Then, to add a feeling for the dynamic nature of the inflationary mechanism, we considered two very simplified models in which some initial price increase triggered a feedback mechanism which carried the economy through a succession of price movements. We also investigated some of the problems associated with combating inflation with monetary and fiscal policies.

The simplified presentation of this chapter should not deceive the student into thinking that the real issues of inflation are correspondingly simple. Several disclaimers must be offered. It is true that particular inflationary periods have been attributed to cost-push or demand-pull sources. In general, the distinction is based on an observation of the general conditions characterizing the labor- and product-markets. For instance, the inflations following World War II and the Korean War are considered to have been attributable to excess demand, primarily because these periods exhibited relatively high levels of employment and output. But the inflation of 1955–57 did not fit this mold. Unemployment was high, and firms had substantial amounts of excess capacity; thus, there was little to substantiate any presumption that excess demand was again the culprit. It was at this point that renewed emphasis started to be placed on supply-side explanations. Some argued that autonomous rises in wages were responsible for the movement of prices; others contended that the blame could be placed on the shift in the composition of demand and the downward rigidity of wages and prices.

These cases may have been relatively amenable to categorization, but one should not get the impression that any inflation is pure in its causes, or that the present inflation and those to come can be so easily relegated to one category or the other. If the world were static, and if we could define and observe the movement of truly exogenous forces, we could pin down the cause of any inflation. But even then, we would often find that *several* factors are at play, on both the supply and the demand side. We would then have to regard the inflation as a mixture of the two basic varieties. But even this oversimplifies the problem. The economy is a dynamic organism, interlaced with virtually thousands of relationships we have found impossible to cover in this chapter. Examining the data generated by the economy over a period of time may tell us *what* has happened, but it is unlikely that it will give us enough information to discern completely *why* it happened.

To be more specific, suppose that we observe a series of upward wage and price adjustments. Can we infer that wages rose autonomously, pulling prices upward? Or do the data indicate that the movement of prices forced wages to follow suit? Certainly, the associated conditions, especially the extent of unemployment, can give us some grounds for sorting out the patterns of behavior, but even the most sophisticated techniques cannot be expected to answer all of our questions, especially if the behavior of the economy differs somewhat from the past. And, again, even if we could identify causes and effects, the causes of a particular inflation may generally be a mixture of reinforcing supply and demand conditions. Samuelson and Solow sum up the conceptual and empirical difficulty in attaching labels to inflations when they lament that "dull as it is to have to embrace eclectic theories, scholars who wished to be realistic would have to steel themselves to doing so."[25]

18.8 Prospects for New Policy Directions

As we become more sophisticated in our diagnoses of inflationary causes, so too must we improve and expand our policy prescriptions. The postwar period has been characterized by the active application of monetary and fiscal tools in the effort to reach price stability. Furthermore, we have seen the intervention of the federal government into the pricing system through a variety of wage-price guidelines and controls. And, although sufficient funding has not been forthcoming, some commitment to manpower training has (at least in principle) been made. Why, then, is the United States now confronted with the most unfavorable combination of inflation and unemployment in recent history? One general view is that the aforementioned policies have not been given a chance, in that their application has been short-lived and weakly enforced. Monetarists, for instance, opposed Phase I of Nixon's New Economic Policy on the grounds that monetary restraint had not been practiced long enough to show any substantial effects. During the period of Phases I through IV, many economists argued that controls were not applied evenly and stringently enough to exhibit any real effect. And labor economists could well point to unwillingness of the executive branch to promote (or even approve) massive job training programs in the late 1960s and early 1970s. Nevertheless, the persistence of adverse times has given rise to the view that economists must broaden their kit of tools in order to deal with the changing structure of the U.S. economy.

It is difficult to discern any general tendencies in the emerging literature on inflation; nonetheless, two arguments seem to be surfacing. First, more attention must be placed on the supply side of the market-

---

[25] Samuelson and Solow, "Anti-Inflation Policy," p. 192.

place. That is, the Keynesian emphasis on the level of aggregate demand must be augmented by a recognition of the importance of those factors which affect the supply of various goods and services and consequently their prices. Second, policy should be based at least partially on an analysis of the microeconomic characteristics of the economy at each point in time. Rather than treating the economy as an amorphous aggregate, we must recognize it as a collection of diverse markets, each with its own problems and each with its own impact on the overall state of the economy.

Keynesian policy was born in a time of depression, and, its early application through the postwar years has been dominated by an effort to maintain high levels of employment. Although the Keynesian prescriptions seem to have worked well during most of this period, they have seen relatively little use as counterinflationary policies; we thus know relatively little about their effectiveness in an inflationary context. Expansionary monetary or fiscal policy is effective in expanding aggregate demand, and thus in decreasing unemployment. And, due to an initial expansion in economic activity, one could expect aggregate supply to increase, thereby reinforcing the favorable effects on unemployment and restraining somewhat the attendant rise in the general price level.

But contractionary policy of the type covered previously may have an adverse effect on aggregate supply. More specifically, policies designed to reduce inflation by cutting back aggregate demand (decreases in the money supply or government expenditures, or tax increases) may depress investment, thus slowing down the growth of the capital stock and causing a decline in aggregate supply. To the extent that this happens, the rate of inflation may not decrease by the desired amount *and* the rate of unemployment may increase by more than expected.

If it is true that monetary and fiscal policy, as practiced in the past, have adverse effects on the supply side, alternative or supplemental policies should be investigated. For instance, policies designed to reduce consumption and government spending could be augmented by policies tailored to encourage investment. Whereas the former policies would have the effect of slowing the growth of aggregate demand, the latter would bolster industrial capacity and lead to an expansion of aggregate supply. The two-pronged policy could, at least in theoretical terms, hold down the rate of inflation with relatively little, if any, loss in employment.

Government expenditures can, of course, be decreased directly; this is a standard policy prescription in times of inflation. Yet, two interrelated problems emerge in this context. First, there are fairly obvious political problems involved in reducing expenditures on any given budget item. Second, budget cuts should be made on a selective basis, with an eye toward specific kinds of expenditures. It may be unwise, for instance, to decrease expenditures on social capital—i.e., those items which add to society's productive capacity. Nor, according to one of our earlier analyses, would it make much sense to diminish the funding of job retraining programs. In general, one could argue that relatively nonproductive items should be the first to be placed on the chopping block.

Tax policies can also be used on a relatively selective basis in order to guard against undesirable effects on aggregate supply. Hendrik Houthakker argues that the corporate tax system should be overhauled to facilitate the financing of new investment.[26] This would involve exempting dividends paid to domestic stockholders from the corporate income tax (which would encourage equity financing of investment) and the establishment of a surcharge on corporations whose profits as a percentage of net worth are in excess of some specified percentage (which would encourage firms to expand their capital stock in order to expand the base of their rate of return). One could also suggest that an investment tax credit (coupled with higher corporate tax rates in order to yield roughly unchanged total tax revenues) could be used to stimulate aggregate supply. Then, in conjunction with these tax policies, personal income taxes could be raised to decrease consumption.

Credit stringency has been used in the past to stem inflation, but this policy typically has taken the form of regulation of the money supply and the consequent raising of interest rates. Unfortunately, this kind of policy can act to discourage investment as well as consumption and, as a result, yield an adverse effect on new capacity. To partially circumvent this problem, policies which have a more direct effect on consumption and a relatively insignificant influence on investment should be used. One possibility would be direct regulation of consumer installment credit through something like the now-defunct Regulation W, which, until its discontinuation in the 1950s, gave the Federal Reserve the power to regulate the maximum allowable term of installment contracts.

The general principle of these approaches to monetary and fiscal policy is that, in periods of high unemployment and rapid inflation,

---

[26]Hendrik, Houthakker, "A Positive Way to Fight Inflation," *The Wall Street Journal,* July 30, 1974, p. 12.

consumption, which enters directly into aggregate demand, should be depressed, whereas investment, which affects both aggregate demand and aggregate supply, should be expanded. The exercise of this selective type of policy makes it all the more important that we achieve a better understanding of the quantitative effects of government decisions on both consumption and investment.

The problems of price and wage rigidity were treated earlier in this chapter, where we discussed the notion of demand-shift inflation. During periods when the structure of demand changes, bottlenecks occur in some industries (for example, the steel industry in 1974) and excess capacity occurs in others. Due to the downward rigidity of wages and prices, the result can be an undesirable mixture of inflation and unemployment. Under these circumstances, the indiscriminate application of monetary and fiscal policy may do little to alleviate these problems. Overall contractionary policy may seriously affect industries with some excess capacity, and thus lead to decreases in employment there with little or no downward movement of prices. It would obviously be more desirable to direct contractionary policy—say, a decrease in government expenditures—to those industries in which excess demand is prevalent. And, to ensure that this is done, demand and supply conditions in individual industries would have to be monitored and considerable discretion would have to be exercised (perhaps through a Cost of Living Council) in choosing the budget items to be cut.

Houthakker suggests some additional policies based on the recognition of microeconomic aspects of the economy.[27] In particular, he suggests that antitrust policies be pursued more vigorously, with the intent of diminishing the kind of concentration of economic power which gives rise to price rigidities. To the extent that markets can be made more competitive, prices will be made more sensitive to the downward pressures of excess supply. Furthermore, he suggests that import restrictions—tariffs and quotas, which tend to restrict the supply of certain foreign-made goods—be relaxed.

As a general commentary on the state of counterinflationary policy, one would have to admit to the need for a broad variety of programs. Monetary and fiscal policy in their current forms are evidently not sufficient to do the job. Instead, the kinds of issues and policies mentioned in this and previous sections will have to be studied and, where appropriate, applied in full force if the lesson of recent years is to be well learned.

---

[27] Ibid.

Suggested Further Reading

Alchian, A. A. "Information Costs, Pricing, and Resource Unemployment." In *Microeconomic Foundation of Employment and Inflation Theory,* edited by E. S. Phelps et al. New York: W. W. Norton, 1970, pp. 27–52.

Ball, R. J. *Inflation and the Theory of Money.* Chicago: Aldine Publishing Co., 1964.

Brechling, F. "Wage Inflation and the Structure of Regional Unemployment." *Journal of Money, Credit, and Banking* 5 (February 1973), 355–79.

Dow, J. C. R. and Dicks-Mireau, L. A. "The Determinants of Wage Inflations: United Kingdom, 1946–56." *Journal of the Royal Statistical Society* 122, Series A (1959), 145–84.

Flanagan, R. "The U.S. Phillips Curve and International Unemployment Rate Differentials." *American Economic Review* 63 (March 1973), 114–31.

Hicks, J. *The Theory of Wages.* New York: Macmillan Co., 1932.

Holt, C. C. "Job Search, Phillips' Wage Relation, and Union Influence: Theory and Evidence." In *Microeconomic Foundation of Employment and Inflation Theory,* edited by E. S. Phelps et al. New York: W. W. Norton, 1970, pp. 53–123.

———— and David, M. H. "The Concept of Vacancies in a Dynamic Theory of the Labor Market." In *Measurement and Interpretation of Job Vacancies.* New York: National Bureau of Economic Research, 1966, pp. 73–141.

Kuska, E. A. "The Simple Analytics of the Phillips Curve." *Economica* 33 (November 1966), 462–67.

Lipsey, R. G. "The Relation Between Unemployment and the Rate of Change of Money Wage Rates in the United Kingdom, 1862–1957: A Further Analysis." *Economica* 25 (February 1960), 1–41.

Oi, W. Y. "Labor as a Quasi-Fixed Factor of Production." *Journal of Political Economy* 70 (December 1962), 538–55.

Phelps, E. S. "Money Wage Dynamics and Labor Market Equilibrium." *Journal of Political Economy* 76 (July–August 1968), Part II, 678–711.

Rees, A. "Wage Determination and Involuntary Unemployment." *Journal of Political Economy* 59 (April 1951), 143–64.

Schultze, C. C. "Recent Inflation in the United States." In *Study of Employment, Growth and Price Levels.* Study Paper No. 1; Joint Economic Committee. Washington, D.C.: Government Printing Office, 1959, pp. 4–16.

Stigler, G. S. "Information in the Labor Market." *Journal of Political Economy,* Supplement no. 5, part 2 (October 1962), 94–105.

Tobin, J. "Inflation and Unemployment." *American Economic Review* 62 (March 1972), 1–18.

Tullock, G. "Inflation, Unemployment and Economic Welfare: Comment." *American Economic Review* 62 (December 1972), 1004.

Waud, R. N. "Inflation, Unemployment, and Economic Welfare." *American Economic Review* 60 (September 1970), 631–41.

Appendix 18.A

Indexation

Much of this chapter has been devoted to the analysis of counterinflationary policies. The need for these policies rests on the observation that inflation creates a number of adverse effects on the economy, many of which stem from the use of money as a standard of deferred payments. In contractual agreements covering future time periods, future receipts (expenditures) are specified in terms of dollars, often with no provision (or, at times, inadequate provision) for changes in the purchasing power of those dollars during the life of the contract. Assuming that inflation is at least partially *unanticipated,* increases in the general price level favor creditors and act to the detriment of debtors.[1] Wage contracts without comprehensive escalator clauses permit real wages to fall during the initial phase of an inflationary period. And, certain government transfer payments like social security and unemployment compensation (which are also contractual arrangements) diminish in real terms as the general price level rises.

Recently, several economists, including Milton Friedman,[2] have argued that the adverse effects of inflation arising from contractual arrangements could be avoided through a policy called *indexation.* Basically, indexation entails the linking of certain contractual obligations to some price index. Under the most comprehensive version of indexation, all contractual obligations would be stated in *real* terms, with payments being adjusted automatically for changes in the value of the price index. For instance, wage contracts would be written in terms of real wages, with a standard escalator clause defining the adjustment of nominal wages to changes in the price index. Loan repayments would be tied to the price index, as would pension benefits, insurance settlements and deposits in financial institutions. Government transfer payments (unemployment compensation, social security payments, welfare benefits, etc.) would be linked to the index. Moreover, tax structures would be defined so that certain statutory provisions, like exemption levels and tax brackets, would be indexed. In most general terms,

---

[1] Note that fully anticipated inflation does not have this effect. See appendix 7.A for a review of this point.

[2] Milton Friedman, "Using Escalators to Help Fight Inflation," *Fortune* (July 1974), p. 94.

money would no longer be a standard for deferred payments; instead, purchasing power ("real money," so to speak) would play this role.

Although the proposal has a utopian ring, its supporters argue that it would yield the same general results as price stability, allowing us to avoid the undesirable effects of inflation on the distribution of income and the allocation of resources. There is little doubt that, under full indexation, inflation would no longer favor debtors at the expense of creditors; individuals would no longer suffer from having fixed incomes in an inflationary economy; and wage-earners would be protected from the adverse effects of general price rises which precede wage increases. And, to the extent that indexation would remove some of the uncertainty of transactions involving contractual agreements, the efficiency of re-source allocation would probably be improved.[3]

Given the perceived advantages of indexation, why hasn't the policy been widely embraced by decision makers? The answer is that critics of the policy have raised a number of issues which cast some doubt on the efficacy of indexation.[4]

First, the implementation of a policy of indexation would require the choice of a single price index to which contractual obligations would be linked. This is not a trivial choice. The coverage of the index (the commodities included) could take a variety of forms. It could encompass existing assets as well as currently produced goods, intermediate as well as final products, investment goods as well as current consumption, and so on.[5]

Moreover, even if the problems surrounding the choice of a bundle of commodities were solved, we would still be confronted with something called the *index number problem*. In this context, the index number problem refers to the fact that price indices computed with fixed weights (base-period quantities) tend to distort the "true" rate of inflation. Changes in the general price level accompanied by changes in *relative* prices would

---

[3] See Jai-Hoon Yang, "The Case for and against Indexation: An Attempt at Perspective," *Federal Reserve Bank of Saint Louis Review* 56 (October 1974), 2–11.

[4] It should be noted that some countries, including Finland, Israel, France, Brazil and the People's Republic of China have used indexing to varying degrees. On this, see ibid., p. 3, for a brief summary and a bibliography covering these experiences. Note also that indexation in a limited form is found in the United States. For instance, many wage contracts have escalator clauses, social security payments are now partially adjusted for increases in the cost of living, and some financial institutions are experimenting with variable interest-rate mortgage contracts.

[5] On this issue, see Jai-Hoon Yang, "The Case for and against Indexation," p. 10; and Armen A. Alchian and Benjamin Klein, "On a Correct Measure of Inflation," *Journal of Money, Credit and Banking* 5 (February 1973), 173–91.

give rise to substitution of relatively cheap goods for relatively expensive ones (thus allowing consumers to avoid some of the brunt of rising prices, but fixed-weight indices ignore this kind of substitution.[6]

Second, the adoption of indexation could lead to substantial transitional costs. Only new contracts would be covered by indexation; existing contracts would not be. Upon the implementation of indexation, the holders of existing debt (e.g., bondholders) could suffer capital losses. The impact of indexation on existing bond prices would, of course, depend upon behavior in financial markets. If inflation is fully anticipated, and future price changes are already reflected in the yields on existing contracts, nonindexed debt would not necessarily be at any competitive disadvantage relative to new, indexed debt.[7] However, if the introduction of indexation were to cause an upward revision of inflationary expectation, or if indexed bonds were considered less risky than existing bonds, the price of existing bonds would be driven downward (i.e., existing debt would have to carry higher yields than indexed bonds to compensate for their relatively high degree of risk).[8] The overall magnitude of these transitional distributional effects is uncertain; but the mere possibility of losses being suffered by some broad segment of the population acts as a strong deterrent to the adoption of indexation.

A third argument against indexation is that it could cause a deterioration in our balance of payments. Critics suggest that indexing makes inflation easier to live with, and this could cause either a greater natural tendency toward rapid inflation or a reduced effort in containing inflation.[9] If either or both of these phenomena occurs, then one would expect an increase in the inflation rate. And, if domestic prices grow more rapidly, domestic goods would become less attractive relative

---

[6]For an analysis of the index number problem, refer to C. E. Ferguson, *Microeconomic Theory* (Homewood, Ill.: R. D. Irwin, 1972), pp. 78–83. It should also be pointed out the variations in the quality of products tend to make price indices less reliable as indicators of pure inflationary price movements. This effect takes two forms. First, some price rises may reflect improvements in the quality of the product(s); to the extent that they do, they do not constitute inflation per se. Furthermore, "true" price increases are sometimes expressed in terms of deterioration of quality at a relatively small decline in price. In the first case, a general price index would tend to overstate the extent of inflation; in the second case, to understate it.

[7]Again, see appendix 7.A for an analysis of the role of price expectations on bond yields.

[8]If indexation applied to only *some* new bond issues (e.g., government bonds, but not private bonds), then the same disadvantages would be incurred by issuers of new nonindexed debt.

[9]See, for example, Murray L. Weidenbaum, "The Case Against 'Indexing,'" *Dun's* (July 1974), p. 11.

to foreign goods, thus causing an unfavorable shift in the balance of payments.[10] The evaluation of this criticism leads us into a tangle of associated issues. There is no strong evidence that indexation would cause a greater inherent tendency toward inflation. In order to argue this point, one must operate within the framework of some particular theory of inflation. And, unfortunately we have already seen that there is no single universally accepted description of the inflationary process. With regard to the impact of indexation on the attitudes of policymakers, more can be said. If indexation does make inflation less costly (if, for example, it diminishes the unfavorable consequences in the areas of income-distribution and allocation, but does not avoid international problems) then perhaps price stability *should* be lowered within the set of policy priorities.

Indeed, proponents of indexation go a step farther by suggesting that policymakers would be even *more* prone to implement counterinflationary policies under indexation. Their reasoning relies partially on the nature of the Phillips curve. As we saw earlier, the curvature of the short-run Phillips curve depends upon the existence of money illusion in the labor market. But if indexation of wage contracts removes money illusion (by specifying contracts in terms of *real* wages), the Phillips curve would be vertical at the "natural" rate of unemployment. If so, they argue, there would no longer be a tendency to accept more inflation in an effort to diminish unemployment; and, in effect, the impetus for reducing inflation would thus be unfettered by any costs in terms of increased unemployment. Policymakers would be more, rather than less, diligent in guarding against inflation.

It is probably fair to say that the general case for indexation suffers from uncertainty with regard to its overall effects. Unlike many of the counterinflationary policies we've analyzed, indexation would constitute a major structural change in economic institutions. But our empirical economic models are relatively useless in forecasting the effects of significant structural changes, since the behavior patterns of economic actors are prone to change drastically and unpredictably in response to such a major alteration in institutions. Far more study, especially of the countries which have adopted some fairly comprehensive form of indexation, will most likely be necessary before large-scale adoption is forthcoming in this country.

---

[10]Actually, this impact on the balance of payments is contingent upon the existence of fixed exchange rates. If exchange rates are flexible, relatively rapid inflation in the U.S. would be accommodated by automatic revisions in the exchange rate relating dollars to foreign currency. But, under fixed exchange rates, inflation at home would be translated, through the exchange-rate mechanism, into higher dollar-prices of foreign goods and services.

Author Index

Subject Index